The
AMC
White
Mountain
Guide

*A Guide to trails in the
mountains of New Hampshire
and adjacent parts of Maine*

Twenty-Third Edition

Published by
The Appalachian Mountain Club
Boston, Massachusetts 02108
1983

EDITIONS

First Edition 1907, Second Edition 1916
Third Edition 1917, Fourth Edition 1920
Fifth Edition 1922, Sixth Edition 1925
Seventh Edition 1928, Eighth Edition 1931
Ninth Edition 1934, Tenth Edition 1936
Eleventh Edition 1940, Twelfth Edition 1946
Thirteenth Edition 1948
Fourteenth Edition 1952
Fifteenth Edition 1955
Sixteenth Edition 1960
Seventeenth Edition 1963
Eighteenth Edition 1966
Nineteenth Edition 1969
Twentieth Edition 1972
Twenty-First Edition 1976
Twenty-Second Edition 1979
Twenty-Third Edition 1983

ISBN 0-910146-48-9

Cover photograph by Paul Mozell

Cover design by Dennis McQuillen

CONTENTS

LIST OF MAPS

MAPS FOLDED IN BLACK FLAP

1. Mt. Monadnock
2. Mt. Cardigan
4. Chocorua-Waterville
5. Franconia
6. Mt. Washington Range
7. Carter-Mahoosuc
8. Pilot Range

Maps 1 and 2 are on back of 7. Map 8 is on back of 5. There is no map number 3.

PAGE MAPS PRINTED IN THIS GUIDE

Due to changes in conditions, use of the information in this book is at the sole risk of the user.

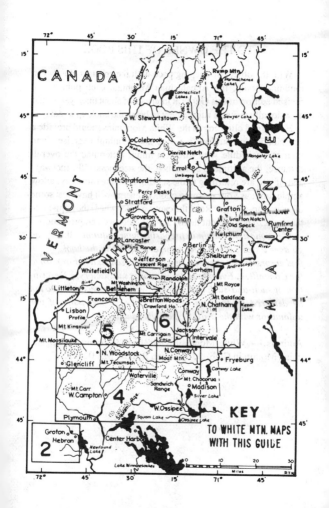

TO THE OWNER OF THIS BOOK

With the object of keeping pace with the constant changes in mountain trails, the Appalachian Mountain Club publishes a revised edition of this Guide at intervals of about three years, and occasionally issues a supplement to bring the book up to date.

Hiking and climbing in the White Mountains should provide a combination of outdoor pleasure and healthful exercise. Plan your trip schedule with safety in mind. Determine the overall distance, the altitude to be reached, the steepness of the footway, and, if you are returning to the starting point the same day, allow ample time, as your morning quota of energy will have lost some of its get-up-and-go. Read the caution notes where they appear in this book. They are put there for your guidance and protection.

We request your help in preparing future editions. When you go over a trail, please check the description in the book. If you find errors or can suggest improvements, send a letter or card to the Committee. Even if the description is satisfactory, "Description of such-and-such trail is o.k.," will be appreciated. Do not be deterred by the lack of experience. The viewpoint of one unfamiliar with the trail is especially valuable.

Address — White Mountain Guidebook Committee, Appalachian Mountain Club, 5 Joy Street, Boston, MA 02108.

In Memoriam
HOWARD M. GOFF, 1894 – 1982

Howie Goff, who passed away in June 1982 at the age of eighty-eight, was editor of this guidebook for almost forty years, serving in that capacity from 1937 to 1976. But this single great service to the Appalachian Mountain Club and to the hiking public was only one of an astounding range and volume of contributions that Howie made throughout his long life. It would scarcely be possible for anyone to travel at all widely in the White Mountains without being touched by one, if not many, of his good deeds. In addition to a term as the AMC's Councillor of Trails, he served on trail work crews and was sign man for the Trail Committee for twenty years. The Boott Spur Trail and the Halls Ledge Trail are largely his trails. He was not content merely to climb the mountains he loved, but worked tirelessly to improve the trails, this guidebook, and the Club, which has taken as its goal the stewardship of the interests of the hiking public and of the mountains themselves.

Howie has passed on, in the fullness of his years and his achievements, but he has left behind an example of dedication and service for those of us who wish to emulate his record of devotion to the mountains we love.

The White Mountain Guidebook Committee dedicates this, the Twenty-Third Edition of the *White Mountain Guide,* to the memory of Howard M. Goff.

Introduction

This book describes hiking trails located, for the most part, in the northern half of New Hampshire and in adjoining parts of Maine. The highest point is Mount Washington, 6288 feet above sea level. The timberline — that is, where the climate becomes so severe that trees cannot survive — occurs at about 5000 feet. A large number of lower mountains, such as Mt. Chocorua, Mt. Cardigan, and Mt. Monadnock, all between 3000 and 4000 feet, also have open, rocky summits with distant views on clear days.

THE WEATHER

The climate gets much cooler, windier, and wetter at higher elevations. Since 1932, there has been a permanent US weather station on top of Mt. Washington, which is under cloud cover about 55 per cent of the time. On an average summer afternoon, the high temperature on the summit is only about 52° F (11° C); in the winter, about 15° F (−9° C). Average winds throughout the day and night are 26 mph in summer and 44 mph in winter. Winds have gusted over 100 mph in every month of the year, over 120 mph at least once in every year 1952 through 1977, and set the world record of 231 mph in April 1934. Over 300 inches of snow fell on the summit in each winter 1969 through 1977, with almost twice as much in 1969. Other mountains also have severe conditions, in proportion to their height and exposure. Mt. Washington averages about 25° F (14° C) cooler than Boston in all seasons, and gets about twice as much precipitation.

Before going above timberline in winter, hikers should build up experience gradually. Section 21, *White Mountains in Winter*, discusses winter hiking. ***Caution.*** Except for Section 21, trail descriptions in this *Guide* are meant to apply in summer conditions (mid-June through September). A reliable source of water in summer at high elevation may be frozen from November through May. Many rescues take place in late winter and early spring, because hikers are unprepared for continuing severe mountain winter conditions. In early May, long after snow is gone from the lowlands, snowshoes or skis may be needed in the mountains. Even at the end of May, snow can remain several feet deep in such places as Mahoosuc Notch or some of the ravines in the Presidential Range.

In the spring, dirt roads may be impassable due to washouts and deep mud until yearly maintenance is done. Trails may not be cleared of fallen trees and brush until late summer, and not all trails are cleared every year. Mosquitoes and black flies are at their worst on windless days in late May and June. Even in midsummer, hikers above treeline should be prepared for cold weatner with a wool sweater, hat, mittens, and a wind parka, which will give comfort on sunny but cool days and protection against sudden storms. By early November, snow tires may be needed on roads above 1000 feet elevation.

STREAM CROSSINGS

Rivers and brooks are often crossed without bridges on White Mountain trails. In normal low water, it is usually possible to jump from rock to rock, perhaps using a stick from the bank for balance. If you need to wade across, wearing boots, but not necessarily socks, is recommended. Higher waters come in the spring as snow melts, in the fall when trees drop their leaves and take up less water, or after heavy rainstorms. Do not plan hikes with potentially hazardous stream crossings during these high-water periods. Rushing current can make swimming extremely hazardous, and several deaths have resulted. If you are cut off from roads by swollen streams, it is better to make a long detour, even if you need to wait and spend a night in the woods. For such unplanned bivouacs, wool sweaters and coats can be supplemented by very lightweight, insulating metallized ''space blankets'' sold in outdoor stores. Flood waters may subside within a few hours, especially in small brooks. It is particularly important not to camp on the far side of a brook from your exit point if the crossing is difficult and heavy rain is predicted.

PROTECTING THE ENVIRONMENT

Carry In — Carry Out

Trash receptacles are not available in trail areas (except at some trailheads), and visitors are asked to bring trash bags and carry out everything — food, paper, glass, cans — they carry in. Cooperation with the "carry in — carry out" program so far has been outstanding, and the concept has grown to "carry out *more* than you carried in." We hope you will join in the effort. Your fellow backcountry users will appreciate it.

Use Special Care Above Timberline

Extreme weather and a short growing season make those areas especially fragile. Just footsteps can destroy the toughest natural cover, so please try to stay on the trail or walk on rocks. And, of course, don't camp above timberline.

Limit the Size of Your Group

The larger the group the greater the impact on the environment and on others. Please limit the size of your groups to a dozen or less.

Guidelines for Backpacking Campers

Those who camp overnight in the backcountry tend to have more of an impact on the land than day hikers do. Repeated camping on one site compacts the soil and makes it difficult for vegetation to survive. Trash may accumulate and trees may be attacked for firewood, and popular campsites begin to resemble disaster areas. How to preserve the mountains for all to enjoy? Two possible methods are: first, to camp in well-prepared, designated sites, supervised by caretakers, or second, to disperse camping over a wide area, out of sight of trails and roads, and to camp with full respect for wilderness values.

Restricted Use Areas (RUAs) and Wilderness Areas

To limit or prevent some of the adverse impacts of concentrated, uncontrolled camping, the US Forest Service (USFS) has adopted regulations for a number of areas in the National Forest. Those areas as of 1982 are listed and shown on a map in Section 22 of this *Guide*. Camping is never allowed above timberline. In RUAs, camping and wood or charcoal fires are not allowed within 200 feet of trails or within ¼ mile of roads, except on designated campsites. For further information see Section 22 and consult any of the USFS, AMC, or other offices listed there, such as the Forest Supervisor in Laconia (603-524-6450) or Pinkham Notch Camp (603-466-2727).

Bring Your Own Tent or Shelter

Shelter buildings are often full, so each group should carry all needed shelter, including whatever poles, stakes, ground insulation, and cord are required. Do not cut boughs or branches for bedding.

Help Preserve Nature's Ground Cover

If a shelter is full, or if you camp away from shelters, try to choose a clear, level site on which to pitch your tent. Site-clearing and ditching around tents are too damaging to soils and vegetation.

Find a Site Out of Sight

As opposed to "concentrated" use at huts or shelters, the object of "dispersed" use is that campers remain unseen. Look for a spot more than ¼ mile off roads, and more than 200 feet off the trail, following any local RUA rules (but dispersed camping has advantages and rewards even where not required by such rules). Use a compass, and check landmarks carefully to find your way to and from your campsite.

Streams — Not Too Close

You will want to find water near your site, but try to put your tent on the same side of the trail as the water, so your path back and forth to the water won't wear a visible track across the main trail. To avoid polluting water supplies, camp at least 200 feet away. Other reasons not to camp too close to a stream or pond are to avoid soil compaction at vulnerable shorelines and to stay above sudden floods.

Don't Be Cut Off

A heavy storm can quickly swell a quiet stream into a rushing torrent. This is especially true during spring runoff, but it can also occur during the summer or fall. In the White Mountains people have been killed trying to cross swollen streams. So, sometimes, it may be important to camp on the side of a river more accessible to civilization.

Use a Portable Stove

In some camping areas, a "human browse line" is quite evident, because people have gathered firewood over the years: limbs are gone from trees, the ground is devoid of dead wood, and vegetation has been trampled as people scoured the area. A stove puts the least pressure on the land. But be careful; stoves can be dangerous.

If You Do Build a Wood Fire . . .

You'll need a campfire permit. In the national forest follow USFS rules (see Section 22). On private land, you need the owner's permission to build a fire, and on state land, you need a state fire permit. Look for wood well away from the site. If you don't disturb the natural vegetation around the site, you will help provide a more enjoyable experience for the next camper. Of course you will put out your fire completely before you leave, but think about dismantling your fireplace so that your fire site is not obvious to others. Make sure, too, that there are no bits of aluminum foil or other unsightly debris left in the ashes.

Water for Drinking and Washing

Wash your dishes and yourself well away from streams, ponds and springs. It's handy to carry a small screen or cloth to filter the dishwater, so you don't leave food remnants strewn about the woods.

Most hikers drink from the streams without ill effect, and

indeed, the pleasure of quaffing a cup of water fresh from a (presumably) pure mountain spring is one of the traditional attractions of the mountains. Unfortunately, in many mountain regions, including the White Mountains, the cysts of the intestinal parasite *giardia* are present in some of the water. A conservative practice is to boil water for 20 minutes or to use an iodine-based disinfectant. Chlorine-based products, such as Halazone, are ineffective in water that contains organic impurities and they deteriorate quickly in the pack. Remember to allow extra contact time (and use twice as many tablets) if the water is very cold.

Think About Human Waste

Keep it at least 200 feet away from water sources. If there are no toilets nearby, dig a trench 6 to 8 inches deep for a latrine and cover it completely when you break camp. The bacteria in the organic layer of the soil will then decompose the waste naturally. (Don't dig the trench too deep, or you will be below the organic layer.)

Hammock Camping

Some campers use hammocks rather than tents. Hanging between trees eliminates even that crushing of groundcover caused by tents. (Hammocks, however, have certain limitations during bug season!) We can all practice low-impact camping by making conscious efforts to preserve the natural forest.

FOLLOWING TRAILS

Most hiking trails are marked with paint on trees or rocks, or (on older trails), with blazes cut into trees. The Appalachian Trail, which crosses most of the higher White Mountains, has vertical rectangular white paint blazes throughout. Side trails off the Appalachian Trail are marked in other colors, such as blue. Above timberline, cairns (piles of rocks) mark the trails. Because hikers have trodden out the vegetation, the footway is usually visible except when it is covered by snow or by fallen leaves. In winter, signs at trailheads and intersections and blazes also are often covered by snow.

There has been logging at one time or another in most of the White Mountains. Trails following or crossing the logging roads require special care at intersections in order to distinguish the trail from diverging roads.

Around shelters or campsites, trodden paths may lead in all directions, so look for signs and paint blazes. If a trail is lost and is not visible to either side, it is usually best to backtrack right away to the last mark seen and look again from there: regularly maintained trails, such as those described in this book, should not just "peter out." Piles of wood or brush are sometimes used to block false trails. Such paths have eroded to the point of becoming rocky stream beds — if a trail seems to disappear at a small brook, it may follow the stream bed.

Caution. Hikers should always carry a compass, and should bear in mind their approximate location on the map. Before entering the woods, make certain which is the north end of the compass needle. Also, remember that the sun, after rising in the east, swings through the south in the middle of the day and sets in the west.

Directions of the compass given in the text are based on *true north* instead of magnetic north, unless otherwise specified. This is important. At the present time there is a deviation of approximately 17 degrees between true north and magnetic north in the general area of the Presidential Range. In the Franconia area, this deviation is 16 degrees, and in the eastern Mahoosucs (Old Speck), it is 17½ degrees. The compass needle points *west* of true north in the northeastern United States. On the maps included with this *Guide,* the longitudinal lines, bottom to top, point to true north. Diagonal light-brown lines, as on the Mt. Washington map, point to magnetic north. In a few places, iron or other mineral deposits may affect compass functioning.

If you become lost from a trail in the White Mountains, it is not necessarily a serious matter. In many instances, retracing your steps will lead you back to the point of departure from the trail. Distances are, as a rule, so short that it is possible to reach a highway in half a day, or at most in a whole day, simply by going downhill, skirting the tops of any dangerous cliffs, until you come upon a river or brook. The stream should then be followed downward. In the Connecticut Lakes, the Upper Androscoggin, and the Magalloway regions described in Section 17, *The North Country*, it would perhaps be safer to follow a compass line for the nearest highway or large stream. Special cautions for dangerous sections of trails appear within the text.

FOR SAFETY AND COMFORT

Let someone else know where you will be hiking. Have the latest guidebook and maps. A good group size is three to four people. Do not let inexperienced people get separated from the group.

Plan to finish your hike with daylight to spare. Hiking after dark, even with flashlights, makes finding trails and crossing streams distinctly harder, and if your flashlight fails, you have a real problem. Remember the shorter days in fall and winter.

Wear comfortable hiking boots. Get the latest weather report and any necessary wilderness entry or campfire permits. If you are going above timberline, carry extra warm and windproof clothing.

Good things to have in your pack for a summer day hike in the White Mountains include: maps, guidebook, water bottle, compass, knife, rain gear, windbreaker, wool sweater(s), hat, waterproof matches, enough food plus extra high-energy foods in reserve (such as chocolate or candy), first aid supplies (including personal medicines, aspirin, bandaids, gauze, and antiseptic), needle and thread, safety pins, parachute cord, trash bag, "mountain money" (toilet paper), and a (small) flashlight with extra batteries.

Bluejeans dry out too slowly in our wet conditions. Most fabrics dry faster than cotton, and wool keeps much of its value even when wet.

For an overnight backpack, you will also need, unless you've made a reservation in an AMC hut, a sleeping bag, pad, tent (shelters are often full), enough lightweight nutritious food, some extra clothes, and probably a stove and fuel. Of course, too much gear can become a burden. At a campsite, you may need to hang up your food to protect it from raccoons or bears.

For emergencies there is a toll-free New Hampshire State Police number 1-800-852-3411. You might want to jot this number down in a handy place, such as the inside front or back cover of this book, along with the AMC Pinkham Notch Camp number (603-466-2727).

THE TREES AND BUSHWHACKING

You can judge your elevation, to an extent, by the vegetation around you. Especially if you want or need to travel off trails, or "bushwhack," a closer acquaintance with the trees can help you to plan your route.

The rich variety of species on the lower slopes diminishes to only a few higher up. In the valleys of the southern White Mountains, at around 1000 feet elevation, some of the most striking trees are the tall white pines, with their needles in 5's. (Smaller ones occasionally occur to about 3000 feet.) A little higher than most white pines, often in ledgy areas, may be some red pines, with thicker twigs and longer needles in 2's. The red maples, with v shaped divisions between leaf lobes, provide autumn glory, as do red oak leaves with their many, irregular, sharp-pointed lobes (white oaks' are rounded).

On some plots in the Hubbard Brook Experimental Forest, between 2000 and 3000 feet above sea level, foresters have found that 90 percent of the trees are either yellow birch (with thin, peeling bark layers), beech (with smooth gray bark on younger trees or limbs), or sugar maple (with u-shaped spaces between its leaf lobes). Sugar maple seedlings apparently prefer to grow under yellow birches, and beech saplings like to grow under sugar maples, while none of the three particularly favors growing under its own kind.

Above about 3000 feet elevation, most of the trees are small evergreens: balsam firs and spruces. If you want to tell them apart, spruce needles have a square cross section and can be rolled between finger and thumb. Balsam needles are flat and do not roll. Hemlocks grow at lower elevations; their needles are flat, like the firs', but shorter.

Near timberline, the small "scrub" or "krummholz" trees grow thickly together and are hard to walk through without a trail, especially uphill, or on ridge crests where they are tangled by the wind. The woods below 3000 feet are more open in all seasons, especially when the leaves are off the trees. So, when bushwhacking, you'll usually go faster if you minimize the distance you travel above 3000 feet. You can often find an old logging road, close to your objective, leading down from about the 2700-foot level to regular trails or roads. There are so many of these old logging roads that only a few of them appear on the maps included with this *Guide*. The first trees to grow into abandoned roads are often white birches, so sometimes an old road will pick up again on the far side of a birch grove.

When bushwhacking on a compass course without other good clues, look at the compass very frequently. Otherwise, for example, while you are trying to slab east along the south side of a descending ridge, you might circle around and end up slabbing west along the north side.

Above timberline, small, delicate alpine flowers can be seen, especially in June in the Alpine Garden on Mt. Washington. Plants, from lichens through trees that grow above about 4000 feet elevation are described in the AMC's *Field Guide to Mountain Flowers of New England*.

SKIING

Some alpine ski trails are described briefly in the text. To locate them, refer to the index under *Skiing*. Except for alpine skiing on Mt. Washington, discussed at the end of Section 1, this *Guide* does not try to cover any kind of skiing (alpine, downhill, or cross-country). Several cross-country (ski-touring) trails are mentioned where they happen to cross hiking trails. They are not indexed.

Abandoned ski trails, owing to their width and their usual zigzag course on steeper slopes, may provide better views than regular summer trails do. On the other hand, they are less shady, the footing may be poor and rough, and some of them cross swampy places that are difficult when not frozen.

On ski trails currently used in winter, summer hiking may promote erosion, a serious concern. Accordingly, the USFS requests that summer hikers not make a practice of using ski trails.

ROCK CLIMBING

Because of extreme hazards to inexperienced or insufficiently equipped climbers or groups, rock climbs are not described in this book. Detailed information concerning a particular route may be obtained from the AMC Mountain Leadership Committee.

Rock climbing is not recommended for hikers in general: it requires special techniques and equipment, and there is greater risk for the unskilled than on trails. Even a slight slip may entail serious consequences. Rock climbing in the White Mountains should not be undertaken except by roped parties under qualified leaders.

OTHER HAZARDS

There are no poisonous snakes or other dangerous animals (except possibly humans) in these mountains. Deer-hunting season is in November, when you'll see many more hunters than deer. The few bears tend to keep well out of sight, except at some popular campsites. Actually, the main risks to look out for on any hiking trip are probably not in the woods at all, but on the highway, going to or from your trailhead.

DISTANCES AND TIMES

The distances and times that appear in the tables at the end of trail descriptions are cumulative from the starting point at the head of each table. Estimated distances are preceded by *est.*

Times are based on a speed of 2 mph, plus an additional half-hour for every 1000 feet gained in elevation. Times are included only to provide a consistent measure for comparison among trails and routes. When no time is given, the route described may be considered a leisurely walk or stroll. With experience, hikers will learn how to correct these standard times for their own normal paces. Bear in mind, however, that if your average pace is faster than the standard time, it will not necessarily be so on trails with steep grades, in wet weather, if you are carrying a heavy pack, or if you are hiking with a group. And in winter, you should roughly double the time it would normally take for you to complete a hike.

The final entry in the distance-time summaries at the end of trail descriptions usually gives the metric equivalent of the total distance, although neither the USGS maps nor the USFS yet use metric measures.

ABBREVIATIONS

The following abbreviations are used in trail descriptions.

hr.	hour(s)
min.	minute(s)
mph	miles per hour
in.	inch(es)
ft.	foot, feet
km.	kilometer(s)
yd.	yard(s)
N.	North (proper name only)

S.	South (proper name only)
E.	East (proper name only)
W.	West (proper name only)
Mt.	Mount (proper name only)
AMC	Appalachian Mountain Club
US	United States
USFS	United States Forest Service
USGS	United States Geological Survey
WMNF	White Mountain National Forest

The following abbreviations are used for organizations that maintain trails, shelters, and other facilities for the public.

AMC	Appalachian Mountain Club
AT	Appalachian Trail
CMC	Chocorua Mountain Club
CTA	Chatham Trails Association
CU	Camp Union
DOC	Dartmouth Outing Club
HA	Hutmen's Association
JCC	Jackson Conservation Commission
MMVSP	Mt. Madison Volunteer Ski Patrol
NHDP	New Hampshire Division of Parks
PEAOC	Phillips Exeter Academy Outing Club
RMC	Randolph Mountain Club
SLA	Squam Lakes Association
SPNHF	Society for the Protection of New Hampshire Forests
SSOC	Sub Sig Outing Club
WMNF	White Mountain National Forest
WODC	Wonalancet Outdoor Club
WVAIA	Waterville Valley Athletic and Improvement Association

The Nancy Pond Trail is currently maintained by Camp Pasquaney and Camp Mowglis maintains several trails in the Cardigan area.

FIRES AND FIRE CLOSURES

Permits to build fires within the WMNF are required except at improved roadside campgrounds, where adequate facilities are provided. Permits can be obtained free of charge from the Supervisor, USFS, Laconia, NH, or from the District Rangers located at Plymouth, Bethlehem, Conway, and Gorham, NH, and Bethel, ME, and from AMC facilities. Campfire permits will be issued for the entire season, except for the Great Gulf and Presidential-Dry River Wilderness Areas. Further information is in Section 22.

During periods when there is a high risk of forest fires, the Forest Supervisor may temporarily close the entire WMNF against public entry. Such general closures apply only as long as the dangerous conditions prevail. Other forest lands throughout New Hampshire or Maine may be closed during similar periods through proclamation by the respective governors. These special closures are given wide publicity so that local residents and visitors alike may realize the dangerous condition of the woods.

MAPS, GUIDES, AND LITERATURE

Extra copies of the maps with the *Guide* may be purchased separately at the AMC Boston and Pinkham Notch offices and at some book and outdoor equipment stores. Elevations of mountain summits not given in the text of this *Guide* may be determined from the maps.

The published topographic quadrangles of the US Geological Survey cover all of New Hampshire. The new USGS 7.5 min. quadrangles are gradually becoming available. Pamphlets published by the WMNF are available free of charge at the Forest Supervisor's Office in Laconia, NH 03246. Other useful maps are: Chocorua Mountain Club Map of the Chocorua Region, NH. Adapted from AMC map of 1966, with panorama from summit of Mt. Chocorua in the margin, published by the CMC. Write to

Chocorua Mountain Club, Box 73, Chocorua, NH 03817, enclosing $1.00.

A detailed map of the Randolph Valley and the Northern Peaks is available (1979 edition) on plastic-coated paper from the Randolph Mountain Club, Randolph, NH 03570. Cost $1.50.

The 1968-69 Navigation Chart of the NH Central Lakes Region shows mountains around Squam, Winnisquam, and Winnipesaukee.

The following may be purchased at the AMC offices at 5 Joy Street, Boston, MA 02108, and at Pinkham Notch Camp: *Monadnock Guide,* covering the history, trails and other features of the area, *Guide to the AT in New Hampshire and Vermont,* and *Guide to the AT in Maine,* published by the Appalachian Trail Conference; *Randolph Paths,* a detailed guide to paths and places around Randolph, published in 1977 by Randolph Mountain Club, Randolph, NH 03570; *Franconia Notch, an In-Depth Guide,* and other guidebooks.

COOPERATION

The AMC earnestly requests that those who use the trails, shelters, and campsites heed the rules of the WMNF, NHDP, and SPNHF (see Section 22), especially those having to do with camping. The same consideration should be shown to private owners.

Trails must not be cut in the WMNF without the approval of the Forest Supervisor at Laconia, NH. The New England Trail Conference (see Section 25) advises that trails should not be blazed or cut elsewhere without consent of the owners and without definite provision for maintenance.

The AMC White Mountain Guide Committee appreciates the comments and suggestions sent in by members of the Club and others, in preparation of this edition. Since the purpose of the *White Mountain Guide* is to furnish accurate details in the text and on the maps, information from any source will be welcome.

If you find inaccuracies, signs missing, obscure places on the trails, or a map that needs correcting, please send report to *White Mountain Guide*, AMC, 5 Joy Street, Boston, MA 02108.

WHITE MOUNTAIN GUIDEBOOK COMMITTEE

Co-editors
Eugene S. Daniell III and Vera V. Smith

Ruth Houghton, *ex-officio*
John E. Auchmoody
D. William and Iris Baird
Lawrence R. Blood
Eugene S. Daniell IV
Benjamin W. English Jr.
John and Margaret Ensor
Joseph J. Hansen
John E. McNamara
Avard Milbury
Kenneth E. Miller
Paul A. Miller
James A. Smith
Stephen and Nina Waite
Edna Welch

SECTION 1

Mount Washington

Mt. Washington (6288 ft.) is the highest peak east of the Mississippi and north of the Carolinas. It was seen from the ocean as early as 1605, and its first recorded ascent was in 1642 by Darby Field and two Indians. It is a huge mountain mass with great ravines cut deep into its sides. Above the ravines are comparatively level stretches called "lawns," which vary in elevation from 5000 to 5500 ft. From these lawns rises the bare, rock-strewn cone or summit, the climate of which is similar to that of northern Labrador. The mountain is on the watershed of three rivers, the Androscoggin, the Connecticut, and the Saco.

This section covers trails on the east slopes of Mt. Washington itself and local trails around the summit. For other approaches see Sections 2 *Northern Peaks*, 3 *Great Gulf*, 4 *Southern Peaks*, and 5 *Montalban Ridge*, which together cover the Presidential Range. For a day hike up Mt. Washington in the summer, popular trails are: from the west, at the Marshfield Station of the cog railway (2700 ft.) via the Ammonoosuc Ravine Trail and Crawford Path (Section 4); or, from the east at Pinkham Notch Camp (2000 ft.) via the Tuckerman Ravine Trail, all the way or via Lion Head.

Most of the Presidential Range is in Restricted Use Areas (camping restricted) and Wilderness Areas, (see Section 22). On the east, in Cutler River drainage (Tuckerman and Huntington Ravines), overnight camping is permitted only at existing shelters, except in winter; see "Hermit Lake Shelters" below.

For those interested in the geological history of Mt. Washington and the Presidential Range, *The Geology of the Mt. Washington Quadrangle* is published by the New Hampshire Department of Resources and Economic Development (603-271-2343).

The visitor who ascends the mountain on foot should carry a compass and should bear in mind that the cog railway on one slope and the Mt. Washington Auto Rd. on another make a line, although a very crooked one, from west to east. If you become

1

lost in a cloud, remember which side of the mountain you are on. Once you have climbed to the upper reaches of the mountain, go north or south, as the case may be, skirting the heads of ravines, and sooner or later you will approach the road or the railroad, landmarks that cannot be missed in the darkest night or the thickest fog, except in winter, when they may be obliterated by snow.

Caution. The appalling and needless loss of life on this mountain has been due largely to the failure of robust hikers to realize that wintry storms of incredible violence occur at times, even during the summer months. Rocks become ice-coated, freezing fog blinds and suffocates, winds of hurricane force exhaust the strongest hikers, and, when they stop to rest, a temperature below freezing completes the tragedy.

If you experience difficult weather, abandon your climb. Storms increase in violence with great rapidity toward the summit. The highest wind velocities ever recorded were attained on Mt. Washington (see the Introduction). Since *the worst is yet to come,* turn back without shame, before it is too late. Don't attempt Mt. Washington if you have coronary problems or are below par physically in any way.

See *The White Mountains in Winter*, Section 21, for detailed information and advice regarding winter climbing.

THE COG RAILWAY

The original Mt. Washington Railroad, known as the cog railway and now extending from the Marshfield station to the summit, was completed in 1869. Its maximum grade, 13½ in. to the yd., is equaled by only one other railroad (excluding funicular roads), that on Pilatus in the Alps. When the cog railway is in operation, walking on the track is not permitted; use the Jewell (Section 2) or the Ammonoosuc Ravine (Section 4) Trail.

There is a parking area below the Marshfield station, owned and operated by the cog railway — fee charged.

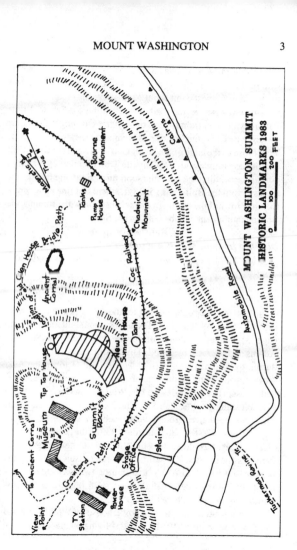

MOUNT WASHINGTON SUMMIT
HISTORIC LANDMARKS 1983

0   100   200 FEET

The cog railway ascends a minor westerly ridge in a nearly straight line to the treeline near Jacob's Ladder (4834 ft.). This trestle, at its highest point about 30 ft. above the mountainside, is the steepest place on the road. Traces of the old Fabyan Bridle Path may be seen from time to time. After crossing the shoulder toward Mt. Clay, the line curves right and crosses the Westside Trail close to the edge of the Great Gulf. Between the Great Gulf and the cog railway lies the Gulfside Trail (Section 2), which, if you are ascending the summit, soon turns right and crosses the tracks. From the Gulf Tank (5638 ft.) there is a fine view across the Gulf toward the Northern Peaks. Just below the summit, the Bourne monument may be seen on the right.

Cog Railway (map 6)

Distance from the Marshfield station

   to Mt. Washington summit: 3 mi., 1 hr. 10 min. via railway

SUMMIT BUILDINGS

No hotel or overnight lodging for the public is available on the summit of Mt. Washington. The new summit building (see map page 3), named in honor of former NH Governor Sherman Adams and operated by the NH Division of Parks and Recreation during the summer season (mid-May to mid-October) has food service, pack room, souvenir shop, public rest rooms, telephone, and a post office. It houses the Mt. Washington Observatory, the Mt. Washington Museum, and facilities for park personnel. There has been a year-round weather observatory on Mt. Washington from 1870 to 1886 and from 1932 to the present.

The Yankee Building was built in 1941 to house transmitter facilities for the first FM station in northern New England. It is now leased by WMTW-TV and houses two-way radio equipment for various state, federal, and local organizations. This building is closed to the public.

The transmitter building and powerhouse for WMTW-TV and WHOM-FM, built in 1954, provides living quarters for station personnel and houses television and microwave equipment. The structure, built to withstand winds of 300 mph, is not open to the public.

The Stage Office, built in 1975 to replace a similar building constructed in 1908, is owned by the Mt. Washington Auto Road Company and used only in connection with their operation.

The first Summit House on Mt. Washington was built in 1852. The first Tip Top House hotel, built in 1853, suffered a fire in 1915. It is now owned by the State of New Hampshire and is part of the Mt. Washington State Park. Plans call for restoring this ancient stone building at a future date. Its use is yet to be decided. At present it is closed to all but park use. The second Summit House, 1873-1908, was destroyed by fire.

THE MOUNT WASHINGTON AUTO ROAD

This road, constructed in 1855-61 and long known as the "Carriage Road," extends from the Glen House site on NH Rte. 16 (Pinkham Notch Highway) to the summit. With long zigzags and an easy grade, it climbs the prominent northeast ridge named for Benjamin Chandler, who died of exposure on the upper part in 1856. Since the upper half is above treeline, it is an interesting way to ascend on foot. The Old Jackson Rd., a hiking trail, is the best approach to the Auto Rd. from Pinkham Notch Camp. Automobiles are charged a toll paid at the foot of the mountain.

The road leaves Rte. 16 opposite the Glen House site (1632 ft.), crosses the Peabody River, and passes the beginning of the Osgood Trail, which diverges right just where the road enters the woods. (There are plans to relocate Rte. 16 about 1.5 mi. north of the Glen House site.) After sharp curves right and then left, just above the 2-mi. mark, the Appalachian Trail crosses. To the right it follows the Madison Gulf Trail (Section 3). "Lowe's Bald Spot," a fine viewpoint about 0.3 mi. from the road, is reached by this trail and a side trail. To the left, the Old Jackson Rd. (trail), after junctions with the Nelson Crag Trail and then

the Raymond Path, leads south to Rte. 16 at Pinkham Notch
Camp. The Halfway House (3840 ft.) is on the right at treeline.
Just above, where there is a fine view to the north, the road skirts
a prominent shoulder, known as the Ledge. A short distance
above this point the Chandler Brook Trail to the Great Gulf
leaves right. Just above the 5-mi. mark, on the right and exactly
at the sharp turn, there are some remarkable folds in the rocks
beside the Auto Rd. At this point, near Cragway *Spring*, the
lower section of the Nelson Crag Trail enters left, and a few yards
above, the upper section diverges left. At about 5.5 mi. the road
passes through the patch of high scrub in which Dr. B.L. Ball
spent two nights in a winter storm in October 1855. A short
distance above the 6-mi. mark, the Wamsutta Trail descends
right to the Great Gulf, and the Alpine Garden Trail diverges left.
The trench-like structures near the road are the remains of the old
Glen House Bridle Path, built in 1853. At the loop of the road at
about 6.5 mi. the Nelson Crag Trail enters left, and just below the
7-mi. mark the Huntington Ravine Trail also enters left. Just
above, in the middle of a lawn known as the "Cow Pasture," the
remains of an old corral are visible. A little beyond on the right
are the cog railway and the Lizzie Bourne monument at the spot
where she perished in September 1855 (the second recorded
fatality on the mountain).

Because of continued theft and destruction of trail signs, they
are now placed on the trails about 100 ft. from the Auto Rd. The
names of some trails that leave the road are painted on a rock at
that point.

There are plans to remove the emergency shelters along the
Auto Rd.

Mt. Washington Auto Rd. (map 6)
Distance from Glen House site (on NH Rte. 16)
    to Mt. Washington Summit: 8 mi. (12.9 km.), 5 hr.

AMC PINKHAM NOTCH CAMP and VICINITY

This camp, originally built in 1920 and greatly enlarged since then, is located on NH Rte. 16 (Pinkham Notch Highway) practically at the height-of-land in the Notch, about 0.8 mi. north of the public parking area near Glen Ellis Falls, about 10 mi. north of Jackson and 11 mi. south of Gorham. It offers food and lodging to the public throughout the year and is managed similarly to the AMC huts (see Section 23, *AMC Activities*). The telephone number is 603-466-2727. Automobiles may be parked at Pinkham Notch Camp.

Concord Trailways offers daily bus service to and from South Station in Boston.

The Tuckerman Ravine Trail, the Lost Pond Trail and the Old Jackson Rd. all start at the camp. The base of the Wildcat Mountain gondola lift, which operates winter and summer, is about 1 mi. north on Rte. 16.

A number of walking trails have been constructed for shorter, easier trips in the Pinkham vicinity. Among these are the Direttissima and the Crew-Cut Trail (see below), and the Square Ledge Trail (Section 14). There are also several ski-touring trails. For information on local ski touring consult personnel at the Camp Trading Post.

Glen Ellis Falls and Crystal Cascade

Glen Ellis Falls are on the Ellis River about 0.8 mi. south of Pinkham Notch Camp. The path leaves the west side of NH Rte. 16 (Pinkham Notch Highway) at the public parking area, passes through a tunnel under the highway to the east side, and leads in about 0.3 mi. to the foot of the main fall, which is about 70 ft. high. Below it are several pools and smaller falls.

Crystal Cascade is easily reached by the Tuckerman Ravine Trail (see below).

The Direttissima (MMVSP)

This trail, which runs between the Glen Boulder Trail and Pinkham Notch Camp, was cut in 1969-71 to avoid hiking on NH Rte. 16 (Pinkham Notch Highway), as well as the sometimes difficult crossing of the Ellis River via Lost Pond Trail. It runs through the woods on the west side of Rte. 16, more or less parallel to the road.

Its start at Pinkham Notch Camp just south of the highway bridge over the Cutler River is indicated by a sign at the edge of the woods. Marked by red paint blazes, the trail turns sharp left about 10 yd. into the woods and follows a cleared area south. It turns slightly west at the end of this clearing and winds generally south, crossing a small brook, skirts through the upper (west) end of a gorge, and then crosses the New River.

The trail continues past an excellent viewpoint looking down the Notch, climbs alongside a cliff, crosses another runoff brook, and ends at the Glen Boulder Trail near the junction of the Chimney Bypass and the Chimney branch of that trail, above the Chimney.

Direttisima Trail (map 6)
Distance from Pinkham Notch Camp
  to Glen Boulder Trail: *est*. 0.6 mi., 35 min.

Crew-Cut Trail, George's Gorge, Liebeskind's Loop (MMVSP)

This trail system, in the woods north of Pinkham Notch Camp and between the Old Jackson Rd. and NH Rte. 16 (Crawford Notch Highway), offers some easy, low-level woods walking through interesting terrain with two good lookout points.

Crew-Cut Trail

The Crew-Cut starts at the Old Jackson Rd., leaving right after a stream crossing near where the abandoned section of the road proper, enters on the right from Rte. 16, and where the Old Jackson Rd. starts to climb steeply. After crossing a stony, dry brook bed it runs generally east-northeast, crossing two runoff brooks, in one of which there is usually *water*. On the east bank of this brook the George's Gorge Trail leaves left, leading up beside the brook, steeply in some places, for example when it passes Chudacoff Falls, until it reaches a knob, from where it descends west to the Old Jackson Rd. in its upper, flat section.

The Crew-Cut continues its same general line, rising gradually through open woods in a long slabbing of the slope and crossing several gullies. It skirts southeast of the steeper rocky outcroppings until it reaches the base of a cliff. At this point the main trail turns sharply right (south) while a very short side trail leads straight ahead and directly up to a lookout, "Lila's Ledge." From this ledge you can look straight in at the Wildcat ski-trail complex, down the Notch over the AMC buildings, and up at Mt. Washington over Huntington Ravine.

The main trail makes a sharp turn around the nose of the cliff and then resumes its generally east-northeast direction. In about 50 ft. Liebeskind's Loop enters left, coming down from the knob at the high point on the George's Gorge Trail. The Crew-Cut continues its descent over a few small ledges and through open woods until it passes east of a small high-level bog formed by an old beaver dam. Shortly thereafter, it goes through open woods again, emerging at the top of the grassy slope on Rte. 16 almost opposite the south end of the Wildcat parking lot.

Crew-Cut Trail

Distance from Old Jackson Rd.

   to NH Rte. 16: *est.* 1 mi., 45 min. to 1 hr.

   (with time allowed for lookout)

Liebeskind's Loop

Liebeskind's Loop, cut in 1974, makes a loop hike possible (using the Crew-Cut, George's Gorge, Loop, and Crew-Cut trails) without resorting to return either by Rte. 16 or by the steep section of the Old Jackson Rd. The Loop leaves right (east) near the top of the George's Gorge Trail just before the latter makes the final short ascent to the knob, where a short spur to the left (south) leads to an excellent view of Wildcat Mountain and Huntington and Tuckerman ravines. It descends to a swampy flat, then rises through a spruce thicket to the top of a cliff, where there is a fine lookout with a good view down Pinkham Notch. Here the trail turns left and runs along the edge of the cliff, finally descending by an easy zigzag in a gully to a beautiful open grove of birches. The cliff above this grove offers interesting possibilities for rock climbers. The trail continues east, descending through two gorges and skirting the east end of rises until it finally climbs a ridge and descends 50 yd. on the other side to join the Crew-Cut Trail just east of Lila's Ledge. The Crew-Cut can then be followed back to the starting point.

This loop hike is best made in the direction described, since the Gorge is most interesting on the ascent and the Loop is more interesting on the descent.

Liebeskind's Loop Trail
Distance from Crew-Cut start

to Crew-Cut start (loop): *est*. 2 mi., 1½-2 hr.

(with time allowed for lookouts)

Old Jackson Road (AMC)

This trail runs north from Pinkham Notch Camp to the Mt. Washington Auto Rd. It is part of the Appalachian Trail and is blazed in white. It diverges right from the Tuckerman Ravine Trail about 50 yd. from the camp. After about 0.3 mi. it begins to ascend steeply and steadily and the Crew-Cut Trail leaves right (east). Upon reaching the height-of-land, where the George's Gorge Trail leaves right (east), the Old Jackson Rd. descends slightly, crosses several brooks, and at a large one takes a sharp left uphill (1977 relocation). After a short, steep climb it slabs along, the Raymond Path enters left, several small brooks are crossed, and then the Nelson Crag Trail enters left. Continuing north the trail climbs slightly, continues through an old gravel pit and meets the Auto Rd. just above the 2-mi. mark, opposite the Madison Gulf Trail.

Old Jackson Rd. (map 6)
Distance from Pinkham Notch Camp
 to Mt. Washington Auto Rd.: 1.8 mi. (2.9 km.), 1¼ hr.

NELSON CRAG TRAIL (AMC)

This trail leaves the Auto Rd. left with the Old Jackson Rd. and Raymond Path, just above the 2-mi. mark and opposite the Madison Gulf Trail. It soon diverges right and bears southwest, then almost due west, climbing steadily with some sharp ascents. After about 1 mi. it rises steeply out of the scrub, emerging on a watershed ridge from which there is an unusual view of Pinkham Notch in both directions. It then bears slightly north, climbs moderately over open ledges, and joins the Auto Rd. near Cragway *Spring,* at the sharp turn about 0.3 mi. above the 5-mi. mark. A few yards above, the trail again diverges left from the Auto Rd. and climbs steeply to the crest of the ridge. It travels over Nelson Crag, crosses the Alpine Garden Trail, passes between two humps and again joins the road at the east corner of the big loop, about 0.5 mi. below the 7-mi. mark.

Nelson Crag Trail (map 6)
Distances from two-mile mark on Auto Rd.
 to about 0.3 mi. above five-mile mark: 1.6 mi., 1 hr. 40 min.
 to about 0.5 mi. below seven-mile mark: 2.6 mi. (4.2 km.),
    2½ hr.

TUCKERMAN RAVINE TRAIL (WMNF)

Tuckerman Ravine is a remarkable glacial cirque in the southeast side of the mountain, named for the botanist Professor Edward Tuckerman.

Below Hermit Lake the tractor road, or Fire Trail, has superseded the original trail, which had become badly eroded after many years of heavy usage.

Information on Hermit Lake camping shelters appears below.

The path leaves the west side of Rte. 16 (Pinkham Notch Highway) at Pinkham Notch Camp 10 mi. north of Jackson. In about 0.3 mi. it crosses a bridge to the south bank of Cutler River. A few yards beyond it turns sharply right and climbs to the best viewpoint of the Crystal Cascade, a few steps off the path, right.

From this point the path bears left, ascends gradually for a short distance and then turns right. At this point Boott Spur Trail leaves left. The Tuckerman Trail continues ahead with two long switchbacks. Above these, the path continues west, ascending by steady grades. At about 1.3 mi. the Huntington Ravine Trail diverges right. A short distance above, the trail crosses two branches of the Cutler River, and then the Huntington Fire Rd., which is the best route to Huntington Ravine in winter, leaves right. Above here, at 2.1 mi., the Raymond Path enters right, at a point where the Tuckerman Trail turns sharply left. About 250 yd. farther, the Boott Spur Link diverges left, and directly opposite the Lion Head Trail diverges right.

Just beyond the buildings, the trail joins the old trail near Hermit Lake. By following the old trail east a few yards to the top of a short rise, a remarkable view is obtained, especially in winter. The cliff on the right is Lion Head, so called because of its appearance from the Glen House site. The more distant crags on the left are the Hanging Cliffs of Boott Spur.

The main trail keeps to the right (north) of the stream. It ascends a well-constructed footway into the floor of the ravine, and finally, at the foot of the headwall, bears right and ascends a steep slope of debris, where the Snow Arch, can be found on the left in the spring, when the snowfield above the Snow Arch usually extends across the trail. The arch is formed by a stream of snow meltwater which flows under the snowfield. The snow in the ravine may persist until late summer, although the arch does not always form. *Caution.* Do not approach too near the arch and *under no circumstances* cross or venture beneath it: one death and some narrow escapes have already resulted. Sections weighing tons may break off at any moment. If the snow extends across the trail, it is better to use the Lion Head Trail. In the spring and fall the WMNF often closes the section of trail up over the headwall because of snow and ice. In the winter this section is impassable except for experienced and well-equipped snow and ice climbers. When ascending the headwall, be careful not to start rocks rolling, since such carelessness may put others in serious danger.

Turning sharp left at the top of the debris slope and traversing under a cliff, the trail emerges from the ravine and climbs almost straight west up a grassy, ledgy slope. About 200 yd. below Tuckerman Junction, the Alpine Garden Trail, which leads to the Lion Head Trail, the Alpine Garden and Mt. Washington Auto Rd., diverges right. At Tuckerman Junction, at the top of the plateau, the Tuckerman Crossover leads almost straight ahead (southwest) to the Crawford Path near the Lakes of the Clouds Hut; the Southside Trail leads west and northwest, skirting the cone to the Davis Path; and the Lawn Cutoff leads left (south) to the Davis Path. The Tuckerman Ravine Trail turns sharp right and, marked by cairns and painted rocks, ascends the rocks to the Auto Rd. near the summit. About a third of the way up the cone, at Cloudwater *Spring*, the Lion Head Trail enters right.

In descending, the trail leaves the right side of the Auto Rd. a few yards below the lower parking area.

Tuckerman Ravine Trail (map 6)
Distances from Pinkham Notch Camp

   to Crystal Cascade: *est.* 0.4 mi.

   to Huntington Ravine Trail: *est.* 1.3 mi., 1 hr.

   to Raymond Path: 2.1 mi., 1¾ hr.

   to Lion Head Trail and Boott Spur Link: 2.3 mi.

   to Hermit Lake shelters: 2.4 mi., 2 hr.

   to Snow Arch: 3.1 mi., 2¾ hr.

   to Tuckerman Junction: 3.6 mi., 3½ hr.

   to Mt. Washington summit: 4.1 mi. (6.6 km.), 4½ hr.

Hermit Lake Shelters

The Hermit Lake Shelters are lean-tos open to the public. Tickets for shelter space must be purchased at Pinkham Notch Camp in person (first come, first served) for a nominal fee. The tickets are nontransferable and nonrefundable. They may be purchased for a maximum of seven consecutive nights. Overnight use is limited to the 86 spaces in the shelters. Ten tent sites for 40 people are available between December 1 and April 1. Fee $1.75 per person per night. Users may no longer kindle charcoal or wood fires; people intending to cook must bring their own small stoves. Day visitors and shelter users alike are *required to carry out all their own trash and garbage*. No receptacles are provided. This operating policy is under continual review, so it can change from time to time. Information is available at the caretaker's residence. There is no warming room open to the public, and refreshments are not sold.

RAYMOND PATH (AMC)

This old trail extends from the Mt. Washington Auto Rd. to the Tuckerman Ravine Trail.

It leaves the Auto Rd. along with the Old Jackson Rd. and the Nelson Crag Trail just above the 2-mi. mark, opposite the Madison Gulf Trail. Soon, the Nelson Crag Trail diverges right. A little farther, so does the Raymond Path. It crosses several streams, first a branch of the Peabody and then branches of the Cutler River. It crosses the Huntington Ravine Trail near the largest stream and ends about 0.5 mi. beyond, at the Tuckerman Ravine Trail.

Raymond Path (map 6)

Distances from Glen House site on NH Rte. 16

   to north terminus of Raymond Path: 2 mi., 1 hr. 10 min.

   to Tuckerman Ravine Trail: 4.4 mi., 2¾ hr.

   to Hermit Lake (via Tuckerman Ravine Trail): 4.7 mi., 3 hr.

   to Mt. Washington summit (via Tuckerman Ravine Trail): 6.4 mi. (10.3 km.), 5½ hr.

HUNTINGTON RAVINE TRAIL (AMC)

This ravine was named in honor of Professor J. H. Huntington in 1871.

Caution. This is the most difficult trail in the White Mountains. Although experienced hikers who are comfortable on steep rock probably will encounter little difficulty when conditions are good, the exposure on several of the ledges is likely to prove extremely unnerving to novices and to those who are uncomfortable in steep places. The trail is very dangerous when wet or icy. Extreme caution must be exercised at all times. Descent by this trail is strongly discouraged. Since retreat under unfavorable conditions can be extremely difficult and hazardous, one should never venture beyond the "Fan" in deteriorating conditions or when weather on the Alpine Garden is likely to be severe. During late fall, winter, and early spring, this trail (and any part of the ravine headwall) should be attempted only by those with full technical ice-climbing gear and training. In particular, the ravine must not be regarded as a viable "escape route" from the Alpine Garden in severe winter conditions.

Between Raymond Path and the boulders, care must be taken to differentiate the trail from a service road that crosses the trail.

The trail diverges right from the Tuckerman Ravine Trail about 1.3 mi. from Pinkham Notch Camp. In about 0.3 mi. it crosses the Cutler River and, in another 150 yd., the brook that drains Huntington Ravine. At about 0.5 mi. from the Tuckerman Ravine Trail, it crosses the Raymond Path. Above this junction it crosses the brook and the Huntington Ravine Fire Rd. several times. In the floor of the ravine there are some interesting boulders near the path; their tops afford good views of the ravine. Beyond the scrubby trees is a steep slope, covered with broken rock, known as the "Fan," whose tip lies at the foot of the deepest gully. To the left of this gully are precipices, the lower is known as the "Pinnacle." After passing through the boulders the path ascends the left side of the Fan for about 60 ft., then turns right, and, marked by yellow blazes on the rocks, crosses a stream and ascends the north (right) side of the Fan to its tip. The trail then climbs the rocks to the right of the main gully. The route follows the line of least difficulty and should be followed carefully over the ledges, which are dangerous, especially when wet. Above the first ledges the trail climbs steeply through scrub and over short sections of rock, with some fairly difficult scrambles, to the top of the headwall where it crosses the Alpine Garden Trail. From this point it ascends gradually to the Mt. Washington Auto Rd. just below the 7-mi. mark.

Huntington Ravine Trail (map 6)

Distances from Pinkham Notch Camp

to Huntington Ravine Trail: 1.3 mi., 1 hr.

to Raymond Path: 1.8 mi., 1 hr. 20 min.

to top of Fan: 3 hr.

to Alpine Garden Trail crossing: 3.3 mi., 4 hr.

to seven-mile mark on Auto Rd.: 3.5 mi., 4 hr. 25 min.

to Mt. Washington Summit (via Auto Rd.): 4.5 mi. (7.2 km.), 5 hr.

RAVINE OF RAYMOND CATARACT

There is no trail up the ravine, just north of Lion Head. Underbrush has completely covered most of a former footway. Water in the ravine may be unfit to drink (summit drainage).

LION HEAD TRAIL (AMC)

This trail diverges right from the Tuckerman Ravine Trail just below Hermit Lake, opposite the foot of the Boott Spur Link. Running north, it diverges from the original trail (used as a winter route) in about 150 yd. and climbs the steep slope by switchbacks, reaching treeline in about 0.5 mi. The trail then bears left, ascends the open slope to the left, and rejoins the original trail about 0.2 mi. farther along, just below the lower

Lion Head. The trail continues over the lower and upper Heads, with impressive views and with little grade over the open spur to the Alpine Garden Trail, which it crosses. After passing through a belt of scrub, it ascends to the Tuckerman Ravine Trail, which it enters at Cloudwater *Spring* about a third of the way up the cone of Mt. Washington.

Lion Head Trail (map 6)

Distance from leaving to rejoining Tuckerman Ravine Trail:
  1.1 mi. (1.8 km.), 1¾ hr.

  Note. The old Lion Head route is closed for summer use due to its steepness and severe erosion. It may be used as a direct winter route when conditions permit.

BOOTT SPUR TRAIL (AMC)

Boott Spur (5500 ft.) is the prominent ridge running south from Mt. Washington, connected by Bigelow Lawn. This was the route for many early ascents of Mt. Washington.

The trail diverges left from the Tuckerman Ravine Trail 350 ft. above the side path to Crystal Cascade, at a sharp right turn. It crosses the John Sherburne Ski Trail, bears right, soon crosses a small brook (*water unreliable*), bears sharp left at the base of a rocky ledge, and, a short distance beyond, makes a sharp right turn and ascends a former logging road, which it leaves in about 0.3 mi. to emerge on a restricted outlook across Pinkham Notch. Descending slightly, the trail shortly makes a sharp right turn, where a side trail (left) leads in 120 ft. to a view east. The trail then passes through some interesting woods, ascends the south side of a small wooded ridge, crosses a south outlook and turns right. It soon reaches a short moist area and ascends (northwest) a steep slope. Halfway up the slope a side trail leads left 300 ft. to a brook (*last water*). At the top of this slope a side trail leads right (east) to an interesting outlook (30 ft.) with the first view of Split Rock on the treeless ridge.

At this junction the trail turns left, continues upward at moderate grades, heads more north, shortly makes a sharp left turn, and comes out on a scrub point with a view of the summit of Mt. Washington and north toward Gorham. Turning more to the west, the trail enters thicker woods and ascends steadily for 0.3 mi. where a short trail right leads to Ravine Outlook, with Lion Head directly in front of the summit. A few steps farther on this side trail, Tuckerman Ravine comes into full view. The main trail continues ahead for 0.1 mi., then emerges from the trees, soon bears left (south) and slabs the ridge to Split Rock, which you can pass through or go around. The trail then turns right, rises steeply over two minor humps to a broad, flat ridge, where Boott Spur Link (right) descends to the Tuckerman Ravine Trail near Hermit Lake. Above this point the trail follows the ridge, which consists of a series of steplike levels and steep slopes. The views of the ravine are excellent, particularly where the path skirts the dangerous Hanging Cliff, 1500 ft. above Hermit Lake. After passing the summit of the Spur, the trail ends at the Davis Path.

Boott Spur Trail (map 6)
Distances from divergence with Tuckerman Ravine Trail
    to first view of Pinkham Notch: 5 mi., 25 min.
    to path to brook: 9 mi., 1 hr.
    to ravine outlook: 1.6 mi., 1 hr. 50 min.
    to Split Rock: 1.9 mi., 2 hr. 10 min.
    to Boott Spur Link: 2.1 mi., 2 hr. 25 min.
    to Davis Path junction: 2.8 mi., 3 hr.
Distances from Pinkham Notch Camp
    to Davis Path junction: 3.3 mi., 3¼ hr.
    to Mt. Washington summit (via Davis and Crawford paths) 5.4 mi. (8.6 km.), 4¾ hr.

Boott Spur Link (AMC)

This trail diverges left from the Tuckerman Ravine Trail just below Hermit Lake, opposite the foot of the Lion Head Trail. It immediately crosses two branches of Cutler River and the John

Sherburne Ski Trail, then runs straight up the side of the ridge very steeply through scrub until it tops the ridge, and ends in a few yards at Boott Spur Trail.

Boott Spur Link (map 6)
Distance from Tuckerman Ravine Trail
   to Boott Spur Trail: .6 mi. (1 km.), ¾ hr.

GLEN BOULDER TRAIL (AMC)

This trail from NH Rte. 16 (Pinkham Notch Highway) to the Davis Path reaches treeline at a low altitude, and in conjunction with the Wildcat Ridge Trail forms the most direct route between Carter Notch and Lakes of the Clouds huts.

The trail, blazed in orange, leaves the west side of Rte. 16 at the parking area near Glen Ellis Falls. It ascends gradually for about 0.3 mi. to the base of a small cliff. You can go up the cliff via the "Chimney Route" or, preferably, take the Chimney Bypass, which goes around to the right of the cliff. After a short, steep climb on the Bypass, the Direttissima from Pinkham Notch Camp enters from the right (north). The Glen Boulder Trail swings south, the Chimney Route enters left, and then a short branch trail leads left to an outlook on the brink of a cliff, which commands a fine view of Wildcat Mountain and Pinkham Notch. The main trail turns west, rises gradually, then steepens, reaching the north bank of a brook draining the minor ravine south of the Gulf of Slides in about another 0.5 mi. Near here, the Avalanche Brook Ski Touring Trail crosses (with blue plastic markers); it is not suitable for hiking. Following the brook, which soon divides, the trail turns southwest, crosses both branches *(water)* about 0.9 mi. from the road. It is level for 200 yd., then climbs rapidly the northeast side of the spur through evergreens, giving views of the minor ravine and spur south of the Gulf of Slides. Leaving the trees, it climbs about 0.3 mi. over open rocks to the Glen Boulder, an immense stone perched on the end of the spur, a familiar landmark for all who travel Rte. 16. The view is wide, from Chocorua around to Mt. Washington, and is particularly fine of Wildcat Mountain.

From the boulder the trail climbs steeply up the open spur, about 0.5 mi., then ascends moderately through high scrub. About 0.8 mi. above the boulder a side trail descends right about 40 yd. to a *spring*. The main trail continues to Slide Peak, the low peak heading the Gulf of Slides, then turns north, descends slightly, soon leaves the scrub, and about 0.3 mi. below the summit of Boott Spur, enters the Davis Path.

Descending, diverge left from the Davis Path at a sign about 0.3 mi. below the summit of the Spur.

Glen Boulder Trail (map 6)

Distances from Glen Ellis parking area on NH Rte. 16

> *to* to outlook: 0.4 mi., 25 min.
> *to* brook crossing: 0.9 mi., 40 min.
> *to* Glen Boulder: 1.5 mi., 1¾ hr.
> *to* spring: 2.2 mi., 2 hr. 25 min.
> *to* Slide Peak: 2.5 mi., 2 hr. 40 min.
> *to* Davis Path junction: 3.1 mi. (5 km.), 3 hr. 10 min.
> *to* Boott Spur summit (via Davis Path): 3.5 mi., 3½ hr.
> *to* Crawford Path junction (via Davis Path): 4.9 mi., 4¼ hr.
> *to* Mt. Washington summit (via Davis and Crawford paths): 5.6 mi., 5 hr.
> *to* to Mt. Washington summit (via Davis Path, Bigelow Lawn Cutoff, and Tuckerman Ravine Trail): 5.1 mi., 4¾ hr.
> *to* Lakes of the Clouds Hut (via Davis Path, Camel Trail and Crawford Path): 5.1 mi., 4 hr. 5 min.

THE GULF OF SLIDES

The broad ravine southeast of Boott Spur is known as the Gulf of Slides from the many landslides and winter avalanches that have scarred its upper slopes. Enclosing the ravine on the south is the spur on which the Glen Boulder is located. The ravine can be reached by the Gulf of Slides Ski Trail (see below).

ALPINE GARDEN TRAIL (AMC)

This trail leads from the Tuckerman Ravine Trail through a series of grassy lawns called the Alpine Garden to the Mt. Washington Auto Rd. It forms a convenient connecting link between the trails on the east side of the mountain. Aside from its beauty, it allows various combinations of routes for those who do not wish to visit the summit.

The tiny alpine flowers, best seen in June, include the five-petaled white Diapensia, the bell-shaped pink-magenta Lapland Rosebay, and rarer blooms. (See the AMC's *Field Guide to Mountain Flowers of New England* and *At Timberline: A Nature Guide to the Mountains of the Northeast*.) No plants should be picked without written USFS permission. Hikers are urged to stay on trails or walk on rocks so as not to kill fragile alpine vegetation.

The trail diverges right from the Tuckerman Ravine Trail a short distance above the ravine headwall, about 200 yd. below Tuckerman Junction. It leads northeast, bearing toward Lion Head, and crosses the Lion Head Trail. About 50 yd. before the crossing is a WMNF sign "Right Gully" with a right arrow, to guide winter hikers and skiers. Beyond the crossing the trail leads north, its general direction, until it ends at the road. It traverses the Alpine Garden and crosses a tiny stream, which is the headwater of Raymond Cataract. (*This water is unfit to drink:* it consists largely of drainage from the summit buildings.) The cataract itself is not visible from the trail, which soon approaches the head of Huntington Ravine and crosses the Huntington Ravine Trail. Here, a little off the trail, there is a fine view of this impressive ravine. Rising to the top of the ridge, the trail crosses the Nelson Crag Tail, then descends and soon enters the old Glen House Bridle Path, constructed in 1853, whose course is still plain although it was abandoned about a century ago. In a short distance the Alpine Garden Trail leads left and in a few yards enters the Auto Rd. a short distance above the 6-mi. mark, and opposite the upper terminus of the Wamsutta Trail.

Alpine Garden Trail (map 6)

Distances from Tuckerman Ravine Trail

to Lion Head Trail crossing: *est.* 0.3 mi.

to Huntington Ravine Trail crossing: *est.* 1.3 mi.

to Auto Rd. junction: 1.8 mi. (2.9 km.), 1 hr.

SOUTHSIDE TRAIL (AMC)

This trail diverges right (west) from Tuckerman Crossover about 10 yd. southwest of Tuckerman Junction and, skirting the southwest side of the cone of Mt. Washington, enters the Davis Path near its junction with the Crawford Path. It forms a link between Tuckerman Ravine and the Westside Trail.

Southside Trail (map 6)

Distance from Tuckerman Crossover

to Davis Path junction: about 0.3 mi., 10 min.

TUCKERMAN CROSSOVER (AMC)

This trail leaves the Tuckerman Ravine Trail left (southwest) at Tuckerman Junction (where the latter trail turns sharply right to ascend the cone). It rises again gradually across Bigelow Lawn, crosses the Davis Path, then descends somewhat steeply to the Crawford Path, which it meets along with the Camel Trail a short distance above the upper Lake of the Clouds. Turning left on the Crawford Path, the Lakes of the Clouds Hut is reached in a few hundred feet.

Tuckerman Crossover (map 6)

Distances from Tuckerman Junction

to Crawford Path junction: 0.8 mi.

to Lakes of the Clouds Hut (via Crawford Path): 0.9 mi. (1.4 km.), ½ hr.

LAWN CUTOFF (AMC)

This trail diverges right from the Davis Path about 0.5 mi. north of Boott Spur and leads north across Bigelow Lawn to the Tuckerman Ravine Trail at Tuckerman Junction. With the Tuckerman Ravine Trail it forms the shortest route from Boott Spur to the summit of Mt. Washington.

Lawn Cutoff (map 6)

Distance from Davis Path

to Tuckerman Ravine Trail junction: 0.4 mi. (0.7 km.), ¼ hr.

CAMEL TRAIL (AMC)

This trail, connecting Boott Spur with the Lakes of the Clouds Hut, takes its name from certain ledges on Boott Spur, which, seen against the skyline, resemble a kneeling camel.

The trail is the right of the two that diverge right (east) from the Crawford Path a short distance above the upper Lake of the Clouds (the Tuckerman Crossover is the left of the diverging trails). It ascends easy grassy slopes, crosses the old location of the Crawford Path, and continues in a practically straight line across the level stretch of Bigelow Lawn. It aims directly toward the ledges forming the "camel," passes under the camel's nose, and joins the Davis Path about 100 yd. northwest of the Lawn Cutoff.

Camel Trail (map 6)

Distance from Crawford Path

to Davis Path junction: 0.7 mi. (1.1 km.), 25 min.

WESTSIDE TRAIL (WMNF)

This trail, partially constructed by pioneer AMC trailmaker J. Rayner Edmands, is wholly above timberline. By avoiding the summit of Mt. Washington, it saves nearly 1 mi. in distance and 700 ft. in elevation between points on the Northern Peaks and on the Crawford Path. The trail diverges left from the Crawford Path, at about 5500 ft., just where the path begins to climb the cone of Mt. Washington, and skirts the cone. It crosses under the Mt. Washington cog railway just before entering the Gulfside trail.

Westside Trail (map 6)
Distance from Crawford Path
   to Gulfside Trail junction: 0.9 mi. (1.4 km.), 35 min.

TRINITY HEIGHTS CONNECTOR

This newly constructed trail allows the Appalachian Trail to make a loop over the summit of Mt. Washington. From the true summit (marked by a large sign) it runs approximately northwest for 0.3 mi. to the Gulfside Trail, not far from its junction with the Crawford Path.

SKIING

For skiers on Mt. Washington, "winter" means December to June. Tuckerman Ravine or the Mt. Washington Auto Rd. offer skiing opportunities throughout this season. The Auto Rd. can be packed, icy, and rough at times, especially after a vehicle has traveled to or from the summit, as when the staff changes shifts at the Mt. Washington Observatory. The areas between the top of the Tuckerman headwall and the summit cone, and Chandler Ridge near the 6-mi. mark on the Auto Rd., afford good spring skiing at all levels, but are hard to reach because of their elevation. Usually, the cog railway resumes operations on May 30, and there is frequently good skiing on the cone for a few weeks after that. Skiing areas in the ravine, in the Gulf of Slides, or on any other part of the mountain above timberline, are subject to wide temperature variations within short periods of time. The difference between corn snow and ice or bathing suits and parkas may be an hour, or even less, when clouds roll in or the afternoon sun drops behind a shoulder of the mountain. Skiers should prepare accordingly.

Tuckerman Ravine

By late February or early March sufficient snow has accumulated in this ravine to provide open-slope skiing at all levels. Because of the nature of the ravine, the snow is pocketed as it falls and blows over the headwall. As it drifts in, slopes of all degrees form. High on the headwall they are very steep; on the floor they are gradual. By the middle of March, when the snow is deepest, the drop from the top of the headwall to the floor is about 800 ft., and climbing on the headwall is hazardous because snowslides are likely.

In the first half of April the snow is well packed and conditions are usually ideal. Descents over the headwall and down the various gullies are only for expert skiers. For intermediate skiers, there are the lower slopes on the headwall and in the gullies for open running under ideal conditions.

During the last half of April the snow settles and melts, crevasses form along the upper stretches of the headwall, and large cracks appear in the floor. Masses of snow and ice that continually break off from the upper gullies and the headwall and roll into the ravine are a hazard. Extreme care should be exercised, and the more dangerous parts of the upper slopes should be avoided. Those who run the headwall should take care to avoid the crevasses.

The skiing season in the ravine continues through to May, and often enough snow is available for persistent skiers until June.

The ravine area and the John Sherburne Ski Trail (see below) are patrolled by the USFS and the Mt. Washington Volunteer Ski Patrol. Sections that are unsafe because of ice or possible avalanches are posted at the shelter area.

John Sherburne Ski Trail (WMNF). This ski trail connects

Tuckerman Ravine to Pinkham Notch Camp. It is named for the late John H. Sherburne, Jr., through whose efforts this trail in large part came about. It leaves NH Rte. 16 (Pinkham Notch Highway) about 200 ft. south of the camp and ascends to the little headwall of the ravine by a zigzag course, keeping at all times left (south) of the Tuckerman Ravine Trail and the Cutler River. Just below Hermit Lake a short side trail leads right to the Hermit Lake Shelters. From the top of the little headwall to the floor of the ravine the trail lies on the north of the stream. It is 10 to 50 ft. wide, and the slope is suitable for expert and intermediate skiers at some points, but less expert skiers can negotiate this trail because of its width. There should be 15 in. of packed snow for good skiing.

Tuckerman Ravine Trail, a graded path 6 to 12 ft. wide, extends from the camp to the Hermit Lake Shelters area. It usually can be climbed on foot by skiers without sealskins or other climbing aids, since the trail is generally well packed by USFS vehicles and heavy hiking traffic. Downhill skiing is not permitted because of the risk it creates for those ascending or descending on foot.

Skiing on the Mount Washington Auto Road

The Auto Rd. offers easy access to the summit and such places as Chandler Ridge. Many portions of the upper half of the road are often blown bare, but the 4 miles from the Halfway House to NH Rte. 16 (Pinkham Notch Highway), a drop of 2200 ft., make a good run from late December to the middle of April for novice and intermediate skiers. Good skiing requires 5 in. of packed snow. However, because of winter truck traffic, the road may be badly rutted and cut up, and consequently poor for skiing. There are plans to remove the emergency shelters along the road.

Old Jackson Rd. With 8 in. of snow, this is a good run for all levels. It may be used as the ski route between Pinkham Notch Camp and the Auto Rd. It drops 650 ft. and can be run in 30 min. The ascent takes 1 hr. Skiers should use the old trail instead of the relocation; enter the Old Jackson Rd. below the 2-mi. mark, about 0.2 mi. below where the relocation and the Madison Gulf Trail meet at the Auto Rd.

Raymond Path. This is not a ski run, but it affords a route between Tuckerman Ravine Trail and the Auto Rd. It is wide on the level sections, but narrow and difficult on the steep pitches. In deep snow, the trail is often obscure. It drops, not uniformly, about 700 ft. toward the north and east.

Gulf of Slides

This area, which is situated somewhat similarly to Tuckerman Ravine, receives a large volume of snow that remains in the ravine, so open-slope skiing is possible well into the spring (April and May). Its slopes, though less severe than those in Tuckerman, are more uniform and avalanche frequently.

Gulf of Slides Ski Trail (WMNF) leaves Rte. 16 about 100 yd. south of Pinkham Notch Camp and ascends west 2200 ft. in about 2.5 mi. to the bowl of the Gulf of Slides.

The Northern Peaks

This name is given to the northern part of the Presidential Range, which extends north and then northeast from Mt. Washington with peaks in the following order: Mt. Clay (5532 ft.), Mt. Jefferson (5715 ft.), Mt. Adams (5798 ft.), Mt. Madison (5363 ft.). Pine Mountain (2404 ft.) stands at the end of the range across the Dolly Copp (Pinkham B) Rd. The four main peaks constitute a great ridge 5 mi. long that averages over 5000 ft. above sea-level, and each of these four peaks rises several hundred feet above the ridge. Two prominent minor summits of Mt. Adams form a part of the crest of the main ridge, Sam Adams (5585 ft.) and John Quincy Adams (about 5470 ft.).

The AMC Mt. Washington Range map (map 6) shows all of the Northern Peaks. The 1979 RMC map of the Randolph Valley and Northern Peaks is available for $2; its larger scale is useful for the dense trail network on the north slopes. The guidebook *Randolph Paths,* 1977 ed., is $1.50 (Randolph Mountain Club, Randolph, NH 03570).

This entire section is a Restricted Use Area, with no camping, wood, or charcoal fires permitted above timberline or within 200 ft. of trails (see Section 22). Hikers are urged to stay on trails when above timberline, to preserve thin soils and fragile alpine plants.

The upper part of the mass of the Northern Peaks is covered with fragments of rock. Above 5000 ft. there are no trees and little scrub. Radiating from this high region are ridges, most important being the Osgood, Howker, and Gordon Ridges of Mt. Madison; Durand and Nowell Ridges and the Israel Ridge, or Emerald Tongue, of Mt. Adams; the Castellated Ridge extending northwest from Mt. Jefferson to Mt. Bowman, the Ridge of the Caps extending westerly and the two Jefferson Knees easterly from Mt. Jefferson; and an unnamed but very salient ridge extending westerly from Mt. Clay. The most important valleys or ravines are the Great Gulf and its offshoots Jefferson Ravine and Madison Gulf, Bumpus Basin, the valley of Snyder Brook, King Ravine, Cascade Ravine, Castle Ravine, and Burt Ravine. All except the Snyder Brook valley, Cascade and Burt ravines are marked examples of the glacial cirque.

In 1860 or 1861, Gordon, the guide, made a partial trail over the peaks to Mt. Washington, and some sections still exist. In 1875-76 Lowe's Path was cut, the branch path through King Ravine was made in 1876, and the Osgood Path was opened in 1878. From 1878 until the beginning of the lumbering in about 1902, Watson, Nowell, Peek, Cook, Sargent, and Hunt led trail-making on the Northern Peaks, and in 1892, J. Rayner Edmands began a system of graded paths. The network of trails they created was greatly damaged by lumbering (1901-06), and some trails were obliterated. The more important ones have since been restored. On the Northern Peaks the USFS now maintains about twenty miles of trails, the AMC about thirty, and the RMC about sixty.

On the Northern Peaks, the Appalachian Trail follows the Gulfside Trail, Osgood Trail, Osgood Cutoff, and Madison Gulf Trail for a total (Clay-Washington col to west Branch of Peabody River) of 8.5 mi.

The Northern Peaks can be reached from the summit of Mt. Washington, from the AMC hut at the Lakes of the Clouds (see Section 4), or, best of all, from the AMC hut at Madison Spring. There are motels at Randolph and Gorham, and overnight cabins at Lowe's (100 yd. east of Lowe's Path), and farther west on US Rte. 2. There is public camping at Dolly Copp Campground and Moose Brook State Park in Gorham.

There is free parking at Pinkham Notch Camp, the Glen House site, Dolly Copp Campground, the Appalachia and Randolph East parking areas, and at Bowman. A nominal parking fee is charged at Lowe's store.

The highest points from which to climb the Northern Peaks, except the summit of Mt. Washington, are the junction of Pine Link and Dolly Copp, also called Pinkham B Rd. (1650 ft); the

2-mi. mark (about 2650 ft.) on the Mt. Washington Auto Rd. where the Madison Gulf Trail begins (see Section 3); Jefferson Notch at the foot of the Caps Ridge Trail (3000 ft.), the easiest point on a road from which to obtain a high summit; and the Marshfield Station of the cog railway, about 2700 ft.

From the Marshfield station, reached by automobile, the foot of the Caps Ridge Trail may be reached via Boundary Line Trail in about an hour.

The Memorial Bridge

This is a memorial to J. Rayner Edmands, Eugene B. Cook, and other pioneer pathmakers — King, Gordon, Lowe, Watson, Peek, Hunt, Nowell, and Sargent. It crosses Cold Brook a little below Cold Brook Fall, which is visible from the bridge. The Link and the Amphibrach Trail use this bridge to cross the stream.

Madison Hut (AMC)

In 1888, at Madison Spring (4825 ft.) a little north of the Adams-Madison col the AMC built a stone hut that was later demolished. The present hut, rebuilt and improved since the fire of 1940, accommodates fifty guests on a coed basis and is open to the public from mid-June to mid-September. For current information contact Reservation Secretary, Pinkham Notch Camp, Box 298, Gorham, NH 03581 (603-466-2727).

Madison Hut (map 6)

Distances from Madison Hut

to Mt. Madison summit: 0.5 mi., ½ hr.

to Mt. Adams summit (via Star Lake Trail): 0.9 mi., 55 min.

to Mt. Jefferson summit: *est.* 2.8 mi., 2 hr. 10 min.

to Mt. Washington summit: *est.* 6.3 mi., 4¼ hr., (3 hr. 10 min. returning)

Distances to Madison Hut

from AMC Pinkham Notch Camp (via Old Jackson Rd. and Madison Gulf Trail): 6.1 mi., 4 hr. 50 min.

> *from* Lakes of the Clouds Hut (via Crawford Path, Westside, and Gulfside trails): 6.8 mi., 4 hr. 40 min.
>
> *from* Appalachia parking lot (via Valley Way): 3.5 mi., 3½ hr.
>
> *from* Glen House site on NH Rte. 16 (via Osgood Trail, Madison Gulf Cutoff, and Madison Gulf Trail): *est.* 5.1 mi., 4½ hr.
>
> *from* Jefferson Notch Road (via Caps Ridge Trail and Mt. Jefferson): 5.1 mi., 4¼ hr.

The Parapet and Star Lake

One-quarter mile south of the hut, and beyond Star Lake "The Parapet," a 4925-ft. rocky ridge at the head of Adams-Madison col overlooking Madison Gulf, affords fine views of Mt. Washington, the Carter Range, the Great Gulf, and the country around Conway. It is reached by the Parapet Trail.

Star Lake, reached by the Star Lake Trail 0.1 mi. from Madison Hut, is a small, shallow body of water among jagged rocks, from which there are good views. The mossy areas around the lake are usually muddy and wet underfoot; visitors should use great care not to damage the vegetation.

Shelters

The Log Cabin (RMC). About 1890 Dr. W. G. Nowell built this cabin on a former campsite at a spring at 3300 ft. altitude, beside Lowe's Path. It is maintained by the RMC and is open to the public. The cabin is closed but it has no stove, cooking utensils, or blankets. There is room for about ten. No wood fires are permitted in the area, and guests are requested to leave the cabin clean and carry out all trash.

The Perch (RMC). This is an open log shelter built on the site of J. Rayner Edmands's shelter of the same name — at about 4200 ft. on the Perch Path, which runs from the Randolph Path to the Israel Ridge Path. It is open to the public and accommodates eight. There are also four tent platforms at the site; the caretaker

at Gray Knob often visits to collect the $1 overnight fee for use of
either the shelter or tent platforms.

Crag Camp (RMC). At the edge of King Ravine near the Spur
Trail (about 4200 ft.), this former private camp of Nelson Smith
is now open to the public at a charge of $2.50 per person per
night. It is a closed cabin, supplied with cooking utensils and a
gas stove in the summer, with room for about fourteen. During
July and August it is maintained by a caretaker. At other times
fees may be sent to the Randolph Mountain Club, Randolph, NH
03570. Wood fires are *not* allowed in the area. Hikers are required
to limit groups to ten and stays to two nights. All trash is to be
carried out. Any infraction of these rules or acts of vandalism
should be reported to the above address.

Gray Knob (Town of Randolph and RMC). This winterized
cabin is on Gray Knob Trail at its junction with Hincks Trail,
near Lowe's Path (about 4400 ft.). It is open to the public at a
charge of $2.50 per person per night. Gray Knob has room for
about twelve and is supplied with a gas stove and cooking
utensils in the summer. There is a caretaker year round. Rules are
the same as for Crag Camp. Reports of infractions may be sent to
the Randolph Mountain Club.

GULFSIDE TRAIL (WMNF)

This trail leads from Madison Hut to the summit of Mt.
Washington. It threads the principal cols, but avoids summits of
the Northern Peaks. Its altitudes range from about 4815 ft. close
to the hut, to 6288 ft., and it affords extensive and varying views.
Barring the slope of Mt. Washington, the highest altitude is 5520
ft. in the Adams-Sam Adams col. The trail is marked by large
cairns, each topped with a yellow-painted stone, is well defined,
and, though care must be used, can be followed even in dense fog
or when obscured by snow. On these heights dangerous winds
and low temperatures are likely to occur with little warning at any
season of the year. If such storms cause serious trouble on the
Gulfside Trail, do not attempt to ascend the cone of Mt. Wash-

ington, where conditions are usually worse. If impossible to go to the hut at Madison Spring or at Lakes of the Clouds, retreat into one of the ravines, using the Jewell Trail to reach the Marshfield station of the cog railway; the Randolph Path for the Perch; Spur Trail for Crag Camp; or Castle Ravine Trail about 0.9 mi. to the protection of Roof Rock. The steel emergency refuge at Edmands Col was removed in 1982. If it is impossible to reach any of the shelters, descend without trail into one of the ravines. A night of discomfort in the woods is better than exposure on the heights, which may prove fatal.

The name Gulfside was given about 1892 by J. Rayner Edmands, who, in that and subsequent years, located and made the greater part of the trail, sometimes following trails that had existed before. All but about 0.8 mi. of the trail was a graded path, some parts paved with carefully placed stones, a work cut short by Edmands's death in 1910. The whole length is part of the Appalachian Trail.

Part I. Madison Hut-Edmands Col

The trail begins at Snyder Brook between Mts. Madison and Adams not more than 30 yd. from the hut. After leading southwest through a patch of scrub, it aims to the right (north) of Mt. John Quincy Adams, ascends a steep, open slope, and near the top of this slope is joined from the right by the Air Line Trail, which coincides with it for a few yards. From here there is a striking view of Mt. Madison.

The path is now on the high plateau between the head of King Ravine and the peak of John Quincy. On the right is a view into the ravine. The Air Line Trail branches left, toward Mt. Adams. Much of the Gulfside Trail for about the next 0.5 mi. is paved with carefully placed stones. It rises gently southwest, curving a little more south, then steepens, and at 0.9 mi. from the hut reaches a grassy lawn in the saddle (5520 ft.) between Mt. Adams and Sam Adams.

Here, where several trails intersect at a spot nicknamed

"Thunderstorm Junction," there is a massive cairn about 10 ft. high. Entering the junction right is the Great Gully Trail, coming up across the slope from the southwest corner of King Ravine. Here also, the Gulfside is crossed by Lowe's Path, ascending from Bowman to the summit of Mt. Adams. A few yards down Lowe's Path, the Spur Trail branches right for Crag Camp. The summit of Mt. Adams is about 0.3 mi. from the junction (left), via Lowe's Path. There is no trail to Sam Adams (5585 ft.), but this peak, marked by a conspicuous cairn, may be reached easily in 0.2 mi. over the rocks from the junction; it affords a good view.

(A cairned trail, known as the "White Trail," runs from Thunderstorm Junction along the ridge south from Sam Adams to a terminus at the Israel Ridge Path where it rejoins the Gulfside about 100 yd. south of Peabody Spring. This is merely to explain the line of cairns that runs roughly parallel to the Gulfside on the ridge to the north: in bad weather stay on the Gulfside.)

Continuing southwest from Thunderstorm Junction and beginning to descend, the Gulfside Trail is joined on the left by the Israel Ridge Path coming down from Lowe's Path, from which it diverges near the summit of Mt. Adams. (Round trip to the summit by either Israel Ridge or Lowe's Path adds about 25 min.) For about 0.5 mi. the Gulfside Trail and Israel Ridge Path coincide. They pass Peabody *Spring* (*unreliable*) just to the right in a small, grassy flat. A few yards beyond *more reliable water* is found at the base of a conspicuous boulder just to the left of the path.

At 1.5 mi. from the hut the Israel Ridge Path diverges right. Near this junction in wet weather there is a small pool called Storm Lake. The Gulfside turns a little left and approaches the edge of Jefferson Ravine, first passing Adams 5, a small peak 2 min. to the left of the trail. This part of the Gulfside was never graded. It is marked by cairns and keeps near the edge of the cliffs, from which there are fine views into the gulf. Descending southwest along the narrow ridge that divides Jefferson Ravine from Castle Ravine, and always leading toward Mt. Jefferson, the trail enters Edmands Col at 2.2 mi. from the hut and 3.5 mi. from the summit of Mt. Washington.

Edmands Col

This col, between Mts. Adams and Jefferson, divides the Connecticut and Androscoggin watersheds. Its 4930-ft. altitude is almost the same as that of the Madison-Adams col at the Parapet, and within 50 ft. of that of the Clay-Jefferson col. Near the site of the former emergency shelter (*dismantled in 1982*) is a bronze tablet in memory of J. Rayner Edmands, who made most of the graded paths on the Northern Peaks. From Edmands Col the Randolph Path leads north into the Randolph valley. The Edmands Col Cutoff leads south about 0.5 mi. to the Six Husbands Trail. Branching from the Randolph Path about 0.1 mi. north of the col are the Cornice, leading west to the Castle Trail, and the Castle Ravine Trail. Thirty yd. south of the col is Gulfside *Spring* (*reliable water*). About 0.2 mi. north near the Castle Ravine Trail is Spaulding *Spring* (*reliable water*).

Gulfside Trail, Part I (map 6)
Distance from Madison Hut
   to Edmands Col: 2.2 mi., 1½ hr.
   to Mt. Jefferson Summit: *est.* 2.7 mi., 2 hr. 10 min.

Part II. Edmands Col-Clay/Jefferson Col

South of Edmands Col the Gulfside Trail ascends steeply southwest over rough rocks, with Jefferson Ravine on the left. It passes flat-topped Dingmaul Rock, from which there is a good view down the gulf, with Mt. Adams on the left. A few yards beyond, the Mt. Jefferson Loop branches right, and leads 0.2 mi. to the summit of Mt. Jefferson (5715 ft.), from which it continues about 0.3 mi. to rejoin the Gulfside at Monticello Lawn. To go over Jefferson by the loop, to Monticello Lawn, will add about 15 min. extra, excluding time spent at summit.

The path now turns southeast and rises less steeply. It crosses the Six Husbands Trail and soon reaches its greatest height on Mt. Jefferson, 5370 ft. Curving southwest and descending a little, it crosses Monticello Lawn, a comparatively smooth, grassy plateau (about 5350 ft.). Here, the Mt. Jefferson Loop rejoins the Gulfside in about 0.3 mi. (13 min.; ascending 20 min.) from the summit. A short distance southwest of the lawn the Cornice enters right from the Caps Ridge Trail.

The Gulfside continues to descend south and southwest. From one point there is a view of the Sphinx down the slope (left). Approaching the Clay-Jefferson col, the ridge and the path turn more south. The Sphinx Trail branches left (east) into the Great Gulf, through a grassy passage between ledges a few yards north of the col.

Part III. Clay/Jefferson Col-Mt. Washington

From this 4965-ft. col two paths lead toward Mt. Washington: the Mt. Clay Loop (a rough trail) to the left, which passes over the summits of Mt. Clay with impressive views into the Great Gulf, and the graded Gulfside Trail, which leads more to the right and avoids the summits. The trails unite beyond Mt. Clay. The Gulfside Trail is the easier and passes close to *water*, but misses the most impressive views.

The Gulfside Trail runs south and rises gradually, slabbing the west side of Mt. Clay. In about 0.3 mi. a loop leads a few steps down to the right to *water*. The path continues about 30 yd. farther to Greenough *Spring* (*more reliable*), then rejoins the Gulfside farther up. The Gulfside continues its slabbing ascent. Just before it gains its highest point, one of the summits of Mt. Clay can be reached by a short climb to the left. Here, from the right, the Jewell Trail enters, ascending from the Marshfield station. The Gulfside swings southeast and descends slightly to the Clay-Washington col (5395 ft.), where the Mt. Clay Loop rejoins it from the left.

There is *no water* in this col. A little to the east is the edge of the Great Gulf, with fine views, especially of the east cliffs of

Mt. Clay. The path continues southeast, rising gradually on Mt. Washington. In about 0.1 mi. the Westside Trail branches right, crosses the cog railway, and leads to the Crawford Path and Lakes of the Clouds Hut. The Gulfside continues southeast between the cog railway and the edge of the Gulf. If you lose the path, follow the railway to the summit. At the extreme south corner of the gulf, the Great Gulf Trail from the left joins the Gulfside from the left, 5.4 mi. from the hut. The Gulfside turns sharp right, crosses the railway, and continuing west joins the Crawford Path just below (north) of the old corral. Just before this junction the Trinity Heights Connector, a link in the Appalachian Trail, leaves left for the summit of Mt. Washington (about 0.2 mi.).

Descending from the summit, the Gulfside Trail coincides with the Crawford Path for 0.3 mi. and turns right just below the old corral.

Gulfside Trail, Parts II and III (map 6)
Distances from Madison Hut

to Air Line Trail junction: 0.3 mi.
to Thunderstorm Junction: 0.9 mi.
to Israel Ridge Path junction: 1 mi.
to Edmands Col: 2.2 mi., 1½ hr.
to North end, Jefferson Loop: 2.4 mi.
to Six Husbands Trail junction: 2.6 mi.
to South end, Jefferson Loop: 3 mi.
to Cornice junction: 3.1 mi.
to North end, Clay Loop: 3.8 mi.
to Jewell Trail junction: 4.5 mi.
to South end, Clay Loop: 4.8 mi.
to Westside Trail junction: 5.0 mi.
to Great Gulf Trail junction: 5.4 mi.
to Mt. Washington summit (via Crawford Path):
    5.7 mi. (9.2 km.), 4 hr.
to Lakes of the Clouds Hut (via Westside Trail and
    Crawford Path): *est.* 6.8 mi., 4 hr. 40 min.

Distances from Mt. Washington Summit

to Great Gulf Trail junction (via Crawford Path) 0.3 mi.

to Jewell Trail junction: 1.2 mi.

to Sphinx Trail junction: 2.1 mi., 1 hr. 5 min.

to Six Husbands Trail junction: 3.1 mi.

to Edmands Col: 3.5 mi., 2 hr.

to Thunderstorm Junction: 4.8 mi., 2 hr. 50 min.

to Air Line Trail junction: 5.4 mi.

to Madison Hut: 5.7 mi. (9.2 km.), 3¼ hr.

Randolph Path (RMC)

This graded path extends southwest from the Dolly Copp Rd. over slopes of Mts. Madison and Adams, and joins the Gulfside Trail in Edmands Col between Mts. Adams and Jefferson. *Brooks* and *springs* supply *water* at short intervals. It was made by J. Rayner Edmands, the part above treeline in 1893 and following years, and the part below during 1897-99. Parts of it were reconstructed in 1978 as a memorial to Christopher Goetze, active RMC member and former editor of *Appalachia*, a journal published by the AMC.

The path begins at the parking space known as Randolph East, 0.2 mi. south of US Rte. 2 on the Dolly Copp Rd. and 0.3 mi. west of the Boston and Maine Railroad crossing. It coincides with the Howker Ridge Trail for approximately 80 yd. west, turns south, crosses the railroad, and 30 yd. beyond diverges right (west); the Howker Ridge Trail continues left (southeast). The Randolph Path keeps south of the power line for about 0.3 mi., where it enters the old location. It then turns southwest, crosses the Sylvan Way in about 0.5 mi., and in about another 0.8 mi. reaches Snyder Brook, where the Inlook Trail and Brookside diverge left. The Brookside and the Randolph Path cross the brook at the same place, then the Brookside diverges right and leads down to the Valley Way. A few yards beyond the brook it is crossed by the Valley Way, coming up from the Appalachia parking area. The Randolph Path soon crosses the

Air Line Trail. At 2 mi. the Short Line, a short cut (1.3 mi.) from the Appalachia parking area, comes in on the right.

The Short Line coincides with the Randolph Path for 0.4 mi., then branches left for King Ravine. The Randolph Path descends slightly and crosses Cold Brook on Sanders Bridge where the Cliffway diverges right. At 3 mi. it crosses the King Ravine Trail at its junction with the Amphibrach. The Randolph Path crosses Spur Brook and in about 100 yd. the Spur Trail leads left and the Randolph Path climbs around the nose of the ridge. Soon two paths to the right lead to the RMC Log Cabin. At about 3.9 mi. from Dolly Copp Rd., Lowe's Path is crossed.

The grade on the Randolph Path moderates. Slabbing the steep west side of Nowell Ridge for about 0.8 mi., the path passes Franconia *Spring*, where there is a view of Mt. Lafayette. At about 4.9 mi. the Perch Path crosses, leading right (southwest) to The Perch and Israel Ridge Path and left (east) to the Gray Knob Trail. There is *water* on the Perch Path a few yards west of the Randolph Path.

Above this junction the Randolph Path rises due south through scrub. *Water* is usually found at a *spring* left. In about 0.5 mi. the scrub ends and Israel Ridge Path enters right (west), ascending from Bowman. Near this junction the Gray Knob Trail from Crag Camp and Gray Knob enters left. From this point the Randolph Path is nearly level to its end at Edmands Col, curving around the head of Castle Ravine. The path is above treeline and visible for a long distance ahead. For a few yards the Israel Ridge Path coincides, then branches left for Mt. Adams. Near the col, right, is Spaulding *Spring* (*reliable water*). The Castle Ravine Trail comes in from the right (northwest) and the Cornice leads west to Castle Trail. In about 0.1 mi. more the Randolph Path joins the Gulfside Trail in Edmands Col.

Randolph Path (map 6)
Distances from Appalachia parking area

to Randolph Path (via Air Line Trail and Short Line Trail or via Amphibrach Trail): *est*. 1.3 mi., 1¼ hr.

to Cliffway junction: *est*. 1.9 mi.

to King Ravine Trail crossing: *est*. 2.3 mi., 2 hr.

to Lowe's Path crossing: *est*. 3.2 mi.

to Perch Path junction: *est*. 4.2 mi., 3½ hr.

to Israel Ridge Path junction: *est*. 4.7 mi., 4 hr.

to Gulfside Trail junction, Edmands Col: *est*. 5.3 mi.
(8.5 km.), 4 hr. 20 min.

to Mt. Jefferson summit (via Gulfside Trail and Jefferson
Loop): *est*. 5.8 mi., 5 hr.

to Mt. Washington summit (via Gulfside Trail and Crawford
Path): *est*. 9.2 mi., 7 hr. 5 min.

to Lakes of the Clouds Hut (via Gulfside Trail,
Westside Trail, and Crawford Path): *est*. 10.5 mi., 7½ hr.

Distances from Randolph East parking area/Dolly Copp Rd.
add 0.7 mi. and ¼ hr. to above

The Cornice (RMC)

This trail, wholly above timberline, leads west from the Randolph Path in Edmands Col, 0.1 mi. north of the Gulfside Trail. After climbing slightly, it slabs around the north and west sides of Mt. Jefferson. It crosses the Castle Trail above the Upper Castle and enters the Caps Ridge Trail above the Upper Cap. It then turns left (east) up the Caps Ridge Trail about 50 ft., again diverges right (south), and climbs gradually to the Gulfside Trail on Monticello Lawn. Because the Cornice avoids the summit of Mt. Jefferson, it serves as an alternate connection — particularly in bad weather — between the Castle and Caps Ridge trails, and between those trails and Edmands Col on the east and Mt. Washington on the south. It is, however, a longer, rougher, and slower route than by the Gulfside Trail or by the Mt. Jefferson Loop: the rock-hopping can be hard on the knees. There is *no water* on the trail.

The Cornice (map 6)

Distances from Randolph Path junction, Edmands Col
to Castle Trail crossing: *est*. 0.5 mi., 40 min.

to Caps Ridge Trail junction: *est.* 1.5 mi., 1 hr. 50 min.
to Gulfside Trail junction: 2 mi. (3.2 km.), 2 hr. 25 min.

Edmands Col Cutoff (RMC)

This important link makes a quick descent possible from Edmands Col into the Great Gulf, a necessity in bad weather. The cutoff leads from the Gulfside Trail and Randolph Path at Edmands Col to Six Husbands Trail, slabbing the cone of Mt. Jefferson. Leaving the col, the cutoff shortly passes a fine *spring,* then rises slightly and begins a rough scramble of about 0.5 mi. over rocks and through scrub — follow cairns. The trail is mostly level, with only a few rises and falls over gullies and good views to the south and of the Great Gulf. The cutoff ends at the Six Husbands Trail about 0.5 below that trail's junction with Gulfside Trail.

Edmands Col Cutoff (map 6)
Distances from Gulfside Trail/Randolph Path junction
to spring: 50 yd.
to Six Husbands Trail: 0.5 mi.

The Link (RMC)

This path "links" the Appalachia parking area with the trails ascending Mts. Adams and Jefferson from the west. It connects with the Amphibrach, Cliffway, Lowe's, and Israel Ridge paths and Castle Ravine, Emerald, Castle, and Caps Ridge trails. The section between the Caps Ridge and Castle trails, although very rough, makes a circuit of the Caps and the Castles possible from Jefferson Notch Rd. It is graded as far as Cascade Brook.

The Link, with the Amphibrach, diverges right from the Air Line about 50 yd. south of its junction with the Valley Way and 100 yd. south of the Appalachia parking area. It runs west about 0.8 mi. to where the Beechwood Way diverges left, and just east of Cold Brook, Sylvan Way enters left. Cold Brook is crossed on the Memorial Bridge where there is a fine view of Cold Brook Fall, which is reached by Sylvan Way. West of the brook, after a few yards, the Amphibrach diverges left.

The Link then follows old logging roads southwest for about 1.5 mi. It enters the WMNF 1.2 mi. from the Appalachia parking area, and at 2 mi. the Cliffway leads east to viewpoints on Nowell Ridge. At about 2.1 mi. the Link turns left and runs south to Lowe's Path, which it crosses at about 2.8 mi. Continuing south about 0.4 mi. it crosses the north branch of the Mystic, and, turning a little to the right, crosses the main Mystic Stream at 3.3 mi. It soon curves left, rounds the western buttress of Nowell Ridge, and running southeast nearly level, enters Cascade Ravine on the mountainside high above the stream. It crosses a slide and keeps the same general direction at nearly the same altitude until it approaches and crosses the brook at 4.1 mi.

Before the Link reaches Cascade Brook, the Israel Ridge Path comes up right from Bowman (about 2.3 mi.) and unites with the Link at 4 mi. from the Appalachia parking area, coincides with it for 100 ft., then branches left for Randolph Path and Mt. Adams. The Cabin-Cascades Trail also intersects the Link just before the brook crossing. On the stream, a little below and a little above the Link, are the first and second cascades. The Link continues southeast for 100 ft., then crosses a slide, rounds the tip of Israel Ridge, and turns south and southeast into Castle Ravine, uniting at 5.1 mi. with the Castle Ravine Trail, with which it coincides for about 0.3 mi. The two trails pass Emerald Trail and cross Castle Brook. Then at 5.4 mi., the Link turns right and ascends west, slabbing the southwest wall of Castle Ravine. In about 0.6 mi. it crosses the Castle Trail below the first Castle at about 4050 ft. It then descends slightly, crosses three small brooks and continues southwest over sections of treacherous roots and hollows for 2.2 mi., slabbing a rough slope to the Caps Ridge Trail, which it enters 0.4 mi. above the Jefferson Notch Rd.

The Link (map 6)

Distances from the Appalachia parking area
  to Cold Brook Fall: *est.* 0.8 mi.

to Cliffway junction: 2 mi.

to Lowe's Path crossing: *est.* 2.8 mi., 1 hr. 40 min.

to Cascade Brook crossing: 4.1 mi., 2½ hr.

to Castle Ravine Trail junction: 5.1 mi., 3 hr. 5 min.

to Emerald Trail junction: 5.3 mi.

to Castle Trail crossing: 5.9 mi., 4¼ hr.

to Caps Ridge Trail: *est.* 8.1 mi. (13 km.), 5¾ hr.

PINE MOUNTAIN

Pine Mountain (2404 ft.), a northeastern spur of the Presidential Range, affords fine views up and down the Androscoggin, up the Moose, and up the Peabody rivers. There are also good views from the south cliff and from ledges along the crest, where the heavy virgin spruce growth was destroyed by fire during 1897-1903.

The 100 acres on the summit of Pine Mountain comprise Douglas Horton Center, a center for renewal and education operated by the New Hampshire Conference of the United Church of Christ (Congregational). The center consists of six buildings and an outdoor chapel on the more precipitous northeast peak. Although public camping is not permitted, day hikers are welcome to appreciate the views from Pine Mountain.

A trail around the south cliff — "Ledge Trail," maintained by the WMNF — gives beautiful views westward. The private road to the center gives easy access (on foot only) to the summit. The center road branches from Dolly Copp Rd. at 1650 ft., a little northwest of the highest point of that road, 2.4 mi. from US Rte. 2 and 1.9 mi. from NH Rte. 16, and opposite the foot of Pine Link. Hikers should watch for automobiles descending on this road. The road runs east across the col, and turns northeast and north to ascend along the west flank of the mountain, where the Ledge Trail branches right to climb around the south cliff and so to the summit. It enters the saddle between two of the summits, and runs south to the south summit. About 1.4 mi. from the highway a side trail leads left to a good *spring*. Opposite this path a shortcut leads right to the south summit.

Pine Mountain (map 6)

Distances to south summit

　from Tractor Rd./Dolly Copp Rd. junction (via Tractor Rd.):
　　1.8 mi., 1 hr.

　from Tractor Rd./Dolly Copp Rd. junction (via Ledge Trail to
　　south cliff): 1.6 mi., 1 hr. 5 min.

MOUNT MADISON

Farthest northeast of the high peaks of the Presidential Range, 5363-ft. Mt. Madison is remarkable for the great drop of over 4000 ft. to the river valleys east and northeast from its summit. The drop to the Androscoggin at Gorham — 4580 ft. in about 6.5 mi. — is probably the closest approach in New England, except at Katahdin, of a larger river to a high mountain. The views of nearby mountains south and southwest, and into the Great Gulf, are very fine. The distant view in these directions is cut off, though Chocorua is visible. In all other directions there is a distant view.

Mt. Madison (map 6)

Distances to summit

　from AMC Pinkham Notch Camp (via Old Jackson Rd.,
　　Osgood Cutoff, and Osgood Trail): *est*. 6.9 mi.,
　　5 hr. 20 min.

　from Glen House site, NH Rte. 16 (via Osgood Trail): 5 mi.,
　　4 hr. 20 min.

　from Glen House site, NH Rte. 16 (via Osgood Trail, Madison
　　Gulf Cutoff, Madison Gulf Trail, and Osgood Trail):
　　est. 5.6 mi., 5 hr.

　from Dolly Copp Campground (via Daniel Webster-Scout
　　Trail and Osgood Trail): *est*. 4 mi., 4 hr. 5 min.

from Appalachia parking area (via Sylvan Way and
   Howker Ridge Trail): 5 mi., 4 hr. 50 min.
from Appalachia parking area (via Valley Way and
   Watson Path): 3.4 mi., 3¾ hr.
from Appalachia parking area (via Valley Way,
   Madison Hut, and Osgood Trail): 3.9 mi.

Osgood Trail (AMC)

Made by B. F. Osgood in 1878, this is the oldest trail now in
use to the summit of Mt. Madison. Above the Osgood Cutoff it is
part of the Appalachian Trail.

Leave NH Rte. 16 (Pinkham Notch Highway) opposite the
Glen House site, and follow the Mt. Washington Auto Rd. across
the Peabody River to the edge of the woods, where a sign (right)
shows the beginning of the trail. The trail gradually climbs the
side of the ridge, then runs level for about 0.5 mi. After crossing
a large brook it follows a former logging road, descends slightly,
and crosses a dry channel of the West Branch. Crossing the West
Branch on a bridge, it intersects the Great Gulf Trail 1.6 mi. from
Rte. 16 (Glen House site) and about 2.3 mi. from Dolly Copp
Campground.

At about 2.3 mi. the Madison Gulf Cutoff diverges left,
affording a more sheltered and shorter (but very steep and difficult) route to Madison Hut. The Osgood Trail turns to the east,
crosses a small brook, and soon begins a steeper ascent. A *spring*
close to the trail on the right is the *last sure water*. Here the
Osgood Cutoff comes in from the left. From this point to Madison Hut the Osgood Trail is part of the Applachian Trail. The
steep ascent continues to treeline at 3.9 mi., where the trail
emerges on the crest of Osgood Ridge. Ahead, on the crest of the
ridge, ten or twelve small, rocky peaks curve to the left in a
crescent toward the summit of Mt. Madison. Cairns mark the
trail over these peaks. Keep on the crest of the ridge. Daniel
Webster-Scout Trail enters right at Osgood Junction, ascending

from Dolly Copp Campground. Here the Parapet Trail diverges
left, slabbing the south side of the cone of Madison, to Madison
Hut. As the Osgood Trail nears the last prominent hump below
the summit and bears more west, it is joined on the right by the
Howker Ridge Trail. It continues west over the summit and
descends to Madison Hut.

In *reverse,* from Mt. Madison the trail runs east about 0.3 mi.
over large fragments of rock to the crest of the southwest ridge of
Mt. Madison, then swings a little north of east and ascends the
ridge a little south of the crest, with the gulf on the right. A few
yards from the summit it turns left, regains the crest of the ridge,
and follows it to the summit, marked by a tall cairn.

Descending toward the Glen House site go east from the
summit, keeping on the crest of the ridge. After about 0.3 mi. the
crest (and trail) curve gradually to the southeast.

Osgood Trail (map 6)
Distances from Glen House site, NH Rte. 16
   to Great Gulf Trail crossing: 1.6 mi., 50 min.
   to Mt. Madison summit: 4.9 mi., 4 hr. 20 min.
   to Madison Hut (via Parapet Trail): 5.4 mi. (8.6 km.),
      4 hr. 40 min.
   to Mt. Madison summit (via Parapet Trail and Madison Hut):
      5.9 mi., 5 hr. 10 min.

Osgood Cutoff (AMC)
   This link, about 0.5 mi. long, provides a convenient route
from Pinkham Notch Camp to the summit of Mt. Madison. Part
of the Appalachian Trail, it leads northeast from the junction of
the Madison Gulf Trail and the Madison Gulf Cutoff to the *spring*
on the Osgood Trail.

Osgood Cutoff (map 6)
Distance from AMC Pinkham Notch Camp
   to Mt. Madison summit (via Old Jackson Rd., Madison Gulf
      Trail, Osgood Cutoff, and Osgood Trail): *est.* 6.9 mi.
      (11 km.), 5 hr. 20 min.

Daniel Webster-Scout Trail (WMNF)

This trail, cut in 1933 by the Boy Scouts, leads from Dolly Copp Campground to Osgood Junction on the Osgood Trail, about halfway between the timberline and the summit of Mt. Madison. It begins on the camp road about 0.8 mi. south of the point where the Dolly Copp Rd. joins the main camp road leading south, and in its course makes several zigzags not shown on the map, though the approximate location is shown. The trail is steep above timberline and, except for the last mile, it is abundantly supplied with *water*.

Daniel Webster-Scout Trail (map 6)

Distances from Dolly Copp Campground

   to *last sure water:* 2.6 mi.

   to Osgood Junction: 3.5 mi.

   to Mt. Madison summit (via Osgood Trail): *est.* 4 mi., 4 hr. 5 min.

   to Madison Hut (via Osgood Trail and Mt. Madison summit): *est.* 4.5 mi., 4 hr. 25 min.

The Parapet Trail (AMC)

This trail, marked with blue paint, leads from Osgood Junction, where the Osgood Trail joins the Daniel Webster-Scout Trail, west to Madison Hut, running nearly on a contour on the south side of the cone of Madison. It meets the Madison Gulf Trail where the latter leaves the scrub at the head of the gulf and continues beside the Parapet to join the Star Lake Trail to Madison Hut. Although above timberline and rough, in bad weather the Parapet Trail is sheltered from northwest winds and saves a climb of about 500 ft. over the summit of Mt. Madison. Use care in rainy weather.

Parapet Trail (map 6)

Distances from Osgood Junction

   to Madison Gulf Trail junction: *est.* 0.6 mi., 20 min.

   to Madison Hut: 1 mi., ½ hr.

Pine Link (AMC)

The Pine Link leads west from the Dolly Copp Rd. near its highest point directly opposite the tractor road to Pine Mountain and 2.4 mi. from US Rte. 2 and 1.9 mi. from NH Rte. 16 (Pinkham Notch Highway). Near it are a *spring* and small parking space. The trail generally follows the crest of a northeast spur of Howker Ridge. Below the outlook a fire in 1968 burned close to the south side of the trail opening fine views east and south. Above the outlook the trail unites with Howker Ridge Trail at the spring south of the second Howk. For about 0.3 mi. the two trails coincide, running southwest through a group of small Howks. At the foot of the highest Howk the trails diverge, Howker Ridge Trail leading left for Mt. Madison summit, and Pine Link, leading right, skirting the upper slopes of Bumpus Basin and high on Gordon Ridge crossing the Watson Path. Then running southwest, nearly level, with many fine views, it contours around the cone of Mt. Madison to Madison Hut.

Descending, start north from hut, soon turning northeast. Time to Dolly Copp Rd., about 2½ hr.

Pine Link (map 6)

Distances from Dolly Copp Rd.

to Howker Ridge Trail junction: *est.* 2.3 mi., 2 hr. 20 min.

to Watson Path crossing: *est.* 3.2 mi.

to Madison Hut: *est.* 3.8 mi., 3½ hr.

Town Line Brook Trail (RMC); Triple Falls

Three beautiful cascades on Town Line Brook just above its crossing of Dolly Copp Rd., 1.6 mi. southeast of the railroad, are known as Triple Falls: Proteus, Erebus, and Evans. The watershed is steep and the rainwater runs off very rapidly, so the falls should be visited during or immediately after a rain.

A good path, close beside the brook, leads from the road to the falls, about 0.1 mi.

Howker Ridge Trail (RMC)

Leading from the Dolly Copp Rd. to the Osgood Trail near the summit of Mt. Madison, this wild, rough trail gives good outlooks at different altitudes and passes three fine cascades.

The trail begins at the parking area known as Randolph East, 0.2 mi. south of US Rte. 2 on Dolly Copp Rd. and 0.3 mi. west of the railroad crossing. It runs with the Randolph Path approximately 80 yd. west, turns south, crosses the railroad, and 30 yd. beyond diverges left (southeast). It runs southeast to the former location of the trail, which it follows up the west bank of Bumpus Brook. The trail passes a cascade (Stairs Fall) that falls into the brook from the east, and at 0.7 mi. it passes Coosauk Fall where Sylvan Way enters from the right. The trail continues a little west of the brook, and the Kelton Trail diverges right. About 1 mi. from the highway the Howker Ridge Trail turns east and at 1900 ft. crosses the brook at the foot of Hitchcock Fall. Then it rises steeply southeast. Howker Ridge curves right, partly enclosing the deep bowl-shaped valley called Bumpus Basin. The trail follows the crest of the ridge, on which are several little peaks called the Howks. The first is a long, narrow ridge covered with woods. In the col south of the first Howk is a *spring* (*water unreliable*). From the second Howk there is a fine view in all directions, especially into Bumpus Basin. South of the Howk the Pine Link enters left (there is a *spring* on the Pine Link about 50 ft. to the east). The two trails coincide for about 0.3 mi., ascend among several Howks in a group, and separate again at the foot of the highest Howk where Pine Link branches right. The Howker Ridge Trail climbs over the highest Howk (about 4200 ft.), descends a little southwest, then ascends steeply to the crest of Osgood Ridge, where it enters the Osgood Trail a few hundred yards from the summit of Mt. Madison.

Howker Ridge Trail (map 6)

Distances from Randolph East parking area, Dolly Copp Rd.

   to Sylvan Way junction: 0.7 mi.

to Hitchcock Fall: 1 mi., 50 min.

to first Howk: 2.3 mi., 2 hr. 10 min.

to second Howk: 3 mi., 2 hr. 50 min.

to Mt. Madison summit (via Osgood Trail): 4.4 mi. (7 km.), 4½ hr.

Distance from Appalachia parking area

add 0.5 mi. and ¼ hr. (via Maple Walk and Sylvan Way)

Kelton Trail (RMC)

This pleasure path branches right from the Howker Ridge Trail about 0.8 mi. from the Dolly Copp Rd. It climbs to Kelton Crag, then ascends, near the northwest arete of the "finger" of Gordon Ridge, to an upper crag at the edge of an old 1921 burn. From both crags there are restricted views, and there is usually *water* between them on the right. Ascending, with good views east, the trail reaches the Overlook at the edge of the unburned woods, and runs west to the Upper Inlook where the Inlook Trail enters (right) from Dome Rock. The Kelton Trail then runs south, nearly level through dense woods, crosses Gordon Rill (*reliable water*), another rill and Snyder Brook, and enters the Brookside 100 yd. below the foot of Salmacis Fall, 2 mi. from the road.

Kelton Trail (map 6)

Distances from Randolph East parking area, Dolly Copp Rd.

to start of Kelton Trail: 0.7 mi.

to Kelton Crag: 1 mi.

to Inlook Trail junction: 1.6 mi., 1½ hr.

to foot of Salmacis Fall: 2 mi. (3.2 km.), 2 hr.

Distances from Appalachia parking area

add 0.5 mi. and ¼ hr. (via Sylvan Way)

Sylvan Way (RMC)

The Sylvan Way leads from the Memorial Bridge over Cold Brook to Howker Ridge Trail at Coosauk Fall. A few yards from the bridge it passes Cold Brook Fall. At 0.1 mi. Beechwood Way crosses. Sylvan Way crosses Air Line at 0.6 mi. and Valley Way at 0.7. Soon, at 0.8 mi., Fallsway crosses, and Maple Walk enters left. Sylvan Way then crosses Snyder Brook and immediately after, the Brookbank. Randolph Path crosses at 1.1 mi. from the Memorial Bridge, and, after a gradual ascent, the Sylvan Way ends at Howker Ridge Trail.

Sylvan Way (map 6)
Distance from Appalachia parking area

to start of Sylvan Way (via Link and Amphibrach Trails): 0.8 mi.

to Howker Ridge Trail junction, Coosauk Fall: 2.6 mi. (4.1 km.)

Fallsway (RMC)

The Fallsway leads from the east end of the Appalachia parking area, goes east for 0.1 mi., and then turns sharply right (south). It immediately crosses the railroad. Soon Brookbank diverges left and Fallsway enters the woods. At 0.4 mi. from the Appalachia parking area, the path passes Gordon Fall and Gordon Fall Loop diverges right. In a few yards Sylvan Way crosses and Maple Walk enters. Lower and Upper Salroc Falls are passed 0.8 mi. from the Appalachia parking area. Soon Fallsway enters Valley Way (below Tama Fall). In a few yards Fallsway leaves Valley Way and passes Tama Fall. Brookbank then enters, and Fallsway ends in a few yards at Valley Way, above Tama Fall.

Fallsway (map 6)
Distance from Appalachia parking area

to Valley Way junction above Tama Fall: 0.9 mi. (1.4 km)

Brookbank (RMC)

Brookbank leads from Fallsway near the railroad, at the edge of the woods. It runs parallel to the railroad for about 0.1 mi., then crosses Snyder Brook, turns sharply right (south), and enters the woods. It runs up the east side of the brook passing

Gordon Fall, Sylvan Way, Upper and Lower Salroc Falls, and Tama Fall. Above Tama Fall it recrosses the brook and reenters Fallsway.

Brookbank (map 6)
Distances from Appalachia parking area
> *to* start of Brookbank (via Fallsway): 0.2 mi.
> *to* Tama Fall: 0.9 mi. (1.4 km)

Maple Walk (RMC) and Gordon Fall Loop (RMC)

The Maple Walk diverges left from Valley Way a few yards from the Appalachia parking area and runs to the junction of Fallsway and Sylvan Way. Gordon Fall Loop diverges right from Fallsway at Gordon Fall and joins Maple Walk about 0.1 mi. from the Appalachia parking area.

Maple Walk and Gordon Fall Loop (map 6)
Distances from Appalachia parking area
> *to* Gordon Fall (via Gordon fall Loop): 0.3 mi.
> *to* Sylvan Way junction: 0.3 mi.

Watson Path (RMC)

The Watson Path, completed by L.M. Watson in 1882, led from the Ravine House to the summit of Mt. Madison. The present path begins at the Scar Trail, leads across the Valley Way and to Bruin Rock, and then follows the original route to the summit.

Branching from the Scar Trail 0.3 mi. from Valley Way, it runs level about 0.2 mi. to the Valley Way, 2.2 mi. from the Appalachia parking area, then at an easy gradient to Bruin Rock, a large, flat-topped boulder on the west bank of Snyder Brook. Here the Brookside enters, coming up the west bank of the stream. The Watson Path crosses the brook at the foot of Duck Fall, but first the Lower Bruin branches to the right, and ascends to join the Valley Way. East of the stream, the Watson Path attacks the steep flank of Gordon Ridge and, slightly more than 3 mi. from the Appalachia parking area, emerges upon the grassy, stony back of the ridge. It crosses Pine Link and ascends to the summit of Mt. Madison over rough and shelving stones.

Watson Path (map 6)

Distances from Appalachia parking area

> *to* Valley Way crossing (via Valley Way and Scar Trail): 2.2 mi., 2 hr.
>
> *to* Bruin Rock: *est.* 2.3 mi.
>
> *to* Pine Link crossing: 3.3 mi.
>
> *to* Mt. Madison summit: 3.5 mi. (5.6 km.), 4 hr.

Valley Way (WMNF)

The direct route from the Appalachia parking area to Madison Hut is preferred in bad weather. Formerly graded throughout, many portions of its upper section have washed, becoming rocky and rough.

The trail, in common with the Air Line, begins at the Appalachia parking area. After crossing the railroad, the Valley Way leads left and Air Line right across the power line location. In a few yards, the Maple Walk diverges left, and about 0.3 mi. from the railroad the trail crosses Sylvan Way. At 0.6 mi., within the WMNF, the Fallsway comes in on the left and soon leaves left for Tama Fall and the Brookbank. It reenters the Valley Way in a few yards and is a short but worthwhile loop.

The Valley Way leads nearer Snyder Brook and is soon joined from the right by Beechwood Way. About 30 yd. above this junction Brookside diverges left and in about 100 yd. the Valley Way crosses the Randolph Path and climbs the ridge at a comfortable grade.

At 1.8 mi. Scar Trail branches right and at 2.2 mi. the Watson Path crosses, leading to the summit of Mt. Madison. The Valley Way slabs the rather steep slopes of Durand Ridge considerably above the stream. At 2.5 mi. the Lower Bruin enters left, coming up from Bruin Rock and Duck Fall. At 2.9 mi. there is a *spring*. At 3 mi. the Upper Bruin, a graded path, branches right, leading in 0.2 mi. to the Air Line at the lower end of the Knife-edge.

The Valley Way steepens and approaches Snyder Brook. The growth is mostly scrub, from which the path emerges close to the stream and near the hut.

Descending, the Valley Way enters the scrub just west of the outlet of Madison Spring.

Valley Way (map 6)
Distances from Appalachia parking area
> *to* Tama Fall (via Fallsway): 0.6 mi.
>
> *to* Randolph Path crossing: *est.* 0.9 mi., 50 min.
>
> *to* Watson Path crossing: *est.* 2.1 mi., 2 hr.
>
> *to* Upper Bruin junction: 3 min., 3 hr.
>
> *to* Madison Hut: 3.5 mi. (5.6 km.), 3½ hr.
>
> *to* Mt. Madison summit (via hut and Osgood Trail): 3.9 mi., 4 hr.

Inlook Trail (RMC)

This path was cut in 1932 from the junction of the Randolph Path and the Brookside east of Snyder Brook. It leads up to the Kelton Trail at the Upper Inlook (about 2700 ft.) near the crest of the finger of Gordon Ridge. There are good outlooks west, north, and east and several "inlooks" up the valley of Snyder Brook to John Quincy and Mt. Adams. The best outlook is at Dome Rock (about 2650 ft.), at the tip of the finger.

Inlook Trail (map 6)
Distances from Appalachia parking area
> *to* start of Inlook Trail (via Valley Way and Brookside Trail): 1 mi.
>
> *to* Dome Rock: 1.5 mi.
>
> *to* Kelton Trail junction: 1.6 mi. (2.5 km.), 1 hr. 35 min.

The Brookside (RMC)

This trail goes up Snyder Brook and offers views of many cascades and pools. It branches left from the Valley Way about 30 yd. above the Beechwood Way and crosses Snyder Brook at the same point as the Randolph Path. East of the brook the Inlook

Trail diverges left. In 0.3 mi. the Brookside recrosses the brook, and then becomes a moderate-to-steep trail to Salmacis Fall, just below which Kelton Trail enters on the left. The Brookside then follows the west side of Snyder Brook through virgin spruce and fir to Bruin Rock (3300 ft.), where it ends at the Watson Path. The brook between Salmacis and Bruin Rock is wild and beautiful, with cascades, mossy rocks, and fine forest.

The Brookside (map 6)

Distances from Appalachia parking area

to start of the Brookside (via Valley Way): *est*. 1 mi.

to Bruin Rock: *est*. 2.3 mi., 2¼ hr.

MOUNT ADAMS

Mt. Adams, at 5798 ft., is second in altitude of the New England summits. With its sharp, clean cut profile, its four lesser summits, its large area above treeline, its great northern ridges (Durand sharp and narrow, Nowell massive and broad-spreading), its four glacial cirques, King Ravine and the three that it shares with its neighbors, and its inspiring views, Mt. Adams perhaps has more interesting features than any other New England mountain except Katahdin. The finest views are across the Great Gulf to Mts. Washington, Jefferson, and Clay.

Mount Adams (map 6)

Distances to Mt. Adams summit

from AMC Pinkham Notch Camp (via Old Jackson Rd., Madison Gulf Trail, and Star Lake Trail): 6.7 mi., 5 hr. 35 min.

from Glen House site on NH Rte. 16 (via Osgood Trail, Madison Gulf Trail, and Star Lake Trail): *est*. 5.5 mi., 5 hr. 5 min.

from Appalachia parking area (via Valley Way and Star Lake Trail): 4.3 mi., 4 hr. 25 min.

from Appalachia parking area (via Air Line Trail): 4.1 mi., 4 hr. 20 min.

from Appalachia parking area (via Air Line Trail, Short Line
   Trail, King Ravine Trail, and Air Line Trail): 4.3 mi., 4¾
   hr.
from Lowe's Store on US Rte. 2 (via Lowe's Path): 4.5 mi., 4
   hr. 20 min.
from Madison Hut (via Star Lake Trail): 0.9 mi., 55 min.

Star Lake Trail (AMC)

This trail leads from Madison Hut to the summit of Mt.
Adams, slabbing the southeast side of John Quincy Adams. It is
often more sheltered from the wind than the Air Line Trail, and,
in the lower part, is well supplied with *water*. It runs south from
the hut, in common with the Parapet Trail, rising gently. In about
0.1 mi. the Parapet Trail branches to the left, passing east of Star
Lake. The Star Lake Trail passes west of the lake and reaches the
Adams-Madison col (about 4925 ft.) about 0.3 mi. from the hut.
Here the Buttress Trail branches left and descends. The Star Lake
Trail continues southwest on the steep southeast slope of John
Quincy. There is usually *water* issuing from the rocks on the
right. The trail continues to slab up the steep east slope of Mt.
Adams to the summit.

Star Lake Trail (map 6)
Distance from Madison Hut
   to Mt. Adams summit: *est*. 0.9 mi., 55 min.

Air Line (AMC)

This is the shortest route from the Appalachia parking area to
Mt. Adams. It was completed in 1885 when Peek, Cook, Sargent, and Watson cut a path from the Ravine House in Randolph
to a previously existing path on the crest of Durand Ridge.

The trail, in common with the Valley Way, begins at the
Appalachia parking area. After crossing the railroad, the Air
Line leads right and Valley Way left across the power line
location. In a few yards the Link and the Amphibrach diverge
right. The Air Line soon crosses Sylvan Way and, about 0.5 mi.

from the Appalachia parking area, crosses Beechwood Way and Beechwood Brook. A little beyond, the Short Line diverges right, and about 0.9 mi. from the Appalachia parking area, the Randolph Path is crossed. *Water* is found just short of 1.5 mi. in a *spring* 100 ft. east of the path (sign). From here the path becomes very steep for 0.5 mi. At 2.3 mi. is an old clearing known as Camp Placid Stream (*water unreliable*). The Scar Trail enters left, coming up from the Valley Way.

At 2.8 mi. the Upper Bruin comes up left from the Valley Way. Here the Air Line leaves the forest and ascends over the bare ledgy crest of Durand Ridge known as the Knife-edge. It passes over crags that drop off sharply into King Ravine on the right and the steep but not precipitous descent into Snyder Glen on the left. At 2.9 mi., just south of the little peak called Needle Rock, the Chemin des Dames comes up from King Ravine. At 3.1 mi. a branch leads left (southeast) 0.3 mi. to Madison Hut, which is visible from this junction in clear weather. *Water* is found on this branch not far from the main path.

The Air Line now departs a little from the edge of the ravine, going left of the jutting crags at the ravine's southeast corner. It rises steeply, and at 3.3 mi. passes the "Gateway" of King Ravine, through which the King Ravine Trail plunges between two crags into that gulf. There is a striking view of Mt. Madison. In a few steps the path enters the Gulfside Trail, turns right, and coincides with it for a few yards, attaining the high plateau at the head of the ravine. Then the Air Line leads to the left (southwest), passing west of Mt. John Quincy Adams, up a rough way over large, angular stones, to the summit of Mt. Adams.

Air Line Trail (map 6)
Distances from Appalachia parking area
to Upper Bruin Trail junction: 2.8 mi., 3 hr.

to King Ravine Trail junction at Gateway: 3.3 mi., 3 hr. 40 min.

to Mt. Adams summit: 4.1 mi. (6.6 km.), 4 hr., 20 min.

to Madison Hut (via branch path): *est.* 3.8 mi., 3 hr. 35 min.

Scar Trail (RMC)

This trail avoids the bad part of the Valley Way and the very steep and rough part of the Air Line on the way to Mt. Adams. It passes through virgin woods and has good outlooks at about 3200 ft. It leads from the Valley Way 1.8 mi. from the Appalachia parking area to the Air Line at an old clearing known as Camp Placid Stream (*water unreliable*) 2.3 mi. from Appalachia. It divides 0.2 mi. from Valley Way; a loop to the right goes over Durand Scar and another viewpoint. The main trail leads left to the beginning of Watson Path, then ascends to unite with the loop.

Scar Trail (map 6)

Distances from Appalachia parking area

> *to* start of Scar Trail (via Valley Way): 1.8 mi.
> *to* Durand Scar (via loop): 2.1 mi.
> *to* Watson Path junction: 2.2 mi.
> *to* Air Line Trail junction: 2.8 mi.
> *to* Mt. Adams summit (via Air Line Trail): *est.* 4.6 mi. (7.3 km.), 4 hr. 40 min.

Distances are the same via main trail or via loop to Durand Scar.

Short Line (RMC)

This graded path leading from the Air Line to the King Ravine Trail below Mossy Fall was made in 1899-1901 by J. Rayner Edmands. It offers easy access to the Randolph Path and to King Ravine from the Appalachia parking area.

The Short Line branches right from the Air Line 0.8 mi. from the Appalachia parking area. At 1.3 mi. from the parking area it unites with the Randolph Path, coincides with it for 0.4 mi., then branches left and leads south up the valley of Cold Brook toward King Ravine, keeping a short distance east of the stream. At 2.8 mi. from the Appalachia parking area, the path joins the King Ravine Trail just below Mossy Fall.

Short Line (map 6)

Distances from Appalachia parking area

> *to* start of Short Line (via Air Line Trail): *est.* 0.8 mi.

to Randolph Path junction: 0.9 mi., 1¼ hr.
to King Ravine Trail junction: *est.* 2.8 mi., 2 hr. 10 min.

King Ravine Trail (RMC)

This branch from Lowe's Path through King Ravine was made by Charles E. Lowe in 1876.

It diverges left from Lowe's Path about 1.8 mi. from US Rte. 2 and rises over a low swell of Nowell Ridge. In 0.8 mi. it crosses Spur Brook below some cascades. In a few yards more it crosses the Randolph Path at its junction with the Amphibrach. Skirting the east spur of Nowell Ridge it enters the ravine and descends slightly. It crosses a western branch of Cold Brook, goes across the lower floor of the ravine, crosses the main stream, and in 0.2 mi. more is joined by the Short Line near the foot of Mossy Fall (*last sure water*). Just above this fall Cold Brook, already a good-sized stream, gushes from beneath the boulders that have fallen into the ravine.

So far the path has been fairly level, rising only 400 ft. in 1.5 mi.; but in the next 0.3 mi. it rises about 550 ft. and gains the upper floor of the ravine (3500 ft). The grandeur of the view of the ravine and to the north warrants a trip to the top of a bank of fallen rocks, even if you go no further. The Chemin des Dames branches left here. From this point to the foot of the headwall, about 0.4 mi., the path winds over and under boulders ranging up to the size of a small house. A short cut called the "Elevated" avoids some of the main boulder-caves. The main trail, the "Subway," 550 ft. long, is more interesting and takes only a few minutes more.

The Great Gully Trail diverges right a little farther south. In a boulder-cave near the foot of the headwall, there is ice throughout the year. About 2.6 mi. from Lowe's Path the ascent of the headwall begins. It is very steep, rising about 1300 ft. in the 0.4 mi. to the "Gateway," where the trail issues from the ravine between two crags, and immediately joins the Air Line close to its junction with the Gulfside Trail. From the Gateway there is a most striking view of Mt. Madison. Madison Hut is in sight, and can be reached by the Gulfside Trail, left. The summit of Mt. Adams is about 0.5 mi. further, by the Air Line.

King Ravine Trail (map 6)

Distances from start of Lowe's Path, US Rte. 2

> *to* start of King Ravine Trail (via Lowe's Path): 1.8 mi., 1 hr. 20 min.
>
> *to* Amphibrach Trail crossing: 2.7 mi., 2 hr.
>
> *to* Short Line Trail junction: 3.4 mi., 2 hr. 35 min.
>
> *to* foot of King Ravine headwall: 4 mi., 3 hr. 40 min.
>
> *to* Air Line Trail junction at Gateway: 4.5 mi., 4½ hr.
>
> *to* Mt. Adams summit (via Air Line Trail): 5.1 mi. (8.2 km.), 5 hr. 10 min.

Distances from Appalachia parking area (via Amphibrach Trail or via Randolph Path and Short Line Trail) *subtract* about 0.8 mi. from distances above.

The Chemin des Dames (RMC)

This trail climbs the east wall of the King Ravine and joins the Air Line Trail above treeline. It is the shortest route out of the ravine. There is *no water,* and the trail is very steep.

Chemin des Dames (map 6)

Distance from King Ravine Trail junction

> *to* Air Line Trail junction: 0.3 mi. (0.5 km.), 40 min.

Great Gully Trail (RMC)

This very steep trail leads up the southwest corner of King Ravine and makes some use of the gully, crossing the brook above a high fall. Near the top of the headwall is a *spring (water unreliable).* After emerging from the ravine the trail runs south to the junction of the Gulfside Trail and Lowe's Path, at Thunderstorm Junction.

Great Gully Trail (map 6)

Distance from King Ravine Trail junction

> *to* Gulfside Trail junction: *est.* 1 mi.

The Amphibrach (RMC)

This trail takes its name from its marking when it was first made, about 1883: three blazes — short, long, and short. It is a good approach to King Ravine or to any point reached via the Randolph Path or the Link, and also, via the Beechwood Way, to points reached by the Short Line, the Air Line, or the Valley Way. It ends at the Randolph Path and King Ravine Trail junction. For descent after dusk the Amphibrach has advantages over narrower footpaths, since this wider logging road is somewhat easier to follow.

The Amphibrach, in common with the Link, diverges right from the Air Line about 50 yd. south of its junction with the Valley Way and 100 yd. south of the Appalachia parking area. It runs west 0.8 mi. to where the Beechwood Way diverges left. Just east of Cold Brook the Sylvan Way enters left. Cold Brook is crossed on the Memorial Bridge. Shortly the Amphibrach turns left where the Link goes straight ahead. Just beyond, a side trail branches left 30 yd. to the foot of Cold Brook Fall. The Amphibrach now follows the course of Cold Brook, ascending west of the stream but generally not in sight of the water, and enters the WMNF. At 1.8 mi., near the confluence of Spur Brook and Cold Brook, the Monaway diverges right. The path crosses Spur Brook on the rocks, ascends the tongue of land between the two brooks, shortly diverges left (east), and climbs gradually, parallel to the badly eroded old trail. The Cliffway is crossed, and at 2.6 mi. the Amphibrach ends at "Pentadoi," the five-way intersection with the Randolph Path and King Ravine Trail.

Amphibrach Trail (map 6)
Distances from Appalachia parking area

to Cold Brook Fall (via Air Line Trail): *est.* 0.8 mi., 20 min.

to Monaway Trail junction: 1.8 mi.

to Randolph Path junction: 2.6 mi. (4.2 km.), 1½ hr.

Spur Trail (RMC)

This trail, cut in 1901 by Charles C. Torrey, leads up the east spur of the Nowell Ridge near the west edge of King Ravine, and at several points gives views into that gulf. The section known as the New Spur proved too steep for the amount of use it received and has been abandoned.

The Spur Trail diverges south from the Randolph Path west of Spur Brook about 100 yd. west of the King Ravine Trail. About 0.3 mi. above the Randolph Path, there is a short branch to Chandler Fall. About 0.3 mi. further up, the Hincks Trail to Gray Knob diverges right from the Spur Trail, and immediately above this point the Spur Trail crosses to the east side of the brook, the *last water* until Crag Camp. It ascends the spur that forms the west wall of King Ravine and goes over the Lower Crag, giving one of the best views of the ravine and an outlook east and north. A little farther on, a short branch leads to the Upper Crag, near which Crag Camp is situated. Here the Gray Knob Trail leads west to Gray Knob, 0.4 mi.

The trail continues up the spur, but not so near the edge of the ravine. It soon reaches the region of scrub and passes a trail that leads east to Knight's Castle, a crag at the edge of the ravine about 0.1 mi. from Spur Trail. Above this junction the trail leaves the scrub, ascends to the east of Adams 4, and merges with Lowe's Path just below the latter's crossing of the Gulfside Trail, or about 20 min. below the summit of Mt. Adams.

Spur Trail (map 6)

Distances from Appalachia parking area

to start of Spur Trail (via Randolph Path): 2.4 mi., 2 hr. 5 min.

to Crag Camp: 3.2 mi., 3 hr. 10 min.

to Mt. Adams summit: 4.6 mi. (7.4 km.), 4½ hr.

Hincks Trail (RMC) and Gray Knob Trail (RMC)

The Hincks Trail diverges right from the Spur Trail about 0.3 mi. above the Chandler Fall side trail and climbs steadily to Gray Knob. The Gray Knob Trail also leads from the Spur Trail, near Crag Camp, nearly on a contour to Gray Knob. The Gray Knob

Trail then continues a few yards to cross Lowe's Path, and some distance beyond, the Perch Path diverges right. Ascending slightly, the Gray Knob Trail joins the Randolph Path near its junction with Israel Ridge Path. Gray Knob Trail is a route from Crag Camp and Gray Knob to Edmands Col without loss of elevation.

Hincks Trail (map 6)
Distance from Spur Trail junction
to Gray Knob: *est.* 0.8 mi., ¾ hr.

Gray Knob Trail (map 6)
Distances from Spur Trail junction, Crag Camp
to Gray Knob: *est.* 0.4 mi., 25 min.
to Randolph Path junction: *est.* 1.4 mi., 1½ hr.

Perch Path (RMC)

This path runs right from the Gray Knob Trail, about 0.3 mi. south of Gray Knob. It descends slightly and, after crossing the Randolph Path, runs about level past the Perch and ends at the Israel Ridge Path.

Perch Path (map 6)
Distances from Gray Knob Trail junction
to Randolph Path crossing: 0.4 mi.
to the Perch: 0.5 mi.
to Israel Ridge Path junction: 0.5 mi. (0.8 km.)
Distance from Gray Knob Camp
to the Perch: 0.8 mi. (1 km.)

Beechwood Way (RMC)

This path starts from the Amphibrach 0.5 mi. from the Air Line. It follows a good logging road with moderate gradients. Just after it crosses Sylvan Way, there is *water* on the left. The path intersects the Air Line Trail and joins the Valley Way just below its junction with the Brookside Trail.

Beechwood Way (map 6)
Distance from Amphibrach Trail junction
to Valley Way junction: 1 mi., 40 min.

Cliffway (RMC)

This pleasure path leads from the Link 1.9 mi. from the Appalachia parking area, over some of the overgrown cliffs and ledges of the low swell of Nowell Ridge, then to Spur Brook Fall. It crosses the Amphibrach, then ends at the Randolph Path just west of Snyder Brook, 2.1 mi. from the Appalachia parking area. The only good view is from White Cliff. Gradients are easy, and much of the trail is level.

Cliffway (map 6)

Distances from Link Trail junction

to White Cliff: 0.7 mi.

to Spur Brook Fall: 1.6 mi.

to Randolph Path junction: 2 mi. (3.2 km.), 1 hr. 10 min.

Monaway, Ladderback Trail, Along the Brink (RMC)

The Monaway leads from the Cliffway near King Cliff to the Amphibrach at the confluence of Cold Brook and Spur Brook (Coldspur Ledges).

Ladderback Trail leads from Cliffway at White Cliff to Monaway 0.2 mi. above the Amphibrach.

A very short loop, Along the Brink, leads from Cliffway to Ladderback Trail via the mossy "brink" of White Cliff, affording good views of the Randolph valley.

Lowe's Path (AMC)

Cut in 1875-76 by Charles E. Lowe and Dr. William G. Nowell, from Lowe's house in Randolph to the summit of Mt. Adams, this is the oldest of the mountain trails that lead from the Randolph valley.

The trail begins on the south side of US Rte. 2 100 yd. west of Lowe's Store, where cars may be parked (a small fee is charged). It follows a broad wood road for 280 ft. and enters the woods right, crosses the railroad track and then the power line location. It ascends through woods at a moderate grade, at first toward the southwest then swinging more south, crosses several small brooks, bears left where it enters the old trail, and in 120 yd. crosses the Link.

In 0.2 mi. the King Ravine Trail branches left. The main path, about 2.3 mi. from US Rte. 2, passes close to the Log Cabin. Here two short spur paths lead left to the Randolph Path. Cabin-Cascade Trail to the Israel Ridge Path in Cascade Ravine (1 mi.) leaves on the right. *Water* is always found at the Log Cabin and midway between the cabin and treeline. About 0.3 mi. above the Log Cabin, Lowe's Path crosses the Randolph Path, and 0.5 mi. farther on the Gray Knob Trail crosses (leading left to Gray Knob). The mile ending at Gray Knob is steep.

The rest of the trail is above treeline and much exposed to wind. Views are very fine. The trail ascends steadily for 0.8 mi. to the summit known as Adams 4, the culminating peak of Nowell Ridge. It descends a little, keeping to the left of Sam Adams. The Spur Trail enters left. Lowe's Path then crosses the Gulfside Trail at Thunderstorm Junction (joined at the same point by the Great Gully Trail), turns a little more easterly, and ascends the summit of Mt. Adams. The Israel Ridge Path enters from the right about 0.2 mi. below the summit.

Lowe's Path (map 6)

Distances from US Rte. 2

to Link Trail crossing: 1.6 mi.

to King Ravine Trail junction: 1.8 mi., 1 hr. 20 min.

to Log Cabin: 2.3 mi., 2 hr.

to Randolph Path crossing: 2.5 mi.

to Gray Knob Trail crossing: 3 mi.

to Adams 4 summit: 3.9 mi.

to Mt. Adams summit: 4.5 mi. (7.2 km.), 4 hr. 20 min.

Israel Ridge Path (RMC)

This trail, which extends from near Bowman NH to Mt. Adams, was constructed as a graded path by J. Rayner Edmands beginning in 1892. Although hurricanes and slides have severely damaged the original trail, and there have been many relocations, the upper part is still one of the finest and most beautiful of the Randolph trails. (Some brook crossings may be difficult in high water.)

From Bowman follow the Castle Trail for 1.3 mi. Here, the Israel Ridge Path branches left and shortly crosses to the east bank of the Israel River. It follows the river for 1.6 mi., then diverges left where the Castle Ravine Trail proceeds straight ahead. The Israel Ridge Path bears southeast up the slope of Nowell Ridge. At 2.5 mi. it unites with the Link, follows it south on a level grade, and enters virgin growth. From this point to treeline, the forest has not been disturbed by lumbering, though slides have done much damage. In a very short distance the Israel Ridge Path branches left from the Link, and a short distance above, the Cabin-Cascades Trail from the Log Cabin enters left.

The first cascade is reached by following the Link a few yards right.

The Israel Ridge Path ascends on the north side of Cascade Brook to the head of the second cascade, where it passes to the south side. It runs southwest, then southeast, making a large zigzag up the steep slope of the ridge called Emerald Tongue or Israel Ridge, between Cascade and Castle brooks.

Soon the path turns sharply east, and Emerald Trail leads in 0.2 mi. to Emerald Bluff, a remarkable outlook, and continues down into Castle Ravine. The Israel Ridge Path zigzags up a rather steep slope where the Perch Path diverges left (east). The main path turns sharply south and ascends to treeline where it joins the Randolph Path 3.8 mi. from Bowman. It is a little north of this junction that the Gray Knob Trail from Gray Knob enters Randolph Path from the left. For a short distance the Randolph Path and Israel Ridge Path coincide. Then, the latter branches to the left and, curving east, ascends the southwest ridge of Mt. Adams, passes to the right of the viewpoint called the Eye and to the left of the summit known as Adams 5, to join the Gulfside Trail near Storm Lake. It coincides with the Gulfside for 0.5 mi., running northeast past Peabody *Spring* and south of Mt. Sam

Adams, aiming for the Adams-Sam Adams col. Before reaching the col the Israel Ridge Path branches right from the Gulfside Trail, and in 0.1 mi. enters Lowe's Path, which leads in 0.2 mi. to the summit of Mt. Adams.

Israel Ridge Path (map 6)

Distances from US Rte. 2, Bowman NH

   to start of Israel Ridge Path (via Castle Trail): *est.* 1.3 mi.
   to Castle Ravine Trail junction: 1.6 mi.
   to Link Trail junction: 2.4 mi., 1¾ hr.
   to Perch Path junction: 3.5 mi., 3 hr.
   to Randolph Path junction: 4 mi., 3 hr. 20 min.
   to Gulfside Trail junction: 4.4 mi., 3 hr. 50 min.
   to Mt. Adams summit: 5.2 mi. (8.4 km.), 4½ hr.
   to Edmands Col (via Randolph Path): 4.4 mi., 3 hr. 40 min.
   to Mt. Washington summit (via Randolph Path and Gulfside Trail): 8.4 mi., 6 hr. 25 min.

Castle Ravine Trail (RMC)

This trail leads through Castle Ravine, to the Randolph Path near Edmands Col.

From Bowman follow the Castle Trail and the Israel Ridge Path to a point 1.6 mi. from Bowman. Here the Israel Ridge Path turns left up a slope, while the Castle Ravine Trail leads straight ahead near the river. It crosses to the west bank (not easy in high water) and soon reaches a point abreast of the Forks of Israel, where Cascade and Castle brooks unite to form Israel River.

The trail crosses to the east bank, passes a fine cascade, and recrosses to the west bank. In general, it follows what is left of the logging road, but where that is too badly eroded, it goes through the woods. After entering Castle Ravine, the trail crosses to the east bank and follows a good logging road high above the brook. After about 0.6 mi. of steady ascent, the Link enters from the left. The two trails coincide for about 0.3 mi. when they cross to the southwest side of the brook in a tract of cool virgin forest beloved of *musca nigra*. Here the Link and the Castle

Ravine Trail pass Emerald Trail, which diverges left for Israel Ridge. The Link then turns right while the Castle Ravine Trail continues up the ravine southwest of the brook. Close to the foot of the headwall it crosses again, and in a few yards. reaches the place where Castle Brook emerges from under the mossy boulders that have fallen from the headwall. At the foot of the headwall, the trail turns left and mounts the steep slope to Roof Rock, under which it passes *(last water)*. This is a good shelter from rain.

Rising steeply southeast, the trail soon winds up a patch of bare rocks, marked by small cairns and dashes of paint, re-entering the scrub at a large cairn. In a few hundred feet it emerges from the scrub at the foot of a steep slide of very loose rock (use caution when descending). It ascends, marked by paint, to the top of the headwall, over rocks and grass, marked by cairns, to Spaulding Spring. It joins the Randolph Path (sign) near Edmands Col.

Descending, leave the Randolph Path (left) at a sign about 0.1 mi. north of Edmands Col, go to Spaulding Spring, then follow cairns north.

Castle Ravine Trail (map 6)

Distances from US Rte. 2, Bowman NH

> *to* start of Castle Ravine Trail (via Castle Trail): *est.* 1.6 mi.
>
> *to* Forks of Israel: *est.* 1.9 mi.
>
> *to* Link Trail junction: *est.* 3 mi., 2 hr. 20 min.
>
> *to* Emerald Trail junction: *est.* 3.2 mi.
>
> *to* Roof Rock, Castle Ravine: *est.* 3.6 mi.
>
> *to* Randolph Path junction, Edmands Col: *est.* 4.3 mi. (6.8 km.), 4 hr. 10 min.

Cabin-Cascades Trail (RMC)

One of the very early AMC trails (1881), Cabin-Cascades leads from the Log Cabin on Lowe's Path to the Israel Ridge Path. It links the Log Cabin and the trails in the vicinity of

Cascade Ravine, as well as the cascades themselves.

The trail begins at the Log Cabin, branching from Lowe's Path, and descends slightly to Israel Ridge Path just above its upper junction with the Link, near the first cascade of Cascade Brook and not far from the second cascade.

Cabin-Cascades Trail (map 6)

Distances from Log Cabin on Lowe's Path

to Israel Ridge Path junction: 1 mi.

to first cascade, Cascade Brook (via Link Trail): 1.1 mi.

to second cascade, Cascade Brook (via Israel Ridge Path): 1.1 mi. (1.7 km.)

Emerald Trail (RMC)

This trail provides a link in an attractive circuit from Bowman, up Israel Ridge, past Emerald Bluff, and down via Castle Ravine. It is steep and rough in spots, but the fine forest above Castle Ravine makes it worth the effort. The trail leaves the Israel Ridge Path high on the ridge about 0.3 mi. below the Perch, and runs level through high scrub for 0.1 mi., where a trail leads straight ahead 25 yd. to Emerald Bluff, an excellent outlook. The main trail bears left and shortly begins the steep and rough descent into Castle Ravine—follow blazes carefully. After 0.5 mi. the trail crosses several brooks, rises slightly, and enters the coinciding Castle Ravine and Link trails, about 0.2 mi. from their lower junction. Follow Castle Ravine Trail down to Israel Ridge Path and Bowman.

Emerald Trail (map 6)

Distances from Israel Ridge Path

to Emerald Bluff: 0.2 mi.

to Castle Ravine Trail/Link Trail junction: 0.7 mi.

Distance round trip from US Rte. 2, Bowman NH

to Bowman NH (via Castle Trail, Israel Ridge Path, Emerald Trail, Castle Ravine Trail, and Castle Trail): *est.* 7.3 mi., 5 hr. 15 min.

MOUNT JEFFERSON

This 5715-ft. mountain has three summits a short distance apart, in line northwest and southeast, the highest in the middle. Perhaps the most striking view is down the Great Gulf with the Carter Range beyond, but there are others—of the Fabyan Plain and down the broad valley of the Israel. The Castellated Ridge, sharpest and most salient of the White Mountain ridges, extends northwest, forming the southwest wall of Castle Ravine. The view of the "Castles" from the village of Bowman is unforgettable. The Caps Ridge, similar in formation, but less striking, extends to the west. The two eastern ridges, Jefferson's "knees," truncated by the Great Gulf, have precipitous wooded slopes and gently sloping tops.

From the summit the Caps Ridge Trail leads west to Jefferson Notch, the Castle Path north then northwest down the Castellated Ridge, and the Mt. Jefferson Loop south to join the Gulfside Trail toward Mt. Clay. The Six Husbands Trail (see Section 3) and the Loop together run east from the summit, the Loop soon branching northeast to join the Gulfside toward Edmands Col, while the Six Husbands Trail continues east over one of the "knees" into the Great Gulf.

South of the peak of Mt. Jefferson is a smooth, grassy plateau called Monticello Lawn, traversed by the Gulfside Trail.

Jefferson Ravine, a glacial gulf tributary to the Great Gulf, has no trail.

Mt. Jefferson (map 6)
Distances to Mt. Jefferson summit
from Glen House site, NH Rte. 16 (via Osgood Trail, Great Gulf Trail, and Six Husbands Trail): *est*. 6.8 mi., 5 hr. 25 min.

from Appalachia parking area (via Randolph Path, Gulfside Trail, and Loop Trail): 6 mi., 5 hr.

from Appalachia parking area (via Link Trail, Castle Ravine Trail, Gulfside Trail, and Loop Trail): 6.8 mi., 5 hr. 35 min.

from US Rte. 2, Bowman NH (via Castle Trail, Israel Ridge
   Path, Randolph Path, Gulfside Trail, and Loop Trail): 4.9
   mi., 4 hr. 20 min.
from US Rte. 2, Bowman NH (via Castle Trail): *est.* 4.8 mi.,
   4¾ hr.
from Jefferson Notch Rd. (via Caps Ridge Trail): *est* 2.4 mi.
   (3.8 km.), 2 hr. 40 min.

Castle Trail (AMC)

Since it was made in 1883-84 by Cook, Sargent, Watson,
Matthews, and Hunt, most of this trail has been relocated. It
leaves US Rte. 2 at Bowman, 3 mi. west of the Appalachia
parking area and 4.2 mi. east of the junction of US Rte. 2 and NH
Rte. 115. Park on the Rte. 2 side of the track, cross the railroad,
and follow the right driveway for 150 yd. to where the trail enters
woods on the right. The trail circles left, crosses a power line,
and at approximately 0.3 mi. crosses the Israel River at the site of
an old footbridge.

At 1.3 mi. the Israel Ridge Path branches left (east). *(Last sure
water* is a short distance along this trail.) The Castle Trail
continues southeast, on the northeast flank of Mt. Bowman. At
2.3 mi. the trail passes a large boulder on the left and becomes
much steeper for the next half mile. At 2.8 mi., near the saddle
between Mt. Bowman and the Castle Ridge, about 3375 ft., it
becomes less steep. The view into the ravine left and toward
Jefferson is quite spectacular. The trail dips slightly, then continues level along the ridge through thick growth. At 3.4 mi. it is
crossed by the Link coming up from Castle Ravine and leading
right to the Caps Ridge Trail. The ridge becomes very narrow
and the trail is steep and rough. After passing over two ledges
with an outlook from each, it reaches the first and most prominent Castle (4455 ft.) 3.6 mi. from Bowman. The view is very
fine. The trail leads on over several lesser crags and ascends to
where the Castellated Ridge joins the main mass of Mt. Jefferson. Above, the Cornice leads northeast to the Randolph Path
near Edmands Col and south to the Caps Ridge and Gulfside

trails. The Castle Trail continues to within a few yards of the summit of Mt. Jefferson, where it connects with the Mt. Jefferson Loop and the Six Husbands and Caps Ridge trails.

Castle Trail (map 6)

Distances from US Rte. 2, Bowman NH

to Israel Ridge Path junction: *est*. 1.3 mi.

to first Castle: *est*. 3.6 mi., 3½ hr.

to Mt. Jefferson summit: *est*. 4.8 mi. (7.6 km.), 4¾ hr.

to Mt. Washington summit (via Jefferson Loop and Gulfside trails): *est*. 8.1 mi., 7 hr.

Jefferson Notch Road: Jefferson Notch

This dirt road leads from the so-called Lower Rd. in Jefferson Highlands through the notch between Mt. Jefferson and the Dartmouth Range to the road to the Marshfield Base Station of the cog railway, officially called the Base Rd. The extension south from the Base Rd. to the Crawford House site is called the Mt. Clinton Rd.

Jefferson Notch Rd. is usually good for driving in summer and early fall. Use caution, since it is winding and narrow in places, and watch out for logging trucks. The beginning of the Caps Ridge Trail at Jefferson Notch (3000 ft.) is the highest point reached by the automobile roads surrounding the Presidential Range, so driving to Jefferson Notch permits the easiest ascent of a high summit. Castellated Ridge can also be reached via the Link Trail.

Jefferson Notch Rd. (map 6)

Distances from Lower Rd. junction

to Jefferson Notch: *est*. 5.5 mi., 2 hr. 40 min.

to Base Rd. junction: *est*. 8.5 mi., 3 hr. 40 min.

to Crawford House site (via Mt. Clinton Rd.): *est*. 12.5 mi.

to Marshfield Station (via Boundary Line Trail): *est*. 8.3 mi., 3 hr. 40 min.

Boundary Line Trail (WMNF)

The trail begins on the north side of the Base Rd. about 0.5 mi.

west of the Marshfield station of the cog railway. It soon crosses Franklin Brook, then the Ammonoosuc River. After heading east 100 yd., it turns north and runs north 1 mi. approximately along a surveyor's line, crossing Clay Brook, to Jefferson Notch Rd., about 1.5 mi. below the Caps Ridge Trail. (Signs may be missing.)

Caps Ridge Trail (AMC)

Because the Caps Ridge Trail starts at an elevation of 3000 ft., it makes possible an easy ascent of Mts. Jefferson, Clay, and Washington, and by the Sphinx Trail (see Section 3) gives access to the upper part of the Great Gulf. It can be reached from the Marshfield station by the Boundary Line Trail.

The Caps Ridge Trail leaves the Jefferson Notch Rd. at the north end of the height-of-land in Jefferson Notch. There is *no water* on the trail but water may be had at Jefferson Brook, which crosses the road 0.5 mi. south from the foot of the trail. About 0.4 mi. from the road the Link diverges left to the Castle Trail. Running east up the Ridge of the Caps, the trail passes an outcrop of granite that has several potholes, presumably formed by torrential streams, showing that the continental ice sheet covered the ridge at this point. About 1.5 mi. from the road the trail emerges from the woods at the lower Cap, a prominent ledge.

The trail follows the narrow crest of the ridge over minor ledges and the upper Cap (4830 ft.). Use care when ascending and descending the Caps: many of the ledges are steep and are slippery when wet.

About 0.1 mi. above the upper Cap the Cornice leads left to the Castle Trail and Edmands Col. By avoiding the summit of Mt. Jefferson the Cornice saves about 500 ft. of climbing, but it is very rough. Fifty feet above, the Cornice again branches right and leads southeast, rising gently, 0.5 mi. to the Gulfside Trail near Monticello Lawn. Hiking time to Mt. Washington, Mt. Clay, or the head of the Great Gulf is 25 min. less via this cutoff than via Jefferson summit. Above the Cornice, the Caps Ridge Trail continues east keeping a little south of the crest of the ridge,

to the summit of Mt. Jefferson where it meets the Castle and Six
Husbands trails and the Mt. Jefferson Loop.

Caps Ridge Trail (map 6)

Distances from Jefferson Notch Rd.

> ***to*** lower Cap: 1.4 mi., 1½ hr.
>
> ***to*** upper Cap: 1.8 mi., 1 hr. 50 min.
>
> ***to*** Mt. Jefferson summit: 2.4 mi. (3.8 km.), 2 hr. 40 min.
>
> ***to*** Gulfside Trail junction (via the Cornice): *est.* 2.2 mi.
>
> ***to*** Sphinx Trail junction (via the Cornice and Gulfside Trail):
> *est.* 2.8 mi.
>
> ***to*** Mt. Washington summit (via the Cornice and Gulfside
> Trail): *est.* 5.3 mi., 4 hr. 25 min.

MOUNT CLAY

Mt. Clay, usually counted as one of the Northern Peaks, is
more properly a northern shoulder of Mt. Washington, corres-
ponding to Boott Spur on the south and Nelson Crag on the
northeast. Its 5532-ft. summit is only 135 ft. above the col that
connects it with the main mass. Mt. Clay's most interesting
feature is the eastern cliffs, which begin close to the summits and
form the west wall of the Great Gulf. The Mt. Clay Loop off the
Gulfside Trail goes over all three summits. The south summit
also can be reached by a short scramble from the Gulfside Trail.

Jewell Trail (WMNF)

This graded trail climbs the ridge that leads west from Mt.
Clay. Named for a Sergeant Jewell, an observer for the Army
Signal Corps on Mt. Washington, it leads from the Marshfield
station (parking area privately owned and operated by the cog
railway) to the Gulfside Trail north of the Clay-Washington col,
and provides an easy ascent of Mt. Washington. In bad weather
the Ammonoosuc Ravine Trail (see Section 4) is safer, since it
leads past the Lakes of the Clouds Hut.

From the Marshfield station the trail immediately crosses the cog railway, then the Ammonoosuc, and zigzags to the crest of the low ridge between the Ammonoosuc and Clay Brook. It descends slightly to the latter, crosses at a fine cascade, switches back northeast up the south flank of the ridge, and winds around its west end. Avoiding the craggy crest, it slabs the north flank and comes out above treeline on the west slope of Mt. Clay. It zigzags up the slope of Mt. Clay and enters the Gulfside Trail 0.3 mi. northwest of the Clay-Washington col. For Mt. Washington, follow the Gulfside right. For Mt. Clay, scramble up the rocks above the junction.

Jewell Trail (map 6)

Distances from the Marshfield Station

to Clay Brook crossing: 0.5 mi.

to Gulfside Trail junction: 3 mi.

to Clay-Washington col (via Gulfside Trail): 3.2 mi.

to Mt. Washington summit (via Gulfside Trail): 4.6 mi. (7.4 km.), 3 hr. 55 min.

SECTION 3

The Great Gulf

This is the valley between Mt. Washington and the Northern Peaks. The views from the walls and from points on the floor of the Great Gulf are among the best in New England.

To preserve its unique scenic values, it was designated a Wilderness Area within the WMNF in 1959. Since 1980, *day-use permits* are no longer required for the Great Gulf Wilderness Area. Permits are, however, required for *overnight use,* with a limit of 60 campers in the Gulf on any night. Contact the USFS, Gorham, NH 03581 (603-466-2713) (see also Section 22). There were formerly shelters in the Great Gulf, but careless campers left trash and damaged vegetation. Following wilderness policy, the USFS dismantled the shelters in 1976 and limited summer camping in the Gulf.

The Great Gulf, from 1100 to 1600 ft. deep, is a typical bowl-shaped gulf for 3.5 mi. from its head, and then becomes a more open valley that extends about 1.5 mi. farther east. It is drained by the West Branch of the Peabody River. Steep slopes and abundant water result in a great number of cascades. The Great Gulf and its tributary gulfs, Madison Gulf, Jefferson Ravine, and the Sphinx, were hollowed out by the action of glaciers, mainly before the last ice age.

The Great Gulf was observed by Darby Field in 1642. The name probably had its origin in 1823 in a casual statement of Ethan Allen Crawford, who, having lost his way in cloudy weather, came to "the edge of a great gulf." A few years later the name began to appear in the literature of the White Mountains. The region was visited in 1829 by Professor J. W. Robbins, but was little known until, in 1881, Benjamin F. Osgood blazed the first trail, from the Osgood Trail to the headwall.

Refer to map 6, the Mt. Washington Range, and the USGS Mt. Washington Quadrangle.

The Appalachian Trail follows the Osgood Trail, the Osgood Cutoff, and the Madison Gulf Trail.

GREAT GULF TRAIL (WMNF)

For use restrictions, see Section 22.

There are plans under consideration to relocate the start of this trail, together with the Osgood Trail, over new bridges to a point on NH Rte. 16 (Pinkham Notch Highway) 1.5 mi. north of the Glen House site.

The Pinkham B or Dolly Copp Rd. branches west from Rte. 16 4.4 mi. southwest of Gorham (Rte. 16 - Rte. 2 junction) and 3.5 mi. north of the Glen House site. It immediately crosses the Peabody River, runs west, passes the entrance to Dolly Copp Campground (left), and about 500 ft. beyond bears right, passes the entrance to the Barnes Field Camping area (right), and runs northwest to Randolph.

To reach the Great Gulf Trail bear left onto the entrance road, and shortly after bear left (south) on the main camp road. The Great Gulf Trail leaves the south side of the road just before reaching the site of the old bridge crossing.

For hikers with automobiles it is better to drive to the Glen House site and enter via the Osgood Trail. This saves 0.7 mi. of walking and may be drier in wet weather.

The Great Gulf Trail follows a logging road south, on the west bank of the Peabody River until it is joined by the West Branch, in about a mile. The trail then continues northwest of the West Branch. At about 2.3 mi. it crosses the Osgood Trail.

The trail soon approaches the West Branch and runs for about 0.3 mi. close to the north bank. Then, diverging from the stream, it ascends to the Bluff, where there is a good view of the Gulf and the mountains around it. The trail follows the edge of the Bluff, descends sharply left, crosses Parapet Brook on a bridge, then continues to the crest of the little ridge that separates Parapet Brook from the West Branch. At the top of this crest the Madison Gulf Trail enters right, and the two trails descend together for a short distance to cross the West Branch, on a suspension bridge. After ascending the steep bank, the Madison Gulf Trail branches left, while the Great Gulf Trail branches right, up the south bank of the river.

In 0.8 mi. the Great Gulf Trail crosses Chandler Brook, and on the far bank the Chandler Brook Trail diverges left and ascends to the Mt. Washington Auto Rd. The trail continues close to the river for more than 0.5 mi., passing in sight of the mouth of the stream that issues from Jefferson Ravine on the north, to join the Six Husbands (right) and Wamsutta (left) trails.

The Great Gulf Trail continues on the southeast bank, then in the bed of the stream, to the foot of a waterfall. Scrambling up to the left of this fall, it crosses a large branch brook and passes left of a beautiful cascade on the main stream. The trail soon crosses to the northwest bank, and in a short distance crosses the brook that descends from the Clay-Jefferson col. At this point the Sphinx Trail, leading to the Gulfside Trail, diverges right. The Great Gulf Trail soon crosses again to the southeast bank of the West Branch, passing waterfalls, including Weetamoo, the finest in the Gulf. There are remarkable views down the Gulf to Mts. Adams and Madison. The trail crosses an eastern tributary and, after a slight ascent, reaches Spaulding Lake, 4250 ft. elevation, 6.3 mi. from the Glen House site, and about 1.5 mi. by trail from the summit of Mt. Washington.

The Great Gulf Trail continues on the east side of the lake, and a little beyond begins to ascend the steep headwall. The trail runs south and southeast, rising 1600 ft. in about 0.5 mi., over fragments of stone, many of which are loose. The way may be poorly marked, because snow slides sweep away cairns, but paint blazes probably will be visible on the rocks. The trail curves a little left until within a few yards of the top of the headwall, then, bearing slightly right, emerges from the gulf and ends at the Gulfside Trail near the cog railway. It is 0.3 mi. to the summit of Mt. Washington by the Gulfside Trail and Crawford Path.

Descending from Mt. Washington, follow the Crawford Path west from the summit. Just below the old corral the Gulfside

Trail diverges right. Follow it north until it crosses the cog
railway. A few yards beyond, where the Gulfside Trail turns
sharp left, the Great Gulf Trail continues straight ahead north a
few yards to the edge of the gulf, and plunges down.

Great Gulf Trail (map 6)

Distances from Glen House site, NH Rte. 16

to Great Gulf Trail junction (via Osgood Trail): 1.6 mi., 50 min.

to Madison Gulf Trail junction: 2.3 mi., 1 hr. 40 min.

to Six Husbands Trail/Wamsutta Trail junction: 4.4 mi., 3 hr.

to Sphinx Trail junction: 5.4 mi., 3 hr. 50 min.

to Spaulding Lake: 6.3 mi., 4½ hr.

to Gulfside Trail junction: 7.1 mi., 6 hr.

to Mt. Washington summit (via Gulfside Trail and Crawford
    Path): 7.5 mi. (12.1 km.), 6 hr. 20 min.

Distances from Dolly Copp Campground

add 0.7 mi. and ½ hr. to above

MADISON GULF TRAIL (AMC)

For use restrictions, see Section 22.

This trail begins at the Mt. Washington Auto Rd. a little more
than 2 mi. from the Glen House site, opposite the Old Jackson
Rd., and descends gently to the West Branch where it meets the
Great Gulf Trail, then ascends along Parapet Brook to the
Parapet, a point 0.3 mi. from Madison Hut. With the Osgood
Trail, the Old Jackson Rd., or the Raymond Path, the Madison
Gulf Trail affords routes to the hut from the Glen House site,
from Pinkham Notch Camp, and from the Hermit Lake shelters
respectively. It is well marked, well protected from storms, and
has plenty of *water*. On the headwall of the Gulf it is very steep
and possibly hazardous. In wet weather, stream crossings and
steep slabs may be a problem. The last mile of the ascent to the
Parapet is rough and very steep, going over several ledge out-
crops, bouldery areas, and a chimney with loose rock. Hikers
with full packs should allow extra time. From the Auto Rd. to

Osgood Cutoff it is part of the Appalachian Trail and so blazed in white; the rest is blazed in blue.

Leave the Auto Rd. after the 2-mile mark, at the end of a straight stretch, via the trail leading north to "Lowe's Bald Spot" opposite the Old Jackson Rd. junction. In a short distance, in a little pass west of Lowe's Bald Spot, the trail to this viewpoint branches right, reaching the summit in 5 min. The view is excellent.

The Madison Gulf Trail bears left and ascends about 75 ft. over a ledge with a limited view, descends rapidly for a short distance, then gently, crossing several water courses. The trail comes within sound of the West Branch of the Peabody River and continues along on contour until it meets the Great Gulf Trail on the south bank. The Madison Gulf Trail turns sharp right and, coinciding with the Great Gulf Trail, descends the steep bank to the West Branch.

Both trails cross a suspension bridge to the north bank, then coincide for a few yards farther up a slope east to the crest of the little ridge that divides Parapet Brook from the West Branch. At this point the Madison Gulf Trail diverges sharply left (northwest) and leads up the ridge. The Great Gulf Trail goes straight ahead northeast. Soon leaving the crest of the ridge, the Madison Gulf Trail crosses to the northeast side of Parapet Brook and is joined on the right by the Madison Gulf Cutoff from the Osgood Trail, affording a route from the Glen House site, about 2.9 mi. below, easier than that via the Bluff. At this junction the Osgood Cutoff continues ahead, leading in 0.5 mi. to the Osgood Trail for Mt. Madison and Madison Hut. The Madison Gulf Trail turns left, continues up the stream, soon crosses to the southwest side, and diverges from the brook, to which it later returns, crossing a small branch brook and turning sharply left just before it reaches the main stream. It soon crosses again to the northeast bank, follows that for a little way, then turns right, ascending steeply with good views.

The trail next turns left, slabbing the mountainside high above the brook, which it approaches again at the mouth of the branch stream from Osgood Ridge. It ascends rapidly between the two brooks, crosses to the west bank of the main stream, then recrosses, and, climbing more gradually, gains the lower floor of the gulf, crosses again, and soon reaches Sylvan Cascade, a fine fall.

The Madison Gulf Trail then ascends to the upper floor of the gulf, where it crosses four brooks. From the floor it rises gradually to Mossy Slide at the foot of the headwall, then ascends very rapidly by a stream.

The trail now turns left, continues near a brook partly hidden among the rocks, then ascends very steeply. Ultimately, it reaches the scrub, emerges on the rocks, and ends at the Parapet Trail. Turn left for the Parapet (400 ft.) and Madison Hut (0.3 mi.), and right for the Osgood Trail (0.6 mi.).

Madison Gulf Trail (map 6)

Distances from Mt. Washington Auto Rd.

to Great Gulf Trail junction: *est.* 2.3 mi., 1¼ hr.

to foot of Madison Gulf headwall: *est.* 4 mi., 3 hr.

to the Parapet: *est.* 4.5 mi., 4 hr.

to Madison Hut (via Osgood Cutoff and Osgood Trail): *est.* 5 mi. (8 km.), 4¼ hr.

Distances from Pinkham Notch Camp

to Madison Hut (via Old Jackson Rd., Madison Gulf Trail, Osgood Cutoff, and Osgood Trail): *est.* 7 mi. (10 km.), 5¾ hr.

to Mt. Madison summit (via Old Jackson Rd., Madison Gulf Trail, Osgood Cutoff, and Osgood Trail): *est.* 7½ mi., 6 hr.

Distance from Hermit Lake Shelters

to Madison Hut (via Raymond Path, Madison Gulf Trail, Osgood Cutoff, and Osgood Trail): *est.* 7.8 mi., 5¾ hr.

CHANDLER BROOK TRAIL (AMC)

About 1 mi. in length, this trail diverges south from the Great Gulf Trail immediately after it crosses Chandler Brook. It follows the brook rather closely, crossing three times. Fine waterfalls can be seen from the trail. From the last crossing the course is southeast. Rising over a confused mass of stones, and keeping west of interesting rock formations, the trail enters the Mt. Washington Auto Rd. near a ledge of white quartz slightly less than 0.5 mi. above the 4-mile post, at the bend above the Halfway House. The trail is blazed in blue.

Descending, look for this white ledge, which is close to the Auto Rd. The trail is marked by cairns here and is visible from the road. For use restrictions, see Section 22.

WAMSUTTA TRAIL (AMC)

Weetamoo was a queen of the Pocasset Indians, and a beautiful waterfall in the Great Gulf bears her name. This trail was named for the first of her six husbands.

The Wamsutta Trail begins at the Great Gulf Trail opposite the start of the Six Husbands Trail, 4.4 mi. from the Glen House site on NH Rte. 16, and ends at the Mt. Washington Auto Rd. immediately above the 6-mile mark, opposite the north end of the Alpine Garden Trail. The Wamsutta Trail is blazed with yellow paint.

Leaving the Great Gulf Trail, the trail runs southwest to a small stream, then ascends gradually. Soon it climbs the very steep and rough northerly spur of Chandler Ridge. Passing a quartz ledge on the right, the trail continues steeply to a small, open knob on the crest of the spur, which offers a good view. It next goes through trees at a gradual ascent, passing a *spring* on the right. Continuing along the crest, the trail emerges at treeline and climbs to the winter shortcut of the Auto Rd. After turning right, it ends in a few yards at the Auto Rd.

Descending from the Auto Rd., be sure to turn left off the winter shortcut.

Wamsutta Trail (map 6)
Distance from Great Gulf Trail junction
   to Auto Rd.: 1.7 mi., 1 hr. 55 min.

SIX HUSBANDS TRAIL (AMC)

This name honors the six successive husbands of Weetamoo. The Six Husbands Trail begins at the Great Gulf Trail at the same point as the Wamsutta Trail, 4.4 mi. from the Glen House site on NH Rte. 16, descends northwest for a few yards, and crosses the West Branch. In times of high water go upstream to a better crossing. The trail bears right away from the West Branch, then ascends gently north until it comes close to the stream that flows from Jefferson Ravine, which it ascends on its southwest bank. At 0.6 mi. the Buttress Trail branches right and crosses the stream. The Six Husbands Trail continues a little farther beside the brook (*last sure water*), turns west and leads under two huge boulders. It ascends by ladders made of two-by-fours and passes near a cavern (10 yd. to left), where snow and ice may be found even in August. The trail soon comes to an overhanging ledge and leads along under its edge for a short distance, ascending again by ladders. It then leads to a crag affording a good view up the gulf, continues steep, and keeps close to the crest of the ridge until it comes out on the north "knee" of Jefferson (view). The ascent becomes easier. Across the bare stretches the trail is marked by cairns. The Edmands Col Cutoff branches right, leading in 0.5 mi. to Edmands Col. Beyond, the trail becomes steeper, begins to climb the cone of Mt. Jefferson, and leads past a snowbank that often lasts well into July. Marked by cairns, the trail crosses the Gulfside Trail and continues west to the summit of Mt. Jefferson, coinciding for the last 100 yd. with the Mt. Jefferson Loop. At the summit it meets the Castle and Caps Ridge trails. The trail is blazed in blue.

In *reverse:* enter the Great Gulf down this steep, difficult trail only in emergency (see also Section 22).

Six Husbands Trail (map 6)
Distances from Great Gulf Trail junction
   to Buttress Trail junction: *est*. 0.5 mi.

to Gulfside Trail crossing: 1.9 mi., 2 hr. 5 min.
to Mt. Jefferson summit: 2.2 mi. (3.5 km.), 2 hr. 25 min.

BUTTRESS TRAIL (AMC)

This is the most direct route from the upper part of the Great Gulf to Madison Hut. The trail, blazed in blue, begins in the ravine between Mts. Adams and Jefferson, leaving the north side of the Six Husbands Trail at a point 0.6 mi. northwest of the Great Gulf Trail. It immediately crosses the brook (*last sure water*) flowing out of Jefferson Ravine, bears right (east) in 0.1 mi., and climbs diagonally across a steep slope of large, loose, angular fragments of rock. Some are easily dislodged, so care must be taken. The trail continues in the same direction, rising gradually along a steep, wooded slope. At the top of this slope, 0.6 mi. from start, the trail turns north across a gently sloping upland covered with trees. There is a *spring (reliable water)* on the left, at about 1 mi. As the trail nears treeline, it passes under a large boulder. At about 1.3 mi. the trail reaches the foot of the steep, rock-covered peak of Mt. Adams. Here, a little left of the trail, a small, ledgy summit provides a fine view.

The trail runs nearly level northwest and then north, passing through patches of scrub, across patches of rock fragments, and crossing two *brooks*. Then, rising slightly through scrub, it passes through a gap between the Parapet and John Quincy, and, just southwest of the lake, it enters Star Lake Trail, which leads in less than 0.3 mi. to Madison Hut.

Buttress Trail (map 6)
Distances from Six Husbands Trail junction
    to Parapet: 1.9 mi.
    to Madison Hut (via Star Lake Trail): 2.1 mi. (3.4 km.), 2 hr.

SPHINX TRAIL (AMC)

This trail derives its name from the profile of a rock formation seen from just below the meadow where *water* is found. The trail is important because it affords the best means of escape for anyone overtaken by storm on Mt. Clay or on the south part of Mt. Jefferson. It diverges east from the Gulfside Trail just north of the Clay-Jefferson col and descends to the Great Gulf Trail. Descending from the col, protection is quickly gained from the rigor of west and northwest winds.

The Sphinx Trail, blazed in blue, branches northwest from the Great Gulf Trail near the crossing of the brook that descends from between Mts. Clay and Jefferson, 5.4 mi. from the Glen House site on NH Rte. 16. It ascends through forest, first gradually, then very steeply. It follows the brook rather closely, using the bed for about 0.3 mi., and passes several small cascades. At 0.6 mi. the trail turns southwest, leaves the brook, and scrambles to a sloping shelf or plateau, partly covered with scrub, through which the trail is cut. A small meadow is crossed, where there is usually *water* under a rock north of the trail. After ascending slightly farther, the Sphinx Trail joins the Gulfside Trail on a level area a little north of the col.

Descending, go from the Clay-Jefferson col a short distance north along the Gulfside Trail. A grassy rock corridor leading east is the beginning of the Sphinx Trail, marked by a sign and cairns.

Sphinx Trail (map 6)
Distance from Great Gulf Trail junction
   to Gulfside Trail junction: *est.* 1 mi., 1¼ hr.

The Southern Peaks

The southern part of the Presidential Range extends southwest from Mt. Washington and includes the following summits, from northeast to southwest: two peaks of Mt. Monroe (highest 5385 ft.); Mt. Franklin (5004 ft.); Mt. Eisenhower, formerly called Mt. Pleasant (4761 ft.); Mt. Pierce or Clinton* (4312 ft.); Mt. Jackson (4052 ft.); and Mt. Webster, formerly called Notch Mountain (3910 ft.). The Ammonoosuc River lies to the northwest, and the Dry River to the southeast. All of the southern peaks and trails in this section are within the Presidential Range Restricted Use Area or regulated Wilderness Area. See Section 22 for additional information.

On trail signs the word "Crawford's" is used to designate the locality near the Crawford railroad depot and the site of the former Crawford House (which burned down in 1977), where the Mt. Clinton Rd. meets US Rte. 302 (Crawford Notch Highway).

Refer to map 6, the Mt. Washington Range.

The Crawford Path (WMNF)

The first section, a footpath leading up Mt. Pierce (Mt. Clinton), was cut in 1819 by Abel Crawford and his son Ethan Allen Crawford. In 1840 Thomas J. Crawford, a younger son of Abel, converted the footpath into a bridle path, although it has not been used for horses for many decades. The trail still follows the original path, except for the section between Mt. Monroe and the Westside Trail. From Mt. Pierce to the summit of Mt. Washington, the Crawford Path is part of the Appalachian Trail, and so it is blazed in white.

Caution. The caution in Section 1 applies with particular force to this trail, because for at least 5 mi. it lies above treeline,

---

*Commonly referred to as Clinton, but legally Pierce, by a 1913 act of the New Hampshire legislature that named the mountain after the only US president from New Hampshire, Franklin Pierce. The name "Mt. Pierce" appears on the USGS maps, "Mt. Clinton" on most signs.

exposed to the full force of all storms. Seven lives have been lost on the Crawford Path through failure to observe proper precautions. Always carry a compass and study the map before starting. If trouble arises on or above Mt. Monroe, use the Lakes of the Clouds Hut or go down the Ammonoosuc Ravine Trail. This is the most dangerous part of the path. If the path should be obscured in cloudy weather, go northwest if you are below Mt. Monroe, west if you are above, descending into the woods and following water. On the southeast nearly all the slopes are more precipitous, and the distance to a highway is much greater.

Because soils are thin and alpine plants are fragile above timberline, climbers are requested to stay on the trail.

The path leaves US Rte. 302 (Crawford Notch Highway) opposite the Crawford House site just south of the junction with the Mt. Clinton Rd. (parking area). About 300 yd. from Rte. 302 a trail leads left to Crawford Cliff (20 min.). The main trail follows the south bank of Gibbs Brook. Gibbs Falls upper and lower are on short side paths left. After leaving the brook the trail ascends steeply for a short distance, then slabs the side of the valley. At 1.8 mi. above the Crawford House site the Mizpah Cutoff diverges east for Mizpah Spring Hut. *Water* is plentiful until the trail leaves the woods near the top of Mt. Pierce. The Webster Cliff Trail, which leads to the summit of Mt. Pierce about 150 yd. south, enters the Crawford Path on the right at treeline.

From Mt. Pierce to Mt. Washington, except for a few bits of scrub, the path is entirely exposed and gives magnificent views in all directions. Cairns and the marks of many feet on the rocks indicate the way. Though the path winds about, for the most part it remains on the top of the ridge, except where it passes Mt. Eisenhower and above the south end of the Mt. Monroe Loop. The general direction in ascending is northeast. There is usually *water* between Mts. Pierce and Eisenhower, nearer the latter. As the path approaches Mt. Eisenhower, the Mt. Eisenhower Loop diverges left, going over the summit of the mountain. The ascent is relatively easy, and the view is so fine that this loop is recommended in good weather. The Crawford Path continues right and slabs through scrub on the southeast side of the mountain: this is the better route in bad weather. In the col between Mts. Eisenhower and Franklin the path passes close to the stagnant Red Pond on the left, and just beyond, the Mt. Eisenhower Loop rejoins the Crawford Path left. A few steps beyond, the Edmands Path also enters left, and then the Mt. Eisenhower Trail from the Dry River enters right. There is a *spring* left just beyond this junction.

From this point to the shoulder called Mt. Franklin, there is a sharp ascent. A few yards to the right (south) of the path along the level ridge is the precipice that forms the side wall of Oakes Gulf. (Consideration is being given to relocating the trail to the northwest side of Mt. Monroe, to mitigate environmental problems on the southeast side. The area between the two ends of the Mt. Monroe Loop is one of great environmental importance and fragility. To protect this area, the most scrupulous care is required on the part of visitors.) South of Mt. Monroe the Mt. Monroe Loop diverges left, rejoining the Crawford Path near the Lakes of the Clouds Hut. Mt. Monroe has two summits, both easily ascended by this loop. There is *water* on the left, just as the Crawford Path reaches the level area at the foot of the higher peaks, and the path continues to Lakes of the Clouds Hut.

The Ammonoosuc Ravine Trail diverges left at the hut and a little farther on, the Dry River Trail diverges right. The Crawford Path crosses the outlet of the larger lake (*last water*) and passes between it and the second lake, where the Camel Trail to Boott Spur and the Tuckerman Crossover to Tuckerman Ravine diverge right. The path then ascends gradually, always some distance below (northwest) of the crest of the ridge. The Davis Path, which here follows the original location of the Crawford Path, enters at the foot of the cone of Mt. Washington. A few yards beyond, the Westside Trail to the Northern Peaks diverges left. The Crawford Path turns straight north, switching back and forth as it climbs the steep cone through a trench in the rocks past the cross and cairn that mark where two hikers died on July 19, 1958. Above the flat where the Gulfside Trail enters left, the Crawford Path passes through the pen in which saddle horses from the Glen House used to be kept, and from there to the summit. It is marked by frequent cairns.

Descending, the path to the corral is on the north side of the railroad track. Beyond the buildings it leads generally northwest, then swings west. Avoid random side paths toward the south and the Gulfside Trail diverging north (right). Those bound for Bretton Woods will probably take the most direct route, Edmands Path, which joins the Crawford Path in the Eisenhower/Franklin col. For the Crawford House site, the Crawford Path is the most direct route. On arriving at Mt. Pierce (Mt. Clinton), many will be tempted to follow the Webster Cliff Trail over Mts. Jackson and Webster. Although this is a delightful route, it is much longer and harder than the direct route, and the difference is decidedly greater than a glance at the map would suggest.

Crawford Path (map 6)

Distances from Crawford House site, US 302 and
Mt. Clinton Rd.

to Mizpah Cutoff junction: 1.8 mi., 1 hr. 20 min.

to Webster Cliff Trail junction: 2.9 mi., 2 hr.

to Mt. Eisenhower Loop junction: 4.4 mi., 2¾ hr.

to Edmands Path junction: 4.7 mi., 2 hr. 55 min.

to Mt. Franklin summit: 5.5 mi., 3¾ hr.

to Mt. Monroe Loop junction (south end): 6 mi., 4 hr. 5 min.

to Lakes of the Clouds Hut: 6.8 mi., 4½ hr.

to Westside Trail junction: 7.7 mi., 5 hr. 20 min.

to Mt. Washington summit: 8.2 mi. (13.2 km.), 6 hr.

Lakes of the Clouds Hut (AMC)

The original stone hut, greatly enlarged since, was built in 1915. It is located on a shelf near the foot of Mt. Monroe about 50 yd. west of the larger lake at an elevation of about 5050 ft. It is reached by the Crawford Path or the Ammonoosuc Ravine Trail, and has accommodations for ninety guests (see Section 23, *Appalachian Mountain Club*). The hut is open to the public from mid-June to mid-September, and closed at all other times. For current information contact Reservation Secretary, Pinkham Notch Camp, Box 298, Gorham, NH 03581 (603-466-2727).

Ammonoosuc Ravine Trail (WMNF)

This trail, which leaves from the Marshfield station of the cog. railway, can be reached on foot from the Jefferson Notch Rd. via the Boundary Line Trail. There is a parking area below the Marshfield station (fee charged).

The Ammonoosuc Ravine Trail, together with the upper section of the Crawford Path, is the shortest route to the summit of Mt. Washington from the west. The views are spectacular. It is the best approach to the Lakes of the Clouds Hut in bad weather, since it lies below treeline to within 100 yd. of the hut.

Ascending by easy grades through open woods the trail follows the south bank of the Ammonoosuc River, and at 1.4 mi. crosses the river on a footbridge to a beautiful pool at the foot of some fine cascades. The trail crosses here to the east bank and begins the steep ascent. After a few hundred yards a side trail right leads about 100 ft. to a spectacular viewpoint at the foot of the gorge. Above this point the main brook falls about 600 ft. down a steep trough in the mountainside at an average angle of 45 degrees. Another brook a short distance to the north does the same, and these two spectacular waterslides meet at the foot of the gorge.

The main trail continues its steep ascent and in about 200 yd. comes within a few feet of the northern of these two brooks a little above their junction. The striking view of the gorge from the precipitous ledge separating the two brooks is worth the scramble out, but it is difficult to find unless the signs are in place. The trail then bears somewhat away from the brook, but soon returns, crosses it, and continues right to the main brook, which it also crosses at a striking viewpoint at the head of the highest fall. After crossing the brook twice more the trail emerges from the scrub and follows a line of cairns directly up some rock slabs, which may be slippery when wet, to the western end of the Lakes of the Clouds Hut.

Ammonoosuc Ravine Trail (map 6)
Distances from the Marshfield station of the cog railway:
to pool at foot of Ammonoosuc Ravine: 1.4 mi., 1 hr.
to side trail to view of falls: 1.6 mi., 1½ hr.
to Lakes of the Clouds Hut: 2.5 mi., 2¾ mi.

Edmands Path (WMNF)

The Edmands Path, leading from the Mt. Clinton Rd. to the Crawford Path in the Eisenhower-Franklin col, is the most comfortable route from the Bretton Woods region to the Southern Peaks and Mt. Washington, and the quickest way to civilization from points on the Crawford Path between Mts. Eisenhower and Monroe. It is a graded path throughout.

The path leaves the east side of the Mt. Clinton Rd. 2.4 mi. north of the Crawford House site and 1.4 mi. south of the junction of US Rte. 302 and the Base Rd. to the Marshfield station. It continues level for approximately 0.4 mi., crosses Abenaki Brook on a footbridge, and turns right on a logging road. After 0.5 mi. more the grade, which has been very gentle thus far, begins to steepen. At 2.3 mi., it crosses a brook at the foot of a small cascade, then quickly crosses two others. Cascade and brooks may be dry in dry weather. The trail then slabs the north face of Mt. Eisenhower at a slight grade, above treeline, to join the Crawford Path in the Eisenhower-Franklin col.

Edmands Path (map 6)
Distance from Mt. Clinton Rd.
to Crawford Path junction: 2.3 mi. (4.7 km.), 2½ hr.

MOUNT WEBSTER AND MOUNT JACKSON

These peaks, the most southerly of the seven southern peaks in the Presidential Range, are ascended either via the Webster-

Jackson Trail from the Crawford Depot, or via the Webster Cliff Trail, which leaves the east side of US Rte. 302 opposite the terminus of the Ethan Pond Trail and goes over the summits of Mts. Webster and Jackson to join the Crawford Path at Mt. Pierce (Mt. Clinton).

Webster-Jackson Trail (AMC)

The trail, blazed in blue, leaves the east side of US Rte. 302 0.1 mi. south of the Crawford Depot and 0.1 mi. north of the Gate of the Notch. The trail to Elephant Head, a ledge overlooking the Notch, leaves right at 0.1 mi. and reaches the ledge in 0.2 mi. The main trail bears a little left toward the brook and rises steadily on the south bank, then bears right (important turn) and up away from the brook at 0.2 mi. where a worn path continues straight ahead. The trail continues up the slope, crosses Little Mossy Brook at 0.3 mi., and continues in the same general direction, nearly level stretches alternating with sharp pitches. At 0.6 mi. from Rte. 302 a short trail (150 ft.) leads right to Bugle Cliff, a massive ledge overlooking Crawford Notch, where the view is well worth the slight extra effort required. The main trail then rises fairly steeply and soon crosses Flume Cascade Brook. About 0.5 mi. beyond the brook, within sound of Silver Cascade Brook, the trail divides, the left branch for Mt. Jackson and the right (straight ahead) for Mt. Webster. Since the two summits are connected by the Webster Cliff Trail, a circuit trip is possible.

Mount Webster

Continuing on the right branch, the trail immediately descends very steeply to the *brook (last sure water)*, which it crosses just below a beautiful cascade and pool. The trail continues straight ahead across the brook. Avoid a worn path leading downstream. The trail then climbs steadily south about 1 mi. to the Webster Cliff Trail, which it follows right about 200 yd. to the ledgy summit of Mt. Webster, where there is an excellent view of Crawford Notch and the mountains to the west and south.

Mount Jackson

Following the left branch of the fork of the Webster-Jackson Trail, the trail is fairly level until it comes within sight of the brook and begins to climb steadily. About 0.5 mi. above the fork, it crosses three branches of the brook in quick succession. Tisdale *Spring (last water, unreliable,* however there is frequently running water 10 to 20 ft. below the spring) is passed at the left (sign), a short distance below the base of the rocky cone, which the trail ascends rapidly. The summit is clear with the best view to be had of the southern peaks.

Webster-Jackson Trail (map 6)

Distances from US Rte. 302

> *to* Elephant Head: 0.1 mi.
>
> *to* Bugle Cliff: 0.6 mi.
>
> *to* Flume Cascade Brook: 0.9 mi.
>
> *to* Mt, Webster Mt. Jackson fork: 1.4 mi., 1 hr.
>
> *to* Silver Cascade Brook: 1.4 mi.
>
> *to* Webster Cliff Trail junction: 2.3 mi.
>
> *to* Mt. Webster summit (via Webster Cliff Trail): 2.5 mi. (3.9 km.), 2¼ hr.
>
> *to* Mt. Jackson summit (via Webster Cliff Trail): 2.7 mi. (4.3 km.), 2½ hr.
>
> *to* US Rte. 302 (via Webster Cliff Trail): 5.3 mi.

Webster Cliff Trail (AMC)

This trail, a part of the Appalachian Trail, leaves the east side of US Rte. 302 (Crawford Notch Highway) opposite the terminus of the Ethan Pond Trail, and leads over Mts. Webster and Jackson to the Crawford Path at Mt. Pierce (Mt. Clinton). The entrance is about 1 mi. south of the Willey House Recreation Area at the Willey House site. It runs nearly east about 400 ft. to the Saco River, which it crosses by a bridge. The trail climbs to the terrace above and gradually ascends the south end of the ridge by a long diagonal through a hardwood forest. The trail grows

steeper and rougher as it approaches the cliffs and swings more to
the north. The trail bears right about 100 yd. below the slide,
switches back and forth up the slope, climbs sunken steps and
goes along left below an open ledge. Above the ledge, it turns left
to a beautiful view down the Notch. After several level yards, the
trail resumes the climb and soon emerges on the south end of the
cliffs a little less than 1.8 mi. from the highway. It then turns
north up the ridge for about 1 mi. at an easier grade, passing a
4-ft. cairn. Before reaching the summit of Mt. Webster, the trail
alternates between woods and open cliff edges, where the finest
views of Crawford Notch are obtained.

The trail then descends slightly toward Mt. Jackson, and in
about 200 yd. the south leg of the Webster-Jackson trail to the
Crawford Depot on Rte. 302 diverges left. The main trail runs
generally north across three gullies to the end of the ridge
connecting Mts. Jackson and Webster. It continues in the same
direction with some further descent, then climbs sharply to the
top of the ridge, runs over three small humps directly toward Mt.
Jackson, and climbs a small gully to the cone. There is *no
reliable water* on the trail. Tisdale *Spring (water unreliable)* is
about 300 yd. below the summit of Mt. Jackson on the north leg
of the Webster-Jackson trail to Rte. 302.

Toward Mt. Pierce, the trail leaves the summit of Mt. Jackson
following a line of cairns running north and descends the ledges
at the north end of the cone quite rapidly into the scrub. The
Nauman Shelters formerly near this point have been removed.
Water is not available here, and there is to be no camping in this
area.

The trail soon emerges to wind through a large meadow with a
good outlook on the right. North of the meadow the trail turns
sharp left, drops into the woods, then continues up and down
along the ridge toward Mt. Pierce. It descends gradually to
Mizpah Spring Hut. Just before the hut, Mizpah Cutoff to the
Crawford Path diverges left (west), and the Mt. Clinton Trail to
Oakes Gulf diverges right (southeast). Continuing past the west

side of the hut, the trail ascends very rapidly for a few hundred yards, coming out at the lowest point of the meadow on the south summit of Mt. Pierce; it passes over the summit, turns somewhat right, and enters the woods. In about 0.3 mi. it emerges into the open on the main summit and follows cairns, cutting through the scrub to the large cairn at the peak. It then descends about 150 yd. in the same direction to the Crawford Path, which it joins at its highest point on the shoulder of Mt. Pierce, just after it leaves the woods.

Webster Cliff Trail (map 6)

Distances from US Rte. 302

to south end of cliffs: *est.* 1.8 mi., 1½ hr.

to Mt. Webster summit: *est.* 2.8 mi., 3 hr.

to Mt. Jackson summit: *est.* 4 mi., 4 hr.

to Mizpah Spring Hut: *est.* 5.8 mi., 5¼ hr.

to Mt. Pierce summit: *est.* 6.5 mi. (10.5 km.), 5¾ hr.

Mizpah Cutoff (AMC)

This trail, which diverges right (east) from the Crawford Path 1.8 mi. above the Crawford House site, climbs the ridge at a moderate grade, passes through a fairly level area, and descends slightly to join the Webster Cliff Trail just before reaching Mizpah Spring Hut.

Mizpah Cutoff (map 6)

Distances from Crawford House site, US Rte. 302

to west end of Mizpah Cutoff (via Crawford Path): 1.8 mi., 1 hr. 20 min.

to Mizpah Spring Hut: 2.5 mi. (4 km.), 2 hr.

Mizpah Spring Hut (AMC)

The newest of the AMC huts was completed in 1965 and is located at about 3800 ft. elevation, on the site formerly occupied by the Mizpah Spring Shelter, at the junction of the Webster Cliff Trail, the Mt. Clinton Trail, and the Mizpah Cutoff. The hut accommodates sixty guests, with sleeping quarters in eight rooms containing from four to ten bunks. This hut is open to the public from mid-June to mid-October. For current information contact Reservation Secretary, Pinkham Notch Camp, Box 298, Gorham, NH 03581 (603-466-2727). There are plans to move the campsite near the hut about 1 mi. west into the Elephant Brook watershed. The campsite has had a caretaker, and a fee is charged in summer.

OAKES GULF AND DRY RIVER

These areas are in the Presidential—Dry River Wilderness Area. (See Section 22.)

Dry River Trail (WMNF)

This trail leaves the east side of US Rte. 302, 0.3 mi. north of the entrance to Dry River Campground. From the highway the trail follows a clearly defined wood road, generally northeast, for 0.5 mi. to its junction with the bed of an old logging railroad. From here the trail follows the railroad bed for 0.4 mi. and stays on the north bank of the river to a point about 1.6 mi. from the highway, where it crosses to the east side on a suspension bridge. (The former Shelter #1 has been removed.) The trail continues on this side of the river, and at 3.0 mi. the Mt. Clinton Trail diverges left for Mizpah Spring Hut. In the next 1.5 mi. the Dry River Trail passes over some rough terrain, alternately climbing the hillside then descending to the valley floor. At approximately 4.5 mi. it turns sharply right, away from its former location, and climbs steeply for a short distance. The Isolation Trail diverges right a short distance beyond Isolation Brook, about 5 mi. from Rte. 302.

The Dry River Trail continues straight, and in about 0.1 mi. crosses another bridge, reaching a small island (formerly the location of Dry River Shelter #2, which was removed in March 1981). After the trail crosses a third bridge over the main river channel, the Mt. Eisenhower Trail diverges sharply left (downstream), and the Dry River Trail turns sharp right (northeast) and soon crosses the Dry River to the southeast bank (no bridge). This crossing may be impassable in times of high water. The trail follows a logging road away from the river and climbs steadily until it is above Dry River Falls. At 5.9 mi. a short side trail leaves left to a viewpoint a few yards away at the top of the falls and a pothole that should not be missed. Above the falls the trail crosses the river again and at 7.1 mi. passes Shelter #3. (It is planned to remove this shelter also by 1983.) The trail continues up through Oakes Gulf toward Mt. Monroe, then swings right up the headwall, passes a small alpine pool, and crosses over the top of the ridge passing south of the larger of the two Lakes of the Clouds to reach the Crawford Path, directly across from the Lakes of the Clouds Hut. The former route of the trail, which passes through an ecological area that is critical and very fragile, should be avoided.

Dry River Trail (map 6)
Distances from US Rte. 302

   to Mt. Clinton Trail junction: 3 mi., 1¾ hr.

   to Crawford Path junction: 10.8 mi. (17.3 km.), 7 hr. 25 min.

Mt. Clinton Trail (WMNF)

This trail diverges left from the Dry River Trail 3.0 mi. from US. Rte. 302, and immediately fords the Dry River. *Note.* This crossing may be impassable in high water. The trail soon begins a steady, generally northwest climb, following a brook, crossing it and several other small brooks many times. The second mile is less steep, but the last mile is mostly a steady climb that ends within about 100 yd. of Mizpah Spring Hut. The Dry River Cutoff enters from the right approximately 0.4 mi. below Mizpah Hut.

Mt. Clinton Trail (map 6)
Distances from Dry River Trail junction

   to Dry River Cutoff: 2.9 mi., 2½ hr.

   to Mizpah Spring Hut: 3.3 mi. (5.3 km.), 2 hr. 50 min.

Mt. Eisenhower Trail (WMNF)

The Mt. Eisenhower Trail diverges left from the Dry River Trail about 5.2 mi. from US Rte. 302, just beyond the third footbridge on the Dry River Trail. In a few steps, it leads right up a steep bank and joins an old logging road, which it follows for some distance. The Dry River Cutoff diverges left at 0.2 mi. The Mt. Eisenhower trail, generally leading north, keeps to the crest of the long ridge that runs south from a point midway between Franklin and Eisenhower. About 2 mi. from the Dry River Trail, the trail contours, and then descends somewhat before beginning the final ascent of the ridge crest by moderate grade, and continues for the most part along the ridge to treeline, joining the Crawford Path in the Eisenhower-Franklin col, 0.1 mi. north of the upper terminus of the Edmands Path.

Mt. Eisenhower Trail (map 6)

Distance from Dry River Trail junction
   to Crawford Path junction: 3 mi. (4.8 km.), 2 hr. 50 min.

Dry River Cutoff (AMC)

This trail diverges left from the Mt. Eisenhower Trail 0.2 mi. from its junction with the Dry River Trail. In approximately 150 yd. it descends steeply and crosses the northern fork of a branch of the Dry River, turns left, and in another 60 yd. crosses the southern fork to its south bank. The trail turns left, then bends right and follows the south bank of the stream in a generally northwest direction. At approximately 0.4 mi. the stream splits and the trail follows a narrow ridge between the two branches for 500 ft., where the stream recombines and the trail crosses to the north bank. It follows the stream, which is for the most part out of sight, at a moderate-to-steep grade until, at approximately 0.8 mi., the trail bends left to the stream. The trail parallels the stream for 40 yd., then crosses to the south bank, which it follows for another 40 yd. before bearing left away from the stream. It climbs at a moderate grade for another 0.3 mi. to the top of the minor ridge extending southeast from Mt. Pierce (Mt. Clinton). For the last 0.5 mi., to its junction with the Mt. Clinton Trail approximately 0.4 mi. below Mizpah Hut, the trail is practically level.

Dry River Cutoff (map 6)
Distance from Mt. Eisenhower Trail junction
   to Mt. Clinton Trail junction: 1.7 mi. (2.7 km.), 1 hr. 20 min.

Montalban Ridge

The Montalban Ridge extends southward from Boott Spur and lies between the Rocky Branch and the Dry River. For convenience, it is subdivided into two parts in this section: the upper Montalban Ridge, which includes Mt. Isolation (4005 ft.), Mt. Davis (3840 ft.), Stairs Mountain (3460 ft.), and Mt. Resolution (3428 ft.); and the lower ridge — or southern Montalbans — which includes Mt. Parker (3015 ft.), Mt. Langdon (2423 ft.), Mt. Pickering (1945 ft.), and Mt. Stanton (1725 ft.). The Bemis Ridge extends southwesterly from Mt. Resolution to Mt. Crawford (3129 ft.), then south to Mt. Hope (2520 ft.) and Hart Ledge (2040 ft.).

The view from Mt. Davis is in the first rank of White Mountain views, and those from Mt. Crawford, Mt. Isolation, and Mt. Parker are scarcely inferior. The Giant Stairs are a wild and picturesque feature of this region. Notchland (formerly Bemis), not far from where the Davis Path begins, is the site of the historic Mt. Crawford House, usually referred to as the first White Mountain hotel.

NORTHERN MONTALBANS

The Davis Path, constructed by Nathaniel P. T. Davis in 1844, was the third bridle path leading up Mt. Washington. It was in use until 1853 or 1854, but soon after became impassable, and eventually went out of existence. It was reopened in 1910. Sections of it leading up Mt. Crawford and Stairs Mountain give some idea of the magnitude of the task Davis performed.

The Montalban Ridge north from Mt. Crawford and the upper Rocky Branch valley, both of which are covered in this section, are in the Presidential-Dry River Wilderness Area. Entry permits are no longer required.

Refer to map 6, the Mt. Washington Range.

DAVIS PATH (AMC)

This path leaves US Rte. 302 on the west side of the Saco River at the suspension footbridge (Bemis Bridge). There is a parking lot on the east side of the highway, about 100 yd. south of Bemis Bridge. Beyond the east end of the bridge, the trail passes through private land. Continue straight east across an overgrown field and a small brook and turn southeast on an embankment. Ignore other branching paths and blazes, which relate to new housing. At about 0.3 mi. the path turns east and enters the woods (WMNF and Wilderness Area) on a logging road. It then crosses a dry brook and, leaving the logging road at the foot of a steep hill 0.8 mi. from Rte. 302, soon enters the old, carefully graded bridle path and begins to ascend the steep ridge connecting Mt. Crawford with Mt. Hope. Attaining the crest, the Davis Path follows this ridge north, mounting over bare ledges with good outlooks. At 2.3 mi. from Rte. 302, at the foot of a large sloping ledge, a trail diverges left for 0.3 mi. to the peaked and higher summit of Mt. Crawford (3129 ft.), from which there is a view worth the extra walk.

From this junction the path turns northeast, descends slightly to the col between the peak and dome of Mt. Crawford, and resumes the ascent. It soon passes over the ledgy shoulder of Crawford Dome and dips to the Crawford-Resolution col. Leaving this col, the path runs north, rises slightly, and keeps close to the same level along the steep west side of Mt. Resolution. The Mt. Parker Trail, which diverges right (east) at 3.8 mi., leads in about 0.6 mi. to the open summit of Mt. Resolution. A trail that branches left at this junction descends a short distance to the AMC Resolution Shelter, an open camp with room for eight, situated on a small branch of Sleeper Brook. (USFS policies call for eventual removal of all shelters from Wilderness Areas, this one probably by 1983.) Ordinarily there is *water* just behind the shelter, but in dry seasons it may be necessary to go down the brook a short distance. In most seasons, this is the first *water* after starting up the grade of Crawford and the last before the site of the former Isolation Shelter.

At 4.1 mi. the path passes just west of the col between Mt. Resolution and Stairs Mountain. Here the Stairs Col Trail to the Rocky Branch diverges right. The path now veers northwest, passing west of the precipitous Giant Stairs, ascending gradually along a steep mountainside, then zigzagging boldly northeast toward the flat top of Stairs Mountain. Shortly before the path reaches the top of the slope, a branch trail leads right a few steps to the "Down-look," a good viewpoint. At the head of the ascent, 4.5 mi. from Rte. 302, a branch trail leads right (southeast) 0.2 mi. to the head of the Giant Stairs (about 3400 ft.) and an inspiring view.

The Davis Path continues down the north ridge of Stairs Mountain for about 1 mi., then runs east in a col for about 200 yd. Turning north again (watch for this turn), it passes over a small rise and descends into another col.

The path next begins to ascend Mt. Davis, whose successive summits are strung along north and south for 2.5 mi., keeping to the west slopes.

At 8.5 mi. a branch trail diverges right (east) to the summit of Mt. Davis (about 3840 ft.), where the view is considered the finest on the Montalban Ridge. This branch trail, marked by cairns, continues southeast to a *spring* (*water unreliable*) 150 or 200 yd. south and a little east of the summit. This side trip requires little more than 10 min. each way, and is well worthwhile in clear weather.

From its junction with this branch trail, the main path descends to the col between Mts. Davis and Isolation, then ascends the latter. At 9.6 mi. a branch trail diverges left, leading in a short distance to the summit (4005 ft.). The open summit provides impressive views in all directions.

At 10.6 mi. the path leads past the site of the former Isolation Shelter and the junction with the east branch of the Isolation

Trail, which leads to the Rocky Branch Valley. There is *water* down the Isolation Trail to the right (east).

Leaving the shelter site, the path climbs a southwest ridge and passes close to two minor summits. At about 0.5 mi. from the shelter site, the west half of the Isolation Trail descends left to the Dry River valley. At about 11.6 mi., just to the left of the path, there is a good view of the headwall of Oakes Gulf with its cascades. Turning northeast, the path reaches treeline (4700 ft.) at about 12 mi., and then passes a *spring* (*water unreliable*). The path, marked by cairns, then leads across a broad, gently sloping lawn and passes close to a rocky summit at 12.5 mi. Here is a good view, and the Glen Boulder Trail joins on the right nearby.

At 12.9 mi. the path passes just west of the summit of Boott Spur (5500 ft.), and the Boott Spur Trail to AMC Pinkham Notch Camp diverges right (east). (The Boott Spur Link leaves the Boott Spur Trail in 0.8 mi. and descends to the Hermit Lake shelters. For overnight use, buy permit in advance at Pinkham Notch Camp; see Section 1.) Turning northwest the path leads along the almost level ridges of Boott Spur and crosses Bigelow Lawn. At 13.5 mi. the Lawn Cutoff diverges right to Tuckerman Junction, affording the shortest but not the easiest route to the summit of Mt. Washington. A short distance farther on, the Camel Trail diverges left (west) to the Lakes of the Clouds Hut.

At 13.9 mi. the Davis Path begins to follow the original location of the Crawford Path, crosses the Tuckerman Crossover, and in about 0.3 mi. is joined on the right by the Southside Trail. A little farther on the Davis Path enters the present Crawford Path, which affords an easy route to the summit of Mt. Washington.

Davis Path (map 6)

Distances from US Rte. 302

to Mt. Crawford summit branch trail junction: *est.* 2.3 mi.

to Crawford Dome: *est.* 2.6 mi.

to Resolution Shelter: 3.8 mi.

to Stairs Col Trail junction: 4.1 mi.

to Giant Stairs branch trail junction: *est.* 4.5 mi.

to Mt. Davis summit branch trail junction: *est.* 8.5 mi.

to Mt. Isolation summit: *est.* 10.4 mi.

to Isolation Trail, east branch junction: *est.* 10.6 mi.

to Glen Boulder Trail junction: *est.* 12.5 mi.

to Boott Spur Trail junction: *est.* 12.9 mi.

to Lawn Cutoff junction: *est.* 13.5 mi.

to Lakes of the Clouds Hut (via Camel Trail): *est.* 14.4 mi.

to Crawford Path junction: *est.* 14.4 mi.

to Mt. Washington summit (via Tuckerman Junction and Tuckerman Ravine Trail): *est.* 14.5 mi.

to Mt. Washington summit (via Crawford Path): *est.* 15 mi. (24.1 km.)

GIANT STAIRS AND STAIRS COL

The Giant Stairs are two great steplike ledges at the south extremity of the ridge of Stairs Mountain. They are quite regular in form and are visible from many points. The view from the top is striking, and the surrounding scenery is wild and unusual. There is no trail to a third and somewhat similar cliff, sometimes called the "Back Stair," east of the main summit. Stairs Col lies between the foot of the Stairs and Mt. Resolution. These points are reached via the Davis Path from US Rte. 302 in Crawford Notch, or via the Rocky Branch and Stairs Col trails from the Rocky Branch valley.

Stairs Col Trail (AMC)

This trail leaves the Rocky Branch Trail left opposite the Rocky Branch Shelter #1 area, and follows an old railroad siding 150 ft. It then turns sharp left, crosses a swampy area, and climbs several yards to a logging road where it enters the Dry River Wilderness Area.

From here nearly to Stairs Col, the trail follows a logging road along the ravine of a brook. The last part is rather steep. (Obtain *water* from the brook, or from one of its tributaries that cross the trail high in the ravine, because there is no permanent water in the col, on Stairs Mountain, or on the Davis Path below the col, except at Resolution Shelter; see Davis Path.) The trail crosses Stairs Col and continues down the west side a short distance until it meets the Davis Path.

Stairs Col Trail (map 6)
Distance from Rocky Branch Trail junction
  to Davis Path junction: 1.9 mi. (3.1 km.), 1 hr. 55 min.
Distances from Stairs Col Trail/Davis Path junction
  to Giant Stairs branch trail (via Davis Path): 0.6 mi., ½ hr.
  to Mt. Resolution summit (via Davis Path and Mt. Parker Trail): *est.* 0.7 mi., ½ hr.
  to Mt. Crawford summit (via Davis Path and branch trail): 2 mi., 1 hr.
  to US Rte. 302 (via Davis Path): 4.1 mi., 2 hr.

ROCKY BRANCH TRAIL (WMNF)

The middle portion of this trail is in the Presidential-Dry River Wilderness Area.

The valley of the Rocky Branch of the Saco River lies between the two longest subsidiary ridges of Mt. Washington — the Montalban Ridge to the west, and the Rocky Branch Ridge to the east.

From just east of the bridge where US Rte. 302 crosses the Rocky Branch, or 1 mi. west of the junction of Rte. 302 and NH Rte. 16, follow the Jericho Rd. — asphalt for about 1 mi., then a good unpaved road — about 4.4 mi. to the beginning of the trail.

The trail immediately crosses Otis Brook and in 0.7 mi. crosses to the west bank of the Rocky Branch. This crossing and the subsequent ones are difficult at high water.

The trail then bears right (northwest) and soon joins an old railroad bed, which it mostly follows from there on. At 1 mi. beyond the river crossing, the Stairs Col Trail diverges left, and a spur trail leads right about 200 ft. to WMNF Rocky Branch Shelter #1 area. (In addition to the shelter there are five 5-person and one 8-person tent platforms.)

The Rocky Branch Trail continues north along the old bed and crosses the main stream four times in the next 2 mi. At the first crossing it enters the Dry River Wilderness Area. Then, continuing generally north along the west bank, and at times on the old railroad bed, the trail reaches the Rocky Branch Shelter #2 in two more miles. (USFS Wilderness policies call for removal of this shelter, probably by 1983.) Just north of the shelter, where the trail crosses to the east bank, the Isolation Trail continues north along the river. The Rocky Branch Trail follows the east bank of the river for a short distance, then swings away right (east) to make an easy climb to a col on the Rocky Branch Ridge. At the height-of-land it leaves the Wilderness Area. From this col the trail follows an old logging road for more than a mile, close to a small brook for part of the distance, slabbing the side of an unnamed hump across the head of the valley of Miles Brook (*water*). Then, leaving the logging road right, it zigzags down the steep slope and, rejoining the logging road, descends at a moderate grade. At about 0.5 mi. from Rte. 16 a ski-touring trail enters from the left and shortly leaves right. The Rocky Branch Trail continues straight and terminates at a new parking lot on Rte. 16, about 400 yd. north of the Dana Place, 5 mi. north of Jackson.

Rocky Branch Trail (map 6)
Distances from Jericho Rd.

   to Stairs Col Trail junction (Rocky Branch Shelter #1):
      1.8 mi., 55 min.
   to Isolation Trail junction (Rocky Branch Shelter #2): 6 mi.,
      3 hr. 10 min.
   to height-of-land (Wilderness Area Boundary): 6.5 mi.,
      3 hr. 40 min.
   to NH Rte. 16: 10 mi. (16.1 km.), 5½ hr.

Isolation Trail (WMNF)

This trail is part of the shortest route from a highway (NH Rte. 16) to Mt. Isolation. From the Rocky Branch Trail just north of Rocky Branch Shelter #2 (to be removed), the Isolation Trail diverges left and follows the river north, with several crossings, for 1 mi. The trail then strikes up a small brook to join the Davis Path at the former site of Isolation Shelter. Coinciding with the Davis Path, it climbs north for about 0.5 mi., then diverges left and descends southwest into Oakes Gulf. The trail finally reaches a branch of the Dry River and terminates at the Dry River Trail, 0.1 mi. south of the site of Dry River Shelter #2.

Isolation Trail (map 6)

Distances from Rocky Branch Trail junction

   to Davis Path junction: 2.5 mi.

   to Dry River Trail junction: *est*. 5.3 mi.

Distances from northeast end Rocky Branch Trail, NH Rte. 16

   to Isolation Trail junction: 4.0 mi., 2¾ hr.

   to Davis Path junction: 6.5 mi., 4½ hr.

   to Mt. Isolation (via Davis Path): 7.5 mi. (11.6 km.), 5 hr.

THE SOUTHERN MONTALBANS

These mountains, with the upper Montalban Ridge, form the longest subsidiary ridge to Mt. Washington.

Mount Langdon Trail (WMNF)

From the four corners at the Bartlett Hotel in Bartlett follow River St. north about 0.5 mi., across the bridge over the Saco. The trail begins at the bend in the road (to the west) just beyond. In about 200 ft. it joins a new logging road and follows it north uphill toward Cave Mountain. The trail to Cave Mountain leaves left in about 0.3 mi. Continue on the main logging road to the WMNF boundary (red paint blazes) at 1 mi., where the logging activity ended and the trail becomes an old logging road. Just beyond the boundary the trail crosses a *brook (last sure water)*. About 0.3 mi. beyond brook the trail bears right, leaving the logging road, and then bears right uphill again, following another old logging road for a short distance.

The Mt. Langdon Trail ascends Oak Ridge through fine oak woods, heads north over the wooded summit, and descends sharply to the Oak Ridge-Parker col, where it bears right at a junction with the Mt. Parker Trail. The Mt. Langdon Trail leads in 0.5 mi. to the WMNF Mt. Langdon Shelter, capacity eight. A short distance down this trail from the junction is the beginning of a *brook (water unreliable)* on the left (north). In dry weather, *water* may be found in pools in brookbed both north and east from the shelter. The summit of Mt. Langdon is reached from the shelter via the Mt. Stanton Trail.

Mt. Langdon Trail (map 6)

Distances from River St., Bartlett NH

   to Oak Ridge: *est.* 2.1 mi.

   to Oak Ridge-Mt. Parker col: *est.* 2.5 mi.

   to Mt. Langdon Shelter: *est.* 3 mi., 2 hr.

   to Mt. Langdon (via Mt. Stanton Trail): 3.7 mi. (5.9 km.), 2¾ hr.

Mount Parker Trail (SSOC)

This trail begins in the Oak Ridge-Mt. Parker col, departing from the Mt. Langdon Trail about 2.5 mi. from Bartlett. (There is *no sure water* on the Parker-Resolution ridge before Resolution Shelter. The *last water* on the Mt. Langdon Trail is from the brook 1 mi. from Bartlett or from near the Mt. Langdon Shelter.)

The Mt. Parker Trail continues straight ahead north in the col from the junction, swinging right through some old blow-downs and then sharp left as it joins an old graded path at a switchback. It follows this, climbing easily with many switchbacks, to an open spot with good views to the southwest. It then slabs to the east of the ridge through beech and oak woods until it reaches the base of some cliffs, where a side path leads left up through a gully to a good viewpoint. Continuing, the trail descends right with a switchback before turning left and climbing steeply onto the main ridge. Heading generally northwest, the trail climbs easily to an outlook to the southwest, then turns right and levels off before the last short, steep climb to the open summit of Mt. Parker, where there are excellent views.

Continuing north, the trail descends to the long ridge between Mt. Parker and Mt. Resolution and passes over three "bumps," alternating between spruce woods and open ledges with good views. It then slabs the west and south sides of the remainder of the ridge until it reaches the southeast corner of Mt. Resolution, where it turns sharp right and zigzags steeply up to the col between the main summit ridge and the south summit (marked "3250" on the map). Here a short branch trail leads left over the open south summit, where there are fine views, and rejoins the main trail in about 100 yd. Beyond this junction the trail winds along the flat top of Mt. Resolution until it reaches a large cairn on an open ledge with excellent views. The true summit is about 200 yd. east-northeast off the trail. From the cairn the trail descends sharply into a gully where it crosses a *brook* (*water unreliable*), then heads northwest down past several ledges, and finally drops steeply to the Davis Path, opposite the branch trail to Resolution Shelter.

Mt. Parker Trail (map 6)
Distances from River St., Bartlett NH

   to start of Mt. Parker Trail (via Mt. Langdon Trail): *est.* 1.3 mi., 1¼ hr.

   to first "bump" Mt. Parker-Mt. Resolution ridge: *est.* 1.9 mi.

   to third "bump" Mt. Parker-Mt. Resolution ridge: *est.* 2.1 mi.

   to Mt. Resolution, south summit branch trail junction: *est.* 3 mi., 2¼ hr.

   to cairn near Mt. Resolution summit: *est.* 3.5 mi., 2 hr. 40 min.

   to Davis Path junction: 4.1 mi. (6.7 km.), 3 hr.

Mount Stanton Trail (SSOC)

Leave the north side of US Rte. 302, 1.8 mi. west of Glen Station and a short distance east of the bridge over the Saco River, and follow an old CCC camp road west about 0.3 mi. past an old covered bridge to a new housing development. At the trail sign the yellow-blazed Mt. Stanton Trail leaves the road on the right (north). It enters the woods on an old logging road, which shortly merges with a new development road. In about 500 ft. it crosses another new road, then continues for about 400 ft. before turning right on a second crossroad. In about 200 ft. the trail enters the woods on the left (sign), and in about another 250 ft. crosses the WMNF boundary (red blazes). Shortly afterward it swings sharply left and climbs moderately to the base of White's Ledge. After a steep climb to the top of the ridge it swings left (west) and follows the crest, open to the south, to another short but very steep climb up the cone of Mt. Stanton to the south summit, where there are excellent views to the south.

The trail swings north over the true summit and descends to the top of a cliff with views to the north. Here the trail swings left and slabs down to the Stanton-Pickering col. Continuing west the trail ascends rapidly, with several switchbacks, to the cone of Mt. Pickering, bears north over the wooded summit, and reaches the top of a ledge with more fine views to the north. At this point the trail swings left, descends to the long ridge between Mt. Pickering and Mt. Langdon, and passes over four interesting humps known as "the Crippies." The last two have open summits with fine views in all directions.

From the last Crippie the trail descends somewhat along the north side of the ridge towards Mt. Langdon, then climbs steeply north along the east side of the mountain, finally swinging left uphill over open slabs, which afford fine views east over the Pickering-Stanton ridge. From the top of the slabs, the trail heads north through the woods to more open slabs with views to the north. The trail then swings sharply left, climbs to the wooded summit cone, which it passes on the right, and comes out on a gravel slope with views to the west. Here it turns right about 100 yd. across the top of the slope, bears northwest and descends rapidly for about 0.5 mi., and runs nearly level about 0.3 mi. to a *brook* (*first water*). Mt. Langdon Shelter, where the Mt. Stanton Trail ends, is a short distance across the brook. In dry weather *water* can be obtained from a larger brook to the right (north) of the shelter. From the shelter to Bartlett is 3 mi. via the Mt. Langdon Trail; to the Davis Path at Resolution Shelter is 4.7 mi. via Mt. Langdon and Mt. Parker trails.

Mt. Stanton Trail (map 6)
Distances from Old CCC Camp Rd., off US Rte. 302
to Mt. Stanton south summit: 1.6 mi., 1 hr. 20 min.
to Mt. Pickering summit: 2.4 mi., 1 hr. 55 min.
to fourth Crippie: 3.6 mi., 2½ mi.
to Mt. Langdon summit: 4.8 mi., 3¼ hr.
to Mt. Langdon trail junction at Mt. Langdon Shelter: 5.5 mi. (8.8 km.), 3 hr. 50 min.

Cave Mountain

Remarkable for the shallow cave near its wooded summit, this 1397-ft. mountain is easily reached from Bartlett by River St., which runs north from the four corners at the Bartlett Hotel and crosses the Saco River. Follow the Mt. Langdon Trail for about 0.3 mi. to the left fork to Cave Mountain. In less than 0.5 mi. this branch trail leads up a steep gravel slope to the cave. A faint trail to the right of the cave leads, after a short scramble, to the top of the cliff in which the cave is located, where there is an excellent view of Bartlett.

Cave Mountain (map 6)
Distances from Mt. Langdon/branch trail junction
to cave: *est.* 0.5 mi.
to Cave Mountain summit: *est.* 0.3 mi.

Hart Ledge

This fine cliff, situated on a bend in the Saco River just above Bartlett, rises more than 1000 ft. above the meadows at its foot and affords commanding views to the east, west, and south.

There is no trail. From Bartlett take the road leading north, cross the bridge to the north bank of the Saco, and turning west proceed about 2 mi. to the house at the second railroad crossing, directly across the ford from Sawyer's Rock. Follow the road north across the railroad tracks and turn left in about 300 ft. at the old Cobb maple sugar mill. In about 0.5 mi., where another road crosses diagonally from the left (and both roads are barricaded), continue straight ahead. In another 0.3 mi., just before a recent borrow pit, turn right (north) uphill. About 0.3 mi. farther, where the road turns sharply left, continue straight north, first on an old road, then through a logged area, into the ravine of a brook (not shown on maps). Follow the ravine up onto the ridge. This route permits an easy line of ascent west of the inaccessible line of crags. Give them plenty of leeway and approach the top from behind, turning right near the crest of the ridge. The distance from the house to the top of the ledge is about 2.3 mi.

Zealand and Twin Mountain Area

This section covers the Willey-Rosebrook Range, the area west across Zealand Notch to N. and S. Twin, including the Ethan Pond Trail, and the Twinway to Galehead Hut, then north to include the mountains between the Little and Zealand rivers, all on map 5, Franconia. The Cherry-Dartmouth Range, on the north side of US Rte. 302 and east of NH Rte. 115, is on map 8, Pilot. Eastern parts of the region overlap map 6, the Mt. Washington Range.

THE WILLEY-ROSEBROOK RANGE

This range forms the west side of Crawford Notch. Its principal peak is Mt. Willey (4302 ft.), on its southern extremity. Running north from Mt. Willey are Mt. Field (4326 ft.), Mt. Avalon (3432 ft.), Mt. Willard (2804 ft.), and Mt. Tom (4047 ft.).

A fire destroyed the former Crawford House hotel in November 1977. It stood at the base of the Avalon and Mt. Willard Trails, opposite the junction of Rte. 302 and Mt. Clinton Rd., near the Crawford Depot. The site area is still referred to as "Crawford's".

Willey-Rosebrook Range (map 5)

Distances from Crawford Depot, US Rte. 302

to Mt. Avalon summit (via Avalon Trail): 2 mi., 1½ hr.

to Mt. Field summit (via Avalon Trail): 3 mi., 2½ hr.

to Mt. Willey summit (via Avalon Trail and Willey Range Trail): *est* 4.3 mi., 3½ hr.

to Willey House Station (via Avalon Trail, Willey Range Trail, and Ethan Pond Trail): *est.* 6.8 mi. (11 km.), 5 hr.

Distances from Zealand Falls Hut

to Willey Range Trail junction (via Twinway, Zealand Trail, and A-Z Trail): *est.* 3.3 mi., 3 hr.

113

to Mt. Field summit (via Twinway, Zealand Trail, A-Z Trail,
and Willey Range Trail): *est.* 4.3 mi., 3½ hr.

to Mt. Willey summit (via Twinway, Zealand Trail,
A-Z Trail, and Willey Range Trail): *est* 5.5 mi., 4½ hr.

to Ethan Pond Trail junction: (via Twinway, Zealand Trail,
A-Z Trail, and Willey Range Trail): *est.* 6.5 mi., 5¼ hr.

to Willey House Station (via Twinway, Zealand Trail,
A-Z Trail, Willey Range Trail, and Ethan Pond Trail):
est. 8 mi., 6 hr.

to Zealand Falls Hut (via Twinway, Zealand Trail, A-Z Trail,
Willey Range Trail, Ethan Pond Trail, Zealand Trail, and
Twinway): *est.* 12.3 mi., 8 hr.

Mount Willard

This low peak (2804 ft.), a spur of the Mt. Field group, is
famous for its view of Crawford Notch. From perhaps no other
point in the mountains can so grand a view be obtained with so
little effort.

The Mt. Willard Trail, formerly a carriage road with wide and
easy grades, leaves the west side of US Rte. 302 at the Crawford
Depot (a former station on the Maine Central Railroad and now
an AMC information center, see Section 23), across from the
north end of Saco Lake, together with the Avalon Trail. After
100 yd. the trail turns left off the Avalon Trail, then continues
level, and soon turns right to begin the ascent. In another 100 yd.
the trail bears right bypassing to the west a severely washed-out
portion of the old road. At 0.6 mi. Centennial Pool (*last sure
water*) is reached (right). Beyond this point the trail bears left,
rejoining the old carriage road, which it follows the remaining
0.7 mi. to the summit ledges.

Mt. Willard Trail (map 5)
Distance from Crawford Depot, US Rte. 302
to Mt. Willard summit: 1.4 mi. (2.3 km.),
1 hr. 10 min. (ascent), ¾ hr. (descent)

Avalon Trail (AMC)

Mt. Avalon, an offshoot of Mt. Field, is about 1500 ft. above the Crawford House site. The summit is ledgy, and the view is excellent.

The trail starts on the west side of US Rte. 302 (Crawford Notch Highway), opposite the north end of Saco Lake, at the Crawford Depot. After 100 yd. the Mt. Willard Trail leaves left. The Avalon Trail ascends gradually and crosses a brook. Beyond this crossing a loop trail leaves left, passes by Beecher and Pearl cascades, and shortly rejoins the main trail. The main trail continues at an easy grade and after another brook crossing (*last sure water*), begins a steeper ascent. At about 1.4 mi. the A-Z Trail to Zealand Falls Hut diverges right. The Avalon Trail continues its steep ascent to the small col just below the Mt. Avalon summit, which is reached by a short side trail left. It then resumes the ascent, affording views to the northeast, and in another mile ends at the Willey Range Trail, 100 yd. north of the summit of Mt. Field.

Avalon Trail (map 5)

Distances from Crawford Depot, US Rte. 302

to Mt. Avalon summit: 2 mi., 1½ hr.

to Mt. Field summit: 3 mi. (4.8 km.), 2½ hr,

A-Z Trail (AMC)

This trail provides a route from the Crawford Depot to Zealand Falls Hut. It diverges right from the Avalon Trail about 1.4 mi. after the start. It crosses a steep gully, then climbs steadily and crosses a small *brook* in 0.5 mi. After a moderately steep climb for another 0.5 mi., the Field-Tom col is reached. Here, the Mt. Tom Spur leaves right. A short distance beyond, the Willey Range Trail leaves left. The A-Z Trail descends rapidly from the col, then moderately for the next 2 mi., generally west, passing through recently logged areas, crossing small brooks, and ends at the Zealand Trail. Turn left (south) on the Zealand Trail, follow it 0.3 mi. to the Twinway, then right on the Twinway for the sharp climb 0.3 mi. to Zealand Falls Hut.

A-Z Trail (map 5)

Distances from Crawford Depot, US Rte. 302

   to start of A-Z Trail (via Avalon Trail): *est.* 1.4 mi., 1 hr.

   to Willey Range Trail junction: 2.3 mi., 2 hr.

   to Zealand Trail junction: 5 mi., 3¾ hr.

   to Zealand Falls Hut (via Zealand Trail and Twinway):
     5.5 mi. (8.9 km.), 4 hr.

Ethan Pond Trail (AMC)

This trail, which is part of the Appalachian Trail, leads from US Rte. 302 to the junction of the Zealand Trail and the Twinway, 0.2 mi. east of Zealand Falls Hut. It passes through a USFS Restricted Use Area (see Section 22).

The trail leaves the west side of US Rte. 302 opposite the Webster Cliff Trail, 1 mi. south of the Willey House site, Crawford Notch State Park, at the foot of the road leading to the former Willey House Station on the Maine Central Railroad. It follows this road 0.3 mi. to a parking area just below the railroad and crosses the track just north of the station. In 0.2 mi. from the railroad, the trail to Ripley Fall diverges left. At about 1.3 mi. the Kedron Flume Trail enters right, and about 0.3 mi. beyond, the Willey Range Trail leaves straight ahead and the Ethan Pond Trail turns left. The trail climbs steadily to the height-of-land, passing from Crawford Notch State Park into the WMNF, continues past *water,* and enters an old logging road. It follows this old road down to a point close to the southeast corner of Ethan Pond (not visible from trail), named for its discoverer, Ethan Allen Crawford, where a side trail right leads in 200 yd. to Ethan Pond Shelter (capacity eight) and tent platforms (capacity twenty). *Water* may be obtained where the side path crosses the inlet brook. About 1.5 mi. beyond, one branch of the Shoal Pond Trail goes straight ahead, and the Ethan Pond Trail bears right. The main trail soon merges into a spur of the old Zealand Valley railroad, which it follows to the main line, where the other branch of the Shoal Pond Trail enters left. In 0.3 mi. the Ethan Pond Trail bears right, crosses the North Fork on a wooden bridge, and then after 0.2 mi. the Thoreau Falls Trail diverges left to continue down the North Fork. The Ethan Pond Trail follows the old railroad grade on a gradual curve into Zealand Notch with its spectacular, fire-scarred walls. At 0.8 mi. beyond the Thoreau Falls Trail junction, the Zeacliff Trail diverges left. The Ethan Pond Trail continues through the notch to meet the south end of the Zealand Trail. Turn sharp left onto the Twinway and follow it for 0.2 mi. to reach Zealand Falls Hut.

Ethan Pond Trail (map 5)

Distances from US Rte. 302/Willey House Station Rd. junction

to Willey House Station: *est.* 0.3 mi.

to Willey Range Trail junction: 1.9 mi., 1 hr. 25 min.

to side trail to Ethan Pond Shelter: 2.8 mi., 1 hr. 50 min.

to Shoal Pond Trail (east branch) junction: 4.4 mi., 2 hr. 40 min.

to Shoal Pond Trail (west branch) junction: 4.8 mi., 2 hr. 50 min.

to Thoreau Falls Trail junction: 5.3 mi., 3 hr.

to Zeacliff Trail junction: 6.1 mi., 3 hr. 25 min.

to Zealand Trail junction: 7.4 mi., 4 hr.

to Zealand Falls Hut (via Zealand Trail and Twinway): 7.6 mi. (12.3 km.), 4 hr. 10 min.

Kedron Flume Trail (AMC)

This steep trail, blazed in blue, extends from the Willey House site in Crawford Notch State Park to the Ethan Pond Trail. It starts near the picnic tables at the south end of the buildings and climbs the slope to the Maine Central Railroad in sight of the path of the old landslide. It crosses the railroad and proceeds diagonally to the left, taking the steep slope at a comfortable grade. About halfway up, the grade lessens somewhat, and the trail crosses Kedron Brook. Above is an interesting flume and below is a waterfall where there is an excellent outlook. The trail continues up the slope, becoming steeper, and ends at the Ethan Pond Trail about 0.3 mi. below that trail's junction with the Willey Range Trail.

Kedron Flume Trail
Distance from Willey House site, US Rte. 302

to Ethan Pond Trail junction: *est.* 1.3 mi., 1 hr.

Willey Range Trail (AMC)

This trail runs over the summits of Mt. Willey and Mt. Field and, with the Ethan Pond, A-Z, and Avalon trails, makes possible various trips over the range between Willey House Station, the Crawford Depot, and Zealand Falls Hut.

The trail continues straight ahead where the Ethan Pond Trail turns left 1.9 mi. from US Rte. 302. It soon crosses Kedron Brook *(last sure water)*, then climbs a very steep and rough slope to the summit of Mt. Willey, coming out on the southeast viewpoint. It circles around the summit to the viewpoint west of the top. The trail descends gradually, keeping on the west of the ridge, loses only 300 ft. in altitude at its low point, then climbs to the summit of Mt. Field. About 100 yd. north of this summit the Avalon Trail diverges right — the direct route to the Crawford Depot — and the Willey Range trail descends gradually northwest about 1 mi. to the A-Z Trail in the Field-Tom col. Turn left on the A-Z Trail for Zealand Falls Hut and right for the Crawford Depot and Rte. 302.

To ascend the range from Zealand Falls Hut, follow the A-Z Trail to the Willey Range Trail, and proceed over that range. A round trip from the hut may be made by turning right at the Ethan Pond Trail and following it back past Ethan Pond Shelter to the hut.

Willey Range Trail
Distances from US Rte. 302/Willey House Station Rd. junction

to start of Willey Range Trail (via Ethan Pond Trail): 1.9 mi, 1 hr. 25 min.

to Mt. Willey summit: *est.* 2.8 mi., 3 hr. 10 min.

to Mt. Field summit: 4 mi., 4 hr. 10 min.

to Crawford Depot, US Rte. 302 (via Avalon Trail) : 7 mi., 5
   hr. 40 min.

to A-Z Trail junction: 5 mi., 5 hr. 10 min.

to Zealand Falls Hut (via A-Z Trail, Zealand Trail, and Twinway): *est.* 8.3 mi., 6 hr. 40 min.

to Crawford Depot, US Rte. 302 (via A-Z Trail and Avalon
   Trail): *est.* 7.3 mi. (11.7 km.), 5 hr. 55 min.

The Rosebrook Range

A northward continuation of the Willey Range, this comprises
Mt. Echo (3084 ft.), Mt. Rosebrook (3007 ft.), and Mt. Oscar
(2748 ft.). There are no trails.

TWIN MOUNTAIN RANGE AND
ADJACENT RIDGES

The principal mountains in the Twin Range, in order from
north to south, are: N. Twin (4769 ft); S. Twin (4926 ft.), Guyot
(4589 ft.), named for the geographer Professor Arnold Guyot;
and Bond (4714 ft.). The Nubble (2712 ft.) is a prominent
shoulder on the north slope of N. Twin. The Cliffs of Bond
(about 4000 ft.) are a series of fine crags and ledges southwest of
Mt. Bond. Zealand Ridge extends northeast from Mt. Guyot to
Zealand Notch, and the Little River Mountains run north from
this ridge, culminating in Mt. Hale (4077 ft.), named for Rev.
Edward Everett Hale. Refer to map 5, Franconia.

Twinway (AMC)

This trail, with white blazes, extends from Galehead Hut to the
junction of the Zealand Trail and the Ethan Pond Trail by way of
Zealand Falls Hut. It is part of the Appalachian Trail. The
Twinway passes through a WMNF Restricted Use Area (see
Section 22). The trail descends for a few yards from Galehead
Hut, then steadily climbs the cone of S. Twin to 50 feet below the
summit cairn. The N. Twin Spur begins here and goes straight

ahead over the highest point, while the Twinway turns right (south), and descends to a col. The grades on the Twinway between S. Twin and Mt. Guyot are very gentle except near the top of S. Twin. The trail then climbs the side of Mt. Guyot until it meets the Bondcliff Trail. Here the Twinway turns left and climbs about 200 yd. to the northwest peak of Mt. Guyot. It descends the long northeast ridge, climbs Zealand Mountain (at the height-of-land a side path marked with a cairn leads left about 0.1 mi. to the wooded summit), bears right, and continues over the ridge to cliffs overlooking Zeacliff Pond. It descends, and soon a side path leads right to a *spring (water unreliable)* on the west side of the pond. After about 0.5 mi. the Zeacliff Trail diverges right. The Twinway continues toward the cliffs overlooking Zealand Notch. A loop trail right about 100 yd. long leads to the edge of the cliffs, where there is a spectacular view of Zealand Notch and the area south. The main trail swings north, meets the other end of the loop trail to the viewpoint, descends down the ridge, and in about 1 mi. crosses Whitewall Brook. Just beyond, the Lend-a-Hand Trail to the summit of Mt. Hale diverges left. A short distance farther, the Twinway passes Zealand Falls Hut, then ends at the junction of Ethan Pond and Zealand trails. There is *no water* between Galehead Hut and Zeacliff Pond, and the spring at Zeacliff Pond is unreliable.

Twinway (map 5)

Distances from Galehead Hut

to S. Twin summit: 0.9 mi., 1 hr. 10 min.

to Mt. Guyot, northwest summit: 3 mi., 2 hr. 25 min.

to Zeacliff Pond spur junction: 5.3 mi., 4 hr.

to Zealand Falls Hut: 7 mi. (11.3 km.), 5 hr. (In reverse direction, Zealand Falls Hut to Galehead Hut, add ½ hr.)

Galehead Hut (AMC)

Galehead Hut, built in 1932, is located at about 3800 ft., on a little hump on the Garfield Ridge. It accommodates thirty-eight and is open to the public from mid-June to mid-September. For the current schedule, contact Reservation Secretary, Pinkham

Notch Camp, Box 298 Gorham, NH 03581 (603-466-2727). For more information about AMC huts, see Section 23.

AMC Galehead Hut (map 5)

Distances to Galehead Hut

from US Rte. 3, Five Corners (via Gale River Trail and Garfield Ridge Trail): 6.4 mi., 4¼ hr.

from Greenleaf Hut (via Greenleaf Trail and Garfield Ridge Trail): 7.6 mi., 6 hr.

from Zealand Falls Hut (via the Twinway): 7 mi., 5½ hr.

Frost Trail (AMC)

This trail leads generally southwest from the Galehead Hut at a moderate grade to the summit of Galehead Mountain (4024 ft.). At about 0.2 mi. the Twin Brook Trail leaves left (south). On the way up there is an excellent viewpoint (south) down the valley of Twin Brook, and from the summit there are fine views of Garfield, the Franconia ridges, and distant mountain ranges.

Frost Trail (map 5)

Distance from Galehead Hut

to Galehead Mountain summit (via Twin Brook Trail): *est.* 0.5 mi.

North Twin Spur (AMC)

This trail leaves the Twinway 50 ft. below the summit of S. Twin, continues over the summit, descends to the col, and climbs to the summit of N. Twin where the N. Twin Trail, coming up from the valley of Little River, enters from the east (right). There is a side trail left to the outlook on N. Twin.

North Twin Spur (map 5)

Distance from the Twinway junction

to N. Twin summit: *est.* 1.3 mi., 1 hr.

North Twin Trail (WMNF)

This trail is reached via a WMNF access road that leaves south from US Rte. 3 about 2.3 mi. west of Twin Mountain and ends in 2.7 mi. at a parking area just after crossing the Little River. The

North Twin Trail begins here, following the old logging railroad
grade and logging roads and crossing the river three times. These
crossings are extremely difficult in high water. The third is the
easiest, and the first two may be avoided by staying on the east
bank and bushwhacking along the brook. At 2.2 mi. the trail
bears right away from the river, follows a small brook for about
0.5 mi., and then breaks right to gain the northeast ridge. Turning southwest, it follows up the broad ridge, moderately at first,
then steeply, before it eases off approaching the rounded summit. There is a superb outlook about 0.3 mi. before reaching the
summit. Then the North Twin Spur, coming over from S. Twin,
enters left, and a short side trail to the west outlook, with fine
views, leaves right.

North Twin Trail (map 5)
Distance from Little River parking area
   to N. Twin summit: 4.5 mi. (7.2 km.), 3¾ hr.

Zeacliff Trail (AMC)

This trail diverges west from the Ethan Pond Trail 0.8 mi.
north of the Thoreau Falls Trail junction. It descends across the
rocks and down the steep slope to Whitewall Brook (*last sure
water*). After crossing the brook it ascends steeply for several
hundred yards, in and adjacent to an overgrown slide.

Above the slide the trail climbs steeply northwest, then more
gradually through an open birch forest to the crest of the ridge,
which it follows nearly to the base of the first cliffs, overlooking
Zealand Notch. It then swings to the left and climbs diagonally
and very steeply to the main ridge behind the cliffs, where it
meets the Twinway. Turn right for the view from the edge of the
cliffs and for Zealand Hut; turn left for Guyot Campsite and for
Galehead Hut.

After turning left (west) on the Twinway, a side path left in
about 0.5 mi. leads down to Zeacliff Pond. Bear right around a
swampy area, through some pines to the old shelter site. Head

directly toward the pond and pass a *spring* (*water unreliable*) before reaching the shore.

Zeacliff Trail (map 5)
Distances from Ethan Pond Trail junction
>*to* Twinway junction: *est.* 1.5 mi., 2 hr.
>*to* Zeacliff Pond (via Twinway): *est.* 2.3 mi. (3.6 km.), 2¼ hr.

Zealand Falls Hut (AMC)
This hut, built in 1932, is located beside Zealand Falls on Whitewall Brook, at the north end of Zealand Notch (2700 ft.). The hut accommodates thirty-six guests and is open for full service in summer and on a caretaker basis in the winter. For current schedules contact Reservation Secretary, Pinkham Notch Camp, Box 298, Gorham, NH 03581 (603-466-2727).

AMC Zealand Falls Hut (map 5)
Distances to Zealand Falls Hut
>*from* Zealand Rd. (via Zealand Trail): 2.7 mi., 1½ hr.
>*from* the Crawford Depot, US Rte. 302 (via Avalon Trail, A-Z Trail, Zealand Trail, and Twinway): 5.5 mi., 4 hr.
>*from* Willey House Station off US Rte. 302 (via Willey Range Trail, A-Z Trail, Zealand Trail, and Twinway): 8 mi., 6½ hr.
>*from* Willey House Station off US Rte. 302 (via Ethan Pond Trail, Zealand Trail, and Twinway): 7.3 mi., 4 hr.
>*from* Galehead Hut (via Twinway): 7 mi., 5 hr.

Zealand Trail (WMNF)
This trail passes through a WMNF Restricted Use Area (see Section 22).

The area traversed by the USFS Zealand Rd. and the Zealand Trail was reduced to a jumble of seared rock and sterile soil by a series of intensely hot forest fires around 1900. It has now made a reasonably complete recovery — a remarkable and outstanding testimony to the infinite healing powers of nature. Nowhere else in New England is there a better example of regeneration after disaster.

The Zealand Trail is reached by following the USFS Zealand Rd. south from Zealand Campground, which is on US Rte. 302, about 2.3 mi. east of Twin Mountain. In 0.5 mi. the Sugarloaf Camping Areas are passed on the right. In 1 mi., at the bridge over the Zealand River, the Sugarloaf Trail leaves right, and in about 2.5 mi. the Hale Brook Trail leaves right for the summit of Mt. Hale. At 3.6 mi. the road ends in a parking area at Hoxie Brook. The Zealand Trail begins here, crossing the brook on a new bridge and following for the most part the road bed of the old Zealand Valley Railroad, rising gently to an area of overgrown meadows and swamps with beaver colonies. At about 2.2 mi. A-Z Trail enters left. The Zealand Trail skirts Zealand Pond (unique for its having beaver dams as well as outlets at both ends) at the north end of Zealand Notch, and ends at 2.5 mi., at the junction of the Ethan Pond Trail and the Twinway. Turn right 0.2 mi. for the steep ascent to Zealand Falls Hut.

Zealand Trail (map 5)

Distances from end of Zealand Rd.

to A-Z Trail junction: 2.2 mi.

to Ethan Pond Trail/Twinway junction: 2.5 mi.

to Zealand Falls Hut (via Twinway): 2.7 mi. (4.3 km.), 1½ hr.

Distance from US Rte. 302/Zealand Rd. junction

to Zealand Falls Hut (via Zealand Rd., Zealand Trail, and Twinway): 6.3 mi.

LITTLE RIVER MOUNTAINS

These peaks form a ridge between the Little and Zealand rivers, extending north from the Zealand Ridge over Mt. Hale and terminating in the bare-topped Sugarloaves, so conspicuous from the highway east of Twin Mountain Village.

Sugarloaf Trail (WMNF)

The trail diverges right from the Zealand Rd. at the bridge over the Zealand River 1 mi. from US Rte. 302. It follows down the river about 0.3 mi. and then climbs gradually for about 0.5 mi., passing a few large boulders before making the abrupt ascent to the col between the North and Middle Sugarloaves. In this col the trail divides. The branch to the left leads in 0.3 mi. to the Middle Loaf (2526 ft.), a popular viewpoint with fine rewards for a modest effort. The branch to the right leads in 0.3 mi. to the North Loaf (2317 ft.). Soon after leaving the col junction, this right branch descends slightly, passes the abandoned trail to Twin Mountain Village on the left, then bears right and ascends the North Loaf from the northwest. The summit ledges afford extensive views.

Sugarloaf Trail (map 5)
Distances from Zealand Rd.
>   *to* Middle Loaf: 1.2 mi. (1.8 km.), 1¼ hr.
>   *to* North Loaf: 1.2 mi. (1.8 km.), 1¼ hr.

Lend-a-Hand Trail (AMC)

This trail diverges right (north) from the Twinway a short distance above Zealand Falls Hut and soon crosses a brook. After climbing gradually for about 0.5 mi. it continues level for about another 0.5 mi., then crosses a wet area. The trail climbs gradually and in 0.8 mi. comes out in the open and steeply ascends the end of a flat ridge, which it follows for 0.5 mi. before the short pitch up to the bare summit of Mt. Hale (4077 ft.). The Hale Brook Trail to Zealand Rd. leaves east (right). Many of the rocks on this summit are strongly magnetic.

Lend-a-Hand Trail (map 5)
Distance from Twinway junction
>   *to* Mt. Hale summit: *est.* 2.5 mi. (4 km.), 2 hr.

Hale Brook Trail (WMNF)

This trail leaves right from Zealand Rd., at a parking area about 2.5 mi. from the Zealand Campground on US Rte. 302, and ends at the bare summit of Mt. Hale (4077 ft.) with excellent views. The trail ascends moderately, crossing Hale Brook twice. After several switchbacks, it passes a small *spring* on the right at 1.7 mi. and crosses another *brook* (*last water*) about 200 ft. beyond. The trail continues through evergreens to the summit.

Hale Brook Trail (map 5)

Distance from Zealand Rd.

to Mt. Hale summit: 2.4 mi. (3.8 km.), 2½ hr.

THE CHERRY-DARTMOUTH RANGE

Cherry Mountain and Mt. Dartmouth make a broad, flat mass, running mainly east and west, between the Ammonoosuc River on the south and Israel River in Jefferson on the north. They contain a number of peaks, several of which have no names. The Cherry Mountain Rd. passes through the high notch that separates the two mountain masses. Refer to map 8, Pilot.

Cherry Mountain Road

This road runs from US Rte. 302 about 0.8 mi. west of the Fabyan Motel to the NH Rte. 115 about 0.5 mi. south of Meadows Railroad Station, passing through the high notch between Cherry Mountain and the Dartmouth Range. Its grades are about the same as those of the Jefferson Notch Rd. At present it is not maintained for regular automobile travel. Just north of the height-of-land, 3.3 mi. north of Rte. 302, the Cherry Mountain Trail leaves on the west.

Cherry Mountain Rd. (map 8)

Distance from US Rte. 302

to NH Rte. 115: *est.* 7.5 mi. (12 km.)

CHERRY MOUNTAIN

The former lookout tower on this 3554-ft. mountain's highest summit, known locally as Mt. Martha, has been removed. Owl's Head, about 1 mi. northeast, has a bare, ledgy top, from which there is a fine view. The two summits are connected by the Martha's Mile Trail.

Cherry Mountain Trail (WMNF)

This trail leaves NH Rte. 115 opposite Lennon Rd., about 2 mi. north of the Rte. 115 and US Rte. 3 junction. Starting as a wood road, it soon enters an old pasture where it keeps left at a fork, ascends at a generally even grade through woods, and passes a *spring* left about halfway up. At a point south of the Cherry Mountain summit, a spur trail leads left (north) about 250 yd. to the summit. From the summit, the Martha's Mile Trail leads 0.8 mi. to Owl's Head.

The Cherry Mountain Trail soon begins to descend and at 1.5 mi. from the junction with the summit spur, the Black Brook Trail leaves right (south) for US Rte. 302. About 0.3 mi. farther down, *water* will be found on a side trail leading left. The main trail continues down the slope and ends at Cherry Mountain Rd. (which is narrow, use care) just north of its height-of-land, 3.3 mi. from Rte. 302.

Cherry Mountain Trail (map 8)

Distances from NH Rte. 115

to Cherry Mountain summit spur trail junction: 1.9 mi., 1 hr. 5 min.

to Cherry Mountain summit (via spur trail): 2.1 mi., 1 hr. 25 min.

to Black Brook Trail junction: 3.2 mi., 2 hr.

to Cherry Mountain Rd. junction: 5.2 mi. (8.4 km.), 3 hr.

Black Brook Trail (WMNF)

This trail, which may be obscure in places, leads north from US Rte. 302 about 0.4 mi. west of the Zealand Campground and 1.8 mi. east of US Rte. 3. At 0.1 mi. it crosses the Maine Central Railroad. At 0.8 mi. bear right up the grade, avoiding the left roadway. At 2 mi. the trail crosses a small *brook (last sure water)*, and after a short distance the trail begins its moderate climb up the south side of Cherry Mountain. It joins the Cherry Mountain Trail about 1.9 mi. below the summit.

Black Brook Trail (map 8)

Distance from US Rte. 302

to Cherry Mountain summit (via Cherry MountainTrail and spur trail): 5.4 mi. (8.7 km.), 3 hr. 40 min.

OWL'S HEAD

Owl's Head Trail (RMC)

This trail leads from NH Rte. 115 to the summit of Owl's Head (3370 ft.). There is no sign to mark the entrance to the trail, which starts from the south side of NH Rte. 115 at the Slide (Mulhearn) Farm. The house is at the end of a driveway several hundred feet long, just west of Slide Brook and 1.3 mi. south of the B&M Railroad crossing at Meadows Post Office.

Behind the house the trail soon goes through a field, with the gully of Slide Brook on the left and then, from the top of the pasture, it follows a logging road. The trail climbs steeply through hardwoods, bears left, crosses the Carroll-Jefferson town line, then turns sharp right and ascends a very steep, overgrown landslide. The trail emerges on the open ledges of Owl's Head just below the summit, where there is an excellent view. There is *no water* above the logging road. From the summit ledges of Owl's Head, Martha's Mile Trail leads to Cherry Mountain.

Owl's Head Trail (map 8)

Distance from Slide Farm, NH Rte. 115

to Owl's Head summit: *est.* 1.9 mi. (3 km.), 2 hr.

Martha's Mile

Martha's Mile is a link trail between the Cherry Mountain Trail and the Owl's Head Trail, connecting these two summits.

This trail leads from NH Rte. 115 to the summit of Owl's Head (3370 ft.). There is no sign to mark entrance to the trail, which starts from the south side of NH Rte. 115 at the Slide (Mulhearn) Farm. The house is at the end of a driveway several hundred feet long, just west of Slide Brook and 1.3 mi. south of the B&M Railroad crossing at Meadows Post Office.

The trail leaves the top of Cherry Mountain in a northeasterly direction and descends gradually for 0.5 mi. keeping to the crest of the ridge. After reaching the bottom of the col, it rises steeply, crosses a narrow ledge, and leads via a switchback to the ledgy summit of Owl's Head.

Martha's Mile Trail (map 8)

Distance from Cherry Mountain summit

to Owl's Head summit: 0.8 mi. (1.3 km.), 2½ hr.

THE DARTMOUTH RANGE

This range comprises eight or more ill-defined summits, bounded roughly on the east by Jefferson Notch Rd. Currently, there are no hiking trails maintained in the range.

PONDICHERRY WILDLIFE REFUGE

This fine 300-acre refuge, mostly in Jefferson with a few acres in Whitefield, is a National Natural Landmark. It consists of Big Cherry Pond (about 90 acres) and Little Cherry Pond (about 25 acres). As "Great Ponds," these are in custody of the state. Surrounding each are bands of open bog and bog-swamp forest belonging to the Audubon Society of New Hampshire.

"Pondicherry" is the old name for Cherry Pond and nearby Cherry Mountain. The refuge is managed jointly by the NH Fish and Game Department and Audubon. Fishing is allowed, but not hunting or trapping. At least fifty kinds of water birds and an ususual variety of mammals have been recorded on the refuge, and several uncommon species of both water and land birds nest there. Pondicherry is also interesting for its vegetation and its spectacular views of the Presidential Range. Best access is east from Whitefield Airport by either the old B&M Railroad right-of-way, which is driveable, and tracks beyond, or the old Maine Central right-of-way off the road from the airport to Rte. 115.

Franconia Range and Mt. Garfield

The Franconia Notch region includes many interesting and accessible natural features such as the Profile (Old Man of the Mountain); Indian Head; Profile, Echo, and Lonesome lakes; the Flume, Pool, and Basin. The Flume and Pool are described in this section, and others in Section 8. The principal peaks of the Franconia Range bordering the Notch on the east are Mt. Lafayette, Mt. Lincoln, Little Haystack Mountain, Mt. Liberty, and Mt. Flume. These high peaks, and Mt. Garfield to the northeast, afford fine, unobstructed views. Between Little Haystack and Lincoln the ridge is narrow with many interesting rock formations. To the west of the Notch are Cannon Mountain and the Kinsman Range. The Franconia Ridge Trail, most of which is above timberline, should not be attempted in bad weather. For trails in this section, refer to map 5, Franconia. All are east of US Rte. 3 and north of the east branch of the Pemigewasset River.

From the Flume area north to Echo Lake, the valley bottom and lower slopes on both sides comprise Franconia Notch State Park.

Construction of Interstate Highway 93 through Franconia Notch may require relocation of the lower portions of many of the trails covered in this section. (Although highway construction is not scheduled to begin before the summer of 1983, some trail work may be started earlier.) Details of proposed trail changes are included with the individual trail descriptions. Inquiring locally may be helpful as work progresses.

Parking in Franconia Notch State Park is currently available at Lafayette Place, at the open space east of Whitehouse Bridge, at the Flume, at Profile Clearing, and at the Tramway. Future plans call for elimination of parking at Whitehouse Bridge, construction of a new hikers' parking lot just north of the Flume, replacement of the present Lafayette Place parking area by new lots on both sides of the highway, and other less extensive changes.

No camping or campfires are allowed, except at designated

areas: anywhere within Franconia Notch State Park, above timberline, within 0.3 mi. of Greenleaf Hut, Liberty Spring or Garfield Ridge Campsites, or within 200 ft. of the following trails: Garfield Ridge, Franconia Ridge, Greenleaf, Old Bridle Path, and Liberty Spring (see Section 22). Roadside campers are currently accommodated at Lafayette Place, where Franconia Notch State Park maintains a 98-unit vehicular-access campground. Following construction of Interstate 93, this campground may be eliminated and a walk-in campsite on the lower reaches of the Old Bridle Path may be built, far enough from the highway to discourage use by persons other than hikers.

The AMC, USFS, and the NH Division of Parks maintain an information booth during summer and on fall weekends at the Old Bridle Path/Falling Waters trailhead to provide information about weather, trail conditions, facilities, and regulations.

MOUNT GARFIELD

Mt. Garfield (4488 ft.) is the culminating point of the long ridge connecting Mt. Lafayette with Twin Mountain. The summit is bare, and the view of the Franconia and Twin ranges particularly fine. The mountain can be climbed most easily from US Rte. 3 via the Garfield Trail.

Garfield Ridge Trail (AMC)

Part of the Appalachian Trail, and so blazed in white, this route traverses the high ridge joining Mt. Lafayette to Twin Mountain. In general, particularly northeast of Mt. Garfield, the footway is rather rough. This should be taken into account in estimating the time you will require for the trip.

The trail starts from the summit of Mt. Lafayette and runs north along the ridge and over the north peak (about 5100 ft.). At 0.3 mi. north of the north peak the Skookumchuck Trail leaves left for US Rte. 3. Swinging northeast, the Garfield Ridge Trail descends to timberline and continues nearly on the crest of the

ridge. The trail passes over a large hump, descending its rough
end to a tangled col, then climbs gradually toward Mt. Garfield.
Near the foot of the cone it passes to the south of Garfield Pond,
then climbs the cone to a point approximately 150 ft. from the
bare summit of Mt. Garfield. The trail descends 0.1 mi. to a
junction, where the Garfield Trail continues straight ahead for
Rte. 3. The Garfield Ridge Trail bears right and descends steeply
northeast and east. At 0.4 mi. beyond the Garfield Trail a side
trail leaves left for the AMC Garfield Ridge Campsite (150 yd.).
There are seven 4-person tent platforms and one 12-person
shelter. A caretaker is in charge during the summer months, and
there is a fee. (See Section 23, *The Appalachian Mountain
Club.*) The main trail continues down and crosses a small brook
before reaching the first col to the east. Just beyond this col,
where *water* will be found, the Franconia Brook Trail leaves
right and descends the valley of Franconia Brook. From this
junction the Garfield Ridge Trail jogs left, and just beyond the
second col, it follows the ridge sometimes north and sometimes
south of the crest, alternately up and down. About 2.4 mi. from
the summit of Mt. Garfield the Gale River Trail enters from the
left, and the Garfield Ridge Trail continues to Galehead Hut.

Garfield Ridge Trail (map 5)

Distances from Mt. Lafayette Summit

 to Mt. Garfield summit: 3.5 mi., 3 hr.

 to Garfield Ridge Campsite (via side trail): 4 mi., 3¼ hr.

 to Franconia Brook Trail junction: 4.7 mi., 3 hr. 40 min.

 to Gale River Trail junction: 6 mi., 4½ hr.

 to Galehead Hut: 6.5 mi. (10.5 km.), 5 hr.

Skookumchuck Trail (WMNF)

This route to the north peak of Mt. Lafayette and the Garfield
Ridge Trail leaves the east side of US Rte. 3 about 300 ft. north
of the junction of Rte. 3 and Interstate 93, about 0.3 mi. north of
Skookumchuck Brook, where there is a small parking lot. Following an old logging road the trail soon heads east, traversing

the steep north bank of the brook. For a little more than a mile the trail climbs steadily, crosses some log bridges and some corduroy, and about 1.3 mi. from the highway turns left climbing steeply out of the brook valley. The grade eases as the trail swings right on an old logging road. It then climbs right up a steep pitch and follows a second, easier grade through fir and birches. After following the crest of the ridge with a clear view of the north peak ahead, the trail descends slightly left and then slabs upward. It emerges from timberline at 3.6 mi. and follows cairns 200 yd. to join the Garfield Ridge Trail 0.3 mi. north of the north peak of Mt. Lafayette.

Skookumchuck Trail (map 5)

Distance from US Rte. 3

   to Garfield Ridge Trail junction: 3.6 mi. (5.9 km.), 3 hr. 5 min.

Garfield Trail (WMNF)

Leave US Rte. 3 on the south side a few yards west of the bridge over the Gale River near Trudeau Rd. and follow the left gravel road 1.2 mi. to the trail's beginning, where the road turns left and crosses a bridge over the south branch of the Gale River. There is a parking area on the right, 110 yd. beyond the bridge. The trail follows a logging road on the west side of the river for 0.3 mi., then bears left and crosses the river and follows an old tractor road. At 0.8 mi. the trail crosses Thompson Brook and, 200 ft. beyond, crosses Spruce Brook and heads generally south. At about 1.8 mi. the trail ascends more steeply and enters a slight depression. It continues to climb several sweeping switchbacks, and, after passing through birch growth, enters an area where spruce predominates, swings left (east) and then due south as it ascends to the junction with the Garfield Ridge Trail. Turn left for Garfield Ridge Campsite. For the summit of Mt. Garfield follow the Garfield Ridge Trail straight ahead 0.1 mi. up the steep rocky cone to a point about 150 ft. north of the summit. The actual summit is to the left, off the trail.

Garfield Trail (map 5)

Distance from south branch bridge, Gale River

   to Mt. Garfield summit (via Garfield Ridge Trail): 4.6 mi. (7.4
      km.), 3½ hr.

Gale River Trail (WMNF)

   Leave US Rte. 3 on a gravel road on the south side opposite the
junction with Trudeau Rd., known locally as "Five Corners."
Bear left at 0.7 mi. (road right leads to Littleton Reservoir), turn
right at 1.3 mi., cross a bridge over the north branch of the Gale
River, and at 1.7 mi. from Rte. 3 the trail begins left at a small
parking area. The trail enters the woods, soon crosses a tributary
of the north branch, continues on the west side of the north
branch of the Gale River, and at about 1.8 mi. crosses to the east
side on a bridge. At about 2.5 mi. the trail crosses to the west side
again, follows an old logging road for about about 0.5 mi.,
crosses the foot of two slides, and shortly turns right at a steeper
grade. The steep climb continues for about 0.5 mi. to the Garfield Ridge Trail. Turn left for Galehead Hut, right for Mt.
Garfield.

   The Gale River Trail lies within the watershed of the north
branch of Gale River, which supplies part of the water for the
town of Littleton. Camping is forbidden and hikers are cautioned
not to pollute the streams.

Gale River Trail (map 5)

*Distances from parking area near north branch bridge, Gale
River*

   to Garfield Ridge Trail junction: 3.7 mi., 2¾ hr.

   to AMC Galehead Hut (via Garfield Ridge Trail): 4.2 mi. (6.8
      km.), 3 hr. 10 min.

THE FRANCONIA RANGE

Mount Lafayette

   Highest of the Franconia Range, this 5242-ft. peak was named

"Great Haystack" on Carrigain's map of 1816. It is most easily climbed from the west, by the Greenleaf Trail or by the Old Bridle Path up to Greenleaf Hut and the Greenleaf Trail. The summit of Mt. Lafayette may also be reached by the Franconia Ridge Trail and the various trails that feed into the ridge trail from US Rte. 3. Avoid the open ridge sections in severe weather. Refer to map 5, Franconia.

Franconia Ridge Trail (AMC)

From the summit of Mt. Lafayette, this trail descends south over rock-strewn slopes to the Lafayette-Lincoln col and continues over the summits of Mt. Lincoln (5089 ft.), Little Haystack Mountain (4513 ft.), Mt. Liberty (4459 ft.), and Mt. Flume (4328 ft.). Between Mt. Lincoln and Little Haystack Mountain, the ridge is narrow in places with slopes on both sides; it may be *dangerous* in wet or windy weather. Much work has been done to define and stabilize the trail and to reduce erosion. Hikers are urged to stay on the trail to save the thin alpine soils and fragile vegetation.

From the west side of Little Haystack Mountain, the Falling Waters Trail leaves for US Rte. 3 at Lafayette Place. At the south end of the Little Haystack summit ridge, the trail descends over rough ledges and enters the woods. Swinging well down the slope to the east, it continues through open woods toward Mt. Liberty. About 0.3 mi. before that peak the Liberty Spring Trail diverges right. There is *water* at Liberty Spring Campsite, 0.3 mi. down this trail; there is *no water* for the next 6 mi. The Franconia Ridge Trail ascends to the rocky summit of Mt. Liberty, then descends about 400 ft. in the next 0.6 mi. to the low point in a rocky gully before beginning a rise of about 275 ft. to the summit of Mt. Flume. At 0.1 mi. beyond the summit the Ridge Trail ends at a junction with the Flume Slide Trail, which leads right to the Liberty Spring Trail and the Whitehouse Bridge area and with the Osseo Trail, which leads straight ahead to the Kancamagus Highway.

From the summit of Mt. Lafayette to the Liberty Spring Trail, the Franconia Ridge Trail is a link in the Appalachian Trail to the Kancamagus Highway.

For a fine one-day circuit, park at Lafayette Place, ascend Falling Waters Trail, go north on Franconia Ridge Trail over Mts. Lincoln to Lafayette, descend Greenleaf Trail to Greenleaf Hut, then return to the starting point via the Old Bridle Path (total 8.1 mi., 7 hr.).

Franconia Ridge Trail (map 5)

Distances from Mt. Lafayette summit

to Mt. Lincoln summit: 1 mi., ¾ hr.

to Little Haystack Mountain summit: 1.7 mi., 1¼ hr.

to Liberty Spring Trail junction: 3.5 mi., 2 hr. 10 min.

to Mt. Liberty summit: 3.8 mi., 2 hr. 25 min.

to Mt. Flume summit: 4.9 mi., 3 hr.

to Flume Slide Trail/Osseo Trail junction: 5 mi. (8 km.), 3 hr. 5 min.

Osseo Trail (AMC)

The Osseo Trail is being relocated, and the new route, to be opened during summer 1983, will run from the Wilderness Trail at about 1 mi. from the Kancamagus Highway to the present Osseo Trail about 0.3 mi. south of the Flume Slide Trail. The trail over Osseo Peak will be closed. The description of the trail before relocation is being retained for use in the interim. Total distance to Mt. Flume from the Kancamagus Highway will be about 4.8 mi.

The Osseo Trail starts from the Kancamagus Highway, 2.9 mi. from Lincoln and 1.6 mi. west of the entrance to the Wilderness Trail, at a small parking area on the north side of the highway. The trail leaves from the northeast corner of the parking lot, enters the woods, and crosses a small brook. The trail bears left at a fork, curves gradually right, crosses Clear Brook, turns generally north, passes a weather bureau rain gauge left, ascends gradually, and later recrosses Clear Brook. It soon bears left and climbs steeply through open beech. Reaching an old logging road, the trail turns right and crosses a large slide. Farther on, where a large boulder left provides a small overhanging shelter, the trail turns sharp left and begins a series of switchbacks to climb the steep east side of Osseo Peak (also known as Whaleback Mountain, 3640 ft.). Just as the trail gains the ridge, a short side path leads left to the edge of a cliff from which there are good views. To the east the peak is wooded, with few outlooks.

The main trail continues in thick growth then takes a straight line north over the ridge, which gradually ascends to join another ridge running west that connects with the Coolidge Mountains. Continuing north, the trail descends a little, bears left, and follows the part of the ridge leading straight toward Mt. Flume, visible in glimpses through the trees. After a sharp rise 0.1 mi. before the summit of Mt. Flume (4328 ft.), the Flume Slide Trail enters from the left, and the Osseo Trail joins the Franconia Ridge Trail.

Osseo Trail (map 5)

Distances from Kancamagus Highway

to Osseo Peak (Whaleback Mountain): *est*. 3.3 mi., 2¾ hr.

to Flume Slide Trail/Franconia Ridge Trail junction: *est*. 5¾ mi. (9.3 km.), 5 hr. 10 min.

Greenleaf Hut (AMC)

Greenleaf Hut is located at the junction of the Old Bridle Path and Greenleaf Trail on Mt. Lafayette, at about 4200 ft., overlooking Eagle Lake. The hut accommodates thirty-six guests. It is 2.1 mi. from US Rte. 3 via the Greenleaf Trail, 1.1 mi. from the summit of Mt. Lafayette, and 7.6 mi. from Galehead Hut. From mid-June through early September, the hut is operated as a full-service facility; for off-season schedules, contact Reservation Secretary, Pinkham Notch Camp, Box 298, Gorham, NH 03581 (603- 466-2727).

Greenleaf Trail (AMC)

The trail, blazed in blue, starts on the east side of US Rte. 3 (Daniel Webster Highway) from the gravel hikers' parking area located just north of the large hard-surfaced parking area in Profile Clearing. (A paved parking lot in approximately the same location is planned in conjunction with construction of Interstate 93 in the area.) The trail enters the woods, passes a small pond, bears right at a large boulder, and runs south parallel to and in sight of Rte. 3. After about 0.3 mi. the trail turns left (east) and ascends more steeply by switchbacks to the original trail, which it joins 20 yd. beyond the upper slide. It then slabs the southwest flank of Eagle Cliff by zigzags. Soon a glimpse of the Profile is obtained, with occasional views of Franconia Notch. At about 1 mi. from and 1000 ft. above the road, the path enters Eagle Pass, a narrow cleft between Eagle Cliff and the mountain proper, which has interesting cliff and rock formations. The nearly level path leads east through the pass. It then swings more south and rises steeply, slabbing a northwest shoulder over loose stones, *slippery* in wet weather. The path emerges on the open top of the shoulder just below Greenleaf Hut, where the Old Bridle Path leaves right for Lafayette Place. From the hut the trail dips slightly, enters the scrub, and passes south of Eagle Lakes, two picturesque shallow tarns (the upper lake is rapidly becoming a bog). The trail rises, emerges from the scrub, ascends at a moderate grade, and somewhat farther, follows rock steps between stone walls. The path bears slightly north and reaches the summit.

From the summit the Garfield Ridge Trail leads north and then northeast to Mt. Garfield, Garfield Ridge Campsite, Galehead Hut and the Twin Range. To the south the Franconia Ridge Trail leads to Liberty Spring Campsite or to the Osseo Trail and the Kancamagus Highway.

Greenleaf Trail (map 5)

Distances from US Rte. 3, gravel parking area Profile Clearing

   to Eagle Pass: 1.1 mi., 1 hr.

to Greenleaf Hut: 2.2 mi., 2 hr. 10 min.
to Mt. Lafayette summit: 3.3 mi. (5.2 km.), 3 hr. 10 min.

Old Bridle Path (AMC)

This trail follows the route of a former bridle path, and it is more scenic than the Greenleaf Trail.

The trail leaves the east side of US Rte. 3 to the left of a gate just across from the entrance to Lafayette Campground. There is an information booth, staffed during the summer and on fall weekends by AMC, USFS, and NH Division of Parks personnel, at the trailhead. (After Interstate 93 has been put through Franconia Notch, a new parking lot east of the highway may serve this trailhead, which may be relocated slightly in the process.) The trail bears northeast into the woods, and ascends at a moderate grade. At 0.7 mi. it turns right for 125 yd. along a level offset, then sharply left, and continues to climb. At another sharp left turn, marking the trail's halfway point, there is a fine view of Mt. Lincoln. Shortly after, the trail reaches open ledges with fine views of Franconia Ridge across Walker Ravine. About 0.3 mi farther, the trail enters a growth of stunted spruce, continues level for about 0.3 mi., with outlooks across Franconia Notch to Cannon Mountain and Lonesome Lake, and then ascends rather steeply over three humps known as "the Agonies" or "Agony Ridge" to Greenleaf Hut.

Old Bridle Path (map 5)
Distance from US Rte. 3, opposite Lafayette Campground
to AMC Greenleaf Hut: 2.5 mi. (4.1 km.), 2 hr. 20 min.

Falling Waters Trail (AMC)

This trail, blazed in blue, leaves the east side of US Rte. 3 opposite Lafayette Campground, beginning in the same location as the Old Bridle Path. (see that description for future relocation of this trailhead).

The trail bears right between several State Park service buildings and follows a broad path generally southeast to Walker

Brook, turns left (east) before crossing it, follows up the north bank for a little, and crosses just below Walker Cascade. The trail leads away from the brook, heads southeast and east, and in 0.5 mi. crosses Dry Brook (use care if water is high), turn left and follows up the south bank to a beautiful cascade known as Stairs Falls. Above the falls the trail passes beneath Sawteeth Ledges and crosses the brook to the north bank just below Swiftwater Falls, which descend 60 ft. in a shady glen. Continuing on the north bank, the trail is a graded switchback for a short distance to an old logging road, which rises gradually in the narrow gorge of Dry Brook. The trail leaves the old road at a steep embankment, ascends in graded sections to Cloudland Falls (80 ft.), and climbs steeply to a viewpoint overlooking the head of the falls and out over the valley toward Mt. Moosilauke on the skyline.

At the head of the falls are two small 25-ft. falls practically facing each other. The one to the south, which emerges from the woods, is on the branch of Dry Brook that runs down from Little Haystack, while the other is on the Mt. Lincoln branch. The trail continues steeply on the north bank of the Mt. Lincoln branch, soon crosses to the south bank, crosses back to the north side, climbs to and follows an old logging road, and recrosses to the south bank.

After a view (cut) to the west, the trail takes the left fork of an old logging road, diverges left again, and ascends the ridge between two drainages via a series of switchbacks. At the south end of the last switchback, a side trail leads south about 100 yd. to the northeast corner of Shining Rock, an exposed granite ledge over 200 ft. high and nearly 800 ft. long. Usually covered with water from springs in the woods above, the cliff shines like a mirror in the sunlight. From this point there are fine views north and west over Franconia Notch. *Caution.* Climbing Shining Rock can be *very dangerous;* do not attempt it without climbing equipment or proper skills. The main trail continues north for a short distance, turns right, and climbs in a nearly straight line to the summit of Little Haystack (4513 ft.).

Descending, this rather steep, twisting trail needs caution. It is *not* recommended in winter.

Falling Waters Trail (map 5)

Distances from US Rte. 3, opposite Lafayette Campground

to Walker Brook: 0.3 mi.

to Dry Brook: 0.8 mi.

to Stairs Falls: 0.9 mi., ½ hr.

to Swiftwater Falls: 1 mi., 35 min.

to Cloudland Falls: 1.4 mi., 1 hr.

to Shining Rock side trail junction: 2.3 mi., 2 hr.

to Franconia Ridge Trail junction, Little Haystack summit: 2.8 mi. (4.5 km.), 2 hr. 35 min.

Liberty Spring Trail (AMC)

This trail extends from the Whitehouse Bridge picnic area — where US Rte. 3 crosses the Pemigewasset River about 0.8 mi. north of the Flume Store — to the Franconia Ridge Trail at a point 0.3 mi. north of the summit of Mt. Liberty (4459 ft.). The trail provides a direct route for long-distance hikers from Kinsman Pond or Lonesome Lake Hut to Mt. Liberty, and is a part of the Appalachian Trail. (Current plans for construction of Interstate 93 provide parking for this trail near the Flume, 0.3 mi. south of Whitehouse Bridge, with a new connector trail or relocation to be built. When this is completed, there will be no parking or other facilities at Whitehouse Bridge.

Go east from the north end of Whitehouse Bridge across the picnic area and cross the brook at the edge of the woods. The trail crosses another brook, occasionally dry, in about 50 ft., slabs northeast through hardwood growth, and in about 0.4 mi. joins the old main logging road from the former Whitehouse mill and soon levels off. About 0.5 mi. from the beginning of the trail, the Flume Slide Trail leaves right (south). The Liberty Spring Trail then bears left, crosses several brooks (one large), heads more southeast, then ascends moderately to a point where it makes a sharp left turn.

Above the sharp turn the trail rises at a moderate grade for some distance, then turns right and climbs more steeply. In places the footing is rough. About 0.6 mi. above the sharp turn a side path leads left to *water*. Some distance farther the trail becomes less steep and soon reaches Liberty Spring Campsite (3800 ft.), the *last sure water* on the ascent. There are twelve tent platforms, with a caretaker during the summer months and there is a fee (see Section 23, *Appalachian Mountain Club*).

The path next ascends fairly steeply through low evergreens and ends in 0.3 mi. at the Franconia Ridge Trail, between Mt. Liberty and Little Haystack. To reach the summit of Mt. Liberty, follow the Franconia Ridge Trail right for about 0.3 mi.

Liberty Spring Trail (map 5)
Distances from US Rte. 3, Whitehouse Bridge

to sharp left turn: 1.3 mi., 1 hr.

to Liberty Spring Campsite: 2.4 mi., 2 hr.

to Franconia Ridge Trail junction: 2.7 mi., 2 hr. 20 min.

to Mt. Liberty summit (via Franconia Ridge Trail): 3 mi. (4.7 km.), 2 hr. 40 min.

Flume Slide Trail (AMC)

The lower terminus of this trail, which, for many years, was located about 150 ft. above the head of the Flume, was moved to the lower section of the Liberty Spring Trail, and may be relocated again with I-93 construction. The Flume Slide Trail leaves the Liberty Spring Trail about 0.5 mi. from Whitehouse Bridge picnic area, on an old logging road, which contours to the right (south). After 200 yd. the trail swings left off the logging road in a more eastern direction and begins a gradual ascent of the southwest shoulder of Mt. Liberty, with occasional descents and rises. In about 100 yd. it crosses a small brook, and about 0.3 mi. farther crosses a slightly larger one. From this point the trail contours for 0.5 mi., until it drops steeply and crosses a large brook on rock steps. After rising from the brookbed, the trail climbs gradually and swings slightly more east. It continues to rise gradually through an old logging area, crossing several brooks. After passing through a swampy area the trail crosses a small brook and turns almost east (sign). From this point the trail should be followed carefully because it makes several brook crossings before leaving the area to ascend to the bottom of the slide. On the slide be careful not to dislodge stones that might endanger climbers below. *In wet weather, extreme caution must be used both in ascending and in descending the slide.* The route over the slide is marked by paint blazes on the ledge. Near the top, the trail enters the woods at the left and climbs steeply in about 0.3 mi. to the Franconia Ridge Trail, a few hundred feet south of the summit of Mt. Flume. The *last reliable water* is the brook some distance below the foot of the slide.

Descending: the average time should be increased for this trail, due to the steepness and slippery footing of the slide.

For a circuit over Mt. Flume (4328 ft.) and Mt. Liberty (4459 ft.) ascend via Liberty Spring and Flume Slide Trails, take the Franconia Ridge Trail over Mt. Liberty, and descend the Liberty Spring Trail (total 8.5 mi., 6 hr.).

Flume Slide Trail (map 5)

Distances from US Rte. 3, Whitehouse Bridge

   to start of Flume Slide Trail (via Liberty Spring Trail): *est.* 0.5 mi., 25 min.

   to foot of slide: *est.* 3.5 mi., 2 hr. 35 min.

   to Franconia Ridge Trail junction: *est.* 4.3 mi., 3 hr. 35 min.

   to Mt. Flume summit (via Franconia Ridge Trail): *est.* 4.4 mi. (7 km.), 3 hr. 40 min.

The Pool

This interesting pothole formation in the Pemigewasset River, over 100 ft. in diameter and 40 ft. deep, can be reached by a path of about 0.5 mi. from the gravel road just south of the Flume Store. There is an admission fee.

The Flume

This narrow gorge, one of the best-known features in the Franconia region, can be reached from the Flume Store by a road and graded trails. It is open for visitors May 30-Oct. 15, and there is an admission fee. Private automobiles are prohibited on the road. Buses are operated by NH Division of Parks. The road is about 0.5 mi. long from the parking area and gate at Flume Store to the Boulder Cabin near Flume Brook. The route beyond is over graded trails and boardwalks with steps. On the way, one can see broad ledges worn smooth by the action of the water and scoured by an avalanche in June 1883, which swept away the famous suspended boulder. Avalanche Falls at the upper end is worth visiting.

Little Coolidge Mountain

This 2403-ft. mountain, at the extreme south end of the Franconia Range, lies north of the village of Lincoln. On its south slope are several ledges from which there are striking views of the Pemigewasset Valley and the villages. There is no maintained trail to the ledges.

Cannon and Kinsman

The trails described in this section are the Kinsman Ridge Trail and, for the most part, those leading to it along its entire length. All are on the west side of US Rte. 3 and north of NH Rte. 112. Refer to map 5, Franconia.

Construction of I-93 through the Franconia Notch will begin in the mid-1980s. Many park changes that will affect trailheads and parking areas are anticipated.

As the work proceeds, contact the AMC and State Parks offices for further information.

CANNON MOUNTAIN (PROFILE MOUNTAIN)

This interesting, dome-shaped 4077-ft. mountain is famous for its wonderful profile known as the Old Man of the Mountain. Forming the west wall of Franconia Notch, its south and east faces are precipitous. Above these are three ledges, which, when viewed from near Profile Lake, form Hawthorne's immortal Great Stone Face. The mountain takes its name from a natural stone table superimposed on a boulder, which, seen from Profile Clearing, resembles a cannon.

Cannon Mountain may be ascended by an aerial tramway. This recently renovated lift, which replaces the first such passenger tramway in North America, extends from a valley station (1995 ft.) just off US Rte. 3 about 0.5 mi. north of the "Old Man," to a mountain station (4002 ft.) just below the main (west) summit. The tramway is operated in winter for skiers. Inquire there for a ski trail guide.

A circuit over Cannon Mountain may be made by following the Kinsman Ridge Trail to Coppermine Col and descending Lonesome Lake Trail to Lafayette Place.

Cannon Mountain Circuit (map 5)
Distances from Kinsman Ridge Trail, northern terminus, off US Rte. 3

   to Coppermine Col (via Kinsman Ridge Trail): *est.* 2.8 mi., 2½ hr.

   to Lonesome Lake Hut (via Lonesome Lake Trail): *est.* 3.9 mi., 3 hr.

   to Lafayette Place (via Lonesome Lake Trail): *est.* 5.4 mi. (8.8 km.), 3 hr. 50 min.

Kinsman Ridge Trail (AMC)

Hikers should carry water from the start on this generally dry trail. About 0.3 mi. south of the tramway station on US Rte. 3, walk directly west on a paved road (large NHDP trail sign) and continue a few yards on a gravel road to the edge of the woods. The trail leaves here (trailhead may change with new road construction) just south of a log cottage, enters the woods, and in a few feet bears sharp left uphill.

The trail climbs at a moderate or steep grade for about 1.3 mi., generally south, with the footway becoming rockier in the upper half; then it levels and passes through a growth of low fir. At the point where it makes a right-angle turn west, an obscure side trail, marked by occasional cairns, continues straight ahead out upon the ledges to the southeast, with a good view of the Franconia Range, then, swinging around northeast and descending, leads in 300 yd. from the junction to "the Cannon," an excellent viewpoint. The main trail, climbing slightly, passes over the east summit (3940 ft.), descends briefly to a col, and ascends the semi-open east flank of the main peak, eventually entering the Rim Trail. Turn right for the tramway terminal and the summit and observation tower.

Turning left at this junction, the Kinsman Ridge Trail soon

leaves the Rim Trail and summit area, and in 0.4 mi. the Hi-Cannon Trail diverges left. The path now descends steeply about 0.5 mi. to Coppermine Col, where the Lonesome Lake Trail diverges left to Lonesome Lake Hut. The Kinsman Ridge Trail leads over the northeast and highest Cannon Ball (3769 ft.), passes northwest of the middle Cannon Ball (about 3660 ft.), goes through a ravine where there is usually *water*, passes over the southwest Cannon Ball (3693 ft.), and over another hump (3812 ft.) to reach Kinsman Junction. Here the Fishin' Jimmy Trail to Lonesome Lake turns sharp left, and the Kinsman Pond Trail to Kinsman Pond Shelter and US Rte. 3 bears slightly left. The Kinsman Ridge Trail turns sharp right at this junction to ascend N. Kinsman; at 0.2 mi. from this junction the Mt. Kinsman Trail leaves right (west). The trail continues up to N. Kinsman, along to S. Kinsman, and then descends to Harrington Pond, where the trail is extremely boggy, losing some 900 ft. in altitude and 1000 ft. more between the pond and where the trail crosses Eliza Brook just below the shelter. The AMC Eliza Brook Shelter is about 150 ft. (right) from the trail after it crosses Eliza Brook. The trail has been relocated west of its former route and now follows the ridge crest between the power line and Mt. Wolf. The Reel Brook Trail ends at the Kinsman Ridge Trail on the ridge crest. A ledge just south of the power line gives fine views in all directions. After crossing the power line, where there are excellent views to the south and southeast, the trail drops gradually down to the old route and traverses Mt. Wolf (see the reverse description for the Kinsman Ridge Trail that follows) to a point about 0.3 mi. west of Gordon Pond, where the Gordon Pond Trail leaves left for NH Rte. 112. From this point, the Kinsman Ridge Trail continues generally southwest over six minor ascents and descents in 2.3 mi. to the Dilly Trail (left), and then to its south terminus on Lost River Rd. (Rte. 112) opposite the entrance to the Beaver Brook Trail, and about 0.5 mi. northwest of the Lost River Reservation. A few yards north of

Rte. 112, an unnamed trail left (east) leads about 0.5 mi. to the reservation's "Ecology Trail."

Kinsman Ridge Trail (map 5)

Distances from northern terminus, off US Rte. 3

   to side trail to "the Cannon" junction: 1.3 mi., 1¼ hr.
   to Rim Trail junction: 2 mi., 1 hr. 50 min.
   to Hi-Cannon Trail junction: 2.4 mi., 2 hr. 5 min.
   to Lonesome Lake Trail junction: 2.7 mi., 2 hr. 20 min.
   to Mt. Kinsman, north peak: *est.* 5.8 mi., 5½ hr.
   to Mt. Kinsman, south peak: *est.* 6.8 mi., 6¼ hr.
   to AMC Eliza Brook Shelter: *est.* 9.5 mi., 8 hr.
   to Gordon Pond Trail junction: *est.* 13.1 mi., 10 hr. 10 min.
   to Dilly Trail junction: *est.* 15.5 mi., 11 hr. 35 min.
   to NH Rte. 112: *est.* 16.5 mi. (26.5 km.), 12 hr.

Kinsman Ridge Trail (AMC) in reverse direction

The portion of this trail from NH Rte. 112 to Kinsman Junction is part of the Appalachian Trail.

The trail leaves the north side of Rte. 112 opposite the north terminus of the Beaver Brook Trail. It bears gradually away from the road for about 0.1 mi., and then bears right uphill rather steeply northeast, through the Society for the Protection of NH Forests' Lost River Reservation. A few yards from the road, it passes an unnamed trail right (east) that leads in about 0.5 mi. to the Lost River Reservation's "Ecology Trail" (see below). The Kinsman Ridge Trail ascends and after about 0.5 mi. turns left, passes the junction with the Dilly Trail at about 1 mi., and then passes over six minor ascents and descents. There are occasional views to the east and north, with one especially good view from the top of a large boulder to the right of the trail. The trail descends from the ridge, crossing a brookbed in which there is usually *water,* to a junction with the Gordon Pond Trail about 0.3 mi. west of Gordon Pond. The Gordon Pond Trail follows the right fork to Gordon Pond and N. Woodstock. The Kinsman

Ridge Trail bears left and after about 0.5 mi. crosses a brook in a gully, climbs steeply, then more gently, to a middle peak of Mt. Wolf, from which there is a fine view south. Then the trail turns east, passing, at an AMC sign marking the main trail, an un-marked side path east to the east summit and a fine 180-degree view east from a rock. The main trail has been relocated west to the ridge line. It descends along the ridge and passes the upper east terminus of the Reel Brook Trail, which enters left from NH Rte. 116. It then runs northeast to the crossing of Eliza Brook. AMC Eliza Brook Shelter (2400 ft.) is about 150 ft. left from the trail just before it crosses Eliza Brook.

The Kinsman Ridge Trail continues up the east bank of Eliza Brook for about 1.3 mi., passing through a logged area. Recrossing the brook (may be last good *water* for some miles), the trail mounts steeply west for about 1.4 mi. to Harrington Pond (3400 ft.). Passing the east end of the little pond on extremely boggy sections of the footway, the trail re-enters the woods on the right (sign), and soon begins a steep slab of the main ridge of S. Kinsman. The grade increases until the path zigzags to a level stretch. After a short, steep ascent through the scrub, with outlooks, the trail emerges on the open summit of S. Kinsman.

The trail continues across a shallow depression and gradually descends the ridge crest to the col between the north and south peaks. Here, there is sometimes *water* to the left of the trail. It then ascends to the summit of the N. Kinsman. Just past the summit a trail to the right leads to the east viewpoint. The main trail continues north, descends the cone rapidly, and the Mt. Kinsman Trail leaves left in 0.4 mi from the N. Kinsman summit. Shortly beyond the foot of the steep descent is Kinsman Junction, where the Fishin' Jimmy Trail continues the Appalachian Trail to Lonesome Lake, and the Kinsman Pond Trail bears right, leading shortly to Kinsman Pond and Kinsman Pond Shelter. **Caution.** *Water* from Kinsman Pond and from the spring in Kinsman Pond Shelter is *not potable*. There is *reliable potable* *water* on the Fishin' Jimmy Trail, about 1 mi. beyond Kinsman Junction.

The Kinsman Ridge Trail bears sharp left at Kinsman Junction, and soon rises abruptly 100 ft. to a hump (3812 ft.) on the ridge. It then continues to the Cannon Balls, the three main humps that constitute the ridge leading to Cannon Mountain. On top of the first Cannon Ball there is a meadow, a little below which, on the trail, *water* may often be found. The trail descends sharply to a deep ravine, where *water* is usually found nearby. The trail slabs north of the second Cannon Ball and enters the next col with very little descent. Over the third Cannon Ball it descends to Coppermine Col, at the base of Cannon Mountain, where the Lonesome Lake Trail leads south 1 mi. to Lonesome Lake Hut (*water* 10 min. down this trail). The Kinsman Ridge Trail then ascends Cannon Mountain, climbing very steeply among and under huge boulders, and at 0.4 mi. from the summit the Hi-Cannon Trail leaves right. The Kinsman Ridge Trail soon bears right following the Rim Trail, leaves (right) where the Rim Trail turns left toward the tramway terminal and, descending over rocks and ledges, and then through scrub, reaches the open ledges of the east summit. Then, turning left, the trail drops steeply to the edge of the woods, descends the mountain, and briefly follows a gravel road to a paved road, to US Rte. 3, 0.2 mi. south of the tramway station.

Kinsman Ridge Trail (map 5)
Distances from southern terminus, NH Rte. 112

   to Dilly Trail junction: 1 mi., 40 min.
   to Gordon Pond Trail junction: 3.4 mi., 2 hr. 20 min.
   to Reel Brook Trail junction: 6.6 mi., 3 hr. 50 min.
   to AMC Eliza Brook Shelter: 7.1 mi., 4 hr. 5 min.
   to Eliza Brook recrossing *(reliable water)*: *est.* 8.3 mi., 4 hr. 55 min.
   to Harrington Pond: *est.* 8.5 mi., 5 hr. 10 min.
   to Mt. Kinsman, south peak: *est.* 9.8 mi., 6 hr. 40 min.
   to Mt. Kinsman, north peak: *est.* 10.8 mi., 7 hr. 25 min.

LONESOME LAKE

This lake is located in a high (2734 ft.), flat area south of Cannon Mountain. There are fine views from its shores. It is most readily approached by the Lonesome Lake Trail, the Basin-Cascades Trail, and/or the Cascade Brook Trail. The walking distance around the lake is about 0.8 mi. The whole area from the notch floor up and beyond the lake is in Franconia Notch State Park. Camping is permitted only at official campgrounds.

Lafayette Place

This clearing on the west side of US Rte. 3 is about 2 mi. south of the tramway and 3.5 mi. north of the Flume Store. It has a campground and a picnic area. There is ample parking space (no time limit, cars left at owners' risk).

The view of the south cliff of Cannon Mountain from the clearing is magnificent. The Lincoln-Franconia town line is just north of the clearing, and 100 yd. farther north, on the east of the highway, is the site of the Mt. Lafayette House, a hotel that burned in 1861.

Lonesome Lake Hut (AMC)

Lonesome Lake Hut, at about 2765 ft., is located on the west shore of Lonesome Lake, with superb views of the Franconia Range. The hut was built in 1964, replacing cabins formerly on the northeast shore. It accommodates forty-six, and is open to the public from mid-June to mid-September. For schedules and information contact Reservation Secretary, Pinkham Notch Camp, Box 298, Gorham, NH 03581 (603-466-2727). The hut may be reached by the Lonesome Lake Trail, the Cascade Brook Trail, the Fishin' Jimmy Trail from Kinsman Junction, or by the Dodge Cutoff from the Hi-Cannon Trail. Camping is not permitted around the hut.

Lonesome Lake Trail (AMC)

This trail may be reached from Lafayette Place as indicated by a prominent swinging sign beside US Rte. 3. From the south end of the picnic area, cross the Pemigewasset on a footbridge; continue directly ahead through the camping area and follow yellow blazes across three camp access roads to where the trail, leaving the campground, bears slightly left. After a short almost-level stretch, the trail begins to climb at a moderate grade. At 0.3 mi. there is *water,* a bridge crossing, and a sharp left turn in the trail. At 0.4 mi. the Hi-Cannon Trail leaves right. From this point the trail is a series of three long switchbacks with a slight descent before reaching a junction with the Cascade Brook Trail (left) and the Dodge Cutoff (right), near the shore of Lonesome Lake. The Cascade Brook Trail is the shortest way to the hut. The Lonesome Lake Trail gives way to a woods trail that continues along the north shore and coincides with part of the Around-Lonesome-Lake Trail, which leaves left at 1.4 mi., leading in 0.3 mi. to Lonesome Lake Hut. (Trails along the north and west shore may be inundated and require some side-stepping.) The main trail continues north and west, at length begins to rise steeply, and ends at the Kinsman Ridge Trail in Coppermine Col, about 0.8 mi. southwest of the main (west) summit of Cannon Mountain.

Lonesome Lake Trail (map 5)

Distances from Lafayette Place picnic area

to Hi-Cannon Trail junction: 0.4 mi., 25 min.

to Cascade Brook Trail junction: 1.2 mi., 1 hr.

to AMC Lonesome Lake Hut (via Cascade Brook Trail and Fishin' Jimmy Trail): 1.5 mi., 1¼ hr.

to AMC Lonesome Lake Hut (via Around-Lonesome-Lake Trail): 1.7 mi., 1 hr. 25 min.

to Kinsman Ridge Trail junction: 2.3 mi. (3.7 km.), 2 hr. 10 min.

Around-Lonesome-Lake Trail (AMC)

This route uses portions of other trails. It has fine views, especially of the Franconia Range. Starting at the junction of the Lonesome Lake and Cascade Brook trails, it follows the latter south along the east shore, turns west and follows the Fishin' Jimmy Trail, crosses the outlet of the lake, and continues ahead where the Fishin' Jimmy Trail bears left to ascend to the hut. The trail continues north along the west side of the lake, crosses several inlet brooks, and meets the Lonesome Lake Trail shortly after entering the woods. Turn right at this point and continue to the entrance of the Cascade Brook Trail, which completes the circuit. On occasion parts of this trail, especially on the west and north shores, are inundated. Careful bushwhacking over higher ground, with the lake as a guide, should prove no great inconvenience.

Around-Lonesome-Lake Trail (map 5)

Distances from Lonesome Lake Trail/Cascade Brook Trail junction

　　to Fishin' Jimmy Trail junction: 0.3 mi.

　　to Lonesome Lake Trail junction: 0.6 mi.

　　to Lonesome Lake Trail/Cascade Brook Trail junction (complete circuit): 0.8 mi. (1.2 km.)

Hi-Cannon Trail (NHDP)

This trail diverges right from the Lonesome Lake Trail 0.4 mi. from Lafayette Campground. In about 500 ft. it crosses a small stream and begins to ascend gradually by switchbacks. At 0.7 mi. the Dodge Cutoff leading to Lonesome Lake enters left at the top of a ridge. At about 1.1 mi. there is a fine outlook across Franconia Notch and the area around Lafayette Campground. About 0.1 mi. farther the trail passes Cliff House (right), a natural rock shelter, soon ascends a ladder, and passes along a cliff edge with a fine view of Lonesome Lake. Then the trail ascends more steeply and roughly to the top of the ridge with a good view of N. and S. Kinsman. At 1.8 mi. the trail ends at its junction with the Kinsman Ridge Trail. Follow the Kinsman Ridge Trail right about 0.4 mi. for the summit of Cannon Mountain.

Hi-Cannon Trail (map 5)
Distances from Lafayette Place picnic area
 to start of Hi-Cannon Trail (via Lonesome Lake Trail): 0.4 mi.
 to Dodge Cutoff junction: 1.1 mi.
 to Kinsman Ridge Trail junction: 2.2 mi.
 to Cannon Mountain summit (via Kinsman Ridge Trail): 2.6 mi. (4.2 km.), 2½ hr.

Dodge Cutoff (NHDP)

This direct 0.3 mi. connection between the Hi-Cannon and Lonesome Lake trails gives access to Cannon Mountain from AMC Lonesome Lake Hut and vice versa. Named in honor of Joe Dodge, a former manager of the AMC hut system, it leaves the Hi-Cannon Trail 0.7 mi from its start and descends gradually (generally southwest) to a flat area, crosses a small stream, then a slight rise and another flat area, to end at the junction of the Lonesome Lake and Cascade Brook trails, 0.3 mi. from Lonesome Lake Hut on the west shore of the lake.

In reverse, the trail bears right about 10 yd. from its beginning.

Profile Lake Trail (NHDP)

This trail leaves the Profile Lake parking area and goes south (a short branch goes up the west side of Profile Lake) along the Pemigewasset River, crossing and recrossing the stream on bridges. Walking is nearly level for almost the entire distance. The trail ends at the Lafayette Campground entrance road, near the large recreation building.

Profile Lake Trail (map 5)
Distance from Profile Lake parking area
 to Lafayette Campground: *est*. 2 mi. (3.3 km.), 1 hr.

Pemi-Trail (NHDP)

This trail extends from Lafayette Campground to the Basin. It follows the west bank of the Pemigewasset River southward at an almost-level grade and ends at the Basin-Cascades Trail about 200 ft. west of the Basin.

Pemi-Trail (map 5)

Distance from Lafayette Campground

   to Basin-Cascades Trail junction: *est.* 2 mi., (3.3 km.), 1 hr.

Basin-Cascades Trail (NHDP)

This trail ascends the beautiful lower half of Cascade Brook and connects with the Cascade Brook Trail. From the Basin on the west side of US Rte. 3 about 1.4 mi. north of the Flume Store, cross two footbridges, first over the Pemigewasset at the Basin, then left by the Basin and over a branch brook. Shortly take the right of three paths, then cross a path and pass a bridge on your right. Next bear left where the Pemi-Trail goes right. Follow blue markers. The trail approaches Cascade Brook and remains on its north bank. Informal side paths lead onto the smooth granite ledges. At one point, about 0.3 mi. from the Basin, the main trail is directly adjacent to the brook. About 125 yd. farther up, a rough side path leads down left to a good view of the 20-ft. Kinsman Falls. Another 40 yd. farther up the main trail, a path to the left leads to a view from the top of the falls. After 500 ft., the main trail crosses a bridge to the south bank of the brook and continues its gradual ascent. In another 0.5 mi. there is a glimpse of upper and lower Rocky Glen Falls, then a closer view of the lower falls. The trail turns left through a little box canyon and in 70 yd. meets the Cascade Brook Trail at a bridge over the brook. For a good view of upper Rocky Glen Falls from above, return cautiously down the brook about 100 ft.

Occasional floods wash out parts of this trail and necessitate relocations.

Basin-Cascades Trail (map 5)
Distances from the Basin, US Rte. 3
to Kinsman Falls: 0.5 mi.
to Cascade Brook Trail junction: 1 mi. (1.6 km.), ¾ hr.

Cascade Brook Trail (AMC)

This trail, a link in the Appalachian Trail, blazed in white, provides a direct route to Mt. Liberty and the adjacent part of Franconia Ridge from the AMC Lonesome Lake Hut. The trail starts from the west side of US Rte. 3 at the south end of Whitehouse Bridge, about 0.8 mi. north of the Flume Store. The trail climbs at a moderate grade, crosses Whitehouse Brook in 0.2 mi., continues generally northwest, and after 1.3 mi. the Basin-Cascades Trail enters right. Just beyond this junction the trail crosses Cascade Brook on a bridge (severely damaged in 1982). About 100 yd. downstream on the Basin-Cascades Trail are some beautiful cascades and pools. The Cascade Brook Trail continues to climb along the northeast bank. At 1.8 mi. the Kinsman Pond Trail diverges left. From this point the trail follows an old logging road to the junction with Fishin' Jimmy Trail at the outlet of Lonesome Lake. Lonesome Lake Hut is 120 yd. to the left. The trail continues east of the lake and ends at the Lonesome Lake Trail in 0.3 mi.

Cascade Brook Trail (map 5)
Distances from Whitehouse Bridge, US Rte. 3
to Kinsman Pond Trail junction: 1.8 mi., 50 min.
to Fishin' Jimmy Trail junction: 2.7 mi., 1 hr. 50 min.
to Lonesome Lake Trail junction: 2.9 mi. (4.7 km.), 2 hr.

Fishin' Jimmy Trail (AMC)

This trail, named for the chief character in a story by Annie Trumbull Slosson, leads from Lonesome Lake to Kinsman Pond. As part of the Appalachian Trail, it is blazed in white. Starting from the Cascade Brook Trail at the outlet (south) of Lonesome Lake, it passes just to the south of Lonesome Lake Hut at 0.1 mi. and begins to slab the ridge, rising sharply at 0.3 mi. There is usually *water* at 0.5 mi. Passing a large rock block (left) at 0.6 mi. and ascending, the trail crosses dried water courses at 0.9 mi., at 1.0 mi., and at 1.1 mi. The trail crosses *reliable water* at 1.2 mi., rises sharply at 1.3 mi., and levels out at 1.6 mi. It ascends over a ledge at 1.8 mi. and levels out again at 2.1 mi., reaching Kinsman Junction and the Kinsman Ridge Trail at 2.3 mi., 0.1 mi. north of Kinsman Pond Shelter.

Water from Kinsman Pond and from the spring at the shelter is not potable. There is no reliable water between Kinsman Junction and S. Kinsman, and little reliable water between Kinsman Junction and Cannon Mountain. Obtain adequate supplies from Lonesome Lake Hut or from the water on the Fishin' Jimmy Trail.

Fishin' Jimmy Trail (map 5)
Distances from Cascade Brook Trail junction
  to Lonesome Lake Hut: 0.1 mi.
  to Kinsman Junction: 2.3 mi. (3.6 km.), 1 hr. 50 min.

Kinsman Pond Trail (AMC)

This trail leaves left from the Cascade Brook Trail 1.8 mi. from Whitehouse Bridge, crosses to the southwest side of the brook in 40 ft., and proceeds west by logging roads. Soon rising, it crosses a small brook at a cascade and reaches virgin forest near a brook. The upper half of the trail is wet, rough, and rocky. The trail now bends northwest, crossing a brook (*last reliable water*), and at 1.9 mi. crosses the outlet of Kinsman Pond not far below the pond itself. The east shore is on the left as the trail approaches and passes Kinsman Pond Shelter. Just beyond, in 0.1 mi., it meets the Kinsman Ridge and Fishin' Jimmy trails at Kinsman Junction. Kinsman Pond Shelter accommodates twelve. *Water* beneath a large rock on the trail about 150 ft. north of the shelter is *not potable*, nor is that in the pond. The nearest *reliable water* is about 1 mi. down the Fishin' Jimmy Trail.

Kinsman Pond Trail (map 5)

Distances from Whitehouse Bridge, US Rte. 3

to start of Kinsman Pond Trail (via Cascade Brook Trail): 1.8 mi., 50 min.

to Kinsman Pond outlet: 3.9 mi., 3 hr.

to Kinsman Pond Shelter: 4.1 mi., 3¼ hr.

to Kinsman Junction: 4.2 mi. (6.8 km.), 3 hr. 20 min.

MOUNT PEMIGEWASSET

On the northwest shoulder of this 2554-ft. mountain is the famous Indian Head, a natural rock profile formed by ledges.

One trail to the summit leaves the Indian Head Cabins driveway, which is on the west side of US Rte. 3 opposite the observation tower, at the most westerly point. It ascends by easy grades through hardwoods, passes near the base of the cliffs on the south side that form the Indian Head, and then climbs a steep gully and approaches the summit from the west. The summit is open and provides a fine view. The walk to the summit is about 1 mi. (1 hr.).

Mt. Pemigewasset Trail (NHDP)

This trail starts from the south end of the parking and picnic areas across US Rte. 3 from the Flume Store, bears left across a small field, enters the woods, and follows a graded path for about 0.5 mi. to the old Mt. Pemigewasset Trail. At about 0.8 mi. the trail approaches but does not cross a brook, and then ascends at a moderate grade, generally west and southwest. It approaches the summit from the north side, and is joined by the trail described above just before reaching the open summit ledges.

Mt. Pemigewasset Trail (map 5)

Distance from parking area opposite Flume Store, US Rte. 3

to Indian Head: *est.* 1.3 mi. (2 km.), 1¼ hr.

Georgiana Falls

These falls, on Harvard Brook, a branch of the Pemigewasset River, are a series of cascades ending in a pool. Leave US Rte. 3 on the west side about 2.5 mi. north of N. Woodstock on a road opposite the Longhorn Restaurant. Fifty yards from Rte. 3 park and cross Hanson Brook (no bridge) and follow a logging road for about 0.2 mi. Just before crossing Harvard Brook turn right on a logging road. Follow the main road, avoiding spurs. In about 0.5 mi. the road turns into a trail that follows Harvard Brook on the north side to Georgiana Falls, where it ends. The last part of the trail goes up the brook on sloping rocks. Above Georgiana Falls there is a series of cascades terminating in Harvard Falls, which are about 0.5 mi. up the brook.

Georgiana Falls (map 5)

Distance from road opposite Longhorn Restaurant, US Rte. 3

to Georgiana Falls: *est.* 1.3 mi. (2 km.)

Gordon Pond Trail (WMNF)

This trail starts opposite and north of Govoni's Restaurant on NH Rte. 112 (Lost River Rd.), 1.8 mi. west of US Rte. 3. It passes between two cottages, bears right in 0.1 mi., follows a level stretch of old railroad bed, crosses open space under a power line, enters the woods, circles gradually around left, and recrosses the power line. From here it follows an old railroad bed for some distance, then continues on logging roads, first on the west and then on the east side of Gordon Pond Brook. Passing to the right of Gordon Falls, it crosses the stream again and reaches Gordon Pond near its outlet. It shortly swings left, ascends at a moderate grade, and ends at the Kinsman Ridge Trail.

Gordon Pond Trail (map 5)

Distances from NH Rte. 112

to Gordon Pond: *est.* 4.5 mi., 2 hr. 50 min.

to Kinsman Ridge Trail junction: 4.8 mi. (7.7 km.), 3¼ hr.

Coppermine Trail (WMNF)

This trail leaves the east side of NH Rte. 116, 3.4 mi. south of Franconia and 7.7 mi. north of the junction of Rtes. 116 and 112 at Bungay Corner. It follows an old road that is passable for automobiles for about 0.8 mi. The trail follows along the left (north) side of Coppermine Brook and finally crosses it. The trail ascends at a somewhat steeper grade, passes the WMNF Coppermine Shelter, and ends at the base of the Bridal Veil Falls. The Coppermine Trail is within a Restricted Use Area (see Section 22).

Coppermine Trail (map 5)

Distance from NH Rte. 116

 to Bridal Veil Falls: 2.5 mi. (4 km.)

Mount Kinsman Trail (WMNF)

This trail leaves the east side of NH Rte. 116, 4 mi. south of Franconia Village and 7 mi. north of the junction of Rtes. 116 and 112 at Bungay Corner. It follows a logging road east into the WMNF and ascends gradually. At a fork in the road bear right (blazes) and bear right at the next fork where one road turns sharp left. At 1.5 mi. the trail passes the WMNF Kinsman Cabin (scheduled for removal) on the left, and the Mt. Kinsman Trail swings sharply right across a brook. The trail crosses a second brook 0.1 mi. farther, and in another 0.2 mi. crosses Flume Brook.

At Flume Brook a branch trail leads right for 0.1 mi. to the head of Kinsman Flume and Profile. At 100 ft. beyond Flume Brook a side path (sign) leads right about 0.2 mi. to Bald Peak, a bare eminence with fine views crowning a west spur of Mt. Kinsman. The main Mt. Kinsman Trail continues sharply left from the Bald Peak spur, heads for the ridge, and meets the Kinsman Ridge Trail 0.2 mi. southwest of Kinsman Junction. The top of N. Kinsman (4275 ft.), 0.4 mi. to the right, affords a fine view. Close by, a short path leads to the cliff on the east overlooking Kinsman Pond. To reach N. and S. Kinsman follow the Kinsman Ridge Trail south.

Descending from the north peak, the trail will be found leaving the west side of the Kinsman Ridge Trail 0.4 mi. north of the summit.

Mt. Kinsman Trail (map 5)
Distances from NH Rte. 116
    to Kinsman Cabin: *est.* 1.5 mi., 1 hr.
    to Flume Brook crossing: 2.1 mi., 1½ hr.
    to Bald Peak spur trail junction: 2.3 mi.
    to Kinsman Ridge Trail junction: *est.* 3.5 mi. (5.5 km.), 3 hr.

Reel Brook Trail (WMNF)

At a point 7 mi. south of Franconia on NH Rte. 116, turn south (east) on a gravel road, plowed in winter. Follow it, generally southeast, for about 0.8 mi to Reel Brook (parking here or 100 yd. back, opposite summer home). The trail starts by crossing Reel Brook, and shortly beyond the Beech Hill Trail diverges right. The trail follows an old logging road near the brook, crosses it twice, and passes under the N. Woodstock-Easton power line between the two crossings. After the second crossing, the trail climbs more steeply, then levels out, leaves the logging road, and climbs generally east to the height-of-land between S. Kinsman and Mt. Wolf (the original "Kinsman Notch"), where it meets the Kinsman Ridge Trail. Turn right for NH Rte. 112 and left for Eliza Brook Shelter.

Reel Brook Trail (map 5)
Distances from NH Rte. 116
    to Beech Hill Trail junction: 0.8 mi., 25 min.
    to Kinsman Ridge Trail junction: *est.* 4 mi. (6.5 km.), 2½ hr.

Beech Hill Trail (WMNF)

The Beech Hill Trail leaves NH Rte. 112 west of Clay Brook and about midway between Wildwood Inn and Wildwood Campground. Portions of this trail may be obscure. It runs northeast across an overgrown pasture, follows an old wood road to Black Brook and up the brook, which it crosses about 1.5 mi. from the highway. Here the trail leaves the wood road, turns generally northwest, soon steeply ascends Beech Hill through a dense growth of small spruce, and levels out on an old wood road. About 1 mi. from the brook it turns more north and passes through the ruins of a camp. It then descends in a straight line on the northwest slope of Beech Hill and ends at the Reel Brook Trail at a point 0.8 mi. from NH Rte. 116.

Beech Hill Trail (map 5)

Distance from NH Rte. 112

   to Reel Brook Trail junction: 4.1 mi. (6.6 km.), 2¼ hr.

MOUNT AGASSIZ

This 2378-ft. mountain, just southeast of Bethlehem and north of Franconia, is topped by a ruined stone structure from which there is an excellent view of the surrounding mountains. A formerly paved road is now used as a trail. The whole mountain is privately owned, but the trail is open to the public.

Mt. Agassiz (map 5)

Distance to Mt. Agassiz summit

   from NH Rte. 142: *est.* 1 mi.

BALD MOUNTAIN AND ARTISTS BLUFF

Bald Mountain (about 2300 ft.) and Artists Bluff (2368 ft.), which fill the north end of Franconia Notch, provide views to the north and down the notch.

To climb Bald Mountain and/or Artists Bluff follow NH Rte. 18 northwest 0.4 mi. from its junction with US Rte. 3 near Echo Lake.

The trail to the summit of Bald Mountain leaves the Roland Peabody Memorial Slope parking area at a point about opposite the entrance. It follows an old carriage road and reaches the top of the ridge in about 0.3 mi. At this point the trail diverges left to the top of Bald Mountain, which is an open rocky summit with a good view. Ten yards beyond the junction where the trail leaves left for Bald Mountain, a trail diverges right and proceeds over the Artists Bluff ridge. A short unmarked trail at the top of a steep gravelly gully diverges left to the top of Artists Bluff. The main trail continues down the gully to the road at Echo Lake beach.

Bald Mountain and Artists Bluff (map 5)

Distances from parking area, NH Rte. 18

to Bald Mountain summit: *est.* 0.4 mi., 20 min.

to Echo Lake (via Artists Bluff): *est.* 0.8 mi., ¾ hr.

THE JOSEPH STORY FAY RESERVATION

This reservation of 150 acres, the gift to the AMC in 1897 of Miss Sarah B. Fay in memory of her father, whose name it bears, is in the towns of Woodstock and Lincoln, just north of the village of N. Woodstock, and lies along both sides of US Rte. 3. It now belongs to the state of New Hampshire.

LOST RIVER

The Lost River Reservation, property of the Society for the Protection of NH Forests, lies 5 mi. west of N. Woodstock on NH Rte. 112. Lost River, one of the tributaries of Moosilauke Brook, flows for nearly 0.5 mi. through a series of caves and large potholes, for the most part underground. At one place it falls 20 ft. within one of the caves, and at another, known as Paradise Falls, 30 ft. in the open air. Trails, walks, and ladders make the caves accessible. In order to protect the forest and caves, the Society began in 1911 to acquire the surrounding land and now owns about 770 acres bordering the highway on both sides for nearly 2.5 mi. The Society maintains a nature garden containing more than 300 indigenous plants. An "Ecology

Trail" circles the inner parking lot area and provides information at numbered and marked sites described in a brochure provided by the Society. There is an admission fee. The reservation is open from May through October. The Appalachian Trail crosses NH Rte. 112 about 0.5 mi. northwest of the reservation buildings, and there is an Appalachian Trail shelter 0.2 mi. south of Rte. 112 on the Beaver Brook Trail.

Note. An unnamed and unmarked trail about 0.5 mi. long connects the southern terminus of the Kinsman Ridge Trail with the Lost River Reservation. It begins a few yards north of Rte. 112 and right of the Kinsman Ridge Trail. It goes east and northeast, roughly paralleling Rte. 112. After a very slight ascent, it descends slightly to the Ecology Trail at the reservation which it joins at about 0.5 mi. Turn right on the Ecology Trail at site 10 and reach the parking lot in about 200 yd. Turn left on the Ecology Trail and reach the Dilly Trail in about 250 yd. Go straight ahead and reach the north edge of the parking lot in about 80 yd.

Dilly Trail (SPNHF)

This trail leaves the northeast corner of the dirt parking area (not the paved area directly beside NH Rte. 112), which is off the road in the Lost River Reservation. At the trailhead there is a sign marked "Dilly Trail .75." The trail is well marked with white paint. At about 100 yd., the trail starts steeply up the cliffs and ledges overlooking the Lost River Reservation, which can be seen at about 0.1 mi. The trail climbs over ledges and begins a series of switchbacks at about 0.3 mi. It reaches the distinctive edge of the ridge at about 0.7 mi., where a branch trail right goes to a lookout over Lost River and to the mountains south of Kinsman Notch. The lookout is about 50 yd. east. The main trail turns sharply left and northwest, passing through open hardwoods and rising slightly with views and glimpses of the country to the northeast, and reaches the junction with the Kinsman Ridge Trail at about 0.8 mi. This junction is marked with white paint on a birch tree and is not easily discernible from the Kinsman Ridge Trail in certain light and leaf conditions. In reverse, the point of descent at the edge of the ridge is marked with white paint both on a tree and on a rock in the trail just below the edge of the ridge, but the point is difficult to see in certain light and leaf conditions.

Dilly Trail (map 5)

Distances from Lost River Reservation parking lot

to lookout over Lost River: *est.* 0.7 mi., 35 min.

to Kinsman Ridge Trail junction: *est.* 0.8 mi., 45 min.

Jericho Road Trail (WMNF)

The Jericho Rd. Trail starts at the height-of-land on the west side of NH Rte. 116, between Easton and NH Rte. 112, near Mud Pond. It follows a horse trail, the old Jericho Rd., north to the summit of Cooley Hill (2600 ft.). At 1.6 mi. an unnamed trail diverges left. Having followed the old Jericho Rd. to Tommy Hall Pasture, the trail leaves the road and traverses the pasture for about 0.5 mi. At about 1.8 mi. the trail starts to follow the height-of-land of the Cooley Hill-Cole Hill range, and finally ends at the foundation of the former Cooley Hill Lookout Tower on the left.

Jericho Rd. Trail (map 5)

Distance from NH Rte. 116

to Cooley Hill summit: 3.3 mi. (5.3 km.), 2½ hr.

Cobble Hill Trail (WMNF)

This trail leaves NH Rte. 112 at a point 0.1 mi. west of Woodsville Reservoir and follows an old road along the west side of Dearth Brook. At 0.7 mi. the abandoned S. Landaff Rd. leaves left. The trail ascends generally north, crosses the height-of-land between Cobble Hill and Moody Ledge, and descends to end at the Landaff Town Rd.

Cobble Hill Trail (map 5)

Distance from NH Rte. 112

to Landaff Town Rd.: 3.5 mi. (5.6 km.), 2¼ hr.

Moosilauke Region

This section includes trails on Mt. Moosilauke and other mountains mostly west and south of it, such as Mt. Cube, Smarts Mountain, the Benton Range area, and the Stinson-Carr-Kineo area. All are south of NH Rte. 112, west of I-93, and north of Plymouth. In this section the Appalachian Trail (AT) crosses the Connecticut River at Hanover and traverses Moose Mountain, Smarts Mountain, Mt. Cube, and Mt. Moosilauke to Lost River. Many trails in this section, blazed in orange and black, are maintained by the Dartmouth Outing Club (DOC). For the AT from Hanover to Glencliff and DOC map, see *Middle Connecticut River Mountains* below. Refer to map 4, Chocorua-Waterville; map 5, Franconia; and USGS quadrangles.

MOUNT MOOSILAUKE

Mt. Moosilauke (4802 ft.) in Benton is easily accessible, and its view is considered by many to be the best in New Hampshire. Two minor summits to the northeast are Mt. Blue and Mt. Jim (4180 ft.). On the east side, between the east and Blue ridges, is Jobildunc Ravine. The upper Baker River flows through the ravine from its source in a marsh that was once Deer Lake.

The stone Tip-Top House built in 1860 was destroyed by fire in 1942. A DOC cabin was removed in 1978. Camping is not permitted anywhere on Mt. Moosilauke. There is a *spring* 400 ft. southeast of the Tip-Top House ruins.

The DOC Ravine Lodge (now closed), southeast of Mt. Moosilauke, is the starting point of several trails. A sand road leaves Rte. 118, 6 mi. north of its junction with NH Rte. 25 and about 6 mi. south of its junction with NH Rte. 112. The road heads generally northwest, then north. Bear right at a fork to the parking area behind Ravine Lodge, 1.5 mi. from Rte. 118. The path down to the Baker River footbridge leaves from the upper left corner of the turnaround.

A Trail Guide to Mt. Moosilauke has been prepared by the
Environmental Studies Division of the DOC, PO Box 9,
Hanover, NH 03755 (603-646-2428) 1978 ed. $3.95, 42 pp.

Beaver Brook Trail (DOC)

This link in the Appalachian Trail, with white blazes, leaves
NH Rte. 112, 0.4 mi. northwest of Lost River (sign). At 0.1 mi.
the trail crosses a bridge over Beaver Brook. A path diverges left
and reaches the DOC Beaver Brook Shelter in 0.1 mi. The main
trail leads toward Beaver Brook, then turns and follows up the
east bank, later rising steeply and passing the Beaver Brook
Cascades, finest in this vicinity (rocks may be slippery). The trail
remains very steep, staying close to the brook and ascending by a
series of granite and wooden steps. After a mile of steep climbing, the trail bears left away from the brook (*last sure water*) and
ascends steeply, alternately following well-worn trails and
brookbeds.

The ascent becomes more gradual, and, 1.9 mi. up, the trail
reaches the summit of the Blue Ridge, at the col between Mt.
Blue and Mt. Jim, where the Asquam-Ridge Trail from the
Ravine Lodge enters left. Here, the Beaver Brook Trail turns
sharply right and west. It skirts the steep slopes of Jobildunc
Ravine, a rough and rocky stretch. The path is built high along
the wall of the ravine with precipitous slopes to the left. After it
veers southwest, *water* may be found at a swampy place where
the trail crosses the beginnings of the Baker River. The trail then
ascends at a moderate grade to the summit.

Beaver Brook Trail (map 4 or map 5)

Distances from NH Rte. 112

to side path to Beaver Brook Shelter: 0.1 mi., 5 min.

to Asquam-Ridge Trail junction: 1.9 mi., 2 hr.

to spring at beginning of Baker River: 2.7 mi.

to Mt. Blue summit: 3.2 mi. (5.1 km.), 3 hr.

Tunnel Brook Trail (WMNF)

To reach the trailhead, take Noxon Rd. southeast from NH Rte. 116 in Benton, just west of Landaff town line, or take the road that heads south from NH Rte. 112 about 0.5 mi. east of its junction with Rte. 116 at Bungay Corner. Just west of a bridge over Tunnel Brook, at the road junction, drive south on Tunnel Brook Rd., a WMNF gravel access road. At 1.6 mi. from the bridge the Benton Trail leaves left (parking). At 2.3 mi., south of a timber bridge, the gravel road ends at a hiker's parking area, and the Tunnel Brook Trail continues south on an old logging road. There are several brook crossings and many beaver dams. The last one is crossed back to the west side of brook. As the trail begins to level off, it reaches Tunnel Brook Slides and Slide Pond, where there are slides on both sides of the trail. Just before descending into the valley of Slide Brook, the trail passes Mud Pond and continues on down to the North and South Rd., following the brook closely for most of the distance. Care should be taken to avoid polluting Slide Brook, water supply of the NH Home for the Elderly, Glencliff.

Tunnel Brook Trail (map 5)

Distances from Noxon Rd.

   to end of gravel road: 2.3 mi.
   to Mud Pond: 4.3 mi.
   to North and South Rd.: 6.5 mi. (10.5 km.)

Benton Trail (WMNF)

Once a bridle path, this trail diverges east from the Tunnel Brook Trail, a gravel road at this point, at a parking area 1.6 mi. south of Noxon Rd. about 3 mi. south of the NH Rte. 112 and NH Rte. 116 junction at Bungay Corner.

The trail descends from the parking lot, crosses a clearing, then Tunnel Brook, and ascends the wooded spur forming the south wall of Little Tunnel Ravine, following the north bank of a brook for a short distance. Watch for arrows and blazes marking trail. About 1.1 mi. a sign indicates the splendid views a few steps to the left of trail. There is a *spring* at 2.1 mi. (*water unreliable*), right of the trail (sign). The trail ascends by moderate grades through a beautiful evergreen forest and reaches treeline about 0.3 mi. below the Mt. Moosilauke summit. From the north end of the broad summit, the trail follows large cairns to the site of the summit house.

Benton Trail (map 5)
Distance from Tunnel Brook Trail junction

   to Mt. Moosilauke summit: 3.5 mi. (5.6 km.), 3 hr.

Glencliff Trail (DOC)

This trail is part of the Appalachian Trail and is blazed in white. Follow the Sanatorium (NH Home for the Elderly) Rd. from its junction with NH Rte. 25 in the center of Glencliff Village (signs) 1.2 mi. north to start of trail. At sign on right side of road, turn right and close gate. Follow the trail across a pasture, continue east, past a cellar hole right, bear left beyond a brook crossing, and enter an open field. The trail follows a path along the right edge, soon reaches a second open field, and follows its left side to the woods at the upper left corner. Hurricane Trail exits right at this point. The trail again crosses the brook to the left bank and passes the ruins of an old camp, ascends more steeply through a pine forest. The trail enters hardwoods, slabs the west face of the south peak of Mt. Moosilauke, rising easily to about 3500 ft., then climbs more rapidly to a point near the summit of the south peak (4560 ft.), where it swings around the north side and joins the Carriage Rd. and S. Peak Trail at the scrub line (4400 ft.), about 1 mi. below the main (north) summit. The S. Peak Trail leads right and climbs gradually 0.2 mi. to the south peak. Continue straight up the road to the main summit. There is a *spring* 400 ft. southwest of the summit.

Glencliff Trail (map 4 or map 5)
Distances from Sanatorium Rd.
  to last sure water: 1.6 mi., 1¼ hr.
  to Carriage Rd. junction: 3 mi., 2½ hr.
  to Mt. Moosilauke north summit: 3.9 mi. (6.3 km.), 3¼ hr.

Hurricane Trail (DOC)

This trail, blazed in double yellow and DOC orange and black markers, leaves to the right off the lower end of the Glencliff Trail, at the top left corner of a pasture. It slabs across the west slope of Hurricane Mountain with a gradual ascent, turns more south, and cuts around south of the summit at 2.3 mi. It bears east again, descends slowly, and approaches Little Brook. The trail parallels the north side of the brook, crosses Big Brook and reaches the Carriage Rd. Turning left it follows the road for 0.3 mi., leaves the road right, heads east, and crosses a small stream and then the Baker River. After this crossing, turn left (north). The Ravine Lodge clearing is about 100 yd. farther.

Hurricane Trail (map 4 or map 5)
Distance from Glencliff Trail junction
  to Ravine Lodge: 5 mi. (8 km.)

The Carriage Road

This former road is no longer passable for vehicles. For approaches from the south, see map 4, Chocorua-Waterville. The Carriage Rd. starts at Breezy Point (1707 ft.) at the Moosilauke Inn, 5 mi. from Warren, 1.8 mi. from NH Rte. 118. After leaving the tar road, pass left of a service building, and continue straight ahead north. The trail ascends the south ridge. It crosses Merrill Brook about 300 ft. after it begins. The trail bears right at a wood road junction, then left where Baker River Trail turns right (east). The trail soon reaches the clearing, continues from the left corner, and soon slabs the east shoulder of Chokecherry

Hill. It bears right at the next fork, soon crosses Little Brook, ascends by easy grades to a junction with the Hurricane Trail (left), at 1.3 mi. A series of switchbacks leads to the Snapper Ski Trail, which enters right at 3.3 mi. At 4.1 mi. the Glencliff Trail and a spur trail that leads 0.2 mi. to the S. Peak of Mt. Moosilauke (4560 ft.) enter left. The road, marked by cairns, follows the windswept ridge about 1 mi. to the main (north) summit. In bad weather this is a dangerous section, and it should not be attempted. About halfway between the south and north peaks is a fine lookout to the right.

The Carriage Rd. (map 4 or map 5)

Distances from Mt. Moosilauke Inn, Breezy Point
 to Snapper Ski Trail junction: 3.3 mi., 2 hr.
 to Glencliff Trail junction: 4.1 mi., 2¾ hr.
 to Mt. Moosilauke, north summit: 5 mi. (8 km.), 3½ hr.

RAVINE LODGE

The following three trails, beginning near the Ravine Lodge, start from the turnaround at the end of the lodge road, follow a common trail downhill to the front of the lodge (not particularly close to it), and cross the Baker River together on a footbridge. For directions to the Ravine Lodge, see "Mount Moosilauke" at the beginning of Section 9.

Gorge Brook Trail (DOC)

This trail, one of the most beautiful on Mt. Moosilauke, provides an almost direct route between the Ravine Lodge and the summit. Ridges shelter most of it from the winds. The trail starts across the Baker River in front of the Ravine Lodge, passing the Asquam-Ridge Trail, which leaves right just across the footbridge. Passing the Snapper Ski Trail at 0.2 mi., it continues on the east side of Gorge Brook, crosses it at 0.4 mi., parallels it on the west bank, at 1 mi. crosses back to the east bank and follows the brook. It then bears right and ascends steeply through fir and mixed hardwood for about 0.3 mi. (The former Gorge Brook Slide Trail has been closed.) The trail then turns slightly left and slabs at a more moderate grade up and along the left side of the east ridge, where there are lookouts onto the Pleiades Slides and across to Mt. Carr and Mt. Kineo. From the timberline follows cairns to the Mt. Moosilauke summit. Drinking water is plentiful until just below the former Gorge Brook Slide Trail junction.

Gorge Brook Trail (map 4 or map 5)

Distance from Ravine Lodge

to Mt. Moosilauke summit: 2.7 mi. (4.3 km.), 2¼ hr.

Snapper Ski Trail (DOC)

This trail, although no longer maintained for skiing, is open to hiking all year round. Cross the Baker River footbridge in front of the Ravine Lodge, and follow the Gorge Brook Trail. The ski trail leaves left at 0.2 mi. and crosses Gorge Brook. The wide trail winds up the mountain, ascending gradually at first and then more steeply, and ends at the Carriage Rd. below south peak. Turn right for Mt. Moosilauke main summit (1.7 mi.).

Snapper Ski Trail (map 4 or map 5)

Distance from Gorge Brook Trail junction

to Carriage Rd. junction: 1.1 mi. (1.8 km.)

Asquam-Ridge Trail (DOC)

This alternative route to Mt. Moosilauke summit begins across the Baker River footbridge in front of the Ravine Lodge and follows the west bank of the river. In 0.4 mi. the trail joins an old logging road, continues gradually uphill, and passes through an abandoned logging camp. At 1.3 mi. the trail recrosses the river and climbs easily on old logging roads. The trail climbs over Mt. Jim (wooded) and ends at the Beaver Brook Trail about midway between Kinsman Notch and Mt. Moosilauke summit.

Asquam-Ridge Trail (map 4)

Distances from Ravine Lodge

to Beaver Brook Trail junction: 3.5 mi.

to Mt. Moosilauke north summit (via Beaver Brook Trail):
4.9 mi. (7.9 km.), 3½ hr.

to NH Rte. 112 (via Beaver Brook Trail): 5.4 mi. (8.6 km.)

MIDDLE CONNECTICUT RIVER MOUNTAINS

These mountains extend along the east bank of the Connecticut River from Haverhill to Claremont. The Dartmouth Outing Club maintains a system of trails covering the region from near Woodstock, Vermont, to Mt. Moosilauke, including about 70 mi. of the Appalachian Trail. DOC operates ten simply equipped shelters for use free to the hiking public. All are close to the Appalachian Trail: Cloudland Shelter, Pomfret, Vermont (16 mi. south of Hanover); Happy Hill open cabin, Norwich, Vermont (5.5 mi. south of Hanover); Velvet Rocks Shelter (1 mi. north of Hanover); Moose Mountain Shelter, on Clark Pond Loop near Harris Junction (0.5 mi. south of the AT); Trapper John Shelter, near Holts Ledge (14 mi. north of Hanover); Smarts Shelter and Ranger Cabin, both near Smarts Mountain summit; Cube Shelter, on the Appalachian Trail just south of Mt. Cube; Wachipauka Pond Shelter, on Webster Slide Mountain above Wachipauka Pond; and Beaver Brook Shelter, at the base of Beaver Brook Trail, Kinsman Notch.

In this subsection, most trails listed are part of the Appalachian Trail. The others — Webster Slide, Smarts 3, Holts Ledge Side Trail, and Clark Pond Loop— have one or both ends on the Appalachian Trail. Trails are listed from northeast to southwest, although within individual trail descriptions, beginning with Holts Ledge Trail, the direction is southwest to northeast.

The DOC has issued a trail map covering the Appalachian Trail from Vermont Rte. 12 to Kinsman Notch, showing shelter locations and mileage (DOC, PO Box 9, Hanover, NH 03755; price 75 cents).

USGS quadrangles cover all this region. Maps with this *Guide* do not.

Town Line Trail (DOC)

From the junction of Glencliff Trail and Sanatorium Rd. go west 0.3 mi. to North and South Rd., then south 0.1 mi. This trail, part of the Appalachian Trail, goes through woods 1.0 mi. to NH Rte. 25 and the start of the Wachipauka Pond Trail.

Town Line Trail (map 4)
Distance from North and South Rd.
   to NH Rte. 25: 1.4 mi. (2.3 km.)

Wachipauka Pond Trail (DOC)

This link in the Appalachian Trail, blazed in white, leaves NH Rte. 25, 1.4 mi. west of Glencliff opposite the Town Line Trail. It rises steeply to the summit of Wyatt Hill, then descends gradually west to the old Appalachian Trail north of Wachipauka Pond. The trail slabs the base of Webster Slide Mountain, and a spur trail to its summit leaves right. The main trail climbs Mt. Mist gradually, passes an excellent outlook east, crosses the wooded summit, and descends gradually to NH Rte. 25C where it crosses a power line. Continuing ahead it passes Ore Hill before crossing through an abandoned mine. At this point the trail leads right (west) down a lumber road to rejoin the former Appalachian Trail. There are long-term plans to replace the lumber-road section when the Appalachian Trail is extended south from the old mine as far as the summit of Mt. Cube.

Wachipauka Pond Trail
(USGS Warren or Rumney)
Distances from Glencliff, NH Rte. 25
   to NH Rte. 25C: *est.* 6 mi.
   to former Appalachian Trail junction: *est.* 7.5 mi. (12 km.)

Webster Slide Mountain

There is a spur trail that leaves the Wachipauka Pond Trail right (north) about 0.3 mi. beyond the pond (trail leaves from old wood road just uphill from Appalachian Trail crossing). It climbs rather steeply for 1 mi. The trail reaches the Webster Slide Mountain summit (2261 ft.), overlooking the pond. A few steps down on the open ledges give even a better view. *Water* must be obtained from the pond.

Webster Slide Mountain
(USGS Warren or Rumney)

Distances from NH Rte. 25

to start of spur trail to summit (via Wachipauka Pond Trail): 1.1 mi.

to Webster Slide Mountain summit (via spur trail): 2.6 mi. (4.2 km.)

Mount Cube

Mt. Cube in Orford is skirted on its north side by NH Rte. 25A. It is an attractive, 2911-ft peak, and the semi-open ledges of the summits offer many viewpoints. The DOC trail, part of the Appalachian Trail, crosses from the north, over both summits, to the west, giving access from north or west.

1. From the north: The trail leaves Rte. 25A about 0.3 mi. west of the Mt. Cube House, a red brick farmhouse at the height-of-land (park in field just off road). It crosses a small field, then follows a lumber road for a short distance to the former location. The trail briefly follows a stream, turns more south, then climbs steeply to the north peak and continues with very slight descent to the higher south summit. Use care in locating trail entrance into woods.

2. From the west: Take the dirt road running south from Rte. 25A 1.7 mi. west of the Mt. Cube House. The trail leaves this road in 1 mi. and reaches Cube Shelter in about 0.2 mi. It climbs steeply up the west flank of the mountain to the southwest ridge, which is then followed directly to the south peak, 1½ mi. (1½ hr.).

Mt. Cube (USGS Mt. Cube)

From the north — distances from NH Rte. 25A

   to Mt. Cube, north peak: *est.* 1.5 mi., 1½ hr.

   to Mt. Cube, south peak: *est.* 2 mi. (3.3 km.), 1¾ hr.

From the west—distance from dirt road off NH Rte. 25A

   to Mt. Cube, south peak: *est.* 1.5 mi., 1½ hr.

Smarts Mountain

This 3240-ft. mountain is south of Mt. Cube and east of Lyme. There is a DOC ranger's cabin near the summit. Telephone lines follow most of the Appalachian Trail. There are interesting views of less-known country.

1. From the southwest: The DOC trail (Ranger Trail), now part of the Appalachian Trail and blazed in white, leaves the Lyme-Dorchester road 3 mi. east of Lyme Center. It starts up a wood road, with brook on the right (east). The road ends at a garage (2.0 mi.), and the trail turns right across the brook. The brook is later recrossed (*last reliable water*), and the grade steepens. There are occasional views to the south and west from the upper reaches of the trail. About 150 yd. before the summit there is stagnant water (*not potable*). Head right 100 ft. to the Mt. Cube shelter. *Potable water* may be found 0.2 mi. north of the ranger cabin, right of the trail.

2. From the north: The trail, part of the Appalachian Trail and blazed in white, starts at "Quinttown," a crossroads reached in 2 mi. by a dirt road that leaves NH Rte. 25A on the right, about 1.5 mi. east of Orfordville. It follows a road south, passable for automobiles for about 0.8 mi. Park at second house on right (abandoned). Soon after crossing Mousley Brook bear left at fork in road (right is DOC Quinttown Trail to Lyme-Dorchester Rd.). The trail passes a private cabin on the left and a shed on the right, follows an old lumber road, and ascends Smarts Mountain by the valley of Mousley Brook. It rises rapidly to a *spring* on the summit ridge, and continues to the summit.

3. From the southeast: Smarts Trail #3 starts at Cummins Pond on the Lyme-Dorchester Rd. and follows old lumber roads

up near Clough Brook and along a ridge to the summit.

Smarts Mountain (USGS Mt. Cube)

From the southwest—distances from Lyme-Dorchester Rd.

   to brook crossing: *est*. 2 mi., 1¼ hr.

   to Smarts Mountain summit: *est*. 3.5 mi. (5.5 km.), 2½ hr.

From the north—distances from Quinttown crossroads

   to Smarts Mountain summit: *est*. 4 mi. (6.5 km.), 3 hr.

   to Mt. Cube Shelter (via Appalachian Trail): 1.7 mi.

From the southeast—distance from Cummins Pond, Lyme-Dorchester Rd.

   to Mt. Cube summit: 4.4 mi. (7.1 km.)

Holts Ledge Trail (DOC)

This trail, part of the Appalachian Trail and blazed in white, is in the towns of Hanover and Lyme. Refer to the USGS Mascoma and Mt. Cube quadrangles. The DOC proposes to relocate the southwest half of the trail up over N. Moose Mountain and ridge. The southwest end of the old route has been at the junction of the Moose Mountain Trail and DOC Ski Loop. The trail heads north on a reasonably level wood road. At 0.6 mi. the DOC Ski Loop diverges east. The Holts Ledge Trail crosses four brooks and reaches a large open field with fine views to the north. It re-enters the woods in 200 ft. on the right side of the field, enters a smaller field 200 ft. farther, and goes into the woods again at the right lower corner. The trail makes a short, steep descent, crosses a brook and a tributary, and bearing right begins a gradual ascent. It levels, passes a small cottage, turns right onto a wood road, passes two other wood roads, finally narrows to a path, and then turns right on a third wood road. Descending gradually, then moderately, the trail reaches a dirt road at 3.6 mi.

Turn right on the road, follow it 0.2 mi., then go left onto a farm road opposite a barn. The trail passes between two fields, soon crosses a bridge and a bar gate, then reaches another dirt road at 4.2 mi. Moose Mountain is visible to the south. The trail climbs a short distance, then levels, and soon becomes a wood road. Turn right from this road at 4.5 mi. onto another wood road. Soon the trail crosses a bridge and the road bears right. The trail continues straight ahead through an open field, past an abandoned shed. It enters a heavy growth of young pines, and turns right. At 5.0 mi. the DOC Holts Ledge Side Trail leaves on the left. The trail soon bears left into woods, crosses another wood road, and rises at a steeper grade from the col between Holts Ledge and Bear Hill, toward the ridge of Holts Ledge. Prior to reaching the highest point, the trail turns right and reaches boundary markers of Dartmouth College land (barbed wire fence). The trail descends gradually to Holts Ledge. From this 800-ft. ledge, the view extends from Mt. Ascutney (3144 ft.) in the south to many mountains east, up to Mt. Moosilauke in the north. Once you reach fence at top of Dartmouth Skiway, the Holts Ledge Trail veers left, down into the woods to a ski trail. At 6.4 mi. DOC Rands Ramble Trail comes in on the left, and then the Papoose Ski Trail at a large boulder. A wood road crosses at 6.7 mi.

The Holts Ledge Trail turns left onto the wood road, passes a *spring* just after leaving the ski trail, and forks left at 6.9 mi. on a lesser-used wood road. The Holts Ledge Side Trail comes in from the left at 7.0 mi. The trail reaches a more traveled wood road. Take right about 0.3 mi. farther at fork in road. The trail continues straight ahead and soon reaches Lyme-Dorchester Rd. at 7.7 mi.

The Appalachian Trail turns right and follows the Lyme-Dorchester Rd., which forks left onto a sand road at 8.3 mi.; right is the Dartmouth Skiway. The DOC Quinttown Trail leaves left at 8.7 mi. After a gradual ascent the DOC Ranger Trail leaves left at 10 mi., just before the first bridge crossing.

Holts Ledge Side Trail

This trail in town of Lyme provides a bypass of Holts Ledge. Refer to the USGS Mt. Cube quadrangle. It leaves the Holts Ledge Trail at 5.0 mi., going north, and soon turns right onto an old wood road, which eventually narrows into a trail as it climbs gradually. The trail passes through a stand of hemlock, crosses two brooks, reaches Dartmouth College property boundary, and then turns left. It descends gradually, passes a large rock, and soon crosses a brook. Rands Ramble leads steeply uphill to Holts Ledge Trail. Continuing the gradual descent, Holts Ledge Side Trail soon ends at 1.3 mi. where it rejoins the Holts Ledge Trail.

Moose Mountain

This long, 2300-ft. ridge in the eastern part of Hanover culminates in the N. Peak, separated from the slightly lower S. Peak by a deep col. Refer to the USGS Mascoma quadrangle. The abandoned Wolfeboro Rd., laid out by Governor Wentworth in 1772 from Wolfeboro to Hanover, runs through this gap. On the S. Peak, a helicopter landing zone was cleared during rescue operations after a plane crash in 1968 on the east slope of S. Peak. There are views east to Goose Pond and Mt. Cardigan.

Moose Mountain Trail (DOC)

From the southwest, this trail, which is part of the Appalachian Trail, heads east from Three Mile Rd. about 1.5 mi. north of Ruddsboro Rd. It crosses a stream, passes S. Moose Mountain, and at about 1.5 mi. reaches the col between S. and N. Moose. At some point (subject to relocation), the trail meets the Holts Ledge Trail which then continues the Appalachian Trail.

From the col, the Clark Pond Loop (old Wolfeboro Rd.) leaves right. Moose Mountain shelter, capacity five, is just east of the col.

Clark Pond Loop (DOC)

This trail at first follows the old Wolfeboro Rd. crossing Moose Mountain at the col between N. and S. Peaks, then passes the Moose Mountain Inn, then an old cemetery 0.1 mi. beyond.

The trail continues straight along a dirt road toward Goose Pond. Descending, it soon crosses Marshall Brook at the north end of Goose Pond. At a road junction, it crosses onto a wood road, soon taking sharp right. Ascending, it soon becomes a dirt road. The trail veers left from the road near the remains of an old farm, follows a telephone line across a field and, bearing right, re-enters the woods. At 5.2 mi. it reaches an asphalt road, follows the road right for 0.5 mi., then turns sharply left on a dirt driveway. The trail turns right onto a wood road and follows it to the outlet of Clark Pond. It veers left and soon picks up another wood road, and bears left at a fork to Clark Pond. The trail follows the eastern edge of Clark Pond, and a sharp left will soon bring you to Clark Pond campsite. *Water* can be obtained from a stream to the east.

North of the campsite, the trail turns right (east) up a ridge, then right at the ridgetop to a semi-open field. Past this field the trail bears right onto another wood road. It renews its ascent, but soon descends toward a level wood road, where it turns left to follow the Mascoma River for 0.4 mi. It turns left again following an irregular ridge through young alders, then descends gradually, crosses a boulder field, and continues along the side of the ridge. Upon reaching the valley floor the trail turns left onto a wood road. The road crosses the river and two tributaries, then turns right on the Lyme-Dorchester Rd. Where the Lyme-Dorchester Rd. soon makes a sharp right, the trail turns sharply left onto a farm road, passing Cummins Pond then heading for Smarts Mountain.

Clark Pond Loop (USGS Mascoma and Mt. Cube)
Distances from Moose Mountain Trail junction

to Clark Pond campsite: 7.8 mi., 4 hr.
to Mascoma River: 9.8 mi.
to Lyme-Dorchester Rd.: 12.7 mi. (20.4 km.)

THE BENTON RANGE

West of Mt. Moosilauke and Mt. Kinsman is the lower Benton Range, extending north and south. On and adjacent to this range is the following group of trails.

Blueberry Mountain Trail (WMNF)

From E. Haverhill, drive north on Lime Kiln Rd. and take second road right at 1.5 mi., then continue 1 mi. from this corner to the start of the Blueberry Mountain Trail, which leaves left at entrance to Page Hill Farm sugar house. After leaving sugar house follow the gravel road 0.5 mi. to the junction with an old road. The trail leads right about 100 yd. before reaching a sawmill, and continues to a small clearing. Beyond the clearing the trail broadens and passes between stone walls. Beyond these the trail narrows, climbs at a moderate grade, and comes out on open ledges with good views. From the rather flat summit (2660 ft.), the trail descends generally south, turns left in about 0.5 mi., and becomes a broad path for the last mile, terminating at the North and South Rd, about 0.8 mi. from the road to the NH Home for the Elderly, 1.4 mi. from Glencliff.

Blueberry Mountain Trail (USGS E. Haverhill)
Distance from Page Hill Farm sugar house, off Lime Kiln Rd.
to North and South Rd.: 4.5 mi. (7.2 km.)

Black Mountain

This 2836-ft. mountain, located in Benton, has ancient lime kilns at its base. East of the summit, near the brink of a precipice, is Tipping Rock. Farther along northeast (arrows painted on ledge) is a *spring (water unreliable)* in a wooded area. The mountain may be ascended by the Black Mountain Trail or by the Chippewa Trail.

Black Mountain Trail (WMNF)

This trail leaves the south side of the town road in Benton, heads generally south, crosses Mardin's field and, as a tractor trail, ascends the north shoulder of Black Mountain, mostly at a moderate grade. It meets the Chippewa Trail a few feet west of the summit, then continues south and southeast, crossing Titus

Brook, then southeast to North and South Rd., 4.1 mi. north of Glencliff.

Black Mountain Trail (USGS E. Haverhill)
Distances from town road, Benton
to Black Mountain summit: 2.3 mi.
to North and South Rd.: 5.9 mi. (9.5 km.)

Chippewa Trail (WMNF)

Turn north off NH Rte. 25 in E. Haverhill onto Lime Kiln Rd. Bear left at a major fork at 1.6 mi. and continue to a point 3.3 mi. from Rte. 25, where the trail begins on left of a parking area. The trail crosses a barbed wire fence, soon descends a small slope, and crosses a wood road. The trail soon turns right on a logging road (left leads to the kilns), bears left at a fork, and then rises steadily to a pasture. It crosses the pasture, generally to the left, enters the woods, and begins the steep ascent toward the ledges. The trail is marked with yellow and white arrows and blazes. The trail ends at its junction with the Black Mountain Trail a few feet west of the summit.

Chippewa Trail (USGS E. Haverhill)
Distance from parking area off Lime Kiln Rd.
to Black Mountain Trail junction: 1.9 mi. (3.1 km.), 1½ hr.

Sugarloaf Mountain

Turn north off Rte. 25 in E. Haverhill, follow Lime Kiln Rd., take second road right at 1.5 mi., then continue 0.8 mi. Turn left and proceed to garage on right. Follow dirt road right 0.6 mi. to small parking area.

The trail, maintained by Camp Walt Whitman, leaves right, beyond open pasture and brook crossing, and follows through woods to an upper pasture. Keep right, and then sharp right across a *brook (last water)*. The trail then slabs moderately to a high pasture, crosses through the middle, turns left at ledges, then bears right up steep shoulder to first of two ladders. Here the trail turns sharp right continuing through woods (use care). The trail then ascends rather steeply to the summit. There are good views of the Benton Range and of Mt. Moosilauke and the trail passes through stands of varied virgin timber on the ascent.

Sugarloaf Mountain (USGS E. Haverhill)
Distance from parking area off Lime Kiln Rd.

to Sugarloaf Mountain summit: *est.* 1.5 mi. (2.5 km.)

STINSON-CARR-KINEO AREA

Stinson Mountain (2870 ft.), Carr Mountain (3470 ft.), and Mt. Kineo (3320 ft.) lie in the angle formed by the Pemigewasset and Baker rivers. Refer to map 4, Chocorua-Waterville.

Stinson Mountain

The USFS fire tower on the summit of this 2880-ft. mountain has had its bottom flight of stairs removed, and its future is in doubt, but excellent views can still be obtained from the summit area. The Stinson Mountain Trail is reached by following the Stinson Lake Rd. from NH Rte. 25 in Rumney. At the foot of the lake, 5.0 mi. from Rte. 25, turn right uphill for 0.8 mi. Turn right again on old Doe Town Rd. to a parking lot at 0.3 mi. on left.

The trail follows an old farm road between stone walls. After passing a cellar hole left, it becomes steeper, entering a logging road at 0.9 mi., where it turns sharp left. At 1.1 mi. there is a junction. Take right fork (left is the old tractor road to the summit, longer and less pleasant). At this fork there is a *brook (water unreliable)*. As the trail climbs by switchbacks, it crosses the old telephone line at 1.5 mi. (restricted view over Stinson Lake) and rejoins the old tractor road just below the summit (note left turn here on descent). Metamorphosed strata make the summit ledges geologically interesting.

Stinson Mountain Trail (map 4)
Distance from parking lot, old Doe Town Rd.

to Stinson Mountain summit: 1.8 mi. (2.9 km.), 1½ hr.

Rattlesnake Mountain Trail (WMNF)

The Rattlesnake Mountain Trail leaves the Ellsworth Rd. to the west at a point 1 mi. north of NH Rte. 25, ascends through stands of white pines and through abandoned farmland, and crosses the ridge just north of Upper Rattlesnake Mountain. At 1.7 mi. the trail enters an old burned-over area, leaving it at 2.5 mi. and intersecting Buffalo Rd. 2.5 mi. west of Rumney village. Refer to map 4, Chocorua-Waterville.

Stevens Brook Trail (WMNF)

This trail leaves the west side of the Ellsworth Rd. about 1 mi. south of Stinson Lake, 4.2 mi. north of NH Rte. 25, and passes through a farmyard. It soon enters the WMNF, crosses a brook, and reaches the height-of-land on Carr Ridge. The trail descends, first west then southwest, crosses a tributary of Stevens Brook on a footbridge about 0.8 mi. below the summit ridge, and joins an old road about 0.6 mi. below the bridge, which is followed to the Buffalo Rd. somewhat east of the bridge over Stevens Brook. There is a fine view from an open field about 0.8 mi. above the Buffalo Rd.

Stevens Brook Trail (map 4)

Distances from Ellsworth Rd.

to height-of-land, Carr Ridge: 2.1 mi., 1¾ hr.
to Buffalo Rd.: 4.4 mi. (7.1 km.), 3 hr.

Carr Mountain Trail (WMNF)

This trail starts at the state fish hatchery, between Wentworth and Warren, just south of Clifford Brook bridge off NH Rte. 25, on an old road section that passes in front of the fish hatchery, opposite an old cemetery. It follows a road passable for automobiles for 0.8 mi., past a house on the left, then through old fields and through a gap in an old stone wall. At 1.5 mi. the trail swings right, crossing into the WMNF at 1.8 mi. The trail turns left at 3.5 mi. near the site of the former summit fire tower. From here the trail descends east, crossing or following the old Carr Mountain telephone line at various points. At 4.6 mi. the trail enters an old logging road and follows it across Sucker Brook, then turns right onto Three Ponds Trail, another logging road, which it follows to Ellsworth Rd. at the northwest end of Stimson Lake.

Carr Mountain Trail (map 4)

Distance from trailhead near Clifford Brook bridge, NH Rte. 25

to Ellsworth Rd. (via Three Ponds Trail): 6.2 mi. (10 km.)

Three Ponds Trail (WMNF)

This trail starts just north of the Sucker Brook bridge on Ellsworth Rd. together with the Carr Mountain Trail, which soon leaves left. The Three Ponds Trail continues on an old logging road up the brook to the Three Ponds. At about 2 mi., on a knoll right overlooking the trail and Middle Pond, is Three Ponds Shelter (WMNF). At 2.2 mi. the Donkey Hill Cutoff leaves right and the Three Ponds Trail swings left, crossing a beaver dam around the upper end of the Middle Pond, and continues north passing to the west of the upper pond. After 1 mi. the trail heads north for 0.5 mi. to a bulldozed logging road, which it follows north for 1 mi., eventually crossing Blodgett Brook and reaching the Hubbard Brook Trail, where a left turn leads in 0.3 mi. to NH Rte. 118, 1.8 mi. east of Breezy Point Rd.

Three Ponds Trail (map 4)

Distances from Ellsworth Rd.

to height-of-land: *est*. 3.5 mi.

to NH Rte. 118 (via Hubbard Brook Trail): *est*. 7 mi. (11.2 km.)

Donkey Hill Cutoff (WMNF)

This trail leaves the east side of the Three Ponds Trail 2.2 mi. from Ellsworth Rd. It heads generally northeast, follows a logging road, and passes east of the upper pond. In about 0.5 mi. it turns southeast, eventually narrows to a path, and ends at the Mt. Kineo Trail, where the latter turns and crosses Brown Brook, about 1.3 mi. from Ellsworth Rd.

Donkey Hill Cutoff (map 4)
Distance from Three Ponds Trail junction
    to Mt. Kineo Trail junction: 0.8 mi. (1.3 km.)

Mount Kineo Trail (WMNF)

This trail starts from the north side of Ellsworth Rd. 100 ft. east of the Brown Brook bridge in the WMNF. It follows Brown Brook, crosses to the west side in about 0.4 mi., and in about 1.3 mi., at the point where the Donkey Hill Cutoff leaves left, bears right and recrosses Brown Brook. From here the trail runs more north, then northeast, and ascends sharply to the height-of-land some distance southeast of the summit of Mt. Kineo. The trail descends toward the northeast, later turns sharp left and leaves the logging road, and ends on a south spur road 0.4 mi. south of the Hubbard Brook Rd.

Mt. Kineo Trail (map 4)
Distances from Ellsworth Rd.
    to Donkey Hill Cutoff: 1.3 mi., ¾ hr.
    to height-of-land: 3.6 mi., 2 hr. 35 min.
    to Hubbard Brook Rd. spur: 4.8 mi. (7.7 km.), 3 hr. 20 min.

Peaked Hill Pond Trail (WMNF)

Peaked Hill Pond lies in a region of deserted farms on the west side of Thornton. Some of the old pastures are not yet overgrown and afford good views.

The trail follows an old highway for the most part. It leaves US Rte. 3 at the 93 Motel in Thornton, north of exit 29 off I-93. Follow road west under I-93, then bear right and pass a sugar house at 0.6 mi. Trail follows cart track through the sugar orchard, and regains the old road near the north end of a level pasture. At 1.2 mi. it leaves the pasture and shortly turns left, rises gradually, then levels off and shortly reaches the north end of the pond.

Peaked Hill Pond Trail (map 4)

Distance from US Rte. 3
   to Peaked Hill Pond: 2.3 mi. (3.7 km.)

Hubbard Brook Trail (WMNF)

The eastern terminus of this trail is on the Hubbard Brook Rd. Hubbard Brook Rd., which leads into the USFS Hubbard Brook Experimental Forest, starts 1.1 mi. west of US Rte. 3 on the north side of Hubbard Brook and crosses to the south side at 3.7 mi. The road leading to the Mt. Kineo Trail branches left at 5.2 mi. Hubbard Brook Rd. crosses back to the north side of the brook, where the Hubbard Brook Trail starts at 6.5 mi., and continues 0.3 mi. to its terminus. The trail leaves the northwest side of the road just after crossing Hubbard Brook from south to north. It parallels the brook, climbs to the height-of-land between Mts. Kineo and Cushman, and crosses the Warren town line. From here, it descends gradually. Beavers are very active in this area, and water may be a problem. The trail continues on a wood road, later crosses the east branch of the Baker River, and ends at NH Rte. 118, 1.8 mi. northeast of Breezy Point Rd.

Hubbard Brook Trail (map 4)

Distances from Hubbard Brook Rd.
   to height-of-land between Mts. Kineo and Cushman: 0.7 mi.
   to NH Rte. 118: 2.2 mi. (3.5 km.)

Mt. Cilley Trail (WMNF)

The original settlement in Woodstock (then Peeling) was about 2 mi. west of the Pemigewasset River, on high ground now called Mt. Cilley. The village was deserted about the time of the Civil War. Since then forests have obscured the views, and all the trail except the Mt. Cilley Trail have been abandoned.

The trail leaves US Rte. 3 about 3 mi. south of N. Woodstock (or north of exit 30 off I-93 on Rte. 3) and follows the location of the ancient highway. At 0.3 mi., the road from the Woodstock water supply enters on the right. At 1 mi. the trail crosses a brook. About 0.5 mi. beyond, just before the trail levels out, old stone walls border both sides, marking what was once the village street of Peeling, but the cellar holes and well-constructed culverts are almost completely covered with vegetation.

The path continues straight ahead on the old village street, descends somewhat through evergreen woods and across a brook. In less than 1 mi., shortly before where the road turns left, the path passes through what appears to be the old village square. Here are the most prominent remains of foundations and walls. The Mt. Cilley Trail continues nearly straight, descends, crosses Jackman Brook (no bridge), and reaches NH Rte. 118, 1.5 mi south of its intersection with NH Rte. 112.

(If you do not plan to walk the complete trail, the route from Rte. 118 to the site of the village is more interesting.)

Mt. Cilley Trail (map 4)

Distances from US Rte. 3

  to brook crossing: 1 mi., 40 min.

  to departure from old village road: 3 mi., 2 hr.

  to NH Rte. 118: 3.8 mi. (6 km.), 2½ hr.

Agassiz Basin

This interesting series of potholes on Moosilauke Brook is easy to reach from N. Woodstock.

Follow NH Rte. 112 for 1.6 mi. west from N. Woodstock then enter the path that leaves left and crosses the stream just beyond. Follow up the south bank about 0.2 mi., recrossing at the bridge.

The Waterville Valley

This section covers the parts of the townships of Waterville Valley and Livermore that are included in the Mad River watershed. The entire watershed, except for about 500 acres on the valley floor, is part of the WMNF, and most of it is in the Waterville Wildlife Management Area. From Campton, NH Rte. 49 runs northeast beside the Mad River, past the WMNF Campton Campground. At about 10 mi. turn left on Rte. 49 to the Mt. Tecumseh Ski Area, passing the WMNF Waterville Campground, or continue straight ahead past a group of lodges and condominiums 1 mi. farther to the Waterville Valley library, Golf and Tennis Club, the Snows Mountain Ski Area and ski-touring center. A road runs west from the library about 0.8 mi. to the WMNF Tripoli Rd. Tripoli Rd. leaves Rte. 49 at the foot of the access road to the Mt. Tecumseh Ski Area, and shortly begins to follow the West Branch of the Mad River northwest to the height-of-land west of Waterville Valley (Thornton Gap, 2300 ft., the pass between Mts. Osceola and Tecumseh), and then westward where it ends at NH Rte. 175 (East Side Rd.) and I-93 in Woodstock. The road is gravel except for paved sections on each end, narrow in places, and winding. Drive slowly and with caution. This road has not been plowed during the winter.

The trails described in this section are for the most part those on Mts. Osceola and Tecumseh, the north and west slopes of Sandwich Mountain, the west and south slopes of Tripyramid, and the trails ascending Scar Ridge or adjacent to its west end. All are east of I-93 and south of the Kancamagus Highway. Refer to map 4, Chocorua-Waterville.

MOUNT OSCEOLA

Mt. Osceola (4326 ft.) lies north of the valley. To its north is the Pemigewasset "Wilderness." Mad River Notch separates Mt. Osceola from Mt. Kancamagus on the east, and Thornton

Gap from Mt. Tecumseh on the southwest. Westward, Scar Ridge joins Mt. Osceola to the low summits near N. Woodstock.

A 30-ft. steel tower (closed to the public) stands on the summit; there are plans to dismantle it.

Mount Osceola Trail (WMNF)

The trail leaves the north side of Tripoli Rd. 7.0 mi. from its west end at Rte. I-93 Exit 31, just west of the height-of-land in Thornton Gap, and 3.8 mi. from Waterville library. It heads northeast, then east for about 0.8 mi., then turns north and climbs by long switchbacks to Breadtray Ridge (views south and southwest), turns east, slabs for about 0.3 mi., passing a *spring (water unreliable)*, then bears left and climbs rather steeply by zigzags, and at about 3 mi. makes a sharp turn right and climbs generally east to the summit.

From the summit of Osceola the trail goes north, then turns east along the crest of the ridge, descends rather steeply to about 3850 ft. at the low point, and ascends the west slope of the E. Peak to its summit (4185 ft.). From the E. Peak the trail turns northeast down a narrow ridge, soon descends, crosses a slide, and descends very steeply through the woods a short distance north, and continues down to the Greeley Ponds Trail near the south end of the upper pond. It should be noted that the E. Peak-Greeley Ponds section of the trail is very steep and eroded, and dangerous in wet weather. There are plans to replace this section by a new trail on the north ridge of the E. Peak from the north trailhead of the E. Pond Trail. When ascending Mt. Osceola from the Greeley Ponds Trail, allow considerable extra time because the climb to the E. Peak is unusually steep.

Mt. Osceola Trail (map 4)

Distances from Tripoli Rd.

to Breadtray Ridge: 1.8 mi.

to Mt. Osceola summit: 3.6 mi. (5.1 km.), 2 hr. 35 min.

to Mt. Osceola, E. Peak: 4.2 mi., 3 hr. 20 min.

to Greeley Ponds Trail junction: 5.4 mi. (8.6 km.), 4 hr.

MOUNT TECUMSEH

This is the highest (4004 ft.) and northernmost summit of the ridges that form the west wall of the valley. Thornton Gap separates it from Mt. Osceola to the northeast; to the west and southwest, long ridges run out toward Woodstock and Thornton.

Mount Tecumseh Ski Area

The Mt. Tecumseh Ski Area is reached by an access road leaving Tripoli Rd. 1.3 mi. north of its junction with NH Rte. 49. The base facilities consist of a complex of buildings and several parking lots. At present no lifts or base facilities are open during the summer.

Mount Tecumseh Trail (WMNF)

This trail ascends the east slope of Mt. Tecumseh. It starts at the Mt. Tecumseh Ski Area parking lots, from the upper right corner as you face uphill. It follows the south side of Tecumseh Brook for 0.4 mi., turns left up the bank, and comes out on the north edge of the ski slope, which it follows uphill for 0.1 mi. The trail enters the woods right and shortly returns to the north edge of the ski slopes, which it follows up for another 0.3 mi. with good views to the east. At a cairn and blazed birch tree, the trail goes right into the woods on an old logging road, and climbs along the south side of the Tecumseh Brook valley to a col where it turns right. Here the Sosman Trail from the top of the ski area enters from the left. About 100 yd. further on (northeast), the Sosman Trail forks left directly to the summit. The Mt. Tecumseh Trail swings right, descends somewhat, and finally climbs steeply to the summit from the back (north).

From the summit the trail heads west, following the boundary line of the Waterville Wildlife Management Area for some distance. It descends north about 300 ft. into a col and then climbs again to the crest of the northern ridge. It turns west along the ridge, descends along the northwest shoulder, and turns right down a logging road into the valley. Near the bottom it turns sharp right, crosses Eastman Brook, and ends on Tripoli Rd., 5.1 mi. west of Waterville Valley. There is *no sure water* on the mountain between the ski area and Eastman Brook.

Note: The USFS has long planned to relocate the eastern part of the trail to avoid the ski slopes. Check locally for starting point of trail and changes in route.

Mt. Tecumseh Trail (map 4)

Distances from Mt. Tecumseh ski area parking lot

to ski slope: 0.4 mi., 20 min.

to re-entering woods: 1 mi., 1 hr.

to Mt. Tecumseh summit: 2.2 mi. (3.5 km.), 2 hr. 10 min.

to Tripoli Rd.: 5.4 mi. (8.6 km.), 3½ hr.

Sosman Trail (WVAIA)

This trail runs north along the ridge for 0.6 mi. from the top of the Tecumseh ski area, then joins the Mt. Tecumseh Trail for about 100 yd., and diverges left on an easier, more direct route to the summit. It is used for ski touring in winter, and, in summer, to make a loop by climbing the Mt. Tecumseh Trail, crossing to the ski area via the Sosman Trail, and descending beneath the upper chair lift past the Schwinde Hutte Restaurant (not open in summer) to the top of the lower chair lift. A work road (sharp right) descends to the bottom of the mountain in 1.5 mi.

WELCH AND DICKEY MOUNTAINS

The fine rocky peak of Welch Mountain (2591 ft.) overlooks the Campton meadows, and forms the west wall of the narrow south gateway to Waterville Valley through which the Mad River flows. The views from the open summit are excellent. Dickey Mountain (2750 ft.), close at hand to the northwest, also has an open summit, with the best views from a fine open ledge and adjacent ledges, about 200 yd. to the north. From Welch Mountain, the trip to these ledges is well worth the extra effort.

There is *no water* on either mountain.

Welch-Dickey Loop Trail (WVAIA)

About 4.5 mi. northeast of Campton Pond dam on NH Rte. 49, the Upper Mad River Road goes northwest across the Mad River. In 0.7 mi. a road, known locally as Orris Rd., diverges right ("Welch Mountain" sign). Follow this road for 0.6 mi. and take a short fork right to a parking area, where the trail begins. Very soon the trail forks. The right branch, leading to Welch Mountain, shortly crosses a brook (*last reliable water*). After heading up the east side of the brook about 0.5 mi., the trail turns sharp right and slabs back to reach the south ridge of Welch Mountain at 0.9 mi. from the start. From here the trail follows its older route over open ledges interspersed with jack pines and dwarf birches. The snow tends to melt from the south-facing ledges in April, earlier than elsewhere in the mountains.

From the open summit of Welch Mountain, the loop to Dickey Mountain drops quickly (use caution) to a wooded col, then rises, working to the left around a high rock slab. Just above this a branch trail leads right to the north outlook from an open ledge.

The main loop continues over the summit of Dickey Mountain and descends another prominent ridge to the southwest, then south, remaining in the open for about 0.8 mi. from the summit. *Caution.* In wet weather some of the ledges may be very slippery. After another 1 mi. through woods, the trail joins a logging road, turns left on the main Dickey Notch logging road (not passable for vehicles), and returns to its starting point.

Welch-Dickey Loop Trail (map 4)

Distances from Orris Rd. parking area

to Welch Mountain summit: *est*. 2 mi. (3 km.), 1¾ hr.

to Dickey Mountain summit: *est*. 2½ mi., 2¼ hr.

to Orris Rd. parking area (complete loop): *est*. 4 mi. (6.5 km.), 3 hr.

SANDWICH MOUNTAIN

Formerly called Sandwich Dome or Black Mountain, this 3993-ft. westernmost summit of the Sandwich Range appears to close the valley on the south. Westward, it looks over the lower Mad River; on the south and southwest, Sandwich Notch separates it from the Campton and Holderness mountains; to the northeast, a high col separates it from Flat Mountain in Waterville, and Cold River has cut a deep ravine between its east shoulder and Flat Mountain in Sandwich.

The summit is double, but all the trails ascend the west peak. The mountain can be climbed by three routes from the Waterville Valley. For the Bennett Street Trail and the Gleason Trail (east side ascent) see Section 12. The Algonquin and Black Mountain Pond trails are in Section 19.

The following two trails start from a parking lot on the east side of NH Rte. 49 about 9 mi. northeast of Campton.

Sandwich Mountain Trail (WMNF)

This trail leaves the southwest corner of the Rte. 49 parking lot, crosses Drakes Brook on a footbridge, climbs gradually south for about 0.3 mi., then turns east and follows the old trail, climbing steeply to Noon Peak. It then follows the curving, gradual ridge, covered with beautiful mosses, and passes several outlooks. There is *water (unreliable)* on the west side of the trail, which soon skirts the east slope of Jennings Peak (3500 ft.). The summit of Jennings Peak, with fine views, 0.3 mi. to the right, is reached by a steep side trail. The main trail swings to the east and climbs through woods. The Drakes Brook Trail enters from the left at 2.5 mi., the Smarts Brook Trail enters from the right at 3.1 mi., and the Algonquin Trail enters right just below the open summit.

Sandwich Mountain Trail (map 4)

Distances from parking area, NH Rte. 49

  to Noon Peak: 1.3 mi., 1¼ hr.

to Jennings Peak: 2.7 mi., 2 hr. 20 min.

to Sandwich Mountain summit: 3.8 mi. (6.1 km.), 3 hr.
10 min.

Drakes Brook Trail (WMNF)

This trail leaves the north side of the Rte. 49 parking lot and
follows a dirt road for 0.5 mi. At this point the trail to Fletcher's
Cascades continues up the road, and the Drakes Brook Trail
leaves right. It crosses Drakes Brook and at 0.9 mi. passes the
remains of a log dam on the left. The trail follows an old logging
road along the brook and at about 2.5 mi. climbs steeply up the
west side of the ravine and joins the Sandwich Mountain Trail
north of Jennings Peak, about 1.3 mi. from the summit of the
mountain.

Drakes Brook Trail (map 4)

Distances from parking area, NH Rte. 49

to Sandwich Mountain Trail junction: 3.2 mi.

to Sandwich Mountain summit (via Sandwich Mountain
Trail): 4.5 mi. (7.2 km.), 3½ hr.

ACTEON RIDGE

Acteon Ridge runs from Jennings Peak to the west over sharp
Sachem Peak (3060 ft.) and ends in the rocky humps of Bald
Knob (2318 ft.), which faces Welch Mountain across the Mad
River Valley. This ridge is occasionally traversed, although
there is no path.

Smarts Brook Trail (WMNF)

Smarts Brook is beautiful in full flow, usually in May and
June. The trail, which roughly parallels the course of the brook,
leaves the east side of NH Rte. 49 from the south end of a parking
area just northeast of the Smarts Brook bridge. It follows a dirt
road, which soon becomes grass-grown, and climbs by very easy
grades roughly parallel to the brook for about 2.5 mi. A series of
large pools and wide ledges in the brook starts at about 1 mi. The

trail passes the site of an old lumber camp and at 2.3 mi. rejoins Smarts Brook. Beyond, it climbs more steeply, following the course of the brook and crossing several small side brooks, then ascends the ridge by a series of switchbacks to join the Sandwich Mountain Trail between Jennings Peak and the summit of Sandwich Mountain. Along the upper part of the trail there are good views of Jennings Peak and the rocky Acteon Ridge.

Smarts Brook Trail (map 4)

Distances from parking area, NH Rte. 49

to pools in Smarts Brook: 1.1 mi.

to Sandwich Mountain Trail junction: 5.1 mi., 3 hr. 40 min.

to Sandwich Mountain summit (via Sandwich Mountain
    Trail): 5.8 mi. (9.3 km.), 4¼ hr.

MOUNT TRIPYRAMID

Mt. Tripyramid (N. Peak 4140 ft., Middle Peak 4110 ft., S. Peak 4090 ft.) stands between the Waterville Valley on the west and the Albany Intervale on the east. The high col of Livermore Pass (2862 ft.) separates it from Mt. Kancamagus on the north. Southward a high ridge joins it to Mt. Whiteface. On the northwest face of the N. Peak, the southwest face of the S. Peak, and the east side of the Middle Peak are the huge slides that are the mountain's chief attraction. The S. Slide fell in 1869 and 1885, the N. in 1885. The S. Slide is actually two distinct parallel slides of about the same length. There is a third, rather short slide, between the upper ends of the two large slides. The rock exposed greatly interested geologists (see *Geology of the Mt. Chocorua Quadrangle,* NH State Development Commission, 1939). For trails ascending the north and east sides of the mountain see Section 12.

Tripyramid Trails

The easier route of ascent from Waterville Valley is up the N. Peak, along the ridge, and down the S. Peak. Ascent of the N. Peak may be made via the N. Slide (summer only), or the Scaur

Ridge and Pine Bend Brook trails.

Note: Yellow paint now marks routes on the slides. Ascent or descent on the slides is extremely rough, and care must be used especially in descending the N. Slide, which is very steep and dangerous when wet or icy.

Tripyramid Trail (WVAIA)

From the Waterville library, follow NH Rte. 49 west over the Mad River. Go right at the fork on USFS Livermore Rd., past a clearing known as Depot Camp (parking) and across a bridge over the Mad River. Livermore Rd. (closed to motor vehicles) continues east, ascending gradually. A trail to Norway Rapids, the Cascades, and back to Waterville leaves right at 1.5 mi. from the parking area. The end of the Tripyramid Trail, leading to S. Tripyramid via the S. Slide, leaves right at 2.3 mi. At 2.8 mi., the road reaches the site of Avalanche Camp, an old logging camp. The road is not maintained beyond this point. At the hairpin turn in the road at 3.3 mi., the eastern end of the Tripyramid Trail, leading to the N. Slide leaves right. It then descends to cross Avalanche Brook (*last reliable water*). A short distance beyond, the trail enters a wood road, which it follows upstream east to the foot of the slide. Yellow paint marks the trail on the slide. From the east corner of the top of its western section (cairn), the trail runs to the summit of N. Peak, giving a view west, north, and east. The Pine Bend Brook Trail joins the Tripyramid Trail about 40 yd. below the north summit.

From the N. Peak the trail (for about 0.5 mi. it coincides with the Pine Bend Brook Trail) over the Middle and S. peaks follows the crest of the ridge heading generally south (follow blazes carefully). Sabbaday Brook Trail leaves left at 0.5 mi. from the N. Peak, Middle Peak is reached at 0.8 mi., and S. Peak (outlook) at 1.2 mi. The trail descends to the top of the S. Slide and down to its west corner. The Sleeper Trail leaves the left (southeast) side of the slide quite near its top. Watch for a sign on a tree. The Tripyramid Trail continues down the S. Slide to its west corner. From here the trail bears right and soon widens into an old logging road, which is followed on the northeast side of Slide Brook back to Livermore Rd., which it reaches after crossing Avalanche Brook. Turn left to return to the parking area.

While this route may be reversed, it is safer to climb the steeper N. Slide and descend the S. Slide.

Tripyramid Trail (map 4)

Distances from Depot Camp parking area, Livermore Rd.

to western end of Tripyramid Trail (Tripyramids via S. Slide): 2.3 mi.

to eastern end of Tripyramid Trail (Tripyramids via N. Slide): 3.3 mi.

to foot of N. Slide: 3.8 mi.

to N. Peak (via N. Slide): 4.5 mi.

to S. Peak: 5.7 mi.

to Livermore Rd. (via S. Slide): 8.1 mi.

to Depot Camp, Livermore Rd. (complete loop): 10.4 mi. (16.8 km.)

Scaur Ridge Trail (WMNF)

The Scaur Ridge Trail leaves the Livermore Rd. right at 0.2 mi. beyond the beginning of the Tripyramid Trail to the N. Slide. It ascends gradually the slope of Scaur Peak, and ends after 1.2 mi. at the Pine Bend Brook Trail (see Section 12), which can be followed to the summit of N. Tripyramid, 2.0 mi. from Livermore Rd.

This is the best route for descent in bad weather, or ascent when there is ice on the shadowed N. Slide.

From the Waterville library on NH Rte. 49, the Cascade Path and cutoff trail to Norway Rapids may be used to reach Livermore Rd., and trails to Mt. Tripyramid. From the library to Livermore Rd. is about 1.3 mi., to S. Tripyramid Trail about 2.3 mi.

Sleeper Trail (SSOC)

This trail follows the high double-domed ridge, called the Sleepers or Sleeper Ridge, that joins Mts. Tripyramid and

Whiteface. The Sleeper Trail leaves the Downes Brook Trail about 1 mi. from the summit of Mt. Whiteface and skirts north of an abandoned beaver pond. The *only sure water* is just north of the junction with the Downes Brook Trail. It soon begins to ascend the E. Sleeper, and there are occasional views to the east and north through the trees. Bearing left of the summit of E. Sleeper the trail turns right on an old road, which it follows for 0.4 mi. and passes some distance southwest of the summit, which is about 0.1 mi. northeast at the height-of-land. Then the trail descends into the col between the Sleepers and passes close to the summit of the W. Sleeper through mature woods. After descending to the Tripyramid col the trail bears west and contours along S. Tripyramid until it enters the eastern of two south slides. Small cairns and yellow blazes mark the winding route on the slide, and the trail climbs steeply to reenter the woods on the opposite side about 100 yd. higher. After 100 yd. through the wooded area the trail enters the large western slide, where it meets the Tripyramid Trail loop. To reach the summit of S. Tripyramid ascend the slide. To reach the Livermore Rd. bear left down the slide, then bear right and follow the trail along the northeast side of Slide Brook. To locate the beginning of the trail on the Tripyramid Slide, look for several small signs on trees at the far east edge of the slide, near its top.

Sleeper Trail (map 4)

Distance from Downes Brook Trail

to S. Slide: *est.* 2.8 mi. (4.4 km.), 2 hr.

MOUNT KANCAMAGUS

Mt. Kancamagus (3728 ft.) is a mass of rounded ridges in the triangular space between Mts. Tripyramid, Osceola, and Huntington. It forms the east wall of Mad River Notch. There are two cliffs with good views facing southwest, but the summits are wooded (except for a clearing for helicopter use in case of forest fire), and there are no trails.

Greeley Ponds Trail (WMNF)

This trail is crossed and recrossed by a ski-touring trail marked with blue diamonds. It starts on the Livermore Rd. at Depot Camp (parking). In about 50 yd. it bears left and follows an old truck road for about 1 mi. to its end, where the trail crosses Mad River on a footbridge. About 0.1 mi. farther, just before crossing Flume Brook, a side trail leads right to the local flume. The main trail continues along the river, with some crossings, to the beautiful Greeley Ponds, between Mt. Osceola and Mt. Kanca-magus. The grade is gradual all the way. The lower pond is reached at 2.9 mi., and at about 3.3 mi. there is a fine *spring* at left, just off the trail. At 3.4 mi. the Mt. Osceola Trail (planned to be closed and replaced) enters from the left, although the sign may be missing. At this junction a loop trail leaves right, crosses the outlet of the upper pond, turns north, continues along the east shore, and rejoins the main trail just north of the pond. The Greeley Ponds Trail continues north, skirts the left (west) side of the upper pond, and ascends gradually for 0.4 mi. to the height-of-land in Mad River Notch. This point is on the boundary of the Waterville Wildlife Management Area (WMNF). The entire Greeley Ponds area is in a Restricted Use Area (see Section 22), and camping is not permitted.

After a short level stretch, the trail descends moderately, crosses two small brooks, then the S. Fork on a bridge, and ends at the Kancamagus Highway, at a sharp turn about 10 mi. east of I-93. The north half of this trail may be relocated west to end with the E. Pond Trail.

Greeley Ponds Trail (map 4)

Distances from Depot Camp parking area, Livermore Rd.

to end of truck road: 1 mi.

to flume side trail junction: 1.2 mi.

to lower Greeley Pond: 2.9 mi.

to upper pond and Mt. Osceola Trail junction: 3.4 mi.

to Kancamagus Highway: 5.1 mi. (8.2 km.)

Livermore Trail (WMNF)

The Livermore Trail leaves from Livermore Rd. Park at the Depot Camp clearing. Beyond, Livermore Rd. is open for WMNF administrative purposes only and closed to motor vehicles. About 50 yd. beyond the gate, the Greeley Ponds Trail bears left. Livermore Rd. crosses a bridge over Mad River, continues east ascending gradually, and at about 2.8 mi. from Depot Camp reaches the site of Avalanche Camp, an old logging camp, where road maintenance ends. About 0.5 mi beyond this there is a hairpin bend, where the Tripyramid Trail to the N. Slide leaves right; 0.2 mi. farther the Scaur Ridge Trail leaves right. The road climbs steeply for some distance, then levels off and reaches the site of Flume Brook Camp, where it ends.

The Livermore Trail begins at this camp and continues on through Livermore Pass (2862 ft.), the col between Mts. Tripyramid and Kancamagus.

After a short but steep drop from the pass, the trail levels off, goes generally north following old lumber roads (watch for a left fork in reverse direction), and ends in about 0.5 mi. at the Kancamagus Highway, about 0.3 mi. southeast of Lily Pond. On the other side of the highway, at a point 0.2 mi. right (east), the Sawyer River Trail leaves for Livermore and US Rte. 302 (Crawford Notch Highway).

Livermore Trail (map 4)

Distances from Depot Camp parking area, Livermore Rd.

to start of Livermore Trail, Flume Brook Camp: *est*. 4 mi.

to Kancamagus Highway: *est*. 7 mi. (11.2 km.)

SHORT WALKS (WVAIA)

A system of local trails is maintained in the valley. Trail information and a map, "Hiking Trails of the Waterville Valley," may be obtained at the service station on NH Rte. 49 opposite the Waterville Campground or at the "Jugtown" store. It should be noted that the hiking trails are frequently intersected by recently cut ski-touring trails, which are marked in black and yellow. A separate map of these is available locally.

Some of the most interesting walks are included here. The Cascade Path, to a series of beautiful waterfalls on Cascade Brook (1.5 mi.); the River Path along the Mad River (about 1.3 mi.); to the Big Boulder on Slide Brook (1 mi.); to Fletcher's Cascade, off the Drakes Brook Trail (1.7 mi.); and to Greeley Ledges, between the Snows Mountain Trail and the top of Snows Mountain ski slopes (0.8 mi.).

The Scaur, a rock outlook between Mad River and Slide Brook with views north, south, and west, may be reached either by a trail leaving the Greeley Ponds road right about 1.6 mi. from the Waterville library, or via the Kettles Path, which leaves Livermore Rd. left about 1.5 mi. from the library. The trail from the Greeley Ponds road to the Scaur (0.5 mi.) includes some very steep pitches; the Kettles Path (1 mi.) climbs much more gradually. The two routes join at the foot of the final climb to the outlook.

On a shoulder of the E. Peak of Osceola are the large Davis Boulders and Goodrich Rock, one of the largest glacial erratics in New Hampshire. They are reached by a trail leaving the Greeley Ponds road left about 1.8 mi. from the library. Distance from Greeley Ponds road to Goodrich Rock is about 1 mi.

The Flume, in the headwaters of Flume Brook, is reached by a side trail about 1.8 mi. long, leaving the Greeley Ponds Trail right about 0.1 mi. from its start (2.3 mi. from the library).

Snows Mountain Trail (WVAIA)

This trail follows the route of the former Woodbury Trail to the shoulder of Snows Mountain, follows the ridge south and east to the summit, and then descends the west slope of the mountain back to Waterville.

The trail leaves the north end of the tennis courts, enters the woods, climbing steeply for 100 yd., then turns left onto a ski slope. It follows the chair lift, to avoid residences. Above the houses it re-enters the wood right, climbing for about another 0.3 mi., then leveling off. At 0.6 mi. a trail leaves left to Greeley Ledges and the top of the ski slope. At 1.1 mi. the Snows Mountain Trail reaches the end of the old Woodbury Trail section and turns right, climbing gradually to Snows Mountain Outlook, which gives a good view west. The ascent continues, passing a large boulder with a view northeast. The trail levels out, then climbs to a high point of the ridge. At 1.8 mi. a side trail leads left 0.1 mi. to a ledge at the summit. The Snows Mountain Trail descends, passing additional viewpoints to the south and west, then continues gradually down the west slope of the mountain, and ends on Upper Greeley Hill Rd., above the swimming pool at Waterville. *Note:* Due to projected residential and ski trail construction, parts of this trail may be difficult to follow.

Snows Mountain Trail (map 4)

Distances from Waterville library

 to Greeley Ledge Trail junction: 0.6 mi.

 to Snows Mountain Outlook: 1.3 mi.

 to Snows Mountain summit: 1.9 mi.

 to Upper Greeley Hill Rd.: 3.4 mi. (5.5 km.)

Kancamagus Ski-Touring Trail (WVAIA)

This trail leaves the Flume Path about 0.3 mi. from the Greeley Ponds Trail, crosses Flume Brook, and follows old lumber roads north and east, gradually ascending the south side of Mt. Kancamagus. It ends at the Livermore Trail, about 0.2 mi. north of the end of Livermore Rd., at the site of the old Flume Brook lumber camp. The trail is cleared primarily for ski touring, but can be used to make a loop walk by returning down Livermore Rd. to its junction with the Greeley Ponds Trail. Total distance is about 8 mi.

SCAR RIDGE

East Pond Trail (WMNF)

This trail leaves Tripoli Rd. to the north, 5.4 mi. east of its intersection with I-93. At 0.4 mi. the trail passes the site of the old Tripoli Mill on the right, opposite which is the beginning of the Little E. Pond Trail. At 0.8 mi. it crosses E. Pond Brook, and at 1.4 mi. skirts the south shore of E. Pond.

The trail leaves the pond at this point, follows old logging roads for 2.2 mi. to the height-of-land on Scar Ridge, then descends northeast along the southeast side of Cheney Brook, crosses Pine Brook at 4.1 mi., and ends on the Kancamagus Highway 50 yd. east of the bridge over Hancock Branch. Total distance is about 5 mi.

Little East Pond Trail (WMNF)

This trail leaves the E. Pond Trail left, 0.4 mi. from Tripoli Rd. opposite the remains of the old Tripoli Mill, and follows an old railroad grade slightly uphill for 0.7 mi. At this point the trail bears sharp right from the end of the railroad grade and continues 1 mi. to Little E. Pond. There is a *spring* right about 0.3 mi. before reaching the pond. Total distance: 1.7 mi. (1 hr. 10 min.)

Russell Crag

This is a south shoulder of Russell Mountain, and at 1640 ft. offers fine views. The former trail, which left from the E. Side Rd., has been abandoned.

RUSSELL POND

Russell Pond (1648 ft.) Campground, in the WMNF, is not far from I-93. The access road leaves the north side of Tripoli Rd. just west of Talford Brook, ascends switchbacks for 2 mi. to the height-of-land, and in the next 0.5 mi. descends to the pond.

LOON MOUNTAIN

A graded but rough path runs from the top of the Loon Mountain ski lift about 1 mi. to the 3075-ft. summit of Loon Mountain.

The Pemigewasset "Wilderness" and Mount Carrigain

This section covers all but a small portion of the region drained by the E. Branch of the Pemigewasset River and includes the poorly defined and extensive area known as the Pemigewasset "Wilderness." It includes also the mountains lying between the E. Branch of the Pemigewasset, the Sawyer River, and the Saco River. More specifically, the region is bounded on the north by the Garfield Ridge, Twinway, and Ethan Pond trails; on the east by US Rte. 302; on the south by the Sawyer River Rd., the Sawyer River Trail, and the Kancamagus Highway, NH Rte. 112 (pronounced Kancamawgus); and on the west side by the Franconia Range. Refer to map 5, Franconia, or to the USGS Crawford Notch and Franconia quadrangles. The history of the logging railroads in this region is recounted in C.F. Belcher's *Logging Railroads of the White Mountains* (available from the AMC).

An 18,560-acre tract of the WMNF was established in 1969 as the "Lincoln Woods Scenic Area" by the USFS. Its approximate boundaries are the Twinway on the north, the Livermore-Lincoln town line on the east, Mts. Anderson and Carrigain and the Desolation and Wilderness trails on the south, and a line from N. Fork Junction to Mt. Bond, the highest point in the area at 4714 ft., on the west.

The principal summits are Mts. Carrigain (4680 ft.), Hancock (4403 ft.), S. Hancock (4274 ft.), Bond (4714 ft.), W. Bond (4526 ft.), and Owl's Head (4023 ft.). There are no AMC huts in the area, but there are two AMC log shelters: Guyot and Desolation. Franconia Brook Campsite, 13 Falls Campsite, Camp 16 Campsite, and Guyot Shelter all have tent platforms. The cabin of the fire tower at the top of Mt. Carrigain was dismantled in the summer of 1978, as was the shelter at 13 Falls; use of the shelter at Franconia Brook Campsite is not permitted.

The whole area has been heavily used in recent years, and it is prudent not to count on finding room in a shelter, particularly on summer or fall weekends. For the past several years, camping has been restricted to designated areas along the Wilderness Trail up to the junction with the Cedar Brook Trail, along the Franconia Brook Trail to the southern junction with the Lincoln Brook Trail, and along the Bondcliff Trail from the Twinway to south of Guyot Shelter, as well as near the Kancamagus Highway and Sawyer River Rd. Camping is not permitted along any trail within Crawford Notch State Park. Current information on Restricted Use Areas can be obtained by writing the USFS (see Section 22) or by stopping at the visitors' centers along the Kancamagus Highway. To preserve the beauty of the region, it is essential that all visitors follow the AMC Guidelines for Backcountry Campers in the introduction to this *Guide*.

The Kancamagus Highway affords the closest approach to the "Wilderness" from the west or south. This road cuts through a vast woodland area and links US Rte. 3 at N. Woodstock directly with NH Rte. 16 and US Rte. 302 at Conway. Its west end is in the village of Lincoln, east of the junction of I-93 and Rte. 112. A description of the eastern end of this road will be found in Section 13. There are no buildings or services of any kind between Loon Mountain and Passaconaway. Big Rock Campground (WMNF) is on the north side of the road, two miles east of the bridge over the E. Branch of the Pemigewasset River.

The Sawyer River Rd. leads to several trails in the east part of the region. This gravel road (sometimes closed to vehicles by a gate) leaves Rte. 302 just north of the Sawyer River bridge and extends southwest up the river past the deserted logging village of Livermore (1.5 mi.) for a distance of 4.0 mi. The north end of the Sawyer Pond Trail (Section 13) is just across the Sawyer River footbridge at the end of the maintained portion of the road. The north end of the Sawyer River Trail is right off the road a short distance beyond a gate at the end of the section of the road normally open for public vehicular travel.

WILDERNESS TRAIL (WMNF)

The Wilderness Trail extends from the Kancamagus Highway for almost 9 mi. up the valley of the E. Branch of the Pemigewasset River. Numerous trails diverge from this central artery, leading to various parts of the Pemigewasset "Wilderness" and to the adjoining mountains. For most of its length, the Wilderness Trail follows the bed of a logging railroad, which last operated in 1948.

The Wilderness Trail leaves the Kancamagus Highway at a large parking area with an information booth, just east of the concrete bridge over the E. Branch, 4.1 mi. from the ranger station at the I-93 exit in Lincoln and about 0.3 mi. beyond the Hancock Picnic Area, which is on the right (south) side of the highway. The trail crosses the E. Branch on a suspension bridge and turns right on the railroad bed. It heads north-northeast, and in about 1 mi. the relocated Osseo Trail (to be opened in the summer of 1983, see Section 7) diverges left. At 2.4 mi. the Black Pond Trail leaves left (west-northwest). At 2.7 mi., the Franconia Brook Campsite, with sixteen tent platforms, is on the left, just before a bridge across Franconia Brook. From the campsite a side trail leads north up the brook 0.4 mi. to Franconia Falls, almost an acre in area and among the finest in the mountains.

The Wilderness Trail crosses Franconia Brook on a footbridge. In about 50 yd., at 2.8 mi., the Franconia Brook Trail climbs the bank on the left (north). Swinging more to the east, the Wilderness Trail reaches the Camp 16 clearing, where there are nine tent platforms, at 5.0 mi. Here the Bondcliff Trail diverges left (north). The Wilderness Trail then crosses Black Brook on a bridge to the left of the old railroad bridge, passes a *spring* left about 0.5 mi. beyond, and in 100 yd. crosses to the south bank of the E. Branch on a 180-ft. suspension bridge. On the far side, the Cedar Brook Trail branches to the right (southwest).

Continuing upstream from the bridge, the Wilderness Trail now skirts the end of the long north ridge of Mt. Hancock, and just after crossing a slide it reaches N. Fork Junction, where the Thoreau Falls Trail diverges left (north), and the main trail continues straight ahead. About 0.8 mi. beyond the junction, the railroad crosses to the north bank, but the Wilderness Trail stays on the south bank, crosses Crystal Brook, and soon regains the old railroad, which has recrossed. After traversing the Camp 18 clearing, the trail veers right into a bypass built in 1971 to avoid two river crossings, crosses Carrigain Branch, and ends at Still-water Junction. Here the Carrigain Notch Trail leads right (southeast) to Desolation Shelter, Carrigain Notch Rd., and the Sawyer River Rd. Also at this junction the Shoal Pond Trail crosses the stream directly ahead (no bridge) and turns left (north).

In the reverse direction, the Wilderness Trail now leaves Stillwater Junction heading away from the stream, whereas it formerly followed the railroad grade along it. Near the suspension bridge, avoid the USFS truck road that follows the southeast bank of the E. Branch from the Wilderness Trail parking lot, which diverges left 200 ft. before the junction with the Cedar Brook Trail.

Wilderness Trail (map 5)

Distances from Kancamagus Highway

to Franconia Brook Campsite: 2.7 mi., 1 hr. 20 min.

to Bondcliff Trail junction: 5mi., 2½ hr.

to suspension bridge at Cedar Brook Trail junction: 5.5 mi., 2¾ hr.

to N. Fork Junction/Thoreau Falls Trail junction: 6.5 mi., 3¼ hr.

to Stillwater Junction: 8.7 mi. (4 hr. 20 min.)

to AMC Desolation Shelter (via Carrigain Notch Trail): 9.3 mi. (15 km.), 4 hr. 40 min.

Black Pond Trail (WMNF)

This trail ascends by an easy grade from the Wilderness Trail to Black Pond, where there is an interesting view of the lower ridges of Mt. Bond from the west shore. Leaving the left (west) side of the Wilderness Trail 2.4 mi. from the Kancamagus Highway, it first follows a former logging railroad spur, crosses a small brook after 50 yd., soon bears left, skirts the north shore of an old ice pond, and then turns right. In 0.2 mi. the trail emerges from the woods, crosses the Camp 7 clearing, and approaches a brook (left). Bearing slightly right up a moderate incline parallel to the brook below, it then descends to cross the outlet brook, which it follows for a short distance and recrosses at a marshy spot. The trail crosses the outlet brook for the last time and follows it to Black Pond. The trail, which is not a through trail, skirts the southwest side of the pond and ends. Three tentsites, marked on the hillside southwest of the pond in 1978, were for temporary research, and have been removed. Black Pond is in a Restricted Use Area, and camping is not permitted (see Section 22). On the reverse route, bear right on the north side of the ice pond to pick up the railroad spur, avoiding the unmarked path that leads toward the Franconia Brook Campsite.

Black Pond Trail (map 5)

Distances from Wilderness Trail junction

   to first crossing of Black Pond outlet brook: 0.6 mi.

   to end of trail at Black Pond: 0.8 mi. (1.4 km.), ½ hr.

FRANCONIA BROOK TRAIL (WMNF)

This trail connects the Pemigewasset "Wilderness" area with the Garfield Ridge. It diverges north up a bank from the Wilderness Trail at a point about 50 yd. east of the footbridge across Franconia Brook, and soon enters an old railroad grade. The trail crosses Camp 9 Brook at 0.4 mi. and again at 0.6 mi. Before the Camp 9 clearing at 1.1 mi., a bypass leads to the right around a pond created by an enthusiastic beaver colony. The trail crosses Camp 9 Brook (bridge), and 0.3 mi. farther, the Lincoln Brook Trail leads left (west). Just before an open swamp on the right, the Franconia Brook Trail continues to ascend gradually on the old railroad grade, passing through clearings that mark the sites of Camps 10, 12, and 13. At 5 mi. it reaches a beautiful waterfall and cascade known as Number 13 Falls. At this point the Franconia Brook Trail turns right, leaves the old railroad grade, and passes the 13 Falls Campsite, where there are six tent platforms. Here the Lincoln Brook Trail re-enters from the left (west), and the Twin Brook Trail branches off to the right. The Franconia Brook Trail continues on an old logging road for about 0.5 mi., then crosses to the west side of the brook. Now climbing somewhat more steeply, it continues along old logging roads to the top of the ridge, where it ends at the Garfield Ridge Trail (part of the Appalachian Trail). This junction is about 1.2 mi. east of Mt. Garfield and about 1.3 mi. west of where the Gale River Trail enters the Garfield Ridge Trail from US Rte. 3.

There is *water* about 200 yd. below the junction with the Garfield Ridge Trail and just before a bend to the right. On the right are a number of old fallen trees and deep sphagnum moss with several pools of clear water under the tree roots.

Franconia Brook Trail (map 5)

Distances from Wilderness Trail junction

to 13 Falls Campsite: 5 mi., 2½ hr.

to Garfield Ridge Trail junction: 7.2 mi. (11.5 km.), 4½ hr.

LINCOLN BROOK TRAIL (WMNF)

This trail begins and ends on the Franconia Brook Trail. Together, these two trails make a complete circuit around the base of the wooded wilderness mountain known as Owl's Head, after the shape of its south end.

Turning left (west) off the Franconia Brook Trail 0.3 mi. north of the bridge at the Camp 9 clearing, 1.4 mi. from the Franconia Brook Trail/Wilderness Trail junction, the Lincoln Brook Trail leads back (southwest) through the woods to join the former route on a railroad bed a short distance before crossing Franconia Brook. In another 0.4 mi. it crosses Lincoln Brook from the north to the south side. These crossings, which may be particularly difficult at high water, can be avoided by bushwhacking up the west banks of Franconia and Lincoln brooks from Franconia Brook Falls, in part following old logging roads. Beyond the Lincoln Brook crossing, the Lincoln Brook Trail follows the brook upstream on a long northward curve. It crosses a small brook at 2.5 mi., the larger Liberty Brook at 2.7 mi. About 50 yd. farther it passes the Camp 11 clearing, and in another 0.3 mi. it crosses Lincoln Brook to the east side. At 3.3 mi. it traverses the base of an old slide from Owl's Head. (Hikers often mistake the Liberty Brook crossing for a crossing of Lincoln Brook, and thus think they have passed the Owl's Head slide when they come to the Lincoln Brook crossing just before the slide.) The trail again crosses Lincoln Brook at 4.2 mi. and continues north, crossing a divide into the Franconia Brook drainage with some glimpses of the northern Franconia Range behind (west) and of Mt. Garfield to the north. The trail descends to cross a west fork of Franconia Brook at 6.5 mi., then bears sharp right and follows down the left bank of the brook, crossing the main stream and rejoining the Franconia Brook Trail at the 13 Falls Campsite.

Lincoln Brook Trail (map 5)

Distance from Franconia Brook Trail junction, Camp 9

   to Franconia Brook Trail junction, 13 Falls Campsite: 6.7 mi.
      (10.8 km.), 3½ hr.

Owl's Head

The true summit of Owl's Head (4023 ft.) can most easily be reached by climbing the slide on the west side of the mountain, starting from the Lincoln Brook Trail at a cairn about 3.3 mi. from the Camp 9 clearing (or about 0.3 mi. beyond the second crossing of Lincoln Brook). There is no officially maintained trail up the slide, which is considerably grown up but still potentially *dangerous,* especially when wet, because of loose rock and smooth ledges. Great care should be taken ascending and descending. In the fall of 1982, occasional cairns marked the way to the top of the slide (about 0.5 mi. from the bottom), where there is a small fountain emerging from the rock a few yards below the woods. From the top of the slide, a well-trod, unmaintained path climbs up to the ridge, with some deviations. After gaining the ridge, it continues north to the summit. The views from the summit are restricted, but a few glimpses of the Bonds and the Franconia Range can be obtained from a short distance to the east and west of the top.

Owl's Head (map 5)

Distances to summit

from cairn on Lincoln Brook Trail (via slide): 1 mi. (1.6 km.), 1 hr. 20 min.

from Kancamagus Highway (via Wilderness Trail, Franconia Brook Trail, Lincoln Brook Trail, and slide): 8.2 mi. (13.2 km.), 4 hr. 50 min.

TWIN BROOK TRAIL (AMC)

Ascending about 1800 ft. in less than 2.5 mi., this trail begins at the Franconia Brook Trail at 13 Falls Campsite and rises gradually east-northeast. At the start, take care to follow blazes at sharp bends, avoiding several old logging roads. After about 0.4 mi., the trail swings more to the north and heads up the valley of Twin Brook, keeping to the left (west) of the brook, which is occasionally audible but not visible. Traversing four distinct "knees" of Galehead Mountain in the next mile, the trail eventually climbs steeply to its terminus on the Frost Trail. Turn right for Galehead Hut. There is *no water* on this trail.

Twin Brook Trail (map 5)

Distances from 13 Falls Campsite

to Frost Trail junction: 2.6 mi., 1¾ hr.

to Galehead Hut (via Frost Trail): 2.8 mi. (3.2 km.), 1 hr. 50 min.

BONDCLIFF TRAIL (AMC)

This trail, blazed in blue, connects the Pemigewasset "Wilderness" with the high summits of the Twin Range (see Section 6). It begins at the Camp 16 clearing about 100 ft. west beyond where the Wilderness Trail crosses Black Brook. The Bondcliff Trail diverges north from the Wilderness Trail, climbs a bank left to a wide logging road after 100 ft., and shortly crosses Black Brook from west to east. It largely follows a series of logging roads, crossing Black Brook eight times in all. Since the second and third crossings are less than 50 yd. apart, they may both be avoided in high water by staying on the east side. The first four crossings may be avoided, with more effort, by staying on the west side from (or to) Camp 16. The *last sure water* comes at the sixth crossing, roughly 2.3 mi. from Camp 16. The eighth and last crossing goes from east to west at the head of a ravine facing south, about 75 ft. after the trail has crossed a steep, sandy slide. If the brook is dry here, *water* can often be found a short distance farther up in the streambed. Thereafter the Bondcliff Trail climbs moderately on old logging roads through woods and scrub, finally swinging north and emerging on the open ridge of Bondcliff (4265 ft.). It then continues along the ridge above and to the east of the cliffs, which have spectacular views. When visibility is poor, keep east if in doubt, since the cliffs are very steep. Beyond the cliffs, the trail dips before climbing steeply through scrub to the summit of Mt. Bond (4714 ft.). It then descends to the Bond-Guyot col, where a side trail leads steeply down right (east) about 0.3 mi. to AMC Guyot Shelter, an open log shelter accommodating twelve, with six tent platforms in addition. The *water* source flows in summer, but not always in colder weather, as in May. The main trail continues up the southeast peak of Mt. Guyot and then descends slightly to the left of the northwest peak, where it meets the Twinway. Turn left here for the Twins and Galehead Hut, or right for Zealand Mountain and Zealand Falls Hut.

In the reverse direction, take care to stay on the trail at the fifth (from the top) crossing of Black Brook; avoid a lumber road that remains on the west side, and cross the stream to the east bank, which the trail climbs steeply for a short distance. (This route — following the west bank — may, however, be preferred in times of high water.)

Bondcliff Trail (map 5)
Distances from Wilderness Trail junction, Camp 16
   to Bondcliff Ridge: *est*. 3.5 mi., 3 hr.
   to Mt. Bond summit: *est*. 4.8 mi., 4 hr.
   to Mt. Guyot summit: *est*. 6 mi. (9.8 km.), 5 hr.

West Bond Ridge

The ridge of West Bond consists of three peaks. The eastern-most and highest (4526 ft.) lies about 0.8 mi. west-northwest of Mt. Bond. A well-worn trail leaves the Bondcliff Trail at a large cairn and sign about 250 yd. south of the junction with the side trail to Guyot Shelter. It strikes southwest through the woods with a slight drop in altitude to the col between Bond and W. Bond before climbing the narrow ridge to the latter summit, which is bare with a fine view.

West Bond (map 5)
Distance from Bondcliff Trail
   to summit, easternmost peak: 0.5 mi. (0.8 km.), 20 min.

THOREAU FALLS TRAIL (WMNF)

This trail connects the Wilderness Trail at N. Fork Junction with the Ethan Pond Trail (Section 6). It diverges left from the Wilderness Trail on a railroad bed and in about 0.4 mi. crosses the E. Branch of the Pemigewasset on a 60-ft. bridge. The trail follows the railroad bed, crossing the N. Fork at 2.1 mi. and again at 2.7 mi. (no bridges). At the edge of a wet area just beyond the upper crossing, the trail turns left to regain the railroad bed. (The two crossings can be avoided by a bypass that leaves the main trail right at the lower crossing; it climbs for about 0.5 mi., passes above a slide area, and descends to rejoin the main trail about 0.1 mi. above the upper crossing. The length of the bypass is about 0.8 mi.) The Thoreau Falls Trail follows the railroad to its end and then a logging road for another 0.9 mi. Climbing steeply on a rough footpath to the right of the falls, it then crosses the N. Fork at the top of Thoreau Falls, which are beautiful with a good flow of water. Leaving the stream, the trail ends shortly at the Ethan Pond Trail, about 0.2 mi. north of the latter's bridge over the N. Fork. Turn left for Zealand Falls Hut and right for Ethan Pond Shelter.

Thoreau Falls Trail (map 5)

Distance from Wilderness Trail junction

to Ethan Pond Trail junction: 5.1 mi. (8.2 km.), 2½ hr.

SHOAL POND TRAIL (AMC)

This trail connects Stillwater Junction and the Ethan Pond Trail. At Stillwater Junction, the trail leads across Anderson Brook on the foundation of an old dam (no bridge), turns left on the railroad bed, and almost immediately leaves it right. Gaining another railroad bed, the trail crosses Shoal Pond Brook; this crossing may be difficult if the water is high. The trail follows the railroad to its end, where there is a pleasant pool to the right in the brook. The trail then follows logging roads, crossing Shoal Pond Brook from west to east, and after about another mile recrossing the brook. A short distance below Shoal Pond, the trail crosses the brook for a last time from west to east. Because of beaver activity, the trail keeps away from the shore east of the pond. About 200 yd. north of Shoal Pond the trail forks; the right (east) fork leads through swampy terrain toward Ethan Pond Shelter, while the left (west) fork leads toward Zealand Falls Hut. By either fork, it is a little less than 0.8 mi. to the Ethan Pond Trail.

Shoal Pond Trail (map 5)

Distances from Stillwater Junction

to Shoal Pond: *est.* 3.5 mi., 2 hr.

to Ethan Pond Trail junction: *est.* 4.3 mi. (6.8 km.), 2 hr. 20 min.

MOUNT CARRIGAIN

Mt. Carrigain (4680 ft.) was named for Philip Carrigain, New Hampshire Secretary of State, 1805-1810, an early mapmaker of the region. The view from the top is considered by many the finest in the White Mountains. Although the cabin on the fire tower was dismantled in summer 1978, an observation platform was completed in 1980 on the remaining section of the tower, which gives an excellent view over the trees.

Signal Ridge Trail (WMNF)

This trail starts at a point on Sawyer River Rd. 2.1 mi. from US Rte. 302, just before a concrete bridge. Since it largely follows the old tractor road to the tower, the grade is moderate. Diverging right (northwest) from the road, the trail crosses Whiteface Brook at 0.2 mi. After a gradual rise of 0.3 mi. it leaves the brook, bears left, and crosses a low divide. After about 1.3 mi. the trail joins a logging road. Roads that cross this one at right angles should not be followed. At 1.7 mi. from the start, the Carrigain Notch Trail diverges right (north). The Signal Ridge Trail soon crosses Carrigain Brook, ascends a gradual slope, and in about 0.5 mi. from the fork begins to rise more steeply. It soon swings to the left up the south side of a valley. When high up it bears right (north), rises less steeply, and slabs the side of the ridge. There is often *water* at two points (3.1 and 3.5 mi.) to the left of the road. When well up it turns left and, after a series of zigzags up the steep slope, comes into the open at the crest of Signal Ridge. The view of the sheer cliffs of Mt. Lowell across Carrigain Notch is notable. From Signal Ridge the path again enters woods and ascends sharply, passing the site of a fire warden's cabin; *water* in the old well *may not be potable*. The trail finally emerges on the wooded summit of the mountain.

Signal Ridge Trail (map 5)

Distances from Sawyer River Rd.

to Carrigain Notch Trail junction: 1.7 mi., 50 min.

to Signal Ridge: 4.5 mi., 3½ hr.

to Mt. Carrigain summit: 5 mi. (8 km.), 4 hr.

Carrigain Notch Trail (AMC)

With the Signal Ridge Trail this trail is the route from the Sawyer River Rd. through Carrigain Notch, connecting with trails to the Zealand Falls Hut, the Twin Range, and the Pemigewasset "Wilderness."

The Carrigain Notch Trail diverges right from the Signal Ridge Trail 1.7 mi. from the Sawyer River Rd. It follows old logging roads, ascending gradually. It crosses Carrigain Brook, follows along the base of Mt. Carrigain, and leads through Carrigain Notch. Several wet areas (some bypasses) attest to beaver activity south of the notch, and in several spots the trail must be followed carefully. About 1.5 mi. from the Signal Ridge Trail, the trail climbs more steeply and in another 0.5 mi. gains the height-of-land, only about 700 ft. above where it diverged from the Signal Ridge Trail. Shortly beyond, the trail again joins old logging roads, with three bypasses to the left (west) of wet areas. About 1.7 mi. north of the notch, the Nancy Pond Trail enters from the right on a logging railroad bed. At this point the Carrigain Notch Trail makes a sharp left turn onto this same railroad bed and follows it about 1 mi. to the site of Camp 20. Here the Desolation Trail continues across the brook, but the Carrigain Notch Trail turns sharply right and descends toward the E. Branch of the Pemigewasset. About 0.2 mi. beyond this junction, the Carrigain Notch Trail passes Desolation Shelter, which is located beside Carrigain Branch and accommodates eight; there is also a tent platform. At Stillwater Junction, the Shoal Pond Trail goes right across Anderson Brook (no bridge), while the Wilderness Trail goes left for the Thoreau Falls, Cedar Brook and Bondcliff trails, and the Kancamagus Highway.

On the reverse route note that at Camp 20 the Desolation Trail goes right and the Carrigain Notch Trail turns sharply left and follows a branch of the railroad for about 1 mi. At this point the Nancy Pond Trail begins, going straight ahead on the railroad bed, but the Carrigain Notch Trail turns sharply right and proceeds to the notch.

Carrigain Notch Trail (map 5)
Distances from Sawyer River Rd.

   to start of Carrigain Notch Trail (via Signal Ridge Trail): 1.7

mi., 50 min.
to Carrigain Notch: 3.8 mi., 2 hr. 40 min.
to Nancy Pond Trail junction: 5.6 mi., 3½ hr.
to Desolation Shelter: 6.5 mi., 4 hr.
to Stillwater Junction: 7.1 mi. (11.5 km.), 4 hr. 20 min.

Desolation Trail (AMC)

This trail leaves the Carrigain Notch Trail at the site of Camp 20, crosses a brook, follows a railroad bed for a short distance, and turns left up a steep bank. Using logging roads for a part of the way, it gradually climbs to the main ridge. Higher up, it follows an old road for some distance. At the top of this road, the trail bears east into virgin timber and climbs through it on a rough way very steeply to the summit. There is *no water* above Camp 20. This trail, with the Carrigain Notch, Shoal Pond, and Ethan Pond trails, forms a direct route between Zealand Falls Hut and Mt. Carrigain (total distance about 10 mi., 5¾ hr.).

Desolation Trail (map 5)
Distances from Carrigain Notch Trail junction, Camp 20
  to upper end of logging roads: 1.3 mi., 1 hr. 10 min.
  to to Mt. Carrigain summit: 1.9 mi. (3 km.), 2 hr. 20 min.
    (*descending* 1¼ hr.)

Carrigain-Hancock Ridge

The ridge line joining Mt. Carrigain and Mt. Hancock has no trail and is rough bushwhacking. (On map 5, Franconia, this line is part of the Lincoln-Livermore town boundary.) Carrigain Pond is just north of the ridge.

SAWYER RIVER TRAIL (WMNF)

This trail turns right off the Sawyer River Rd. a short distance beyond the bridge over the Sawyer River and about 0.2 mi. beyond the gate marking the end of public travel, 4 mi. from US Rte. 302. It follows an older road, washed in places, on the south side of the stream below a heavily lumbered area, for 1 mi. to an overgrown clearing (Hayshed Field) on the edge of a lumbered area. The Hancock Notch Trail leaves here on the right. Continuing in the woods straight ahead and leaving the lumbered area, the Sawyer River Trail gradually swings left (south) and follows an old logging railroad bed across an imperceptible divide in the flat region west of Green's Cliff. It crosses Meadow Brook (this section may be very wet) and follows the right (west) bank of this stream for some distance before curving gradually right (southwest) to cross the Swift River (can be very difficult in high water) at about 3.5 mi. from the start. The trail now leaves the railroad bed and follows an old logging road, turning due south and ending at the Kancamagus Highway, about 0.3 mi. southeast of Lily Pond. The Livermore Trail leaves 0.2 mi. west on the other side of the highway for Livermore Pass and Waterville.

Sawyer River Trail (map 5)

Distance from Sawyer River Rd.

   to Kancamagus Highway: 4.5 mi. (7.2 km.), 2 hr. 40 min.

HANCOCK NOTCH TRAIL (WMNF)

This trail leads from the Kancamagus Highway through Hancock Notch between Mt. Hancock and Mt. Huntington before descending along the Sawyer River to the Sawyer River Trail. With the Cedar Brook Trail, it affords the most-used access to Mt. Hancock.

The trail starts at the hairpin turn on the Kancamagus Highway about 0.9 mi. north of the northern terminus of the Greely Ponds Trail and about 8.5 mi. east of the ranger station at the I-93 exit in Lincoln. It follows a railroad bed, crossing a brook at 0.6 mi. and gradually approaching the north fork of the Hancock Branch. It crosses two brooks in less than 0.1 mi. and follows old logging roads generally east to northeast up a gentle grade to the Cedar Brook Trail (turn left on this trail and cross a small brook for Mt. Hancock). The Hancock Notch Trail rises somewhat more

steeply for about 0.8 mi. to the notch. East of the notch it passes
through a dense stand of spruce on a somewhat rougher footway,
descending quite rapidly at times. Crossing to the north side of
the Sawyer River, then back to the south, the trail then diverges
from the river, passes by an open boggy place, and following
logging roads crosses a south branch of the river. Descending,
the trail crosses the Sawyer River twice and follows newer
logging roads to its end at the Sawyer River Trail at Hayshed
Field, an overgrown clearing about 1 mi. from the Sawyer River
Rd. *Caution.* River crossings may be very difficult during high
water. In the *reverse direction*, be sure to avoid a snowmobile
trail leading right beyond the first river crossing.

Hancock Notch Trail (map 5)

Distances from Kancamagus Highway

   to Cedar Brook Trail junction: 1.8 mi., 55 min.

   to Hancock Notch: 2.5 mi., 1½ hr.

   to Sawyer River Trail junction: 6.3 mi., 2 hr. 25 min.

   to Sawyer River Rd. (via Sawyer River Trail): 7.4 mi. (11.9
   km.), 4 hr.

CEDAR BROOK TRAIL (WMNF)

With the Hancock Notch Trail, this trail affords the most direct
route to Mt. Hancock. It begins on the Hancock Notch Trail 1.8
mi. from the Kancamagus Highway, turns left across a small
brook, and climbs about 0.3 mi. to the first of five crossings of
Hancock Branch; the lowest two crossings are close together and
can be avoided by staying on the near bank. Following logging
roads past the upper three crossings, the trail passes the beginning of the Hancock Loop 150 yd. beyond the fifth crossing.

Climbing more steeply to the height-of-land between Mt.
Hancock and Mt. Hitchcock, the Cedar Brook Trail then de-
scends on logging roads with a long swing right to Slide Brook.
Passing Camp 24A, the trail continues on logging roads down to
Camp 24, from which it descends on a railroad bed northwest and

then east to the Wilderness Trail at the south end of the suspension bridge. Avoid the USFS truck road that branches left 0.5 mi. before the junction with the Wilderness Trail.

In the reverse direction, avoid the USFS access road that descends to the right about 0.5 mi. from the suspension bridge and leads along the south and east banks of the E. Branch to end at the Kancamagus Highway at the northwest corner of the parking area for the Wilderness Trail. At Camp 24, the railroad bed ends in Cedar Brook, while the trail jogs left up a bank to a logging road.

Cedar Brook Trail (map 5)

Distances from Kancamagus Highway

to start of Cedar Brook Trail (via Hancock Notch Trail): 1.8 mi.

to Hancock Loop Trail junction: 2.5 mi.

to height-of-land between Mts. Hancock and Hitchcock: 3 mi.

to Camp 24A: 4.2 mi.

to Camp 24: 5.8 mi.

to Wilderness Trail junction: 7.5 mi. (12 km.), 3 hr. 50 min.

MOUNT HANCOCK

Mt. Hancock has two major peaks (north peak 4403 ft.; south peak 4274 ft.) and a number of lesser summits. The ascent of the mountain was at one time more or less arduous. The Kancamagus Highway and subsequent trail-cutting made the mountain readily accessible.

Hancock Loop Trail (AMC)

This route to the Hancock summits leaves the Cedar Brook Trail on the right (east) about 0.8 mi. north of Hancock Notch Trail, about 150 yds. north of the fifth brook-crossing on the Cedar Brook Trail. This is about 2.5 mi. from the Kancamagus Highway via the Hancock Notch and Cedar Brook trails. Following an old logging road, the trail soon recrosses the main brook, and then encounters a steep rocky brookbed and a wet area. Keeping south of the main brook, some distance away from it and considerably higher, the trail continues its gradual ascent and reaches Loop Junction at about 1 mi. from the start. From this point the circuit over the two main summits of Mt. Hancock can be made in either direction.

North Link

The North Link leaves Junction Loop by diverging left from the lumber road and descending at an angle. It crosses a dry brookbed, where the foot of a large slide is visible about 150 ft. to the left. The ascent begins, first at a moderate grade slabbing the hillside, then straight up and always to the right of the slide. Near the top, the trail veers west and becomes less steep. From the wooded north summit (4403 ft.) a side path leads left a short distance to a fine view south, of the Sandwich Range, Osceola, etc.

Ridge Link

The Ridge Link from N. to S. Hancock starts out almost due north. After about 220 ft. a side trail leads right about 120 ft. to a facsimile of Plymouth Rock, which affords a somewhat overgrown view of Mt. Carrigain and the Presidential Range. Then the Ridge Link curves right, east, and then south, and traverses the ridge with several minor ups and downs to the south peak.

South Link

From Loop Junction, the South Link continues along the logging road for about another 0.1 mi., where the road peters out and a trail swings right up the hillside. The climb to the south summit (4274 ft.) is unrelievedly steep. On the other side of the summit, a short trail descends slightly to a fine viewpoint overlooking the Sawyer River valley to the southeast.

Hancock Loop Trail (map 5)

Distances from Cedar Brook Trail junction

   to Loop Junction: 1 mi., 50 min.

   to Mt. Hancock, north peak (via North Link): 1.8 mi. (2.8 km.), 1 hr. 50 min.

to Mt., Hancock, south peak (via North Link and Ridge Link): 3.1 mi. (4.9 km.), 2 hr. 50 min.

to Mt. Hancock, south peak (via South Link): 1.4 mi. (2.3 km.), 1 hr. 35 min.

to Cedar Brook Trail junction (complete loop): 4.5 mi. (7.3 km.), 4 hr. 10 min. in either direction

MOUNTS LOWELL, ANDERSON, NANCY, AND BEMIS

Mt. Lowell (3743 ft.), Mt. Anderson (3722 ft.), Mt. Nancy (3906 ft.), and Mt. Bemis (3706 ft.) are a group of peaks northeast of Carrigain Notch that form the watershed between the Saco and the E. Branch of the Pemigewasset. The region is notable for its concentration of four ponds at an altitude of about 3100 ft. and for a stand of virgin spruce, just south of Nancy Pond on the north slopes of Duck Pond Mountain, said to be one of the two largest remaining areas of virgin timber in the state. In October 1964, the USFS established in this region the Nancy Brook Scenic Area of 460 acres, to be maintained as nearly as possible in an undisturbed condition.

Nancy Pond Trail (Pasquaney Camp/WMNF)

The trail leaves the west side of US Rte. 302, 1.0 mi. north of the Sawyer River Rd. It follows a wood road for about 0.3 mi., where it bears left off the road and in 0.1 mi. crosses Halfway Brook. About 0.1 mi. beyond the brook, the trail intersects a logging road. Keep right and proceed northwest 0.6 mi. to a large cairn built in the road shortly before a stream crossing. The Nancy Pond Trail leaves the logging road left here, and climbs abruptly to the top of a ridge. Passing through some blow-down areas, it proceeds along the ridge through a spruce grove, briefly shelves along the shoulder, and drops down to cross Nancy Brook. On the far side it picks up another logging road, which it follows upstream with several reroutings due to washouts and slides. Near the base of Nancy Cascades, at about 2.2 mi. from the start, the trail recrosses to the south bank. At this point a side trail leads down right to a pool at the base of the lowest cascade, but the main trail bears left and makes three switchbacks, each time returning to a viewpoint on the cascades, which are several hundred feet high. Snow may remain in this area quite late in the spring. From the top of the headwall, the trail winds through the moss-carpeted virgin spruce forest past a small overgrown tarn to the northeast shore of Nancy Pond, 4 acres in area. Continuing along the north shore, the trail crosses the swamp at the upper end and continues over the height-of-land that divides Saco from Pemigewasset drainage, to Little Norcross Pond. Skirting the north shore, it then climbs over another small rise to Norcross Pond (7 acres). Again hugging the north shore, it proceeds to a ledgy natural dam at the west end, where there is a commanding view of the Pemigewasset "Wilderness" and beyond to the Franconia Range.

Continuing west after crossing the stream at the outlet of Norcross Pond, the Nancy Pond Trail now follows a logging road on a gradual descent. There is *water* at a *spring* (iron pipe) on the south side of the trail about 1.2 mi. from Norcross Pond. After another 0.8 mi. the trail veers right, crosses Norcross Brook and shortly swings left onto a railroad bed. After about 0.5 mi. it crosses Anderson Brook and then passes along the south side of the Camp 19 clearing. Continuing on the railroad bed for another 0.3 mi., the trail then turns sharply left and soon recrosses the combined Norcross and Anderson brooks. On the far side, another railroad bed is followed for about 0.5 mi. The trail then bears right on the railroad and crosses Notch Brook. A few yards farther on, it ends at a point where the Carrigain Notch Trail enters the railroad bed from the left (southeast). The latter trail continues straight ahead (west) on the railroad bed toward Desolation Shelter and Stillwater Junction.

In the reverse direction, note that the Carrigain Notch Trail makes a sharp right turn just where the Nancy Pond Trail begins. At Norcross Pond, the trail turns right along the north bank of the pond, while the logging road continues directly ahead. Near Rte. 302, within sight of buildings, the trail turns right off the logging road it has been following, crosses Halfway Brook, and proceeds to the road.

Nancy Pond Trail (map 5)
Distances from US Rte. 302

> *to* foot of Nancy Cascades: 2.2 mi., 1 hr. 40 min.
> *to* Nancy Pond: 3.3 mi., 2¾ hr.
> *to* Norcross Pond outlet: 4 mi., 3 hr. 10 min.
> *to* Carrigain Notch Trail junction: 7 mi., 4 hr. 40 min.
> *to* Desolation Shelter (via Carrigain Notch Trail): 8.2 mi. (13.2 km.), 5¼ hr.

ARETHUSA-RIPLEY FALLS AREA

The steep west side of Crawford Notch is cut by several brooks; in times of high water, the waterfalls on these can be quite spectacular. A network of trails connects some of these waterfalls and affords the opportunity for a series of shorter day hikes.

Arethusa Falls Trail (NHDP)

From the Arethusa Falls parking lot on the west side of US Rte. 302 the trail crosses the railroad and leads south (left) for 50 yd., where it turns right into the woods. It follows old roads above the north bank of Bemis Brook until it crosses the brook shortly below the falls. These are over 200 ft. high, the highest in the state.

Arethusa Falls Trail (map 5)
Distance from parking area, US Rte. 302

> *to* Arethusa Falls: *est.* 1.3 mi., 55 min.

Bemis Brook Trail (NHDP)

This alternate route to Arethusa Falls departs left from the Arethusa Falls Trail 0.3 mi. from its start at the railroad, angles toward the brook, and then follows close to the brook. Passing Fawn Pool, Coliseum Falls, the Bemis Brook Falls, it then climbs steeply up the bank to rejoin the Arethusa Falls Trail.

Bemis Brook Trail (map 5)

Distance from depart Arethusa Falls Trail

to rejoin Arethusa Falls Trail: 0.6 mi. (1 km.), 40 min.

Arethusa-Ripley Falls Trail (AMC/NHDP)

These two spectacular spots in Crawford Notch are connected by a trail that starts at the end of the Arethusa Falls Trail just below the falls. It immediately recrosses the brook and slabs away from the falls up the side of the valley on a graded path. It then doubles back on the south side of a smaller brook, which it shortly crosses. A rougher path leads northeast across several small watercourses to the plateau behind Frankenstein Cliff. Turning east, the trail shortly passes the junction of the Frankenstein Cliff Trail and again heads north across the plateau. With various views of Mt. Webster, Crawford Notch, and Mt. Willey, the trail drops gradually and then more steeply on switchbacks to Avalanche Brook at the foot of Ripley Falls, which are about 100 ft. high. In dry weather, the brook is rather low. The rocks just off the path near the falls are slippery and should be avoided. Crossing the brook at the foot of the falls, the path rises slightly to the east for 0.4 mi. to join the Ethan Pond Trail 0.2 mi. from the Willey House Station; continue straight ahead for that destination.

Arethusa-Ripley Falls Trail (map 5)

Distances from Arethusa Falls parking area, US Rte. 302

to start of Arethusa-Ripley Falls Trail (via Arethusa Falls Trail): *est*. 1.3 mi., 55 min.

to Frankenstein Cliff Trail junction: *est*. 2.3 mi.

to Ripley Falls: *est*. 3.4 mi.

to Ethan Pond Trail junction: 3.8 mi.

to Willey House Station, US Rte. 302 (via Ethan Pond Trail): 3.9 mi. (6.2 km.), 2 hr. 25 min.

Frankenstein Cliff Trail (NHDP)

Frankenstein Cliff, a prominent feature from the highway, juts out from the tableland south of Mt. Willey and affords excellent views of the lower part of Crawford Notch.

The trail leaves the west side of US Rte. 302 just south of the bridge over the Saco River, and south of the entrance to the Dry River Campground. It briefly follows an old logging road and then climbs to the Frankenstein Cutoff and passes under the Frankenstein railroad trestle near the south abutment. It continues on switchbacks and stone steplike formations through the woods beneath the cliffs and up to the ridge, rather steep in places. It then passes through open hardwood forest, crossing a streambed where there is usually *water*. It passes through a fine area of spruce and balsam to an outlook similar to that on Mt. Willard, with a view south in the notch.

Leaving the outlook, the trail ascends gradually through a fine stand of spruce in a west-northwest direction, skirting the top of the cliffs, with views of the valley and Mt. Bemis, and passing just south of the summit marked "2451" on map 5. At one point there is a view of Arethusa Falls far up at the head of the valley. Near the height-of-land the trail levels off, then descends the ridge for a short distance, and winds gradually to where it meets the Arethusa-Ripley Falls Trail.

Frankenstein Cliff Trail (map 5)

Distances from US Rte. 302

to railroad trestle: 0.2 mi.

to Frankenstein Cliff: 0.9 mi.

to Arethusa-Ripley Falls Trail junction: 1.8 mi. (2.9 km.), 1½ hr.

Frankenstein Cutoff (NHDP)

This connection between the Frankenstein Cliff Trail just below the trestle and the Arethusa Falls Trail at the parking lot follows below (east of) the railroad embankment.

This trail provides a circuit, going up the trail to Arethusa

Falls, recrossing Bemis Brook, continuing up the slope on the Arethusa-Ripley Falls Trail and bearing right on the Frankenstein Cliff Trail and descending to and under the railroad trestle to the cutoff and then back to the parking area. Trespassing on the railroad is strictly prohibited, as is use of the tracks as a footway.

Frankenstein Cutoff (map 5)

Distance from Frankenstein Cliff Trail

>   *to* Arethusa Falls parking area, US Rte. 302: 0.5 mi. (0.8 km.), ¼ hr.

Mount Chocorua and the Sandwich Range

The Sandwich Range extends about 30 mi. westward, from near Conway on the Saco River to Campton on the Pemigewasset. Rising somewhat abruptly from the lake country to summits of 4000 ft., its views combine mountain and water scenery. The north peak of Mt. Tripyramid (4140 ft.) is the highest in the range.

The conspicuous and picturesque rocky cone at the east end of the range is Mt. Chocorua (3475 ft.). To the west is the irregular ledgy mass of Mt. Paugus (3200 ft.), and beyond it Mt. Passaconaway, a graceful wooded peak (4060 ft.). Southwest of Mt. Passaconaway lies Mt. Whiteface (4015 ft.), with bare cliffs south of its summit. Farther in the same direction, Flat Mountain (3300 ft.) connects Mt. Whiteface with the prominent wooded ridge of Sandwich Mountain (also known as Sandwich Dome or Black Mountain, 3993 ft.). This is flanked on the south by Mt. Israel in Sandwich and on the southwest by Mt. Weetamoo (2548 ft.). in Campton. Mt. Tripyramid, northwest of Mt. Whiteface, separates the valley of the Mad River in Waterville Valley from that of the Swift River in Albany. Practically all of Mt. Chocorua, Mt. Paugus, Mt. Passaconaway, Mt. Whiteface, and Mt. Tripyramid are in the WMNF.

For trails to Tripyramid and Sandwich Mountain from the west, see Section 10, The Waterville Valley. For Sandwich Mountain from the south, and Mt. Israel, see Section 19, Lakes Region.

The Chocorua Mountain Club, Wonalancet Outdoor Club, and WMNF maintain most of the trails in this area. Those of the CMC are marked by yellow signs and occasional yellow paint on the trails. The WODC trails have blue blazes and signs. Open shelters will be found near the summits of Mts. Chocorua, Paugus, Passaconaway, and Whiteface.

Refer to map 4, Chocorua-Waterville, which shows the entire Sandwich Range.

The Chocorua-Paugus region is accurately shown on a contour map issued by the CMC (9th ed., 1976) with a panorama from Mt. Chocorua (Chocorua Mountain Club, Box 73, Chocorua, NH 03817, $1.00). The trails in the Paugus-Passaconaway-Whiteface region are shown on a map issued by the WODC (1976).

MOUNT CHOCORUA

Mt. Chocorua (3475 ft.) is abundantly supplied with trails. The Piper Trail, beginning at the Piper Trail Restaurant on NH Rte. 16 about 3 mi. north of Chocorua Lake, is the popular way of ascent from the east side. From the west side take either the easier Liberty Trail or the more attractive Brook Trail. From the Kancamagus Highway, take the Champney Falls Trail.

On the descent, it is sometimes difficult to locate these trails at the top of the mountain. Go 50 yd. southwest from the summit by the only marked trail, down a small gully to the first junction. The trails on the open rocks are marked with orange paint and all junctions are signed with WMNF signs.

Piper Trail (WMNF)

This popular trail was first blazed years ago by Joshua Piper. Starting at the Piper Trail Cabins and Restaurant on NH Rte. 16 (sign, fee for parking), it leads across an open field. The Weetamoo Trail diverges left 0.8 mi. from the start, and at 1.3 mi. from Rte. 16 the Nickerson Ledge Trail (sign) leaves right (north) to the ledge 0.3 mi. distant and 300 ft. up, with a fine though limited view of the peak of Mt. Chocorua.

After crossing Chocorua River (a small brook at this point) at 2.0 mi., the trail then makes a rather sharp left turn, ascends moderately for 0.6 mi., then turns sharply right. It goes over a series of switchbacks, stone steps, and paving for approximately

0.2 mi. A spur trail leaves left, leading in 0.2 mi. to Camp Penacook (WMNF), an open shelter which accommodates six to eight, and a tent platform that also accommodates six to eight. There is *water* 0.1 mi. below the shelter to the south of the trail. The Piper Trail turns sharp right from the Camp Penacook spur trail, with more stone steps and paving, crossing open ledges with spectacular views to the north, east, and south. The Champney Falls Trail bears right and in another 0.2 mi. the West Side Trail (sometimes referred to — and signed as — a part of the Liberty Trail) joins the Piper Trail, and the latter continues over open ledges to the summit. The trail is marked with yellow paint. In bad weather it may be safer to use the West Side and Brook trails to reach the summit, since the Piper Trail is quite exposed.

Descending, go 50 yd. southwest from the summit, following the only marked trail, to a junction with a sign, then north, skirting the peak, to the open ridge. At the junction with the Champney Falls Trail keep right (east) for the base

Piper Trail (map 4)

Distances from NH Rte. 16, Piper Trail Cabins

   to Nickerson Ledge Trail junction: 1.3 mi., 1 hr.
   to Chocorua River crossing: 2.0 mi., 1½ hr.
   to Camp Penacook spur trail junction: 2.9 mi., 2 hr. 25 min.
   to Champney Falls Trail junction: 3.6 mi., 3 hr.
   to West Side (Liberty) Trail junction: 3.7 mi., 3 hr. 5 min.
   to Mt. Chocorua summit: 4.1 mi. (6.6 km.), 3 hr. 25 min.

Nickerson Ledge Trail (WMNF)

This trail, in combination with the Weetamoo Trail, offers an attractive circuit with maximum walking above treeline. The circuit includes Carter Ledge, the Three Sisters, the summit cone of Mt. Chocorua, and Bald Mountain.

The trail branches right (north) from the Piper Trail nearly 1.3 mi. from NH Rte. 16, ascends sharply for 300 ft. to Nickerson Ledge 0.3 mi. away, with a limited view of the peak. It then turns left (northwest) for about 0.5 mi. to end at the Carter Ledge Trail, which leads left to Middle Sister Trail.

Nickerson Ledge Trail (map 4)

Distances from NH Rte. 16, Piper Trail Cabins

to Nickerson Ledge (via Piper Trail): 1.6 mi.

to Carter Ledge (via Carter Ledge Trail): 3 mi.

to Middle Sister Trail junction (via Carter Ledge Trail): *est.* 4.3 mi.

to Mt. Chocorua summit (via Carter Ledge Trail and Middle Sister Trail): 5.5 mi. (8.9 km.), 4 hr. 10 min.

Weetamoo Trail (CMC)

This attractive and varied trail connects the lower end of the Piper Trail with the Hammond Trail. Relocated in 1980, the Weetamoo Trail now diverges left from the Piper Trail 0.8 mi. from NH Rte. 16. At 0.4 mi. the trail crosses Chocorua River, then follows it for 0.1 mi. with a view of the summit. After crossing an old logging road, the trail then crosses a small stream (*last sure water*). Soon there is a fine view of Carter Ledge and Middle Sister. Vistas have been opened with views of Middle Sister and Mt. Chocorua at 1.4 mi., and views south and east of lakes and ponds at 1.6 mi. and 1.8 mi. from the Piper Trail. At 1.6 mi. Weetamoo Rock, an immense boulder, lies to the left of the trail. Here, crossing the old route, follow new 2″ × 6″ paint blazes. At 2.0 mi. the Hammond Trail is reached. A sharp right leads to the Mt. Chocorua summit in 1.6 mi.

Weetamoo Trail (map 4)

Distances from NH Rte. 16, Piper Trail Cabins

to start of Weetamoo Trail (via Piper Trail): 0.8 mi., ½ hr.

to Hammond Trail junction: 2.8 mi., 2¼ hr.

to Mt. Chocorua summit (via Hammond Trail): 4.4 mi. (7.1 km.), 3 hr. 40 min.

Hammond Trail (CMC)

About 1.5 mi. north of the Chocorua Lake bridge, leave NH Rte. 16 on the left (west), opposite a large erratic boulder and follow narrow dirt road. Parking area is on right in about 0.5 mi. The Hammond Trail crosses Stony Brook (*last sure water*) twice in about 0.5 mi. About 0.5 mi. north of the second crossing the trail crosses a bulldozed firelane. The trail ascends a ridge called Bald Mountain and follows its rocky crest, marked on the ledges by yellow paint. The Weetamoo Trail comes in from the right not far beyond Bald Mountain. The Hammond Trail bears generally northwest and in about another 0.5 mi. ends at the Liberty Trail, which can be followed to the summit.

Hammond Trail (map 4)

Distances from parking area off NH Rte. 16

to Bald Mountain: 1.8 mi., 1½ hr.

to Liberty Trail junction: 3.1 mi., 2¼ hr.

to Mt. Chocorua summit (via Liberty Trail): *est.* 4 mi. (6.5 km.), 3¼ hr. (*descending* 2½ hr.)

Liberty Trail (WMNF)

This very old path was improved somewhat by James Liberty in 1887, and further developed as a toll bridle path by David Knowles and Newell Forrest in 1892. Knowles built a two-story Peak House in 1892, which was blown down in September 1915. The stone stable was rebuilt by the CMC in 1924 and named the Jim Liberty Shelter. This lasted till 1932, when the spring winds blew off the roof. In 1934 the WMNF replaced it with an enclosed cabin with stove and six bunks.

The trail is reached by the Paugus Mill Rd., which branches north from Fowler's Mill Rd. between Chocorua Lake and NH Rte. 113A from Tamworth to Wonalancet. The eastern terminus of Fowler's Mill Rd. is at NH Rte. 16, where a small bridge crosses the watercourse between the large and small Chocorua lakes, while the western end branches northeast just north of the bridge over Paugus Brook on Rte. 113A. The Paugus Mill Rd. branches north just east of the bridge over Paugus Brook (sign). A short distance after leaving Fowler's Mill Rd., Paugus Mill Rd. passes a small house on the site of the old Durrell Farm, where it turns sharp left, and in 0.7 mi. reaches a parking area where the Liberty Trail branches right. (The Bolles Trail leaves this road left about 0.1 mi. past the gate, and the Brook Trail leaves the road right about 0.3 mi. from the gate.) From this point the Liberty Trail mostly follows the former bridle path. The Hammond Trail joins the Liberty Trail on the high shoulder of the mountain about 0.5 mi. below the Jim Liberty Cabin.

Some 30 yd. southwest of the cabin there may be a small pool of *water* in the rock. There is a small brook 200 yd. northeast down a branch trail (sign). The Liberty Trail swings to the left (west) at the foot of a ledge and, often blasted out of the rock, encircles the southwest side of the cone on a gradual ascent and meets the Brook Trail a few yards away from the latter's junction with the Bee Line Trail. For the summit, the Brook Trail leads east over the ledges (yellow paint), then northeast (left) to the junction of Piper Trail left (north) and sign, then on to the summit. The summit can be avoided during bad weather by following the West Side Trail beyond the point where the Bee Line Trail enters. The West Side Trail runs north around the west side of the summit cone to the Piper Trail.

Liberty Trail (map 4)
Distances from Paugus Mill Rd. parking area
   to Jim Liberty Cabin: 3.3 mi., 2 ½ hr.
   to Mt. Chocorua summit (via Brook Trail): 3.8 mi. (6.1 km.), 3 hr. 10 min.

Brook Trail (CMC)

This trail, cut by the country people to avoid paying toll on the Liberty Trail, is perhaps the most beautiful trail on Mt. Chocorua. From the Liberty Trail parking area on Paugus Mill Rd., continue north on new lumbering road. After 0.2 mi. bear right on gravel road, where the Bolles Trail goes straight. Then after about 0.1 mi., the Brook Trail bears right (east) at a bridge over Claybank Brook, and follows old logging roads through stands of hemlock and second-growth hardwood. The Brook Trail continues well into the ravine, sometimes at a distance from the brook, ascending by moderate grades, crossing two small brooks. Finally, the trail swings to the left across the brook (*last sure water*) and climbs sharply through spruces and hardwoods to the steep, open ledges of the Farlow Ridge, where it is marked with cairns and yellow paint. At the treeline, the Liberty Trail comes in on the right, and the Bee Line Trail a few yards beyond on the left. In about 200 yd. the West Side Trail continues north and the Brook Trail goes east over the ledges where it swings northeast (left) to the junction with the Piper Trail left (sign), then east to the summit through a small gully.

Descending, keep to the left at the junction of the West Side Trail and Bee Line Trail and bear right 10 yd. farther, leaving the Liberty Trail on the left.

Brook Trail (map 4)

Distances from Paugus Mill Rd. parking area

to last brook: 2.3 mi., 1 hr. 40 min.

to Mt. Chocorua summit: 3.5 mi. (5.6 km.), 3 hr. (*descending* 2¼ hr).

Bee Line Trail (CMC)

The Chocorua section of this trail leaves right from the Bolles Trail 1.2 mi. north of the Paugus Mill Rd. parking area. The trail follows an old lumber road northeast up a valley and crosses a brook twice (*last sure water*). Beyond the second crossing it climbs to a small group of spruce. On the north edge of this it joins a steep slide, which it follows to within 100 yd. of its junction with the coinciding Brook and Liberty trails. Yellow paint marks the trail on the ledges. *Caution.* The open ledges are extremely hazardous when they are wet or icy.

Descending, keep to the left at the junction of the West Side Trail. Follow the coinciding Brook and Liberty trails for about 200 yd. to the upper end of the Bee Line Trail (yellow paint) on the right, marked by a yellow sign and only a few yards before the Brook Trail leaves right from the Liberty Trail. The first part must be followed with care.

Bee Line Trail (map 4)
Distances from Paugus Mill Rd. parking area
   to start of Bee Line Trail (via Bolles Trail): 2 mi., 1 hr.
   to Mt. Chocorua summit (via Brook Trail): 4.1 mi.
     (6.6 km.), 3¼ hr. (*descending* 2¼ hr.)

Champney Falls Trail (WMNF)

This trail is named for Benjamin Champney, pioneer White
Mountain artist (1817-1907). The falls are meager in dry seasons. The area within a quarter of a mile of each side of this trail
is a Restricted Use Area as far as Champney Falls (see Section
22).

The trail (sign) leaves the Kancamagus Highway where Twin
Brook crosses the road, 11.5 mi. from NH Rte. 16 in Conway.
The Bolles Trail to the Paugus Mill site is 250 yd. to the west. By
easy grades the trail follows a lumber road about 0.3 mi. to
Champney Brook. The trail follows the west bank of the brook
for about a mile, then climbs along the high west bank of the
stream.

The main trail now rises by comparatively easy but constant
grades higher and higher above the brookbed. At 1.2 mi. a side
trail left leads in 0.3 mi. to the bottom of Champney Falls, climbs
steps along their west side to the top, and returns to the main trail
1.5 mi. from the Kancamagus Highway. From the bottom of the
falls a path leads left 200 ft. to Pitcher Falls. There is a good
lookout to Mt. Carrigain from a cleared spot along the main trail
at 1.4 mi. Well up on the mountain, on the right (west) side of the
trail, a good *spring* issues from broken ledges. Just beyond, the
trail ascends by a series of zigzags. Shortly after entering a stand
of spruce a cutoff left leads in 0.3 mi. to the Middle Sister Trail.
Just under 0.3 mi. beyond this junction the Middle Sister Trail
leaves left. The Champney Falls Trail ends at its junction with
the Piper Trail, about 100 yd. farther.

Champney Falls Trail (map 4)
Distances from Kancamagus Highway
> *to* foot of Champney Falls: 1.5 mi., 1 hr.
> *to* spring: 2.4 mi., 2 hr.
> *to* Piper Trail junction: 3.1 mi., 2 hr. 40 min.
> *to* Mt. Chocorua summit (via Piper Trail): 3.6 mi. (5.8 km.),
>   3 hr. 10 min.

Middle Sister Trail (WMNF)

The open ledgy northern spurs of Mt. Chocorua are only slightly lower than the summit.

Middle Sister Trail leaves NH Rte. 16 at the WMNF White Ledge Campground. It branches left (west) from the short roadway into the camp (sign) and follows a lumber road over the flat col between Chocorua and White Ledge. It crosses Hobbs Brook, then ascends more and more steeply to a small col between Three Sisters ridge and Blue Mountain, where the trail turns sharp left (southwest) and soon ascends the northeast spur of the Third Sister, largely on open ledges. Near the top the Carter Ledge Trail joins on the left (southeast). Crossing a small dip beyond the Third Sister, the trail reaches the summit of the Middle Sister (3330 ft.). The trail continues across ledges (yellow paint) to a cutoff right to the Champney Falls Trail, and continues ahead about 0.4 mi. to its terminus on the Champney Falls Trail. Turn left for the Piper Trail (100 yd.) and the summit of Mt. Chocorua, 0.5 mi.

Middle Sister Trail (map 4)
Distances from White Ledge Campground, NH Rte. 16
> *to* Middle Sister summit: 4.2 mi.
> *to* Champney Falls Trail junction: 4.7 mi. (7.5 km.)

Carter Ledge Trail (WMNF)

This trail provides an attractive alternate route from White

Ledge Campground to Middle Sister. It runs from the west end of a short loop road west of the main camp roadway near NH Rte. 16. Ascending very gradually, it is joined by the Nickerson Ledge Trail near the foot of the great open Carter Ledge, which it ascends steeply. Near the top the trail passes a colony of Jack Pine, *Pinus Banksiana*, one of four known New Hampshire stands. Beyond the flat top of the ledge it ascends the Third Sister steeply to join Middle Sister Trail, just north of the Middle Sister summit.

Carter Ledge Trail (map 6)

Distances from White Ledge Campground, NH Rte. 16

   to Nickerson Ledge Trail junction: 2 mi., 1½ hr.

   to Middle Sister summit (via Middle Sister Trail): *est*. 4 mi. (6.5 km.), 3¼ hr.

White Ledge Loop Trail (WMNF)

White Ledge (about 2010 ft.) is a bluff just east of the Three Sisters of Mt. Chocorua. The top gives a fine view south and east. This loop trail has east and west branches, both starting from the south. A complete loop begins and ends at White Ledge Campground.

The east branch of the trail can also be entered from NH Rte. 16 opposite Pine Knoll Camp (1.5 mi. northeast of the Piper Trail). From here the trail follows an old town road. After 0.5 mi. the east branch of the trail from the campground enters on the left (it is also 0.5 mi. to this point from the campground). The trail continues northwest along the old town road, passing an old building site. Then turning north and northeast, it passes through a high notch, with the main bluff of White Ledge on the left. Beyond it, in an old overgrown pasture area, the trail turns around left toward the west, then southwest, and leads up the east end of White Ledge, over a smooth ledge to the summit (view). From here the west branch of the trail descends 1.6 mi. to the campground.

White Ledge Loop Trail (map 4)
Distances from White Ledge Campground off NH Rte. 16
to fork of east and west branches: 0.2 mi.
to trail from Pine Knoll Camp junction (via east branch):
  0.5 mi.
to White Ledge summit: 2.7 mi., 2 hr.
to White Ledge Campground (complete loop): 4.3 mi.
  (7 km.), 2 hr. 50 min.

Bickford Path (WODC)

The Bickford Path offers a route from Wonalancet to the Paugus Mill site, the Bolles Trail and the Bee Line trails up Mts. Chocorua and Paugus. The trail, marked with blue paint, must be followed with care. East of the Bolles Trail it is extremely obscure. The Bickford Path leaves NH Rte. 113A just east of the height-of-land and about 0.8 mi. from Wonalancet Farm (sign). In an easy 0.5 mi. it reaches a spur of Mt. Mexico. The trail descends to a field near the home of James Breasted, passes around the lower end of a horse corral, and then continues across overgrown fields. It is marked with blue paint on rocks, which must be followed with care. The trail enters the woods on the east side of the field, climbs a wooded ridge, and descends. It meets the Old Paugus Trail on the left. The two cross Whitin Brook together and meet the Bolles Trail.

Bickford Path (map 4)
Distance from NH Rte. 113A
to Old Paugus Trail junction (Paugus Mill site): 1.9 mi. (3.1 km.), 1¼ hr.

Bolles Trail (WMNF)

This old logging road from Tamworth to Albany, between Mts. Paugus and Chocorua, was reopened by Frank Bolles in 1891 and called the "Lost Trail." The north end of the Bolles Trail is 250 yd. west of Twin Brook on the Kancamagus Highway.

From the south, start at the Fowler's Mill Rd. parking area, where the Liberty Trail diverges right and the Brook Trail begins. Follow the Brook Trail 0.1 mi. from this junction to the start of the Bolles Trail. It crosses the Paugus Brook in 0.2 mi. At 0.3 mi. beyond this crossing there is a junction with the Old Paugus Trail and the Bickford Path on the left. The Bickford Path (obscure) leaves to the right 100 yd. farther. A half-mile beyond, just before crossing Paugus Brook, the Bee Line Cutoff to Mt. Paugus leaves left. In 0.8 mi. more, the Bee Line Trail from Mt. Chocorua to Mt. Paugus is crossed. The Bolles Trail again crosses Paugus Brook 2 mi. from the Paugus Mill site, and, at the point where several old lumber roads diverge, follows the one that leads northwest. It then diverges to the right (northeast) from a blind road, crosses a small gully, and steeply ascends the sandy head slope of the valley. At the divide, for a view north, one must scramble up a small burned knoll on the left of the trail. Proceeding northeast the trail enters the head of an old logging road in the green growth and descends sharply to Twin Brook, which it crosses and recrosses repeatedly, until the brook finally turns sharply east about 0.3 mi. from the Kancamagus Highway. There is *water* except on the highest part of the trail.

Bolles Trail (map 4)

Distances from Paugus Mill Rd. parking area

   to start of Bolles Trail (via Brook Trail): 0.2 mi.

   to Old Paugus Trail junction (Paugus Mill site): 0.7 mi.

   to Bee Line Cutoff junction: 1.2 mi.

   to Bee Line Trail crossing: 2 mi., 1 hr.

   to Kancamagus Highway: 5.7 mi. (9.1 km.), 3 hr. 25 min.

MOUNT PAUGUS

This low (3200 ft.) but rugged mountain was named by Lucy Larcom for the Pequawket chief who led in the battle of Lovewell's Pond. It was formerly also called "Old Shag." The summit is wooded but 600 yd. south of it is another eminence with bare ledges giving limited outlooks (about 3100 ft.) where all trails end. The mountain is separated from NH Rte. 113A by the ridge of Mt. Mexico. Whitin Brook lies between Mts. Mexico and Paugus. Trails ascend Mt. Paugus from the southeast and from the west, affording in combination an interesting circuit.

Bee Line Trail (CMC)

The Paugus section of this trail forms a continuation of the Bee Line Trail from Mt. Chocorua (see above). Leaving the Bolles Trail, the Bee Line Trail crosses Paugus Brook and then a narrow ridge. About 0.2 mi. farther Bee Line Cutoff departs left (southeast) on an old lumber road and joins the Bolles Trail about 0.5 mi. above the Paugus Mill site. (The cutoff provides a shortcut on the way from the Paugus Mill site to Mt. Paugus summit via the Bee Line Trail, but it is somewhat obscure.) Beyond the junction with the cutoff, the Bee Line Trail follows old lumber roads up the steep side of the mountain to the Old Paugus Trail near the top of the ridge. All junctions are marked by CMC signs. *Water* is available, after leaving the Paugus Valley, at a brook above the junction of the branches; at a tiny brook to the right, at the base of a grove of spruces well up the ridge; and at the pool at CMC Old Shag Camp, an open log shelter. None of these sources is completely reliable.

Descending, the junction with Old Paugus Trail is indicated by a sign. The Bee Line Trail turns left downhill.

Bee Line Trail (map 4)

Distances from Paugus Mill Rd. parking area

to Bee Line Cutoff junction (via Bolles Trail): 1.2 mi., 35 min.

to Bolles Trail-Bee Line Trail crossing: 2 mi., 1 hr.

to Mt. Paugus summit (via Bee Line Cutoff): 3.5 mi., 3 hr.

Old Paugus Trail (CMC)

The Old Paugus Trail is reached from the Paugus Mill Rd. parking area via the Brook and Bolles trails. At 0.7 mi. north of the trailhead, just below the Paugus Mill site, the Old Paugus

Trail turns left off the Bolles Trail and crosses Whitin Brook, forking right where the Bickford Path goes left. The Old Paugus Trail soon crosses to the north side of Whitin Brook and at the beginning of the Whitin Brook Trail turns sharply right up the side of the valley to the north , where it is joined by the Big Rock Cave Trail. A few yards beyond is a good *spring* on the left (west). The trail then leads up a steep, gravelly cut to the base of a cliff, which it skirts to the northeast. After traversing a spruce forest it is joined by the Bee Line Trail from the right (east) and then ascends sharply over several ledges. At 0.2 mi. below the Mt. Paugus summit ledges is Old Shag Camp (CMC) on a short branch trail to the north (sign) with a swampy area to the west. "High Altitude" beavers have caused havoc with what was once a small, clear stream. This is the *last water*. The trail ends where it meets the Lawrence Trail at a cairn on a ledge 600 yd. south of the true summit. Ledges near the summit may be dangerous when wet or icy.

Descending, the trail will be found east of the cairn (sign). Keep right at the junction with Bee Line Trail.

Old Paugus Trail (map 4)

Distances from Paugus Mill Rd. parking area

to start of Old Paugus Trail (via Bolles Trail): 0.7 mi., 20 min.

to Whitin Brook Trail junction: 1.8 mi., 1¼ hr.

to Bee Line Trail junction: 2.9 mi., 2¼ hr.

to Mt. Paugus summit ledges: 3.7 mi. (5.9 km.), 3 hr.
  (*descending* 2 hr. 10 min.)

Old Shag Camp (CMC)

Old Shag Camp is sheltered among spruces near the small beaver dam just below (2960 ft.) and east of the summit ledges of Mt. Paugus. It is reached by a short side trail (sign) that branches to the right off the Old Paugus Trail ascending to the summit ledges. It is an open log shelter, accommodating six. Nearby *water* is poor because of beaver activity; a blue-blazed trail leads 0.3 mi. to a better source.

Whitin Brook Trail (CMC)

This trail makes possible a day-trip circuit of great scenic beauty: ascending Mt. Paugus by the Old Paugus Trail, down over the Overhang along the Lawrence Trail, continuing through spruce woods to the Cabin Trail, and along the Cabin Trail to the Whitin Brook Trail. The Whitin Brook Trail descends from this junction to the east (left) through woods to Whitin Brook, which it follows back down to the Old Paugus Trail. The Big Rock Cave Trail is crossed 0.2 mi. before the Old Paugus Trail junction.

In ascending, start from the point where the Old Paugus Trail diverges north (right) from the Whitin Brook Trail. The Big Rock Cave Trail crosses in 0.2 mi. Just below the site of a logging camp, the Whitin Brook Trail bears right along edge of brook, joining the logging road beyond the camp. It then climbs through spruce to Whitin Ridge at the junction with the Cabin Trail.

Whitin Brook Trail (map 4)

Distances from Paugus Mill Rd. parking area

> *to* start of Whitin Brook Trail (via Bolles Trail and Old Paugus Trail): 1.8 mi., 1¼ hr.
> *to* Whitin Ridge: 3.4 mi., 2 hr. 20 min.
> *to* Mt. Paugus summit ledges (via Cabin Trail and Lawrence Trail): 3.9 mi. (6.3 km.), 3 hr.

Big Rock Cave Trail (WODC)

This trail is reached by an old logging road leaving NH Rte. 113A 0.3 mi. east of Wonalancet Farm (sign). At about 0.4 mi. Cabin Trail diverges left, while Big Rock Cave Trail continues straight ahead, following logging roads. All junctions are marked with blue paint and arrows, which should be followed with care. Halfway up the ridge, the trail leaves a logging road and continues as a blazed trail over the broad crest of Mt. Mexico to Big Rock Cave. Beyond the cave it descends to Whitin Brook about 0.2 mi. north. The trail crosses the Whitin Brook Trail, which leads east to the Paugus Mill site, and ascends north and east 0.3 mi. to end at the Old Paugus Trail. From Wonalancet, Mt. Paugus may be ascended by this route, returning by the Lawrence Trail and Kelley Trail.

Big Rock Cave Trail (map 4)

Distances from NH Rte. 113A

   to Big Rock Cave: *est*. 1.8 mi., 1½ hr.

   to Old Paugus Trail junction: *est*. 2.3 mi. (3.5 km.), 2 hr.

Lawrence Trail (WODC)

This trail leaves the upper end of the Old Mast Rd. (trail) about 2.5 mi. from the Ferncroft Rd. parking area, at junction with the Square Ledge and Walden trails. From this junction the Lawrence Trail heads east and in 0.3 mi. reaches Paugus Pass, where it is joined on the left (north) by the Oliverian Brook Trail from Albany Intervale and on the right (south) by the Kelley Trail. In another 0.3 mi. the Lawrence Trail reaches the Cabin Trail junction. Crossing to the east side of the ridge, it passes a *spring* on the north of the trail about 0.1 mi. beyond the Cabin Trail, and descends to the base of the Overhang (2100 ft.). From there it passes along the face of high, wooded cliffs, ascending, very steeply in places, a total of 420 ft. The trail follows the path of a rock slide, then descends 130 ft. into a hollow along the brook-bed. There is usually *water*, either in the trail or a few yards down the principal brookbed. The section of the trail between the overhang and the brookbed is rough and has steeper parts than any other trail on the Sandwich Range. It is marked with faded blue spots, which should be followed with care. A steep gravelly ascent leads through spruce woods to the upper plateau of Mt. Paugus, which the trail crosses to the highest edge of the south summit, marked by a cairn.

PAUGUS PASS AND VICINITY

Paugus Pass is a low point (2200 ft.) on the ridge connecting Mt. Passaconaway and the Wonalancet Range on the west with Mts. Paugus and Mexico on the east. The Lawrence Trail crosses it from west to east. The Kelley Trail ascends the valley to the south, and the Oliverian Brook Trail to the north. Both join the Lawrence Trail at the same point in the pass. The pass is also conveniently reached by the Old Mast Rd. (trail).

Cabin Trail (WODC)

This trail offers a route to Mt. Paugus via Whitin Ridge and the Lawrence Trail from the Wonalancet Farm district. The trail is reached by a short road leaving NH Rte. 113A about 0.3 mi. east of Wonalancet Farm (sign). Turn right at the first fork of the road and left just before it reaches a summer residence. Shortly after this the Big Rock Cave Trail diverges right. The Cabin Trail ascends to the height-of-land through open woods and is joined by Whitin Brook Trail. The Cabin Trail stays to the left on the side of Whitin Ridge for 0.4 mi. to its end at the Lawrence Trail. Follow the Lawrence Trail right for Mt. Paugus and left for Paugus Pass.

Cabin Trail (map 4)

Distances from NH Rte. 113A

to Whitin Brook Trail junction: *est.* 2.1 mi., 1½ hr.

to Mt. Paugus summit (via Lawrence Trail): *est.* 4.3 mi. (6.8 km.), 3½ hr.

Kelley Trail (WODC)

This trail leads to Paugus Pass en route for Albany Intervale and offers a route to Mt. Paugus via the Lawrence Trail. Giving access to interesting falls, bluffs, and wooded slopes in the ravine of Cold Brook, it leaves the new Ferncroft Rd. parking area and follows a well-constructed logging road (unauthorized vehicles prohibited) for the first 0.8 mi. It slabs up the ravine on the left, descending to the gully before the height-of-land. Here it joins the Lawrence and Oliverian Brook trails in Paugus Pass.

Kelley Trail (map 4)

Distance from Ferncroft Rd. parking area

to Lawrence Trail junction: *est.* 2.5 mi. (4 km.), 1¾ hr.

Oliverian Brook Trail (WMNF)

This trail, which runs from the Kancamagus Highway to
Paugus Pass, replaced the north part of the Old Mast Rd., which
was in large part destroyed by logging. Numerous old sections of
corduroy and ruined bridges have been replaced by ground trails.
With any of the southern trails described, it offers an easy route
between Wonalancet and the Albany Intervale region.

The trail leaves the Kancamagus Highway 0.2 mi. west of
Oliverian Brook and leads south up the west side of the stream.
At about 2 mi. the Passaconaway Cutoff diverges right (southwest). The Oliverian Brook Trail continues south and at 2.2 mi.
crosses a branch of Oliverian Brook from the west. A half-mile
farther on it crosses Oliverian Brook itself for the first of several
times in the course of a mile. This district is swampy. Just
beyond the swamp the Square Ledge Branch Trail diverges right
(sign) shortly after the trail crosses Square Ledge Brook. The
trail then crosses Oliverian Brook twice more and begins the
climb to Paugus Pass in earnest: the total altitude gain is about
950 ft.

The trail intersects the Lawrence Trail in the pass, from which
the most direct route to the Ferncroft parking area is by the Kelley
Trail. For Wonalancet Farm it is nearer to follow the Lawrence
Trail left, and then turn right down the Cabin Trail.

Oliverian Brook Trail (map 4)

Distances from Kancamagus Highway

to Square Ledge Branch Trail junction: 3.3 mi., 2 hr.

to Paugus Pass: 4.3 mi. (6.9 km.), 2¾ hr.

to NH Rte. 113A (via Kelley Trail): *est.* 6.8 mi., 3¾ hr.

Old Mast Road (WODC)

The Old Mast Rd. is said to have been built for hauling out the
tallest timbers as masts for the British navy. The south end of the
trail leaves from the Ferncroft Rd. parking area (park in designated area near the junction). Take the left gated road adjacent
to the parking area. In 0.3 mi. a brook is reached and the

Wonalancet Range Trail diverges left. The Old Mast Rd. continues straight ahead, ascending at an easy grade, skirting the east slope of Mt. Wonalancet. Follow the blue blazes along the line of the old lumber road. In about 2.3 mi. the Walden Trail to Mt. Passaconaway diverges left, the Lawrence Trail to Mt. Paugus diverges right, and the Square Ledge Trail continues straight ahead. The latter may be followed to Mt. Passaconaway or to Albany Intervale via Square Ledge Branch and Oliverian Brook trails.

Old Mast Rd. (map 4)

Distance from Ferncroft Rd. parking area

  to Lawrence Trail/Walden Trail junction: *est*. 2.3 mi. (3.5 km.), 1½ hr.

MOUNT PASSACONAWAY

This 4060-ft. mountain is named for the great chief of the Penacooks who ruled at the time the Pilgrims landed. It is densely wooded, but there are views from three outlooks practically at the summit. One, the true summit, can easily be reached by a short side trail where there is a view to the south. An arm of the mountain extends southeast to a 3140-ft sub-peak, unnamed on maps, sometimes called Mt. Hedgehog, although another Hedgehog Mountain is on the north ridge. To the east of the 3140-ft. peak is Paugus Pass, and the Wonalancet Range, with Mt. Hibbard and Mt. Wonalancet, extends to the southwest. Square Ledge is to the north of this arm, somewhat separated from it. Another ridge runs southwest to join the north ridge of Mt. Whiteface. The east spurs give Mt. Passaconaway the characteristic, step-like profile it has when viewed from the lake country to the south. From the south it can be ascended directly from Ferncroft or over the Wonalancet Range. From Albany Intervale to the north it can be ascended either directly or by longer routes over Square Ledge.

Dicey's Mill Trail (WODC)

The Dicey's Mill Trail was the earliest to be laid out on the mountain. Use the Ferncroft Rd. parking area and walk northwest on the unpaved Ferncroft Rd., which becomes a wood road after passing the last house. (The gate is not intended to keep out hikers.) The trail soon turns sharply right and climbs steeply for a short distance around a curve known as the "S." keeping some distance east of the main stream. The Wiggin Trail to Mt. Whiteface leaves on the left shortly. The site of Dicey's Mill (1980 ft.) is reached as the trail approaches Wonalancet Brook. The trail crosses to the west bank of the stream, and the steep part begins. It climbs the side of a ridge through some hardwoods with occasional views of the Wonalancet Range. At the ridge top the Rollins Trail from Mt. Whiteface enters left (at 3300 ft.). The Dicey's Mill Trail then climbs through a rough area and enters some spruce woods. Shortly before it reaches Camp Rich, where there is a fine *spring*, the East Loop diverges right (east) to join the Walden Trail. The Dicey's Mill Trail bears right (northeast) a short distance above this junction, about 20 yd. below the camp, and climbs to the west outlook, which is close to the top. A short trail leads to the east outlook and the start of Walden Trail. The true summit is reached by a short trail diverging to the right (south). There is an outlook to the south.

Camp Rich (WODC) is on the southwest side of the mountain on the Dicey's Mill Trail at about 3500 ft. elevation. It is an open, unequipped log shelter for eight.

Dicey's Mill Trail (map 4)

Distances from Ferncroft Rd. parking area

to Wiggin Trail junction: *est.* 2 mi., 1¼ hr.

to Rollins Trail junction: *est.* 3.8 mi., 2 hr. 50 min.

to Mt. Passaconaway summit: *est.* 4.3 mi. (6.8 km.), 3½ hr. (*descending* 2½ hr.)

Rollins Trail (WODC)

This trail from Mt. Whiteface to Mt. Passaconaway is rough in parts, with many ups and downs that are not evident from the contours on the map. Starting from the south summit of Mt. Whiteface just beyond and to the left (northwest) of the highest rock as one faces away from the cliff, the trail dips into the col beyond (north), passing Camp Shehadi. Here the Downes Brook Trail branches left connecting in 1 mi. with the Sleeper Trail for Mt. Tripyramid. From the camp the Rollins Trail climbs to the true, wooded summit of Mt. Whiteface, then follows the high, curving ridge with a series of small humps. This ridge forms the rim of a broad ravine known as "The Bowl." Shortly after leaving the col at the edge of the ravine, the trail passes a ledge at the base of which there is a small pool that sometimes contains *water*. At about 2.1 mi. from Mt. Whiteface, the Rollins Trail ends at the Dicey's Mill Trail approximately 0.3 mi. below Camp Rich. Follow the Dicey's Mill Trail to Mt. Passaconaway or Dicey's Mill Trail, and the East Loop to the Walden Trail.

Rollins Trail (map 4)

Distances from Mt. Whiteface, south summit

    to Camp Shehadi: *est.* 0.2 mi.

    to Mt. Whiteface, true summit; *est* 0.3 mi.

    to Dicey's Mill Trail junction: *est.* 2.1 mi. (3.5 km.), 1¾ hr.

Walden Trail (WODC)

This trail runs from the Old Mast Rd. to the east outlook on Mt. Passaconaway. It is a long and difficult route up from Wonalancet but the most direct route from Mt. Paugus. Its lower end can be reached from Wonalancet by the Old Mast Rd., which it leaves on the west (left) just north of the height-of-land. After leaving the Old Mast Rd., the trail ascends the steep east side of the Wonalancet Range. Near the top of the range often called Mt. Hedgehog (3140 ft.), the Wonalancet Range Trail diverges left (south). The Walden Trail swings right, descends, and crosses a deep col. At the bottom of the col the trail passes *water* and climbs an unnamed shoulder, the steepest and roughest part of the trail. The blue blazes should be followed with care, avoiding abandoned routes blocked by wood or brush piled at intersections. The trail descends the west side of the shoulder and, after crossing a col, is joined by the Square Ledge Trail right. Shortly the East Loop diverges left. This may be followed as an alternative route to the summit of Mt. Passaconaway via Camp Rich, where there is a *spring*. The Walden Trail branches right up the mountain, crosses a rocky brookbed where there is sometimes *water*, climbs to the cone by a steep gully, and comes out at the east outlook. A short trail leads to the west outlook.

Walden Trail (map 4)

Distances from Ferncroft Rd. parking area

    to start of Walden Trail (via Old Mast Rd.): *est.* 2.4 mi., 1½ hr.

    to 3140-ft. summit, Wonalancet Range: *est.* 3.3 mi., 2¼ hr.

    to Mt. Passaconaway summit: *est.* 5 mi. (8 km.), 4 hr.

Passaconaway Cutoff (WMNF)

The Passaconaway Cutoff branches to the southwest from the Oliverian Brook Trail about 2 mi. south of the Kancamagus Highway. In about 2 more mi. and about a mile from the summit of Mt. Passaconaway it joins the Square Ledge Trail, which can be followed west to the Walden Trail and so to the top.

Leaving the Oliverian Brook Trail, the cutoff follows an old logging road for about 0.5 mi., then turns sharp left off the logging road, and within 100 yd. drops to a major tributary of Oliverian Brook, which it immediately crosses. The trail follows another logging road on the other side in a southwest direction. In about 0.5 mi. more, just before returning to the brook, the trail turns sharp left and climbs steeply up the hillside to the crest of a small narrow ridge. The cliffs of Hedgehog Mountain are visible backward through the trees. From here the trail has been re-located away from the brook. There is *no water* on this section of the new trail.

Passaconaway Cutoff (map 4)

Distances from Kancamagus Highway

    to start of Passaconaway Cutoff (via Oliverian Brook Trail): *est.* 2 mi., 50 min.

to Square Ledge Trail junction: *est*. 4 mi., 2½ hr.
to Mt. Passaconaway summit (via Square Ledge Trail and
   Walden Trail): *est*. 5 mi. (8 km.), 4 hr.

THE WONALANCET RANGE

This small range is a southwest ridge of Mt. Passaconaway. It
consists of three low, rounded summits, from southwest to
northeast: Wonalancet proper (about 2800 ft.), Hibbard (2900
ft.), and the highest, sometimes called Hedgehog, (3140 ft.).
The summits are all wooded, but there are ledges that offer good
views, especially of the Ossipee Mountains and Lake Winnipesaukee to the south and east.

Wonalancet Range Trail (WODC)

From the Ferncroft Rd. parking area off NH Rte. 113A, follow
the Old Mast Rd. north to the first brook. The Wonalancet Range
Trail branches left (sign) just before the brook crossing. It leaves
the brook and slabs across the slope to an old lumber road. It soon
leaves the wood road and slowly ascends the east side of Wonalancet. Just under the ledges *water* is sometimes found. The trail
skirts right of the steeper ledges and comes out near the top. From
here there is a good view to the south and east. The trail continues
over the wooded summit of Mt. Wonalancet, along the ridge to
Mt. Hibbard, where there is a good view to the southwest, then to
the 3140-ft. high point. Just beyond, the Wonalancet Range Trail
ends at its junction with the Walden Trail. Follow the Walden
Trail left to ascend Mt. Passaconaway, right to descend to the
Old Mast Rd. and return to the parking area.

Wonalancet Range Trail (map 4)

Distances from Ferncroft Rd. parking area

to Mt. Wonalancet summit: *est*. 1.8 mi., 1½ hr.
to 3140-ft. high point: *est*. 3.5 mi., 3 hr.
to Ferncroft Rd. parking area (via Walden Trail and Old Mast
   Rd.): *est*. 6.8 mi. (11 km.), 4½ hr.

SQUARE LEDGE

This is a bold, rocky promontory about 1 mi. to the north of the southeast arm of Mt. Passaconaway.

From the Kancamagus Highway about 0.5 mi. west of the WMNF Passaconaway Information Station (Albany Intervale), Square Ledge is reached by following the Oliverian Brook Trail 3.3 mi. to the Square Ledge Branch Trail, which branches sharply west (right) and ascends to meet the Square Ledge Trail, which leads to the ledge.

Square Ledge (map 4)

Distance to Square Ledge
   from Kancamagus Highway (via Oliverian Brook Trail, Square Ledge Branch Trail, and Square Ledge Trail): 4.2 mi. (6.8 km.), 2¾ hr.

Square Ledge Trail (WODC)

This trail starts at the junction of the Old Mast Rd. and the Lawrence Trail. It descends from the height-of-land, crossing two small brooks, just before the second of which the Square Ledge Branch Trail diverges east (right) to join the Oliverian Brook Trail. A short distance farther, the main trail makes a sharp turn west (left) to ascend the ledge. It bears east for a short distance, then climbs steeply to the summit. A spur leads off the trail 20 yd. to a ledge with a fine view across the valley. Leaving the ledge the trail ascends an unnamed hump, and then descends to a brook valley, where at the site of a logging camp, the Passaconaway Cutoff to the Kancamagus Highway diverges right. There is usually *water* in the brook. The trail follows an old lumber road, crosses a slide, and climbs steeply to meet the Walden Trail, which may be followed to the summit of Mt. Passaconaway.

Square Ledge Trail (map 4)

Distances from Old Mast Rd./Lawrence Trail junction
   to Square Ledge: *est.* 1.5 mi., 1 hr.
   to Walden Trail junction: *est.* 3.3 mi. (5.3 km.), 2½ hr.

HEDGEHOG MOUNTAIN

This small, 2520-ft. mountain is situated north of Mt. Passaconaway, between the latter and the Swift River Valley. It should be distinguished from the 3140-ft. summit that is sometimes called "Mt. Hedgehog" in the Wonalancet Range not more than 3 mi. away (in a direct line). Hedgehog Mountain separates the valley of Oliverian Brook on its east from that of Downes Brook on its west. There is a ravine on the northeast side of the mountain. Allen's Ledge on its lower north lip gives views to the east and north. Ledges near the summit and on the east shoulder give interesting views in other directions.

UNH Trail (WMNF)

This is a loop trail onto Hedgehog Mountain that leaves the south side of the Kancamagus Highway at a wood road about 0.3 mi. east of the WMNF Passaconaway Campground. About 200 yd. south of the highway there is a fork. The left fork goes to the E. Ledges (2 mi.). The right fork is the trail to Allen's Ledge (1 mi.) and the summit (2 mi.). On approaching Allen's Ledge the trail to the summit turns sharp right (south) 100 ft. before and in sight of Allen's Ledge.

The left fork follows an old logging road. At just over 1.0 mi. the trail ascends moderately over a softwood ridge. A small *stream (reliable water),* is crossed at 1.6 mi. The trail shortly swings left (yellow paint on the rocks) to a view north and east, then bears right to reach the summit of the E. Ledges with fine views south and east.

The trail from the E. Ledges to the summit (1 mi.) follows along the top of the cliffs on the south face, enters the woods under the steep ledgy south side of the summit, and bears gradually toward the north onto the west slope of the summit, which it climbs in a short series of switchbacks to join the trail from Allen's Ledge at the summit.

UNH Trail (map 4)

Distances from Kancamagus Highway

   to Hedgehog Mountain summit via left fork and E. Ledges: 3 mi.

   to Hedgehog Mountain summit via right fork and Allen's Ledge: 2 mi.

   to Kancamagus Highway (round trip via E. Ledges, summit, and Allen's Ledge): 5 mi. (8 km.), 4 hr.

MOUNT POTASH

Mt. Potash (2660 ft.) separates the valley of Downes Brook on its east from that of Sabbaday Brook on its west. A ledge on a prominent hump on its northeast shoulder gives views to the east and northeast. The summit is open and ledgy and affords excellent views of the valley and surrounding mountains in all directions.

Mount Potash Trail (WMNF)

Start on the Downes Brook Trail, which leaves the Kancamagus Highway on the south side opposite the entrance to the Passaconaway Campground. In 0.1 mi. the Mt. Potash Trail leaves sharp right and, heading generally southwest, shortly crosses Downes Brook. After crossing the brook the trail bears slightly left. In about 1.5 mi. it emerges on open ledges on the shoulder of the mountain. Leaving the ledges, turn sharply right into the woods. The route over the open ledges below the summit is marked with yellow paint. In descending, use caution in following the marked route on the rock slabs just below the summit.

Mt. Potash Trail (map 4)

Distances from Kancamagus Highway

   to Mt. Potash shoulder (via Downes Brook Trail): *est.* 1.5 mi., 1¼ hr.

   to Mt. Potash summit: *est.* 2 mi., 1¾ hr.

MOUNT WHITEFACE

Mt. Whiteface doubtless received its name because of the precipitous ledges south of its open summit. The backbone of this 4015-ft. mountain runs northeast, continuing as a prominent ridge connecting it with Mt. Passaconaway. The Rollins Trail lies on this ridge. There are two ridges on the south; the Blueberry Ledge Trail is on the easterly one, and the McCrillis Trail is on the westerly. Sleeper Ridge, upon which are two rounded humps, runs northwest toward Mt. Tripyramid.

The highest point on the mountain is wooded. Nearly as high is a magnificent viewpoint about 0.5 mi. south of it, at the top of the precipices. There is a *spring (water unreliable)* near a ledgy summit a few yards northeast on the Blueberry Ledge Trail. Camp Heermance and Camp Shehadi are open shelters near the summit.

A memorial tablet to the Reverend Martin Luther King, Jr., was dedicated at the viewpoint on Good Friday 1968, but later removed by persons and for reasons unknown.

Blueberry Ledge Trail (WODC)

The usual route to ascend Mt. Whiteface from Wonalancet, this trail was opened in 1899. Marked with blue paint, it leaves from the Ferncroft Rd. parking area in Wonalancet(park in designated area). Walk northwest along Ferncroft Rd. past the first private house. At the second private house, cross the brook on "Squirrel Bridge" and continue along a private unpaved road. Follow the main dirt road, avoiding driveways, for about 0.1 mi. to an open area near a house. The main trail enters the woods (sign) and follows an old road, soon crossing the abandoned Quimby Hill ski slope. In 100 yd. the Blueberry Ledge Cutoff diverges right to rejoin the main trail at the ledges. (In 0.4 mi. pass on left signs for the McCrillis Trail, now badly overgrown on the north half, which formerly connected to the McCrillis Trail that ascends Whiteface from Whiteface Intervale.)

The Blueberry Ledge Trail continues along flat ground past a swampy area and then climbs to the open ledges where it is marked by blazes and cairns. Above, it ascends gently through open hardwoods and then rises steeply to Wonalancet Outlook (about 3000 ft.). It next climbs sharply to the top of the ridge, drops slightly into a hollow to a junction with the Wiggin Trail on the right, and ascends a rough and somewhat difficult rocky ridge to the summit.

Descending, the top of the trail will be found about 8 yd. back from the top of the cliff on the east side. It passes a *spring (water unreliable)* about 20 yd. southeast of Camp Heermance.

Blueberry Ledge Trail (map 4)

Distances from Ferncroft Rd. parking area

   to foot of ledges: 0.9 mi., ¾ hr.

   to Mt. Whiteface summit (cliff top): 3.6 mi. (5.8 km.), 3½ hr.

Camp Heermance (WODC)

This camp was built in 1912 and rebuilt in 1932. It is in a partially sheltered spot near the summit of Mt. Whiteface, about 20 yd. north of the *spring (water unreliable)* at the top of Blueberry Ledge Trail. It is an open shelter accommodating six.

Camp Shehadi (WODC)

This shelter for six replaced an earlier shelter here in 1930. It is at the junction of the Rollins and Downes Brook trails, 0.2 mi. north of the open ledges on Mt. Whiteface. The *nearest reliable water* is some distance down the Downes Brook Trail.

Wiggin Trail (WODC)

This trail, cut in 1895, leaves the Dicey's Mill Trail on the left a short distance south of the old mill site. It crosses the stream and, bearing left, ascends a little knoll, crosses a small brook, and bears right again. Very steep in parts, it justifies its nickname, "The Fire Escape." It joins the Blueberry Ledge Trail about 0.5 mi. below the summit of Mt. Whiteface.

Wiggin Trail (map 4)

Distances from Ferncroft Rd. parking area

> *to* start of Wiggin Trail (via Dicey's Mill Trail): *est.* 1.8 mi., 1 hr. 10 min.
>
> *to* Blueberry Ledge Trail junction: *est.* 3 mi., 2¾ hr.
>
> *to* Mt. Whiteface summit (via Blueberry Ledge Trail): *est.* 3.5 mi. (5.5 km.), 3½ hr.

McCrillis Trail (WMNF)

There are two trails in the Whiteface-Wonalancet region designated by this name. One trail (now completely overgrown and posted "No Trespassing," in the west half) once connected Whiteface Intervale to the lower end of the Blueberry Ledge Trail in Wonalancet. The trail described here is the second one, which leads to the summit of Mt. Whiteface from Whiteface Intervale, This trail initially follows the Flat Mountain Pond Trail, which leaves the Whiteface Intervale Rd. near the bridge over White Brook and the road to a brick house. The McCrillis Trail leaves the Flat Mountain Pond Trail at 0.5 mi. from the start, follows the west bank of White Brook, crosses a tributary, then follows a logging road. It climbs noticeably until it passes the first ridge, then runs nearly level for about 0.5 mi. At about 1.3 mi. it crosses the Waterville town line (WMNF boundary). In another 0.3 mi. it descends very gradually into a swampy area where a brook starts, and where there may be *water* in wet seasons. The trail then ascends for about 1.3 mi. to the first ledges, which are about at the level of the bottom of the cliffs and almost due west from them. Cairns mark the trail across the rocks. It ascends steeply north through small spruce and crosses a narrow ledge to the east ending only about 50 yd. from the Mt. Whiteface summit. At the east end the great cliffs fall away to the south, providing fine views. The trail reaches the south summit from the southwest.

Descending, walk from the highest rock southwest 40 yd. to the lower edge of the top ledges, visible from the south summit;

turn right (west) 10 yd. along a rock to the small patch of conifers and follow the blazes.

McCrillis Trail (map 4)

Distances from Whiteface Intervale Rd.

> *to* start of McCrillis Trail (via Flat Mountain Pond Trail): 0.5 mi.
>
> *to* Mt. Whiteface south summit (cliff top): 3.6 mi. (5.8 km.), 3¼ hr.

Downes Brook Trail (WMNF)

The summit of Mt. Whiteface may be reached from the Albany Intervale by going over Mt. Passaconaway or, more directly, by the Downes Brook Trail. The trail leaves the Kancamagus Highway on the south side, opposite the entrance to the WMNF Passaconaway Campground. It follows the valley of Downes Brook, generally south and southwest. At about 0.1 mi. the trail to Mt. Potash leaves right. The Downes Brook Trail crosses the brook four times in the first 2 mi. It continues up the valley, crossing the brook repeatedly, taking the branch leading toward the brook at every fork. Farther on, it follows an old slide, which destroyed the old logging road, but beyond the slide it resumes the old road on the west bank of the brook. The trail ascends to the broad plateau between Mt. Tripyramid and Mt. Whiteface, where it meets the southeast terminus of the Sleeper Trail. Follow the Sleeper Trail left (east) for Camp Shehadi, the Rollins Trail, and the summit of Mt. Whiteface.

Downes Brook Trail (map 4)

Distances from Kancamagus Highway

> *to* Sleeper Trail junction: *est.* 5 mi.
>
> *to* Mt. Whiteface summit (via Sleeper Trail) *est.* 6 mi. (9.5 km.), 4½ hr.

Sleeper Trail

The Sleeper Trail to Mt. Tripyramid is described in Section 10.

FLAT MOUNTAIN PONDS

The two ponds (2311 ft.) are connected by a narrow water area, with a dam at the south end. They lie about 2.5 mi. southwest of Mt. Whiteface, between the two low summits of Flat Mountain. One rounded summit (2940 ft.) is southeast of the ponds. The north summit (3300 ft.) is 2 mi. west. The area is recovering from lumbering begun in 1920 and an extensive fire in 1923. There is a WMNF shelter (capacity eight) at the south end of the ponds.

The ponds may be reached by ascending the Guinea Pond Trail to the northeast from the Sandwich Notch Rd. (see Section 19) from the Bennett Street Trail, or by the Flat Mountain Pond Trail.

Flat Mountain Pond Trail (WMNF)

The trail to the ponds leaves Whiteface Intervale Rd. near the bridge over White Brook and the road to a brick house. The trail enters the woods where at 0.5 mi. the McCrillis Trail to the summit of Mt. Whiteface leaves right. The trail shortly follows an old wood road and in about 0.3 mi. comes in sight of White-face River (left). About 1.3 mi. beyond, at a clearing, it crosses a branch stream and bears left following the main river. The trail continues to follow the stream, bearing generally northwest and crossing several tributaries. Near the source of the stream on the side of Flat Mountain, the trail crosses to the west bank and ascends a ridge, crossing two more tributaries. It follows the ridge until it reaches the burned-over divide at the top, and a short distance farther, a swampy area at the east end of upper Flat Mountain Pond. The trail continues around the north and then the west side of the ponds, and at their south end coincides with an old logging railroad.

At this point a side trail left (east) leads in 50 yd. to the WMNF Flat Mountain Pond Shelter. The trail then continues along the old logging railroad bed, makes several brook crossings, crosses

the Bennett Street Trail, then the Gleason Trail. It continues
south, still along the railroad bed, to a junction with the Guinea
Pond Trail, at which point it turns sharp left (east), leaves the
railroad, and soon descends with the Guinea Pond Trail to Jose's
bridge. Jose's bridge may also be reached by turning left on
either the Bennett Street or Gleason trails.

Flat Mountain Pond Trail (map 4)

Distances from Whiteface Intervale Rd.

   to McCrillis Trail junction: 0.5 mi., ¼ hr.

   to Flat Mountain Pond: 4.2 mi., 2¾ hr.

   to Guinea Pond Trail junction: 8.1 mi., 4¾ hr.

   to Jose's bridge: 9 mi. (14.5 km.), 5 hr.

SANDWICH MOUNTAIN

This 3993-ft. mountain, also known as Black Mountain, a
name also given to a lower peak on the ridge southwest, is
described in Section 10. It may be climbed from the west by trails
starting on the Mad River Rd. or the Sandwich Notch Rd. (see
Section 19). The two trails next described reach the summit from
the east side.

Bennett Street Trail (WODC)

At the upper end of Bennett Street at Jose's bridge, proceed
west on the road where the sign points to the WMNF. The
Bennett Street Trail leaves right in 300 yd. The junction is
marked with blue paint. It is a series of logging roads, with
connecting links of trail, and is marked throughout by blue
blazes, which should be followed with care, especially descending. This trail is overgrown, particularly in the middle sections
(1982). The route follows a logging road on the southwest bank
of Cold Brook, crossing several small streams flowing east. In
0.5 mi. the Gleason Trail diverges left. After a little over 1 mi.
the Bennett Street Trail leaves Cold Brook, ascends a smaller
stream, and then climbs steeply about 0.5 mi. to Flat Mountain

Pond Trail, which follows an abandoned lumber railroad bed. Cross the railroad and ascend a steep bank. The Bennett Street Trail then ascends for about 0.5 mi. through hardwood and spruce to a logging road, which follows right (north) and soon comes to a fine *spring*. It follows the logging road for about 1.5 mi., crossing two small streams, then climbs by connecting logging roads to the depression between the south spur and the main summit of Sandwich Mountain. Here the Gleason Trail enters left. The trail crosses a ridge of the east, wooded summit and after 0.3 mi. reaches a *spring (water unreliable)*. At the spring, turn left on an old logging road, which reaches the site of an old cabin in about 0.1 mi. (there is occasionally *water* under a rock 20 yd. northeast), and the summit 0.1 mi. beyond.

Descending, the trail leads northeast from the grassy place just south of the summit (sign "Whiteface Intervale"). Below, at the railroad, turn left (north) 30 yd. to a turn to the right down the bank.

Bennett Street Trail (map 4)
Distance from Bennett St., Jose's bridge
  to Sandwich Mountain summit: *est.* 4 mi., 3-4 hr.

Gleason Trail (AMC)

This trail branches left from the Bennett Street Trail at 0.8 mi., follows an old logging road through a hardwood forest, crosses a stream, then crosses several recently used logging roads. At 0.5 mi. the trail crosses Flat Mountain Pond Trail (abandoned railroad, no signs) follows a logging road very briefly, then branches right until it shortly meets another logging road. It goes left along this road, takes a fork right, and climbs moderately for about 0.5 mi., sometimes along logging roads, until it comes to a *spring* by the main brook down the east side of the mountain. Here it turns right and within 0.2 mi. climbs steeply to another logging road, follows it left briefly, climbs steeply again to another logging road, and goes right on it for a short distance. The trail then angles left and climbs through conifers. After another mile the trail ascends gradually for 0.4 mi. to its junction with the Bennett Street Trail near the col between the eastern ridge of Sandwich Mountain and its summit.

Descending, follow the Bennett Street Trail for about 0.5 mi. Shortly after crossing the eastern ridge of the mountain, the Gleason Trail diverges right.

Gleason Trail (map 4)

Distances from lower junction with Bennett Street Trail

to upper junction with Bennett Street Trail: 2.1 mi., 2¼ hr.

to Sandwich Mountain summit (via Bennett Street Trail from upper junction): *est.* 2.6 mi., 2¾ hr.

MOUNT TRIPYRAMID

Besides the well-known north and south slides on this mountain (see Section 10), two smaller ones come down from the ridge north of the middle peak into a branch of Sabbaday Brook. Either offers a route of ascent from Passaconaway and the chance for a strong climber to cross to Waterville. The trails on the west side are described in Section 10. From the Passaconaway Campground a ridge, whose north slope blends so closely with the slope of N. Tripyramid that it can be distinguished only by looking carefully on a clear day, lies between the observer and Mt. Tripyramid. Parties have ascended this ridge only to find themselves still separated from Mt. Tripyramid by a long, scrubby ridge, hence the name "The Foolkiller."

Sabbaday Brook Trail (WMNF)

The Sabbaday Brook Trail leaves the Kancamagus Highway on the south about 100 yd. west of the bridge across Sabbaday Brook at the WMNF Sabbaday Falls picnic area. In 0.4 mi. a short path left leads down to Sabbaday Falls, a picturesque series of cascades in a narrow flume. The area within a quarter-mile of each side of this trail as far as the falls is in a Restricted Use Area (see Section 22).

The main trail for Mt. Tripyramid continues up the west bank of the brook. In the next 0.8 mi. it crosses the brook three times (the first two can be avoided by staying on the west bank of the brook for 0.1 mi.) and then follows an old logging road on the east side for about 2 mi. At about 2100 ft. the trail turns sharply right, descends, crosses Sabbaday Brook (fourth crossing), and continues on this (now north) side of the main stream up the valley between Mt. Tripyramid and the south end of the Foolkiller for about 0.8 mi., gradually turning in a more northerly direction. A short distance beyond a slide on the Foolkiller at the right, and after crossing the brook for the last time, the Tripyramid slides are seen on the left. The slide to the right (north) occurred in 1924.

The trail ascends the first and older slide and leads to its upper left corner. *Caution.* The slide up Tripyramid is dangerous for travel in wet weather, due to loose rock and sand. The path shortly enters thicker woods, and after some distance ends at the upper terminus of the Pine Bend Brook Trail in the col between the north and middle peaks of Mt. Tripyramid, at a point 0.3 mi. north of the middle peak. There is *no water* beyond the foot of the slide.

Sabbaday Brook Trail (map 4)
Distances from Kancamagus Highway

to Sabbaday Falls: 0.4 mi., ¼ hr.

to fourth crossing, Sabbaday Brook: 3 mi., 2 hr.

to Pine Bend Brook Trail junction: 4.3 mi., 3¼ hr.

to Mt. Tripyramid, North Peak (via Pine Bend Brook Trail): 4.8 mi. (7.7 km.), 3¾ hr.

Pine Bend Brook Trail (WMNF)

This trail leaves the Kancamagus Highway 2.4 mi. west of the WMNF Passaconaway Campground, shortly enters the old railroad grade, then leaves it left to follow old logging roads up Pine Bend Brook for about 1.5 mi. (*last sure water*). It then turns right, descending gently to another brook, which it follows up for about 0.5 mi. Leaving this brook *(water unreliable)* it bears left, climbs more steeply up an easterly spur of the main ridge, and follows the crest of this spur to the main ridge connecting N. Tripyramid and Scaur Peak. On the ridge the Scaur Ridge Trail leaves right (west) for the Livermore Rd. and Waterville Valley. From this junction the trail ascends generally southeast to the summit of N. Tripyramid, continues ahead along the ridge, and ends at the upper terminus of the Sabbaday Brook Trail, at a point 0.5 mi. south of the north peak.

Pine Bend Brook Trail (map 4)

Distances from Kancamagus Highway

   to Scaur Ridge Trail junction: 3 mi., 2 hr. 10 min.

   to Mt. Tripyramid, North Peak: 3.8 mi., 2 hr. 50 min.

   to Sabbaday Brook Trail junction: 4.3 mi. (6.9 km.), 3¼ hr.

Conway, Bartlett, and Jackson

North Conway, Intervale, Bartlett, and Jackson are convenient climbing centers in the upper Saco Valley area. From them US Rte. 302 (Crawford Notch Highway) leads to Crawford Notch, NH Rte. 16 (Pinkham Notch Highway) to Pinkham Notch and the Mt. Washington Range, and NH Rte. 112 (Kancamagus Highway) to trails on the north side of the Sandwich Range. The trails in the Jackson area are the last group in this section. Refer to map 7, Carter-Mahoosuc; map 4, Chocorua-Waterville; and map 6, the Mt. Washington Range, or to the USGS North Conway quad.

MOUNT KEARSARGE NORTH AND BARTLETT MOUNTAIN

Mt. Kearsarge North (3268 ft.), formerly called Pequawket, is in Bartlett and Chatham, the town line being near the summit. The view from the summit is one of the best in the mountains.

The Pequawkets were a famous tribe of Indians who once inhabited the intervales of Conway and Fryeburg. The mountain first appeared on the map under the name Kearsarge in 1784. It did not become the official name of the mountain, however, until 1957.

The fire tower on the summit was erected in 1951. There is a *spring* about 100 yd. below the summit on the abandoned telephone line that parallels the Mt. Kearsarge North Trail near the summit. The Weeks Brook Trail also ascends the mountain, from the east side (see Section 15).

Bartlett Mountain (2661 ft.) is a part of the same mountain mass, extending westward toward Intervale. The lower range of hills extending northeast from the summit includes Mt. Shaw (2566 ft.) and the Gemini (2493 ft. and 2495 ft. respectively). The Green Hills of Conway — Hurricane Mountain (2101 ft.), Black Cap Mountain (2370 ft.), Peaked Mountain (1734 ft.),

Middle Mountain (1850 ft.), Cranmore Mountain (1700 ft.), and Rattlesnake Mountain (1550 ft.) — stretch away to the south.

Mt. Kearsarge North Trail (WMNF)

This trail to the summit of Mt. Kearsarge North leaves the north side of Hurricane Mountain Rd. 0.4 mi. east of Kearsarge Village. It heads generally north and gains only 200 ft. in altitude in the first 0.5 mi. It then becomes steeper, passes a *spring* about halfway up, and about 0.5 mi. beyond reaches some ledges with views south. After crossing the saddle between Mt. Kearsarge North and Bartlett Mountain, the trail bears well around to the north side of the mountain, then south again, and, marked by cairns and paint, climbs the bare ledges to the summit.

Mt. Kearsarge North Trail (map 7)

Distances from Hurricane Mountain Rd.

to ledges: 2 mi., 1 hr., 50 min.

to Mt. Kearsarge North summit: 3 mi. (4.8 km.), 2¾ hr.

THE GREEN HILLS

The names and altitudes of this range of small mountains that stretch south from Mt. Kearsarge North are listed above. They may be traversed without trails, although trails lead from Hurricane Mountain Rd. to Hurricane and Black Cap mountains. The Skimobile is on Cranmore Mountain.

Hurricane Mountain Road

The western terminus of this paved road leaves NH Rte. 16 in Intervale just north of the railroad crossing, rises steeply at first, and then goes straight ahead through Kearsarge Village and soon begins the rather steep climb over the ridge. It descends to the S. Chatham Rd. about 2 mi. southwest of Kimball Ponds.

Hurricane Mountain Rd. (map 7)

Distances from NH Rte. 16, Intervale

to Kearsarge Village: 1.5 mi.

to height-of-land: 4 mi.
to S. Chatham Rd.: 6 mi. (9.6 km.)

Hurricane Mountain

Just west of the height-of-land on Hurricane Mountain Rd., a road, reported to be somewhat overgrown, leaves the north side. Follow this for about 0.3 mi. and bear right onto trail that leads to open ledges and the north end of the wooded summit. (Total distance: about 0.5 mi.)

Black Cap Mountain

This bare summit affords the best views in the Green Hills range. A few steps west of the height-of-land on Hurricane Mountain Rd. a sign on the south side indicates the trail. It passes through spruce, then beech forest. At the foot of the ledges a trail leaves right for the Cranmore Skimobile. There is no *water* on the trail. (Total distance: 1.2 mi.)

Peaked Hill

This 1734-ft. sharp, rocky knoll, bare except for a few small pines, affords good views. From NH Rte. 16 near North Conway, take Artist's Falls Rd., then right on Woodland Rd. to its end at a small reservoir (parking). The start of the trail is marked by a cairn below the fence on the downstream side of the reservoir. In 25 yd. it crosses the brook at a small flume, continues straight for a few yards, then bears rather sharply left and continues ahead. Almost level at first, after bearing right, it ascends fairly steeply to the top of the first ledges. Just below the crest at a large cairn a loop along the ledges diverges sharp right, and the main trail continues straight. The ledge loop is by far the more attractive and best way to ascend. It follows along the top of the ledges for about 0.3 mi., then in a small hollow at a fallen pine swings left, ascending steeply over ledges, through a narrow belt of woods, and over ledges again to an almost level grassy shelf. Here it shortly turns left, descending slightly to a wooded hollow, where it meets the main trail indicated by a small arrow worded "down." Another arrow worded "top" indicates the short continuation to the summit. In returning, it is better to follow the main trail, more gradual and well marked by cairns and some ribbons, to the junction with the loop. (Total distance about 2 mi., 2 hr. round trip.)

MOAT MOUNTAIN

This long irregular ridge lies west of the Saco River nearly opposite N. Conway. N. Moat (3201 ft.), the top of Red Ridge (2750 ft.), Middle Moat (2802 ft.), and S. Moat (2772 ft.) make up the main ridge. All were completely burned over several decades ago. There are still numerous open ledges with fine views. A shoulder consisting of several clustered peaks to the west is known as W. Moat (Big Attitash), and is reached by the Attitash Trail. Refer to map 4, Chocorua-Waterville, and to the USGS N. Conway quadrangle.

Moat Mountain Trail (WMNF)

This trail reaches the highest summit, N. Moat, from the east. (See the lower right corner of map 6, the Mt. Washington Range, for the start of the trail.) From Conway take Passaconaway Rd., or from N. Conway take the road just north of the Eastern Slope Inn. Drive west across the Saco River. Take West Side Rd. north to 0.7 mi. north of the road to Cathedral Ledge. Turn left into gravel road between farm fields and park. Continue on foot about 0.5 mi. to the clearing just below Diana's Baths mill site. The main path leaves the upper end of the clearing, close to the Baths, by a logging road, which follows the north bank of Lucy Brook for about 0.5 mi. and then forks (sign). The left branch (Red Ridge Trail) crosses the brook and continues to Red Ridge; the right is the main trail to N. Moat.

The Moat Mountain Trail crosses a swampy area, follows the south bank of Lucy Brook for 1 mi., then turns abruptly left, uphill away from the stream (*last sure water*), while the Attitash Trail continues straight ahead to W. Moat. In about 0.3 mi. the trail emerges and follows yellow blazes over some ledges. The trail continues up through the woods. After passing through scrub on the shoulder at the foot of the cone a path leads west (right) 50 yd. to a *spring* (*water unreliable*).

From the summit of N. Moat the trail descends southeast to about 2630 ft., then climbs easily to the top of Red Ridge (2750 ft.), where the Red Ridge Trail leaves left (east) for Lucy Brook and Diana's Baths. The Moat Mountain Trail continues generally southeast, descending to a col (2450 ft.) before continuing up to Middle Moat and down the ridge for about 0.5 mi. to S. Moat, from where it descends to Dugway Rd.

To locate the southern (Dugway Rd.) trailhead, from opposite NH Rte. 153 in Conway, drive north on Passaconaway Rd., which becomes West Side Rd. Go left at a fork, then left on Still Rd. which becomes Dugway Rd. The Moat Mountain Trail leaves Dugway Rd. about 3.5 mi. from Conway (sign).

Moat Mountain Trail (map 6, map 4)

Distances from West Side Rd.

to Diana's Baths: *est.* 0.5 mi., ¼ hr.

to Red Ridge Trail junction: 1.1 mi., ½ hr.

to last sure water: est. 2.3 mi., 1 ¼ hr.

to N. Moat Mountain summit: *est.* 4.3 mi., 3 hr.

to top of Red Ridge: *est.* 5.5 mi., 3 ¾ hr.

to Middle Moat Mountain summit: *est.* 6.5 mi., 4 ½ hr.

to S. Moat Mountain summit: *est.* 7.3 mi., 5 hr.

to Dugway Rd.: *est.* 9.5 mi. (15.3 km.), 6 ¼ hr.

Red Ridge Trail (WMNF)

This trail branches left from the Moat Mountain Trail 0.6 mi. from Diana's Baths and immediately crosses Lucy Brook. It runs generally south by west up a gentle grade, reaching Red Ridge Link on the left in about 0.7 mi., then continues almost level. At about 1.5 mi. from the Moat Mountain Trail the trail turns right (west), just before a red-blazed WMNF boundary. An old road and an abandoned trail continue ahead. This area is covered with rounded stones, and a branch of Moat Brook flows underground here, at least in some periods. The trail follows the brookbed up for about 0.5 mi., then crosses the brook (*last sure water*) and ascends the wooded slope of Red Ridge, rather steeply for the first 0.3 mi. Passing alternately through scrub and over ledges, it emerges and winds up the crest of the bare ridge to its top, where it rejoins the Moat Mountain Trail on the main Moat ridge at an unnamed subpeak (2750 ft.).

Red Ridge Trail (map 4)

Distances from West Side Rd.

to start of Red Ridge Trail (via Moat Mountain Trail): 1.1 mi., ½ hr.

to Red Ridge Link Trail junction: 1.8 mi., 1 hr.

to right turn uphill at WMNF boundary: 2.6 mi., 1 ½ hr.

to Moat Mountain Trail junction: 4.7 mi. (7.6 km.), 3 ½ hr.

WEST MOAT MOUNTAIN

This mountain, called Big Attitash on the USGS N. Conway quandrangle, has several summits, the three highest are 2938, 2882 and 2884 ft. The most easterly is the highest; it is wooded to the top and separated from N. Moat by a deep, wooded col. The other summits bear patches of the original forest but for the most part have been burned and logged. The present growth, containing much spruce, permits only partial views. From a scenic standpoint, N. Moat is far superior. The mountain may be reached from Diana's Baths or from the Bear Notch Rd. by the Attitash Trail.

Attitash Trail (WMNF)

The Attitash Trail is the route from Bear Notch Rd. over Table Mountain and W. Moat Mountain to Diana's Baths. It leaves Bear Notch Rd. on an old logging road at Louisville Brook, about 2.5 mi. south of Bartlett. In about 0.3 mi. the trail turns right, leaving the logging road, and ascends close to Louisville Brook (right) for some distance. It continues to climb in a southerly direction to the col between Bear and Table mountains where, turning left, it follows the route of the former Bear Mountain Trail. It then bears sharp left (north), then shortly right (east), and passes close to but south of the summit of Table Mountain (2663 ft.). Its south ledges offer fine views. A little farther the trail turns left (northeast) and follows along a broad ridge toward a peak labeled "2884" on map 4. About a mile farther the trail passes left of the summit of W. Moat, turns right, crosses peak "2938," and descends in an easterly direction into the col between W. Moat and N. Moat, where it turns northeast, descends sharply for about a mile, and crosses Lucy Brook four times, the fourth shortly before it ends where the Moat Mountain Trail enters right on the south side of Lucy Brook

Attitash Trail (map 4, map 6)
Distances from Bear Notch Rd.
    to Bear Mountain - Table Mountain col: *est.* 2 mi.
    to Diana's Baths (via Moat Mountain Trail): *est.* 8 mi.
    to West Side Rd. (via Moat Mountain Trail): *est.* 8.5 mi.

MOUNT ATTITASH

This 2518-ft. mountain, called Little Attitash on the USGS quadrangle, is the highest point on a long, curving ridge that continues the W. Moat ridge north and northeast to end in Humphrey's Ledge. The Attitash ski area is on the north slope, with the entrance on US Rte. 302.

Humphrey's Ledge

This is the end of the long northeast ridge of Attitash. The former trail to Pitman's Arch, a shallow cave in the face of Humphrey's Ledge, is completely overgrown.

WHITE HORSE AND CATHEDRAL LEDGES

These semidetached bluffs offer fine views from their precipitous eastern faces. White Horse Ledge (1455 ft.) may be ascended around the south and west sides from Echo Lake State
Park using the White Horse Ledge Trail — probably the most
interesting route. Alternatively, it may be ascended from Echo
Lake State Park using either the east or the west section of the
White Horse Trail, the Bryce Path Link, the Bryce Path, and the
northern section of the White Horse Trail — the shortest,
steepest route. From Cathedral Ledge Rd., the Bryce Path may
also be followed directly to its junction with the White Horse
Trail. From the West Side Rd., White Horse Ledge can be
reached using the Moat Mountain, Red Ridge, Red Ridge Link,
and White Horse Trails — the longest, easiest route.

The easiest route up Cathedral Ledge (1145 ft.) is by Cathedral
Ledge Rd. (cars can be driven to the summit), 0.9 mi.

White Horse Trail (NHDP)

This trail, marked by yellow blazes, begins at the rear (east) of
the parking lot at Echo Lake State Park. (To reach Echo Lake
State Park from N. Conway, take the road just north of the
Eastern Slope Inn, cross the Saco, bear left on West Side Rd.,
and soon enter park on right.) Shortly the west arm of the Echo
Lake Trail turns off right at a sign, and the White Horse Trail
continues straight ahead 0.4 mi. to the boulders at the south end
of the ledge. After leveling off, it descends slightly, slabs the
ridge, then climbs fairly steeply in loops to join a wood road,
which it follows right, gradually ascending for about 0.5 mi. to
the junction with the Red Ridge Link. Here it turns right, goes up
sharply, then levels and reaches the summit ledges in 0.2 mi. The
trail continues, turning sharp left, descends along the crest of the
north ledge and through the woods to a junction (sign) with the
Bryce Path. You can either follow the Bryce Path left to the top of
Cathedral Ledge, or descend steeply to the right to the base and
the Bryce Path Link, which leads back to Echo Lake.

White Horse Trail (map 4)
Distances from Echo Lake Park parking area
> *to* Red Ridge Link Trail junction: 1.5 mi.
> *to* White Horse Ledge summit: 1.7 mi.
> *to* Bryce Path junction: 2.3 mi.
> *to* Bryce Path Link Trail junction (via Bryce Path): 2.5 mi.
> *to* Echo Lake parking area (via Bryce Path Link): 2.9 mi.
>   (4.7 km.)

Red Ridge Link Trail *(NHDP)*

This trail links the White Horse Trail with the Red Ridge Trail, offering a route to the top of White Horse Ledge from Diana's Baths, in combination with the Moat Mountain, Red Ridge, and White Horse trails. It is 0.5 mi. long, of moderate grade, and well marked by orange blazes. Ascending, it traverses open hemlock forest and then younger growth. It leaves the Red Ridge Trail at a sign about 0.8 mi. beyond the junction with the Moat Mountain Trail, and ends at the White Horse Trail 0.2 mi. below the summit ledges.

Red Ridge Link Trail (map 4)
Distances from West Side Rd.
> *to* start of Red Ridge Link Trail (via Moat Mountain and Red Ridge trails): 1.8 mi.
> *to* White Horse Trail junction: 2.2 mi.
> *to* White Horse Ledge summit (via White Horse Trail): 2.4 mi. (3.9 km.), 1 hr. 40 min.

The Bryce Path *(NHDP)*

This path starts inside the Echo Lake-Cathedral Ledge State Park at the foot of a hill between the two ledges and leads to the summit of Cathedral Ledge. Signs start at the park entrance on West Side Rd., where a road leads west about 0.3 mi. to a fork. The right (north) fork is the automobile road to summit of Cathedral Ledge. Take the left (south) fork to the edge of the woods (parking). The Bryce Path enters the woods and passes trails merging in from the left. At 0.2 mi. the Bryce Link from

Echo Lake comes in on the left and the rock climbers' trail up White Horse Ledge goes straight ahead. (The ledges are extremely dangerous; this trail is not maintained by the State Park Authority.) The Bryce Path for the ledges turns right, passes near the foundation of an old sugar house, and goes directly uphill about 0.4 mi., bears right, then right again where the White Horse Trail leaves left. This right fork swings north through a flat, wooded upland, and after about 0.5 mi. comes directly to the south slope of Cathedral Ledge, which it ascends to the summit.

Bryce Path (map 6, map 4)
Distances from fork at base of Cathedral Ledge Rd.
   to Bryce Path Link Trail junction: 0.2 mi.
   to White Horse Trail junction: 0.5 mi.
   to Cathedral Ledge summit: 1.1 mi., 1 hr.

THE KANCAMAGUS HIGHWAY AND SWIFT RIVER VALLEY

The scenic Kancamagus (pronounced Kancamawgus) Highway, a section of NH Rte. 112, connects Conway on the east with Lincoln on the west, a distance of approximately 34 mi. Its east end on NH Rte. 16 in Conway is marked by a conspicuous sign. The WMNF Saco District Headquarters is at this junction. The Kancamagus Highway is on WMNF land for nearly its entire length. There are no gas stations or other service facilities. It may be closed to through traffic during extreme winter storms. The area for a half-mile on both sides of the highway is a Restricted Use Area, and camping is permitted only at designated camping areas (see Section 22).

The eastern portion of the highway from Conway to the height-of-land gives access to the Swift River Valley and Passaconaway, also known as Albany Intervale. Trails on the north slopes of the Sandwich Range and the Livermore Trail to Waterville Valley leave the south side of the highway. To the north of the highway lie Moat Mountain, Mt. Tremont, and several lesser peaks. Their trails are described in this section.

Dugway Rd. is an alternative route from Conway. It passes the Moat Mountain Trail at 3.5 mi. from Conway, follows the north bank of the Swift River, and passes the WMNF Covered Bridge Campground and the Boulder Loop Trail at about 7 mi. Shortly thereafter at a fork the Dugway Rd. turns left, crosses the Swift River on a covered bridge, and joins the Kancamagus Highway on the south bank, at the WMNF Blackberry Crossing Campground.

Continuing west and climbing gradually, the Kancamagus Highway passes two WMNF scenic areas. The Champney Falls and Bolles trails are on the left (south) about 11 mi. from Conway. At about 13 mi. Bear Notch Rd. from Bartlett enters on the right (north). The WMNF Jigger Johnson Campground is about 0.3 mi. west of this junction and the WMNF Passaconaway Information Station about 0.5 mi. west (inquire here about the short nature trail). The Oliverian Brook Trail is on the south of the highway about 1 mi. west of the junction. The Sawyer Pond Trail is on the right (north) about 1.5 mi. west of the junction. The UNH Trail is on the left (south) about 2 mi. west of the junction, the WMNF Passaconaway Campground on the right (north), and the Downes Brook Trail on the left (south).

The Sabbaday Brook Trail starts at a picnic area west of Sabbaday Brook. The Pine Bend Brook Trail is on the south about 18 mi. from Conway. The Sawyer River Trail leaves right (north) about 20 mi. from Conway, and 0.2 mi. farther along the Livermore Trail leaves left (south). Beyond Lily Pond the highway skirts the northeast and north slopes of Mt. Kancamagus, climbing to an altitude of 2855 ft. (Kancamagus Pass) where, at the height-of-land, the Clifford L. Graham Wangan ground (WMNF) offers excellent views north and east. Descending west there is another spectacular view, of Mt. Osceola and mountains south and west. The western end of the highway is described in Section 11.

Boulder Loop Trail (WMNF)

This is a loop nature trail near the WMNF Covered Bridge Campground, with access to the ledges north of it. It leaves Dugway Rd. (north side) near the campground road. At 0.1 mi. the trail forks. The left fork soon passes a large boulder (left) then climbs gradually for a mile. At 1.2 mi. a spur trail right (south) leads 0.2 mi. to ledges from which there is a fine view of Mt. Passaconaway, Mt. Chocorua, and Middle Sister Mountain. The main trail continues around ledges, descends toward Big Brook, continues right below the ledges, passes a boulder (left), and then completes the loop 0.1 mi. from the starting point.

Boulder Loop Trail (map 4)

Distances from Dugway Rd.

to fork: 0.1 mi.

to spur trail to ledges junction: 1.2 mi.

to Dugway Rd. (complete loop): 2.7 mi.

Sawyer Pond Trail (WMNF)

The trail leaves the north side of NH Rte. 112 (Kancamagus Highway) about 0.5 mi. east of the WMNF Passaconaway Campground and 1.5 mi. west of Bear Notch Rd. In 0.3 mi. it fords Swift River (no bridge, difficult at high water). The trail continues northwest, and at 1.1 mi., the Brunel Trail leaves right for Owl Cliff. The trail skirts the west slope of Birch Hill, descends gently, and crosses a logging road. It then passes over a divide east of Green's Cliff. Approaching Sawyer Pond it descends more to the north and turns sharp left in a small clearing near the west side of Sawyer Pond, where it crosses the outlet brook. A short detour may be necessary because of beaver activity in the outlet brook. Beyond the outlet, a side path (right) leads in 0.2 mi. to Sawyer Pond Shelter and five tent platforms on the northwest side of the pond. The shelter accommodates eight. The trail, now leading more west, continues down an old logging road, crosses the outlet brook, continues west about on contour, and ends at the footbridge over the Sawyer River. Across the bridge is the end of the Sawyer River Rd. 4.0 mi.

southwest of US Rte. 302.

Turn left for the Sawyer River and Hancock Notch trails across the footbridge.

From the shelter, the area for a quarter-mile on each side of the trail is a Restricted Use Area, and no camping is permitted.

Sawyer Pond Trail (map 4)

Distances from Kancamagus Highway

to Brunel Trail junction: 1.1 mi., 35 min.

to Sawyer Pond: 4.7 mi., 2 ½ hr.

to Sawyer River Rd.: 5.7 mi. (9.2 km.), 3 ¼ hr.

Church Pond Loop Trail (WMNF)

This trail starts from the far end of the west loop road around Passaconaway Campground (sign) and crosses the Swift River at a point where the stream usually can be waded easily. In less than 100 yd. it crosses an old bed of the Swift River, and 100 yd. farther comes out at the southeast corner of an old field (sign). Here there is a choice of two routes. The shorter (left at the sign) follows an old logging road across the field, bears right into the woods, becomes a footpath, crosses two open bogs, and emerges on a knoll overlooking Church Pond. The longer (right at the sign) follows a logging road into the woods. Shortly take the right fork, which leads in about 200 yd. to an old trail. Turn left on the old trail that skirts the bog and joins the other branch of the loop on the knoll. Both trails are wet at times.

Church Pond Loop (map 4)

Distances to Church Pond

from Passaconaway Campground via left branch: *est*. 1 mi.

from Passaconaway Campground via right branch: *est*. 1.5 mi.

GREEN'S CLIFF

This 2903-ft. summit, northwest of Albany Intervale, bears a series of interesting cliffs on its south and east faces, with several views from ledges near the summit, but there is no trail.

BEAR MOUNTAIN NOTCH AND VICINITY

This notch (about 1750 ft.) lies between Bear Mountain on the southeast and Bartlett Haystacks on the northwest. It offers a convenient route between Bartlett and Albany Intervale. Late in the last century it was traversed by a lumber railroad. Afterward the Bear Mountain Notch Trail used part of the old roadbed; both have been replaced by the Bear Notch (Bartlett-Passaconaway) Rd.

Bear Notch Road (WMNF)

This 9.3 mi. road closely follows the line of the old railroad north of Bear Mountain Notch. Its highest point is 1000 ft. above Bartlett, and it was greatly improved in 1969 when magnificent outlooks were cleared.

In approaching the road from Bartlett, turn south from US Rte. 302 at the Bartlett Hotel, cross the railroad and continue south. At 2.5 mi. south of Bartlett the Attitash Trail leaves left. The road ends at the Kancamagus Highway at the Albany Intervale, about 13 mi. west of Conway.

A WMNF access road that leaves Bear Notch Rd. on the west about 1 mi. north of the Kancamagus Highway leads into the Rob Brook watershed. This road will probably be closed by a locked gate during the summer.

The WMNF Bartlett Experimental Forest occupies a large area on the slopes of Bear Mountain and the Bartlett Haystacks. Bear Notch Rd. runs close to the east and south borders of the reservation. The area for a quarter-mile on both sides of the road is a Restricted Use Area, and no camping is permitted.

MOUNT TREMONT

This 3384-ft. mountain, crossed by the Bartlett-Livermore boundary line, lies south of the big bend in the Saco River, west of Bartlett. It is a narrow ridge, running north and south, with three conspicuous summits, of which the south is the highest. Still farther south is a fourth summit, Owl Cliff (2951 ft.). There are numerous open ledges with fine views.

Brunel Trail (WMNF)

This trail leaves the Sawyer Pond Trail on the northeast (right) 1.1 mi. from the Kancamagus Highway, and proceeds east and north. Upon reaching the bed of the abandoned Bartlett and Albany railroad, the Brunel Trail turns sharply northwest (left) and follows the railroad through an area that was logged in the 1960s. The trail meets a WMNF access road at the end of the maintained section, 2.6 mi. from the Bear Notch Rd. The Brunel Trail follows the access road east for 0.1 mi., then leaves the road at a sign and turns northeast into the woods. It climbs gradually for about 0.5 mi. and crosses two shallow gullies or Rob Brook tributaries (*last water*). Beyond, the grade becomes steeper, and large boulders signify the approach to the east end of Owl Cliff.

The trail then ascends steeply to a point east of the rocky cliff. Turning sharply west (left), it follows the ridge with occasional outlooks across small rocky openings. A side trail left leads in about 0.3 mi. to an outlook at an old fire burn with good views to the south and west. The main trail bears right, crosses the ridge and descends through woods to the col between Owl Cliff and Mt. Tremont. After leaving the col the trail climbs steadily, swinging northwest where it comes out on the summit ledges of Mt. Tremont, where there are excellent views in all directions.

Owl Cliff can also be ascended starting from the WMNF access road, at the end of the maintained section, where the Brunel Trail leaves right (north), 2.6 mi. from Bear Notch Rd.

Brunel Trail (map 4)

Distances from WMNF access road/Brunel Trail junction
to Owl Cliff: 2.2 mi., 1 ¾ hr.

to Mt. Tremont summit: 3.5 mi. (5.6 km.), 2 hr. 35 min.

Mt. Tremont Trail (PEAOC)

This trail leaves the south side of US Rte. 302 3.0 mi. west of the Bartlett Hotel and 1 mi. west of Sawyer Rock. It follows the west side of Stony Brook for nearly 1 mi., swings right, climbs steeply a short distance, then levels off and crosses a logging road. At about 1.5 mi. it descends to cross Stony Brook (*last water*). The trail then climbs the steep northeast side of the mountain by zigzags, passes through virgin woods, and approaches the summit from the north. The ascent is fairly steep in the final 200 yd. before turning left onto the summit rocks. The view is excellent in all directions.

Mt. Tremont Trail (USGS N. Conway)

Distances from US Rte. 302

to Mt. Tremont summit: *est.* 3.5 mi.

Bartlett Haystacks

This 3000-ft. mountain, often called Mt. Silver Spring, has at least four summits, one of the southerly ones being the highest. A ledge near the summit affords a spectacular view. There is no trail, but an ascent can be made from the height-of-land on Bear Notch Rd.

JACKSON AREA

Jackson is situated at the junction of the Ellis River, flowing from Pinkham Notch, and the Wildcat River, flowing from Notch. It is closely surrounded by mountains of moderate height. Carter Notch, the eastern and southern sides of Mt. Washington, the Montalban Ridge, Black Mountain, Iron Mountain, Double-head, and Mt. Kearsarge North are easily accessible. Refer to map 7, Carter-Mahoosuc.

Jackson Falls, on the Wildcat River just above the village, are a picturesque succession of cataracts, and NH Rte. 16B (Carter Notch Rd.) passes along their entire length on the west.

The Jackson Ski-Touring Foundation trails coincide with portions of some of the hiking trails in this area, but their signs should not be construed as regular hiking trail markers. A map is available (charge) at their headquarters, Jackson, NH 03846.

Winniweta Falls Trail (WMNF)

Leaving the west side of NH Rte. 16 (Pinkham Notch Highway) 3 mi. north of the bridge over the Ellis River in Jackson, the trail descends to cross the Ellis River (difficult in high water). After entering the woods the trail follows a logging road up the north bank of Miles Brook to a sign, where the trail turns left from the road and soon reaches the falls. (Total distance: 1 mi.)

The ledges south of Miles Brook, visible from Rte. 16, may be reached by crossing Miles Brook at Winniweta Falls and climbing, without a trail, the slope west of the ledges on Popple Mountain. When well up, turn east to the ledges where the view north and east is excellent. (Total distance: 1 mi., ½ hr.)

Hutmen's Trail (HA)

This trail crosses the flat ridge between Spruce Mountain on the south and Wildcat Mountain on the north, from NH Rte. 16 to NH Rte. 16B (Carter Notch Rd.). It leaves the east side of Rte. 16 4.2 mi. north of Jackson and 5.6 mi. south of Pinkham Notch Camp. The trail crosses a small field, begins to ascend the moderately steep west slope of Spruce Mountain, and shortly approaches a small brook (right). After about 0.4 mi. it begins to level, bears away (left) from the brook, turns more north, and shortly crosses another brook (bridge). The trail then goes through an old spruce and softwood area, nearly level, bears right (east) as it reaches the height-of-land, and passes along the south edge of an old pasture (left). It continues on a level grade for another 0.3 mi. through woods, then begins to descend at a moderate grade, crosses Marsh Brook, and follows a logging road with a steep bank right. It continues almost straight to emerge from the woods and pass in front of a summer cottage, which has a fine view of Black Mountain and down the valley to

Kearsarge North. The trail continues on a farm road for about 0.1 mi. to end at Rte. 16B (Carter Notch Rd.) at the Fernald Cottages.

Hutmen's Trail (map 7)

Distance from NH Rte. 16

> *to* NH Rte. 16B (Carter Notch Rd.): *est.* 2.3 mi. (3.5 km.),
> 1½ hr.

Hall's Ledge Trail (HA)

This trail starts on the east side of NH Rte. 16 opposite the Dana Place inn, 5 mi. north of Jackson. It follows a woods path at a nearly level grade, crosses a small brook, and shortly approaches another brook on the right (*last water*). The trail then bears slightly left and climbs the moderately steep bank on the north side of some cascades. It bears away from the brook and in about 0.1 mi. begins a short, steep ascent. From the top of this rise it runs generally north and northeast through fine woods with intervals of level stretches and slight rises, until it reaches a section of spruce a short distance below the ledge. Through this softwood area the ascent is only moderate. The ledge, on the left, is small, overgrown, and at the end of a straight, almost level stretch of about 100 yd., Mt. Washington, Boott Spur, and the Gulf of Slides may be seen through the trees.

Beginning 50 ft. beyond Hall's Ledge and from this point following cairns which have been placed where old logging roads come together, the trail descends to NH Rte. 16B (Carter Notch Rd.). From the first cairn the logging road descends slightly, passes a fine outlook toward Mt. Washington, shortly bears right uphill, then left, and at 0.4 mi. at a sharp right turn, the long descent begins. The road passes the Wildcat Reservation plaque (right) and a side road enters right about 0.3 mi. beyond. From this point the road descends about 0.7 mi. to end at Carter Notch Rd. Turn right for Jackson, left for Carter Notch (Wildcat River Trail) or Wild River area (Bog Brook Trail).

Hall's Ledge Trail (map 7)

Distances from NH Rte. 16

   to cascades: 0.3 mi.

   to Hall's Ledge: 1.6 mi., 1¼ hr.

   to Wildcat Reservation plaque: *est.* 2.4 mi., 1 hr. 50 min.

   to NH Rte. 16B (Carter Notch Rd.): *est.* 4.2 mi., 2½ hr.

BLACK MOUNTAIN

This mountain is a long ridge with about seven summits. It continues the line of the Carter Range south of Carter Dome, from which it is separated by Perkins Notch. The south summit, the only one not wooded, which has a fine view, is called the knoll.

Black Mountain Ski Trail (WMNF)

This trail leaves the east (right) side of NH Rte. 16B (Carter Notch Rd.) at a sign 3.3 mi. north of Jackson village. It ascends through a series of open pastures, connected by short lengths of trail, to the ridge just a few yards south of the 2758-ft. summit. There is a WMNF cabin, with stove, which accommodates twelve, on the west slope of the mountain to the south of this trail about 0.5 mi. from the top of the ridge.

Black Mountain Ski Trail (map 7)

Distance from NH Rte. 16B (Carter Notch Rd.)

   to WMNF Black Mountain Cabin: 2 mi. (3.2 km.)

MOUNT DOUBLEHEAD

The north peak (3056 ft.) is wooded to the top, but there is a fine view from the ledges 100 ft. east of the WMNF cabin. The south peak (2938 ft.) consists of a short ridge running east and west, divided into three minor humps, with ledges on each affording good views. The north and south peaks are connected by a trail, with the low point in the col at about 2720 ft. The WMNF cabin on the north peak contains eight bunks and a stove.

Doublehead Ski Trail (WMNF)

This trail starts from the east (left) side of Dundee Rd. 2.4 mi. from Jackson and 0.4 mi. beyond the Black Mountain Rd. sign. It enters the woods, swings left, and becomes steeper. At 0.6 mi. it bears slightly left for the north peak, and the Old Path leaves right. The ski trail ascends by a zigzag route on the west slope to the summit of N. Doublehead, terminating at the WMNF Doublehead Cabin. There is *no water* at the cabin; the nearest *water* is alongside the trail about halfway down. Beyond the cabin door, a path leads in 100 ft. to a good view of the Mountain Pond area.

Doublehead Ski Trail (map 7)

Distance from Dundee Rd.

   to WMNF Doublehead Cabin: 1.8 mi. (2.9 km.)

Old Path (JCC)

This trail leaves the Doublehead Ski Trail right at 0.6 mi. from Dundee Rd. It passes a brook left in 50 yd., rises at a moderate grade for about 0.1 mi., then steepens somewhat until it reaches the height-of-land in the col between the peaks at 0.6 mi. Turn left for the north peak, and right for the south peak. The latter comes out on a fine ledge looking west.

Old Path (map 7)

Distance from Doublehead Ski Trail junction

   to N. Doublehead summit: 1.0 mi. (1.6 km.)

New Path (JCC)

This trail is steep in its upper half, but it has better views than the Old Path. It starts left from Dundee Rd. about 0.5 mi. beyond the Doublehead Ski Trail, 2.9 mi. from Jackson, opposite a driveway. The trail declines slightly as it leaves the road and in 200 ft. bears right, then left, and follows a logging road at a slight upgrade. At 0.3 mi. from the road bear left and in about 100 yd. descend slightly and cross a dry brookbed. Proceed uphill for 100 yd. and bear right at a cairn. About 0.2 mi. from this point the trail crosses a small, almost flat ledge with a good view, and crosses a similar open ledge about 100 yd. beyond. From here the trail begins the steep climb to the summit, approaching it from the southeast slope. It meets the ridge path at a point between two open ledges. Turn right for the east view, or left for the west view and the trail that connects the Doublehead summits.

New Path (map 7)

Distances from Dundee Rd.

to first open ledge: 0.6 mi.

to S. Peak, Doublehead Mountain: *est.* 1.3 mi. (2 km.), 1¼ hr.

THE EAST BRANCH COUNTRY

This region, drained by the East Branch of the Saco River, lies between the mountains east of Jackson and those west of Chatham. A lumber railroad formerly ran up the river from Lower Bartlett, with a branch up Slippery Brook, the chief tributary. It is now almost completely within the WMNF.

The most convenient approach is by Slippery Brook Rd. in lower Bartlett, which leaves NH Rte. 16A on the east side, continues up the East Branch valley, then up the Slippery Brook valley to about 1 mi. above the western terminus of the Mountain Pond Trail.

A USFS road leaves the west side of Slippery Brook Rd. just beyond the entrance to the East Branch Trail, runs above and more or less parallel to the trail, until it turns left, crosses the East Branch Trail and the East Branch, bears right, continues on contour, passes the lower end of the Bald Land Trail (left), bears right, and ends at the East Branch Trail. The WMNF has constructed a stream-gauging station at the East Branch crossing.

The area for a quarter-mile on both sides of the Slippery Brook Rd. within the WMNF, and the branch that leaves its west side, is a Restricted Use Area, and no camping is permitted.

East Branch Trail (WMNF)

From NH Rte. 16A in lower Bartlett (between Glen and Intervale), follow Town Hall Rd. east, which becomes Slippery Brook Rd. This trail leaves Slippery Brook Rd. about 4.5 mi. from the Rte. 16A junction and near the confluence of Slippery Brook and the East Branch of the Saco. The trail starts from the west side of the road, descends to cross Slippery Brook, then enters and follows an old railroad bed on the east side of the East Branch. At 2 mi. a WMNF road that connects with Slippery Brook Rd. crosses the trail. Beyond this point, after leaving the roadbed for a while and then regaining it, the trail crosses the East Branch three times well to the north of Mt. Doublehead. The last crossing (east to west side) is at a stretch of still water. In a few yards the WMNF road enters left and ends. The trail then crosses Gulf Brook. Within 0.1 mi. the trail leaves the railroad bed and follows old logging roads. About 1.3 mi. north of the junction with the end of the WMNF road, the East Branch Trail crosses Black Brook and shortly bears northwest away from the river, and climbs by easy grades to a divide between Black Mountain and a prominent peak on a southwest ridge of N. Baldface. Toward the height-of-land *water (unreliable)* is found on the left. The logging road dwindles to a trail, passes through a patch of spruce, and descends 0.3 mi. to its junction with the Wild River Trail on the south bank of Wild River. Turn right for Gilead or N. Chatham; left for the shelter in Perkins Notch, or for Carter Notch or Jackson via Perkins Notch.

East Branch Trail (map 7)

Distances from Slippery Brook Rd.

to WMNF road: 3.3 mi., 1¾ hr.

to height-of-land: *est*. 6.6 mi., 3 hr. 50 min.

to Wild River Trail junction: 8.0 mi. (12.9 km.), 4½ hr.

Mountain Pond

Mountain Pond is a crescent-shaped body of water about three-quarters of a mile long by half a mile wide, entirely surrounded by woods and overlooked by Mts. Baldface, Shaw, and Doublehead. It drains west into a tributary of Slippery Brook. On its north shore is a WMNF shelter. The Mountain Pond Trail is described in Section 15.

Slippery Brook Trail (WMNF)

From Rte. 16A in Lower Bartlett (between Glen and Inter-vale), follow Town Hall Rd. east, which becomes (gravel) Slip-pery Brook Rd., to the gate at 7.2 mi. The trail begins 200 yd. north of the locked gate and continues up the east side of Slippery Brook. At 1.9 mi., just after crossing a small brook, the Bradley Brook Trail leaves right. The trail soon crosses the brook four times and slabs more steeply up the west slope of Eastman Mountain, crossing a brook (*water unreliable*) west of the col. At the height-of-land between S. Baldface and Eastman mountains, the Baldface Knob Trail leaves left, and the Eastman Mountain Trail leaves right. Beyond this junction the trail descends rather steadily through the woods, generally a little north of east, crosses several small brooks, and farther on, after a short, steep descent, crosses a branch of Chandler Brook. It then continues at a more moderate grade down to its terminus at the Baldface Circle Trail. NH Rte. 113 is 0.3 mi. right. (For reverse route see Section 15.)

Slippery Brook Trail (map 7)
Distances from gate at end of Slippery Brook Rd.
> *to* Bradley Brook Trail junction: 1.9 mi., 1 hr. 10 min.
> *to* Baldface Knob/Eastman Mountain trails junction: 3.9 mi.,
>   2 hr. 25 min.
> *to* Baldface Circle Trail junction: 6.8 mi. (10.9 km.), 4¼ hr.

S. Baldface Mountain

S. Baldface Mountain may be reached from Jackson or Lower Bartlett by driving up Slippery Brook Rd. from NH Rte. 16A to its end, and then following the Slippery Brook Trail to the col between Eastman Mountain and S. Baldface. From the col, the Baldface Knob Trail leaves left (north) going directly to the

Baldface Circle Trail, which is followed left (west) to the summit
of S. Baldface.

S. Baldface Mountain (map 7)

Distance to summit

   from gate at end of Slippery Brook Rd. (via Slippery Brook
     Trail, Baldface Knob Trail, and Baldface Circle Trail): 5.4
     mi. (8.6 km.), 3 hr. 25 min.

Bald Land Trail (WMNF)

   This trail follows an old roadway from Black Mountain Rd. to
the East Branch through the divide between Black Mountain and
Doublehead Mountain. It gives easy access to the upper part of
the East Branch valley from Jackson.

   The trail begins at the end of Black Mountain Rd. and continues straight ahead. At 0.4 mi. the trail diverges right, immediately crosses Great Brook, and follows an old roadway with
a stone wall on the right. At 0.7 mi. it leaves the stone wall and
begins a slight uphill grade, swings more northeast, and at the
height-of-land crosses a disused pasture and re-enters the woods.
(Take care at this point because a ski-touring trail diverges left.)
The Bald Land Trail continues straight and begins a long, moderate descent. When it is well down in the valley of the East
Branch, the trail turns left, crosses a former logging road, and
soon ends at a WMNF road that leads right to Slippery Brook Rd.
Follow this road left 0.2 mi. to the East Branch Trail and
continue north on the East Branch Trail about 4.7 mi. for the
Wild River Trail.

Bald Land Trail (map 7)

Distances from Black Mountain Rd.

   to height-of-land: 1.5 mi., ¾ hr.

   to East Branch Trail junction: 2.5 mi. (4 km.), 1¼ hr.

THE THORN MOUNTAIN RANGE

   This range includes the three low summits east of Jackson
village: Tin Mountain (2025 ft.) on the north, Middle Mountain

(1910 ft.), and Thorn Mountain (2287 ft.) at the south. Thorn Hill (1440 ft.) lies southwest from Thorn Mountain across Thorn Hill Rd.

Thorn Mountain via Thorn Hill Road

This is the shortest way from Jackson. Ascend Thorn Hill Rd. about 1 mi. to a driveway opposite open field on right (look for Thorn Mountain Trail sign). The entire trail is on private property. Cars should be parked in an area 0.1 mi. farther up the road. Turn left (east) into driveway (through large evergreens) from which the trail leaves on the right. It ascends gradually through young trees and bushes, then enters the spruces and rises more steeply, especially near the summit. There is *no water*. Descending, the trail is located just north of the lower part of the ledges.

Thorn Mountain (map 7)

Distance to summit

from Thorn Hill Rd.: *est.* 1 mi., 1 hr.

Tin Mountain

The chief objects of interest on this 2025-ft. mountain are the abandoned tin mines. Private home construction in the area, however, has curtailed public access.

IRON MOUNTAIN

Iron Mountain (2716 ft.) lies southwest of Jackson between the Ellis and the Rocky Branch rivers. Of several summits and long ledgy ridges, the most prominent runs a little north of east, and ends in a conspicuous 1305-ft. cliff called Duck's Head, from its shape as seen from nearby pastures. Abandoned iron mines are located on the Jericho side.

A line of cairns may be followed down (south) from the summit for about 0.8 mi. to where a short trail leaves right (west) to the cliffs — well worth seeing, and a fine view west and south. The cairns, and some blazes, continue down to the abandoned iron mines on the Jericho side.

Iron Mountain Trail (JCC)

Follow the Iron Mountain Rd., which leaves the west side of NH Rte. 16 near the golf links, just south of the bridge over the Ellis River in Jackson. It is one lane and rather steep, with fine views to the north, especially of some of the mountains in the Presidential Range. The trail to the summit starts at the end of the road, behind a summer home (Hayes Farm) at the height-of-land. It slabs the northwest face of the ridge at a moderately steep grade, and later follows its crest generally south to the summit. There is *no water* on the trail.

Iron Mountain Trail (map 7)

Distance from end of Iron Mountain Rd.

to Iron Mountain summit: 1.3 mi. (2.1 km.), 1 hr.

SPRUCE MOUNTAIN

This mountain comprises three summits on the long ridge running south from Wildcat Mountain. The middle peak (2272 ft.) is the highest, but the south peak (2220 ft.) is the one usually climbed. It is slightly wooded, but there are views in all directions from scattered ledges, those to the north and east being the best.

The mountain is usually ascended from Spruce Mountain Lodge, on the west side of the Carter Notch Rd., about 2.5 mi. north of Jackson.

EAGLE MOUNTAIN

This low (1615 ft.) craggy peak forming the end of the long ridge running south from Wildcat Mountain may be reached from the Eagle Mountain House on Carter Notch Rd. The trail that followed the old logging road south from behind the hotel is reported to be obscure. (Total distance: about 1 mi., ¾ hr.)

The Carter-Moriah Range

The Carter-Moriah Range lies east of Mt. Washington and the northern peaks. It is made up of Mt. Surprise (2225 ft.), Mt. Moriah (4049 ft.), Shelburne Moriah Mountain (3748 ft.), Imp Mountain (3708 ft.), N. Carter Mountain (4539 ft.), Middle Carter Mountain (4621 ft.), S. Carter Mountain (4458 ft.), Mt. Hight (4690 ft.), Carter Dome (4832 ft.), and Wildcat Mountain A (4422 ft.) through E (4041 ft.).

Trails described in this section are in the Carter-Moriah Range and its slopes. All are south of US Rte. 2 and east of NH Rte. 16. All trails that leave west from Wild River Rd. and the Wild River Trail are described, as well as four trails that ascend the range from the east and the south—Basin, Black Angel, East Branch, and Bog Brook trails.

SHELBURNE MORIAH MOUNTAIN

This 3748-ft. peak is the most northerly of the range. It has many ledges traversed by the Kenduskeag Trail that offer fine views.

Shelburne Trail (WMNF)

This trail, from Shelburne to Wild River Rd., was relocated in 1981 to begin near Connor Brook rather than Clement Brook. Drive about 9 mi. east of Gorham on US Rte. 2 to the west end of an abandoned wayside area immediately west of the Maine/New Hampshire border. Go about 0.1 mi. into this area and take a good dirt road right for 0.6 mi. to the end of the maintained section. The trail begins here and follows the continuation of the road. At 0.3 mi. the trail reaches the WMNF boundary, and at 0.7 mi. another logging road branches right. At 2.2 mi., the trail turns left into the woods. At 2.7 mi. the trail reaches the junction with the abandoned section and begins to climb. At 4.6 mi. the trail crosses a very small stream twice, and shortly reaches the

height-of-land where it meets the eastern terminus of the
Kenduskeag Trail. (Follow this trail right for the summit of
Shelburne Moriah Mountain.) The Shelburne Trail continues
over the height-of-land and descends rapidly. At 6.9 mi. the trail
turns left and follows a logging road east down the valley of Bull
Brook, crosses a branch of the brook, crosses Wild River farther
on, and ends at Wild River Rd. Turn left on the road for Hastings
and US Rte. 2, or right for Wild River Campground and the Wild
River Trail.

There are plans in the future to extend the access road 0.4 mi.
to move the trailhead parking into WMNF. When this occurs,
subtract 0.4 mi. from all distances.

Shelburne Trail (map 7)

Distances from end of maintained dirt road
   to height-of-land: 4.8 mi., 3 hr. 25 min.
   to Wild River Rd.: 7.9 mi. (12.6 km.), 5 hr.

Kenduskeag Trail (WMNF)

Named for an Abenaki word meaning ''a pleasant walk,'' this
trail begins at the height-of-land on the Shelburne Trail 4.5 mi.
south of US Rte. 2 and follows the Moriah ridge west to Mt.
Moriah. It starts in a northerly direction, immediately swings
west, and climbs steeply to the summit of Shelburne Moriah
Mountain, where there are fine views of the Androscoggin and
Wild River valleys from an almost level ledge, that is several
acres in area. The trail descends gradually along the ridge to the
col between Shelburne Moriah and Middle Moriah mountains,
where the Rattle River Trail from Rte. 2 enters right. From here,
the Kenduskeag Trail is part of the Appalachian Trail and enters a
Restricted Use Area (see Section 22). It rises steeply through
downed trees, skirts the south slope of the heavily wooded peak
of Middle Moriah Mountain about 100 ft. below the summit. It
heads generally southwest, steep for about the last 0.3 mi., and
ends at the Carter-Moriah Trail about 150 yd. from the summit
ledge of Mt. Moriah.

Kenduskeag Trail (map 7)
Distances from Shelburne Trail junction
  to Shelburne Moriah Mountain summit: 1.4 mi., 1 hr.
  to Rattle River Trail junction: 2.6 mi., 1 hr. 50 min.
  to Mt. Moriah summit: 3.9 mi. (6.3 km.), 3 hr.

Rattle River Trail (WMNF)

A link in the Appalachian Trail, this trail leaves US Rte. 2 near the east end of the bridge over Rattle River, about 300 yd. east of the North Road intersection and 3.7 mi. east of Gorham. It leads generally south, following a logging road on the east side of the stream. At about 0.5 mi., it crosses a tributary. At 1.6 mi. it passes the WMNF Rattle River Shelter (left), and at about 2 mi., it crosses and soon recrosses the Rattle River. At about 3 mi., it descends right, again crosses the Rattle River, and, continuing almost due south, begins the rather long, steep climb to a wooded col between Shelburne Moriah and Middle Moriah mountains where it ends at the Kenduskeag Trail. Turn right for Mt. Moriah. Except for a short stretch of private land at the beginning, this trail is all within a Restricted Use Area (see Section 22).

In reverse direction, for those following the Appalachian Trail, upon reaching Rte. 2 turn left and in 0.2 mi. turn right on North Rd., and follow it 0.2 mi. to a dirt road left, which leads 0.3 mi. to Centennial Trail (see Section 16).

Rattle River Trail (map 7)
Distances from US Rte. 2
  to WMNF Rattle River Shelter: 1.6 mi., 1 hr.
  to Kenduskeag Trail junction: 4.2 mi. (6.8 km.), 3½ hr.

Mount Evans

This 1455-ft. mountain, south of the Androscoggin River in the western part of Shelburne, affords fine views of Mt. Washington and the Northern Peaks and good views up and down the river and across to the Mahoosuc Range. It is on private property. Drive east from Gorham on US Rte. 2 about 2.8 mi. to the first dirt road right beyond former Twin Gables Cottages (no sign). The road is nearly opposite but prior to Reflection Pond and Shadow Pool. Park beside Rte. 2 and walk into the road (posted against vehicular access) about 120 yd. to a yarding area for lumbering operations beyond the power line clearing. Bearing right, follow the road out the southwest corner of this area. In about 100 yd., the road reaches a small spring and branches. Follow the less-used left branch for another 100 yd. and again branch left, crossing the stream a second time. The trail now climbs and reaches the crest of a narrow ridge in about 50 yd. Turn right to follow the crest south through a cutting area, where the trail may be obscure. A short distance above the top of the ridge and near the summit the trail steepens and divides, the left branch leading to the lookout on to the Mahoosuc Range and valley below. The right branch (straight ahead) goes to a western ledge that affords the best view of the Northern Peaks, and from which the summit is reached left over open ledges. The top is smooth ledges with scattered conifers, and there is a large boulder, which is, perhaps, the actual summit.

Mt. Evans (map 7)

Distance from US Rte. 2
   to Mt. Evans summit: 0.7 mi. (1.1 km.), 35 min.

CARTER-MORIAH TRAIL (AMC)

Carter-Moriah Trail. Gorham to Mount Moriah
   Water should be carried from the start of this dry ridge trail.
This section is blazed in blue.

To reach this trail, go east from Gorham on US Rte. 2, cross the Peabody River, then the railroad track, and turn sharp right on a road immediately after the railroad crossing. Follow the road up the east bank of the river to its end. The trail entrance is on the left. (On foot from Gorham follow the road that leaves the east side of NH Rte. 16 just south of the railroad tracks. Bear right in 0.1 mi. on Mill St. In 0.1 mi. more a path left leads across the Peabody River on a footbridge. Turn right here and follow the road to its end where the Carter-Moriah Trail enters the woods left.)

The trail then follows logging roads. After 0.5 mi. it follows the crest of a ridge south, and at 2 mi. the trail reaches open ledges with fine views. In 100 yd. more, it reaches the top of the shoulder called Mt. Surprise, where there is a tiny box canyon. About 250 yd. beyond Mt. Surprise, in a flat area among beeches, a side trail leads left past a cairn to a dry brookbed that can be followed about 200 yd. downhill to *water* (*unreliable*).

The main trail then ascends open ledges. There is sometimes *water* in a swampy section on the trail 1 mi. beyond Mt. Surprise. The trail continues over wooded knolls and ledges to 50 yd. from the summit of Mt. Moriah, where a short spur trail leaves right for the summit. There is sometimes *water* just south of the summit, at the foot of the ledge. The summit is open, with views in every direction.

Carter-Moriah Trail. Mount Moriah to North Carter

From the Mt. Moriah summit spur trail junction, the Carter-Moriah Trail descends straight in about 100 yd. to a junction with the Kenduskeag Trail, which leaves left for Shelburne Moriah Mountain. The Carter-Moriah Trail turns right (southwest). From this junction the trail is part of the Appalachian Trail and has white blazes. Then the trail follows the ridge crest south over open ledges. At 0.9 mi. from Mt. Moriah, reaching the top of some small cliffs, the trail turns west and descends. At the low point on the ridge between Mt. Moriah and Imp Mountain, the Moriah Brook Trail enters left, and 100 ft. later the Stony Brook Trail enters right. At about 2 mi. from Mt. Moriah a spur trail leads down and right a short distance to Imp Shelter and tent sites. In summer there is a caretaker, and a fee is charged. There is *water* in a brook above the shelter. The Carter-Moriah Trail continues 0.5 mi. generally southwest and up the steep climb to

N. Carter. There is sometimes *water* just before the grade steepens.

Carter-Moriah Trail. *North Carter to Carter Dome*

From open summits in this section, on clear midmornings, the Atlantic reflects the sun on the southeast horizon behind Sebago Lake.

The path continues south, winding along the crest of the ridge, with excellent views of Wild River Valley and the Presidentials. At 0.3 mi. beyond N. Carter summit, the N. Carter Trail diverges right. Less than 1 mi. beyond N. Carter the trail crosses several boggy depressions and may be wet. Just beyond the largest of these, the trail leads through scrub just to the left of the summit of Mt. Lethe, with restricted views. The trail continues south about 0.3 mi. to Middle Carter, passes over a number of knolls and summits, and reaches wooded S. Carter. It then descends over 500 ft. to Zeta Pass, where there is *water* at the lowest point, near the path. Here the Carter Dome Trail enters right and the two coincide for about 0.2 mi.

Continuing south the Carter-Moriah Trail soon branches left, and ascends steeply 700 ft. to Mt. Hight, approaching the open summit, with superb, extensive views, from the west. The trail then descends about 150 ft. before climbing southwest through scrub to rejoin the graded Carter Dome Trail. A short distance beyond, the Black Angel Trail leaves left (east) for the Wild River crossing at Spider Bridge. In 0.5 mi. the Carter-Moriah Trail reaches the flat, sandy summit of Carter Dome which bears the remains of the foundation of the former fire tower. The Rainbow Trail leaves this summit for Perkins Notch.

Carter-Moriah Trail. *Carter Dome to Carter Notch*

The trail descends southwest 1400 ft. in 1.5 mi. About 0.5 mi. down, a short path leads right (west) to a *spring* (*water unreliable*). About 1 mi. down, another leads left (south) to a ledge with a fine view of the notch and south country. From this point the trail is very steep. It meets the Nineteen-Mile Brook Trail on the shore of the larger Carter Lake. Carter Notch Hut is about 500 ft. to the left (south). Except for a small part at the beginning, this trail is all within a Restricted Use Area (see Section 22).

Carter-Moriah Trail (map 7)

Distances from end of dirt road off US Rte. 2

to Mt. Surprise summit: 2 mi., 1¾ hr.

to Mt. Moriah summit: 4.5 mi., 4 hr.

to Moriah Brook Trail and Stony Brook Trail junctions: 6 mi., 4¾ hr.

to Imp Shelter spur trail junction: 6.5 mi., 5 hr. 10 min.

to N. Carter summit: 8.2 mi., 6½ hr.

to N. Carter Trail junction: 8.5 mi., 6 hr. 40 min.

to Middle Carter summit: 9.1 mi., 7 hr. 10 min.

to S. Carter summit: 10.4 mi., 8 hr.

to Mt. Hight summit: 11.8 mi., 9 hr. 10 min.

to Black Angel Trail junction: 12.5 mi., 9½ hr.

to Carter Dome summit: 12.8 mi., 9 hr. 50 min.

to Carter Notch Hut: 14.3 mi. (23 km.), 10 hr. 50 min.

(*In reverse direction*: 9 hr. 40 min.)

Stony Brook Trail (WMNF)

This trail leaves NH Rte. 16 just south of the bridge over the Peabody River about 2 mi. south of Gorham (park off highway at east side parking area). The trail begins as a road bearing right. Within the first 0.2 mi., the trail passes a camp (left), then bears left, crosses a brook in a culvert, and passes directly in front of a second camp (right). The trail passes around a chain gate and then through a recently logged area with several branching side trails. It continues straight, marked by arrows, and in about 2 mi. passes the site of an old logging camp, then crosses a branch of Stony Brook and rises sharply. At 3 mi. it crosses a brook on ledges. The trail reaches the ridge crest in 3.5 mi., where it ends at the Carter-Moriah Trail. The upper half of this trail is within a Restricted Use Area (see Section 22). Turn left (north) for Mt.

Moriah, and right (south) for Imp Shelter, the Carters, and Carter Notch Hut. Continue ahead on the Moriah Brook Trail for the Wild River Trail.

Stony Brook Trail (map 7)

Distance from NH Rte. 16

   to Carter-Moriah Trail junction: 3.5 mi. (5.6 km.), 3 hr.

Imp Profile

This is a fine 3175-ft. cliff on a west spur of N. Carter. The profile is best seen from the Dolly Copp Rd. at the monument marking the site of the Dolly Copp house.

Imp Trail (WMNF)

This trail has north and south branches that form a loop. It makes a fine circuit in either direction. The north branch leads over a good viewpoint (near "Imp Face" on map 4). It begins on NH Rte. 16, 2.6 mi. north of the Mt. Washington Auto Rd. and 5.4 mi. south of Gorham. The trail heads east, and goes up the south rim of the Imp Brook valley, through a pleasant stand of hemlocks. After about 0.8 mi., it crosses the brook, slabs north up a ridge, and follows its crest, nearly level for some distance. There is sometimes *water* on this flat stretch. The trail slabs more steeply up the north side of the ridge and continues nearly to the bottom of a ravine northeast of the cliff. It then turns right and circles steeply to the viewpoint.

From the cliff, the trail skirts the edge of the Imp Brook ravine and crosses a large *brook* in about 0.3 mi. Becoming rough, it continues generally south to where the North Carter Trail diverges left. The Imp Trail turns right and descends a logging road generally southwest, and, just before reaching Cowboy Brook, turns northwest. After crossing another brook, in about 0.8 mi., it follows an old logging road north down to cross a small brook; it then immediately crosses a larger brook, turns sharp left, runs west-southwest about level for 75 yd. and ends at Rte. 16, 5.7

mi. south of Gorham and only 0.3 mi. south of the beginning of the trail. Imp Trail is within a Restricted Use Area (see Section 22).

Imp Trail (map 7)

Distances from northern terminus, NH Rte. 16
  to viewpoint: 2.2 mi. (1 hr. 55 min.)
  to North Carter Trail junction: 3.1 mi.
  to NH Rte. 16: 6 mi. (9.7 km.), 4 hr. 50 min.

Distances from southern terminus, NH Rte. 16
  to North Carter Trail junction: 2.9 mi.
  to viewpoint: 3.8 mi.
  to NH Rte. 16: 6 mi. (9.7 km.)

North Carter Trail (WMNF)

This trail leaves the Imp Trail 0.9 mi. southeast of Imp Face, climbs steadily at moderate and steep grades, generally east, and enters the Carter-Moriah Trail a short distance south of the summit of N. Carter. The entire North Carter Trail is within a Restricted Use Area (see Section 22).

North Carter Trail (map 7)

Distance from Imp Trail junction
  to N. Carter summit (via Carter-Moriah Trail): 1.2 mi. (1.8 km.), 1½ hr.

CARTER NOTCH

This deep cleft between Carter Dome and Wildcat Mountain includes some of the finest scenery in this region. The highest point of the notch, about 3450 ft., overlooks two small, beautiful lakes. From the west shore of the larger, the impressive cliffs of Wildcat Mountain rise vertically nearly 1000 ft. To the northeast, Carter Dome rises steeply; from its side juts the immense boulder called Pulpit Rock. Large sections of the cliffs on each side have fallen into the notch to form caves that are interesting to

explore, and where ice sometimes remains well through the
summer. The Carter Notch area is a Restricted Use Area (see
Section 22).

Carter Dome from Carter Notch

To reach the summit of Carter Dome from Carter Notch, use
the Carter-Moriah Trail, which leaves the notch just east of the
overflow brook between the lakes. It climbs steeply at first, then
more gradually. Just beyond the steep section, a rough trail
(right) leads to a ledge beside Pulpit Rock. If you attempt to
climb the rock do so only *with great caution*. About 1 mi. from
the notch a side trail descends steeply left about 100 ft. to *water*
(*unreliable*). (Distance from Carter Notch Hut to Carter Dome
summit: 1.5 mi., 1½ hr.)

Boulders on Carter Dome

A rough trail over the ''Rampart,'' or barrier of rocks south of
Carter Notch, leaves the Wildcat River Trail about 150 yd. south
of Carter Notch Hut and runs east over the huge rocks, where
there is a good view toward Jackson. Among the rocks many
boulder-caves invite exploration (use caution).

Wildcat Mountain from Carter Notch

To reach the summit of Wildcat Mountain from Carter Notch
use the Wildcat Ridge Trail, which branches west from the
Nineteen-Mile Brook Trail about 0.3 mi. north of the hut (*water*
just above this junction). The ascent is steep with several
switchbacks. Just beyond the summit, there is a side path that
leads 50 ft. left to the ''East View.'' (Distance from Carter Notch
Hut to Wildcat Mountain summit: *est.* 1.3 mi., 1 hr. 10 min.)

North Chatham from Carter Notch

To reach N. Chatham from Carter Notch, follow the Wildcat
River Trail toward Jackson for 1.8 mi., until, just after crossing
the Wildcat River, it meets the Wild River Trail and turns sharp

right. Follow the Wild River Trail through Perkins Notch and down the Wild River valley to the Eagle Link Trail. Follow the Eagle Link to Eagle Crag and follow the Baldface Circle Trail straight ahead down to N. Chatham. To reach the summit of N. Baldface, turn right on the Baldface Circle Trail at Eagle Crag. (Distance from Carter Notch to N. Chatham: 13 mi., 6¾ hr.)

Carter Notch Hut (AMC)

The AMC constructed this stone hut in 1914. It is located about 100 ft. south of the smaller lake at 3450 ft. altitude, at the southern terminus of the Nineteen-Mile Brook Trail and the northern terminus of the Wildcat River Trail. The hut, with two bunkhouses, accommodates forty. It is open from mid-June to mid-September, and in the winter with a caretaker. For current rates and schedule, contact Reservation Secretary, Pinkham Notch Camp, Box 298, Gorham, NH 03581 (603-466-2727)

Nineteen-Mile Brook Trail (WMNF)

The trail leaves NH Rte. 16 on the north bank of Nineteen-Mile Brook, 7 mi. south of Gorham and 1 mi. north of the Glen House site. It heads southeast and east, along the northeast bank of the brook. Cars may park at the entrance of this trail or south of the brook on the west side of Rte. 16. (In winter, park at off-highway clearing on west side of Rte. 16, 300 yd. south of trailhead.) The trail stays on the same bank, passing beautiful birches, until the Carter Dome Trail through Zeta Pass diverges left, 1.9 mi. from Rte. 16. The Nineteen-Mile Brook Trail leaves the graded path, crosses a bridge over a brook, and enters the woods directly ahead. At 2.2 mi. it crosses another brook on a bridge, bears more to the south, and climbs directly toward the notch. At 3.5 mi. from Rte. 16 the trail reaches the height-of-land, and the Wildcat Ridge Trail diverges right. The trail, now a part of the Appalachian Trail, descends left, and in about 0.1 mi. reaches the shore of the larger of the lakes near Carter Notch Hut. At this point there is a *spring* (*water unreliable*) left of the trail.

The Carter-Moriah Trail shortly diverges left, and just beyond, the Nineteen-Mile Brook Trail passes between the two lakes and reaches the hut on a slight upgrade. The trail is well supplied with *water*. It is within a Restricted Use Area (see Section 22).

(It is planned to build a new parking lot about 0.5 mi. farther north on the west side of Rte. 16, just beyond Camp Dodge. New connectors to the Great Gulf Trail across the Peabody River and the Nineteen-Mile Brook Trail would start here.)

Nineteen-Mile Brook Trail (map 7)

Distances from NH Rte. 16

   to Carter Dome Trail junction: 1.9 mi. (1¼ hr.)

   to Wildcat Ridge Trail junction and height-of-land: 3.5 mi., 2¼ hr.

   to Carter Notch Hut: 3.8 mi. (6.1 km.), 2½ hr.

Carter Dome Trail (WMNF)

This graded trail leaves the Nineteen-Mile Brook Trail 1.9 mi. from NH Rte. 16. After 0.8 mi. it turns left, crosses a fork of Nineteen-Mile Brook, and begins a steeper ascent. The trail climbs by several switchbacks to join the Carter-Moriah Trail at Zeta Pass, between S. Carter and Mt. Hight. It turns right with the Carter-Moriah Trail for 0.2 mi., then bears right again and slabs the west side of Mt. Hight. In the col beyond Mt. Hight it rejoins the Carter-Moriah Trail. Just south of this point the Black Angel Trail leaves left, and the Carter Dome Trail continues to Carter Dome. The last *water* (*unreliable*) is on the right at Zeta Pass. This trail is within a Restricted Use Area (see Section 22).

Carter Dome Trail (map 7)

Distances from Nineteen-Mile Brook Trail junction

   to Zeta Pass and Carter Moriah Trail junction: 1.9 mi., 1¾ hr.

   to Carter Dome summit: 3.3 mi. (5.3 km.), 3 hr.

Wildcat River Trail (AMC)

This trail begins on the Carter Notch Rd., 5 mi. from NH Rte. 16B in Jackson, or about 1.3 mi. beyond the end of pavement.

The trail initially coincides with, and is signed, the Bog Brook Trail. It begins at a point where the road branches sharp left uphill. Park here and follow a less-used dirt road right. Camps are passed at 200 and 300 yd. on the left. At 0.1 mi. the Bog Brook and Wildcat River trails officially begin at a Bog Brook Trail sign at a right fork in the road. In 25 yd., the trail enters the woods (right) just before a former turnaround. Running nearly level, it crosses the Little Wildcat Brook, then another brook, and then the Wildcat River. In 25 yd. the trail climbs and turns sharp left. In about 50 yd. the Bog Brook Trail leaves right. The Wildcat River Trail continues ahead and soon emerges into a grassy opening with a view of the mountains that form Carter Notch. In 0.5 mi. the trail turns right, ascending slightly, then descending. It remains entirely on the east bank of the Wildcat and crosses a large tributary, Bog Brook. A mile beyond, the Wild River Trail leaves right. Turning left for 0.3 mi. the trail crosses the Wildcat River. After a short ascent it bears right, and climbs more steeply the remaining 1.5 mi. to the notch. From the Wild River Trail to Carter Notch, the altitude gain is about 1100 ft.

Wildcat River Trail (map 7)

Distances from Bog Brook Trail sign at road fork

   to Little Wildcat Brook crossing: 0.3 mi.

   to first crossing, Wildcat River: 0.6 mi.

   to Bog Brook crossing: 1.8 mi., 50 min.

   to Wild River Trail junction: 2.8 mi., 1¾ hr.

   to Carter Notch Hut: 4.5 mi. (7.2 km.), 3½ hr.

WILDCAT MOUNTAIN

This 4397-ft. mountain is a long ridge comprising about ten more or less definite summits, the highest of which is that nearest Carter Notch. The five highest, which are the only ones crossed by the trail, are designated *A, B, C, D,* and *E,* in order from east to west.

Wildcat Ridge Trail (AMC)

This trail, a link in the Appalachian Trail, may be longer and harder than one would suppose. Between some of the main cols and lettered summits are several smaller cols and summits that are not evident from the map contours. Hikers starting from AMC Pinkham Notch Camp should enter the trail via Lost Pond Trail. Both have white blazes.

The trail starts on the east side of NH Rte. 16 opposite the parking area for Glen Ellis Falls, and leads east across the stream to a target. There is no bridge. In about 0.1 mi. the Lost Pond Trail enters left, and the trail shortly begins the steep rise up the end of the ridge (use care on all ledge areas), crossing two open ledges, both with excellent views of Mt. Washington across Pinkham Notch. Above the second ledge the trail rises steeply again over ledges, and goes over a rocky, scrub-covered prominence at the end of the ridge. At the top is undoubtedly the finest view obtainable of the southeast face of Mt. Washington. To the north of the main trail midway through a steep rise is a side path to a *spring (last sure water)*.

Soon after entering the woods, the trail climbs summit *E* (4041 ft.), the first on the main ridge. The trail turns sharply north, descends into a col, and passes close to the east end of the Wildcat gondola lift terminal building (views, *no water* available). From here the trail ascends summit *D*, where there is a wooden view platform and a graded footpath from the gondola terminal area enters left. Summits *E* and *D* are sometimes called "The Wild Kittens."

The trail then swings more to the east around the north slope of summit *D* and descends into the deep Wildcat col, at the head of Little Wildcat Brook. The trail next crosses a slightly higher col and ascends the long ridge to summit *C*, open at the top, with the best view from a ledge about 100 ft. to the right of the trail. Beyond this summit is another col and then an easy rise, with a swampy place where there is sometimes *water*. Crossing the little wooded summit *B*, the trail soon reaches the highest point on Wildcat Mountain. The "East View" is a few steps to the right. The trail soon descends steeply 1 mi. Follow the Nineteen-Mile Brook Trail right 0.3 mi. through Carter Notch for the Carter Notch Hut. In the reverse direction, hikers going to Pinkham Notch Camp should turn right on Lost Pond Trail 0.1 mi. from highway, to avoid crossing the Ellis River. The entire Wildcat Ridge Trail is within a Restricted Use Area (see Section 22).

Wildcat Ridge Trail (map 7)

Distances from NH Rte. 16

to first ledge: 0.5 mi., 35 min.

to second ledge: 0.8 mi., 1 hr.

to view of Mt. Washington, southeast face: 1.5 mi., 2 hr. 10 min.

to summit *E:* 2 mi., 2 hr. 40 min.

to summit *D:* 2.3 mi., 3¼ hr.

to Wildcat col: 3 mi., 3 hr. 35 min.

to summit *C:* 3.8 mi., 4 hr. 25 min.

to Wildcat Mountain, main summit: 4.7 mi., 5¼ hr.

to Nineteen-Mile Brook Trail junction: 5.7 mi.

to Carter Notch Hut (via Nineteen-Mile Brook Trail): *est.* 6 mi. (8.8 km.), 6 hr.

Distance from Carter Notch Hut

to NH Rte. 16: 6 mi., 5 hr. 10 min.

Lost Pond Trail (AMC)

This trail is part of the Appalachian Trail and so blazed in white. It was built to avoid highway walking between Pinkham Notch Camp and the start of the Wildcat Ridge Trail, and to eliminate the difficult and sometimes dangerous crossing of the Ellis River at the beginning of the Wildcat Ridge Trail. It leaves NH Rte. 16 almost opposite Pinkham Notch Camp, crosses a bridge over the Ellis River, and turns south. A side trail leads left to Square Ledge. Bearing right, the Lost Pond Trail follows the Ellis, soon joined by the larger Cutler River. The trail follows the east bank for 0.3 mi., then leaves it and climbs at a moderate grade to the pond. It follows the east shore (good views), descends slightly, and joins the Wildcat Ridge Trail 0.1 mi. from its start. This trail is within a Restricted Use Area (see Section 22).

Lost Pond Trail (map 7)

Distance from NH Rte. 16

    to Wildcat Ridge Trail junction: 1 mi.

Square Ledge Trail

This trail diverges left from the Lost Pond Trail at the east end of the footbridge crossing Ellis River, where the latter trail turns south. It ascends in about 0.1 mi. to a ledge which, though overgrown, offers a fine view of Pinkham Notch Camp. The trail then continues north and joins a ski trail heading northeast to a clearing, where it turns right (east) and climbs moderately, passing Hangover Rock. It then climbs to the base of Square Ledge and ascends steeply via a V-slot about 50 yd. to an outlook that has excellent views of Pinkham Notch and Mt. Washington. This trail is within a Restricted Use Area (see Section 22).

Square Ledge Trail (map 7)

Distance from Lost Pond Trail junction

    to Square Ledge: *est.* 0.5 mi., ½ hr.

Thompson Falls (WMNF)

This is a series of high falls on a brook flowing from Wildcat Mountain. Except in wet seasons, the brook is apt to be rather low, but the falls are well worth visiting for the excellent views of Mt. Washington and its ravines from the large sloping ledges that the brook flows over.

Cross the bridge to the Wildcat Ski Area on the east side of the parking area. Turn left and follow the Nature Trail left (north); continue ahead where a branch leaves left (0.1 mi.) and also where a loop leaves right and returns. Leaving the Nature Trail, the trail to the falls crosses a small stream and a maintenance road. It then leads up the south side of the brook to the foot of the first fall, crosses to the north side above the fall, bears right, and continues for another 0.3 mi. (Distance from bridge crossing to end of trail: 0.8 mi.)

WILD RIVER FOREST

This tract of about 35,000 acres, comprising the greater part of Bean's Purchase, is now part of the WMNF. It is drained by Wild River, which was once paralleled by a lumber railroad.

Perkins Notch

Perkins Notch lies between Carter Dome and Black Mountain. It gives convenient access to the Wild River region from the south or from Carter Notch, and makes it possible to go, in a long day's hike, to N. Chatham or even to Gilead, Maine. There is a WMNF shelter on the southeast side of Wild River and just south of the pond, with bunk space for six.

Wild River Road and Trail (WMNF)

Wild River Road leaves NH/ME Rte. 113 just south of the bridge over Evans Brook at Hastings. It is a good automobile road as far as the Wild River Campground, 5.7 mi. from Hastings. There is a fork in the road at the campground bulletin board and water pump. Follow the right branch to a parking area. The Basin Trail leaves left for Rim Junction, and the Wild River Trail leaves straight ahead for Spider Bridge.

The Wild River Trail leaves the parking area at the far southwest edge of the campground, 5.8 mi. from Hastings, following an unmaintained continuation of Wild River Rd. It continues generally southwest and on the south bank of Wild River. At 0.4 mi. the Moriah Brook Trail leaves right. About 2.3 mi. farther the Black Angel Trail enters left and coincides with the Wild River Trail as both turn west and cross to the west side of Wild River on Spider Bridge. Just across the bridge the Highwater

Trail leaves right for Hastings and the Wild River Trail and Black
Angel Trail turn left. In 0.1 mi. the Black Angel Trail leaves
right for Carter Dome. The Wild River Trail continues generally
southwest, passes Spruce Brook Shelter (right), then crosses
Spruce Brook. Just before crossing Red Brook, it leaves the old
railroad bed and bears right. About 1 mi. after crossing Red
Brook the Eagle Link leaves left for Eagle Crag, and in another
0.4 mi. the trail crosses to the south bank of Wild River. About
0.5 mi. beyond this crossing the East Branch Trail leaves left, the
Wild River Trail soon crosses the Wild River to the north bank,
and recrosses for the last time in about 0.4 mi.

The trail skirts the south side of No-Ketchum Pond, passes
WMNF Perkins Notch Shelter, heads more west, and begins a
gradual climb into Perkins Notch. About 0.3 mi. beyond the
shelter the Rainbow Trail leaves right for Carter Dome, and
about 0.6 mi. farther on the Bog Brook Trail leaves left for Carter
Notch Rd. From this junction the trail descends gradually through
the woods for about 1 mi. and ends at the Wildcat River Trail.
Continue right for Carter Notch Hut; turn left for Jackson. The
Wild River Rd. and the initial portion of the Wild River Trail
that uses the unmaintained extension of Wild River Rd. are
within a Restricted Use Area (see Section 22).

Wild River Trail (map 7)

Distances from Wild River Campground parking area

   to Moriah Brook Trail junction: 0.4 mi.

   to Spider Bridge, Black Angel Trail junction, Highwater Trail
      junction: 2.7 mi., 1½ hr.

   to Eagle Link Trail junction: 5.4 mi., 3 hr. 10 min.

   to East Branch Trail junction: 6.4 mi., 3 hr. 50 min.

   to Perkins Notch Shelter: 7 mi., 4¼ hr.

   to Rainbow Trail junction: 7.4 mi., 4½ hr.

   to Bog Brook Trail junction: 8.2 mi., 5 hr.

   to Wildcat River Trail junction: 9.4 mi. (15.1 km.), 5 hr. 35
      min.

   to Carter Notch Hut (via Wildcat River Trail): 11.2 mi., 6 hr.
      55 min.

Hastings Trail (WMNF)

This trail starts at a parking lot at the junction of NH/ME Rte. 113 and Wild River Rd. approximately 300 ft. south of Evans Brook bridge at Hastings. It crosses Wild River on the 180-ft. suspension footbridge. On the west bank the Highwater Trail leaves left heading upriver for Spider Bridge. The main trail now enters the woods. It follows a logging road generally north, and farther on the remnants of an abandoned telephone line. It follows an old narrow logging road, then descends (right) onto an old broad logging road for about 0.3 mi., and (right) onto a private dirt road for about 0.4 mi. It ends 200 ft. inside the east end of an abandoned wayside area on US Rte. 2 immediately west of the ME/NH border and about 9.2 mi. east of Gorham and 2 mi. west of Gilead.

Hastings Trail (map 7)

Distance from ME/NH Rte. 113
    to US Rte. 2: 2.6 mi. (4.1 km.), 1 hr. 20 min.

Highwater Trail (WMNF)

This is an attractive trail of easy to moderate grades. It leaves the Hastings Trail left (south) at Hastings on the west bank of the Wild River. It follows an old logging road that bears away from the river at about 0.8 mi. In another 0.5 mi. the trail bears left from the logging road, crosses the ME/NH state line and continues up the river. Heading generally southwest it crosses Martins Brook and a mile beyond follows a logging road to cross the Shelburne Trail. The trail crosses Bull Brook and in about 1 mi. reaches the footbridge where the Moriah Brook Trail crosses Wild River. The trail joins the Moriah Brook Trail for a time. It turns sharp right in 0.1 mi., and 0.4 mi. farther leaves the Moriah Brook Trail (left) to cross Moriah Brook. The trail continues on top of a steep bank, then crosses and follows logging roads for short distances at a time. It crosses Cypress Brook and 0.1 mi. beyond ends at the Black Angel Trail. Turn left to cross the Wild River on Spider Bridge. Most of the Highwater Trail is within a Restricted Use Area (see Section 22).

Highwater Trail (map 7)

Distances from Hastings Trail junction

to Martins Brook crossing: 3.7 mi., 1 hr. 40 min.

to Shelburne Trail crossing: 5 mi., 2½ hr.

to Moriah Brook Trail junction, Wild River footbridge: 6.1
mi., 3 hr.

to Black Angel Trail junction, Spider Bridge: 8.9 mi. (14.3
km.), 4 hr. 25 min.

Basin Trail (WMNF)

This attractive trail of easy to moderate grades is the quickest
and easiest access to the crest of the ridge between Mt. Meader
and W. Royce Mountain. It leaves the Wild River Road (left) 5.8
mi. from Hastings at Wild River Campground (for directions to
trailheads, see Wild River Trail description). At first it follows
an old lumber road. At 0.4 mi. where the road swings right, the
trail continues straight ahead and soon approaches the southwest
bank of Blue Brook, which it follows for about 0.8 mi. At 1.3 mi.
from the start it crosses the brook at the foot of a pretty cascade
and then follows the northeast bank, in 0.2 mi. passing opposite a
very striking cliff to the south of the brook. The trail leaves the
brook, and crosses another small one, then climbs somewhat
more steeply. At 2 mi. from the start a side trail branches right
0.3 mi. to Blue Brook Shelter, and the main trail soon crosses the
Basin Rim Trail at Rim Junction. From there the trail descends to
a parking area on Basin Pond, an impoundment created for flood
protection near the WMNF Cold River Campground (see Section
15).

Basin Trail (map 7)

Distances from Wild River Campground parking area

to Rim Junction: 2.2 mi.

to Basin Pond parking area: 4.5 mi.

to NH/ME Rte. 113: 5.2 mi. (8.4 km.), 3¼ hr.

Moriah Brook Trail (WMNF)

This trail leaves the Wild River Trail on the right, about 0.4 mi. from the Wild River Campground. It soon crosses the Wild River on a footbridge, where it joins the Highwater Trail. The trail turns left and follows the river bank about 0.1 mi., turns sharp right and generally follows the course of the former lumber railroad up Moriah Brook. At 0.4 mi. along the railroad bed the Highwater Trail leaves left. At the first brook crossing 1.3 mi. from the start of the Moriah Brook Trail, it is well worthwhile to follow the stream southeast a short distance to Moriah Gorge. Beyond this first crossing the trail more or less parallels the brook in part on the old railroad bed for about 1.3 mi., then crosses to the north side and continues in a northwest direction. It passes through an old burn where occasional stumps are still visible, and then rises steeply, crosses and recrosses the brook, passes through a swampy area, and ends at the junction of the Carter-Moriah Trail and the Stony Brook Trail, at the lowest point between Mt. Moriah and Imp Mountain. To reach Imp Shelter turn left on the Carter-Moriah Trail.

Moriah Brook Trail (map 7)

Distances from Wild River Trail junction
>   *to* Carter-Moriah Trail junction: 5.3 mi., 4 hr.
>   *to* NH Rte. 16 (via Stony Brook Trail): 8.8 mi. (14.2 km.),
>   6 hr.

Black Angel Trail (WMNF)

This trail starts at Rim Junction and descends gradually southwest 0.5 mi. to the Blue Brook Shelter, where there is a junction with a branch trail that runs north for 0.3 mi. to connect with the Basin Trail 0.3 mi. west of Rim Junction. From Blue Brook Shelter the Black Angel Trail, while ascending southwest to a wooded height-of-land, gains 600 ft. in altitude. After crossing this high point the trail descends southwest to an old logging road, and follows it generally west for 1.4 mi. down the Cedar Brook valley, remaining on the north side of the stream and making several obvious shortcuts at curves. The trail then leaves the logging road, turns more north, and joins the Wild River Trail to cross Wild River on Spider Bridge. Just across the bridge the Highwater Trail leaves right for Hastings, and the Wild River Trail continues ahead. The Black Angel Trail turns left, turns right in 0.1 mi., and rises slowly through open woods and small growth. About 1.5 mi. up from the Wild River the grade steepens; at 2.2 mi. the trail crosses the north branch of Spruce Brook, and about 0.5 mi. beyond enters virgin timber. The grade lessens as the trail slabs the east slope of Mt. Hight, passes lookout points on its south-southeast slope, turns southwest, and ends at the Carter-Moriah Trail, 0.3 mi. north of the summit of Carter Dome.

Black Angel Trail (map 7)

Distances from Rim Junction

to Blue Brook Shelter: 0.5 mi.

to Wild River Trail junction, Spider Bridge: 2.7 mi., 1 hr. 40 min.

to brook crossing: 4.9 mi.

to Carter-Moriah Trail junction: 7.5 mi., 5 hr. 25 min.

to Carter Dome summit (via Carter-Moriah Trail): 7.8 mi. (12.6 km.), 5 hr. 40 min.

East Branch Trail (WMNF)

This trail leaves south from the Wild River Trail close to where it crosses the Wild River at the foot of the hill east of Perkins Notch. After a short climb it crosses the height-of-land between Black Mountain and an unnamed spur of N. Baldface, then follows old logging roads down along the west bank of the East Branch of the Saco River. About 3 mi. from Wild River the trail reaches an old railroad bed. Farther along, the WMNF East Branch Rd. leads 0.2 mi. right to the Bald Land Trail, and also to the Slippery Brook Rd. A short distance beyond this point the trail reaches the East Branch and crosses it three times in about 0.4 mi. Shortly after the third crossing the trail crosses the East Branch Rd. 9 (left for Slippery Brook Rd.). The trail follows the east bank, on and off on the old railroad bed. After about 3 mi. on the east bank it turns sharply right off the railroad bed. It follows a logging road, crosses Slippery Brook, and ends at the Slippery Brook Rd. about 4.5 mi. from NH Rte. 16 in Lower Bartlett. For reverse route see Section 13.

East Branch Trail (map 7)

Distances from Wild River Trail junction

   to WMNF East Branch Rd.: 4.7 mi., 2¾ hr.

   to Slippery Brook Rd.: 8 mi. (12.9 km.), 4 hr. 20 min.

Rainbow Trail (WMNF)

The Rainbow Trail leaves the Wild River Trail at the east end of Perkins Notch about 0.4 mi. west of the WMNF shelter near No-Ketchum Pond. It ascends the southeast slope of Carter Dome, in a generally northwest direction, with a moderate grade, rising 2250 ft. in 2.5 mi. from the floor of Perkins Notch. From a false summit near the Dome (excellent viewpoint), the trail descends slightly then rises to the actual summit of Carter Dome and ends at the Carter-Moriah Trail.

Rainbow Trail (map 7)

Distance from Wild River Trail junction

   to Carter-Moriah Trail junction: 2.5 mi. (4.0 km.), 2½ hr.

Bog Brook Trail (WMNF)

This trail leaves the south side of Wild River Trail about 1.3 mi. west of No-Ketchum Pond. Follow arrows and WMNF blazes across a beaver dam. The trail descends at a moderate grade, generally south-southwest, to its junction with the Wildcat River Trail, just before the latter turns sharp right and crosses the Wildcat River. The two trails coincide from this point to the Carter Notch Rd.

Bog Brook Trail (map 7)

Distances from Wild River Trail junction

to Wildcat River Trail junction: 2.1 mi., 1 hr. 10 min.

to Carter Notch Rd.: 2.7 mi., 1 hr. 25 min.

to Jackson (via Carter Notch Rd.): 8 mi. (12.8 km.), 4 hr.

Chatham-Evans Notch

This district lies in the valley of Cold River on the east boundary of New Hampshire. The valley floor is not over 600 ft. above sea level. NH/Me Rte. 113, from Stow, ME to Gilead, ME, roughly divides the trail area in half. The principal mountains are Eastman (2936 ft.), S. Baldface (3569 ft.), N. Baldface (3591 ft.), Eagle Crag (3060 ft.), Mt. Meader (2783 ft.), W. Royce Mountain (3202 ft.), E. Royce Mountain (3115 ft.), Mt. Caribou (2828 ft.), Speckled Mountain (2877 ft.), and Blueberry Mountain (1820+ ft.). Mt. Kearsarge North (3268 ft.) may be climbed by the Weeks Brook Trail.

The trails in this section are south of US Rte. 2, east of the Wild River, and east of the East Branch of the Saco River. Refer to map 7, Carter-Mahoosuc.

The area along the Wild River from Hastings to the slide on the Wild River Trail is a Restricted Use Area (see Section 22).

The AMC Cold River Camp is in N. Chatham. Two WMNF campgrounds, Basin and Cold River, are at the north end of the valley, on the west side of Rte. 113 about 0.3 mi. west of the ME/NH border. The WMNF Hastings Campground entrance is 0.2 mi. south of the junction of Rte. 113 and Wild River Rd. Wild River Campground (WMNF) is reached by Wild River Rd. It is about 5 mi. southwest of the junction of Wild River Rd. and Rte. 113. The Kimball Ponds offer opportunities for fishing.

Due to a destructive windstorm in December 1980, the following trails remained closed to the public in summer 1982: Albany Mountain, Albany Notch, Albany Brook, Big Deer Hill, Conant, Bradley Brook, Horseshoe Pond, Little Deer Hill, Mountain Pond, Shell Pond, and Province Brook (north end). The Evans Notch Ranger District in Bethel, ME, advises that some of these will be opened in summer 1983, but some not until 1984. The District Ranger suggests that interested parties contact his office before planning to use these trails.

N. Chatham can be reached by car from Conway, NH (25

mi.), from Fryeburg, ME (17 mi.), and from Gilead, ME (12 mi.), via NH/ME Rte. 113, the Evans Notch Rd. There are through trails from Carter Notch, Carter Dome, and N. Lovell, ME. Chatham, hereafter called Chatham Center to distinguish it from N. Chatham and S. Chatham, may be reached on foot from Lower Bartlett. S. Chatham may be reached from Intervale or Kearsarge Village by Hurricane Mountain Rd.

KEARSARGE NORTH

Weeks Brook Trail (WMNF)

Leaving the highway south of S. Chatham, about 100 ft. south of Weeks Brook, this trail follows the south side of a branch of the brook for about 0.2 mi., crosses the brook on a wooden bridge, follows a lumber road up the north side, and enters woods in approximately 1 mi., at lumbering operation clearing (watch carefully for arrow). In another 0.5 mi., the trail approaches Shingle Pond from the south and passes it on the right (east) side. The trail shortly crosses another branch of the brook, turns left, and ascends rather steeply to the col between Rickers Knoll and Kearsarge North, where there is a small bog pond. The trail turns left here and ascends steeply to the summit.

Weeks Brook Trail (map 7)

Distance from highway south of S. Chatham
  to Mt. Kearsarge North summit: 4.7 mi. (7.6 km.), 3 ½ hr.

Province Brook Trail (WMNF)

Trail closed north of shelter: see page 317.

This trail begins at the north end of Peaked Hill Rd., which intersects the highway south of S. Chatham 0.6 mi. north of Weeks Brook. The trail heads northwest up Province Brook and crosses the brook shortly before reaching Province Pond. There is a WMNF shelter at the pond. From this point it bears north and to the east of Mt. Shaw and ends at a dirt road that parallels

Langdon Brook coming up from (west of) Chatham Center.

Province Brook Trail (map 7)

Distances from north end of Peaked Hill Rd.

to Province Pond: 1.4 mi.

to Province Pond Shelter: 1.6 mi.

to dirt road parallel to Langdon Brook: 3.7 mi. (6 km.), 2 hr. 35 min.

Mountain Pond Trail (WMNF)

Trail closed: see page 317.

This trail is the most direct route from Chatham Center to Jackson or Lower Bartlett. Follow Butter Hill Rd., which runs northwest from opposite the cemetery in Chatham Center, for 1 mi. to a dirt road (left). Follow the dirt road to McDonough Brook, where cars may be parked. The trail begins here, crosses the brook, and then turns right into the woods. It follows a logging road, climbs steadily for some distance but levels before reaching the pond. The Mountain Pond Trail follows the north shore, past a good *spring* and a WMNF shelter. A branch known as the Mountain Pond Cabin Trail (WMNF) leads left around the south side of pond and shortly unites west of the pond with north branch. In about 0.3 mi., these trails terminate at Slippery Brook Rd. Turn left for Jackson, Intervale, and Bartlett (in 6.6 mi. this road, now called Town Hall Rd., intersects NH Rte. 16A).

Mountain Pond Trail (map 7)

Distances from McDonough Brook parking area

to Mountain Pond Shelter: 2.7 mi., 1 hr. 55 min.

to Slippery Brook Rd.: 3.6 mi. (5.8 km.), 2 hr. 20 min.

SABLE, CHANDLER, AND EASTMAN MOUNTAINS

Former trails over the summits of Sable (3540 ft.) and Chandler (3330 ft.) have been abandoned. Eastman Mountain summit (2936 ft.) may be reached by the Eastman Mountain Trail.

Eastman Mountain Trail (CTA)

This trail leaves the south side of the Slippery Brook Trail at the height-of-land in the col between Eastman Mountain and S. Baldface, opposite the lower terminus of the Baldface Knob Trail. The trail first descends slightly through spruce then deciduous growth, and rises quite steeply onto the northerly ridge, where outlook points provide fine views of S. Baldface and Sable mountains. It continues generally southeast to the first and higher of the two summits, which has a rewarding 360-degree view. For experienced hikers, a bushwhack of about 15 min., in a generally south direction, leads to the lower (southern) summit along an abandoned section of trail that formerly ascended the mountain from the south side. This secondary summit is partially wooded, but has good outlooks in several directions. The trail to the main summit is well marked with blazes and cairns. The nearest *water* is at a brook crossing about 0.5 mi. east of the col on the Slippery Brook Trail.

Eastman Mountain Trail (map 7)

Distance from Slippery Brook Trail

to Eastman Mountain, north summit: *est.* 0.8 mi., ¾ hr.

Bradley Brook Trail (WMNF)

Trail closed: see page 317.

Turn west off NH/ME Rte. 113 on a paved road just south of large brick house shortly north of the junction of Rte. 113 and Chatham Rd., north of Chatham Center. This road is 2.3 mi. south of the AMC Cold River Camp entrance. Follow this road about 1 mi., crossing the bridge over Bradley Brook at 0.6 mi., and turn right on an old town road just before a gate. It may be best to park cars off the road at this point. Continue on the old road about 0.3 mi. to where Bradley Brook Trail leaves left (northwest). The trail turns sharp right in about 50 yd. and shortly bears left away from a stone wall (right). It ascends gradually through young mixed hardwoods and enters thicker woods. The trail, climbing generally southwest, follows the south side of Bradley Brook, later crosses McDonough Brook, slabs around the south side of the summit of

Eastman Mountain, crosses a logging road, and shortly ends at the Slippery Brook Trail, about 1.8 mi. west of the col between Eastman and S. Baldface. Turn left for Slippery Brook Rd. (1.9 mi.), or right for the Baldfaces.

Bradley Brook Trail (map 7)

Distance from old town road at start of trail

   to Slippery Brook Trail junction: 2.5 mi., 2 hr.

Slippery Brook Trail (WMNF)

This trail leaves the Baldface Circle Trail on the south 0.3 mi. from NH/ME Rte. 113. It soon crosses a branch of Chandler Brook, ascends generally southwest through woods, crosses another branch brook, and crosses the col between S. Baldface and Eastman, where the Baldface Knob Trail leaves right (north) for S. Baldface, and the Eastman Mountain Trail leaves left (south). The Slippery Brook Trail soon descends to Slippery Brook, which it crosses six times. Shortly after the last crossing, on the east bank, the Bradley Brook Trail leaves left. After nearly 2 mi. on the east bank, the trail ends at Slippery Brook Rd., 200 yd. north of locked gate. For lower Bartlett continue 7.2 mi. down Slippery Brook Rd., which becomes Town Hall Rd., to NH Rte. 16A.

Slippery Brook Trail (map 7)

Distances from NH Rte. 113

   to start of Slippery Brook Trail (via Baldface Circle Trail): *est.* 0.3 mi.

   to Baldface Knob Trail and Eastman Mountain Trail junction: *est.* 3.3 mi., 2 hr. 40 min.

   to Bradley Brook Trail junction: 5.3 mi., 3 ¼ hr.

   to Slippery Brook Rd.: 7.2 mi. (11.5 km.), 4 ¼ hr.

TO WILD RIVER AND CARTER RANGE

The Wild River Forest, lying between the Carters and the Baldface-Royce Range, is described in the Carter-Moriah section. It may be approached at several points from N. Chatham. Its southern part is reached via the Eagle Link Trail, which is the most direct route to Carter Notch and Jackson via Perkins Notch. The central part is reached by the Basin Trail and the northern part, at Hastings, by NH/ME Rte. 113.

Carter Notch and Jackson via Perkins Notch

Carter Notch is reached by way of the Eagle Link Trail. At the Eagle Link-Wild River Trail junction turn left (south), follow the Wild River Trail through Perkins Notch down to the Wildcat River Trail, and follow that north to Carter Notch.

Carter Notch via Perkins Notch (map 7)

Distances from start of Baldface Circle Trail

   to Wild River Trail junction (via Eagle Link): 6.4 mi., 4 hr.

   to Wildcat River Trail junction (via Wild River Trail): 10.4 mi., 6 hr.

   to Carter Notch (via Wildcat River Trail): 12.1 mi. (19.5 km.), 7½ hr.

Jackson is reached by following the Carter Notch route through Perkins Notch to Bog Brook Trail, which is then followed south to the Carter Notch Rd., which leads to Jackson. This route from N. Chatham to Jackson is longer and harder than the route via Slippery Brook Trail, but it is more attractive.

Jackson via Perkins Notch (map 7)

Distances from start of Baldface Circle Trail

   to Bog Brook Trail junction (via Wild River Trail): 9.2 mi., 6 hr.

   to Carter Notch Rd.: 11.9 mi. (19.1 km.), 7 hr.

   to Jackson: 17.2 mi.

THE BALDFACE RANGE

This range includes two prominent summits, S. Baldface (3569 ft.) and N. Baldface (3591 ft.). With Eagle Crag (3060 ft.), a buttress on the ridge northeast of the latter, these summits enclose a cirque-like valley on their east. Mt. Meader on the north, and

Sable, Chandler, and Eastman mountains on the south, are parts of the same mountain mass. There is a WMNF shelter just below the ledges on S. Baldface.

Baldface Circle Trail (AMC)

This trail is recommended as probably the most attractive in the N. Chatham Region. The mountains were swept by fire in 1903, which denuded their summits and upper slopes, so that for about 4 mi. the trail affords unobstructed views. The trail is blazed in blue. The circle proper begins and ends at the junction of the main trail from NH/ME Rte. 113 and a short trail to Emerald Pool.

From Rte. 113 the path starts at the south end of a parking area on the west side of the road just south of the bridge over Charles Brook, 0.2 mi. north of the AMC Cold River Camp driveway. Slippery Brook Trail leaves on the left, 0.3 mi. from the highway, and the Baldface Circle Trail continues straight to the junction, known as Circle Junction, 0.7 mi. from Rte. 113.

A short trail leaves right at this junction and in about 0.3 mi. reaches Emerald Pool, worth seeing.

Baldface Circle Trail via South Baldface

From the junction the trail runs southwest, then turns south, crosses a brook, and climbs a grade to where it enters an old logging road, which it follows for almost a mile. At 0.4 mi. from the junction a trail leads off to Chandler Gorge 0.3 mi., and 0.1 mi. beyond, the older Bigelow Path leaves on the left for the same point. About 2 mi. from the junction the trail swings around the south side of Spruce Knoll to Last Chance *Spring (last water, unreliable)*. About 100 ft. southeast of the spring is the WMNF S. Baldface Shelter. Above the spring the trail up the ledges, marked by cairns and blue blazes, is very steep for about 0.5 mi. On the broad shoulder below the final summit of S. Baldface, the Baldface Knob Trail to Slippery Brook Trail leaves left (south). The Baldface Circle Trail then ascends to the summit of S. Baldface and, bearing right, follows a broad ridge, mostly in the open, to the summit of N. Baldface. Descending from the summit the trail turns more northeast and again follows a broad, open ridge toward Eagle Crag. At 0.9 mi. from the summit of N. Baldface, the Bicknell Ridge Trail leaves right, a scenic route to the valley. Just 0.3 mi. beyond this point is a junction where Eagle Link leaves left (west) for Wild River Trail, the Meader Ridge Trail continues straight ahead (north) for Eagle Crag and Mt. Meader, and the Baldface Circle Trail turns sharp right and descends steeply.

There is *no water* between Last Chance Spring and a small *spring (water unreliable)* on the north side of N. Baldface. There is *water*, except in very dry times, 0.6 mi. below the Crag.

Baldface Circle Trail via S. Baldface (map 7)
Distances from NH/ME Rte. 113

> *to* Circle Junction: 0.7 mi., 25 mi.
> *to* Last Chance Spring and S. Baldface Shelter: 2.5 mi., 2 hr.
> *to* top of ledges: 2.9 mi., 2 ½ hr.
> *to* Baldface Knob Trail junction: 3.1 mi., 3 hr.
> *to* S. Baldface summit: 3.6 mi., 3 hr. 20 min.
> *to* N. Baldface summit: 4.7 mi., 4 ¼ hr.
> *to* Bicknell Ridge Trail junction: 5.6 mi., 4 ¾ hr.
> *to* Eagle Link Trail junction: 5.9 mi., 5 hr. 10 min.
> *to* Circle Junction: 8.9 mi., 6 ½ hr.
> *to* NH/ME Rte. 113: 9.5 mi. (15.3 km.), 6 hr. 55 min.

Baldface Circle Trail via Eagle Crag

From Circle Junction continue straight ahead, then bear right, cross to the north bank of Charles Brook, bear left upstream, pass Mossy Slide (left). The trail rises steadily through a hardwood forest to the foot of Eagle Crag, passing several brooks. The *last water (unreliable in dry seasons)* is 0.6 mi. before Eagle Crag. The Bicknell Ridge Trail leaves left, and 0.1 mi. beyond, 0.6 mi. from Circle Junction, the trail crosses a branch of Charles Brook. At 1.3 mi. from the junction a side trail to Eagle Cascade leaves left and, after crossing the brook above the falls, continues up through the woods to end at the Bicknell Ridge Trail. The Baldface Circle Trail to Eagle Crag continues straight ahead and soon begins the steep climb up the ledges to the bare ridges. About 0.2 mi. south of the top of the crag, the Baldface Circle Trail turns left (south) at a right angle, the Eagle Link continues straight (west), and the Meader Ridge Trail diverges right (north). The Bicknell Ridge Trail leaves left 0.3 mi. south of this junction. There is a small *spring (water unreliable)* on the trail at the base of the cone of N. Baldface. From N. Baldface the trail swings southeast on the skyline to S. Baldface, then descends east to ledges, then steeply down to treeline, Last Chance Spring, S. Baldface Shelter, and from there down through the woods to Circle Junction and to NH/ME Rte. 113.

Baldface Circle Trail via Eagle Crag (map 7)
Distances from NH/ME Rte. 113

> *to* Circle Junction: 0.7 mi., 25 min.
>
> *to* Bicknell Ridge Trail (lower end) junction: 1.3 mi., 50 min.
>
> *to* Eagle Cascade Trail. 2 mi., 1 hr. 20 min.
>
> *to* Eagle Link Trail, Meader Ridge Trail junction: 3.6 mi., 3 hr.
>
> *to* Bicknell Ridge Trail (upper end) junction: 3.9 mi., 3¼ hr.
>
> *to* N. Baldface summit: 4.8 mi., 4 hr.
>
> *to* S. Baldface summit: 5.9 mi., 4 hr. 50 min.
>
> *to* Circle Junction: 8.9 mi., 6 ½ hr.
>
> *to* NH/ME Rte. 113: 9.5 mi. (15.3 km.), 6 hr. 55 min.

Baldface Knob Trail (WMNF)

This trail leaves north of the Slippery Brook Trail in the col between Eastman and S. Baldface, opposite the beginning of the Eastman Mountain Trail. It climbs to Baldface Knob and continues along the open ridge to end at the Baldface Circle Trail, on the broad shoulder below the final summit of S. Baldface. Turn left on the Baldface Circle Trail for the summit.

Baldface Knob Trail (map 7)
Distances from NH/ME Rte. 113

> *to* start of Baldface Knob Trail (via Slippery Brook Trail): *est.* 3.3 mi., 2 hr. 40 min.
>
> *to* Baldface Circle Trail junction: *est.* 4.5 mi., 3 hr. 55 min.

to S. Baldface summit (via Baldface Circle Trail): *est*. 5 mi.
(8 km.), 4 hr. 25 min.

Eagle Link Trail (AMC)

This trail leaves the Wild River Trail on the east side, 5.4 mi.
southwest of Wild River Campground, and follows what was
formerly a section of the Wild River Trail northeast for 0.5 mi. It
shortly crosses the Wild River, then bears sharp right, and
ascends generally east at a moderate grade, crosses a large brook,
slabs the north slope of N. Baldface, and ends at the junction of
the Baldface Circle and Meader Ridge trails, 0.2 mi. south of
Eagle Crag. Follow the Baldface Circle Trail straight ahead for
the shortest way to ME/NH Rte. 113 in N. Chatham. Turn right
for the Bicknell Ridge Trail or N. Baldface.

Eagle Link Trail (map 7)

Distances from Wild River Trail junction

to Wild River crossing: 0.5 mi., ¼ hr.

to Baldface Circle Trail/Meader Ridge Trail junction: 2.8 mi.
2 hr.

to NH/ME Rte. 113, N. Chatham (via Baldface Circle Trail):
6.4 mi. (10.2 km.), 4¼ hr.

Bicknell Ridge Trail (CTA)

This trail diverges left from the northern branch of the Baldface Circle Trail 1.3 mi. from NH/ME Rte. 113 and immediately
crosses Charles Brook. It ascends gradually through second-
growth hardwood. After about a mile, it turns more west, rises
more rapidly along the south side of Bicknell Ridge, and, just
before the first ledges, crosses a brookbed where there is usually
water among the boulders. Soon after the trail emerges on the
open ledges, the Eagle Cascade side trail leaves right. From here
the trail mostly travels over broad open ledges with excellent
views. It meets the Baldface Circle Trail on the ridge 0.9 mi.
north of the summit of N. Baldface and 0.3 mi. south of Eagle
Link.

Bicknell Ridge Trail (map 7)
Distances from NH/ME Rte. 113

> *to* start of Bicknell Ridge Trail (via Baldface Circle Trail, north
> branch): 1.3 mi.
> *to* Eagle Cascade side trail junction: 2.7 mi.
> *to* Baldface Circle Trail junction: 3.7 mi. (5.9 km.), 3 hr.

Bicknell Ridge may also be reached by ascending the Baldface
Circle Trail farther toward Eagle Crag and turning left on the side
trail that leads to Eagle Cascade. Cross the brook above the
cascade and follow the trail about 0.4 mi. to Bicknell Ridge
Trail. (Distance from Rte. 113 via Eagle Cascade side trail to
upper junction Bicknell Ridge Trail and Baldface Circle Trail:
about 4.1 mi., 3¼ hr.)

MOUNT MEADER

Mt. Meader is a 2783-ft. summit in the ridge connecting the
Baldfaces and Royces. A prominent shoulder juts east from the
mountain into the Cold River valley. Open ledges near the
summit make the climb worthwhile, and the trail ascending the
shoulder permits a circuit route in either direction.

Mount Meader Trail (AMC)

The trail leaves the west side of NH/ME Rte. 113 in N.
Chatham about 0.5 mi. north of the entrance to the Baldface
Circle Trail and the bridge over the Charles Brook. It follows a
logging road that stays on the north side of Mill Brook and
crosses a branch brook at 0.8 mi. The trail continues mostly on an
old road for nearly a mile, then bears right and begins a steep
climb of about 0.5 mi. up the heel of the ridge. Coming out on
open ledges with fine views, it reaches a slightly lower false
summit of Mt. Meader in 0.2 mi., where it joins the Basin Rim
and Meader Ridge trails.

Mt. Meader Trail (map 7)

Distance from NH Rte. 113

   to Meader Ridge Trail junction: 2.9 mi. (4.7 km.), 2 hr. 25
   min.

Meader Ridge Trail (AMC)

   From its junction with the Mt. Meader Trail on the false
summit of Mt. Meader, the Meader Ridge Trail descends slightly
in a southwest direction, crosses a small brook (*water unreliable*), and in 0.2 mi. reaches the true summit (2783 ft.). Descending again, with a small intervening ascent, it passes several
good viewpoints to the east. At a sign, a short branch trail to the
west leads up to a large open ledge with fine views to the west
(branch trail may be overgrown). The Meader Ridge Trail
reaches the deepest col of the ridge (2620 ft.) 0.4 mi. from the
summit and crosses a fairly reliable small brook. (Sometimes
there is also *water* upstream a short distance in a swampy place
called the Bear Traps.) The trail now climbs about 0.5 mi. to a
high intermediate peak (2878 ft.), and descends 0.3 mi. to
another col (2760 ft.). Climbing again, it emerges from timberline in 0.4 mi., passes over the summit of Eagle Crag, and
then descends slightly 0.2 mi. to meet the Baldface Circle and
Eagle Link trails.

Meader Ridge Trail (map 7)

Distances from Mt. Meader Trail junction

   to deep col: 0.6 mi.

   to Baldface Circle Trail/Eagle Link Trail junction: 2.0 mi.
   (3.2 km.), 1¼ hr.

Basin Rim Trail (AMC)

   Connecting the summits of Mt. Meader and W. Royce Mountain, this trail leaves the Mt. Meader Trail at its highest point, just
east of the summit. It descends north over the ledges and, just
after crossing a small brook, reaches a col near Ragged Jacket, a
prominent hump. Slabbing the east side of the Jacket, without

going over the summit, the trail soon descends steeply from ledge to ledge down the north slope to the main col of the ridge (1850 ft.). From there it rises gradually over ledges to Rim Junction, passing a magnificent viewpoint at the edge of the cliffs on the east. At Rim Junction it crosses the Basin Trail. In about 0.3 mi. there is a view east over the great cliff of the Basin Rim. Passing west of the prominent southeast knee of W. Royce, the trail climbs, with only short intervening descents, to the summit of W. Royce, where it ends at the Royce Trail. There is a *brook* (*water unreliable*) 0.6 mi. before the summit of W. Royce.

Basin Rim Trail (map 7)
Distances from Mt. Meader Trail junction
   to Rim Junction: 1.2 mi., 40 min.
   to W. Royce Mountain summit: 3.7 mi. (5.9 km.), 2¾ hr.

Basin Trail (WMNF)

This trail leads from the WMNF Basin Pond parking area. The access road is on the west side of NH/ME Rte. 113, north of N. Chatham. The trail enters the woods, crosses numerous brooks, and in approximately 0.3 mi. meets and continues on an old logging road. It crosses a small clearing, two small brooks, and bears right. At 1.0 mi. from the parking area a side trail leads left about 0.3 mi. to Hermit Falls; it rejoins the main trail at 1.2 mi. At 1.1 mi., the main trail turns left uphill from logging road. After crossing a wide, stony *brook* (*last sure water*) 0.4 mi. from this turn, it soon reaches the base of a great cliff and climbs very steeply along its foot and left side to the ridge and Rim Junction, where it meets the Basin Rim and Black Angel trails. (Follow the Black Angel Trail 0.4 mi. to reach Blue Brook Shelter.) Follow the Basin Rim Trail north for less than 0.3 mi. to reach a fine viewpoint at the top of the cliff that overhangs the Basin.

From Rim Junction the Basin Trail descends northwest. A side trail leaves left for Blue Brook Shelter 0.3 mi. from Rim Junction. The trail crosses and follows Blue Brook rather closely, then bears away north, crosses a planked boardwalk over a wet area, and ends at the WMNF Wild River Campground on Wild River Rd., 5 mi. south of NH/ME Rte. 113.

Basin Trail (map 7)

Distances from Basin Pond parking area

   to Rim Junction: 2.3 mi., 2 hr.

   to Blue Brook Shelter (via Black Angel Trail): 2.7 mi., 2¼ hr.

   to Blue Brook Shelter (via side trail): 3 mi., 2 hr. 25 min.

   to Wild River Campground: 4.5 mi. (7.2 km.), 3 hr. 35 min.

MOUNT ROYCE

This mountain, situated north of N. Chatham, has two distinct summits, E. Royce (3115 ft.) and W. Royce (3202 ft.).

Royce Trail (AMC)

Leave the west side of NH/ME Rte. 113 about 75 ft. above the entrance to the Brickett place (about 0.3 mi. north of the access road to the WMNF Cold River Campground) and follow a narrow road about 0.3 mi. Cross the Cold River and bear right on trail, which is blazed in blue. In 1.1 mi. the trail crosses and recrosses the river, then, crossing the south branch of Mad River, it rises more steeply and soon passes Mad River Falls. A side trail leads left 70 ft. to a viewpoint. The trail becomes rather rough, with large boulders, and rises steeply under the imposing ledges for which this mountain is famous. At 1 mi. from the falls, the Laughing Lion Trail enters right, and at a height-of-land 0.2 mi. beyond, after a very steep ascent, the Royce Connector Trail to E. Royce branches right. For W. Royce, trail bears left at this junction and descends somewhat, then climbs to the height-of-land between the peaks, where the Burnt Mill Brook Trail to Wild River Rd. leaves slightly right while the Royce Trail turns abruptly left (west) and ascends the steep wall of the col. It then continues by easy grades over ledges and through stunted spruce to the summit, where it meets the Basin Rim Trail. There is usually *water* between the Royce Connector Trail and the Burnt Mill Brook Trail.

Royce Trail (map 7)

Distances from NH/ME Rte. 113

 to Mad River Falls: 1.6 mi., 1 hr.

 to Laughing Lion Trail junction: 2.6 mi., 2 hr.

 to Royce Connector Trail junction: 2.8 mi., 2 hr. 20 min.

 to W. Royce summit: 4.0 mi. (6.4 km.), 3½ hr.

Royce Connector Trail

This short trail connects the Royce Trail and the E. Royce Trail. (Distance from Royce Trail junction to E. Royce Trail junction: 0.1 mi.)

Burnt Mill Brook Trail (WMNF)

This trail gives access to the Royces from the north. It leaves Wild River Rd. at the south end of Burnt Mill Brook bridge, 2.7 mi. south from NH/ME Rte. 113. It ascends logging roads south for 1.2 mi. and then bears southeast, climbing more steeply and crossing the brook three times, to the col between E. and W. Royce, where it meets the Royce Trail. Watch carefully for trail to W. Royce, which leaves sharply right at the height-of-land.

Burnt Mill Brook Trail (map 7)

Distance from Wild River Rd.

 to Royce Trail junction: 2 mi. (3.2 km.), 1 hr. 50 min.

East Royce Trail (AMC)

This trail, blazed in blue, leaves the west side of NH/ME Rte. 113 just north of the height-of-land, about 0.3 mi. north of the Laughing Lion outlook, and 3 mi. north of the Brickett Place. It immediately crosses Evans Brook and ascends steeply, crossing several other brooks in the first half-mile. At a final brook crossing at 1 mi. (*last water*) the Royce Connector Trail for W. Royce enters from the left. The E. Royce Trail emerges on open ledges at about 1.1 mi., reaches an open subsidiary summit at 1.3

mi., and the true summit, also bare, 0.1 mi. farther. A spur trail can be followed over several more ledges to a large open ledge with a beautiful outlook to the north and west.

East Royce Trail (map 7)
Distance from NH/ME Rte. 113

to E. Royce summit: 1.4 mi. (2.3 km.), 1 hr. 50 min.

Laughing Lion Trail (CTA)

This trail leaves the west side of NH/ME Rte. 113 just north of a roadside picnic area, about 2 mi. north of the Brickett Place. It descends in a northerly direction to Cold River, then ascends steeply, mostly southwest and west, with occasional fine views down the valley. The trail continues northerly at a mostly steep grade, leveling off just before it ends at the Royce Trail, south of the col between E. and W. Royce. Turn right for the summits of E. or W. Royce.

Laughing Lion Trail (map 7)
Distances from NH/ME Rte. 113

to Royce Trail junction: 1 mi., 1 hr.

to E. Royce summit (via Royce Trail): 1.8 mi. (2.9 km.), 2 hr.

THE ROOST

This small, 1300-ft. hill, near Hastings, permits fine views of the Wild River Valley, the Evans Brook Valley, and many mountains.

Roost Trail (WMNF)

This trail leaves the east side of NH/ME Rte. 113 from the north end of the lower north bridge over Evans Brook at Hastings. It ascends a steep bank for 100 ft., then bears right (east) and ascends gradually along a wooded ridge, crosses a *brook* (*water unreliable*) at 0.3 mi., rises somewhat more steeply at its upper end, and emerges on a small rock ledge. A side trail descends east through woods to spacious open ledges where the views are excellent. The main trail continues, descends generally southeast at a moderate grade, crosses a small brook, and swings back west on an old road to return to Rte. 113 just south of the upper (south) bridge over Evans Brook at Hastings.

Roost Trail (map 7)
Distances from north trailhead, NH/ME Rte. 113

   to the Roost: 0.5 mi. (25 min.)

   to south trailhead, Rte. 113: 1.3 mi. (2.1 km.), 50 min.

Wheeler Brook Trail (WMNF)

This trail leaves the south side of US Rte. 2 about 2.3 mi. east of the junction of NH/ME Rte. 113 and Rte. 2. It follows the west side of Wheeler Brook, crosses the brook several times, and, keeping generally to an old logging road, rises about 1400 ft. to its highest point, along the northwest slope of Peabody Mountain (there is no trail to the wooded summit). The trail descends generally southwest and ends at logging operation near Little Lary Brook Rd. Because of the logging, care should be exercised in following the trail to the road, especially when hiking in the reverse direction, since the last 400 yd. or so of the trail have been obliterated. From the end of the trail at Little Lary Brook Rd., it is 1.3 mi. to the junction with Rte. 113, 6.8 mi. north of the Brickett Place and 3.5 mi. south of the Rte. 2 and Rte. 113 intersection.

Wheeler Brook Trail (map 7)
Distances from NH/ME Rte. 113

   to Little Lary Brook Rd.: 3.4 mi. (5.5 km.), 3 hr.

   to Rte. 113 (via Little Lary Brook Rd.): 4.7 mi., 3 hr. 40 min.

MOUNT CARIBOU

This 2828-ft. mountain, called Calabo in the Walling map of Oxford County (1853), is in the town of Mason, ME. The bare, ledgy summit affords excellent views. The Caribou and Mud Brook trails make a pleasant loop.

Caribou Trail (WMNF)

The trail leaves the east side of NH/ME Rte. 113 about 6.2 mi. north of the Brickett Place. There is parking space for several cars at the trailhead. The trail immediately crosses Morrison Brook and follows it for about 2.3 mi., crossing and recrossing several times. One crossing, at 1.6 mi., is at the head of Kees Falls, a 25-ft. waterfall. The trail levels off at the height-of-land as it crosses the col between Gammon Mountain and Mt. Caribou. Here the Mud Brook Trail leaves right for the summit of Mt. Caribou, passing Caribou Shelter and Caribou Spring (*water unreliable*) in 0.3 mi. The Caribou Trail continues ahead at the junction, descends more rapidly, and turns northeast toward the valley of Bog Brook, east of Peabody Mountain. The trail ends at Bog Rd., which leads to Rte. 2, 1.5 mi. west of W. Bethel. (Sign at junction of Bog Rd. and Rte. 2 reads STEAM RAILROAD-IANA.)

Caribou Trail (map 7)

Distances from NH/ME Rte. 113

to Mud Brook Trail junction: 2.7 mi., 2 hr.

to Mt. Caribou summit: 3.2 mi., 2½ hr.

to Bog Rd.: 5.2 mi. (8.4 km.), 4 hr.

to US Rte. 2: 8 mi., 5¼ hr.

Mud Brook Trail (WMNF)

This trail leaves NH/ME Rte. 113, 5.5 mi. north of the Brickett Place, 2 mi. south of the bridge at Hastings, and just north of the Mud Brook bridge. It runs generally east along the north side of Mud Brook, rising gradually for 1.8 mi., then crossing a branch brook and swinging more steeply left (north). The trail crosses several smaller brooks and, 1 mi. from the beginning of the steep ascent, comes out on a small bare knob with excellent views east. There is a short descent into a small ravine, where *water* may be found. The trail then emerges above timberline and crosses ledges for about 0.3 mi. to the summit of Mt. Caribou. It descends north, passes Caribou Spring (*water unreliable*) left, Caribou Shelter right 200 ft. farther, and meets the Caribou Trail in the col.

Mud Brook Trail (map 7)

Distances from NH/ME Rte. 113

   to Mt. Caribou summit: 3.1 mi., 2 hr. 20 min.

   to Caribou Trail junction: 3.6 mi. (5.8 km.), 2 hr. 35 min.

Haystack Notch Trail (WMNF)

The shortest route from Hastings to Mason, this trail starts on the east side of NH/ME Rte. 113, 4.6 mi. north of the Brickett Place. It runs generally east, easy going with little climbing, through Haystack Notch and down the valley of the west branch of the Pleasant River to meet the Miles Notch Trail at an old road heading northeast to a paved road that leads generally north-northwest to W. Bethel on US Rte. 2, across from the Post Office.

Haystack Notch Trail (map 7)

Distances from NH/ME Rte. 113

   to Miles Notch Trail junction: 5.2 mi. (8.4 km.), 3 hr.

   to W. Bethel (via old dirt road and paved road): 6.4 mi.

Miles Notch Trail (WMNF)

This trail begins in Stoneham, ME where the Great Brook Trail leads left. Access to the trailhead is from N. Lovell, ME. From ME Rte. 5N, go left for 1.9 mi. on a road marked "Evergreen Valley." Turn right on a road just before a bridge with a sign "F & R Ames" at corner. The trailhead is 1.5 mi. from this corner. The trail leads generally north and, after about 0.3 mi., turns abruptly left on a blue-blazed trail. It climbs for about a mile, then again makes an abrupt left turn, leaving the blue blazes. The trail crosses a branch of Beaver Brook, becomes much steeper after another mile, and passes through Miles Notch, where the Red Rock Trail leaves left (west) for the summit of Speckled Mountain. From Miles Notch it descends along Miles Brook to the terminus of the Haystack Notch Trail.

From here an old road may be followed out to the road that leads generally north-northwest to W. Bethel on US Rte. 2, across from the Post Office.

Miles Notch Trail (map 7)

Distances from trailhead, N. Lovell, ME

   to Red Rock Trail junction: 3.7 mi., 2¾ hr.

   to Haystack Notch Trail, old road junction: 6.1 mi. (9.8 km.), 4½ hr.

SPECKLED MOUNTAIN

This 2877-ft. mountain lies northeast of N. Chatham, NH, in Stoneham, ME. It is one of at least three mountains in Maine that have been known by this name. The summit's open ledges have excellent views in all directions. There is a WMNF observation tower (no longer staffed) on the summit and a *spring* about 0.1 mi. north of the tower.

Blueberry Ridge Trail (CTA)

This trail leaves the Bickford Brook Trail at a sign 0.6 mi. beyond the trailhead at the Brickett Place on NH/ME Rte. 113. It descends to cross Bickford Brook, then ascends southeast to an open area just over the crest of Blueberry Ridge, where the White Cairn Trail leaves right. The Stone House Trail comes in 0.2 mi. farther on the right, only a few steps beyond the top of Blueberry Mountain. A half-mile overlook loop with excellent views to the south leaves the Blueberry Ridge Trail shortly after the White Cairn junction and rejoins it shortly before the Stone House junction. From the junction with the Stone House Trail, marked by signs and a large cairn, the Blueberry Ridge Trail to Speckled Mountain bears left and descends to a *spring (water unreliable)*, a short distance from the trail on the left (north). The trail turns sharply right here, continues over ledges marked by cairns, through occasional patches of woods and over several humps.

Above the top of the Rattlesnake Brook ravine the trail ends at the Bickford Brook Trail in a shallow col about 0.5 mi. below the summit of Speckled Mountain. The Bickford Brook Trail leads somewhat more steeply through woods and over ledges to the rocky top. (The Blueberry Ridge Trail may also be reached from Shell Pond Rd. via the Stone House or White Cairn trails.)

Blueberry Ridge Trail (map 7)

Distances from the Brickett Place, NH/ME Rte. 113

to start of Blueberry Ridge Trail (via Bickford Brook Trail): 0.6 mi., ½ hr.

to Blueberry Mountain, Stone House Trail junction: 1.5 mi., 1½ hr.

to spring: 1.8 mi., 1¾ hr.

to Bickford Brook Trail junction: 3.7 mi., 2 hr. 50 min.

to Speckled Mountain summit (via Bickford Brook Trail): 4.1 mi. (6.6 km.), 3 hr. 20 min.

Bickford Brook Trail (WMNF)

This trail extends from the Brickett Place on NH/ME Rte. 113 to the top of Speckled Mountain. The trail enters the woods near the garage. The WMNF service road to Speckled Mountain enters left at 0.3 mi., and the two coincide for about 2.5 mi. In 0.4 mi. the Blueberry Ridge Trail leaves right (east) for Bickford Slides. Another path leaves right 0.2 mi. farther for the upper end of the Slides, forming a loop. A third path to the Upper Slides leaves right at 0.2 mi. above the second (upper loop) path. The Bickford Brook Trail crosses a branch of the brook, then bears slightly left and ascends more steeply. The *last sure water* is at a logging camp site. Farther up on the ridge the Spruce Hill Trail enters left. The trail then passes west and north of the summit of Ames Mountain and into the col between Ames and Speckled mountains, where the Blueberry Ridge Trail enters again right. The trail then continues upward about 0.5 mi. more to the summit.

Bickford Brook Trail (map 7)
Distances from the Brickett Place, NH/ME Rte. 113
   to Blueberry Ridge Trail, lower junction: 0.6 mi.
   to Spruce Hill Trail junction: 2.8 mi.
   to Blueberry Ridge Trail, upper junction: 3.5 mi.
   to Speckled Mountain summit: 4.1 mi. (6.6 km.), 3¼ hr.

Spruce Hill Trail (WMNF)

In combination with the Bickford Brook Trail, this trail is the shortest route to Speckled Mountain. It leaves the east side of NH/ME Rte. 113, 0.6 mi. north of Laughing Lion Trail and 2.8 mi. north of the Brickett Place. It ascends generally southeast through woods (with excellent views of Evans Notch) to the summit of Spruce Hill, descends to a subsidiary col, then climbs to connect with the Bickford Brook Trail.

Spruce Hill Trail (map 7)
Distance from NH/ME Rte. 113
   to Bickford Brook Trail junction: 1.8 mi. (2.9 km.), 1¼ hr.

Cold Brook Trail (WMNF)

Access to the Cold Brook Trail is from ME Rte. 5N in N. Lovell, ME, by following a road with a sign "Evergreen Valley" for 2 mi., taking the first right after a bridge with Evergreen Valley sign, and continuing 0.4 mi. farther. The WMNF sign is on the paved road, but a gravel road may be followed for 0.5 mi. to a parking area. Trail goes about 1 mi. through a current lumbering operation, then turns left at house marked "Sugar Hill," the Duncan McIntosh House. The trail climbs the Cold Brook valley, passes west of Sugarloaf Mountain, and ascends the south side of Speckled Mountain. It emerges on open ledges about 1.5 mi. south of the summit. With excellent views for the next mile, the trail ends at the summit.

Cold Brook Trail (map 7)
Distance from trailhead, N. Lovell, ME
   to Speckled Mountain summit: 4.7 mi. (7.6 km.), 3 hr. 20 min.

Red Rock Trail (WMNF)

This trail, with fine views of the mountains in this section of Maine, leaves west from the Miles Notch Trail in Miles Notch, bears northwest, shortly west and ascends Red Rock Mountain. It then follows the ridge to Butters Mountain with several changes in elevation. Just beyond, in the col, the Great Brook Trail diverges southeast descending to W. Stoneham. The trail then turns south, soon crosses the summit of Durgin Mountain, and bears southwest to the summit of Speckled Mountain. There is a *spring* near the trail about 0.1 mi. east of the observation tower.

Red Rock Trail (map 7)

Distances from Miles Notch Trail junction

   to Great Brook Trail junction: 3.3 mi.

   to Speckled Mountain summit: 5.5 mi. (8.9 km.), 3¼ hr.

Great Brook Trail (WMNF)

This trail begins in Stoneham, ME, where the Miles Notch Trail leaves right (northeast). Access to the trailhead is from N. Lovell. From ME Rte. 5N, turn left at road marked "Evergreen Valley" and follow it for 1.9 mi. Turn right on a road just before bridge marked with sign "F & R Ames." The trailhead is 1.5 mi. from this corner. The trail continues up the old road about 1.5 mi. through open woods and crosses Great Brook. It leaves the old road, follows Great Brook, mostly northwest, becoming steeper in the last 0.5 mi., reaches the ridge, and joins the Red Rock Trail in the col between Butters and Durgin mountains.

Great Brook Trail (map 7)

Distances from trailhead, N. Lovell, ME

   to Red Rock Trail junction: *est.* 3.8 mi.

   to Speckled Mountain summit (via Red Rock Trail): 6 mi. (9.6 km.), 3 hr. 55 min.

ALBANY MOUNTAIN

Views from the open summit ledges are excellent in all directions. The area is just off the east side of map 7, Carter-Mahoosuc. Refer to the USGS Bethel or the E. Stoneham quadrangle.

Albany Notch Trail (WMNF)

Trail closed due to storm damage: see page 317.

From US Rte. 2 at W. Bethel, go south on ME Rte. 7 about 6 mi. to ME Rte. 18, which leads south about 1 mi. to the WMNF Crocker Pond Campground. About halfway, the Albany Notch Trail leaves right (southwest). Park off the road. The trail is wide and almost level for the first mile. At 0.6 mi., just before a small brook crossing, the Albany Mountain Trail leaves left (south). The Albany Notch Trail ascends to the height-of-land. Beyond there, at 1.7 mi., another trail goes left (east) and connects with the Albany Mountain Trail. The Albany Notch Trail continues south to old wood roads and ME Rte. 5.

Albany Notch Trail
USGS Bethel or E. Stoneham
Distances from ME Rte. 18
to Albany Mountain Trail junction: 0.6 mi.
to connector trail junction: 1.7 mi.
to ME Rte. 5: *est.* 3.8 mi. (6 km.), 1 hr. 55 min.

Albany Mountain Trail (WMNF)

Trail closed due to storm damage: see page 317.

Leaving from the Albany Notch Trail, this trail ascends the north slope of Albany Mountain. About 0.5 mi. below the summit, a trail branches right (west), leading in 0.5 mi. to the Albany Notch Trail on the south side of the notch. The Albany Mountain Trail continues ahead and shortly enters the open summit area. From this point the trail is well cairned and leads directly to the summit. (There are many side paths made by blueberry pickers.)

Albany Mountain Trail
USGS Bethel or E. Stoneham

Distances from ME Rte. 18

to start of Albany Mountain Trail (via Albany Notch Trail):
0.6 mi.

to Albany Mountain summit: 2 mi. (3.2 km.), 1 hr. 25 min.

BLUEBERRY MOUNTAIN

This 1820-ft. mountain is a long, flat, outlying spur running southwest from Speckled Mountain. The top is mostly one big ledge, with sparse and stunted trees. Numerous open spaces afford excellent views, especially from the southwest ledges on the summit. There is *water* in many places at the top except in dry seasons.

Stone House Trail (CTA)

This trail and the White Cairn Trail are reached from the Shell Pond Rd., which leaves NH/ME Rte. 113 on the east side, about a mile north of Cold River Camp. A padlocked steel gate on Shell Pond Rd. 1.1 mi. in from Rte. 113 makes it necessary to park cars at that point.

The trail leaves left 0.5 mi. beyond the gate, east of an open shed, follows a logging road, and approaches Rattlesnake Brook. Off-trail, downstream from an old logging road bridge, is Rattlesnake Flume, a gorge worth visiting. At a point 0.2 mi. upstream from the flume, the logging road bears uphill left, and the trail continues straight ahead. Just beyond, a side trail descends right about 150 yd. to Rattlesnake Pool, at the foot of a small cascade. In about 0.3 mi. the trail bears left on a still older logging road and at 1 mi. begins to climb, straight and steep, generally northwest, to the top of the ridge, where it ends at the Blueberry Ridge Trail, only a few steps from the top of Blueberry Mountain. At the junction bear right for Speckled Mountain, or turn left to descend via the White Cairn Trail (0.2 mi.), or via the Blueberry Ridge Trail, Bickford Slide, and the Bickford Brook

Trail to the Brickett Place on NH/ME Rte. 113. (Blueberry Mountain can also be ascended by the Blueberry Ridge Trail, described under Speckled Mountain.)

Stone House Trail (map 7)

Distances from Shell Pond Rd.

   to Rattlesnake Flume: 0.2 mi.

   to Blueberry Mountain summit: 1.3 mi. (2.1 km.), 1½ hr.

White Cairn Trail (CTA)

This trail provides access to the open ledge on Blueberry Mountain and, with the Stone House Trail, makes an easy half-day circuit. The trail leaves Shell Pond Rd. 0.2 mi. beyond the locked gate at a small clearing. It follows old logging roads north and west to an upland meadow, then climbs steeply up the right (east) margin of the cliffs seen from the road, to a broad view of the Baldfaces and Royces. Following the crest of the cliffs to the west, the trail turns north, traversing open ledges and scrub growth along a line of cairns to end at a junction with the Blueberry Ridge Trail, 0.2 mi. west of the upper terminus of the Stone House Trail. A short side trail crosses the upper ledges to the right (east) to a second outlook.

White Cairn Trail (map 7)

Distances from Shell Pond Rd.

   to cliffs: *est.* 1 mi., 1 hr.

   to Blueberry Ridge Trail junction: *est.* 1.5 mi., 1½ hr.

TO KEZAR LAKE

Shell Pond Trail (WMNF)

   Trail closed due to storm damage: see page 317.

Drive about 0.7 mi. north of N. Chatham on NH Rte. 113 and turn right on Shell Pond Rd. Cross a bridge over the Cold River, bear right and continue 1.1 mi. to a locked steel gate where cars must be parked. Follow the road about 0.5 mi. to the Stone House. Shell Pond Trail starts just beyond the house (sign), goes southeast across a level field, bears left then right, and crosses Rattlesnake Brook in about 0.4 mi. It enters the woods east of the latter and passes north of Shell Pond. It ascends gradually, crossing a brook, and ends at Deer Hill Rd., 1.2 mi. from the Stone House.

Shell Pond Trail (map 7)

Distances from gate on Shell Pond Rd.

   to Stone House: *est.* 0.5 mi.

   to Deer Hill Rd.: *est.* 1.8 mi. (2.9 km.), 1 hr.

Horseshoe Pond Trail (WMNF)

   Trail closed due to storm damage: see page 317.

   This trail starts from Deer Hill Rd., 1.1 mi. east of the Shell Pond trailhead, at a cairn at the edge of a parking area at a bend in the road. It heads south past the Styles grave, enclosed by a stone wall, to the north shore of Horseshoe Pond. Near the pond a side trail leads right (west) to join the Conant Trail.

   From 0.5 mi. farther east on Deer Hill Rd., Chadbourne Rd. leads southwest to the northeast shore of Horseshoe Pond. About midway, old abandoned town roads lead easterly to the paved road near the west shore of Kezar Lake.

DEER HILL AND LITTLE DEER HILL

   Trail closed due to storm damage: see page 317.

   Deer Hill, often called Big Deer, is located in Stow, ME, across the Cold River, east of the AMC Cold River Camp. The views from the east and south ledges are excellent. Little Deer, a lower hill west of Deer Hill that rises only about 600 ft. above the valley, gives fine views of the valley and the Baldfaces from its summit ledges.

Little Deer Hill

   Trail closed due to storm damage: see page 317.

   This trail starts at the dam at the AMC Cold River Camp. After crossing the stream it remains level for a short distance, then rises slowly, crosses a logging road, and climbs at a moderate grade through the woods. It crosses two open ledges with views of the valley, then ascends through a short woods section before reaching the open summit. At the summit bear left for Big Deer Hill, or continue ahead and descend an alternate (shorter but very steep) loop, to reach the trail from Big Deer at the base.

Little Deer Hill may also be reached from the south by way of the unsigned road that branches east from NH Rte. 113 about 0.5 mi. south of the AMC Cold River Camp and just south of Chandler Brook. Just beyond the bridge bear left and follow the road across the field and up a slight rise to the woods. About 0.1 mi. after entering the woods the trail to Little Deer and Big Deer diverges sharp right (watch for this turn). This trail entrance may be reached from Cold River Camp by following the wood road right just after crossing the river at the dam.

Little Deer Hill (map 7)
Distance from dam at AMC Cold River Camp
to Little Deer Hill summit: 0.6 mi. (1 km.), ½ hr.

Big Deer Hill
Trail closed due to storm damage: see page 317.

Big Deer Hill (1220 ft.) may be reached by following the Little Deer trail from Cold River Camp over Little Deer, leaving the northeast corner of the summit ledge and descending into the col, where there is a *spring* just east of the trail. The trail then ascends gradually, generally east, to the Big Deer summit. A few steps east of the summit there is a viewpoint, and 0.3 mi. south the trail crosses another outlook, then descends through woods. A trail leaves left (south) for Deer Hill Spring ("Bubbling Spring"). Just beyond the junction the trail swings right (east) and for a short distance passes through scrub in a previously clearcut area. It descends through woods, crosses an old road, and a small brook in a shallow gully, shortly bears left, then sharp left at a junction, where a right turn leads up to Little Deer Hill. From this junction the trail runs nearly level out to the wood road on the east side of the Cold River. Bear right for Cold River Camp, and sharp left for the bridge over Cold River and out to NH Rte. 113.

Big Deer Hill (map 7)

Distances from dam at AMC Cold River Camp

to Big Deer Hill summit: 1.4 mi., 1¼ hr.

to Cold River Camp: 3.0 mi. (4.8 km.), 2¼ hr.

PINE, LORD, AND HARNDON HILLS

These three hills lie east of N. Chatham. Although they are not high, their open ledges and pastures afford interesting views.

Conant Trail (CTA)

Trail closed due to storm damage: see page 317.

Turn east off NH Rte. 113 just south of Chandler Brook, cross the Cold River, bear right (southeast) across a field up a short rise, and continue straight on Deer Hill Rd. for 1.5 mi. from Rte. 113. Turn right and about 100 yd. farther park on left in large cleared area.

From this point travel east, cross Colton Brook (Colton Dam is located several hundred yards to the right from here), and continue to where the trail divides. (This is a circle trail; the following description is for the route from south to north.) To the right, the trail follows Hemp Hill Rd. for about 0.8 mi. to an old cellar hole on the Johnson Place. Leaving Hemp Hill Rd. on the left (east) side, the trail ascends gradually to an outlook over the Cold River Valley, turns more northeast, and climbs to the top of Pine Hill and along the ridge, where there are views from open ledges.

Continuing straight toward Lord Hill, the trail descends, crosses a brook, then a logging road, rises slightly, and soon comes out on the Lord Hill ledges overlooking Horseshoe Pond. The trail then turns left, climbs about halfway to the top of a ledge, and enters woods on the right. It soon emerges into an abandoned pasture, where a side trail 1.2 mi. long leads right to the west shore of Horseshoe Pond, and then to a sandy beach at the north end. The Conant Trail continues ahead for 0.3 mi., turns left, slabs the south side of Harndon Hill, past a *spring (water unreliable)* to a cellar hole, then passes down Harndon Hill Rd. It shortly enters a logging road, which leads back to Hemp Hill Rd.

Conant Trail (map 7)

Distances from Colton Dam parking area

   to Hemp Hill Rd. circle junction: 0.2 mi.

   to top of Pine Hill: 1.3 mi.

   to Lord Hill ledges: 2.2 mi.

   to Horseshoe Pond side trail junction: 2.3 mi.

   to Hemp Hill Rd. circle junction: 4 mi. (6.2 km.), 2 hr. 50 min.

MINOR POINTS OF INTEREST
IN NORTH CHATHAM

Chandler Gorge, Fall, and Flumes

   The beautiful rocky gorge on Chandler Brook is reached from the S. Baldface branch of the Baldface Circle Trail. The Chandler Gorge Trail leaves the S. Baldface Circle Trail on the left 0.4 mi. above Circle Junction, and runs generally south about 0.4 mi. It enters the gorge at a point where it is easy to go up to the fall, or by stepping across the brook, to view the two flumes through which the stream descends. The older Bigelow Path leaves the Baldface Circle Trail slightly farther up and runs to the same point. (Distance from NH Rte. 113: 1.6 mi., 1¼ hr.)

Bickford Slides

   Between Blueberry Mountain and the west ridge of Speckled Mountain, Bickford Brook twice passes a series of flumes, falls, and boulders of unusual beauty. There are three routes to the slides from the Bickford Brook Trail. (1) The Blueberry Ridge Trail leaves right at 0.6 mi. from the Brickett Place, leading in 0.1 mi. to the upper end of the lower slide; (2) a path leaves right at 0.8 mi., leading in 0.1 mi. to the lower end of the upper slide and crosses the brook; and (3) a path leaves right at about 1 mi. for the upper end of the upper slide, crosses the brook, and descends on the high bank of the gorge. Path #2 joins path #3 after crossing below the upper slide, and the trail continues down to the Blueberry Ridge Trail, making a loop of 0.8 mi. (Round-trip distance from the Brickett Place, visiting both slides: *est.* 2.3 mi., 1 hr. 35 min.)

On the way to Speckled Mountain by the Bickford Brook Trail a detour to visit the upper slide adds about 0.3 mi. Descending Blueberry Mountain, the Blueberry Ridge Trail crosses Bickford Brook at the upper end of the lower slide.

Cold River

A path turns left (northwest) from the dam across the river from the AMC Cold River Camp, leads along the east bank of Cold River, across the outlet brook from Shell Pond, and ends at Shell Pond Rd. (Distance: 1.1 mi.)

Shell Pond

There is no cleared trail around this shallow pond. The circuit — a rough scramble — may be made by means of an overgrown trail, which leaves the Shell Pond Trail, right, a few yards beyond the Rattlesnake Brook crossing and bears southeast toward the shore of the pond. Upon reaching the southwest end of the pond turn north, cross Shell Pond Brook, the outlet from the pond, and return to Shell Pond Rd. (Round-trip distance from Shell Pond Rd.: 1 mi.)

Deer Hill Spring

Trail closed due to storm damage: see page 317.

Deer Hill Spring is an interesting shallow pool with air bubbles rising through a small light-colored sand area.

Turn east on the road that leaves NH Rte. 113, 0.7 mi. south of the AMC Cold River Camp entrance and just south of bridge over

Chandler Brook. Cross the Cold River and continue on Deer Hill Rd. Park at a turnout in about 1.4 mi. The trail leaves left (north) and ascends easily north and northeast for about 0.6 mi. Bear right at a cairn and descend southeast and east 0.1 mi. to the spring, which is also called Bubbling Spring. (Distance from parking area: 0.7 mi.)

A short cutoff from this trail to Big Deer leaves left (north) about 75 ft. before the trail turns right to descend to the spring. The cutoff ascends gradually through spruce, then a fine stand of birch, heads generally west and northwest through mixed growth, and ends at the trail leading to Big Deer (south side) about 100 ft. above an abandoned mica mine. Turn right for the summit of Big Deer. Turn left to descend to the wood road on the east side of Cold River. (Length of cutoff: 0.2 mi.)

JOCKEY CAP

This ledge near Fryeburg, ME, rises perpendicularly some 200 ft. above the valley and offers an excellent view in all directions. At the top, a bronze profile of the surrounding summits stands as a monument to Robert E. Peary. A trail leaves the north side of US Rte. 302, 1 mi. east of Fryeburg through a gateway between a store and the former Jockey Cap Cabins. It soon reaches Molly Lockett's cave, named for the last of the Pequawket Indians who is said to have used it for a shelter. Trail makes a sharp left turn at the cave and then divides. The left branch continues ahead, circling to the west; the right branch turns abruptly right and climbs steeply, hugging west side of ledge. Care should be taken in descending, since there are many side paths that do not necessarily lead back to the cabins. (Round trip by either route: 25 min.)

STARKS MOUNTAIN

The most traveled and scenic route up this 1020-ft. mountain near Fryeburg is along a ski trail. To reach the trailhead, follow

US Rte. 302 to a point 1 mi. southwest of the intersection where NH/ME Rte. 113 branches northwest, and turn southeast at State of Maine Information Center. Cross the railroad tracks and turn left on a dirt road to the parking area at the base of the ski trail. Distance from Rte. 302 to parking area is 0.8 mi. Bear right up ski slope to end of ski trail, through a wooded area, and then over open ledges to the summit. (Distance: 0.5 mi., ½ hr.)

PLEASANT MOUNTAIN, MAINE

Pleasant Mountain has had extensive logging. See the *AMC Maine Mountain Guide* for trail descriptions.

This 2007-ft. mountain, east of Fryeburg in Denmark, ME, commands an unusual view. There is a 60-ft. fire tower on the summit. Entrance to a ski area on the north peak is 0.7 mi. from US Rte. 302. (Refer to the USGS Fryeburg quadrangle.)

SABATTUS MOUNTAIN

This low (1280 ft.) peak in Center Lovell, ME, has an almost vertical ledgy face on its southwest aspect that affords superb and impressive views of the countryside from Pleasant Mountain, ME to the Baldfaces. The trail is reached by following ME Rte. 5 North from a Lovell building marked "Lovell Town House 1796." (Do not confuse this with the building marked "Town of Lovell Selectman's Offices.") Take the first right, Sabattus Rd., (paved), 0.1 mi. north of the Town House, and continue straight to a fork, 1.6 mi. from Rte. 5. Bear right at the fork for 0.3 mi. on a dirt road past a private residence to a small parking area left. The trail, indicated by a large "S" on a tree, leaves opposite the parking area. It climbs by easy grades past the old fire tower site to open summit ledges. Excellent views to south and west. (Round trip: 1 hr.)

Mahoosuc Range Area

This section includes the region along the Maine-New Hampshire border from Lake Umbagog southward to the big loop of the Androscoggin River from Gorham to Bethel. It is drained principally by this river and its branches. The Mahoosuc Trail extends the entire length of the Mahoosuc Range, from Gorham to Old Speck, and there are numerous side trails. All of the trails in this section are east of NH Rte. 16 and north of US Rte. 2.

Grafton Notch State Park includes the ridge crest in Maine from the New Hampshire border up through N. Baldpate. The rest of the land in this section is owned mainly by the Brown Company and other paper companies. Hiking is permitted through their courtesy. State laws restrict wood and charcoal fires to designated sites (shelters and Trident Col); for permits, contact state fire wardens. Please camp only at these sites. (Elsewhere, only stoves are permitted.)

ALPINE CASCADES

The Alpine Cascades on Cascade Brook, which flow from the northwest slope of Cascade Mountain, are an attractive sight except in dry seasons. As you approach Berlin from Gorham on NH Rte. 16, note the Cascade Paper Mill off to the right. From the railroad crossing drive 0.7 mi. and take sharp right turn onto Watson St., continue a short distance to its end, and park in the area near the railroad bridge. Cross the railroad bridge, follow the track south about 0.4 mi. to a point near the Cascade Mill, and follow a footpath off left. This path divides. The right branch leads about 100 yd. to the foot of Cascade Falls; the left branch ascends about 0.3 mi. across a power line to an old reservoir where there is a nice view down the Androscoggin Valley.

The reservoir may also be reached by going to the south from the end of Burgess St. on the Berlin East Side, and following an old dirt road for about 1 mi. A trail descends from the reservoir to the Alpine Cascades.

FROM BERLIN VIA SUCCESS POND ROAD

Success Pond Rd. runs from Berlin to Success Pond, about 14 mi. The entrance to the road may be reached by going north on NH Rte. 16 through Berlin, then crossing the Androscoggin River. (Berlin Mills Bridge was closed in 1979. However, another bridge farther north is open.) Go south, then turn left on a dirt road. Success Pond Rd. is the widest of several dirt roads and heads directly east through the mill yard. Watch for large trucks. The road may be closed at times during the winter or the mud season. Trailheads may sometimes be obscure due to recent logging activity.

Success Trail (AMC)

Mt. Success (3590 ft.), in Success, NH (reached also from Shelburne on the south via the Austin Brook and Mahoosuc trails), is accessible from Success Pond Rd.

The trail leaves right about 5.4 mi. from the beginning of the road, where there is a small brook at the right. It crosses the brook and ascends a logging road. Within 0.1 mi. take the right fork. The trail enters the woods 0.3 mi. beyond, where it makes a left turn. At 0.8 mi. the trail jogs right. Somewhat over 2 mi. from Success Pond Rd., at the top of the ridge, the trail passes a side path to an outlook and turns right. It descends about 200 yd., then bears left and ascends the shallow ravine above (*water*), reaching the Mahoosuc Trail in about 0.3 mi. Follow the Mahoosuc Trail about 0.9 mi. right to the summit.

Success Trail (map 7)

Distances from Success Pond Rd.

to Mahoosuc Trail junction: *est*. 3 mi.

to Mt. Success summit (via Mahoosuc Trail): *est*. 3.5 mi. (5.5 km.), 2¼ hr.

Carlo Col Trail (AMC)

The trail leaves Success Pond Rd. about 8.2 mi. from its beginning in a flat, open area with the sharp peak of Mt. Goose Eye visible to the east-southeast. Coinciding at first with the Goose Eye Trail, it follows a level lane for 250 ft., then branches right and climbs 150 ft. to a broad logging road, which it follows east for 0.8 mi., with little gain in elevation. Turning left off the road at a log yard, the trail immediately crosses the main brook, continues near it for about 0.3 mi., then turns obliquely left away from the brook and follows a branch road with a steeper rise. It crosses back to the south, over the north and south branches of the main brook, and bends east up the rather steep south bank of the south branch to its head at Carlo Col Shelter (*last water* for several miles). Continuing up the dry ravine, the trail ends at the Mahoosuc Trail about 0.3 mi. beyond the shelter, in a small box canyon known as Carlo Col, the first col on the ridge southwest of Mt. Carlo.

Carlo Col Trail (map 7)

Distance from Success Pond Rd.

to Mahoosuc Trail junction: 2.6 mi. (4.1 km.), 1½ hr.

Goose Eye Trail (AMC)

Mt. Goose Eye (3860 ft.) is ascended from Success Pond Rd. and also by the Mahoosuc Trail. The origin of the name of this mountain is debated: some claim it to be "Goose High," because the geese in their flights from the Rangeleys are said just to clear its top.

The trail leaves Success Pond Rd. about 8.2 mi. from its beginning, at the same trailhead as the Carlo Col Trail. It heads east, then swings left to northeast, crossing brooks about 0.3 and 0.5 mi. from the road. It follows logging roads, crosses others, makes a wide right turn, and begins the ascent. The grade increases to the top of a subsidiary ridge, where the trail bears left and crosses to the shoulder of the main peak, emerging from the woods on a short, steep, rocky ridge just below (north of) the bare west summit, the main peak of Goose Eye. *Caution.* Just as the trail leaves the woods, it ascends about 30 ft. up a steep ledge, where one must use care, and then continues over bare ledge to the summit.

About 200 yd. east of the summit the trail ends at the Mahoosuc Trail. Bear right (south) for Mt. Carlo, or continue east to the east and north peaks of Goose Eye.

Goose Eye Trail (map 7)

Distance from Success Pond Rd.

to Mt. Goose Eye, main summit: 3 mi. (4.8 km.), 2 hr. 20 min.

Notch Trail (AMC)

The trail to Mahoosuc Notch leaves right, at a clearing about 11 mi. from the beginning of the Success Pond Rd. Watch carefully for blazes. The trail follows a logging road about 0.5 mi. to a small brook (right). It takes the right fork of the road across the brook and soon passes a clearing and cabin on the right. The trail bears left from the road about 50 yd. beyond the cabin and then proceeds up through the woods, soon reaching beaver ponds, which it skirts on the left side. This section of the trail is very muddy and badly eroded in places. About 0.5 mi. farther, near the height-of-land, it meets the Mahoosuc Trail. At this point the valley, which has been an ordinary one, changes sharply to a chamber formation similar to the Ice Gulch in Randolph, NH, and the high cliffs of the notch, which have not been visible at all on the lower part of the trail, come in sight.

The Mahoosuc Trail, descending from Fulling Mill Mountain, enters here at the right and continues on east through Mahoosuc Notch.

Notch Trail (map 7)

Distance from Success Pond Rd.

to Mahoosuc Trail junction: *est.* 2.8 mi. (4.5 km.), 1¾ hr.

Speck Pond Trail (AMC)

Success Pond Rd. forks about 12 mi. from its beginning. Follow the right fork about 0.8 mi. to where the trail leaves right. It follows a logging road for 200 yd., then bears right into the woods. At about 0.5 mi. it recrosses the logging road in a clearing before following a series of old logging roads through woods at easy grades for about 2 mi. It then climbs steeply for 1 mi. to a lookout near the northwest summit of Mahoosuc Arm. The trail continues generally east, more or less on contour, on the north slope of the arm but below the top of the ridge, then rises to about 3700 ft. The May Cutoff to Mahoosuc Arm from the Mahoosuc Trail enters right at this point. The Speck Pond Trail then turns northeast and descends to the north end of Speck Pond to end at Speck Pond Campsite. Camping is supervised by a caretaker during the summer months to prevent damage to the area's fragile soils. A fee is charged for camping during summer.

Speck Pond Trail (map 7)

Distance from Success Pond Rd.

to Speck Pond Campsite: *est*. 3.3 mi. (5.3 km.), 2 hr. 40 min.

MAHOOSUC TRAIL (AMC)

This AMC trail extends the entire length of the range from Gorham, NH to the summit of Old Speck. Beyond its junction with the Centennial Trail, the Mahoosuc Trail is a section of the Appalachian Trail. There are four shelters — Gentian Pond, Carlo Col, Full Goose, and Speck Pond, with tent platforms and caretakers at several sites. Camping is carefully regulated to protect fragile soils, vegetation, and water purity, and a $2 fee (1982) is charged. This is a rugged trail, with many ups and downs, some rocky. Mahoosuc Notch is regarded by many who have hiked the entire length of the Appalachian Trail as the most difficult mile. It can be hazardous in wet or icy conditions and can remain impassable through the end of May. *Hikers are cautioned not to rely on finding water except where indicated.*

Mahoosuc Trail, Part I. Gorham to Mount Hayes

Since this section of the Mahoosuc Trail is no longer part of the Appalachian Trail, most of its blazes are blue rather than white. To reach the trail, cross the Androscoggin River by the footbridge under the Boston & Maine Railroad bridge 1.3 mi. north of the Gorham post office on NH Rte. 16 to Berlin. On the east bank follow the road to the right (southeast) along the river for 0.6 mi., then cross the canal through the open upper level of the powerhouse (left of entrance). Beyond, keep straight ahead about 100 yd. to the woods at the east end of the dam, where the trail sign will be found. Turn left and follow an old road north along the side of the canal for 125 yd. and then turn right uphill. At 0.2 mi. from this turn the trail crosses beneath a power line; on entering the clearing, bear right for 30 ft. and then turn left up across it. Just after entering the woods the trail bears right and reaches, but does not cross a brook, follows it closely for 100 yd., ascends at only a slight grade for about 0.3 mi. to where a side trail to Mascot Pond leads right 0.2 mi. to the pond, just below the cliffs seen prominently from Gorham. The Mahoosuc Trail ascends a brook valley, which it crosses and recrosses four times. About 2.5 mi. from the Boston & Maine bridge, it passes Popsy Spring on the left and soon emerges on the southwest side of the flat, ledgy summit of Mt. Hayes (2566 ft.). At the top of the steep climb, an unmarked footway leads a few yards right to the best viewpoint south over the valley. A cairn marks the true summit of Mt. Hayes.

Mahoosuc Trail, Gorham to Mt. Hayes (map 7)
Distance from NH Rte. 16
   to Mt. Hayes summit: 3.1 mi. (5.1 km.), 2 hr. 20 min.

Mahoosuc Trail, Part II. Mount Hayes to Gentian Pond

The trail passes over the flat summit of Mt. Hayes, and in 0.2 mi., the upper terminus (right) of the Centennial Trail, on open ledges with good views north. From here the Mahoosuc Trail is part of the Appalachian Trail, marked with white blazes. It

descends north to the col between Mt. Hayes and Cascade
Mountain. (There is sometimes *water* in this col, either on the
trail or a few yards to the east.) The trail then ascends Cascade
Mountain by a southwest ridge, emerging on a bare summit ledge
(2606 ft.). It turns back sharply into the woods, descending
gradually northeast and east to the east end of the mountain. It
enters a fine forest and descends rapidly beside cliffs and ledges
to Trident Col. A side path leads left about 200 yd. to Trident Col
tent site, with space for four tents. *Water* is available about 50
yd. below (west of) the site.

The bare ledges of the rocky cone to the east of Trident Col
repay a scramble to the top. About 0.3 mi. beyond the col the trail
enters an old logging road, follows it for 100 yd., then branches
left, descends to the southeast, and slabs the ridge past the foot of
this peak, of a second similar peak, and of the peak just west of
Page Pond, which together form the Trident. The trail crosses
three or four brooks, one of which at least should have *water*,
then it ascends to Page Pond.

The trail passes the south end of the pond, crosses a beaver
dam, and climbs gradually, then steeply, to the summit of
Wocket Ledge, a spur from Bald Cap Dome. The fine view from
some ledges 50 ft. to the northwest, reached by a side trail,
should not be missed. The Mahoosuc Trail descends east, crosses
the upper left branch of Peabody Brook, then climbs around the
nose of a small ridge and descends gradually to the head of
Dream Lake. The trail bears left here, then right around the north
end of the lake and crosses the inlet brook. Just beyond, the
Peabody Brook Trail leaves right.

From the Peabody Brook Trail junction, the Mahoosuc Trail
follows a lumber road left 100 yd. It soon recrosses the inlet
brook, passes over a slight divide into the watershed of Austin
Brook, ascends through some swampy places, and descends to
Moss Pond. It continues past the west shore of the pond and
follows an old logging road down the outlet brook. About 0.3 mi.
below Moss Pond the trail turns abruptly right downhill from the

logging road to Gentian Pond, skirts the southwest shore of the pond, crosses a small brook first, then soon drops to cross the outlet brook. A few yards beyond are the Gentian Pond Shelter (capacity 20) and tent sites, and the Austin Brook Trail diverges right for North Rd. in Shelburne.

Mahoosuc Trail, Mt. Hayes to Gentian Pond (map 7)
Distances from Mt. Hayes summit
  to Centennial Trail junction: 0.2 mi.
  to Cascade Mountain summit: 2.1 mi., 1 ¼ hr.
  to Trident Col tent site: 3.5 mi., 2 hr.
  to Page Pond: 4.3 mi., 2 hr. 40 min.
  to Wocket Ledge: 5 mi., 3 ½ hr.
  to Dream Lake, inlet brook crossing: 6.1 mi., 4 hr.
  to Gentian Pond Shelter: 8.3 mi. (13.3 km.), 5 hr. 40 min.

Mahoosuc Trail, Part III. Gentian Pond to Carlo Col

From Gentian Pond Shelter the trail climbs about 0.5 mi. to the top of the steep ridge, whose ledges overlook the pond from the east, then descends more gradually. About 0.5 mi. farther it passes through a col, climbs over two steep humps, with *water* in the col beyond the second hump, and then begins to ascend the southwest side of Mt. Success. The grade is steep and the footing is rough for about the next 0.5 mi. The trail climbs over open ledges with an outlook to the southwest, passes through a belt of high scrub, and finally comes out on the summit of Mt. Success.

The trail turns sharp left here and descends through scrub then forest to the sag between Mt. Success and an unnamed peak marked "3345" on map 7, where the Success Trail diverges left. The main trail climbs slightly, slabs the east side of "3345", and then descends in a general northeast direction to a rough col. The trail then rises steadily, passes a tree marked with ME-NH border signs, and climbs up and down two cols that resemble box ravines. The second (east) col, 0.7 mi. from the ME-NH border, is known as Carlo Col. The Carlo Col Trail to Success Pond Rd.

diverges left here, and the Carlo Col Shelter is located at the head of a *brook* about 0.3 mi. down the Carlo Col Trail.

Mahoosuc Trail, Gentian Pond to Carlo Col (map 7)
Distances from Gentian Pond Shelter
to Mt. Success summit: 2.9 mi., 2 hr. 50 min.
to Success Trail junction: 3.5 mi., 3 hr. 20 min.
to Carlo Col Trail junction: 5.4 mi. (8.7 km.), 5 hr. 20 min.

Mahoosuc Trail, Part IV. Carlo Col to Mahoosuc Notch

From Carlo Col the trail climbs steadily to the bare southwest summit of Mt. Carlo with an excellent view. It then passes to the south of the wooded northeast summit, descends northeast, through a mountain meadow where there is usually *water*, to the col. The trail turns more north and climbs the steep side of Mt. Goose Eye. *Hikers should use care on the ledges.* The trail emerges on an open ridge about 200 yd. east of the main (west) peak, which is reached by the Goose Eye Trail. The Mahoosuc Trail then turns sharply to the right (east) and follows the bare ridge crest about 200 yd. to the scrub. It continues in the same direction through the col and climbs steeply through woods and open areas to the bare summit of the east peak of Mt. Goose Eye, where it turns sharply north down the bare ridge, and enters the scrub at the east side of the open space. Beyond the col the trail runs in the open nearly to the foot of the north peak, except for two interesting box ravines, where there is often *water*. At the foot of the north peak the trail passes through a patch of woods, then climbs directly to the summit. Here it turns east along the ridge crest and swings northeast down the steep slope, winding through several patches of scrub. At the foot of the steep slope it enters the woods, slabs the west face of the ridge, and descends to the col. Full Goose Shelter is located on a shelf here. There is a *spring* 100 ft. behind (east of) the shelter. The trail then turns sharply left and ascends, coming into the open about 0.3 mi. below the summit of the south peak of Fulling Mill Mountain. At this peak the trail turns sharply left, runs a few hundred yards through a meadow, and descends northwest through woods, first gradually then steeply, to the head of Mahoosuc Notch. Here the Notch Trail to Success Pond Rd. diverges sharply left (southwest).

Mahoosuc Trail, Carlo Col to Mahoosuc Notch (map 7)
Distances from Carlo Col Trail junction
>   *to* Mt. Carlo, southwest summit: 0.4 mi., ½ hr.
>   *to* Mt. Goose Eye, west peak: 1.7 mi., 2 hr.
>   *to* Mt. Goose Eye, east peak: 2.2 mi., 2 hr. 25 min.
>   *to* Mt. Goose Eye, north peak: 3.2 mi., 2¾ hr.
>   *to* Full Goose Shelter: 4.3 mi., 3¼ hr.
>   *to* Fulling Mill Mountain: 4.8 mi., 3 hr. 25 min.
>   *to* head of Mahoosuc Notch, Notch Trail junction: 5.9 mi. (9.4 km.), 4 hr. 10 min.

Mahoosuc Trail, Part V. Mahoosuc Notch to Grafton Notch

From the head of Mahoosuc Notch the trail turns sharply right (northeast) and descends the length of the narrow notch along a rough footway, passing through a number of boulder caverns, some with narrow openings where progress will be slow and where ice remains into the summer. The trail is blazed on the rocks with white paint. Great care should be exercised in the notch on account of slippery rocks and dangerous holes. Heavy backpacks will impede progress considerably. *Caution.* Mahoosuc Notch may be impassable through early June because of snow; snowshoes may not help.

At the lower end of the notch the trail leaves the brook, bears left, ascends gradually, and, after slabbing the eastern end of Mahoosuc Mountain for about 0.5 mi., follows the old logging road leading up the valley of Notch 2 for about 150 yd., then crosses to the north side of a brook, where there are some interesting waterfalls. The ledges below the falls are very steep, slippery, and dangerous.

The trail then ascends, winds along rocks and ledges, and

climbs through fine forest, in general slabbing the ridge of
Mahoosuc Arm at a very steep angle. A little more than halfway
up it passes the head of a little flume, in which there is sometimes
water. Near the top of Mahoosuc Arm the trail travels along
ledges and deer runs to the bare summit. The May Cutoff to the
Speck Pond Trail leaves left here. The Mahoosuc Trail follows
the open, winding ridge for about 0.5 mi., southeast, northeast,
and north, then drops steeply about 0.3 mi. to Speck Pond, about
3500 ft., said to be the highest pond in Maine. It is bordered with
thick woods. The trail crosses the outlet brook and continues
around the east side of the pond about 0.3 mi. to Speck Pond
Campsite (in summer, there is a caretaker and a fee for overnight
camping). The Speck Pond Trail descends from here to Success
Pond Rd.

The trail then climbs about 0.3 mi. to the southeast end of the
next hump on the ridge, passes over it, and slabs the east face of a
small second hump. In the gully beyond, a few yards east of the
trail, there is a *spring*. The trail climbs to the open shoulder of
Old Speck. The footway is definite up this open ridge, and hikers
need only to keep on the crest. Near the top of the shoulder the
trail bears right, re-enters the woods, and follows the wooded
crest about 0.5 mi. to the summit of Old Speck. Along the crest is
a series of blue blazes that mark the boundary of the Grafton
Notch State Park. At a point 0.3 mi. before reaching the summit,
the Old Speck Trail (part of the Appalachian Trail) leads left in
3.5 mi. to Grafton Notch.

Note: hikers carrying large packs should allow extra time to go
through Mahoosuc Notch.

Mahoosuc Trail, Mahoosuc Notch to Grafton Notch (map 7)
Distances from head of Mahoosuc Notch, Notch Trail
junction

   to foot of Mahoosuc Notch: 1 mi., 1 hr. 50 min.

   to Mahoosuc Arm summit: 2.5 mi., 3 ½ hr.

   to Speck Pond outlet crossing: 3.1 mi., 4 hr.

   to Speck Pond Shelter: 3.4 mi., 4 hr. 10 min.

to Old Speck Trail junction: 4.2 mi., 5 ¼ hr.
to Old Speck summit: 4.6 mi. (7.4 km.), 5 ½ hr.
Mahoosuc Trail, Total Length (map 7)
Distance from Gorham, NH
to Old Speck summit: 27.3 mi. (43.9 km.)

GRAFTON NOTCH

This general area, including the 3132-acre Grafton Notch State Park and climbs in the vicinity, is described in the *AMC Maine Mountain Guide*. The two trails that appear below are well inside Maine, but they are described in this book because the AMC maintains them.

Old Speck and Old Speck Trail (AMC)

Old Speck (4180 ft.) in Grafton, ME, called that to distinguish it from the "Speckled Mountains" in Stoneham, ME and in Peru, ME, is the third highest peak in the state.

The Old Speck Trail, part of the Appalachian Trail and so blazed in white, leaves ME Rte. 26 near the height-of-land, about 2.7 mi. northwest of Screw Auger Falls, where the road is level and there is a state park parking area with the sign "Hiking Trails" on the west side of the road. The trail ascends the scenic north ridge of Old Speck. From the north side of the parking lot follow the left trail (the right trail goes to Baldpate Mountain). In 0.1 mi., the Eyebrow Trail leaves right to circle an 800-ft. cliff shaped like an eyebrow. The Old Speck Trail crosses a brook and soon begins to climb, following a series of switchbacks to approach the falls on Cascade Brook. Above the falls the trail, now heading more north, crosses the brook for the last time (*last water*). Beyond the brook there are views along the top of the Eyebrow. The Old Speck Trail passes the upper terminus of the Eyebrow Trail on the right about 0.1 mi. beyond the brook crossing. The main trail bears left, ascends gradually to the N. Ridge where it bears more left, and follows the ridge, which has views southwest. At about 3300 ft. the trail turns southeast toward the summit, and at about 3600 ft. the Link Trail leaves left and descends 0.3 mi. to a brook, the old fire warden's cabin site, and the lower terminus of the East Spur Trail. The Old Speck Trail turns more south and ascends to end at the Mahoosuc Trail, 0.3 mi. west of the summit. Follow the Mahoosuc Trail 1.2 mi. right for Speck Pond Shelter. The summit, to the left, is flat and wooded, and the best views are from the observation tower.

Descending, leave the easterly end of the summit through scrub by following the East Spur Trail to open, smooth rock slopes on East Spur, then down over the ledges, through short patches of scrub, keeping near the south edge. About halfway down is Tri-Boulder Cave — the largest boulder is white and can be seen from above. At the lower end of the spur, where the cliffs fall off to Grafton Notch, the trail turns sharp left, northwest, slabbing the mountain, and ends at the site of the warden's cabin and the lower terminus of the Link Trail (blue blazes). The view from the spur toward the east and south is particularly good. *Ascending* the Link Trail, avoid the abandoned Fire Warden's Trail (formerly the Appalachian Trail) by following the blue blazes on a bearing just east of south. The East Spur Trail is not recommended in wet weather.

Old Speck Trail (map 7)

Distances from parking area off ME Rte. 26

to first brook crossing: 0.3 mi.

to last brook crossing: 1.1 mi.

to Eyebrow Trail junction, upper terminus: 1.2 mi.

to Link Trail junction: 3.1 mi., 2 hr. 40 min.

to Mahoosuc Trail junction: 3.5 mi., 3 hr. 10 min.

to Old Speck summit (via Mahoosuc Trail): 3.9 mi. (6.3 km.), 3 hr. 25 min.

BALDPATE MOUNTAIN

Baldpate Mountain, formerly called Bear River Whitecap or Saddleback, is just east of Grafton Notch. The higher E. Peak (3812 ft.) is open with excellent views. The W. Peak (3680 ft.), almost a mile to the southwest by trail, is covered with scrub but has good views. The shoulder (3000 ft.) to the southeast is called Mt. Hittie. Refer to the USGS Old Speck Mountain quadrangle.

Baldpate Mountain Trail (AMC)

This trail, part of the Appalachian Trail and so blazed in white, leaves the north side of the state park parking area off ME Rte. 26, the same trailhead as the Old Speck Trail. It soon crosses Rte. 26 and in 0.3 mi. it crosses a brook and passes Grafton Notch Shelter. The trail climbs steeply for a short distance beside the brook, bears right on a wood road, and ascends gradually to where a blue-blazed side trail leads right about 0.5 mi. to Table Rock, with fine views of Old Speck and down the Bear River Valley. The Baldpate Mountain Trail ascends steadily, then more steeply , to the west knob of Baldpate, with good views to the northwest. The trail then slabs the north side of the knob to a ridge extending toward the W. Peak, soon descends to a brook (*water unreliable*), then climbs steeply with rough footing to the W. Peak, which is covered with scrub growth but has good views in almost all directions. The trail, turning in a more northerly direction, loses only about 240 ft. altitude before it climbs to the E. Peak.

From this summit the trail descends northerly to the open top of Little Baldpate Mountain, and continues down the ridge, bearing right (northeast) in about 0.5 mi. After about 1 mi. the trail reaches, but does not cross Frye Brook. Later it crosses a branch brook, passes a series of waterfalls and cascades, then

Frye Brook Shelter, and reaches Andover-B Hill Rd. about 0.3 mi. farther. Turn right (east) for Andover.

Baldpate Mountain Trail
(USGS Old Speck Mountain quadrangle)

Distances from parking area off ME Rte. 26
to W. Peak summit: 2.8 mi., 2 hr. 20 min.
to E. Peak summit: 3.7 mi., 3 ¼ hr.
to Andover-B Hill Rd. junction: 7.4 mi. (11.9 km.), 5 ½ hr.

Lead Mine Bridge Reservation

This 155-acre public reservation lies on both sides of the Androscoggin River, where the Lead Mine Bridge crosses, half-way between Gorham and Shelburne.

FROM SHELBURNE

North Road

Trails leading from Shelburne into the Mahoosuc area all start at North Rd., which turns north off US Rte. 2 about 3.5 mi. east of Gorham, crosses the Androscoggin River on the Lead Mine Bridge at a small dam and power plant, and continues east along the north side of the Androscroggin Valley into Maine, rejoining Rte. 2 about 1 mi. north of Bethel. Cross roads connect with Rte. 2 via bridges at Shelburne and Gilead. There is little traffic on North Rd., so it is pleasant for driving or walking. Along with 275 yd. on Rte. 2, North Rd. links the Appalachian Trail between the Rattle River and Centennial trails. For the Rattle River Trail turn west on Rte. 2 and north on North Rd. for about 0.7 mi. to Hogan Rd., a dirt road on the left, to reach the Centennial Trail.

North Rd. Link, Appalachian Trail (map 7)
Distances from Rattle River Trail
to North Rd.: 0.2 mi.
to Hogan Rd.: 0.9 mi.

Centennial Trail (AMC)

The Centennial Trail is a relocation of a section of the Appalachian Trail that the AMC constructed in 1976, its centennial year.

Follow North Rd. 0.7 mi. north from its western end and turn left onto dirt road (Hogan Rd.). Follow it 0.3 mi. to a parking area left. Parking is also permitted at the junction of North and Hogan roads. Please avoid blocking the road.

The trail, blazed in white, leaves north from Hogan Rd., turns left into the woods, heading generally northwest. After 135 ft. it bears left up a steep bank, levels off, and reaches stone steps in 0.1 mi. The trail ascends rather steeply, then more gradually, with a limited view of the Androscoggin River. It turns left onto a wood road and crosses a brook at about 1.2 mi. (*last reliable water*). The trail then crosses a recent logging road and at 1.6 mi. turns sharply right — the ledge to the left has fine views of the Moriahs and Mt. Washington. It soon descends into a small valley, then ascends to open ledges with a fine view of the Mahoosuc Range and the Androscoggin Valley to the right. At 3.3 mi. the trail reaches an easterly summit of Mt. Hayes, where there is an excellent view of the Carter-Moriah Range and Northern Presidentials from open ledges. The trail descends slightly, then ascends across a series of open ledges to end at the Mahoosuc Trail at 3.7 mi. Mt. Hayes is 0.2 mi. left with fine views. The Appalachian Trail at this point follows the Mahoosuc Trail toward Cascade Mountain, 1.9 mi. right.

Centennial Trail (map 7)

Distance from Hogan Rd.

to Mahoosuc Trail junction: 3.7 mi. (6 km.), 2 hr. 35 min.

Peabody Brook Trail (AMC)

There is no overnight parking at the base of this trail, which is no longer part of the Appalachian Trail. The trail, blazed in blue, leaves the north side of the North Rd. in Shelburne, 1.3 mi. from

US Rte. 2. It passes between two cottages and continues as a
logging road, almost level until after crossing Peabody Brook at
0.2 mi. The trail, still a logging road, heads generally north along
the brook and bears left at 0.8 mi., where a newer logging road
bears right. About 100 yd. beyond, the road becomes a trail, and
soon begins to ascend moderately. At 1.2 mi. a path leaves left
and descends about 0.5 mi. to Giant Falls. The trail rises more
steeply, and at 1.5 mi. there is a good view (left) of Mts.
Washington and Adams through open trees. The trail climbs a
short ladder just beyond. About 0.5 mi. farther, it crosses the east
branch of the brook, then recrosses in 0.3 mi. From here the trail
is nearly level and enters a rather broad open area, making a
sharp left turn in about 0.4 mi. Soon Dream Lake is seen left. The
Dryad Fall Trail leaves right, 0.2 mi. beyond the sharp turn. The
Peabody Brook Trail ends at the Mahoosuc Trail, 120 yd. from
this junction.

Peabody Brook Trail (map 7)
Distances from North Rd.
    to Giant Falls path junction: 1.2 mi.
    to Dryad Fall Trail junction: 3 mi.
    to Mahoosuc Trail junction: 3.1 mi. (4.9 km.), 2 hr. 20 min.

Austin Brook Trail (AMC)

The Brown Company's Mill Brook Rd., a good logging road,
has bypassed the lower end of this trail so cars can be driven in for
a mile, perhaps farther, depending upon the condition of the road
(it has been reported that this road is sometimes gated). Park off
the road. Austin Brook is also known as Mill Brook.

From US Rte. 2 in the center of Shelburne, take the road that
goes northeast, across the Androscoggin River and turn left on
North Rd. Mill Brook Rd. leaves right almost immediately. Bear
left on the main road at several forks. In about 0.5 mi., at the site
of a cabin (left), go straight ahead where an old road goes left
along the brook and a new logging road goes right. Park here or
continue about 1 mi., past where the Austin Brook Trail (coming

from its official starting point on North Rd., see below) joins in from the left, and park at a stream crossing. Beyond the crossing, the Dryad Fall Trail leaves left. About 0.3 mi. farther, take the left fork of the road. The Austin Brook Trail continues along the logging road, which soon turns sharp right. From this point follow arrows at branch roads, bearing right.

In about 0.8 mi. the trail crosses the brook that drains Gentian Pond, crosses a clearing, enters a logging road, soon bears left away from it, and begins the rather steep climb of about 0.5 mi. to the Mahoosuc Trail at Gentian Pond Shelter. (Distance from Mill Brook Rd. parking area to pond: about 2.5 mi., 2 hr.)

The Austin Brook Trail officially begins on North Rd., nearly 0.5 mi. west of Mill Brook Rd., just to the west of Austin Brook. The entrance is through a gate on private land on the north side of North Rd. The trail follows the west side of Austin Brook, passing between the garage (left) and a summer camp called "The Wigwam" (right) about 0.3 mi. from the road. Then the trail turns sharply left, ascends a small bank, and continues about 0.5 mi. to Austin Brook, which it crosses to reach Mill Brook Rd., the logging road mentioned in the first paragraph. Turn left on the logging road, and continue ahead past the start of the Dryad Fall Trail, as explained above.

Austin Brook Trail (map 7)
Distances from North Rd.
> *to* Mill Brook Rd. junction: *est.* 1.3 mi.
> *to* Gentian Pond: 3.3 mi. (5.3 km.), 2 ½ hr.

Dryad Fall Trail (AMC)

Dryad Fall, one of the highest cascades in the mountains, is particularly interesting for a few days after a rainstorm, since its several cascades fall at least 300 ft. over steep ledges.

The trail is blazed in orange. It starts from Mill Brook Rd., the same logging road described for the Austin Brook Trail. Access to the trailhead is either via Mill Brook Rd. about 2.6 mi. in from North Rd., or via the Austin Brook Trail to Mill Brook Rd. The trail leaves left and gradually ascends old logging roads through woods for about 0.5 mi. It then drops down, right, to Dryad Brook, which it follows nearly to the base of the falls. From here the trail climbs steeply northeast of the falls. After rising several hundred feet with good views of the falls, the trail bears right and joins a logging road. It ascends left on this road, which soon meets another logging road. It follows this road left, crossing Dryad Brook above the falls and climbing left. The trail then heads generally west for 0.8 mi., until it slabs off obliquely right. From here almost to Dream Lake it goes through woods, generally west, rising at a moderate grade.

At the crest of the ridge the trail again meets a logging road, then descends to end at the Peabody Brook Trail. Turn right and follow the trail for about 100 yd. to the Mahoosuc Trail.

Descending, watch carefully for where the trail turns down steeply right off the logging road above the falls.

Dryad Fall Trail (map 7)

Distances from Mill Brook Rd.

to Dryad Fall: *est*. 0.8 mi.

to Dream Lake: *est*. 1.5 mi. (2.5 km.), 1 hr. 25 min.

Lary Flume

This is a wild chasm in the south slope of the Mahoosuc Range that resembles the Ice Gulch and Devils Hopyard, with many boulder caves and one fissure cave.

There is no trail, but experienced climbers have followed up the brook that may be reached by going east where the Austin Brook Trail begins its last 0.5 mi. of ascent to Gentian Pond.

LOCAL TRAILS

The town of Shelburne maintains a network of fire trails on the southern Mahoosuc slopes, giving access to the scenic local hills and mountains, such as Middle Mountain and Mts. Crag, Cabot, and Ingalls. Inquire locally of R. Finnson, or at the Philbrook Farm Inn on North Rd., for the current status of these trails.

Middle Mountain

Follow a rough road that leaves North Rd. on the north just east of Gates Brook, 2.4 mi. from the west junction of North Rd. and US Rte. 2. Continue on this road, which becomes a lumber road, for about 0.8 mi., past a trail right that leads to Mt. Crag at 0.4 mi., then take a left branch that leads up the ravine between First and Middle mountains. At the height-of-land between them, a branch trail turns right and climbs, at first steeply, along the ridge to the bare summit of Middle Mountain (1998 ft.), with fine views. The other branch descends west to the Peabody Brook Trail.

Mount Crag

This little 1415-ft. mountain is easily climbed and it offers a fine view up and down the Androscoggin Valley. It has two trails.

(1) Take the road described for the ascent of Middle Mountain. The trail leaves this road 0.4 mi. from North Rd., on the right, and climbs steeply to the ledges.

(2) Follow the Austin Brook Trail about 0.3 mi. in from North Rd., then go left on the Yellow Trail to Mt. Crag.

The Yellow Trail

This trail gives convenient access to the Austin Brook Trail and Mt. Crag from the Philbrook Farm Inn on North Rd. It leads west from the north end of the access road behind the cottages connected with the inn. The trail coincides with the Red Trail (see Mt. Cabot) for 50 yd., then branches left and leads west on a practically level grade. It crosses several wood roads, Mill Brook Rd. and Austin Brook, and the Austin Brook Trail, then heads generally northwest (yellow circle blazes) to the summit of Mt. Crag.

Mount Cabot

Running south and southeast from Mt. Success is a range of mountains of diminishing height — Mts. Ingalls and Cabot,

Crow's Nest, and Hark Hill. Several trails, distinguished by color, start from the access road at the Philbrook Farm Inn on North Rd. The easternmost is the White Trail, which leads to Crow's Nest. The Blue and Red trails both lead to the summit of Mt. Cabot, making a loop trip possible. The Yellow Trail slabs west to Mt. Crag and provides access to Mt. Ingalls via the Scudder Trail.

White Trail (Crow's Nest)

The White Trail is best reached from the dirt road east of the Philbrook Farm Inn that starts immediately west of the fire pond. Follow this road to the first cottage where the White Trail turns right by a large rock. Shortly, the Wiggin Rock Trail leaves left while the White Trail climbs east along an old logging road for a mile, and then makes a short, steep ascent to the wooded summit. The trail ends a few yards farther at a limited viewpoint to the northeast.

Orange Trail

From the junction with the White Trail, the Orange Trail climbs steeply for about 0.3 mi. to Wiggin Rock, a small ledge with a view southeast across the Androscoggin Valley. Beyond the viewpoint, the trail drops steeply for about 0.3 mi. to the Blue Trail.

Blue Trail (Mt. Cabot)

Starting from the gravel road immediately to the west of the Philbrook Farm Inn, the Blue Trail follows a good wood road, passes the Orange (Wiggin Rock) Trail on the right, and turns right on another old road shortly before it reaches an old reservoir. The Blue Trail continues much of the way on logging roads at an easy grade to a boundary marker, beyond which the trail climbs more steeply for about 0.3 mi. to the summit and the Red Trail.

The summit is wooded, but a ledge on the right shortly before the summit gives a view east, and an orange-blazed trail from the summit leads left to an open ledge with views southwest.

Red Trail (Mt. Cabot)

From the access road west of the Philbrook Farm Inn, the Red Trail bears left from the Blue Trail, coinciding with the Yellow Trail for 50 yd. It continues on a series of logging roads, passing a trail to a viewpoint on the right, crossing a small brook, circling around, and finally climbing steeply to approach Mt. Cabot from the north. The Judson Pond Trail, blazed yellow, leads left (downhill) shortly before the Red Trail reaches the summit and the junction with the Blue Trail. The summit is wooded, but a view southwest is reached by following the orange-blazed viewpoint trail for 100 yd. west. An eastward view may be obtained by following the Blue Trail a short distance, to a ledge in sight on the left.

Judson Pond Trail

The Judson Pond Trail is a connecting trail that leads from the Red Trail 0.1 mi. northwest of the summit of Mt. Cabot 0.2 mi. to the Ingalls-Cabot col and junction with the Scudder Trail. It turns sharp right in the col, circling northeast on contour, climbing only slightly to cross Little Ingalls Brook in about 0.3 mi. From there the trail drops another 0.3 mi. to Judson Pond, a tiny body of water attractive because of its secluded location.

Scudder Trail-Mount Ingalls

The Scudder Trail provides access to the ledges and summit of 2253-ft. Mt. Ingalls. It is reached from US Rte. 2 in central Shelburne by taking the bridge across the Androscoggin River, then turning left on North Rd. for 50 yd. to Mill Brook logging road. The Scudder Trail turns right off the logging road about 0.5 mi. from North Rd. and leads to the Ingalls-Cabot col and the

Judson Pond Trail. There is no water on the trail, but *water* may be found by following the Judson Pond Trail northeast about 0.3 mi. to Little Ingalls Brook.

The Scudder Trail, blazed white, turns sharp left at the col and soon comes out on a ledge on the west side of the ridge with views over the Androscoggin Valley. The trail climbs back eastward, passing the blue blazes of a Brown Company boundary in a ravine beneath a high cliff. The trail wanders back and forth, emerging on open ledges on both sides of the ridge, and finally circling an extensive ledge with views southwest. It then climbs steeply about 0.3 mi. to the wooded summit of Mt. Ingalls, covered with blowdown from the 1980 storm.

Scudder Trail (map 7)
Distances from North Rd.

> *to* start of Scudder Trail (via Mill Brook Rd.): 0.5 mi.
> *to* Ingalls-Cabot col: 1.8 mi., 1 hr. 10 min.
> *to* lower ledges: 2 mi., 1 hr. 20 min.
> *to* upper ledges: 3 mi., 2 hr. 10 min.
> *to* Mt. Ingalls summit: 3.5 mi. (5.6 km.), 2 hr. 35 min.

SECTION 17

The North Country

From the Presidential Range a vast wooded region extends sixty-five miles north to the Canadian border. It varies in width from twenty-five miles at the southern end to less than fifteen at Pittsburg. Its natural boundaries are the Israel and Moose rivers on the south, the Androscoggin and the Magalloway on the east, and the Connecticut on the west.

In the southern quarter of this region, south of the Upper Ammonoosuc River or of NH Rtes. 110 and 110A between the towns of Groveton and Milan, the mountains are still relatively high — two just over 4000 ft. — and grouped compactly into ranges, like those farther south. Above this line lies the true North Country, a region very similar to the adjacent section of Maine. The mountains become lower — very few exceed 3500 ft. — mostly with wooded summits. The noteworthy peaks, for example the Percys, Mt. Magalloway, Rump Mountain, and Mt. Aziscoos, are scattered, separated by long stretches of less interesting terrain. Although the main backbone of the White Mountains, the divide between the Connecticut River and the streams and lakes to the east, continues north through this country all the way to the Canadian border, it is for the most part ill-defined with no outstanding summit other than Dixville Peak. Except for Dixville Notch, there is little rugged mountain scenery, but there are several large lakes.

South of the Upper Ammonoosuc good roads are always within a reasonable distance, and the interior, most of which is within the WMNF, has a well-developed trail system. In the great tract to the north only a few mountains, even those over 3000 ft. high, have trails.

There are only three main highways. US Rte. 3 follows the Connecticut Valley to its uppermost headwaters, in the Connecticut Lakes near the Canadian border. An alternate road between Colebrook and Pittsburg is the scenic NH Rte. 145. On the east side NH Rte. 16, which continues as ME Rte. 16, accompanies the Androscoggin and Magalloway rivers north to the outlet of Lake Aziscoos, where it swings east to the Rangeley Lakes district. NH Rte. 26, the only east-west road north of the Upper Ammonoosuc, crosses from Colebrook to Errol through Dixville Notch.

Even secondary roads are few and short, although logging has created an intricate system of privately built and maintained main-haul gravel roads and winter truck roads. The vast interior of the country is a wilderness of great forests. The lack of highways, trails, settlements, and striking landmarks makes this region difficult or even dangerous to inexperienced hikers attempting longer trips without guides. On the other hand, people competent in the woods may find the area's remoteness its chief attraction.

Much of the land in this area, particularly north of NH Rte. 110, is privately owned, managed for the continuous production of veneer logs and pulpwood. Logging operations often radically alter the trail system from year to year. Obtain specific information about current conditions, particularly for areas other than trails mentioned in this section, in advance. Contact the State District Chief Conservation Officer, William Hastings in Gorham, or one of the State District Fire Chiefs, Richard Belmore in Lancaster, for the region south of Rte. 110, or Burham Judd in Pittsburg, for country north of Rte. 110. Woodland managers for the principal landowners are: John Bork, Brown Company, Berlin; Allison Merrill, Dartmouth College, Hanover; John Barfield, St. Regis Paper Company, West Stewartstown; Rhoades Sawyer, International Paper Company, Stratford; and Harold Mountain, Diamond International, Groveton.

The descriptions that follow begin at the Moose-Israel valley just north of the Presidential Range and work north to the Canadian border. For the North Country proper, descriptions are of necessity highly selective, dealing with a mountain here and there while passing over large areas without comment. Refer to map 8, Pilot.

CRESCENT RANGE

The Crescent Range is north of Randolph and west of Berlin. The chief summits from southwest to northeast are: Boy Mountain, Randolph Mountain, Mt. Crescent, Black Crescent Mountain, Mt. Jericho, and Mt. Forist. In addition to map 8, refer to the RMC map of the Randolph Valley and the Northern Peaks and to the USGS Mt. Washington and Gorham quadrangles.

Active (1982) lumbering on the south slopes of the Crescent Range may cause temporary interruptions of some of the following trails. Watch carefully for markers.

Boy Mountain

Boy Mountain (2240 ft.) is located east of Jefferson Highlands. The trail leaves the north side of US Rte. 2 just west of the junction with the Jefferson Notch Rd. and about 0.3 mi. east of the Tower Inn site. It crosses a meadow just left of an orchard, crosses an electric fence twice, and enters the woods east of the Carter-Bridgman barn (sign: "Bois Mtn."). Signs and arrows mark the path, which follows logging roads to an open ledge near the summit. There is a good view of the Dartmouth Range and the Southern Presidentials. (Distance: about 1 mi., 1½ hr.)

Local Paths in Randolph

The town of Randolph consists of two sections, the lower section is along Durand Rd., which was formerly US Rte. 2, in the Moose River valley. Lowe's Store and Ravine House site are located in this lower section. The upper section of Randolph is situated on Randolph Hill, reached by Randolph Hill Rd. Randolph Hill (about 1830 ft.) is a plateau that extends southeast from the foot of Mt. Crescent. Views of the Northern Peaks are very fine. On the south slope of the hill, connecting the two sections of the town and providing access from various points to major mountain trails, is a well-developed network of paths, maintained by the Randolph Mountain Club (RMC). These are described in detail in the RMC publication *Randolph Paths* and are shown on that club's map of the Northern Peaks and Randolph Valley.

LOOKOUT LEDGE

This 2240-ft. granite cliff on a knob of the southeast ridge of Mt. Randolph has a unique and probably the best view into King Ravine. It is reached by Pasture Path, Ledge Trail, Sargent Path, and Crescent Ridge Trail. The ledge is on private property. No fires are permitted.

Pasture Path (RMC)

This trail leads from Randolph Hill Rd. to the Ledge Trail. The Pasture Path begins at the Randolph Hill Rd. about 0.1 mi. above Stearns Rd. and runs west through old pastures and woods, using parts of Stearns Rd., Glover Spring Rd., and High Acres Rd., passing the Diagonal, Wood Path, E Z Way, and Bee Line trails. Below High Acres the path leaves High Acres Rd., passes through ancient forest and then light woods. Grassy Lane diverges right, and the Pasture Path enters young second growth and turns sharply left. The Notchway diverges here, and the Pasture Path continues across several tributaries of Carlton Brook and ascends to meet the Ledge Trail below Lookout Ledge.

Pasture Path (map 8)

Distances from Randolph Hill Rd.

to Glover Spring Rd. junction: 1.2 mi.

to Notchway junction: 1.9 mi.

to Lookout Ledge (via Ledge Trail): 2.8 mi., 1 hr. 40 min.

Ledge Trail (RMC)

Leading from the Ravine House site to Lookout Ledge, this trail forms a steep but direct route to the outlook. At the west end of the site, look for a trail sign on the driveway. Follow blazes across a rocky slope above which the Eusden house is visible.

The trail soon leaves the yard and, rising steadily northwest, climbs through deep and beautiful woods to the notch, where the Notchway diverges right for Randolph Hill. The Ledge Trail turns sharp left, steepens, and leaves the woods to follow an overgrown lumber road through second growth where it shortly intersects the Pasture Path. The trail re-enters the woods, climbs steeply over some rocks, and then descends slightly, passing the Eyrie, a small outlook, and continues on a few yards to end at the Crescent Ridge Trail. Just below is Lookout Ledge.

Ledge Trail (map 8)

Distances from Ravine House site, US Rte. 2

   to Notchway junction: 0.7 mi.

   to Pasture Path junction: 1.1 mi.

   to Lookout Ledge: 1.3 mi. (2.1 km.)

Sargent Path

This is the most direct route to Lookout Ledge, as well as the steepest. It is maintained by the Cutters. Leave Durand Rd. at the sign "1916" opposite a dark-red cottage 0.8 mi. west of the Ravine House site and 0.9 mi. east of Randolph Spring. The path rises steadily to the ledge, where it meets Ledge and Crescent Ridge trails. This trail is little used, but well blazed, and it can be followed with caution.

Sargent Path (map 8)

Distance from Durand Rd.

   to Lookout Ledge: 0.8 mi. (1.3 km.), 50 min.

Notchway (RMC)

This connecting path leads 0.9 mi. from the Ledge Trail to the Pasture Path about 0.5 mi. west of the Mt. Crescent House site. The Notchway leaves the Ledge Trail at the notch, ascends slightly, passes through a lumbered area, old forest, and a swamp, crosses three tributaries of Carlton Brook, and then rises to a relocation. Follow arrows left to a logging road and from there to the Pasture Path.

Notchway (map 8)

Distance from Ledge Trail

   to Pasture Path: 0.4 mi., 20 min.

Crescent Ridge Trail (RMC)

This trail branches right from the Mt. Crescent Trail 1.1 mi. from Randolph Hill Rd. and crosses the east flank of the mountain. From there it turns west and climbs directly to the north outlook, where it again meets the Mt. Crescent Trail. Continuing southwest, it descends gradually, crossing Carlton Brook, to Carlton Notch, where it crosses the Carlton Notch Trail. The Crescent Ridge Trail then follows a ridge that extends to the southwest, past Lafayette View, an outlook with an excellent view of King Ravine, Mts. Madison, Adams, and Jefferson. The ridge drops abruptly here to the col north of Randolph Mountain. The trail descends to this col, crosses the headwaters of a branch of Carlton Brook, and climbs over Randolph Mountain. Finally the trail descends steeply on an old lumber road to the Ledge Trail just above Lookout Ledge.

Crescent Ridge Trail (map 8)

Distances from Randolph Hill Rd.

   to Mt. Crescent, north outlook (via Mt. Crescent Trail): 1.8 mi.

   to Carlton Notch Trail junction: 2.6 mi.

   to Lafayette View: 3.3 mi.

   to Randolph Mountain summit: 3.9 mi.

   to Lookout Ledge: 4.8 mi. (7.7 km.), 3½ hr.

MOUNT CRESCENT

Mt. Crescent, northwest of Randolph Hill, derives its name from the shape of the 3230-ft. summit. It is ascended by the Crescent Ridge and the Mt. Crescent trails.

Mount Crescent Trail (RMC)

This trail begins at Randolph Hill Rd., about 0.3 mi. west of the Mt. Crescent House site opposite the head of Grassy Lane. It coincides for 0.1 mi. with Cook Path, which then branches right. The Mt. Crescent Trail continues on the logging road for another 0.1 mi. until the junction with the Carlton Notch Trail, where it turns right and begins to ascend the mountain.

At 0.3 mi. from Randolph Hill Rd. Boothman Spring Cutoff enters, and the main trail steepens. At 0.7 mi. it passes Castleview Loop, which leads in about 50 yd. to Castleview Rock. At 1.1 mi. the Crescent Ridge Trail branches right for the north summit of Mt. Crescent. The Mt. Crescent Trail continues left, northwest to the south viewpoint and then to the south summit of Mt. Crescent where there is a glimpse of the Northern Peaks. The path continues for 0.2 mi. to the north summit, also wooded, from which the Pliny and Pilot ranges can be seen across the broad valley of the Upper Ammonoosuc. The trail ends here, at its second junction with Crescent Ridge Trail. There is *no water* on the trail. An alternate way to the upper part of Mt. Crescent is via the Crescent Ridge Trail.

Mt. Crescent Trail (map 8)
Distances from Randolph Hill Rd.

> *to* Mt. Crescent, south summit: 1.5 mi.
>
> *to* Mt. Crescent, north summit: 1.7 mi. (2.7 km.), 1 hr. 40 min.

Castleview Loop (RMC)

The Castleview Loop diverges left from the Mt. Crescent Trail 0.7 mi. from Randolph Hill Rd. In a few feet a side trail leaves left to Castleview Rock, an interesting boulder. The main trail descends gently through light woods, passing Castleview Ledge, which is named for its unique view of the Castellated Ridge of Mt. Jefferson. Entering thick forest the loop then descends steeply and in about 0.3 mi. ends at the Carlton Notch Trail near the Mt. Crescent Water Co. Reservoir.

Castleview Loop (map 8)
Distances from Mt. Crescent Trail junction
   to Castleview Rock: 0.1 mi.
   to Castleview Ledge: 0.2 mi.
   to Carlton Notch Trail junction: 0.4 mi. (0.6 km.), ¼ hr.

Boothman Spring Cutoff (RMC)

This shortcut gives access to the Ice Gulch and Mt. Crescent from the Mt. Crescent House site on Randolph Hill Rd., a good starting point with parking space. The trail is level throughout, leading from the old hotel driveway (sign), through a field, then into the woods. At 0.2 mi. from the end of the field the cutoff passes Boothman Spring (*last sure water*). It soon crosses Cook Path to the Ice Gulch, then a lumber road, and ends at the Mt. Crescent Trail.

Boothman Spring Cutoff (map 8)
Distances from Mt. Crescent House site, Randolph Hill Rd.
   to Cook Path crossing: 0.4 mi.
   to Mt. Crescent Trail junction: 0.5 mi. (8 km.), 20 min.

POND OF SAFETY

This small but attractive pond north of the Crescent Range in the town of Randolph derived its name as follows. During the Revolution several Continental soldiers, who differed with the authorities as to the terms of their enlistment, retired to this isolated region and remained as long as there was danger of their being apprehended as deserters.

The pond may be reached from the Kilkenny area by the WMNF Pond of Safety Trail, from Randolph Hill by the Carlton Notch Trail, or from Jefferson by Stag Hollow Rd.

For Stag Hollow Rd., follow Ingerson Rd., which leaves US

Rte. 2 just west of the junction with NH Rte. 115, for about 1 mi.
to where the Ingerson Rd. turns left (west). Stag Hollow Rd.,
rebuilt for logging operations, continues straight, rising through
recent cuttings to the height-of-land between the Crescent and
Pliny ranges. From here the road gradually nears the south and
east sides of the pond, crosses an outlet brook, and reaches a
branch road left, which leads 0.2 mi. to the southeast shore of the
pond. Continue straight ahead for the Carlton Notch Trail to
Randolph Hill. This area has heavy snowmobile traffic in winter.

Pond of Safety Trail (WMNF)

This trail leaves Bog Dam Rd. (WMNF Rd. 15) 7.9 mi. south
of its eastern junction with York Pond Rd. (WMNF Rd. 13). It
leads generally southwest, crosses a stream of the Upper Ammonoosuc, ascends gradually and leaves the WMNF, descends a
low ridge, then ascends gradually toward the Pond of Safety. It
passes east and southeast of the pond to Stag Hollow Rd. at its
junction with the Carlton Notch Trail. Turn right (west) at this
junction for the south side of the pond (side road 0.1 mi.) and
Ingerson Rd. (3.8 mi.).

Pond of Safety Trail (map 8)
Distance from Bog Dam Rd.
   to Stag Hollow Rd.: 2.9 mi. (4.7 km.), 1¾ hr.

Carlton Notch Trail (RMC)

The Carlton Notch Trail leads from the Mt. Crescent Trail,
through the Randolph-Crescent col on Crescent Ridge, to the
Pond of Safety.

The trail starts on Mt. Crescent Trail 0.1 mi. above the Cook
Path junction and 0.2 mi. from Randolph Hill Rd., where Mt.
Crescent Trail leaves the logging road right. Stay on the road for
the Carlton Notch Trail (sign). The trail rises gently on the road
for a time and reaches the Mt. Crescent Water Co. Reservoir
(*water*) and the Castleview Loop about 0.5 mi. from Randolph

Hill Rd. The trail soon begins a half-mile ascent up a steep slope
to the top of the divide, Carlton Notch, where it crosses Crescent
Ridge Trail.

From Carlton Notch the trail descends gently through the head
of lumbering, and soon enters the main lumber road. It turns left
and follows this road and then others north, northeast, and finally
west down into the valley to Stag Hollow Rd. Follow this road
left a short distance for a branch road that leads right to the pond.

Carlton Notch Trail (map 8)

Distances from Randolph Hill Rd.

   to start of Carlton Notch Trail (via Mt. Crescent Trail): 0.2 mi.
   to reservoir: 0.5 mi.
   to Carlton Notch: 1.4 mi.
   to Stag Hollow Rd.: 3.7 mi.
   to Pond of Safety (via Stag Hollow Rd. and side trail): 4.0 mi.
      (6.4 km.), 2 hr.

ICE GULCH

The Ice Gulch is a deep cut on the southeast slope of the
Crescent Range, between Mt. Crescent and Black Crescent
Mountain. The bed of the gulch is strewn with great boulders that
lie in picturesque confusion, similar in many respects to those
scattered over the floor of King Ravine. Among the boulders are
many caves, some with perpetual ice. Springs and the melting ice
form the headwaters of Moose Brook.

Two paths lead to the gulch: Cook Path to the head, and Ice
Gulch Path to the foot and from there through the gulch. A short
loop, Peboamauk Loop, follows Moose Brook past Peboamauk
Fall and several fine springs back to Ice Gulch Path.

Cook Path (RMC)

This trail begins on Randolph Hill Rd. opposite Grassy Lane,
about 0.3 mi. west of the Mt. Crescent House site. It coincides
with the Mt. Crescent Trail for about 0.1 mi., then branches

right, passing an old trail and then the Boothman Spring Cutoff, a shortcut. It ascends then descends to the head of Ice Gulch, where Ice Gulch Path enters from the Ice Gulch. Follow signs for the Ice Gulch.

Cook Path (map 8)

Distances from Randolph Hill Rd.

to Boothman Spring Cutoff junction: 0.4 mi.

to head of Ice Gulch, Ice Gulch Path junction: 2.6 mi. (4.2 km.), 2 hr.

Ice Gulch Path (RMC)

This path is the descent route from Cook Path through the Ice Gulch and back to Randolph Hill Rd.

From the head of the Ice Gulch, the descent is steep to ''the Vestibule,'' where there is an excellent *spring*. The way down the gulch is rough, and hikers should be careful. The general direction is southeast with views toward Gorham, and down the gulch. At the foot of the gulch the trail passes Fairy *Spring*, and just below the Peboamauk Loop leaves left. The Ice Gulch Path goes right, passes through a marshy area and curves right at the site of the ''Marked Birch,'' where Peboamauk Loop re-enters the trail from Peboamauk Fall. The path leads south about 2 mi., across several brooks and through the field of Sky Meadow Farm to Randolph Hill Rd., about 0.4 mi. east of the Mt. Crescent House site.

Ice Gulch Path (map 8)

Distances from Cook Path junction, head of Ice Gulch

to site of ''Marked Birch'': 1.4 mi.

to Randolph Hill Rd.: 3.4 mi. (5.5 km.), 2 hr.

Peboamauk Loop (RMC)

This loop of the Ice Gulch passes a fine cascade and travels beside a pleasant stream. On the ascent, after branching right from the Ice Gulch Path, the trail descends steeply to Peboamauk Fall (Winter's Home) then rises steeply and follows Moose

Brook for about 0.3 mi., ending at the foot of the gulch just below Fairy *Spring*, where it re-enters the Ice Gulch Path.

Peboamauk Loop (map 8)

Distances from Ice Gulch Path, lower junction
   to Peboamauk Fall: 0.1 mi., ¼ hr.
   to Ice Gulch Path, upper junction: 0.3 mi., ¼ hr.

BLACK CRESCENT MOUNTAIN

There are no trails on this 3265-ft. mountain, located north-northeast of Mt. Crescent. It can be ascended without trail from the head of the Ice Gulch, or from Peboamauk Fall. The upper part of a large slide on the south side of the mountain has an excellent view.

JERICHO MOUNTAIN

The partially overgrown summit of this 2483-ft. mountain, also known as Black Mountain, offers a fine view east to the Mahoosucs and an attractive, though obstructed prospect of the Carter Range and the Northern Presidentials. The trail is no longer maintained and may be obscure.

In Berlin follow Second Ave. to its south end, then turn right up Haskell St. to its end. The trail leaves west (house on left is Number 31 Haskell) and continues for 0.1 mi. through a clearing to where an arrow painted on a rock points left into the woods. After traversing a short boggy area, turn right on a woods road, which travels generally west at a gentle grade. At 1.5 mi. a trail branches right for Mt. Forist. In 0.3 mi. the road turns sharp right (arrow) and the summit trail, overgrown but with faded yellow blazes, continues ahead to the summit, about 0.6 mi. farther southwest. *Descending,* follow a small rock dike northeast until the first blazes are found.

Jericho Mountain (map 8)

Distance to summit
   from Haskell St., Berlin: 2.4 mi. (3.9 km.), 1¾ hr.

MOUNT FORIST

This 2046-ft. mountain, also known as Elephant Mountain because of its shape, rises abruptly on the west edge of Berlin. It was named for Merrill C. Forist, an early settler. There are several approaches to the summit on the elephant's "head," or to the outlook on its "rear end." One of the better ways begins at the upper end of Madigan St. (Follow NH Rte. 110 southeast out of Berlin. Madigan St. is a part of this road. When you reach Madigan St., follow it to its upper end where the trail begins.) Follow the trail for about 50 yd. to the base of the cliff (trail may be obscure), turn left, and follow the base about 50 yd. to an old slide, now mostly grown over. The trail leads up the mountain at a rather steep angle to a point about halfway between the elephant's head and its tail. Bear left and follow the trail to the summit on the "head," where there is a nice view of Berlin and the Androscoggin Valley toward Gorham.

Mt. Forist (map 8)

Distance to summit
   from Madigan St., Berlin: *est.* 0.6 mi., ¾ hr.

PLINY AND PILOT RANGES

These are essentially one mountain mass, extending north and south between the Israel and Upper Ammonoosuc rivers just east of Lancaster. The Pliny Range forms the semicircular southern end of this mass; its chief summits are Mt. Starr King, Mt. Waumbek, and Mt. Weeks. Across Willard Notch from Mt. Weeks the Pilot Range begins, containing Terrace Mountain, Mt. Cabot (the highest peak in the entire North Country), and Hutchins Mountain, often known as Mt. Pilot. A spur that extends northeast from Mt. Cabot carries the Bulge and the Horn.

Refer to map 8, Pilot, to the USGS Mt. Washington and Percy quadrangles, or to the Starr King-Waumbek section of the RMC map of the Randolph Valley and the Northern Peaks.

The USFS has begun a ridge-top trail across the major peaks of this section. When this is completed, most of the present trails that originate at York Pond will be partially or completely abandoned. At present (1983), the new trail has been opened from South Pond to Unknown Pond, with backcountry campsites at Rogers Ledge and Unknown Pond.

MOUNT STARR KING

This 3913-ft. mountain is located northeast of Jefferson village. It is named for the author of "The White Hills." The summit is wooded, but views have been cleared in several directions.

Starr King Trail (RMC)

Enter the road directly across US Rte. 2 from the former entrance to the Waumbek Inn. Continue north on a wood road avoiding a right branch about 100 yd. along past a ruined spring house, right, in about 200 yd. (*spring* on the right 100 yd. farther, on a side trail). Follow a logging road uphill for about 0.3 mi. The trail then turns right off the road and climbs the west slope of the mountain for almost 0.8 mi., then north to traverse the west flank for about 1 mi. The trail passes two *springs* (left down then right up) about three-quarters of the way over this section.

Leaving the traverse, the trail turns right and climbs to the summit in another 150 yd. About 50 yd. before the summit, a trail to the left leads about 50 yd. to *water* (*unreliable*). The trail continues another 60 yd. to an excellent cleared viewpoint south and west, the site of a former shelter. It winds southeast and then east along the ridge descending slightly to the col, then rising in about 0.7 mi. to the wooded summit of Mt. Waumbek.

Starr King Trail (map 8)
Distances from US Rte. 2
  to beginning of traverse: 1.6 mi., 1 hr. 35 min.

to Mt. Starr King summit: 2.8 mi., 2 hr. 40 min.
to Mt. Waumbek summit: 3.8 mi. (6.2 km.), 3 hr. 20 min.

MOUNT WAUMBEK

Immediately east of Mt. Starr King, Mt. Waumbek is the highest point of the Pliny Range. It was formerly called Pliny Major. The Starr King Trail leads to the summit.

Priscilla Brook Trail

Maintenance and location of this trail in the future are in doubt.

The trail leaves the Ingerson Rd. in Jefferson just east of Priscilla Brook. It follows logging roads and crosses private land and is apt to be wet and badly eroded. Follow a logging road east of the brook for about 1.5 mi., then cross a major tributary brook and continue northeast on a logging road around the base of Mt. Waumbek to the height-of-land between Mt. Waumbek and Mt. Pliny. For S. Weeks Mountain ("3885" on map 8) follow marked town boundary north until marking ends, then set compass course due north and bushwhack.

Priscilla Brook Trail (map 8)

Distances from Ingerson Rd., Jefferson

to brook crossing: 1.4 mi.
to height-of-land: 2.7 mi. (4.3 km.), 2 hr. 10 min.

Landing Camp Trail (WMNF)

This trail diverges east from the Upper Ammonoosuc Trail about 1.3 mi. southwest of Bog Dam, runs east nearly level for about 0.4 mi., crosses an open flat, rises over a knoll, bears right and crosses a small stream. The trail turns more south, crosses three small streams in less than 1 mi., soon bears left, and passes through the ruins of Camp 18. It ascends east through wooded area and ends at the west side of Bog Dam Rd. (WMNF Rd. 15), about 6.2 mi. south of its eastern junction with York Pond Rd.

(WMNF Rd. 13).

Landing Camp Trail (map 8)

Distance from Upper Ammonoosuc Trail junction
   to Bog Dam Rd.: 2.2 mi. (3.5 km.), 1 hr.

Upper Ammonoosuc Trail (WMNF)

This trail leaves the west side of Bog Dam Rd. (WMNF Rd. 15) 4.1 mi. south of its eastern junction with the York Pond Rd. (WMNF Rd. 13). It leads generally southwest, crosses a brook at 0.4 mi., and reaches the site of Bog Dam at 0.8 mi. The Landing Camp Trail diverges left (east) at 1.6 mi. for Bog Dam Rd. About 0.2 mi. farther, the trail crosses the Upper Ammonoosuc River, and in another 0.3 mi. Keenan Brook. It soon ascends a slight grade, recrosses Keenan Brook, and ends at Bog Dam Rd. 5.3 mi. south of its junction with the York Pond Rd.

Upper Ammonoosuc Trail (map 8)

Distance from Bog Dam Rd.
   to Landing Camp Trail junction: 1.6 mi., 50 min.

MOUNT WEEKS

Located northeast of Mt. Waumbek, this 3890-ft. mountain has three distinct peaks. The north peak may be climbed from the height-of-land in Willard Notch (see York Pond Trail below). There is no trail and the summit is wooded with no views.

The south peak may be climbed from the Priscilla Brook Trail. Again, there is no trail to be summit, but there is a view to the north.

York Pond Trail (WMNF)

This trail connects the Berlin Fish Hatchery at York Pond with Lancaster via Willard Notch, which is between Terrace Mountain and Mt. Weeks. It is a snowmobile through-trail between Berlin and Lancaster and its condition has deteriorated. It is obscure in parts of the middle section.

From the fish hatchery (just beyond the upper house on the road there is a gate, which may be locked) follow York Pond Rd. (WMNF Rd. 13) 1 mi. The trail (sign) leaves the left (south) side of the road. It first follows an old logging railroad bed, across a number of small streams and past the (abandoned) Bunnell Notch Trail (right) at about 0.4 mi. After about 0.5 mi. of swampy area, the trail swings gradually south up a hardwood ridge. It dips, then rises again on the slope of Mt. Weeks, and slabs the south side of the notch, staying well above the height-of-land. As it descends, it enters an area of logging roads and swamps. Most of the junctions on the logging roads are marked with either arrows or signs, but the footway may be obscure.

At 4.6 mi. the trail crosses Garland Brook. Within the next 0.6 mi. it recrosses the brook and one of its major tributaries, then becomes a main-haul road. After 1.3 mi. the trail leaves the road right (sign). The main-haul road may be followed to Arthur White Rd. The York Pond Trail follows an older road to join the Bunnell Notch Trail near its western end. Turn left (west) for Heath's Gate (also called "White's Farm").

York Pond Trail (map 8)

Distances from York Pond Rd.

to Bunnell Notch Trail junction: 0.4 mi.

to height-of-land: 2.5 mi., 1¾ hr.

to first crossing, Garland Brook: 4.6 mi.

to main-haul road: 5.3 mi.

to Bunnell Notch Trail junction, western end: 7 mi.

to Heath's Gate ("White's Farm"): 7.5 mi. (12 km.), 4¼ hr.

TERRACE MOUNTAIN

Northwest of Mt. Weeks and south of Mt. Cabot, Terrace Mountain (3640 ft.) is named for its appearance when seen from the west. The former trail from Bunnell Notch to the summit has been abandoned.

Bunnell Notch Trail

This trail was closed by the WMNF in 1980 east of the Mt. Cabot Trail.

The trail cuts the arc of the York Pond Trail and shortens the distance between Lancaster and the Berlin National Fish Hatchery at York Pond by 1.7 mi. It also provides access to the Mt. Cabot Trail.

There are plans to relocate to the northwest the section of this trail from Arthur White Rd. to the height-of-land and the Mt. Cabot Trail. The present trail and the section from the height-of-land east to the York Pond Trail are slated for closure.

From Jefferson, turn onto North Rd. about 0.3 mi. west of the junction of US Rte. 2 and NH Rte. 116. After 2.3 mi. turn right onto Gore Rd. for 1.7 mi., then right on Pleasant Valley Rd. for 0.8 mi. to the Arthur White Rd. Follow this to parking (sign), about 50 yd. before the end of the road at ''Heath's Gate.'' Do not park in the turnaround.

From Heath's Gate, the York Pond Trail (sign Mt. Cabot Trail) follows a badly eroded logging road through old pastures 0.4 mi. to the Kilkenny railroad bed, where it turns right (southeast) along the railroad bed and the Bunnell Notch Trail begins. It follows the road east for about 0.5 mi., then follows an older logging road for another 0.3 mi. Where the road bears left the trail bears right (sign) passing the WMNF boundary 0.3 mi. beyond (sign). Just under 1 mi. farther it crosses Bunnell Brook. The Mt. Cabot Trail diverges left (north) 100 ft. beyond. The Bunnell Notch Trail is abandoned and obscure beyond this point, but it may be followed through the notch to its junction with the York Pond Trail 0.3 mi. from York Pond Rd.

Bunnell Notch Trail (map 8)

Distances from ''Heath's Gate,'' A. White Rd.

to start of Bunnell Notch Trail (via York Pond Trail): 0.4 mi., 20 min.

to WMNF boundary: 1.3 mi.

to Mt. Cabot Trail junction: 2.2 mi. (3.5 km.), 1 hr. 40 min.

MOUNT CABOT

Located north of Bunnell Notch, Mt. Cabot's 4180-ft. summit is wooded with no views, but outlooks east and west have been cleared from the fire tower base 0.3 mi. southeast of the true summit.

Mount Cabot Trail (WMNF)

The trail leaves the Bunnell Notch Trail 2.3 mi. east of Heath's Gate (also called "White's Farm") and 2.9 mi. west of the York Pond Rd. The Mt. Cabot Trail/Bunnell Notch Trail junction is about 100 ft. east of the only major stream crossing on the west side of the height-of-land between Mt. Cabot and the north peak of Terrace Mountain. (There is *no water* beyond this brook.)

The trail climbs generally north to northeast for 0.5 mi., then swings right and ascends for 0.1 mi. to a rocky outlook facing southwest. From here the trail turns northeast again and climbs through evergreens to a cabin. Beyond (sign) the trail is rougher and leads north through a shallow sag, then gradually up to the true summit (sign).

There are plans to relocate this trail and the Bunnell Notch Trail northwest to the height-of-land.

Mt. Cabot Trail (map 8)

Distances from Bunnell Notch Trail junction

to outlook: 0.6 mi.

to cabin: 1.3 mi., 1 hr. 25 min.

to Mt. Cabot summit: 1.7 mi. (2.7 km.), 1 hr. 40 min.

The Bulge and the Horn

These peaks (3920 ft. and 3905 ft.) lie just north of Mt. Cabot in the Pilot Range. There are no trails, but they may be reached via the ridge that joins them to Mt. Cabot. In general, the south-facing slopes are open hardwoods while the north-facing ones are spruce. The Bulge is wooded with no views, while the Horn is bare with views in all directions.

Climbing from the east, follow the Unknown Pond Trail about 2 mi., then find the stream coming in from the west. Follow upstream to the small unnamed pond (located at the "H" in "Horn" on map 8, Pilot). From the pond, the Horn is in sight. Climb toward it, swinging left higher up to avoid the cliffs.

KILKENNY AREA

The district lying immediately north of the Crescent Range and east of the Pliny and Pilot ranges is a small, mostly wooded area of much attraction. While there are no important peaks, the Devils Hopyard deserves a visit, and the view from Rogers Ledge is one of the most striking in the entire White Mountains.

The center of this area is accessible by York Pond Rd. (WMNF Rd. 13) to the Berlin Fish Hatchery at York Pond and by Bog Dam Rd. (WMNF Rd. 15), which makes a 15.5 mi. loop south of the area. York Pond Rd. leaves NH Rte. 110 7.2 mi. northwest of Berlin and about 4.5 mi. southeast of W. Milan.

There are gates between the various areas of the fish hatchery that may be locked from early afternoon until morning. Therefore, it is advisable to consult with the hatchery office about taking cars beyond that point.

The following trails are nearly all in the country north of York Pond. For those running south see the Crescent Range, and for those to the southwest see the Pliny/Pilot ranges. Refer to map 8, Pilot, to the USGS Percy quadrangle, and to the USFS map of the WMNF.

Many of the trails in this section are slated for eventual abandonment, to be replaced by a trail connecting the South Ponds to Mt. Cabot.

WEST MILAN TRAIL (WMNF)

This trail runs between York Pond Rd. (WMNF Rd. 13) and W. Milan, along an old railroad bed on the west bank of the

Upper Ammonoosuc River. There is heavy snowmobile traffic in winter. At W. Milan take the road that turns southwest from NH Rte. 110 about 0.1 mi. south of the railway crossing and follow it across the river and south about 1.5 mi. to its end at a farmhouse. (This point may also be reached by taking the road that leaves Rte. 110 on the west 1 mi. south of W. Milan and joins the preceding road a little north of its end.) The trail begins here. In just under 1 mi. it meets and coincides with another short section of road, at the beginning of which an abandoned trail leaves right (west) uphill. The trail crosses Higgins Brook, and at about 2.3 mi. passes an old logging camp. It crosses three small brooks in the next 0.5 mi., then Fifield Brook. A mile beyond, the trail crosses Fogg Brook. About 0.8 mi. farther it crosses another brook and then ends at the York Pond Rd. just west of the bridge over the Upper Ammonoosuc River, 1.7 mi. from Rte. 110.

West Milan Trail (map 8)

Distance from farmhouse
   to York Pond Rd.: 5.5 mi. (8.9 km.), 2½ hr.

MILL BROOK TRAIL (WMNF)

Formerly a through-route from Stark village to York Pond, this trail has been abandoned by the USFS from the height-of-land to Stark. Logging has obscured the footway in this area.

From the Berlin Fish Hatchery at York Pond the trail ascends along Cold Brook for about 1.3 mi., then diverges east (right) up a side stream, passes the foot of Rogers Ledge, and terminates at the height-of-land on the low divide between Rogers Ledge and Mt. Cabot.

Mill Brook Trail (map 8)

Distance from York Pond
   to end of maintained trail at height-of-land: 3.6 mi. (5.8 km.), 2¼ hr.

DEVILS HOPYARD

This picturesque gorge on a brook that empties into South Ponds resembles the Ice Gulch, but is shorter and narrower. The small stream is for the most part completely out of sight beneath moss-covered boulders, while sheer ledges overhang above. (Use caution if rocks are wet from rain and covered with moss.)

Devils Hopyard Trail

The trail begins at South Ponds Recreational Area (*Note:* The road from NH Rte. 110 to South Ponds, about 2 mi. long, has a gate locked to the public except from about July 1 to Labor Day, before 8:00 P.M.). The trail leads south skirting the west side of the pond, crosses the outlet brook in 0.6 mi., passes the entrance to an abandoned trail, and at 0.7 mi. crosses the outlet brook to the north side.

In the next 0.1 mi. the trail enters the hopyard and after about 0.4 mi. rises steeply at its west end. Be careful climbing at this steep section—the rocks are slippery. (This is a dead-end trail.)

Devils Hopyard Trail (map 8)

Distance from South Ponds
    to Devils Hopyard: 0.8 mi., 25 min.

UNKNOWN POND TRAIL

Trail maintenance ended in 1975, but the footway is well defined and easy to follow. The trail begins on York Pond Rd. (WMNF Rd. 13), 1.5 mi. west of the fish hatchery. (Just west of the upper house at the hatchery there is a gate, which may be locked.) The path follows Unknown Pond Brook northwest for 3.3 mi., passing east of the pond. It then descends north to the Mill Brook Rd. and Stark.

Unknown Pond Trail (map 8)

Distances from York Pond Rd.
    to Unknown Pond: 3.3 mi., 2 hr.
    to Mill Brook Rd.: 7 mi. (11.2 km.), 4 hr.

ROGERS LEDGE

Rogers Ledge (2945 ft.) is in the center of the Kilkenny district, about 3.5 mi. north-northwest of York Pond. The entire southwest face of the ledge is a cliff and the view from the top includes the Kilkenny area, the Pilot Range, the Mahoosucs and the Presidential Range.

A trail (may be obscure) leaves the Mill Brook Trail 3.9 mi. north of York Pond, swings east (right) to the south of the open face and climbs 0.7 mi. to the summit.

The Youth Conservation Corps has been working on a trail from the South Ponds Recreation Area off NH Rte. 110 in W. Milan to Rogers Ledge. Inquire locally for current status and directions.

UPPER CONNECTICUT RIVER REGION

The mountains treated here are widely scattered peaks, selected chiefly because of their accessibility. Refer to the USGS quadrangles mentioned under specific peaks.

PERCY PEAKS

These twin peaks, north of Stark on the Upper Ammonoosuc River, are the most conspicuous mountains in the northern view from Mt. Washington. The summit of the north peak (3418 ft.) is bare, expect for low scrub; that of the south peak (3200 ft., no maintained trails) is wooded, but there are several good viewpoints. Refer to the USGS Percy quadrangle.

West Side Trail

A short, direct route up N. Percy from the west, this trail must be followed with some care. The upper slabs are steep and exposed. Extreme caution is advised in wet weather.

Leaving NH Rte. 110, 2.6 mi. east of Groveton, go north on Emerson Rd. 2.2 mi. to Emerson School Corner (marked on

USGS map), the beginning of Nash Stream Rd. (sign). Follow this road for 2.8 mi. to a large rock on the east side of the road (several cairns). The trail leaves directly south of this rock.

The trail follows logging roads that generally parallel Slide Brook. At 0.6 mi. the trail approaches the brook (*last sure water*), then bears left up the north bank and follows the ridge above the main stream for 0.4 mi. It crosses a small gully, turns left, and begins to climb steeply. The beginning of the Notch Trail is reached in 0.3 mi. Lower sections of the slabs are mossy and slippery when wet, and the trail swings right (south) through the woods to avoid the worst places. About 80 yd. above the Notch Trail junction, it crosses to the left (north) side of the slab. Follow the paint blazes carefully. Above here slabs become steeper, and views begin to appear. Descend southwest from the summit, meeting the paint blazes in about 150 ft.

West Side Trail (USGS Percy quadrangle)
Distances from Nash Stream Rd.
   to Notch Trail junction: 1.2 mi., 1 hr. 10 min.
   to N. Percy summit: 1.7 mi. (2.7 km.), 1 hr. 55 min.

Notch Trail

This trail, an alternative to the West Side Trail, avoids the steep, exposed slabs near the summit. It diverges right from the West Side Trail 0.1 mi. above the base of the first open slab (sign), traverses several ledges staying north of the low point in the notch, and reaches the summit slabs from the south. There are good views in all directions from the summit.

Notch Trail (USGS Percy quadrangle)
Distance from West Side Trail junction
   to N. Percy summit: 1 mi. (1.6 km.), 1 hr.

DEVILS SLIDE

This sheer cliff west of Stark rises 740 ft. above the valley. From NH Rte. 110 take Stark Rd. north to Stark and go west about 0.5 mi. along the north side of the river. There is no trail.

SUGARLOAF MOUNTAIN

East of N. Stratford, at the head of Nash Stream, this 3701-ft. summit, topped by a fire tower, commands interesting views, particularly of the Percy Peaks. Refer to the USGS Percy and Guildhall, VT quadrangles.

The summit trail, in good condition, leaves Nash Stream Rd. left (west) 8.9 mi. from its beginning, or 0.1 mi. beyond the crossing of the main stream. The trail follows a logging road that ascends the east side of the mountain by a rather direct route. (Distance: Nash Stream Rd. to fire warden's cabin: about 2 mi.; to summit, about 2.5 mi.: 2 hr., 10 min.)

DIXVILLE MOUNTAINS

This well-integrated group of mountains, clustered about Dixville Notch, about midway between Colebrook and Errol, is reached from NH Rte. 26, which passes through the notch. The more important peaks of the group are Mt. Abenaki, Cave Mountain, Dixville Peak, Mt. Gloriette, and Mt. Sanguinari. The Balsams Hotel has prepared a trail guide to this area, which is available at the information booth on Rte. 26 across from the hotel access road. Refer to the USGS Dixville quadrangle.

DIXVILLE NOTCH

Between Mts. Sanguinari (north) and Gloriette (south), with the Mohawk River flowing west and Clear Stream east, Dixville Notch (1990 ft.) is less than 2 mi. long, with a steep grade on each side, and only wide enough at the summit to admit the highway. The cliffs, formed of vertical strata, are impressively jagged. To the south from the highest point, high up on these cliffs, is the Profile.

Just west of the high point on the north side of the road is Lake Gloriette, an artificial lake formed by the headwaters of the Mohawk River. It is on the grounds of the Balsams Hotel, which owns most of the land west of the ridge line on both sides of the road.

From a parking area just east of Lake Gloriette there is a trail to Table Rock, which has a panoramic view of the notch. About 1 mi. east of the Balsams, near a picnic area north of the highway, is a small but attractive flume (sign). The trail is very short. A little farther east on the south side of the highway is a second picnic area from which a slightly longer trail leads to Huntingdon Cascades.

MOUNT GLORIETTE

Forming the south side of the notch, this 2780-ft. mountain includes the rock formations Table Rock, Old King, Third Cliff, and Profile Cliff. There are paths to all of them, but only that to Table Rock is clearly marked.

Table Rock

This cliff juts out from the north side of Mt. Gloriette south of the highway. Formed of vertical rock slabs, it is less than 10 ft. wide at its narrowest and extends over 100 ft. from the shoulder of the mountain. The view is extensive. The most direct approach is from the parking area east of Lake Gloriette. Beginning at a sign, the path ascends steeply for about ¼ mi. to the ridge, turns right, and in a few yards emerges on the cliff. The vertical drop is about 700 ft.

A branch path to the left (east), where the trail meets the crest of the ridge, passes a cleft known as the Ice Cave and approaches the cliffs known as Old King, Profile Cliff, and Third Cliff. There are no signs, and several intersecting footways. A path from Table Rock to NH Rte. 26 near the east end of the Wilderness Ski Area access road provides an alternate descent route, or it may be used for ascent by those for whom the direct route is too steep. There is a sign for this path at the edge of the woods just east of the access road, and the trail is marked with signs, though not clearly at the upper end. To descend by this route, enter the woods above Table Rock, avoid a path west, and take the next right (west) fork, which is marked with an obscure dark-green XC sign. The correct of several paths has "Table Rock" signs on it facing in the reverse direction.

Table Rock (USGS Dixville quadrangle)

Distances from Lake Gloriette parking area, NH Rte. 26
to Table Rock: 0.3 mi.
to path near east end, ski area access road: 0.4 mi.
to NH Rte. 26 (via path): 0.7 mi. (1.1 km.)

DIXVILLE PEAK

Dixville Peak at 3482 ft. is the highest mountain in the vicinity of Dixville Notch. It is wooded to the summit, and the former trails have been abandoned.

MOUNT SANGUINARI

This 2748-ft. mountain forms the north wall of Dixville Notch. Its name derives from the color of its cliffs at sunset.

Sanguinari Ridge Trail

This trail starts at the Flume Brook Picnic Area of the Dixville Notch State Wayside, a rest area off NH Rte. 16. It climbs a scenic ridge, following an old 1920s trail in places, as well as the blue-blazed State Park boundary. The trail is mostly through balsam and spruce forest with some hardwoods. Along the ridge crest and overlooking the notch are some outlook points with views of Table Rock and Old King Cliffs, and toward Errol and the Mahoosuc Range in Maine. The most spectacular view is from a rocky pinnacle (1 mi.) overlooking Lake Gloriette and the Balsams Hotel. The trail descends past Index Rock by graded switchbacks to the entrance road into the Balsams. It is marked with long pale-yellow paint blazes and directional signs.

Sanguinari Ridge Trail (USGS Dixville quadrangle)
Distance from Flume Brook Picnic Area
   to the Balsams Hotel entrance rd.: 1.5 mi. (2.5 km.), 1 hr. 40
   min.

CONNECTICUT LAKES REGION

Some 10 mi. above Colebrook the Connecticut River Valley
bends northeast and, just beyond the village of Beecher Falls,
VT, comes wholly within New Hampshire. Between its source
near the Canadian line and the village of Pittsburg, the river
passes through a chain of lakes of increasing size, numbered first
to fourth, in upstream order from the south. A high dam at
Pittsburg created Lake Francis at the lowest lake, before First
Lake, and dams are responsible for the present sizes of both First
and Second Lakes. First Lake, 5.5 mi. long and 2.5 mi. at its
broadest, and Lake Francis are the largest bodies of water in New
Hampshire north of the main ranges.

US Rte. 3 passes close to all of the lakes except Fourth,
crossing the river from west to east between Second and Third
and eventually entering Canada. It is the only road of any
consequence in the entire region. Refer to USGS Second Lake,
Indian Stream, and Moose Bog quadrangles.

MOUNT MAGALLOWAY

Located east of First Connecticut Lake, this 3360-ft. mountain
overlooks the Middle Branch of the Dead Diamond River.

Turn southeast from US. Rte. 3 just northeast of Coon Brook,
4.7 mi. from the First Connecticut Dam. Drive a gravel road 1.4
mi. to the Connecticut River bridge. Take the right fork just
beyond the bridge and follow small signs ("Lookout Tower").
Drive 0.9 mi. to a second fork, then left 0.7 mi. to a third fork.
Go left at the third fork, crossing the height-of-land on a good
gravel road. At 2.4 mi. from the third fork (signs), take a road

right. Drive 1.8 mi. to a clearcut area. The road continues but it is rough, suitable only for four-wheel-drive vehicles. Follow this jeep road 1.6 mi. to a cabin, avoiding a branch road right (west). Jeep road ends a few yards short of the cabin in a grassy turnaround, from which follow the left track (sign). (Right track, which is not marked, leads through a wet area to the lower end of the Bobcat Trail.)

Beyond the cabin the rough jeep track passes a *spring* and ascends steeply to the summit, passing the upper end of the Bobcat Trail in 0.6 mi., and reaching the fire tower in 0.7 mi.

Mt. Magalloway (USGS Second Lake, Indian Stream,
Moose Bog quadrangles)

Distances from US Rte. 3 and road at Coon Brook junction
  to third fork: 5.4 mi.
  to clear-cut area: 7.2 mi.

Distances from clearcut area
  to cabin: 1.6 mi., 45 min.
  to fire tower, Mt. Magalloway summit: 2.3 mi. (3.7 km.), 1½ hr.

Bobcat Trail

The Bobcat Trail follows the ridge west of the fire tower and rejoins the jeep track described above near the turnaround below the cabin. It is steep but more attractive than the jeep track.

Bobcat Trail (USGS Second Lake quadrangle)
Distances from fire tower, Mt. Magalloway summit

to upper end of Bobcat Trail: 0.1 mi.

to lower end of Bobcat Trail (near turnaround): 0.5 mi. (0.8 km.)

RUMP MOUNTAIN

Located in Maine just east of the New Hampshire border, 7 mi. south of the Canadian line, Rump Mountain (3647 ft.) was formerly known as Mt. Carmel or Camel's Rump, from its appearance from the southwest. This attractive but remote mountain has views of three states and Quebec Province, and in clear weather, possibly of Mt. Katahdin.

Rump Mountain is on land now owned by the Boise-Cascade Corporation. Although Boise-Cascade does not object to hikers crossing its land, there are restrictions on vehicle travel and camping. Contact the corporation's Woods Department, Rumford, ME or its district forester, Bradford Wyman in W. Milan, NH.

DEER MOUNTAIN

Located west of the Connecticut River, between Second and Third Lakes, 3005-ft. Deer Mountain with its fire tower commands interesting views of the Perry Stream and Indian Stream valleys, of the range of hills forming the international boundary, and of the neighboring villages in Quebec.

Deer Mountain Trail (NHDP)
The lower part of this trail has been much disturbed by logging. Ask at Moose Falls Campground for current conditions.

Leave US Rte. 3 on a gravel logging road south of the northernmost highway bridge across the Connecticut River and just south of Moose Falls Campground. Go west 0.6 mi. to a cleared area and look for a trail sign west at the upper edge of the clearing. In the next 0.6 mi. bear right at three forks, crossing the stream three times. Watch for orange and blue tape and signs of an old telephone line. At 0.6 mi. from the gravel road go left (west) just before the main skidder road enters a large clearcut area: the sign here is not obvious. The trail passes a good *spring* about 1 mi. beyond this point and the warden's cabins in another 0.3 mi. The fire tower is 0.3 mi. beyond; it is not staffed and is kept locked. Views may be had from the upper levels.

Deer Mountain Trail

Distances from US Rte. 3

   to clearing: 0.6 mi.

   to left fork: 1.2 mi.

   to spring: 2.2 mi.

   to fire warden's cabins: 2.6 mi.

   to fire tower, Deer Mountain summit: 2.9 mi. (4.6 km.), 1 hr.
    55 min.

FOURTH LAKE

This little pond, northwest of Third Lake and just south of the Canadian line, is the ultimate source of the Connecticut River. Once considered as remote a spot as the mountains had to offer, it is now accessible from US Rte. 3

From the US customs station at the height-of-land on Rte. 3, follow the international boundary uphill to the west. The boundary is a wide swath cut through the forest and marked at irregular intervals by brass discs set in concrete. It is cleared at ten-year intervals (last in 1975), and some discs are not readily visible. At marker 484-15 (0.6 mi., ½ hr.), enter the woods left, bearing south-southwest. The lake will be found in 0.1 mi. There is a snowmobile sign at this point, and the route is marked with orange tape, although there is no obvious footway. Paths diverge into the woods from markers 13 and 14 also, and may be followed. They all intersect before reaching the lake. (Distance from US Rte. 3 to Fourth Lake: 0.7 mi.)

UPPER ANDROSCOGGIN AND
MAGALLOWAY REGION

CAMBRIDGE BLACK MOUNTAIN

Cambridge Black Mountain, northeast of Milan, may be reached by bushwhacking from logging roads owned by the James River Corporation. Entry can be gained from Milan, Berlin, or Upton. Roads are good-quality gravel but are not signed. Use topographic maps (USGS Milan quadrangle), and be on the lookout for logging and road-building activity. Consult with the Woods Department in Berlin for further information.

SIGNAL MOUNTAIN

Signal Mountain (2673 ft.) is west-southwest of Errol. Refer to the USGS Errol quadrangle.

From NH Rte. 16 in the Thirteen Mile Woods between Dummer and Errol, turn west on a gravel road that enters just south of the steel bridge at Seven Islands. This is the road to Millsfield Pond, and it passes south of Signal Mountain. At 5.3 mi. from Rte. 16 go right (north) at a sharp fork (snowmobile signs) and continue 1.2 mi. to a grassy turnout (snowmobile sign "Signal Mt.").

The path follows a number of intersecting logging roads. At 1 mi. there is a three-forked junction; take the left (east) fork (signs "Trail" and "Lookout Tower"). The trail reaches the ridge from the northeast and swings west and southwest toward the summit. At 1.4 mi. take right fork (sign), and at 1.5 mi., where the cart track ends, continue ahead (sign). The path traverses the north slope in two long switchbacks and reaches the warden's cabin from the northwest, passing two spring holes just below. The fire tower is just beyond. There is a view of Millsfield Pond from behind the cabin, and good views from the fire tower; several steps are missing, however, and others are rotten.

Descending. Watch intersections carefully since there are several diverging tracks and no signs. (Distance from grassy turnaround to Signal Mountain summit: 1.7 mi., 1 hr. 20 min.)

DIAMOND RIVER REGION

Between Errol and Wilsons Mills the Diamond River enters the Magalloway from the west. The Swift Diamond on the south and the Dead Diamond on the north come together to form the Diamond River in the Dartmouth College Grant only a few miles from the Magalloway River. Branches of the Dead Diamond extend well up into the Connecticut Lakes region. Refer to the USGS Errol quadrangle.

Immediately below the confluence of its two branches, the Diamond enters a wild and beautiful gorge cut between the Diamond Peaks on the north and Mt. Dustan on the south. This valley is served by a private logging road, open to walking, but not to automobile travel without a permit.

At 8.5 mi. north of Errol or 0.5 mi. before reaching the Maine state line, a gravel road leaves NH Rte. 16 on the west near a small cemetery. The gatehouse is reached in 1.0 mi. Hikers may leave their cars there, cross the Diamond River on a logging bridge, and proceed up through the gorge. Good viewpoints are reached in about 0.5 mi., the Dartmouth Peaks Camp at the confluence of the rivers in 1 mi., and the Management Center at 1.5 mi. Hellgate, another scenic gorge, is reached 12.5 mi. from the gatehouse.

Paths have been cut from the Management Center to the ledges on the Diamond Peaks and from Hellgate to the ledges, a 2-mi. loop that has been much disrupted by recent logging. For further information, call the gatehouse, listed under Dartmouth College in the Berlin telephone directory, or write to Allison Merrill, Dartmouth College, Hanover, NH 03755.

DIAMOND PEAKS

These two small elevations (2071 ft.) between the Dead Diamond and Magalloway rivers together compose a nearly semicircular ridge. Their attractive feature is a high cliff on the concave side of the ridge, facing south. The sharp semidetached east peak has a bare summit, and the long and flat west peak has many viewpoints from the brink of the cliff. They may be reached by a path from the Dartmouth Management Center (above).

Mount Cardigan Area

This region, between Interstates 89 and 93, includes Mt. Cardigan (3121 ft.), Plymouth Mountain (2187 ft.), Ragged Mountain (2240 ft.), and Mt. Kearsarge (2937 ft.).

MOUNT CARDIGAN

The outstanding peak of west central New Hampshire, Mt. Cardigan is located in Orange (near Canaan) and Alexandria (near Bristol). There are excellent views from the steep-sided rock dome of "Old Baldy" itself, as well as from the S. Peak (also noted for its blueberries in season) and from Firescrew, the north peak, named for a spiral of fire and smoke that rose from it during a conflagration in 1855. Though relatively low, Cardigan has a variety of terrain and trails that vary from gentle woods walks to the West Ridge Trail — a traditional first "big mountain climb" for children — to the Holt Trail, with upper ledges that are among the more difficult scrambles in New England. From the east, a fine circuit can be made by ascending Cardigan by the Holt, Cathedral Forest, and Clark trails (or by taking the much more challenging Holt Trail all the way), and returning over Firescrew via the Mowglis and Manning trails.

Most of the mountain is within a state reservation of over 5000 acres. Adjacent to the park is the AMC's 1000-acre Cardigan Reservation, which occupies much of "Shem Valley" and portions of the east slopes of the mountain. The AMC Cardigan Lodge, which has a main lodge, a cottage, a campground and "Hi-Cabin," provides meals and lodging to the public during the summer season. Nearby Newfound Lake, with Wellington State Park, offers swimming, boating, and fishing. For reservations and local trail information, contact Manager, AMC Cardigan Lodge, RFD, Bristol, NH 03222 (603-744-8011). The usual approach is from Bristol, easily accessible from I-93. Turn left (west) from NH Rte. 3A at the stone church at the foot of

Newfound Lake, continue straight ahead through the crossroad at 1.9 mi., bear right at 3.1 mi., and turn left at 6.3 mi. At 7.4 mi. from the church, turn right on a gravel road, then bear right at 7.5 mi. at the "Red Schoolhouse," and continue to lodge at 8.9 mi. This road is plowed in winter, but must be driven with great care.

Many of the trails on Mt. Cardigan are heavily used and well beaten; others, noted in the individual descriptions, are lightly used, sparsely marked, and receive little maintenance. They may be difficult to follow in the early part of the season when a footway is not clearly established, or in fall when covered by leaves. Although these trails are not recommended for the inexperienced, experienced hikers with map and compass may follow them fairly easily. Refer to map 2, Mt. Cardigan, and to the USGS Cardigan quadrangle.

West Ridge Trail (NHDP)

This is the main trail to Mt. Cardigan from the west, the shortest and easiest route to the summit.

From NH Rte. 118 about 0.5 mi. north of Canaan, turn right at a large Cardigan State Park sign. Bear right 2.7 mi. from Rte. 118, shortly after crossing Orange Brook. At 3.4 mi. bear left to parking area at 4.1 mi., where there are picnic tables and restrooms. The well-beaten trail starts at a sign in the parking area. It crosses a service road, and just beyond, the South Ridge Trail diverges right at a sharp turn in the West Ridge Trail. The trail passes a well and a brook, both left, climbs to a junction with the Skyland Trail right, then crosses a bridge and reaches the Hermitage, a small open shelter. At the shelter the Hurricane Gap Trail diverges right (no sign) for Hi-Cabin and the Clark Trail (*water* 200 yd. above shelter), and shortly beyond, a branch of the South Ridge Trail leads right to the warden's cabin. From here the West Ridge Trail ascends marked ledges to end at the Clark Trail just below the summit.

West Ridge Trail (map 2)
Distances from Cardigan State Park parking area
> *to* South Ridge Trail junction: 0.4 mi.
> *to* Hermitage Shelter: 1 mi.
> *to* Mt. Cardigan summit (via Clark Trail): 1.4 mi. (2.3 km.), 1¼ hr.

South Ridge Trail

This trail provides access to Mt. Cardigan, S. Peak and Rimrock, and with the West Ridge Trail makes a scenic loop. It diverges right from the West Ridge Trail 0.4 mi. from the State Park parking area, crosses a brook and climbs, rather steeply at times, to Rimrock, where it crosses the Skyland Trail. (*Descending,* follow the left of two lines of cairns on the ledge below Rimrock.) The trail continues across marked ledges, passing the summit of S. Peak, where a poorly marked spur descends to the Hurricane Gap Trail. The South Ridge Trail turns left and descends to cross the Hurricane Gap Trail, then turns sharp right at a junction (left is the branch trail to the W. Ridge Trail at the Hermitage Shelter, 0.2 mi.), and continues to the warden's cabin where it ends at the Clark Trail.

South Ridge Trail (map 2)
Distances from West Ridge Trail junction
> *to* Rimrock: 0.7 mi.
> *to* Mt. Cardigan, S. Peak: 1 mi.
> *to* Clark Trail junction: 1.3 mi. (2.1 km.), 1 hr.

Loop from Cardigan State Park parking area
> *via* West Ridge, Clark, and South Ridge Trails: 3.4 mi. (5.4 km.), 2½ hr.

Orange Cove Trail

This trail provides a direct approach from the west to Mowglis Trail, Cilley's Cave, Hanging Rocks, and Crag Shelter. Follow

directions above for West Ridge Trail, but bear left 2.7 mi. from
NH Rte. 118, immediately after crossing Orange Brook. Follow
this road 1.2 mi. to end of pavement. This trail (no sign) is the old
Groton-Orange road and it is easy to follow. It passes the State
Park boundary, bears left at a fork, and climbs easily past a large
beaver pond to end at the Mowglis Trail in the col between
Cilley's Cave and Cataloochee Mountain. Follow the Mowglis
Trail straight on the old road to Groton, or bear sharp right for
Cilley's Cave and Mt. Cardigan.

Orange Cove Trail (map 2)

Distances from end of paved road

 to beaver pond: 1.0 mi.

 to Mowglis Trail junction: 1.6 mi. (2.5 km.), 1 hr.

Mowglis Trail

 From Hebron village on Newfound Lake take Sculptured
Rocks Rd. west and follow signs to Sculptured Rocks State
Geological Site on the Cockermouth River, an interesting glacial
gorge with potholes and a popular picnic spot with a swimming
hole. Continue 1 mi. past the picnic area to just beyond the white
bridge over Atwell Brook. The trail (no sign) follows the old
Groton-Orange road, which forks left along Atwell Brook, ascending at a moderate grade to a junction with the Orange Cove
Trail in the col between Cilley's Cave and Cataloochee Mountain. The Orange Cove Trail continues ahead on the old road, and
the Mowglis Trail turns left and climbs briefly to a junction with
the Elwell Trail. Soon after this junction a spur trail (sign) leads
left 80 yd. to Cilley's Cave, a lonely, rocky retreat, where it is
said a hermit once lived, and about 0.3 mi. farther, another spur
leads left to Hanging Rocks.

 Hanging Rocks is a glacial formation of unusual beauty that
forms a natural shelter. About 100 yd. from the Mowglis Trail
the spur forks. The right fork leads 0.1 mi. across the top of the
ledge, with a fine view east, and the left fork descends 0.1 mi.
among the rocks at the foot of the ledge. The connecting link at

the far end of these two paths is obscure and requires a fairly difficult scramble.

The Mowglis Trail then ascends more steeply past Crag Shelter (an open shelter accommodating fifteen, maintained by Camp Mowglis) to an outlook north, where the trail turns sharp right and climbs to the summit of Firescrew to meet the Manning Trail. It descends across wide ledges deeply marked by glacial action, passes a side trail left (0.2 mi. long, 200-ft. descent) to Grotto Cave and a smaller boulder cave, marked by a sign painted on the rocks, then ascends steeply to the summit of Mt. Cardigan.

Mowglis Trail (map 2)

Distances from Sculptured Rocks Road

to state park boundary: 2.4 mi.

to Orange Cove Trail junction: 3.5 mi.

to Elwell Trail: 3.7 mi.

to Cilley's Cave spur trail: 3.8 mi.

to Hanging Rocks spur trail: 4.1 mi.

to Crag Shelter: 4.6 mi.

to Firescrew summit: 5.1 mi.

to Grotto Cave spur trail: 5.5 mi.

to Mt. Cardigan summit: 5.7 mi. (9.2 km.), 4 hr.

Elwell Trail

This trail extends over 10 mi. from Newfound Lake to the Mowglis Trail, 2 mi. north of Mt. Cardigan. The trail begins on W. Shore Rd. directly opposite the entrance to Wellington State Park. It passes a spur trail that leads left 0.2 mi. to Goose Pond, crosses the open summit of Little Sugarloaf, continues along the ridge, and finally climbs steeply to the summit of Sugarloaf. About 100 yd. past this summit the trail turns sharp left, descends steeply, then runs fairly level across the old Hebron-Alexandria turnpike. It then climbs by steep switchbacks, with rough footing, to the summit ridge of Bear Mountain, where there are several fine outlooks across Newfound Lake. The Elwell Trail continues along the ridge, passes under power lines, and crosses the Welton Falls Trail. It ascends gradually with occasional steep pitches, past several fine outlooks, to the summit of Oregon Mountain. The trail descends sharply to a junction with the Carter Gibbs Trail (right) and the Old Dicey (left), then crosses a brook and climbs gradually to the summit of Mowglis Mountain, where there is a memorial tablet for Colonel Elwell Alcott, for whom this trail is named, on the right. It descends again to the next col, where the Back 80 Trail diverges left for Cardigan Lodge, then climbs to a spur trail leading left 130 yd. to Cilley's Cave (sign), and descends slightly to end at the Mowglis Trail. Between Sugarloaf Mountain and the Back 80 Trail junction, the Elwell Trail is sparingly marked and must be followed with great care.

Elwell Trail (map 2)
Distances from W. Shore Rd.

to Goose Pond spur trail: 0.5 mi.

to Little Sugarloaf Mountain summit: 0.8 mi.

to Sugarloaf Mountain summit: 1.7 mi.

to old Hebron-Alexandria Turnpike crossing: 2.3 mi.

to Bear Mountain summit ridge: 3.3 mi.

to Welton Falls Trail crossing: 4.8 mi.

to Oregon Mountain summit: 7.6 mi.

to Old Dicey Rd./Carter Gibbs Trail junction: 7.9 mi.

to Mowglis Mountain summit: 8.9 mi.

to Back 80 Trail junction: 9.9 mi.

to Mowglis Trail junction: 10.6 mi. (17 km.), 7¼ hr.

Carter Gibbs Trail

This trail leaves Sculptured Rocks Rd. (no sign) at a small gravel turnout on the south side, 0.2 mi. east of the Sculptured Rocks parking area. It follows a gravel road for about 0.5 mi., then turns left where a right fork crosses Dane Brook on a snowmobile bridge. In another 0.3 mi. it bears right at a fork and follows an old logging road that gradually peters out. The trail then climbs more steeply to the height-of-land between Oregon Mountain and Mowglis Mountain, where a side path (sign) leads right 0.2 mi. to an outlook on Carter's Knob. The main trail then descends sharply to the Elwell Trail opposite the upper terminus of the Old Dicey Rd.

Carter Gibbs Trail (map 2)
Distances from Sculptured Rocks Rd.

   to Carter Knob spur trail: 2.7 mi.

   to Elwell Trail junction: 3.0 mi. (4.8 km.), 2¼ hr.

Welton Falls Trail

This trail provides a route from Hebron to the Elwell Trail and Welton Falls Rd. It has been extensively rerouted so trail markings must be followed with great care.

The trail diverges left from Hobart Hill Rd. 0.8 mi. from the village square in Hebron. The only sign at the trailhead is a small Mowglis Trail marker. The trail follows an old road across a brook through a ruined farm, then slabs the hillside to another old road. It turns left and ascends this road, passing under power lines, and crosses the Elwell Trail at the top of the ridge. Descending, it soon joins old logging roads and follows them past a ruined camp, where it crosses a better road diagonally to an open field, where stacks of decaying wood serve as cairns. Becoming a trail again, it descends across a brook, on and off old roads, and continues to a gravel road at the edge of a field (parking). The gravel road continues to Welton Falls Rd. just north of the bridge over Fowler River. This point can also be reached by following the route described for Cardigan Lodge. Bear right 6.3 mi. from the stone church and continue 0.8 mi., just across the bridge.

Welton Falls Trail (map 2)
Distances from Hobart Hill Rd.

   to Elwell Trail crossing: 1.5 mi.

   to gravel road junction: 3.2 mi.

   to Welton Falls Rd. (via gravel road): 3.3 mi. (5.3 km.), 2 hr.

Old Dicey Road

Follow the route for Cardigan Lodge but bear right 6.3 mi. from the stone church. Follow the road for another 1.2 mi. Where the good road turns sharp right uphill, continue straight ahead another 0.1 mi. to a parking area at a washed-out bridge. Follow the road, which is the Old Dicey Rd., across a brook. At 0.2 mi. the Manning Trail diverges left on a cart track, while the Old Dicey Rd. continues to a clearing. Here the Back 80 Loop continues straight ahead, and the Old Dicey Rd. turns right and climbs past an old shack and cellar hole, along a small brook, to end at the Elwell Trail opposite the south terminus of the Carter Gibbs Trail.

Old Dicey Rd. (map 2)

Distances from parking area

   to Manning Trail junction: 0.2 mi.

   to Back 80 Loop junction: 1.1 mi.

   to Elwell Trail junction: 2 mi. (3.3 km.), 1½ hr.

Back 80 Loop

This short trail connects the Old Dicey Rd. with the Back 80 Trail and makes a circuit to Welton Falls possible from Cardigan Lodge. It follows an old road straight ahead from the clearing where the Old Dicey Rd. turns right, then bears left, soon crosses two brooks, and ascends across another brook and the 93Z Ski Trail to meet the Back 80 Trail at a cellar hole.

Back 80 Loop (map 2)

Distances from Old Dicey Rd. junction

   to 93Z Ski Trail crossing: 0.6 mi.

   to Back 80 Trail junction: 0.8 mi. (1.2 km.), 35 min.

Back 80 Trail

This trail diverges right from the Holt Trail about 100 yd. west of Cardigan Lodge and follows an old logging road. At 0.3 mi. the Short Circuit Ski Trail diverges right, and about 0.5 mi. farther the trail turns sharp right where the Alleeway Ski Trail turns left and reaches a cellar hole. The trail to the right is the

Back 80 Loop to Welton Falls; the Back 80 Trail turns left (follow the trail with care from here on). It crosses the 93Z Ski Trail, then a brook at a scenic little waterfall. It turns sharp left at a corner post at the east corner of Back 80 Lot and runs along the northern border of the lot. The trail goes around a flowage from a beaver dam, which may force a detour through the woods, passes a junction with the Duke's Link Ski Trail, then turns sharp right, crosses a brook, turns left, and follows the brook and the edge of another beaver pond to the back corner post (marked Draper-NHFS-AMC). The trail then ascends gradually across a brook to end at the Elwell Trail in the col between Mowglis Mountain and Cilley's Cave.

Back 80 Trail (map 2)
Distances from Holt Trail junction
to Back 80 Loop junction: 0.8 mi.
to corner post, east corner Back 80 Lot: 1.2 mi.
to Duke's Link Ski Trail junction: 1.8 mi.
to Elwell Trail junction: 2.4 mi. (3.9 km.), 1½ hr.

Manning Trail
This trail diverges left from the Old Dicey Rd. 0.2 mi. from the parking area near a washed-out bridge on Welton Falls Rd., follows a cart path to the Fowler River, crosses on stones, and enters the Welton Falls Reservation (NHDP). It continues up-river to a deep, mossy ravine and the main falls. There are many attractive falls and rapids, as well as spectacular potholes, above and below the main falls. From Welton Falls the trail climbs and descends several small ridges, usually in sight of the river, to a junction with the Hiawata Trail. The Manning Trail turns right at this junction, crosses the river without a bridge (difficult at high water) and ascends to a plateau, where it passes through a planted grove of spruces. It crosses the 93Z Ski Trail, then descends through a picnic area to Cardigan Lodge. (To reach the Manning Trail from the lodge, ascend through a picnic area to the road at right of the fireplace.)

The Manning Trail continues past the lodge, coincides with

the Holt Trail for 0.3 mi., then diverges right, passes the old Holt cellar hole, turns right at an arrow, and climbs through the woods to the first ledges. It passes a *spring (water unreliable)*, then climbs again to a great open ledge where the Duke's Ski Trail enters right, then diverges right at the head of the ledge. The Manning Trail turns left through scrubby woods, ascending at times steeply, until it reaches ledges where the Duke's rejoins from the right. The trail follows cairns and paint markings across flat ledges to the cairn where it ends at the Mowglis Trail, just below the summit of Firescrew. Cardigan summit is to the left on Mowglis Trail.

Manning Trail (map 2)
Distances from Old Dicey Rd. junction
   to Welton Falls: 0.3 mi.
   to Hiawata Trail junction: 1.1 mi.
   to Cardigan Lodge: 1.6 mi., 1 hr.
   to Duke's Ski Trail, first junction: 3.5 mi.
   to Mowglis Trail junction: 4 mi. (6.4 km.), 3 hr.
Distance from Cardigan Lodge
   to Mt. Cardigan summit (via Manning Trail and Mowglis Trail): 3.0 mi. (4.8 km.), 2½ hr.

Hiawata Trail
This trail connects the Manning Trail with the Shem Valley Rd. 0.4 mi. east of the lodge (sign), and is used at high water to avoid the difficult crossing of Fowler River on the Manning Trail to Welton Falls.

Hiawata Trail (map 2)
Distance from Shem Valley Rd.
   to Manning Trail junction: 0.3 mi. (0.5 km.)
Distance from Cardigan Lodge
   to Welton Falls: 1.4 mi. (2.3 km.), ¾ hr.

Elizabeth Holt Trail
This is the shortest, but far from the easiest, route from Cardigan Lodge to the summit of Mt. Cardigan. The climb up the

steep upper ledges is more difficult than any other trail in this section. It is *dangerous* in wet or icy weather.

From Cardigan Lodge the Holt Trail follows a gravel road to a junction with the Manning Trail, then a lumber road almost to the Bailey Brook bridge. There it diverges right, and the Alexandria Ski Trail continues straight. The Holt Trail stays on the north bank of the brook, then crosses at the head of Elizabeth Falls to rejoin the Alexandria Ski Trail near Grand Junction. The Cathedral Forest Trail (Holt-Clark Cutoff) diverges left, providing an easier ascent of Mt. Cardigan via Cathedral Forest and the Clark Trail. The Alexandria Ski Trail also diverges left here, and shortly beyond the Alleeway Ski Trail diverges right. The Holt Trail continues along Bailey Brook to a point directly under the summit, climbs steeply on a rocky path through woods, then emerges on open ledges and makes a rapid, sporty, and very steep ascent over marked ledges to the summit.

Holt Trail (map 2)

Distances from Cardigan Lodge

  to Grand Junction: 1.1 mi.

  to Mt. Cardigan summit: 2.2 mi. (3.6 km.), 2 hr.

Cathedral Forest Trail (Holt-Clark Cutoff)

This trail leads left from the Holt Trail at Grand Junction to the Clark Trail in the Cathedral Forest. About 100 yd. above the junction the Vistamont Trail branches left to Gilman Mountain. Ascending in graded switchbacks past the huge dead trunk of the Giant of the Forest, the trail joins the Clark Trail at a large cairn, providing the easiest route to the summit of Cardigan from the east.

Cathedral Forest Trail (map 2)

Distances from Holt Trail, Grand Junction

  to Clark Trail junction: 0.6 mi.

  to Mt. Cardigan summit (via Clark Trail): 1.5 mi. (2.4 km.)

Clark Trail

The official beginning of this trail is on the Shem Valley Rd. 0.6 mi. east of Cardigan Lodge, but most hikers will find it more convenient to enter via the Woodland Trail from the Lodge. The trail proper starts at the top of a ledgy ridge, opposite "Shim Knoll," and follows a rough dirt road left (sign: "Williams") past a summer residence. Just over Clark Brook the Woodland Trail enters right. The two trails together ascend a logging road at a moderate grade to the point where the Woodland Trail turns sharp left on the logging road, and the Clark Trail continues straight ahead on an older road. It passes an old cellar hole, enters the state reservation at a level grade in a beautiful forest, then climbs rather steeply until it crosses the Vistamont Trail. The grade becomes more gradual, and the Clark Trail reaches the Cathedral Forest, where the Cathedral Forest Trail enters from the right. As the trail continues a moderate ascent, the Alexandria Ski Trail enters right near P. J. Ledge, and 30 yd. farther the Hurricane Gap Trail leaves left for Hi-Cabin and the Hermitage Shelter. The Clark Trail continues past a side trail left that leads to a *spring* and Hi-Cabin, then climbs on ledges and through scrub to the warden's cabin, where it meets the South Ridge Trail. It turns right and follows marked ledges steeply to the summit.

Clark Trail (map 2)

Distances from Shem Valley Rd.

to Woodland Trail, first junction: 0.5 mi.

to Woodland Trail, second junction: 1.1 mi.

to Vistamont Trail crossing: 1.9 mi.

to Cathedral Forest Trail junction: 2.2 mi.

to Hurricane Gap Trail junction: 2.5 mi.

to warden's cabin: 2.9 mi.

to Mt. Cardigan summit: 3.1 mi. (5 km.), 2½ hr.

Hurricane Gap Trail

This trail connects the east and west sides of the mountain through the col between Cardigan and S. Peak. It leaves the Clark Trail just above P. J. Ledge, passes an unsigned spur right to a *spring*, then reaches the AMC Hi-Cabin, where another spur trail leads right 60 yd. to the *spring* and 40 yd. farther to the Clark Trail. It climbs past a spur that leads 0.1 mi. left to S. Peak, then crosses the South Ridge Trail at the height-of-land, and descends to the West Ridge Trail at the Hermitage. (*Reliable water* 200 yd. above the Hermitage.)

Hurricane Gap Trail (map 2)

Distances from Clark Trail junction

   to AMC Hi-Cabin: 0.1 mi.

   to South Ridge Trail crossing: 0.4 mi.

   to West Ridge Trail junction: 0.6 mi. (0.9 km.), ½ hr.

Vistamont Trail

This trail connects the Holt Trail with the Skyland Trail at Gilman Mountain. It leaves the Cathedral Forest Trail left about 100 yd. above Grand Junction, and rises over a low ridge where it crosses the Clark Trail. It then drops to cross a branch of Clark Brook, and ascends by switchbacks up the east spur of Gilman Mountain (USGS Orange Mountain), climbing moderately on open ledges to the Skyland Trail 80 yd. southeast of the rocky summit of Gilman Mountain (fine views).

Vistamont Trail (map 2)

Distances from Cathedral Forest Trail junction

   to Clark Trail crossing: 0.6 mi.

   to Skyland Trail junction: 1.6 mi. (2.6 km.), 1 hr. 20 min.

Distance from Cardigan Lodge

   to Gilman Mountain summit (via Holt, Cathedral Forest, Vistamont, and Skyland trails): 2.8 mi. (4.5 km.), 2¼ hr.

Woodland Trail (Skyland Cutoff)

This trail runs from Cardigan Lodge to the Skyland Trail near the summit of Church Mountain. It leaves the parking lot to the left of the pond, crosses the outlet brook on a bridge, and passes the east entrance of the Kimball Ski Trail. It continues through woods past the Brock Farm cellar hole and field, then turns right on the Clark Trail, with which it coincides for some distance. It then turns sharp left on a logging road and descends across a brook, and climbs to a large beaver pond. From here on the trail is harder to follow and great care must be used. It ascends along the inlet brook, crosses it, and doubles back along the edge of the pond, then climbs moderately past a corner post marked "Draper" in a boggy area near a large boulder. Finally it rises more steeply to end at the Skyland Trail at the northwest shoulder of Church Mountain.

Woodland Trail (map 2)

Distances from parking area, Cardigan Lodge

to Clark Trail junction: 0.6 mi.

to Clark Trail departure: 1.2 mi.

to beaver pond: 2.1 mi.

to Skyland Trail junction: 3.3 mi. (5.2 km.), 2¼ hr.

Skyland Trail

This trail runs from Alexandria Four Corners to the West Ridge Trail just below the Hermitage. It follows the western and southern boundaries of Shem Valley, and in 4.5 mi. crosses five of the six peaks that extend south and southeast from Cardigan summit. It is lightly marked for much of its distance, and, particularly between Brown Mountain and Gilman Mountain, must be followed with great care. It is, however, a very scenic route.

The trail starts at Alexandria Four Corners, reached by following signs from the stone church at the foot of Newfound Lake to Alexandria village. Continue through the village on the main road, which turns sharp right, then left, pass under power lines and then, as the main road turns sharp left for Danbury, continue straight for about 4 mi. to the corner (sign: "Rosie's Rd."). Best parking is here; do not block roads above.

The trail follows the road right (north) from the corner and soon bears left at a fork. At about 0.3 mi. it turns sharp left (arrow) on a short road to a clearing, and ascends moderately to the edge of a logged area and a house. It climbs almost to the wooded summit of Brown Mountain, then turns left and crosses the col to the summit of Church Mountain (2280 ft.), where there is an outlook. It continues past a junction (right) with the Woodland Trail coming from Cardigan Lodge, then follows the ridge top over Grafton Knob (2200 ft.) and Crane Mountain (2420 ft.), with good views from several ledges near the summit. The Skyland Trail continues to Gilman Mountain, where the Vistamont Trail enters 80 yd. before the summit. There are fine views from the summit ledges. The trail descends to a col, then climbs fairly steeply to Rimrock where it crosses the South Ridge Trail. It descends along a ledge (follow the right of two lines of cairns) and soon enters the West Ridge Trail just below the Hermitage Shelter.

Skyland Trail (map 2)
Distances from Alexandria Four Corners

   to Church Mountain summit: 1.1 mi.

   to Woodland Trail junction: 1.3 mi.

   to Crane Mountain summit: 2.1 mi.

   to Vistamont Trail junction: 3.3 mi.

   to Rimrock: 4.3 mi.

   to West Ridge Trail junction: 4.6 mi. (7.3 km.), 3¼ hr.

SKI TRAILS AT CARDIGAN LODGE

The AMC maintains a number of ski trails in the woods around Cardigan Lodge, in addition to many hiking trails which can be skied. A map available at the lodge shows most of these trails and their ratings (novice cross-country to expert alpine on the ledges of Cardigan and Firescrew). The following trails — cut as alpine trails in the days before modern tows became common — were not constructed to withstand summer use, and hikers are requested not to use them.

Alexandria Ski Trail

This trail coincides with the Holt Trail along old roads 0.8 mi. to Bailey Brook bridge, then crosses the bridge and runs along the south bank 0.3 mi. to Grand Junction. (The section from the bridge to Grand Junction may be used by hikers.) It then climbs a wide, steep, curving course for 0.6 mi. to the Clark Trail at P. J. Ledge.

Kimball Ski Trail

This trail may be entered from the Woodland Trail 0.1 mi. from Cardigan Lodge, or from the Holt Trail 0.1 mi. from the lodge. The routes join at about 0.5 mi., and the trail climbs to a ledgy ridgecrest (sign). An old route (no well-defined trail) led left from here down to the Clark pastures and the Clark Trail. The main trail bears right and descends to Grand Junction. (Total length: about 1.5 mi.)

Duke's Ski Trail

Named for Duke Dimitri von Leuchtenberg, who scouted its location, this trail leaves the Holt Trail about 0.2 mi. from Cardigan Lodge, ascends the open ski slope, then climbs to the high ridge that forms the north slope of Shem Valley. It joins the Manning Trail on the lower ledges of Firescrew, diverges right, then rejoins above. (Total length: about 2 mi.)

Alleeway Ski Trail

This trail leaves the Holt Trail just above Grand Junction and runs across the Manning Trail and Duke's Ski Trail to the Back 80 Trail just below a cellar hole, where the Back 80 Trail Loop enters. (Total length: about 1.5 mi.)

Duke's Link Ski Trail

This trail connects the Duke's Ski Trail with the Back 80 Trail just below the upper beaver pond. (Total length: about 1 mi.)

93Z Ski Trail

This trail leaves the Shem Valley Rd. about 0.3 mi. east of the lodge, following a logging road that crosses the Manning Trail in a spruce grove. It continues past a junction with the Short Circuit Ski Trail, crosses the Back 80 Loop, and ends at the Back 80 Trail above a cellar hole. (Total length: about 1.5 mi.)

Short Circuit Ski Trail —

This short link runs about 0.3 mi. from the 93Z Ski Trail to the Back 80 Trail.

PLYMOUTH MOUNTAIN

This mountain lies in Plymouth, northeast of Newfound Lake. The true summit (2187 ft.) is wooded, but nearby open ledges afford excellent views. Refer to the USGS Holderness quadrangle.

At the crossroads on NH Rte. 3A near the head of Newfound Lake, where the lake shore road to Hebron Village runs west, go east on Pike Hill Rd. and bear left at first fork. Park just past this fork on the left because the road may be impassable beyond. About 1.1 mi. past the fork after a rough bridge over a brook, the trail leaves right on an old logging road (sign). The trail is marked with Camp Mowglis stencilled signs. It crosses a brook (use care), follows another old road upward, turns sharp left where an unsigned branch trail enters right, and ascends to an outlook over Newfound Lake.

(*Descending,* turn sharp right to avoid a branch trail that is almost straight ahead and better signed at this point. This trail is rather obscure and connects to old roads that lead back to Pike Hill Rd.) It becomes less steep, crosses a false summit, and climbs to the true summit (sign). From here an open ledge 30 yd. straight ahead (east) provides fine views of Franconia Notch and the White Mountains, while a line of cairns leads right (south-west) to an outlook over Newfound Lake to Mt. Cardigan.

Plymouth Mountain (USGS Holderness quadrangle)
Distances from US Rte. 3A

   to fork: 0.2 mi.

   to start of summit trail: 1.4 mi., 1 hr.

   to Plymouth Mountain summit: 2.9 mi. (4.6 km.), 2¼ hr.

RAGGED MOUNTAIN

This 2240-ft. mountain lies in the towns of Andover and Danbury. It is well named, a large, irregular, rugged mass, most of which is heavily wooded. There are several peaks of nearly equal height with numerous ledgy outlooks. The Bulkhead is a precipitous buttress on the east side. The Ragged Mountain Ski Area, off NH Rte. 104 in Danbury, is on the slightly lower W. Peak. Refer to the USGS Mt. Kearsarge quadrangle.

The mountain has a number of trails. The best approach is probably from the ski area. From the base ascend diagonally to the left of the T-Bar lift, or follow less steep slopes further left. These two routes unite in a flat area, and a narrow ski trail soon diverges left, slabs around the east side of the W. Peak and turns sharp right to the summit. At this turn a ski trail, Wilson's Wonder, descends left, slabbing the ridge and curves into the col. An unsigned yellow-blazed trail diverges left there, descends slightly, climbs steeply, then moderately to where both paths rejoin, just east of the "West Top" (W. Peak on some signs), which has fine views south. The ridge path continues past a trail junction, then past another junction with a logging road (which descends past a spur trail to Balanced Rock to join the Wilson's Wonder ski trail to Proctor). The trail then ascends past a *spring* to the summit (restricted views) and continues to the "Old Top," with the finest views on the mountain.

Ragged Mountain (USGS Mt. Kearsarge quadrangle)
Distances from Ragged Mountain ski area parking lot
   to Wilson's Wonder ski trail junction: 1 mi.
   to yellow-blazed trail in col (via Wilson's Wonder Trail): 1.3
      mi.
   to Ragged Mountain summit: 2.1 mi.
   to Old Top: 2.4 mi. (3.8 km.), 2 hr.

MOUNT KEARSARGE

Mt. Kearsarge is located in Warner, Wilmot, Andover, and Salisbury. This 2937-ft. mountain has a bare summit with fine views in all directions. Mt. Kearsarge probably was discovered shortly after the Pilgrims landed. On a very early map (Gardner's) it appears as "Carasaiga," but since Carrigain's map of 1816 "Kearsarge" has remained the accepted spelling. On the summit are a fire tower and an airways beacon, on separate and prominent ledges about 30 yd. apart, and a fire warden's cabin near the tower. From the cabin an orange-blazed trail leads down about 0.1 mi. to a *spring*. Refer to the USGS Mt. Kearsarge quadrangle.

Wilmot (Northside) Trail

From NH Rte. 11 between Wilmot Flat and Elkins, take the Kearsarge Valley Rd. south, then follow signs to Winslow State Park and the site of the old Winslow House (caretaker's cabin, picnic area, *water,* and parking space; modest admission fee). The trail starts from the parking area to the left of a service garage. It is well beaten and marked with red paint. The trail crosses under power lines and climbs moderately to a fork. (The left branch rejoins above and is slightly shorter but rougher.) The right branch climbs more steeply past Halfway Rock, slabs upward to an outlook north, then turns south and ascends over bare ledges, marked with orange paint, to the summit.

Wilmot Trail (USGS Mt. Kearsarge quadrangle)
Distance from parking area, Winslow State Park
  to Mt. Kearsarge summit: 1.1 mi. (1.8 km.), 1 hr. 5 min.

Warner (Southside) Trail

Leave NH Rte. 103 in Warner and follow signs to the toll gate at Rollins State Park. A small fee is charged, and the gate is often closed on weekdays before Memorial Day and after Labor Day. There is a picnic area with tables, fireplaces, and *water*. The road then mainly follows the route of the old carriage road along the crest of Mission Ridge and ends at a parking area 3.7 mi. above the toll gate. There are more picnic tables and fireplaces here, but *no water*.

The trail follows the old carriage road, now badly eroded, to a ledge with a fine view. (An unsigned, red-blazed trail, 0.1 mi. longer and rough, bypasses the worst section of the old road to the right and rejoins at the outlook.) The trail then swings left and rises to the foot of the summit ledges, where there are toilets. An orange-blazed trail diverges sharp right, a direct route to the warden's cabin and a *spring*. The main trail, blazed in silver, continues across the ledges to the beacon and tower.

From the west end of the parking area, an unsigned trail starts as a cart track to the foot of the ledges and, marked with red paint on the rocks, climbs steeply to the top. Faded paint blazes lead along sparsely wooded ledges toward the tower, then to the main trail just below the beacon.

Warner Trail (USGS Mt. Kearsarge quadrangle)
Distances from parking area, Rollins State Park
  to Mt. Kearsarge summit (via carriage road): 0.6 mi. (1 km.), 25 min.
  to Mt. Kearsarge summit (via ledges): 0.5 mi. (0.8 km.), 25 min.

The Lakes Region and Southeast

Around Squam Lake and Lake Winnipesaukee are ranges between 2000 and 3000 ft. with fine views of the lakes and mountains. To the east, beyond Ossipee Lake, is Green Mountain (1907 ft.) in Effingham. In the southeastern quarter of the state, east of I-93 and south of the lakes, are scattered low mountains.

Although many of the trails are heavily used and well beaten, some are not officially maintained, and the condition of footways and markings can vary greatly. Hikers should exercise extra caution in following them.

SQUAM LAKE AREA

In the vicinity of Squam Lake, the low peaks of the Squam Range to the north, Mt. Israel to the northeast, and Red Hill to the east have nice views. Most of the trails are maintained by the Squam Lakes Association and are blazed with yellow paint. Refer to map 4, Chocorua-Waterville. There is a Squam Lakes Association *Trails Guide (*Squam Lakes Association, Plymouth, NH 03264). For short walks see *25 Walks in the Lakes Region* by Paul H. Blaisdell (New Hampshire Publishing, Somersworth, 1977).

THE RATTLESNAKES

W. Rattlesnake (1220 ft.) and E. Rattlesnake (1280 ft.) are two low mountains near the north end of Squam Lake. The view to the south from W. Rattlesnake is especially fine. The latter may be climbed directly from NH Rte. 113 via the Old Bridle Path or from the road to Rockywold and Deephaven camps, which lie to the south of the mountains.

Old Bridle Path (SLA)

This trail leads to W. Rattlesnake from NH Rte. 113 between Center Sandwich and Holderness. It starts 0.5 mi. northeast of the road to Rockywold and Deephaven camps and directly opposite the entrance to the Mt. Morgan Trail (parking) and follows an old cart road to the summit. Descending, the entrance to this trail is slightly northwest of the cliffs at a sign.

Old Bridle Path (map 4)

Distance from NH Rte. 113

to W. Rattlesnake summit: 0.9 mi. (1.4 km.), ½ hr.

Ramsey Trail (SLA)

This trail to W. Rattlesnake leaves the road to Rockywold and Deephaven camps or NH Rte. 113 100 yd. east of the entrance to the camps (sign). It soon takes a sharp right (the Undercut Trail continues straight ahead to Rte. 113 and the Old Bridle Path). It is well marked to the top, but steep in places.

Ramsey Trail (map 4)

Distances from Rockywold-Deephaven camps road

to W. Rattlesnake summit: 0.5 mi. (0.8 km.), ½ hr.

Pasture Trail (SLA)

This trail leads to W. Rattlesnake from Rockywold and Deephaven camps. Continue east on the road to Rockywold and Deephaven camps (off NH Rte. 113) past the entrance to the camps to the trailhead, about 100 yd. east of the entrance to Pinehurst Farm. The trail leads uphill past farm buildings and bears right through an overgrown field. After the trail turns left at 0.1 mi., the E. Rattlesnake Trail branches right. Just beyond, the Pasture Trail bears left, the Col Trail continues straight ahead. The Pasture Trail then climbs to the summit.

Pasture Trail (map 4)

Distance from Rockywold-Deephaven camps road

to W. Rattlesnake summit: 0.5 mi. (0.8 km.), ½ hr.

Col Trail (SLA)

This trail continues straight where the Pasture Trail (see above) bears left 0.1 mi. from the Rockywold-Deephaven camps road, just beyond where the E. Rattlesnake Trail branches right. It meets the Ridge Trail halfway between E. and W. Rattlesnake. The Col Trail jogs right a short distance on the Ridge Trail, then turns left ("Saddle" sign). It descends, passes east of a large beaver pond, joins a wood road, and reaches NH Rte. 113 about 1 mi. east of the Old Bridle Path trailhead and 0.3 mi. west of Metcalf Rd.

Col Trail (map 4)

Distances from Pasture Trail junction
   to Ridge Trail junction: 0.5 mi.
   to NH Rte. 113: 1.6 mi. (2.6 km.)

Ridge Trail (SLA)

This trail connects W. and E. Rattlesnake. It begins just northeast of the summit of W. Rattlesnake and descends gradually. At 0.4 mi. the Col Trail comes in from the right, and just beyond leaves again to the left. The Ridge Trail ascends. The E. Rattlesnake Trail enters right at 0.7 mi., and the Ridge Trail reaches the summit of E. Rattlesnake at 0.8 mi.

Ridge Trail (map 4)

Distance from W. Rattlesnake summit
   to E. Rattlesnake summit: 0.8 mi. (1.3 km.)

East Rattlesnake Trail (SLA)

This trail branches right from the Pasture Trail (above) 0.1 mi. from the road. It ascends steadily to the Ridge Trail. To the right 0.1 mi. is a view to the southeast.

E. Rattlesnake Trail (map 4)

Distance from Rockywold-Deephaven camps road
   to E. Rattlesnake summit (via Pasture Trail and E. Rattlesnake Trail): 0.6 mi. (1.3 km.)

Butterworth Trail (SLA)

This trail leads to E. Rattlesnake from NH Rte. 113. About 5 mi. west of Center Sandwich and 1.9 mi. northeast of the Rockywold-Deephaven camps road, take Metcalf Rd. leaving the south side, and proceed to trail entrance right 0.5 mi. The trail ascends the northeast slope of the mountain in nearly a direct line to the summit. For a view, continue south to an open ledge.

Butterworth Trail (map 4)

Distance from Metcalf Rd.

  to open ledge: 0.8 mi. (1.3 km.)

SQUAM RANGE

The Squam Range is a long ridge that stretches from the Sandwich Notch Rd. to Holderness. It is northwest of NH Rte. 113 and roughly parallel to it. The most frequently climbed peaks are Mt. Morgan (2243 ft.) and Mt. Percival (2235 ft.). Cotton Mountain (1170 ft.) and Mt. Livermore (1497 ft.) afford views principally to the south and east.

"Old Highway" Trail (SLA)

At 1.3 mi. northeast of Holderness and 0.1 mi. beyond a sand pit, NH Rte. 113 turns right and this trail continues straight ahead. A century ago, it was the highway. The western portion is no longer passable for four-wheel-drive vehicles. It leads to the Prescott and Old Mountain Road trails.

Prescott Trail (SLA)

This trail to Mt. Livermore turns left off the "Old Highway" Trail 0.8 mi. from NH Rte. 113, just beyond an old cemetery. It follows a logging road, then turns left 90 yd. beyond a small clearing. At 1.5 mi. a steep shortcut to the summit leaves right. Beyond, the main trail climbs switchbacks over a low ridge and descends to the Crawford-Ridgepole Trail, which enters left at 1.8 mi. From this point the two trails ascend together via switchbacks, and just below the summit they turn sharp right and ascend steeply to the top.

Descending, the Crawford-Ridgepole Trail heading south and the Prescott Trail leave the summit together, descend to the west along an old stone wall, and turn left onto an old bridle trail. After 0.4 mi. the Crawford-Ridgepole Trail leaves on the right. From the top, the shortcut descends steeply to the east.

Prescott Trail (map 4)

Distances from NH Rte. 113

to start of Prescott Trail (via Old Highway Trail): 0.8 mi.

to Crawford-Ridgepole Trail junction: 1.8 mi.

to Mt. Livermore summit: 2.2 mi. (3.5 km.)

Old Mountain Road Trail (SLA-Webster)

This trail leads up from the Old Highway Trail, 1.1 mi. from its western end at NH Rte. 113, to the Crawford-Ridgepole Trail at the low point between Mt. Livermore and Mt. Webster.

Old Mountain Road Trail (map 4)

Distance from Old Highway Trail junction

to Crawford-Ridgepole Trail junction: 0.9 mi. (1.4 km.)

Mount Morgan Trail (SLA)

This trail leaves the west side of NH Rte. 113, 0.5 mi. northeast of the road leading to Rockywold and Deephaven camps. From the small clearing (parking), the trail follows a logging road, turning off left almost immediately. There is usually *water* on the right at 1.3 mi. The trail bears right at a fork and soon begins the steeper ascent of the southeast slope of the mountain. At 1.7 mi. the Crawford-Ridgepole Trail leaves left for Mt. Webster. The main trail continues to climb. At 1.9 mi. an alternate route, left, not currently maintained, led up ledges (ladders missing). Straight ahead the trail makes an easier ascent, meeting the Crawford-Ridgepole Trail from Mt. Percival. A side trail leads left to the clifftop viewpoint and summit.

For an interesting round trip follow the Crawford-Ridgepole

Trail northeast to Mt. Percival (0.8 mi.) and descend the Mt. Percival Trail.

Mt. Morgan Trail (map 4)
Distance from NH Rte. 113
  to Mt. Morgan summit: 2.1 mi. (3.4 km.), 1½ hr.

Mount Percival Trail (SLA)

The trail leaves the north side of NH Rte. 113, 0.9 mi. northeast of the Rockywold-Deephaven camps road. It follows a logging road through two stone walls to an overgrown field. It reaches a log yard and then enters the woods, forking right off a logging road. The trail follows a generally northwest direction. There is *water* at a brook crossing in 0.9 mi., and at 1.2 mi. a fork leads left to *water*. The upper portion of the trail is steep, and near the top an alternate route leads left through a cave and over cliffs to the summit.

Descending, near the bottom, just below the clearing, a trail sharp right leads down 0.4 mi. to the lower end of the Mt. Morgan Trail.

Mt. Percival Trail (map 4)
Distance from NH Rte. 113
  to Mt. Percival summit: 1.9 mi. (3.1 km.), ° 1½ hr.

Doublehead Trail (SLA)

This trail descends from the Crawford-Ridgepole Trail to NH Rte. 113, 2.1 mi. from Sandwich Notch Rd. and 2.4 mi. east of the Mt. Percival Trail. It leaves the Crawford-Ridgepole Trail to the south, 100 yd. west of the summit of E. Doublehead.

The trail descends over some ledges, then follows close by a stream, crossing it several times. It passes through a stone wall at 0.7 mi. and another at 1.0 mi., just after an old trail diverges left. Shortly beyond, bear right as a wood road enters left. Later bear left as another road enters right. Pass through a third stone wall at 1.3 mi., then descend through a grown-over field. At 1.4 mi. turn left onto a dirt road and continue straight until the trail passes through a farmyard and ends at NH Rte. 113, 2.8 mi. east of the Mt. Morgan Trail and 3.4 mi. west of the Rte. 113 and NH Rte. 109 junction in Sandwich.

Doublehead Trail (map 4)
Distance from Crawford-Ridgepole Trail junction
  to NH Rte. 113: 2.4 mi. (3.9 km.), 1¼ hr.

Crawford-Ridgepole Trail (SLA)

This trail follows the backbone of the Squam Range, from Sandwich Notch to Mt. Livermore. There is *no reliable water*. The trail starts on the Sandwich Notch Rd. 0.5 mi. beyond Beede Falls (Cow Cave) and 2.0 mi. from the power line along the Beebe River.

From the road (sign) it ascends steeply, crosses an unnamed wooded peak, and continues along the ridge to Doublehead (2176 ft.). Just beyond the east peak, at 2.1 mi., the trail turns right and descends where the Doublehead Trail diverges left past a viewpoint and down to NH Rte. 113. Continuing much of the way over open ledges, the Crawford-Ridgepole Trail passes a side trail to Uncle Paul's Potholes at 3.1 mi. and crosses Mt. Squam (2200 ft.) and Mt. Percival (2235 ft.). It joins the Mt. Morgan Trail at 5.4 mi. Side trails lead right to Mt. Morgan summit (2243 ft.) and a clifftop viewpoint. To continue, descend the Mt. Morgan Trail for 0.4 mi., then branch right at 5.7 mi., cross a level area, and bear right at a fork. Care should be taken to follow the SLA blazes. Two viewpoints overlooking the lake are passed. At 9.6 mi. the trail crosses the Old Mountain Rd. and continues 0.4 mi. to the summit of Mt. Livermore (view).

The trail descends west from Mt. Livermore along a stone wall and turns left onto an old bridle path. It branches right from the Prescott Trail at 10.4 mi., picks up a logging road, continues straight when the latter turns right, crosses a *stream*, and descends to a *brook* at the bottom of the Cotton-Livermore col. It then ascends steadily up Cotton Mountain (1170 ft., limited views). The trail continues to Mt. Fayal (1050 ft.) where it joins the Gephart Trail just northwest of the summit. The Gephart (west) and Davison (east) trails both connect Mt. Fayal to the Squam Lakes Science Center just west of the center of Holderness.

Crawford-Ridgepole Trail (map 4)
Distances from Sandwich Notch Rd.

to W. Doublehead summit: 2.2 mi., 2 hr.

to Mt. Squam summit: 3.2 mi., 2½ hr.

to Mt. Percival summit: 4.5 mi.

to Mt. Morgan summit: 5.3 mi., 4 hr.

to Mt. Livermore summit: 10 mi.

to Cotton Mountain summit: 11.3 mi. (18.2 km.)

SANDWICH NOTCH AREA

The Sandwich Notch Area includes Mt. Israel (2620 ft.) and two trails on Sandwich Dome (3993 ft.).

Sandwich Notch Road

This interesting dirt road through the wilderness is quite passable, but steep in places. It runs northwest from Sandwich to NH Rte. 49 between Campton and Waterville, in the Mad River Valley. Beede Falls (Cow Cave), in the Sandwich town park, are worth a visit. Refer to map 4, Chocorua-Waterville.

From NH Rte. 113 in Center Sandwich, take the road northwest from the village to Diamond Ledge. Bear left at the first fork up the hill. Pass the Chicks Corner Rd. on the left and Dale Rd. on the right. Keep left at the next fork, and from here on the road is unmistakable. The right-hand road at the fork just mentioned leads to the Mead Explorer Base Camp, trailhead for the Wentworth Trail up Mt. Israel.

Sandwich Notch Rd. (map 4)
Distances from NH Rte. 113 junction, Sandwich

to Mead Explorer Base Camp road junction: 2.6 mi.

to Beede Falls (Cow Cave): 3.4 mi.

to Crawford-Ridgepole Trail: 3.9 mi.
to Guinea Pond Trail: 5.7 mi.
to Algonquin Trail: 7.3 mi.
to NH Rte. 49: 11 mi. (17.7 km.)

Wentworth Trail (SLA)

This trail ascends Mt. Israel from the southwest, with splendid views of the lake region and the Sandwich Range.

The trail is reached by following the road to the Mead Explorer Base Camp, which leaves Sandwich Notch Rd. 2.6 mi. northwest of Sandwich. Drive straight in (parking). The trail, blazed in yellow, leads directly uphill, following an old cart path through an opening in a stone wall 0.3 mi. above the camp. It turns right, slabs the hillside above the wall, and crosses several brookbeds before turning left. At the foot of a cliff it turns left, passes an outlook on the left at 1.4 mi., then climbs to a ridge, which it follows to the right. It soon comes out on the open ledges of the west summit of Mt. Israel, with fine views to the north. The trail continues along the ridge to the main peak, passing the Mead Trail on the left just before the summit. The best views are from the ledges 80 yd. east of the summit.

Wentworth Trail (map 4)

Distance from end of road to Mead Base Camp
   to Mt. Israel summit: 2 mi. (3.2 km.), 1½ hr.

Mead Trail (SLA)

This trail links the summit of Mt. Israel and the Guinea Pond Trail. It diverges from the Wentworth Trail right (north) a short distance west of the east peak of Mt. Israel, and descends the north slope at a moderate grade, passing a *spring (water unreliable)* in 0.1 mi. on the right. There is *reliable water* about 0.3 mi. farther on the left. The trail follows an old lumber road down the east bank of the brook, crosses it at 0.8 mi., and later bears left, crossing a tributary at 1.4 mi. The trail later crosses a power line, and ends at the Guinea Pond Trail.

Mead Trail (map 4)
Distance from Mt. Israel summit
  to Guinea Pond Trail junction: 1.7 mi. (2.7 km.), 1 hr.

Black Mountain Pond Trail (SLA)

This trail leaves the north side of the Guinea Pond Trail 1.6 mi. east of Sandwich Notch Rd., opposite the lower terminus of the Mead Trail. It crosses the Beebe River and continues generally north to the west bank of the brook from Black Mountain Pond. Just below two beaver dams, a relocated section crosses to the east bank and soon rejoins the old trail. The trail climbs at a moderate grade and crosses a logging road. At 1.9 mi. a side trail leads left to a (wet-season) waterfall. Near the pond, the trail crosses to the west bank, ascends, and skirts the south shore of Black Mountain Pond on a wooded bluff. At 2.4 mi. it passes an eight-person shelter on the west end.

The trail leaves the pond at the inlet brook at the north end. It passes among beaver ponds, climbs through a small stand of virgin spruce, then ascends steeply. Above the lower ledge at 2.8 mi., there is sometimes *water* on the left below the trail. The trail continues through woods and over ledges to end at the Algonquin Trail.

Black Mountain Pond Trail (map 4)
Distances from Guinea Pond Trail junction
  to shelter, Black Mountain Pond: 2.4 mi., 2 hr.
  to Algonquin Trail junction: 3.5 mi. (5.6 km.), 3 hr.

Guinea Pond Trail (WMNF)

This trail leaves the east side of Sandwich Notch Rd. just south of the bridge over the Beebe River. After crossing under a power line, the trail follows the south side of the river on a nearly level grade. At about 1.3 mi. there is a bypass around the south side of a large beaver pond. At 1.6 mi. the Mead Trail leaves right, and the Black Mountain Pond Trail leaves left. At 1.8 mi., a side trail left leads 300 yd. to Guinea Pond. The main trail passes south of

Guinea Pond, bears left at a fork, and follows the railroad bed on contour. At 4.0 mi. it meets the Flat Mountain Pond Trail, turns sharp right onto a logging road, and descends steeply for a short distance. It passes through a logged area, then a junction with the Bennett Street Trail (left), and ends 300 yd. farther at Jose's bridge.

Guinea Pond Trail (map 4)
Distances from Sandwich Notch Rd.

to Mead Trail/Black Mountain Trail junction: 1.6 mi., ¾ hr.

to Bennett Street Trail junction: 4.6 mi. (7.4 km.), 2½ hr.

Algonquin Trail (SLA)

This trail ascends Sandwich Dome via the southwest shoulder, with many extensive views from open ledges.

The trail leaves the north side of Sandwich Notch Rd. 1.5 mi. from the power line along the Beebe River and 3.7 mi. from NH Rte. 49. It follows an old lumber road across a brook and through a small boggy area. A little farther, at 0.9 mi., the trail turns left off the road, and climbs for about 0.5 mi. through hardwoods. At 1.8 mi., it crosses a tiny *stream,* ascends to a col, turns right, and climbs the Black Mountain ridge, largely in the open, with splendid views on all sides. At 2.7 mi., just before the ridge crest, the Black Mountain Pond Trail diverges right. A short distance beyond, the Algonquin Trail emerges on a ledge overlooking the pond. It crosses the wooded summit of Black Mountain (3460 ft.), descends slightly to a ledge with views to the north, and then drops to a col. From here it follows a wooded ridge to scattered open ledges on Sandwich Mountain, and after a short climb through woods terminates just below the summit at the Sandwich Mountain Trail from Waterville Valley.

Algonquin Trail (map 4)
Distance from Sandwich Notch Rd.

to Sandwich Mountain summit: 4.5 mi. (7.2 km.), 3½ hr.
  (*descending* 2½ hr.)

RED HILL

Located north of Center Harbor, Red Hill has two summits.
There is a fine lake view, especially of Squam, from a fire tower
on the higher one (2029 ft.). Refer to map 4, Chocorua-
Waterville, and the USGS Winnipesaukee and Chocorua
quadrangles.

Eagle Cliff Trail (SLA)

In Center Harbor from NH Rte. 25 go northwest on Bean Rd.
This trail leaves on the right, 5.2 mi. from Center Harbor, and
0.4 mi. northeast of the Sandwich-Moultonboro town line. The
entrance is difficult to see from the road: it is a well-worn path
through a thicket in a depression just north of a red farmhouse. It
climbs through an overgrown field, enters the woods, and ascends steeply to Eagle Cliff at 0.4 mi.

From the upper ledge, the trail enters the woods and continues
along the ridge to the fire tower on Red Hill. There is a limited
view from the top of the first knoll at 0.7 mi. The trail descends
steeply to a col, crosses another knoll, and shortly begins to
ascend steadily through fine woods. It levels out and meets the
Red Hill Trail just below the summit of Red Hill.

Descending, the trail to Eagle Cliff diverges right from the
graded Red Hill Trail just below the fire warden's cabin (sign).

Eagle Cliff Trail (map 4)

Distances from Bean Hill Rd.

  to Eagle Cliff: 0.4 mi., ½ hr.

  to Red Hill fire tower: 2.3 mi. (3.7 km.), 2 hr.

Red Hill Trail

In Center Harbor from NH Rte. 25 go northwest on Bean Rd.
After 1.6 mi. take a road on the right that passes between
Wakondah (Round) Pond and Kanasatka Lake. A road enters
right, and then 1.3 mi. from Bean Rd. the trail leaves right (sign
and parking).

The trail, a jeep road, soon makes a sharp right turn uphill and crosses a brook in about 0.3 mi. At 0.4 mi. it swings left around a cellar hole. At 1.0 mi. there is a piped *spring* left. The Eagle Cliff Trail enters left just before the fire warden's cabin on Red Hill.

Red Hill Trail (map 4)
Distance from parking area, road between Wakondah Pond and Kanasatka Lake

   to Red Hill summit: 1.7 mi. (2.7 km.), 1¼ hr.

OSSIPEE MOUNTAINS

These mountains, located just north of Lake Winnipesaukee, occupy a nearly circular tract about 9 miles in diameter. Mt. Shaw (2975 ft.), the highest of the Ossipees, is accessible from NH Rte. 171. Refer to map 1, Chocorua-Waterville. Also see the USGS Chocorua, Ossipee Lake, Winnipesaukee, and Wolfeboro quadrangles, which corner near the center of the Ossipee Mountains. The Chocorua and Winnipesaukee quadrangles show the locations of many of the old carriage roads of the Plant Estate, now called Castle in the Clouds.

Mount Shaw Trail
The trail begins at a dirt road on the north side of NH Rte. 171, 3.7 mi. east of the junction of NH Rte. 109 and Rte. 171, 3.8 mi. west of Tuftonboro, 9.7 mi. west of the junction of Rte. 171 and NH Rte. 28 in Ossipee, and just east of a road from Melvin Village and a bridge over Fields Brook. The trail goes over private land; permission to use the trail may be obtained at the white farmhouse just west of the Fields Brook bridge. The trail follows the dirt road north 0.3 mi. to a hemlock grove, left, where there is a waterfall. The trail detours above the stream around a washout. At about 0.5 mi. from the waterfall it joins a logging road and crosses a side stream on a bridge. Beyond, it passes through an old logging camp clearing. Just beyond this, bear left and pass through a deep cut. In another 200 yd. the trail leaves the logging road left at a cairn and follows the east bank of Fields Brook.

About 1 mi. from the waterfall, the trail crosses to the west bank and, farther up, to the east bank (*last sure water*). Soon it climbs steeply out of the ravine to join an old carriage road. Turn right and pass a side trail, right, which leads in 5 min. to an open knob ("Black Snout", not the same as Black Snout Mountain) with good views over Lake Winnipesaukee. Down the side trail 300 yd., the Banana Trail enters left. Immediately after the side trail, the Thunderbird Trail enters right. The Mt. Shaw Trail continues on the carriage road about 0.5 mi. to the summit. At the carriage road turnaround on the summit the Gorilla Trail enters left.

Descending, the trail leaves the left side of the old carriage road about 5 min. below the side trail to the open knob.

Mt. Shaw Trail (USGS Winnipesaukee quadrangle)
Distances from NH Rte. 171

to second brook crossing: *est.* 2 mi., 1½ hr.
to old carriage road junction: *est.* 2.5 mi., 2 hr.
to Mt. Shaw summit: *est.* 3.3 mi. (5.2 km.), 2¾ hr.

Bald Peak Trail

The trail begins on NH Rte. 171, at the Moultonboro-Tuftonboro town line, about 0.5 mi. west of the Mt. Shaw trailhead at the Fields Brook bridge. Follow the dirt road into a gravel pit. Facing Bald Peak, descend to the lower right corner of the pit (northeast) and turn sharp left onto a dirt road. This road crosses a small brook. Take the left fork as the road enters the wood and follow the yellow blazes. The trail ascends steeply. It passes near a brook on the lower ledge, and in 1 mi. reaches Bald Peak from which there are fine views of Lake Winnipesaukee.

Descending, the trail leaves Bald Peak to the east through a wide V in the rock, a short distance above (north of) an old carriage road turnaround.

It is possible to continue to the summit of Mt. Shaw following old roads of the Plant Estate (suggested for the ascent). The distance is about 3.8 mi., much of which is uninteresting. From

the ledges on Bald Peak, follow the old road as it descends gradually for about 0.3 mi. along the west slope of the ridge. In less than 0.5 mi., at a small, grassy clearing, it meets a hairpin turn. Bear right uphill. It soon begins a steady ascent of about 0.8 mi., and then follows for a short distance along the ridge above Bald Peak.

As the road approaches a brook, bear left uphill. After crossing continue straight uphill. Less than 0.5 mi. above the stream, another Plant Estate road enters left just before a small, stagnant pond right. After another 0.8 mi., and 3 mi. from Bald Peak, the Mt. Shaw Trail enters right. The summit is about 0.8 mi. farther on.

Bald Peak Trail (USGS Winnipesaukee quadrangle)
Distances from NH Rte. 171

to Bald Peak: *est.* 1 mi., 1 hr.

to Mt. Shaw Trail junction (via Plant Estate roads): *est.* 4 mi., 3 hr.

to Mt. Shaw summit (via Mt. Shaw Trail): *est.* 4.8 mi. (7.6 km.), 3¾ hr.

Thunderbird Trail

Follow a paved road that branches to the north off NH Rte. 171 0.7 mi. west of Tuftonboro. In 1 mi. a road to Sentinel Lodge leaves right. In 1.4 mi. the paved road becomes a dirt road and passes some farms. The main road, which leads to Camp Merrowvista, turns sharp right 1.8 mi. from Rte. 171. A country road continues straight ahead (northwest). The trail begins at this corner and follows the country road. At 0.2 mi. a road leaves left, which is the start of the Banana Trail. The Thunderbird Trail continues straight along the wood road, ascending slightly. In about 0.5 mi., it passes two clearings, right. The trail continues on the wood road, which soon ascends and passes close to a stream at the head of a cascade where there is a small campsite. A short distance beyond, where the dirt road bears left and crosses the brook on a bridge, the Thunderbird Trail continues straight,

ascending another wood road. About 1 mi. from **the** clearings the wood road ends at a small brook (*water unre**liable**; reliable water* a short distance upstream).

Beyond, the trail is blazed and a well-worn **pathw**ay is evident. Hikers accustomed to "standardized" trail**s** will find this one poorly cleared, but it is easy to follow. The **trail** slabs up the side of the valley, steeply in places. About 1 mi. **from** the end of the wood road, the trail ends at the old carriage ro**ad**, which is the Mt. Shaw Trail. A few feet to the left is a trail **that** leads to an open knob with a good view ("Black Snout") and **to** the Banana Trail. Follow the Mt. Shaw Trail right a little ove**r 0**.5 mi. for the summit of Mt. Shaw.

Thunderbird Trail (USGS Wolfeboro qu**ad**rangle)
*Distances from trailhead off road to Camp Merro**w**vista*

to Mt. Shaw Trail (old carriage road) junction: *est.* 2.5 mi., 2 hr.
to Mt. Shaw summit (via Mt. Shaw Trail): *est.* 3 mi. (4.8 km.), 2½ hr.

Banana Trail

This trail starts from the Thunderbird Trail. (**For** directions to the Thunderbird trailhead, see above.) Follow **the** Thunderbird Trail 0.2 mi. and turn left onto a wood road **opp**osite a house, which is the beginning of the Banana Trail. **The** road shortly crosses a stream, turns right along the stream, **turns** left, and another wood road enters left. Go straight, past **sev**eral houses, and then the trail leaves left. From here on, the **trail** is blazed in yellow, but recent construction may render the **lower** part obscure. Follow a wood road with a stream on the **right**. At 0.9 mi. from the Thunderbird Trail junction, the road **leaves** the stream (*last water*) and ascends to open ledges known **as** Blueberry Mountain, with a nice view of Dan Hole Pond, **at** about 1.6 mi. Beyond Blueberry Mountain, the Banana Trail is well blazed but not well worn and obscure in places. Follow cairns **to** the top of the ledges. At 1.8 mi., enter the woods at a sign **and** descend to a col, then climb steeply up the open knob known **as** "Black

Snout." The trail ends at the side trail to "Black Snout" (0.2 mi. to the left). To the right 300 yd. is the old carriage road, which is the Mt. Shaw Trail to the summit of Mt. Shaw.

Banana Trail (USGS Wolfeboro quadrangle)
Distance from Thunderbird Trail junction
   to Mt. Shaw Trail (old carriage road) junction: 3.4 mi. (5.4 km.), 2¾ hr.

Gorilla Trail

This trail runs about 4.5 mi. from the summit of Mt. Shaw to Camp Merrowvista. The trail starts east of the old carriage road turnaround on the summit of Mt. Shaw and follows the ridge eastward. It is well blazed but rather rough in places, with many boulders. The trail ends at Camp Merrowvista, which is located about 2.3 mi. from NH Rte. 171, 0.5 mi. beyond the start of the Thunderbird Trail.

Gorilla Trail (USGS Wolfeboro quadrangle)
Distance from Mt. Shaw summit
   to Camp Merrowvista: *est.* 4.5 mi. (7.2 km.), 3½ hr.

MOUNT MAJOR

This 1784-ft. mountain is located in Alton, east of the Belknap Mountains. It has excellent views over Lake Winnipesaukee. Refer to the USGS Winnipesaukee quadrangle.

The north approach is from a parking area (large sign) on NH Rte. 114, 2 mi. north of Alton Bay and 1.7 mi. from the NH Rte. 11 junction with NH Rte. 11D. The trail follows a lumber road west for 0.7 mi., then diverges sharp left on a path marked with dark-blue paint. It climbs steeply through second growth and over ledges to the ruins of a stone hut at the top. At several points there are one or more alternate paths, all of which lead to the summit.

The south approach follows a road west from NH Rte. 11 at its junction with NH Rte. 11D, 2.4 mi. north of Alton Bay. This

road ends in 1.1 mi. at buildings and a gravel pit. Ask a Mr. Boudrow for permission to park here; in any case do not block the pit entrance. The trail starts to left of the pit and circles its back on an old road. At 0.6 mi. it forks right and approaches a brook, then continues to the bottom of the ledges, which it ascends to the summit. Note the route carefully for descent because the trail is not well marked on the ledges. The line of light-blue blazes on these ledges is an obscure trail to the south summit of Straightback Mountain, not the Mt. Major Trail.

Mt. Major (USGS Winnipesaukee quadrangle)

Distances to Mt. Major summit

from parking area, NH Rte. 11 (north approach): 1.5 mi. (2.4 km.), 1 hr. 20 min.

from gravel pit off NH Rte. 11 (south approach): 1.6 mi. (2.6 km.), 1 hr. 20 min.

THE BELKNAP RANGE

The Belknap Mountains are an isolated range in the town of Gilford. The principal peaks, from north to south, are Mt. Rowe (1660 ft.), Gunstock Mountain (2220 ft.), Belknap Mountain (2384 ft.), and Piper Mountain (2020 ft.). A fire tower on Belknap and an observation tower on Gunstock, as well as numerous scattered ledges on all the peaks, provide fine views of Lake Winnipesaukee, the Ossipee and Sandwich ranges, and Mt. Washington. Principal trailheads are at the Gunstock Recreation Area (east side) and the Belknap Carriage Road (west side). The East Gilford Trail also ascends from the east. Paths along the ridge connect all four summits. Refer to the USGS Winnipesaukee quadrangle.

Gunstock Recreation Area

This is a four-season recreation area off NH Rte. 11A, operated by Belknap County. It includes a major downhill ski area located on Mt. Rowe and Gunstock Mountain, and a 420-site camp-

ground. Ellacoya State Beach on Lake Winnipesaukee is nearby. The chair lift on Gunstock Mountain operates on weekends and holidays in summer. A map of hiking trails is available at the base lodge.

MOUNT ROWE

Try-Me Trail

To ascend Mt. Rowe (1660 ft.), from the Gunstock parking area go right under the single chair lift, ascend the novice slope, pass around a fence, and follow a ski trail to the top of the lift just below the summit. The Ridge Trail begins at the summit. In descending, take ski trail to the left from the lift station.

Try-Me Trail (USGS Winnipesaukee quadrangle)

Distance from Gunstock parking area

to Mt. Rowe summit: 0.9 mi. (1.4 km.), 50 min.

Ridge Trail

From the summit of Rowe Mountain, this blue-blazed trail follows the ridge south, crossing ledges and blueberry fields, through the saddle, ascends to a ski trail, and soon joins the Flintlock Trail. (*Descending,* turn left on ski trail at Ridge Trail sign, then shortly follow the arrow left into the woods.) The Ridge and the Flintlock trails coincide to the summit of Gunstock Mountain along the right edge of the ski trails. The Ridge Trail continues south on the right edge of the ski trails, then turns right into woods (watch carefully for arrow) and descends to the col where the Blue Dot Trail enters right. It then ascends Belknap Mountain and ends at the Red Trail just before the summit.

Ridge Trail (USGS Winnipesaukee quadrangle)

Distances from Mt. Rowe summit

to Flintlock Trail junction: 0.7 mi.

to Gunstock Mountain summit: 1.6 mi., 1 hr. 10 min.

to Blue Dot Trail junction: 2 mi.

to Belknap Mountain summit: 2.5 mi. (4.1 km.), 1 hr. 50 min.

GUNSTOCK MOUNTAIN

Flintlock Trail

From the Gunstock parking area go left (south) to a large stone fireplace (trail signs). This trail follows a service road that curves right upward and crosses under the chair lift. The Ridge Trail enters as a ski trail from the right about halfway up, and the trails coincide to the Gunstock Mountain summit (2220 ft.), always keeping to the right on ski trails. *Descending,* keep to the left edge of the ski trails until the Ridge Trail enters (sign), then bear right on the service road.

Flintlock Trail (USGS Winnipesaukee quadrangle)

Distances from Gunstock parking area

to Ridge Trail junction: 0.8 mi.

to Gunstock Mountain summit: 1.7 mi. (2.7 km.), 1½ hr.

Brook Trail

Although officially maintained, this yellow-blazed trail may be relatively obscure and must be followed with care. From the right of the stone fireplace south of the Gunstock parking area it diverges left from the Flintlock Trail and follows a fairly level ski trail. When another ski trail enters left, the Brook Trail turns sharp left into the woods (sign), and crosses, then roughly parallels the brook. (A ski trail to the right across the brook, often in sight, is easy to locate and ascend if you lose the Brook Trail.) Eventually the Brook Trail enters a ski trail, which it follows to the Ridge Trail just south of the summit. *Descending,* follow the Ridge Trail toward Belknap Mountain just past a small pond on the left, then turn left (yellow arrow) and follow a ski trail, turn left on another ski trail (arrow), and enter the woods on left (arrow). These arrows are in less-than-obvious locations, and must be looked for.

Brook Trail (USGS Winnipesaukee quadrangle)

Distance from Gunstock parking area

to Ridge Trail junction, Gunstock Mountain summit: 1.6 mi. (2.6 km.), 1½ hr.

BELKNAP MOUNTAIN

Belknap Carriage Road

To reach this road, which provides access to all the trails on the west side of the Belknap Range, leave NH Rte. 11A at Gilford Village and follow Belknap Mountain Road south, bearing left at 0.8 mi. and right at 1.4 mi. At 2.4 mi. the Belknap Carriage Road forks left and leads to a parking area. Various relatively easy loop hikes may be made from this trailhead. For the Green, Red, and Blue Dot trails, follow the road up to the fire warden's garage (signs on wall). The Piper Cutoff is a short distance down the road.

Blue Dot Trail

This trail runs to the Belknap-Gunstock col, from which either peak may be ascended via the Ridge Trail. It follows the road past the Red and Green trails, descends slightly to cross a brook, then diverges right and climbs the Ridge Trail.

Blue Dot Trail (USGS Winnipesaukee quadrangle)

Distances from Belknap Carriage Road parking area

to Ridge Trail junction, Belknap-Gunstock col: 0.6 mi., 25 min.

to Gunstock Mountain summit (via Ridge Trail): 0.9 mi. (1.5 km.), ¾ hr.

to Belknap Mountain summit (via Ridge Trail): 1.1 mi. (1.8 km.), 55 min.

Green Trail

This is the shortest route to Belknap Mountain. It leaves the road behind the garage and crosses a service road and telephone line. There are several alternate paths (including the road), any of which may be followed to the warden's cabin, where there is a *well,* and to the tower at the summit.

Green Trail (USGS Winnipesaukee quadrangle)

Distance from Belknap Carriage Road parking area

to Belknap Mountain summit: 0.7 mi. (1.1 km.), 40 min.

Red Trail

This less steep, more scenic route to the summit leaves the road just beyond the Green Trail and climbs past a good outlook (west) to the summit.

Red Trail (USGS Winnipesaukee quadrangle)
Distance from Belknap Carriage Road parking area
   to Belknap Mountain summit: 0.8 mi. (1.3 km.), ¾ hr.

East Gilford Trail

To reach this trail, perhaps the most attractive on the range, turn right off NH Rte. 11A 1.7 mi. south of the Gunstock Recreation Area road on Bickford Rd. Turn left on Wood Rd. and park near a house at the end of the road. The trail follows a cart track at the left of the house (sign), circles around to the right, and bears right at fork. Halfway up, near a brook on the right, the trail turns sharp left and climbs more steeply to the first outlook over Lake Winnipesaukee. It then continues at a moderate grade, mostly on ledges, and joins the Piper Trail. The two trails coincide for the final 0.2 mi. to Belknap Mountain summit.

East Gilford Trail (USGS Winnipesaukee quadrangle)
Distance from Wood Rd.
   to Belknap Mountain summit: 2.1 mi. (3.4 km.), 1 hr. 40 min.

PIPER MOUNTAIN

Piper Trail

A continuation of the Ridge Trail, this white-blazed trail leaves the summit of Belknap Mountain together with the E. Gilford Trail, then diverges right and drops to the Belknap-Piper col. This part of the trail must be followed with care. At the col the Piper Cutoff comes in right from the Belknap Carriage Road. The Piper Trail ascends along the ridge of Piper Mountain and ends at a large cairn. The true summit (2020 ft.) is 0.2 mi. south across open blueberry fields.

Piper Trail (USGS Winnipesaukee quadrangle)
Distances from Ridge Trail junction, Belknap Mountain summit

to Belknap-Piper col: 0.8 mi.

to Piper Mountain, true summit: 1.5 mi. (2.4 km.), 50 min.

Piper Cutoff

This well-beaten but unsigned trail (yellow-blazed at present) leaves the Belknap Carriage Road below the last bridge at a yellow-blazed birch, then climbs to meet the Piper Trail in the Belknap-Piper col. Either peak may be ascended via the Piper Trail.

Piper Cutoff (USGS Winnipesaukee quadrangle)
Distances from Belknap Carriage Road parking area

to Piper Trail junction, Belknap-Piper col: 0.4 mi., ¼ hr.

to Piper Mountain summit (via Piper Trail): 1.1 mi. (1.8 km.), ¾ hr.

to Belknap Mountain summit (via Piper Trail): 1.2 mi. (1.9 km.), 55 min.

GREEN MOUNTAIN

Green Mountain is an isolated 1907-ft. peak in the town of Effingham. The state owns fifteen acres on the summit, which has a 50-ft. fire tower with an extended view. Refer to the USGS Ossipee Lake quadrangle.

From the junction of NH Rte. 25 and NH Rte. 153 northbound in Effingham Falls, follow Rte. 25 west for 0.2 mi., then turn left at a church (fire lookout sign). Follow this road for 1.2 mi., then turn left again on High Watch Rd. The trail (a road closed by a chain) is 1.4 mi. farther on the right, just past High Watch Farm. The trail ascends moderately on this road to the fire warden's garage, then leaves left and climbs, sometimes steeply, to Green Mountain summit.

Green Mountain (USGS Ossipee Lake quadrangle)
Distances from High Watch Rd.

to fire warden's garage: 0.5 mi.

to Green Mountain summit: 1.4 mi. (2.2 km.), 1¼ hr.

BLUE JOB MOUNTAIN

Blue Job Mountain (1356 ft.) is part of the Blue Hill Range, located in Strafford and Farmington. There are picnic tables, fireplaces, and an excellent view from a fire tower on the summit. Refer to the USGS Alton quadrangle.

From the intersection of US Rte. 202 and NH Rte. 11 in Rochester, follow NH Rte. 202A west for 2.8 mi., then bear right to Strafford Corner. (Or, follow Rte. 202A 3.6 mi. east from its junction with NH Rte. 126 in Center Strafford, then turn left to Strafford Corner, 4.8 mi. by either route). Continue to parking (8.3 mi. from either starting point), opposite a disintegrating farmhouse. The trail, marked with red paint, follows a cart track through a blueberry field into woods to a junction with an unmarked path left that leads steeply to the summit following a telephone line. The trail bears right, passes a *well* with hand pump, and turns sharp left to the summit.

Blue Job Mountain (USGS Alton quadrangle)
Distance from parking area

to Blue Job Mountain summit: 0.4 mi. (0.7 km.), 25 min.

FORT MOUNTAIN

Fort Mountain (1413 ft.) is located in Epsom. The summit is a bare ledge with good views north, west, and south. Refer to the USGS Gossville quadrangle.

From NH Rte. 28 south of Epsom, take the road east to Short Falls and New Rye. Follow it for 1 mi. to a crossroads. Continue straight for another mile, then turn left on Swamp Rd. After about 1.5 mi., turn left at a white house. Continue for 0.2 mi., then at a red house bear right. Follow this road 0.1 mi. to a jeep road on left. Limited parking here.

There are two routes, which meet about halfway up and coincide to the summit. A bike trail forks right from the jeep road 50 yd. north of the parking place and climbs to a junction with an old hiking trail. This old trail is more attractive but harder to find. It runs straight from the end of the paved road past the last house and follows a cart track that bends left through overgrown fields. The trail crosses a stone wall and immediately angles left uphill (avoid a false path straight ahead). The trail ascends past the junction with the bike trail (descending, this junction is easy to miss), crosses an open ledge with a view north, and approaches the summit from the northwest.

Fort Mountain (USGS Gossville quadrangle)

Distance to Fort Mountain summit

  from parking area (via bike trail or via old hiking trail): 1.1 mi.
    (1.8 km.), 55 min.

PAWTUCKAWAY MOUNTAINS

The Pawtuckaways in Nottingham comprise a group of three parallel ridges, all contained within Pawtuckaway State Park. Refer to the USGS Pawtuckaway quadrangle.

The best access to the mountains is from the State Park off NH Rte. 156. Trails are reached by following road to beach, passing toll booth, and then passing a pond left. Take a sharp left directly after the pond and follow the trail to base of S. Mountain. Trail maps are usually available at the State Park.

The mountains may also be reached from NH Rte. 107 between Deerfield and Raymond (3.1 mi. north of NH Rte. 101) where there is a fire lookout sign. The road leads east, becoming dirt after 1 mi. Bear right at 1.2 mi., and reach the south junction of a loop road at 2.3 mi. This road is rough and at times eroded.

South Mountain

This 908-ft. peak bears a fire tower (now closed) with an extended view of Great Bay and the hills of southern NH, and an occasional glimpse of Mt. Washington. From the south loop road junction continue straight for 0.2 mi., then bear left 0.8 mi. to the former location of the ranger's camp (behind which there is a tiny old graveyard). The trail leaves just beyond on the right and climbs steeply to open summit ledges. At a small service building just below the summit, where the trail turns sharp right, a side trail turns left to a *spring* and continues to the "Indian Steps" and open ledges north-northwest of the tower. (The trail may be obscure.)

South Mountain (USGS Pawtuckaway quadrangle)
Distance from south junction, loop road
to summit tower, South Mountain: 0.4 mi. (0.6 km.), 25 min.

Boulder Natural Area and North Mountain

In the valley east of North Mountain there is an extraordinary collection of huge boulders and several other unusual and interesting rock formations. From the former location of the ranger's camp continue 0.8 mi. to the north loop junction (1.3 mi. left from the south loop junction), then bear right for another 0.5 mi. As the road bears up to the right, there are two obscure trailheads on the left. The left trail leads over a bridge to a good *spring*, and the trail to the boulders runs under a large fallen tree (may have a small sign "Boulders"). It descends gradually 0.2 mi. to the boulders. The trail is sparingly blazed with white paint and must be followed with care. Just beyond the boulders the trail turns sharp left at a junction (sign on tree, "Dead Pond") and continues to the pond. (Straight ahead from this junction a white-blazed trail leads around a beaver pond — detours upslope may be necessary — and past some rock formations to the road. Turn right on the road to loop back to the starting point.) At Dead Pond the trail turns left and climbs steeply to the Devil's Den (a crevice in the rocks to the left of the trail) and an outlook right.

From here the trail is difficult to follow and is recommended only for experienced hikers with topographic map and compass. It slabs steeply up the north side of the ridge and, marked with cairns, continues roughly along the top to a small col below boulder cliffs. It climbs a switchback to an outlook where there is Public Service Company reflector. A faint trail continues along the ridge to the overgrown summit.

Boulder Natural Area/North Mountain
(USGS Pawtuckaway quadrangle)

Distances from trailhead
to junction just past boulders: 0.2 mi.
to Dead Pond: 0.6 mi.
to Devil's Den: 0.7 mi.
to North Mountain summit: 1.5 mi. (2.5 km.), 1¼ hr.

Distances from junction just past boulders
to road (via beaver pond): 0.5 mi.
to trailhead: 1.1 mi. (1.8 km.), 35 min.

Monadnock and the Southwest

In the southwest quarter of New Hampshire, south of I-89 and west of I-93, are scattered mountains. Mt. Monadnock (3165 ft.) is by far the most popular.

On some other, less frequented mountains in the area, not all trails are officially maintained, and some may be hard to find and follow.

MOUNT MONADNOCK (GRAND MONADNOCK)

Mt. Monadnock lies in Dublin and Jaffrey, about 10 mi. north of the Massachusetts border. It is an isolated mountain, 3165 ft. above sea level and 1500 to 2000 ft. above the surrounding country. The upper 500 ft. is open ledges, bared by ancient forest fires. Mt. Washington is visible when it has snow cover. There are six well-marked trails to the summit and a network of connecting and secondary trails on the east, south, and west sides of the main peak. Condition of some of these secondary trails varies from year to year. Inquire about the condition of secondary trails from State Park personnel. All trails listed in this section were very well maintained and almost all had signs (1982). Refer to map 1, Grand Monadnock, and to the USGS Monadnock quadrangle.

Reservation on Mount Monadnock

The public reservation on the mountain now comprises about 5000 contiguous acres cooperatively administered by the state, the town of Jaffrey, the Association to Protect Mt. Monadnock, and the Society for the Protection of NH Forests. The public reservation extends from NH Rte. 124 on the south across the summit to NH Rte. 101 on the Dublin side.

At the Monadnock State Park, just off Memorial Rd., the state maintains picnic grounds, a refreshment stand, a parking lot, and a public campground (fees charged for each). Camping is not permitted on the mountain.

A former toll road, now closed to automobiles, is still open for hikers. There is limited parking at the base, but no facilities. It leaves Rte. 124, 5 mi. west of Jaffrey and 4 mi. east of Troy, near the height-of-land. It climbs about 1.3 mi. to the site of the Halfway House hotel on the west flank of the south ridge at about 2100 ft. The White Arrow Trail, the most direct route to the summit from this area, and many other trails start near the Halfway House, which is a good base for circuit trips.

White Arrow Trail

One of the older routes to the summit, this trail begins at the top of the toll road, near the site of the Halfway House hotel. It is marked by painted white arrows. It runs north, crosses a brook, passes the picnic grounds, and bearing slightly east, immediately begins to climb steeply through the woods on a broad, rocky way. In about 0.3 mi. Quarter-Way Spring (*water*) is located on the left.

An unmaintained trail leads right to a *spring (water unreliable)* at treeline (no sign).

The trail bears left here and starts to ascend the ledges. Just below the last stretch to the summit there is an interesting scramble up an inclined chimney. Emerging from this narrow gully the trail turns right for the summit a few yards away.

White Arrow Trail (map 1)
Distance from Halfway House site

to Mt. Monadnock summit: 1 mi. (1.6 km.), 1 hr. (*descending ½ hr.*)

Dublin Path (SPNHF)

From the flagpole in Dublin go west on NH Rte. 101. At 0.4 mi. bear left on Lake Rd. At 1.6 mi., end of lake, go straight. Bear left at 2.0 mi. and 2.1 mi. At 2.5 mi., opposite the golf pavilion, go left downhill on Old Troy Rd., through crossroad, to small clearing on right at 4.0 mi., where there is parking space. (Beyond the houses at 3.4 mi. the road becomes narrow and poor; it may be impassable when muddy.) The trail, marked with white D's, starts opposite the clearing and climbs to the tip of the ridge, passing a *spring (water unreliable)* at 1 mi. It follows the ridge over slabs, passes another *spring (water unreliable)* at the foot of a rock at 1.8 mi., and emerges above timberline. The Marlboro Trail joins just beyond a prominent cap of rock, a false summit. The Dublin Path continues to meet the White Arrow Trail 150 ft. below the true summit.

Dublin Path (map 1)

Distances from Old Troy Rd.

   to Marlboro Trail junction: 1 mi.

   to White Arrow Trail junction, Mt. Monadnock summit: 2.2 mi. (3.5 km.)

Pumpelly Trail (SPNHF and AMC)

Follow NH Rte. 101 west from Dublin and turn left on Lake Rd. (sign). The trail leaves the road left at 0.4 mi., opposite a log cabin on the pond, 75 yd. east of where the road reaches the shore. The trailhead is marked with a wooden sign on a post. The trail is wide for 120 yd., then turns right into a narrow path through a stone wall (small cairn and sign). It crosses the summit of Oak Hill then turns right and mounts the steep north end of Dublin Ridge. There is a *spring* on the south side of the trail near the foot of the steep pitch. The trail zigzags up and emerges on the open shoulder of the mountain about 2 mi. from the summit. For about the first 0.3 mi. on the ridge, the trail winds among the rocks and scrubby spruces and firs, always following the ridge top. About 1 mi. from the summit, it comes out on bare, glaciated rocks. For the remaining distance it is marked by large cairns. From a saddle (2700 ft.), about 0.3 mi. north of the dominant summit on the ridge, a line of cairns and yellow blazes that leads left is the Cascade Link, a direct descent toward the reservation and Jaffrey.

The Pumpelly Trail continues along the ridge. Just before it reaches the Sarcophagus, a huge rectangular boulder in plain view, the Spellman Trail enters left. About 0.3 mi. beyond the Sarcophagus the Red Spot-Old Ski Trail enters left, and soon after, a northeast extension of the Smith Connecting Trail, marked with yellow spots and cairns, leaves left for the White Dot and White Cross trails and from there to Bald Rock and into the complex of trails that radiate from the Halfway House site.

The Pumpelly Trail, marked by cairns, continues over ledges to the summit. Glacial striations are plainly visible on many of the ledges.

(*Descending*, look for a large white arrow on summit rock marked Pumpelly Trail. There are few cairns for the first 200 yd. and care must be taken to locate the first one. In several cases cairns are rather small.)

Pumpelly Trail (map 1)

Distances from Lake Rd.

to Cascade Link junction: *est.* 2.8 mi.

to Spellman Trail junction: *est.* 3.5 mi.

to Red Spot Trail junction: *est.* 3.8 mi.

to Mt. Monadnock summit: *est.* 4.5 mi. (7.3 km.), 3½ hr.

White Dot and White Cross Trails

These two trails have a common origin, coincide for their first 0.8 mi., then separate, but rejoin for the last 0.3 mi. to the summit.

Both trails start on a broad jeep road near the warden's office at the west end of Poole Memorial Rd. in Monadnock State Park. They descend slightly and cross a small brook. At about 0.6 mi. the Spruce Link, a cutoff that rejoins the White Cross Trail above Falcon Spring, leaves left. The White Dot and White Cross trails then climb gradually 0.2 mi. through woods to a junction with the Cascade Link at Falcon *Spring* (*water reliable* about 25 yd. left of the trail).

The White Dot Trail goes straight from the Falcon Spring junction, northwest up the steep ridge, and emerges in about 0.5

mi. on the bare plateau near treeline. It crosses an old trail that runs north to the Red Spot Trail, then climbs the ledges through meager evergreens badly damaged by a forest fire. Another branch trail connecting with the Red Spot Trail leaves right 100 yd. farther, and 200 yd. beyond, the White Dot Trail crosses the Smith Connecting Trail, which circles the east side of the summit cone from the Halfway House site to the Pumpelly Trail. In a few feet the south branch of the Red Spot Trail enters right, and the White Dot rejoins the White Cross Trail to continue up slanting ledges to the summit.

The White Cross Trail leaves left at Falcon Spring junction and slabs gradually uphill behind the spring. In a short distance the Spruce Link enters on the left and the White Cross Trail turns sharply right and starts to climb at moderate grades over boulders left by an old slide. It passes through a burn (fine views back to the east and south across a ravine called Dingle Dell) and finally reaches the flat southeast shoulder. It soon emerges from sparse evergreens on the ledges. The Smith Connecting Trail crosses, and a few feet farther the White Cross rejoins the White Dot Trail to continue to the summit. Above this junction the trail is most frequently marked with white dots rather than white crosses.

The White Dot Trail is steeper, but not appreciably shorter than the White Cross. Views from the White Cross are more interesting. There is *no sure water* on either trail above Falcon Spring.

White Dot Trail (map 1)

Distances from Poole Memorial Rd.

to Falcon Spring and Cascade Link junction: 0.7 mi.

to White Cross Trail, upper junction: 1.8 mi.

to Mt. Monadnock summit: 2 mi. (3.2 km.), 1¾ hr. (*descending* 1 hr.)

White Cross Trail (map 1)

Distances from Poole Memorial Rd.

to Falcon Spring: 0.7 mi.

to White Dot Trail, upper junction: 1.9 mi.

to Mt. Monadnock summit: 2.1 mi. (3.4 km.), 1¾ hr. (*descending* 1 hr.)

The Harling Trail (SPNHF)

This trail begins on the highway leading from Jaffrey to Dublin just north of the second of two brooks that are about 0.5 mi. north of the Monadnock Bible Conference, formerly called "the Ark." The beginning of the trail, not signed, is now a private drive to a new residence. *Please do not obstruct the driveway.* There is room for two or three cars to park opposite the trail entrance. The trail follows a logging road, bearing left before the house, across partially cut-over land. About 0.5 mi. from the highway the logging road veers right, but the trail stays west on the traces of an old wood road, marked by small cairns. It reaches the Cascade Link a short distance north of the Falcon Spring junction. At the junction, follow the Cascade Link right for the Red Spot, Spellman, and Pumpelly trails.

Harling Trail (map 1)
Distance from Jaffrey-to-Dublin road
to Cascade Link junction: 1.1 mi. (1.7 km.)

Cascade Link (AMC)

This trail runs between Falcon Spring junction and the Pumpelly Trail, slabbing gradually upward, south to north. With the Pumpelly Trail it is an interesting descent from the summit to the State Park. With either the Spellman Trail or the Red Spot Trail it offers the sportiest and most varied ascents from the east side of the mountain.

The Cascade Link starts at the Falcon Spring junction, reached by the White Dot and White Cross trails. It runs northeast, descends slightly, and passes through spruce woods to a brook and the little cascades for which this trail is named. At about 0.3 mi. it crosses the brook and climbs gradually along its east side, rising about 300 ft. before it leaves the brook (*last sure water* for those following the Red Spot Trail or the Spellman Trail). The trail winds over some ledges in thick woods. About 0.3 mi. from the brook crossing, just before an old east-west stone wall, the Birchtoft Trail enters right and, 100 ft. beyond, the Red Spot

leaves left for Dublin Ridge and the Pumpelly Trail. About 100
yd. beyond the wall the Spellman Trail leaves left for the steepest
(700 ft. in about 0.5 mi.) climb on the mountain, up to the
Pumpelly Trail just north of the Sarcophagus. (The Spellman
Trail is a good scramble in its middle section, with excellent
views back to the east. This trail is difficult to follow when snow
covers the white dots that mark the route on the rocks, because in
winding about to avoid the worst ledges, the trail does not always
follow a clear line.)

About 0.1 mi. beyond the wall, the Cascade Link turns left
over a knob with a wide view. It passes through woods across a
small brook, which it follows closely along the east bank to
where the brook rises, close to the boundary between Dublin and
Jaffrey. From there, prominent cairns mark the Cascade Link
over open ledges to a saddle on the Dublin Ridge (2700 ft.),
where it ends at the Pumpelly Trail. (The Pumpelly Trail is a
picturesque descent with many outlooks. It is marked with yellow paint blazes.)

Cascade Link (map 1)

Distance from White Cross and White Dot trails junction,
Falcon Spring

   to Pumpelly Trail junction: 1.5 mi. (2.5 km.), 1½ hr.

Birchtoft Trail

This trail leaves the Monadnock Recreation Area located on
the Jaffrey Center-Dublin Rd. 1 mi. north of Poole Memorial Rd.

The Monadnock Recreation Area campground is privately
owned. There is a parking fee, and hikers are requested to
register at the lodge office. Follow the recreation area entrance
road a short distance. Turn left on the first driveway and follow it
100 yd. to the shore of Gilson Pond (parking). The trail (sign)
skirts the east and south shores of the pond and ascends by easy
grades to end at the Cascade Link Trail, 100 ft. south of its
junction with the Red Spot Trail.

Birchtoft Trail (map 1)
Distance from Gilson Pond
　to Cascade Link Trail junction: *est*. 2 mi. (3.2 km.)

Marlboro Trail (SPNHF)

This is one of the older trails to the summit, dating to 1850 or earlier. Follow NH Rte. 124 west from Jaffrey, past roads to Monadnock State Park and the Halfway House hotel site. Take the first dirt road on the right, 0.6 mi. west of Perkins Pond. Follow this road 0.7 mi. to a small clearing on left and old cellar hole (parking). The trail follows a wood road for about 0.5 mi. to an east-west wall, then up the steep nose of the ridge to the open ledges. It is marked with cairns and white M's to its junction with the Dublin Path, about 0.3 mi. west of the summit.

The *Marian Trail* leaves the Marlboro Trail on the right at the ledges known as the Stone House at (2350 ft.), 0.3 mi. from the Marlboro Trail-Dublin Path junction. A short but steep connecting trail to the left (east) 0.8 mi. after the Marlboro Trail-Marian Trail junction leads to Monte Rosa. The Marian Trail, now called the Mossy Brook Trail, continues ahead (south) 0.8 mi. to join the old toll road south of the Halfway House site. The *Dutscher Point Trail* (sign) leaves right from here to a view that is rather obscured in summer. The Bear Pit, so named because a bear was once reputedly trapped in the quagmire, is a depression to the west of the Mossy Brook Trail, about 25 yd. north of its junction with the Dutscher Point Trail.

Marlboro Trail (map 1)
Distance from parking area, road west of Perkins Pond
　to Dublin Path junction: 2.2 mi. (3.5 km.), 2 hr.

Halfway House Site Region

There are good, varied walks here. One of the finest scenic trails on Mt. Monadnock is the *Cliff Walk Trail,* marked with white C's, which runs along the south and east edge of the south ridge, from Hello Rock to Bald Rock, past splendid viewpoints, notably Thoreau's Seat, Emerson's Seat, and What Cheer Point, and historical points, such as the Graphite Mine (left), which was in operation about 1850. Several paths lead up to the Cliff Walk from the Halfway House site. One is the *Hello Rock Trail,* which leaves the Halfway House clearing at the southeast corner between the road and Moses Spring. It ascends gradually to Hello Rock through a fine forest. A few yards from the start the *Thoreau Trail* diverges left and leads north to the Cliff Walk Trail. Hello Rock may also be reached from the south via the *Cliff View Trail,* which leaves the Parker Trail about 0.3 mi. from the toll road.

From Bald Rock, the *Smith Connecting Trail,* marked with yellow S's, descends a short distance, soon passes Coffee Pot Corner, and shortly reaches the "Four Spots," a trail junction. The Smith Connecting Trail goes right at this junction, eventually crosses the White Cross Trail, then the White Dot Trail, and ends at the Pumpelly Trail. The trail that forks left at the Four Spots junction climbs with little grade to join the Sidefoot Trail, which soon reaches the White Arrow Trail.

The *Sidefoot Trail* is an excellent alternative to the lower part of the White Arrow Trail and it avoids some of the heavy traffic on that trail. To reach the Sidefoot Trail, climb the bank in the center of the Halfway House clearing and follow a path there a few yards into the woods to a trail junction. The Sidefoot Trail leaves left at this junction to join the White Arrow Trail at Halfway Spring. (Distance from Halfway House site to White Arrow Trail junction: 0.5 mi.)

Three (signs) trails in close succession — the *Do Drop Trail,* the *Novle Trail,* and the *Hedgehog Trail* — leave to the right of the Sidefoot Trail and climb steeply to the Cliff Walk.

The *Fairy Spring Trail* leaves the picnic grove at the north end of the Halfway House clearing and climbs to the peak of Monte Rosa, past the foundation of Fassett's "Mountain House" and Fairy Spring. At the peak, a branch trail (yellow dots) descends steeply to the Tooth, a large pointed boulder, and continues to the *Smith Summit Trail* (white dots), which leads gradually around the west side to the summit in slightly more than 0.5 mi. A short side trail to the top of the "Black Precipice" (sign) soon leaves to the right, providing a view of the "Amphitheater." A rewarding round trip to the summit combines the Cliff Walk Trail with the Monte Rosa trails.

Parker Trail (SPNHF)

This trail begins at Monadnock State Park on the west side of the outlet brook from the reservoir and heads west across the south slope of the mountain. It maintains a gentle grade and provides easy walking through heavy woods. It joins the toll road about 0.5 mi. below the Halfway House site. This trail has signs at both ends and is blazed with yellow paint.

Parker Trail (map 1)

Distance from west side of reservoir outlet brook

to Halfway House site toll road: 1.6 mi. (2.6 km.), 40 min.

The Lost Farm Trail

This trail branches right from the Parker Trail 0.3 mi. from the State Park and leads in 1.1 mi. to Emerson's Seat on the Cliff Walk Trail. A fine circuit walk from the park headquarters combines this trail with the Cliff Walk, the Smith Connecting Trail, and either the White Cross or the White Dot trails.

METACOMET-MONADNOCK TRAIL

This trail, 160 miles long, begins in the Hanging Hills of Meriden, Connecticut, and runs north along the trap rock ridge that borders the Connecticut River. It traverses Mt. Tom and the Holyoke Range, passes over the Northfield Hills, Mt. Grace, Little Monadnock, and Gap Mountain, and terminates at Grand Monadnock. The New Hampshire section, marked by white rectangular paint blazes, is easy to follow.

The Metacomet-Monadnock Trail enters New Hampshire at
the intersection of Bliss Rd. and NH/MA Rte. 32, about halfway
between Richmond NH and W. Royalston MA. It follows Rte.
32 north a short distance to Greenwoods Rd. which it follows for
about 0.3 mi., then enters the woods left, and continues to NH
Rte. 119. The trail turns right on Rte. 119 and follows it for 170
yd., then turns left and climbs Grassy Hill. It crosses a log bridge
over Tully Brook in approximately 0.5 mi. The trail continues,
partly along old tote roads, through interesting hardwoods and
mixed forest, for about 1 mi. to the base of Little Monadnock
Mountain, at the grass-grown Old Troy Rd. It ascends the southwest slope of the mountain, crossing ledges near the summit with
extensive views back over Grassy Hill to Mt. Grace, Crag
Mountain, and Mt. Toby. A side trail (right) about 0.3 mi. from
the summit leads about 1 mi. down to Rhododendron State Park.
(This park may also be reached by a paved road from Rte. 119 a
short distance west of Fitzwilliam.) From the summit (1883 ft.)
the trail continues straight down the north ridge and soon passes
another trail on the right that leads down to Monadnock State
Park.

The Metacomet-Monadnock Trail enters Troy, turns southeast
along the main street for about 0.5 mi. to the NH Rte. 12
intersection, then turns left into Quarry Rd. The trail takes a right
fork onto an abandoned road that leads over Fern Hill. The trail
takes a sharp turn left over a wall, descends through thick pine
woods, crosses a swampy brook, and reaches the foot of Gap
Mountain. The trail climbs about 1 mi. to the 1800-ft. summit,
which has open pastures with excellent views, particularly of
Grand Monadnock.

The trail descends from the summit west then north, crosses a
brook at the foot of the mountain, and turns left on a wood road,
which it follows for about 0.5 mi. to Monadnock St. (Jaffrey
Rd.) at the foot of Perkins Pond. It crosses this asphalt road and
enters a dirt road opposite, which leads through the barnyard of
E. Hill Farm. Turning north the trail passes over the ledgy

summit of Bigelow Hill, descends steeply at first, and emerges at NH Rte. 124, directly opposite a dirt road that leads in 0.7 mi. to the start of the Marlboro Trail to Mt. Monadnock.

(The Berkshire Chapter of the AMC has published a guide to the Metacomet-Monadnock Trail in Massachusetts and New Hampshire with more detailed descriptions and maps. Available from the AMC, 5 Joy St., Boston, MA 02108.)

Metacomet-Monadnock Trail

Distances from NH state line

to NH Rte. 119 junction: 4 mi.

to Little Monadnock Mountain summit: 7.8 mi

to Troy, NH Post Office: 11 mi.

to Gap Mountain summit: 13.6 mi.

to Monadnock St. crossing: 15.4 mi.

to NH Rte. 24 junction: 16.8 mi.

to Mt. Monadnock summit (via Marlboro Trail): 19.9 mi. (32 km.)

MONADNOCK – SUNAPEE GREENWAY
(AMC and SPNHF)

The Monadnock – Sunapee Greenway is a continuous trail that runs for 51 miles, mostly along ridge tops, between these two major peaks in southwest New Hampshire. Because a large part of this trail is located on private property, users should be particularly aware that they are guests and avoid thoughtless behavior that could jeopardize this privilege. (A guide to the Monadnock – Sunapee Greenway is available from the AMC or the Society for the Protection of NH Forests.)

WAPACK TRAIL

This is for the most part a skyline trail that follows the ridge of the Wapack Range for approximately 21 miles. It runs from Watatic Mountain in Ashburnham, MA, over Barrett and Tem-

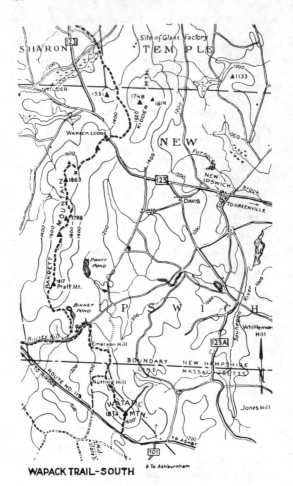

WAPACK TRAIL-SOUTH

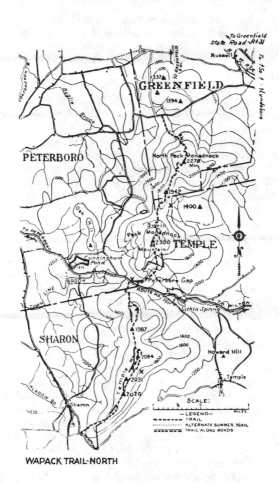

WAPACK TRAIL-NORTH

ple mountains and across the Pack Monadnocks in New Hampshire. There are many open ledges with fine views, and the spruce forest is similar to that of a more northern region. The trail is blazed with yellow triangles and marked by cairns on open ledges.

Wapack Trail, Section I. Watatic Mountain

There are three approaches from the south to the start of the Wapack Trail:

(1) The trail leaves from MA Rte. 119, 0.7 mi. west of the MA Rte. 101 junction northeast of Ashburnham. It climbs steeply, following power and telephone lines to the summit tower on Watatic Mountain, which has a sweeping view. The trail descends northwest through spruce woods that are a state bird sanctuary, then crosses pastures over Nutting Hill to a junction near cellar holes (obscured by bushes) that mark the Nutting Place, settled by James Spaulding just before the Revolution and continued by his son-in-law, Jonas Nutting, until about 1840.

(2) Follow an old ski trail that leaves MA Rte. 119, 1.5 mi. west of the Rte. 101 junction. The trail leads along an old road (bear left at a fork) up through overgrown pastures and spruce forest to the trail junction on Nutting Hill near the cellar holes.

From the Nutting Hill junction the trail follows a long-abandoned road north into beech woods and in about 0.5 mi. crosses an east-west wall on the Massachusetts-New Hampshire border. A few yards west of the trail, close to the wall, are two stone monuments, one erected in 1834.

The trail continues north for about 0.3 mi. past an obscure junction with another old road on the right, bears left slightly downhill (west by north), then turns right at a small clearing about 0.3 mi. farther. In about another 0.5 mi. it reaches Binney Hill Rd. (no longer maintained). The trail turns left (west) on this road and follows it for 1000 ft., then bears right (north).

(3) The third approach is to follow Binney Hill Rd. north from Rte. 119 to the trail junction described above. The Nutting Hill

section of the trail and Binney Hill Rd. can be skied. Binney Hill Rd. can be driven for only about 0.3 mi. in from Rte. 119, and parking is limited because of private residences.

Wapack Trail, Section II. Barrett Mountain

The Barrett Mountain section of the Wapack Trail runs from Binney Hill Rd. to Wapack Lodge on NH Rte. 123. Shortly after leaving Binney Hill Rd., the trail crosses a small brook, then skirts the Binney Ponds near their west shores. (Flooding from beaver dams may require a detour here.) There is usually good drinking *water* at the north end of the Binney Ponds, just before the trail begins to climb Barrett Mountain. The trail traverses the ridge of Barrett Mountain, nearly 3 mi. long and partly wooded, with four summits (highest 1881 ft.) and numerous outlooks. Two private trails intersect the Wapack Trail along this ridge so hikers should be especially careful to identify the Wapack Trail at any junctions. In the saddle between the third and fourth summits, the trail crosses the location of one of the oldest roads from Massachusetts to the hill towns, "The Boston Road," built in 1753. The trail ascends an outlying knoll, then descends to Wapack Lodge located on Rte. 123, on the site of a house built in 1776 by Deacon John Brown of Concord, MA. (Accommodations and meals are *not* available, and the lodge is no longer identified by a sign.)

Wapack Trail, Section III. Kidder Mountain

The Wapack Trail next crosses the lower western slopes of Kidder Mountain. From Wapack Lodge it crosses the highway and enters the woods opposite the lodge driveway. In about 0.6 mi. the trail turns left on an old roadway with bordering stone walls and crosses under a power line 150 yd. beyond. (A poor, blue-blazed side trail leads right from here along the power lines, then left into the woods to the summit of Kidder Mountain, about 1.5 mi.) The Wapack Trail descends to a junction with a gravel road from the left at a pond on the right. It turns right onto a wood road, crosses the pond outlet, and ascends gradually to the Wildcat Hill-Conant Hill saddle, where there is an old homestead to the right. The trail descends gradually, still on the old roadway, crosses the beaver pond outlet on the right at 0.6 mi. and a stream at about 1 mi., and in another 130 yd. reaches a junction with Sharon Rd.

Wapack Trail, Section IV. Temple Mountain

The trail continues straight ahead along Sharon Rd. for 0.4 mi., bears right at a fork, then turns right 100 ft. beyond to follow a dirt road for a short distance before entering the woods. (From Sharon Rd. north the trail passes through private land known as Avelinda Forest. Please observe the no fires-no smoking rules posted in the forest.) The trail then ascends the south end of Temple Mountain, which has several bare summits. The highest, Holt Peak (2084 ft.), however, is broad, wooded, and viewless. A short distance south of Holt Peak, the trail crosses a stone wall, then turns sharp left and parallels the wall a short distance before climbing to the summit. (An alternate route, marked by old red blazes, continues straight ahead beyond the wall, swings to the east of the summit, and rejoins the main trail about 0.3 mi. north of the summit.) The trail follows the ridge, which has wide views, especially toward Grand Monadnock. Stone monuments mark the Sharon-Temple town line, which also follows this ridge. From the north summit the trail descends through the Temple Mountain ski area to NH Rte. 101 in Peterboro Gap, a few yards east of the road up South Pack Monadnock, which leaves Rte. 101 at the height-of-land. The Temple Mountain section of the trail can be skied, preferably from south to north in order to descend through the cleared ski slopes.

Wapack Trail, Section V. Pack Monadnock

This extended ridge ("pack" is an Indian word for "little") culminates in open peaks, South Pack (2300 ft.) and North Pack (2278 ft.). It lies between Peterborough and Temple, NH, a well-known landmark in southern New Hampshire and eastern Massachusetts. On the summit of South Pack is a small state reservation, General James Miller Park. (To reach the park, drive up the road that starts at the parking lot located just off NH Rte. 101, about 100 yd. west of the Temple Mountain parking lot.)

The Wapack Trail crosses Rte. 101 just east of the State Park sign, enters the woods, and reaches a trail junction 25 yd. east of the park area (sign, "Foot Trails," at east end of area). The blue-blazed trail right is the former route of the Wapack Trail. (It slabs the east side of the mountain, then climbs moderately past two radio towers to the automobile road just below the summit at a small sign, "Parking Lot." Continuing north from the summit road — sign, "Wapack" — it joins the present Wapack Trail, enters left at remnants of the Peterborough Merchants' cairn.) The present Wapack Trail is substantially more difficult than the former route, particularly for descent. It continues north from the trail junction near the parking area, crosses the automobile road and immediately attacks a steep ledge. Turning northwest it skirts the crest of ledges with views southwest and passes two crevice caves. The trail turns east through woods and over ledges, crosses a hollow, and slabs north parallel to the automobile road through a beautiful hemlock forest. It ascends to the Peterborough Merchants' cairn and the junction with the former Wapack Trail on a ledge 0.1 mi. north of the South Pack summit. (In this area a trail marked with yellow C's is encountered several times.)

The Wapack Trail leads down the wooded north slope past a *spring,* over the semiopen "Middle Peak" to another *spring,* where it turns sharp right and ascends directly to the summit of North Pack. This ledgy peak provides fine views of central New Hampshire, the Contoocook River valley, and, on a clear day, of Mt. Washington and other White Mountain peaks. The trail descends north, northwest, then north through overgrown pastures, past *reliable water* halfway down, and ends at Old Mountain Rd., 2.6 mi. west of NH Rte. 31 (via Old Mountain Rd. to Russell Station Rd.).

Wapack Trail

Distances from MA Rte. 119 west of Ashby, MA

to Watatic Mountain summit: 0.5 mi., ½ hr.

to road at the south foot of Barrett Mountain: 2.6 mi., 2 hr.

to S. Barrett Mountain summit: 4.5 mi., 3¼ hr.

to Middle Barrett Mountain summit: 5.6 mi., 4 hr.

to N. Barrett Mountain summit: 7 mi., 5 hr.

to Wapack Lodge, NH Rte. 123: 8.5 mi., 6 hr.

to road at south foot of Temple Mountain: 10.8 mi., 7 hr.

to Temple Mountain, main summit (Holt Peak): 13.5 mi., 9 hr.

to NH Rte. 101, at foot of South Pack Monadnock: 15.5 mi., 10¼ hr.

to South Pack summit: 17 mi., 11½ hr.

to North Pack summit: 19.5 mi., 12¾ hr.

to Old Mountain Rd. junction, foot of N. Pack: *est.* 21 mi. (33.6 km.), 13¾ hr.

UNCANOONUC MOUNTAIN

This twin-peaked mountain is situated in Goffstown. Refer to the USGS Pinardville quadrangle.

North Peak

From NH Rte. 114 in Goffstown, just east of the junction with NH Rte. 13, follow Mountain Rd. south and bear left at 0.9 mi. The trailhead (somewhat hard to find) is on the right at 1.4 mi. The trail is marked with white circles. It passes through a stone wall and approaches the 1324-ft. summit. A nearby side path leads down to a view of Manchester.

At 0.4 mi. from the start of the first trail, just beyond Goffstown Water Works Rd., turn right on a wood road. In a depression near a shed, climb a bank right, and follow a white-blazed trail that leads moderately then steeply to a jeep trail at a large scrub pine just southwest of the summit.

Uncanoonuc Mountain, N. Peak
(USGS Pinardville quadrangle)

Distances to summit:
   from trailhead via first trail: 0.6 mi. (1 km.), 40 min.
   from trailhead via second trail: 0.7 mi. (1.2 km.), 40 min.

South Peak

From NH Rte. 114 in Goffstown, 0.6 mi. east of the junction with NH Rte. 13, follow Wallace Rd. south 1.4 mi. to Mountain Base Rd. Follow Mountain Base Rd. 1 mi. to the Uncanoonuc Mountain Association picnic grounds. ("No Trespassing" signs do not apply to hikers.) The trail follows the road along the south shore of the pond, then forks left just past a white cottage. (This route is extremely obscure and, in fact, should be regarded as a bushwhack. It is included here only as an alternative to the unattractive trestle.)

The old trestle of the Uncanoonuc Mountain railroad ascends directly from the picnic grounds to just below the summit (1310 ft.) on the perimeter road. (*Descending*, go east to a house; the trestle is on the left.)

Uncanoonuc Mountain, S. Peak
(USGS Pinardville quadrangle)

Distance from picnic grounds
   to summit via trestle: 0.6 mi. (0.9 km.), 40 min.

LYNDEBOROUGH MOUNTAINS

The Lyndeborough Mountains form a large irregular mass in the northwest part of Lyndeborough. Rose Mountain (1720 ft.) at the northwest end of the range is the highest, and Winn Mountain (1676 ft.) to the southwest also provides outstanding views. The mountains are best reached by taking Lyndeborough Center Rd. from NH Rte. 31 in S. Lyndeborough for 1.3 mi., then turning left. Pavement ends 1.0 mi. from Center Rd., and a rough dirt road continues. Roads lead right toward Rose Mountain at 1.6 mi., and left toward Winn Mountain at 2.1 mi. There are no maintained trails, but travel through blueberry fields, present and past, is generally easy. Refer to the USGS Peterborough quadrangle.

CROTCHED MOUNTAIN

Crotched Mountain is in Francestown and Bennington with a south spur in Greenfield. The fire tower on the 2040-ft. summit is now abandoned and probably unsafe to climb, but there are excellent views from scattered ledges around the summit. Refer to the USGS Peterborough and Hillsboro quadrangles.

Greenfield Trail (CU)

From NH Rte. 31, 0.9 mi. north of Greenfield follow a road with the sign "Crotched Mountain Rehabilitation Center." Pass Gilbert Verney Drive on right 1.4 mi. from Rte. 31 and park 0.1 mi. farther where there is a gated road on the left. ("No Trespassing" signs do not apply to hikers.) There is no trail sign, but the trail is a gravel road. Take a left fork almost immediately, then left at a sign, and continue on road through overgrown blueberry barrens. Shortly after entering larger trees, take the left fork (sign) where road ends. The trail passes a spur trail to *reliable water,* and continues to Lookout Rock, which has an excellent view west and south and an impressive view of Mt. Monadnock. The Bennington Trail soon enters left at a stone wall, and the two trails coincide to the summit.

Greenfield Trail

(USGS Peterborough and Hillsboro quadrangles)

Distances from parking area

to Bennington Trail junction: 1.4 mi.

to Crotched Mountain summit: 1.8 mi. (2.9 km.), 1 hr. 20 min.

Bennington Trail (CU)

From NH Rte. 31, 1.6 mi. south of Bennington, take the road with signs "Summus Mons Campground" and "Mountain Rd."

for 0.5 mi. to the campground entrance. The trail follows a dirt road right (sign), which may be passable for cars for 0.2 mi. The trail turns sharp right here (sign) and follows an old logging road to a double cairn and sign, where it turns left. Follow it with care. It passes a *spring* (*water reliable*), then begins to climb more steeply to a junction with the Greenfield Trail. The two trails then coincide to the summit.

Bennington Trail
(USGS Peterborough and Hillsboro quadrangles)
Distances from campground entrance
   to Greenfield Trail junction: 1.2 mi.
   to Crotched Mountain summit: 1.6 mi. (2.5 km.), 1 hr. 20 min.

Francestown Trail (CU)

This trail begins at the Crotched Mountain Ski Area, off NH Rte. 47 west of Francestown. It starts as a driveway to the left of the lodge, just above the novice slope (sign "Sugar Run" on building) It goes left of the equipment garage and becomes a service road, which crosses under the chair lift and circles back to the top of the lift, then climbs to the base of a wooden stairway that leads to the summit.

Francestown Trail
(USGS Peterborough and Hillsboro quadrangles)
Distance from Crotched Mountain parking area
   to Crotched Mountain summit: 1.2 mi. (1.9 km.), 1 hr.

MOUNT SUNAPEE

This irregular, massive, 2720-ft. mountain is in Newbury at the south end of Lake Sunapee. The mountain is heavily wooded, but Lake Solitude is unique for a high elevation, remoteness, and beauty of setting. Nearby are a spring and cliffs that rise 300 ft. to White Ledge, where there is a fine view southeast over the wild country of the Merrimack-Connecticut watershed. Refer to the USGS Sunapee quadrangle.

Mt. Sunapee State Park is on NH Rte. 103, 7 mi. east of Newport. There is a state-owned ski area on the north slope of the mountain. A hikers' map is available at the lodge.

The mountain is easily climbed via the ski slopes (about 1.5 mi.). It is the northern terminus of the Monadnock-Sunapee Greenway. A trail, part of the Greenway, leads from the summit 1.6 mi. to Lake Solitude and connects to the Andrews Brook Trail from the east, and the Five Summers Trail from Pillsbury State Park in Washington.

White Mountains in Winter

According to Ticknor's *White Mountains,* published in 1887, the higher peaks of New Hampshire "seem to have received the name of White Mountains from the sailors off the coast, to whom they were a landmark and a mystery lifting their crowns of brilliant snow against the blue sky from October until June." Winter on the lower trails in the White Mountains may require only snowshoes and some warm clothing. But above timberline, conditions are often such that the equipment and experience needed to deal with them are of a different magnitude. Helpful information can be found in "Don't Die on the Mountain," by Dan H. Allen ($1, available from the AMC) and *Winter Hiking and Camping* by John A. Danielson (1982, Adirondack Mountain Club).

WINTER WEATHER

The conditions on the Presidential Range in winter are as severe as any in North America south of the mountains of Alaska and the Yukon Territory. On Mt. Washington summit in winter, winds *average* 44 mph, and daily high temperatures average 9° C. There are few calm days. The Mt. Washington Observatory, established in 1932, has often reported wind velocities in excess of 100 mph, and on April 12, 1934, a gust of 231 mph was timed. Temperatures are often below zero, record low for the present station being −46° F. The combination of high wind and low temperature has such a cooling effect that the worst conditions on Mt. Washington are approximately equal to the worst reported from Antarctica, despite the much greater cold in the latter region. Extremely severe storms also can come up suddenly and unexpectedly.

The winter of 1968-69 was the severest on record. New avalanches occurred on Lion Head and on Mt. Madison, in Madison Gulf, and in King and Ammonoosuc ravines. During the storm of February 24-26, 1969, the observatory recorded a snowfall of 97.8 inches. Within a 24-hour period during that storm, a total of 49.3 inches was recorded, a record for the mountain and for all weather observation stations in the United States. The previous 24-hour record (also nationwide) was February 10-11, 1969, when 40.6 inches was measured. The total snowfall from July 1, 1968, to June 30, 1969, was 566.4 inches, 222 inches more than the previous record.

PHYSICAL FITNESS, CLOTHING, AND EQUIPMENT

Severe weather and unfavorable snow conditions, for example deep powder below treeline or a breakable crust above, may put a climbing party to its ultimate test of physical fitness. People should not climb at this time of the year unless they have prepared by recent regular exercise, such as running, to face these adverse conditions. A safe size for a party is not less than three, or preferably four. Above treeline, they should stay close together at all times.

For a full day with a full pack, a hiker will need around 5500 calories. Candy, mintcake, and the like provide quick energy. Fats, like butter, provide prolonged energy.

A compass, map, and this *Guide*, well studied in advance, are more important than ever.

Clothing should be carefully chosen. Ordinarily, while climbing to timberline, relatively little should be worn, and the body should be suitably ventilated. Overdressing increases the possibility that clothing will become damp with perspiration. Once activity decreases or exposure increases, perspiration is the greatest cause of chill. Wool clothing is best for all winter hiking and climbing because of its insulating value, wet or dry. With two or three layers of wool clothing, winter hikers can better regulate body temperature when moving or resting. Wind parkas, alone or with wool depending on conditions, provide further versatility for body temperature maintenance. Cotton clothing, especially bluejeans, is not adequate, not safe, and not comfortable for winter hiking, skiing, or camping.

Parkas filled with down or with some synthetics provide excellent insulation for camping and some above-timberline hiking, but they are usually too hot and restrictive for hikers with packs. Down has the disadvantage of losing much of its insulating value if it becomes wet with snow, rain, or perspiration. High-loft fiberfills do not lose so much of their value when wet. In the White Mountains, where the weather can change very fast, hikers should always have rain gear and, if camping, a tent fly.

Hikers exposed to the wind, especially above timberline, are almost certain to want extra clothing, which must include a parka, warm mittens, and a face mask and goggles or a snorkel hood to avoid frostbite. Provisions for additional dry clothing should take into consideration the possibility that caps and mittens may be blown away.

Summer boots should not be used. Cold weather military boots — "Mickey Mouse" boots — are excellent as long as the felt inside them remains dry. For boots with removable liners, spare dry liners should be carried.

Crampons and snowshoes with creepers attached beneath the bindings are essential. During a trip, it may be necessary to switch from snowshoes to crampons and back several times, and these changes will be less agonizing if the equipment can be easily removed from or attached to the pack. It is vital to try on, try out, and adjust all equipment in a relatively warm place in advance. Camping equipment, such as stoves with pumps, also should be tried out in advance in winter conditions. If crampons might be needed on the upper half of a steep slope (as on Lion Head), it is better to put them on at the bottom.

Extra supplies, in addition to clothing and food, should include sun goggles and means to repair broken bindings and cope with possible emergencies. Strong nylon twine, rawhide, a knife, matches, and flashlights or, preferably, a headlamp, a first aid kit, and extra quick-energy food would be very useful at such times.

Finally, some people tend to overlook the possibility that they may get thirsty. Snow is not a good source of water because it requires energy to melt. It is advisable to carry a canteen of water, wrapped in a wool shirt or sock to keep it from freezing. Use a wide-mouthed water bottle. In the coldest weather, carry it next to the body. Dehydration is a more serious problem in winter than in summer in the mountains.

HYPOTHERMIA

Any winter emergency is likely to involve hypothermia or exposure. Hypothermia — the inability to stay warm because of injury, exhaustion, lack of sufficient food, and inadequate or wet clothing — is a very serious danger. The symptoms are uncontrolled shivering, impaired speech and movement, lowered body temperature, and drowsiness. The result is death, unless the victim (who usually does not understand the situation) is re-warmed. The victim should be given dry clothing and placed in a sleeping bag with someone else in it, then quick-energy food, and, when full consciousness is regained, something warm (not hot) to drink. Do not rewarm too quickly. Stay with the victim until help arrives. Many winter rescues in the White Mountains involve hypothermia victims.

Accordingly, a well-equipped party will carry at least one sleeping bag, a foam pad, and perhaps a tent shell, even on day trips.

INJURIES

Injuries are both more likely and more threatening in winter. An injured person unable to walk should be placed in a sleeping bag if possible. If outside help is needed for rescue, fill out an accident report form on the back of a map. At least one person should stay with the victim while another goes for help, which is why parties should have at least three or four people.

REGISTERING

Winter hikers or climbers who leave from Pinkham Notch or from the Appalachia parking area should register at Pinkham Notch Camp, at Lowe's Store, or with John H. Boothman (WMNF Forest Warden) in Randolph. Note: On the summit of Mt. Washington, no buildings are open to the public in winter.

SNOWSHOEING

Each snowshoer should carry an ice axe or at least a ski pole. Since many trails are hard to find, it's a good idea to hike a trail in the summer or fall before doing it in winter. Take account of the short winter days: set a "turn around" time and stick to it, and carry lights. In general, don't split the group unless an emergency requires it, or unless each subgroup is strong enough on its own — which will not usually be the case, since the most common motive for splitting up is that some members are weaker.

Allow at least double the time needed to hike the same trail in summer. With full backpacks and fresh snow, a party may cover only 5 miles a day.

Air pockets can form under small fir or spruce trees that may be completely covered by snow, setting "spruce traps" for unwary hikers, especially those without snowshoes.

In summer or fall, it's nice to take circular hikes — going up one trail, crossing two or more summits, and descending another trail. In winter, you should be very sure you can find your trail for the descent. If you descend on the same trail you went up, you can usually follow your own tracks out unless, as occasionally happens, the wind has covered them with snow. But a different trail for the descent can cause problems if no one else has broken it out since the last snowfall, especially if the trail is steep and you try to follow it at the end of a relatively long hike on a short winter's day. (For example, don't plan to circle up the Old Bridle Path to Lafayette, Lincoln, and down the Falling Waters Trail.)

If in doubt, do consult this *Guide* and maps.

ABOVE TIMBERLINE

Winter hiking above the trees requires redoubled caution. On an average winter day in the White Mountains, the winds will be too strong. Ice axe and crampon experience under qualified instruction are mandatory, along with a good amount of below-timberline winter hiking.

WINTER CAMPING

Camping out in the winter in the White Mountains, with temperatures that can be $-20°$ F. or below, involves serious risk of frostbite and hypothermia, even for individuals who appear to be fully equipped. This is even truer at high elevations. Camping above timberline is extremely dangerous. It should be noted that the USFS has removed the Edmands Col emergency shelter, which had been improperly used for planned overnights.

As with rock climbing, it is doubtful that adequate skills for winter camping can be learned from a book, and this book does not presume to teach such skills.

WINTER TRAVEL

In the early 1960s, a trip to timberline in the winter often was a struggle in itself. But year-long use of trails in the 1970s and 1980s has been substantial. Frequently, a beaten path can be found heading toward most of the high peaks. A nice winter Saturday may find over a dozen people plodding up the Old Bridle Path to Lafayette. The danger is that it looks too easy, which leads to overestimating what is possible and underestimating the equipment required.

Obviously, many trails are infrequently used, and climbing just after a heavy snowfall can be like the "good" old days. If you have the option, avoid trails that ascend steeply or slab along a river valley. Steep slopes and the areas below them are subject to avalanches. Moderate grades, shortness, and shelter from the prevailing west winds are considerations in choosing a route. Among preferred snowshoe trails are: on Mt. Moosilauke, the Gorge Brook Trail; the Lonesome Lake and Fishin' Jimmy trails; the Liberty Spring Trail; on Mt. Lafayette, the Old Bridle Path; the Crawford Path up to Mt. Clinton; and the 19-Mile Brook and Carter Dome trails.

Sometimes trails are hard to follow even at the bottom. In a hardwood forest it is sometimes difficult in winter to tell where the trail does *not* go (this does not apply to the old logging railroads of the Pemigewasset "Wilderness"). Higher up, the snow may be so deep that the evidence of a cleared trail lies beneath the snow. Above timberline, trail signs and even the big cairns on the Gulfside Trail and the Crawford Path may be buried. In very deep snow, without a packed trail to follow, it would, for instance, be hard to locate and follow the Falling Waters Trail as it descends the broad ridge off Little Haystack.

Caution. In the Presidential Range, many ravines — the Great Gulf, Madison and Oakes gulfs, Raymond Cataract, the Gulf of Slides, and Castle, Huntington, Jefferson, King, and Tuckerman ravines — have open ice and snow slopes, with the accompanying danger of avalanche, that require a knowledge of technical climbing, which this chapter does not presume to give. Stay out until you have acquired the necessary skills. Ravines may be officially closed — even to qualified climbers — by the USFS during some periods of avalanche danger.

The most variable factor in winter hiking is the weather. Under no circumstances should you proceed or continue above treeline if conditions are deteriorating. To do so is to take a risk in which the odds are heavily against you. The cone of Mt. Washington in particular is no place to be in bad winter weather. During white-out conditions, features of the terrain vanish, including such a seemingly obvious landmark as the Mt. Washington Auto Rd. Do not count on finding the cog railway either. Therefore, to circle the cone looking for either one makes little sense. In the face of bad weather, the only safe direction is down (with great caution and navigational care).

AMMONOOSUC RAVINE TRAIL

Because the road into the Marshfield station of the cog railway is not plowed, this trail is seldom used in the winter. However, a few notes for the descent are given here in case a climbing party is trapped by bad weather in the vicinity of the Lakes of the Clouds Hut.

The start from the hut is down a small ridge dividing two depressions and then into the right or more easterly of these. The direction is fixed exactly by a prominent slide showing as a broad band of snow on an opposite ridge of Mt. Washington; in a storm lay a compass course directly toward magnetic north. Once in the depression, follow the brookbed down to the first waterfall. Go around this, steeply, on the right (northeast) to the head of the big gorge. Here, on the right, a side trail leads right to the main trail. The main trail then descends on the right of the gorge to a pool at its foot, where it crosses to the left bank. Then the brook itself can probably be followed for some distance; in case of open water the trail lies for the most part on the left (south) bank and near at hand.

SKIING

For alpine skiing on Mt. Washington, see the end of Section 1. For cross-country skiing (ski touring), suitable trails are occasionally mentioned in this *Guide*, but a separate book is needed for adequate information.

National and State Areas

WHITE MOUNTAIN NATIONAL FOREST (WMNF)

Most of the higher White Mountains are within or adjoin the White Mountain National Forest (WMNF). In the Presidential Range, the Great Gulf and Dry River-Davis Path areas within the WMNF have been set aside for preservation as Wilderness Areas. A free wilderness permit is required for overnight camping in the Great Gulf Wilderness from June 15 to September 15. Also, camping and fires are restricted to designated sites in a number of Restricted Use Areas (RUAs) in the Forest, described below and shown on the map, pp. 490-491. By protecting the plants, water, soil, and wildlife of the White Mountains, these areas should help to provide a higher quality experience for the visitor

CAMPFIRE PERMITS

The laws of the states of Maine and New Hampshire and regulations of the Secretary of Agriculture require that permits be obtained to build campfires anywhere in the WMNF, except at improved roadside campgrounds maintained by the USFS, where no campfire permits are required. Permits are not required to use portable stoves. Campfire permits are not required when snow is on the ground. Permits may be obtained from the District Forest Rangers or other WMNF offices, or from AMC huts or offices listed below. Applications may be made personally, by letter, or by telephone, any time before the planned trip.

WMNF OFFICES AND RANGER DISTRICTS (R.D.'s)

Ammonoosuc R.D., Trudeau Rd., Bethlehem, NH 03574 (just north of US Rte. 3 opposite Gale River Rd.). Tel. 603-869-2626.

Androscoggin R.D., 80 Glen Rd., Gorham, NH 03581 (at south end of town along NH Rte. 16). Tel. 603-466-2713.

Evans Notch R.D., Bridge St., Bethel, ME 04217. Tel. 207-834-2134.

Pemigewasset R.D., 127 Highland St., Plymouth, NH 03264 (out to west of town). Tel. 603-536-1310.

Saco R.D., Kancamagus Highway (RFD 1, Box 94), Conway, NH 03818 (near east end of highway). Tel. 603-447-5448.

Forest Supervisor, P.O. Box 638, Laconia, NH 03246. Tel. 603-524-6450.

The Androscoggin Ranger District has been open seven days a week in the summer from about 8:00 A.M. to 5:00 P.M. or later. The Saco Ranger District Visitors' Center is open in the summer seven days a week, as follows: 8:00 A.M. to 5:30 P.M. Monday through Thursday; 8:00 A.M. to 10:00 P.M. Friday and Saturday; and 9:00 A.M. to 5:30 P.M. on Sunday. Otherwise, the offices are open during normal business hours.

The WMNF also has information centers on the Kancamagus Highway in Passaconaway and at the west end in Lincoln, and in Campton. Campfire and wilderness entry permits as well as other information are available there as well as at Ranger District offices. The Lincoln Center has been open seven days a week for most of the year from about 9:00 A.M. to 7:00 P.M.

AMC OFFICES

Fire permits and further information are also available from the AMC at Pinkham Notch Camp, Gorham, NH (603-466-2727), 7:30 A.M. to 10:00 P.M. seven days a week, and on summer days, at the Old Bridle Path trailhead in Franconia Notch. Fire permits are also available from the USFS and from fire wardens. Information can also be obtained at AMC huts during their operating season and from the caretakers of shelter sites.

FIRE AND CAMPING REGULATIONS

The use of portable stoves is encouraged and does not require a permit. Operate stoves with reasonable caution. Wood or charcoal campfires require permits and must be made in safe, sheltered places and not in leaves or rotten wood, or against logs, trees, or stumps. Before you build a fire, clear a space at least 5 ft. in radius of all flammable material down to the mineral soil. Under no circumstances should a fire be left unattended. All fires must be completely extinguished with earth or water before you leave a campsite, even temporarily. Firewood may be obtained only from dead trees. Green trees may be cut only with a permit from the District Rangers.

All camp refuse should be carried out *(Carry in/Carry out)*, and when you break camp the site must be made tidy and attractive. No rubbish or refuse should be thrown into any stream, spring, pond, or into or beside any road or path. Bathing and washing clothes or dishes is absolutely prohibited in certain streams that are used for domestic water supply by neighboring towns. Hunting and fishing must conform to the laws of the state in which the lands are situated. The policy of the USFS is to make all campsites available for the general public instead of leasing them to individuals for private use. Sites are available on a first-come, first-served basis.

For more detailed camping guidelines, see the Introduction.

WILDERNESS AREAS

The national Wilderness Preservation system, which included the Great Gulf, was established in 1964 with passage of the Wilderness Act. The Presidential Range-Dry River Wilderness was created in 1974, and in 1979 numerous additional areas within the WMNF were also proposed for Wilderness Act protection.

Permits are now required only for overnight camping in the Great Gulf Wilderness Area. They may be obtained from the Androscoggin Ranger District office in Gorham, NH 03581 (603-466-2281) from May 1 to October 31, or at Dolly Copp Campground from July 1 to Labor Day. No permits are required for day use in either the Great Gulf or the Presidential-Dry River Wilderness Areas. Permits for overnight camping are not required in the Presidential-Dry River Wilderness Area.

Shelter buildings are contrary to Wilderness Act policy, so eventual dismantling of all shelters in Wilderness Areas is planned.

Great Gulf Wilderness

This area includes some 5552 acres of WMNF land, see map, pp. 490-491.

Beginning on the north side of the Mt. Washington Auto Rd. at a point about 0.8 mi. up from NH Rte. 16, the boundary generally follows the road to about 0.5 mi. below the summit of Mt. Washington, turns right along the Gulfside Trail, then goes over Mt. Adams to Madison Hut, along the Osgood Trail over Mt. Madison and down to the Great Gulf Trail, turns east for a short distance and then right (south) to the Auto Rd.

The Gulfside and Osgood trails (except for a short segment) are just *outside* the Great Gulf Wilderness.

Presidential-Dry River Wilderness

This area includes the Dry River valley and parts of the Montalban Ridge, see map, p. 491. Its boundary is, in general, as follows: beginning at the New Hampshire Division of Parks-WMNF boundary on the Webster Cliff Trail, it follows that trail, then the Crawford Path to where the line turns south at the base of Mt. Washington summit cone, and goes just southwest of the Glen Boulder Trail, follows the Rocky Branch Ridge down to where the line turns west across Mt. Crawford, and then north along the WMNF boundary to the Webster Cliff Trail. The

Webster Cliff Trail and Crawford Path are entirely in the Presidential RUA, but just outside the Presidential-Dry River Wilderness Area.

RESTRICTED USE AREAS (RUAs)

Overnight camping is permitted in almost all of the WMNF. The object of the RUA program is not to hinder backpackers and campers, but to disperse their use of the land so that people can enjoy themselves in a clean and healthy environment without causing deterioration of natural resources. Overnight camping and fires are therefore regulated to limit damage in some areas of the WMNF that are threatened by overuse and misuse. Following are the current RUA regulations in 1982. Contact the USFS in Laconia, NH (603-524-6450), or any Ranger District office for up-to-date information. Ask for a current *Restricted Use Area Map*.

In summary, the 1982 RUA rules call for *no camping and no wood or charcoal fires:*

1. *above timberline* (where trees are less than 8 ft. in height);
2. *within 200 ft. of certain trails,* except at designated sites;
3. *within a quarter mile of certain roads, rivers, and sites,* except in or on campgrounds, shelters, and designated sites.

Stoves are permitted for day use, even in RUAs. RUAs as of 1982 are listed below, but the list may change from year to year, since new areas may need this protection and old ones may not. Because hikers and backpackers have cooperated with RUA rules, many trails once designated as RUAs are no longer under formal restrictions. However, common sense and self-imposed restrictions are still necessary to prevent trailside damage.

The RUAs, Wilderness Areas, and other regulated areas as of 1982 are numbered as on the map, pp. 490-491. RUA boundaries and approved overnight sites within RUAs are indicated by prominent signs. Specific rules are posted at each site.

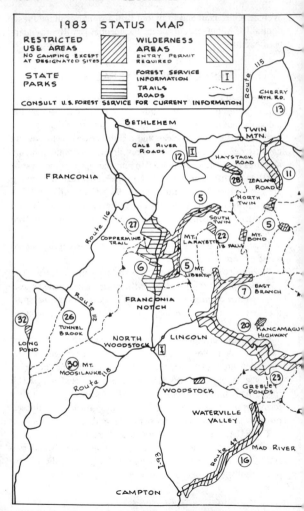

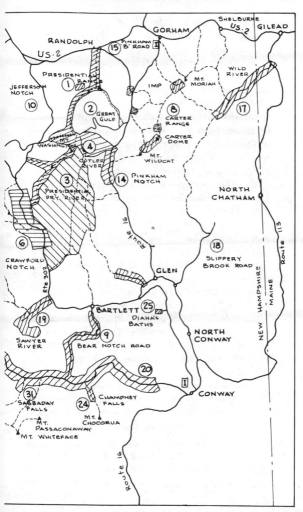

Use Regulations for Specific RUAs

1. *Presidential Range RUA. No camping, no wood or charcoal fires above timberline* (where trees are less than 8 ft. high). *No camping, no wood or charcoal fires within 200 ft. of trails,* except at shelters, in huts, and at Mizpah-Nauman campsite. *Removal, without permission, of any tree, plant, or shrub is prohibited.*

2. *Great Gulf Wilderness.* See the beginning of Section 22.

3. *Presidential-Dry River Wilderness. No camping, no wood or charcoal fires above timberline* (where trees are less than 8 ft. high). *No camping, no wood or charcoal fires within 200 ft. of trails,* except at designated sites.

4. *Cutler River Drainage RUA* (Tuckerman and Huntington Ravines). *No camping allowed year-round* except at Harvard Mountain Club Cabin in Huntington Ravine and at Hermit Lake Shelters in Tuckerman Ravine. *No campfires.* Stoves only. Tickets for shelters in Tuckerman Ravine are sold on first-come, first-served basis at Pinkham Notch Camp. *Inquire* before hiking in to the ravine. There is a caretaker at Hermit Lake.

5. *Franconia-Crawford RUA. No camping, wood or charcoal fires above timberline* (where trees are less than 8 ft. high). *No camping, no wood or charcoal fires within 200 ft. of trails* or within a quarter-mile of designated campsites except on sites themselves. *No camping at Thoreau Falls.* Overnight use is permitted at huts, but there is *no camping around huts.*

   Camping and wood or charcoal fires *permitted* at Liberty Spring, Garfield Ridge, and Guyot campsites. Fee and caretakers. Camping and wood or charcoal fires *permitted* at Ethan Pond Campsite. No fee and no caretaker.

6. *Franconia and Crawford notches* (NH state parks). Franconia Notch State Park 603-823-5563; Crawford Notch State Park 603-374-2272. *No camping, no wood or charcoal fires* are allowed in the state parks except at Lafayette

Campground in Franconia Notch and the Dry River Campground in Crawford Notch. Fees. AMC Lonesome Lake Hut: *no camping around hut.*

7. ***East Branch-Pemigewasset River RUA.*** *No camping, no wood or charcoal fires* within ¼ mi. of river. Overnight use, wood or charcoal fires *permitted* at Franconia Brook and Camp 16 campsites. No fee. Specific rules posted at each site.

8. ***Carter Range RUA.*** *No camping, no wood or charcoal fires above timberline* (where trees are less than 8 ft. high), or *within 200 ft. of several trails* (see map). Overnight use *permitted* in Carter Notch Hut, but *no camping* around hut, and at Imp Shelter, caretaker and fee.

9. ***Greeley Ponds Scenic Area.*** This is a *day-use area only. No camping or fires* year-round within this area and all land within a quarter-mile on either side of the Greeley Ponds Trail between the Scenic Area and NH Rte. 112 (Kancamagus Highway).

10. *No camping or fires* along **Tripoli Rd. near Eastman Brook.** Specific rules posted at sites.

11. ***Hancock Trail,*** portions of which receive heavy use—*no camping or fires.* Specific rules posted at sites.

12. ***Rocky Branch Trail,*** portions along Rocky Branch River. *No camping or fires.* Specific rules posted at sites.

No camping, no wood or charcoal fires within a quarter-mile of the following roads except at campgrounds that are designated sites (fees charged).

ROAD	CAMPGROUNDS
13. Bear Notch Rd.	none
14. Zealand Rd. — Ammonoosuc River	Zealand, Sugarloaf
15. NH Rte. 16 — Pinkham Notch	Dolly Copp, Barnes Field
16. Mad River — Tripoli Rd.	Campton, Waterville

17. Wild River Rd.   Wild River, Hastings
18. Sawyer River Rd.   Sawyer Pond Shelter and
                                      tent platforms (no fee)
19. Kancamagus Highway   Covered Bridge, Blackberry
    (within ½ mi.)   Crossing, Passaconaway, Big
                                      Rock, Jigger Johnson (fees)

No camping, no wood or charcoal fires within the following areas except at designated sites indicated.

AREA (see map)	DESIGNATED SITES
20. 13 Falls	Tent platforms
21. Champney Falls	none
22. Diana's Bath	none
23. Haystack Road (within ¼ mi.)	none
24. South Pond*	none
25. Sabbaday Falls	none
26. Long Pond, islands	none

This completes the list of RUAs as of 1982. Again, contact the USFS (603-524-6450) for current status, or consult up-to-date RUA map.

SCENIC AREAS

The USFS has established nine scenic areas in the WMNF. These areas are designated to preserve lands of outstanding or unique natural beauty. Information may be obtained by writing to the Forest Supervisor, WMNF, Laconia, NH 03246. The present areas, with size in acres, are:

Gibbs Brook (900)	Nancy Brook (460)
Greeley Ponds (810)	Pinkham Notch (5600)
Lafayette Brook (99)	Rocky Gorge (70)
Lincoln Woods (18,560)	Sawyer Pond (1130)
Snyder Brook (36)	

---

*South Pond, #24, is to the north, off our 2-page map.

NATIONAL FOREST — BACKGROUND

Under the Weeks Act, and subsequent legislation passed by the states of Maine and New Hampshire, the USFS was authorized to purchase approximately 850,000 acres in the White Mountains and adjoining regions. The total area of the WMNF, including lands acquired and approved for purchase, is currently about 752,000 acres, of which about 47,000 acres are in the state of Maine.

As lands are acquired they are placed under the care of the USFS, and their immediate supervision is delegated to the Forest Supervisor, whose office is at Laconia, New Hampshire. Anyone who plans to camp in the WMNF, to buy timber, or to use the resources of the Forest in other ways, should communicate with a District Ranger in person, by mail, or by telephone.

It is important to remember that this is not a National Park, but a National Forest. Parks are established primarily for preservation and recreation. National Forests are managed for multiple use. In the administration of National Forests the following objectives are considered: recreation development, timber production, watershed protection, and wildlife propagation. It is the policy of the USFS to manage logging operations so that trails, streams, camping-places, and other spots of public interest are protected. Mountain recreation has been identified as the most important resource in the WMNF.

To preserve the rare alpine flora of the Mt. Washington Range and to assure that the natural conditions on the upper slopes of the WMNF are maintained, removal of any tree, shrub, or plant without permission is prohibited. See the AMC's *Field Guide to Mountain Flowers of New England*.

The boundaries of the WMNF are usually marked wherever they cross roads or trails. The printed notice faces outward from the Forest. Throughout the mountains red-painted corner posts and blazes indicate either WMNF boundaries or the boundaries of various tracts acquired.

PUBLIC CAMPS AND SHELTERS

Public campgrounds for motor camping in the WMNF for the districts in Sections 1 through 20 of this *Guide* are listed below. There is also a table that describes WMNF trailside shelters and tent sites for campers on foot.

IMPROVED WMNF ROADSIDE CAMPGROUNDS	*SECTION OF GUIDE*
White Ledge	Sandwich Range
Passaconaway	Sandwich Range
Blackberry Crossing	Conway
Dugway	Conway
Covered Bridge	Conway
Jigger Johnson	Conway
Cold River	Chatham-Evans Notch
Hastings	Chatham-Evans Notch
Dolly Copp	Northern Peaks
Wild River	Carter-Moriah
Sugarloaf #1 and #2	Zealand, Twin Mountain
Zealand	Zealand, Twin Mountain
Wildwood	Kinsman
Waterville	Waterville
Campton	Waterville
Russell Pond	Waterville
Oliverian	Moosilauke
Big Rock	Pemigewasset
Crocker Pond	Chatham-Evans Notch
Basin Pond	Chatham-Evans Notch

Trailside Shelters and Tent Sites

Shelters are overnight accommodations for persons carrying their own bedding and cooking supplies. The more popular shelters are often full, so bring tents or tarps. Dishwashing should be done at a location away from any surface water. Please heed the rules of neatness, sanitation, and fire prevention, and carry out everything — food, paper, glass, cans, etc. — that you carry in. Do your part to keep the backcountry clean. (See the Introduction for more detailed guidlines.)

Around many shelters or sites are tent platforms or tent pads, providing camping areas for numbers of people given in parentheses in the table below. Less formalized tent sites are also often available, but they may be scarce.

Please note that the facilities listed below are described as follows:

C — Cabin and capacity

S — Shelter and capacity

T — Tent site and capacity

*** No tents at Hermit Lake. Shelters only. Charge. Tickets only at Pinkham Notch Camp.

† — Caretaker at site in summer

Contact Pinkham Notch Camp, Gorham, NH 03581 (1-603-466-2727), for up-to-date information on shelters, tent sites, huts, and trails.

Guide Section	Facility	Capacity	Maintaining Organization	Trail
1	Hermit Lake Shelters***	86	AMC	Tuckerman Ravine
2	The Log Cabin	C-10	RMC	Lowe's Path
2	Crag Camp	C-14	RMC	Near Spur Trail
2	Gray Knob	C-12	Town of Randolph	Near Lowe's Path
2	The Perch	S-8	RMC	Perch Path
4	Nauman	T-16	AMC	At Mizpah
5	Resolution	S-8	AMC	Davis Path
5	Mt. Langdon	S-8	WMNF	Mt. Langdon
5	Rocky Branch No. 1	S-8 T-20	WMNF	Rocky Branch
5	Rocky Branch No. 2	S-10	WMNF	Rocky Branch
6	Ethan Pond	S-8 T-20	AMC	Ethan Pond
7	Liberty Spring†	T-48	AMC	Liberty Spring
7	Garfield Ridge†	S-10 T-40	AMC	Garfield Ridge

Guide Section	Facility	Capacity	Maintaining Organization	Trail
8	Coppermine	S-7	WMNF	Coppermine
8	Kinsman Pond†	S-12	AMC	Kinsman Pond
		T-25		
8	Eliza Brook	S-8	AMC	Kinsman Ridge
9	Beaver Brook	S-6	DOC	Beaver Brook
	Three Ponds	S-10	WMNF	Three Ponds
11	Desolation	S-8	AMC	Carrigain Notch
		T-4		
11	Guyot†	S-12	AMC	Bondcliff
		T-24		
11	Franconia Brook	T-64	WMNF	Wilderness
11	Camp 16	T-40	WMNF	Wilderness
11	13 Falls	T-24	WMNF	Franconia Brook
12	Camp Heermance	S-6	WODC	Blueberry Ledge
12	Camp Shehadi	S-6	WODC	Rollins
12	Camp Penacook	S-8	WMNF	Piper
		T-4		
12	Jim Liberty Cabin	C-6	WMNF	Liberty (Choc.)
12	Old Shag Camp	S-6	CMC	Old Paugus
12	Camp Rich	S-8	WODC	Dicey's Mill
12	Flat Mountain Pond	S-8	WMNF	Flat Mountain Pond
13	Black Mountain Cabin	C-12	WMNF	Black Mountain Ski
13	N. Doublehead Cabin	C-8	WMNF	N. Doublehead Ski
13	Sawyer Pond	S-8	WMNF	Sawyer Pond
		T-20		
14	Imp†	S-12	AMC	Carter-Moriah
14	Perkins Notch	S-6	WMNF	Wild River
14	Rattle River	S-10	WMNF	Rattle River
14	Spruce Brook	S-5	WMNF	Wild River
14	Blue Brook	S-8	WMNF	Black Angel
15	Mountain Pond	S-8	WMNF	Mountain Pond
15	Wild River	S-5	WMNF	Wild River Campground
15	Province Pond	S-5	WMNF	Province Brook
15	S. Baldface	S-5	WMNF	Baldface Circle
15	Caribou	S-5	WMNF	Mud Brook
16	Trident Col	T-8	AMC	Mahoosuc
16	Gentian Pond	S-14	AMC	Mahoosuc
16	Carlo Col	S-14	AMC	Mahoosuc
16	Full Goose	S-10	AMC	Mahoosuc
16	Speck Pond	S-12	AMC	Mahoosuc
		T-10		
19	Black Mountain Pond	S-8	SLA	Black Mountain Pond

THE APPALACHIAN TRAIL (AT)

This 2,035-mile footpath, running from Springer Mountain, Georgia to Katahdin in Maine, traverses the backbone of the White Mountains in a southwest to northeast direction from Hanover, NH to Grafton Notch, ME, approximately 154 miles within New Hampshire. Its route traverses most of the major peaks and ranges of the White Mountains, following many historic, heavily used local and circuit hiking routes. Persons interested in following this section as a continuous path should consult the Appalachian Trail Conference's guidebook, *Guide to the Appalachian Trail in New Hamsphire and Vermont*. In 1978, new USFS signs were posted at trail junctions on the AT, giving distances (some of which, unfortunately, were incorrect). Information on the Appalachian Trail and the several guidebooks which cover its entire length can be secured from the Appalachian Trial Conference, P.O. Box 236, Harper's Ferry, WV 25425.

With the passage of Public Law 90-543 "The National Trails System Act," by Congress on October 2, 1968, the Appalachian Trail became the first federally protected footpath in this country and was officially designated the Appalachian National Scenic Trail. Under this act the Appalachian Trail is administered primarily as a footpath by the Secretary of Interior in consultation with the Secretary of Agriculture and representatives of the several states through which it passes. In addition, an Advisory Council for the Appalachian National Scenic Trail was appointed by the Secretary of Interior. It includes representatives of each of the states and the several hiking clubs recommended by the Appalachian Trail Conference.

STATE PARKS

Franconia Notch State Park on US Rte. 3 has long ranked among the state's foremost attractions for summer and winter recreation. Its principal features are the Old Man of the Mountains, the aerial passenger tramway to the summit of Cannon Mountain, the Flume (a natural gorge 800 feet long), Profile and Echo lakes. Also in the notch are numerous hiking trails, described in Sections 7 and 8 of this *Guide,* and an extensive network of ski trails and lifts on the north slopes of Cannon Mountain. There is overnight camping and day use at Lafayette Campground. The camping season is from Memorial Day to mid-October. The campground manager's office is on the premises.

Construction of I-93 through the park will begin in the mid-1980s. Many park changes that will affect trailheads and parking areas are anticipated. Contact AMC and state park offices for further information.

Bear Brook State Park is located off NH Rte. 28 in Allenstown. Its facilities include a large day-use area with family picnic grounds, a group picnic area with large shelter, a waterfront, and a bathhouse. A campground with 81 tent sites, located 5 miles from the park entrance, is open from mid-May to mid-October. There is a charge. The campground manager's office is on the premises. A Nature Center supervised by the Audubon Society of New Hampshire offers field trips in the park, a museum with numerous changing exhibits, games, and free nature movies. It is open from early July through Labor Day.

Mt. Sunapee State Park (2194 acres) off NH Rte. 103 in Newbury is a year-round recreation center with four passenger gondolas to the 2700-foot summit (summer and fall only), several trails including the one to Lake Solitude beginning near the summit (see Section 20). There is a swimming beach on Lake Sunapee.

As of 1982, the state of New Hampshire had 181 distinct and separate areas comprising over 110,000 acres under the jurisdiction of the State Department of Resources and Economic Development. State parks are supervised by the Director of Parks in the New Hampshire Parks Division; forest properties by the Director of Forests and Lands. Offices are in the State House Annex, Concord, NH 03301.

In Crawford Notch on US Rte. 302, camping is available from mid-May to mid-October at Dry River Campground, with 30 tent sites, 3 miles south of the park buildings. There is a charge. Natural attractions (see Sections 4 and 11) are Mts. Webster, Willard, and Willey, Arethusa Falls — reached by a side road 3 miles south of the Willey House site, and by a trail (about a mile to the falls) — Silver and Flume cascades, and Frankenstein Cliff.

Other State Campgrounds

The following New Hampshire state parks also provide campgrounds near hiking trails.

Pillsbury State Park, Washington. 20 tent sites. Open late June to Labor Day. There is a charge.

Monadnock State Park, Jaffrey (see Section 20). Campground with 21 tent sites situated at the end of Memorial Rd., from which trails lead to the mountain. Seven youth group sites. Open April 16 to November 11. There is a charge.

White Lake State Park, Tamworth. Two campgrounds, 173 sites, bathing beach. Open mid-May to mid-October. There is a charge.

Moose Brook State Park, Gorham. Excellent campground and bathing in park, 42 tent sites. Open mid-June to Labor Day. Trails in park connecting to Randolph trails. There is a charge.

Milan Hill State Park, Milan. State road from Milan Hill Rd., ample facilities for day use and overnight camping near fire tower. Twelve tent sites. Open late June to Labor Day. There is a charge.

Coleman State Park, Stewartstown. On Little Diamond Pond. 12 mi. east of Colebrook, off NH Rte. 26 and an unnumbered road. Picnicking, campground with 30 tent sites. Camping season, open mid-June to mid-October. There is a charge.

Greenfield State Park, 1 mi. west of Greenfield via NH Rte. 136. Camping season, mid-May to mid-October. Full time after Memorial Day. Beach and bathhouse, picknicking, camping. 252 sites. There is a charge.

Pawtuckaway State Park, Nottingham, 3½ mi. north of junction of NH Rtes. 101 and 156 in Raymond. Beach and bathhouse, picnicking, camping. 170 tent sites. Camping season mid-May to mid-October. There is a charge.

Lake Francis State Park, Pittsburg. On Connecticut River at inlet to Lake Francis. On River Rd. off US Rte. 3 approximately 7 mi. north of Pittsburg. 36 tent sites. No swimming available. Open mid-May to end of hunting season. There is a charge.

In state campgrounds, tent sites cannot be reserved. Campers must appear at the park office to register. The camping period is limited to TWO WEEKS from mid-June to Labor Day. Extensions may be obtained before and after that period at the discretion of park managers. Anyone camping in a state park must have a tent or a camping unit. Camping with only a sleeping bag is not permitted. Write NH Division of Parks and Recreation, Concord, NH 03301 for information on camping in state parks.

STATE FORESTS

State forests include: Connecticut Lakes, 1548 acres, through which US Rte. 3 extends for 9 mi. to the Canadian Border. Picnic and camping facilities available.

Other state forests located on or near trails described in this book are as follows: Merriman Reservation on Mt. Bartlett, Conway Common lands, Green Mountain in Effingham, Livermore Falls, Campton, Black Mountain in Haverhill, Mt. Cardigan, Welton Falls in Alexandria, Mt. Kearsarge in Merrimack

County, Mt. Monadnock in Jaffrey, Pawtuckaway Reservation in Nottingham, Miller Park, summit of N. Pack Monadnock, Peterborough, Annett Forest in Rindge and Sharon. The Fox Forest, which is for research and partly a bird sanctuary, is a mile north of Hillsboro Post Office. Several miles of trails are maintained. Hemenway Reservation in Tamworth includes summer facilities for the Algonquin Council of Boy Scouts in Framingham, Massachusetts. Gile Forest (6700 acres) in Springfield is bisected by NH Rte. 4A and has many local foot trails. Pine River State Forest (3000 acres) in Ossipee and Effingham has local trails including approximately 3 mi. along this very scenic river. Bear Brook State Forest (9400 acres) in Allenstown has local hiking trails, cross-country skiing, camping and day use facilities in season. Pisgah Wilderness State Park (13,000 acres) in Chesterfield and Winchester has many miles of local hiking trails and several small lakes and ponds. Pillsbury State Park in Washington and Sunapee State Park, Newbury, are joined by a corridor along the Sunapee mountain ridge, with group camping facilities at the Sunapee end and family camping at Pillsbury.

OTHER MOUNTAIN RESERVATIONS

The 5000-acre reservation on Grand Monadnock is owned in part by the Town of Jaffrey, State of New Hampshire, and the Society for Protection of New Hampshire Forests (SPNHF). A state park is located at the mountain base.

The Lost River Reservation in Kinsman Notch is owned and operated by the SPNHF.

For further information on the Society and its properties write to the SPNHF, 54 Portsmouth St., Concord, NH 03301.

For AMC reservations see the next section.

The Appalachian Mountain Club and Its Activities

The Appalachian Mountain Club (AMC) was organized in 1876 and was subsequently incorporated both in Massachusetts and in New Hampshire. It is the oldest, and largest, mountain club in the United States. It has made substantial contributions to various branches of geography, and has taken a leading part in efforts to preserve the beauty and economic value of the mountains and forests, and to promote backcountry research and education. It has built and maintains about 400 miles of foot trails and 20 shelters in New Hampshire and Maine.

The Club publishes a semiannual magazine, *Appalachia*, a monthly *Bulletin*, guidebooks, and other books.

AMC headquarters are in its own building, 5 Joy Street, Boston, Massachusetts. The information center and library are open to the public Monday through Friday, from 9:00 A.M. to 5:00 P.M. The information center is a resource for questions about trails and camping. It also sells guidebooks and books on outdoor recreation published by other publishers as well as by the AMC. Club-sponsored lectures, meetings, and social gatherings are held in Boston. The AMC also sponsors weekly outings and longer excursions, including some to foreign countries. Chapters in Maine, eastern New York, the Catskills, greater Philadelphia (Delaware Valley Chapter), New Hampshire, Connecticut, Rhode Island (Narragansett Chapter), Vermont, and Massachusetts (Worcester, Boston, Southeastern Massachusetts, and Berkshire chapters) also hold outings and meetings. There is opportunity to participate in trail clearing, skiing, canoeing, rock climbing, and other outdoor activities, in addition to hiking.

The Club now has more than 28,000 members. It invites all who love the woods and mountains and wish to contribute to their protection to join. Membership is open to the public upon completion of an application form and payment of an initial fee and annual dues. Information on membership, as well as the names and addresses of the secretaries of local chapters, may be obtained by writing to the Appalachian Mountain Club, 5 Joy St., Boston, MA 02108, or by telephoning (617-523-0636).

AMC Trails

Development, construction, and maintenance of backcountry trails and facilities have been a major focus of the AMC's public-service efforts since the Club's inception in 1876. Today, through twelve chapters, numerous camps, and its trails program, the AMC is responsible for maintaining and managing nearly 1000 miles of trails, including over 250 miles of the Appalachian Trail, many miles of ski trails, and more than twenty shelters and tent sites throughout the Northeast. The largest portion of these is in the White Mountain area of New Hampshire and Maine, where the AMC maintains over 100 hiking trails with an aggregate length of some 350 miles.

In general, trails are maintained to provide a clear pathway while protecting and minimizing damage to the environment. Some may offer rough and difficult passage. The Club reserves the right to discontinue any without notice, and expressly disclaims any legal responsibility for the condition of its trails at any time.

As a well-known and respected authority on hiking trails, the AMC works cooperatively with many federal, state, and local agencies, corporate and private landowners, and numerous other trail clubs and outdoor organizations.

AMC trails are maintained through the coordinated efforts of many members who volunteer their labor, and trails program staff and seasonal crew. Most of the difficult major construction projects are handled by the AMC trail crew, based in the White Mountains, which began operations in 1917 and is probably the oldest professional crew in the nation. Hikers can help maintain trails by donating their time for various projects and regularly scheduled volunteer trips with the AMC chapters and at AMC camps.

Funding for the AMC's trail and shelter maintenance comes primarily from membership dues, publication sales, fees from AMC facilities, and private and corporate donations. A Club-wide volunteer trails committee works closely with staff and other committees to develop program policy, budgets, and priorities.

For more information on any aspect of the Club's trail and shelter efforts, contact AMC Trails Program, Pinkham Notch Camp, Box 298, Gorham, NH 03581, or AMC Trails Program, 5 Joy St., Boston, MA 02108.

Comments on the AMC's trail work and information on problems you encounter when hiking or camping are always welcome.

AMC Hiker Shuttle

Shuttle service is available between Pinkham Notch Camp and major trailheads throughout the White Mountain National Forest. Connecting public transportation to Boston and points south via Concord Trailways is available through the ticket agency at Pinkham Notch Camp.

The shuttle operates daily from mid-June through Labor Day. Reservations are suggested. For additional information on fares and current schedule, write or call Reservations, AMC, Pinkham Notch Camp, PO Box 298, Gorham, NH 03581 (603-466-2727).

AMC Huts

There are eight AMC huts spaced a day's hike apart along the Appalachian Trail. They span the White Mountains from Lonesome Lake west to Carter Notch, and range in surroundings from lowland deciduous woods to alpine tundra. Each hut is operated by young men and women who pack in much of the food and supplies. Hearty meals prepared by the crew are served family-style at specific hours; bunks, blankets, and pillows are provided. All huts are open from mid-June through Labor Day. Many huts are open during the spring and fall on a caretaker basis. During caretaker season, the hut stove and utensils are available for use, but each guest must bring a sleeping bag and food. Zealand Falls and Carter Notch remain open on caretaker service through the winter.

All huts are open to the public; AMC members receive a discount on lodging. Reservations and deposits are necessary to guarantee space. For complete information, write or call Reservations, AMC Pinkham Notch Camp, Box 298, Gorham, NH 03581 (603-466-2727).

Pinkham Notch Camp

Pinkham Notch Camp is a unique mountain facility in the heart of the White Mountain National Forest. It is located along NH Rte. 16, twenty miles north of N. Conway, with public transportation via Concord Trailways available to the front door. The Joe Dodge Center, which accommodates over 100 guests in rooms with two, three, or four bunks, also offers a library that commands a spectacular view of the nearby Wildcat Ridge, and a living room where accounts of the day's activities can be shared by an open fireplace. The Center features a 65-seat conference room equipped with audio-visual facilities.

The Trading Post, a popular meeting place for hikers, has been a center of AMC recreational and educational activities since 1920. Weekend workshops, seminars, and lectures are conducted throughout the year. The building houses a dining room, and an information desk where basic equipment and guidebooks are available. The pack-up room downstairs is open 24 hours a day for hikers to stop in, relax, shower, and repack their gear.

Crawford Notch Hostel

Low-cost, self-service lodging is available in historic Crawford Notch. The main hostel holds 30 people in one large bunkroom. There are also a kitchen, bathrooms, and a common area. Three adjacent cabins accommodate 8 persons each.

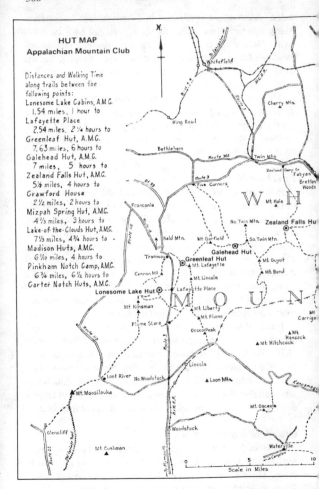

HUT MAP
Appalachian Mountain Club

Distances and Walking Time
along trails between the
following points:
Lonesome Lake Cabins, A.M.C.
   1.54 miles, 1 hour to
Lafayette Place
   2.54 miles, 2¼ hours to
Greenleaf Hut, A.M.C.
   7.63 miles, 6 hours to
Galehead Hut, A.M.C.
   7 miles, 5 hours to
Zealand Falls Hut, A.M.C.
   5½ miles, 4 hours to
Crawford House
   2½ miles, 2 hours to
Mizpah Spring Hut, A.M.C.
   4⅔ miles, 3 hours to
Lake-of-the-Clouds Hut, A.M.C.
   7½ miles, 4¾ hours to
Madison Huts, A.M.C.
   6 1/10 miles, 4 hours to
Pinkham Notch Camp, A.M.C.
   6¾ miles, 6½ hours to
Carter Notch Huts, A.M.C.

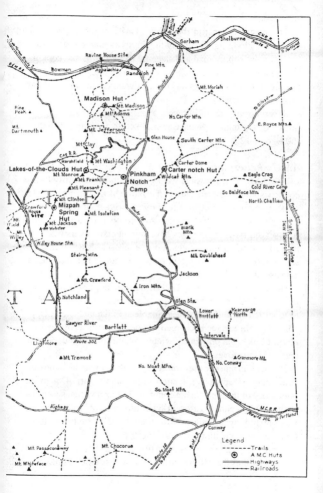

Legend

Trails — ------
AMC Huts — ⊙
Highways — ═══
Railroads — ┼┼┼┼

The hostel is open to the public. AMC members receive a discount on lodging. Overnight lodging is available year-round. Guests must supply food and sleeping bags; stoves and cooking equipment are provided. The hostel is an excellent choice for families and small groups and offers a wide range of hiking and outdoor experiences.

Reservations are encouraged. Please write or call Reservations, AMC Pinkham Notch Camp, Box 298, Gorham NH 03581 (603-466-2727).

AMC Shelters and Tent Sites

The AMC is responsible for 15 of the more than fifty backcountry shelters and tent sites in the White Mountain area. These sites are maintained cooperatively with private landowners and state and federal land agencies. All are open on a first-come, first-served basis. Some sites have summer caretakers who collect an overnight fee to help defray expenses. Most sites have shelters, a few have only tent platforms, and some have both. The use of stoves is encouraged.

Hermit Lake Shelters in Tuckerman Ravine, also maintained by the AMC, have limited space available on a first-come, first-served basis. Tickets are available at Pinkham Notch Camp. An overnight use fee is charged. Some tenting is available near Hermit Lake, but only in the winter. Wood fires are not permitted, so bring stoves.

Shelter and tent site users must supply their own food, cooking equipment, sleeping bag, foam pad, and tent or tarp. Due to the popularity of the area, do not count on finding a vacant space in a shelter. Be prepared to use tent sites or to camp off-trail, which is feasible and legal in much of the area. Check with the AMC or USFS about regulations prior to your trip.

Please help keep the sites clean by carrying out all of your own trash as well as that left by others who are less thoughtful.

AMC Reservations and Private Camps

The Club owns two reservations in New Hampshire for the benefit of the public. Madison Spring Reservation, with Madison Hut, is one acre.

The Cardigan Reservation, located in Alexandria, New Hampshire, contains almost 1000 acres of pasture and woodland on the north and east slopes of Mt. Cardigan. About sixty persons can be comfortably accommodated in the two lodges. It is open to the public on a seasonal basis. Reservations should be made with the Manager, Cardigan Lodge, RFD, Bristol, New Hampshire 03222 (603-744-8011).

The following camps, each under its own committee, afford comfortable summer vacations for AMC members, their guests, and friends of the Club. August Camp, where guests live in tents, changes its location from year to year. Cold River Camp is in N. Chatham, New Hampshire. Echo Lake Camp is on Mt. Desert Island, Maine. Ponkapoag Camp is in the Blue Hills Reservation near Boston, Massachusetts. Three-Mile Island Camp is on Lake Winnipesaukee, New Hampshire, and Wonalancet Cabin is in Wonalancet, New Hampshire. The Club also operates six campgrounds.

SECTION 24

Four Thousand Footers and Hundred Highest

For those who want to climb all the higher summits, a Four Thousand Footer Committee has compiled lists of the highest mountains in New Hampshire and New England.

The Four Thousand Footer Club

Organized in 1957, the Four Thousand Footer Club of the White Mountains has introduced its members to some mountain peaks and areas not usually visited by the average climber.

Prerequisite for membership in the Four Thousand Footer Club is climbing on foot to and from the forty-eight summits that are on the official list. (Upon completing the official list, contact the Four Thousand Footer Committee, Appalachian Mountain Club, 5 Joy Street, Boston MA 02108, for details about membership.)

Criteria for mountains on the official list are: (1) each peak must be 4000 ft. high, and (2) each peak must rise a clear 200 ft. above the low point of its connecting ridge with a 4000-ft. neighbor. This latter qualification eliminates such 4000-ft. peaks as Clay, Franklin, N. Carter, Guyot, Little Haystack, S. Tripyramid, Lethe, Blue, and Jim. By now, all forty-eight Four Thousand Footers are reached by well-defined trails, although the path to Owl's Head and some shorter spur trails to other summits are not officially maintained.

After climbing each Four Thousand Footer, please record the date of the ascent, companions, if any, and other remarks.

(Since publication of a new USGS map for the Waterville area, the committee has determined that the W. Peak of Tecumseh no longer qualifies for the New England Hundred Highest list. This peak has been replaced by Bondcliff, which is therefore also added to the 4000-Footer list, bringing the total number of peaks on that list to forty-eight. Until April 1, 1985, climbers may

512

ascend either W. Tecumseh or Bondcliff for the New England Hundred Highest Club. In order to qualify for the White Mountain Four Thousand Footer Club or the New England Four Thousand Footer Club, ascending Bondcliff will be optional until that date.)

The official list follows:

Mountain	Elevation (feet)	New Elevation**
1. Washington	6288	—
2. Adams	5798	—
3. Jefferson	5715	—
4. Monroe	5385	—
5. Madison	5363	—
6. Lafayette	5249	5240*
7. Lincoln	5108	5089
8. S. Twin	4926	4902
9. Carter Dome	4843	4832
10. Moosilauke	4810	4802
11. N. Twin	4769	4761
12. Eisenhower (Pleasant)	4761	—
13. Bond	4714	4698
14. Carrigain	4680	—
15. Middle Carter	4621	4600*
16. Bond, W. Peak	4526	4520*
17. Garfield	4488	4480*
18. Liberty	4460	4459
19. S. Carter	4458	4420*
20. Hancock	4403	—
21. Wildcat	4397	4422
22. S. Kinsman	4363	4358
23. Flume	4327	4328
24. Field	4326	—
25. Osceola	4326	4320*

Mountain	Elevation (feet)	New Elevation**
26. Pierce (Clinton)	4310	—
27. Willey	4302	—
28. Zealand	4301	4240*
29. N. Kinsman	4275	4293
30. Hancock, S. Peak	4274	—
31. Bondcliff***	4240*	4265
32. Osceola, E. Peak	4185	4156
33. Cabot	4160*	—
34. Tripyramid, N. Peak	4140	—
35. Tripyramid, Middle Peak	4110	—
36. Cannon (Profile)	4077	4080*
37. Hale	4077	4054
38. Passaconaway	4060	—
39. Jackson	4052	—
40. Tom	4047	—
41. Moriah	4047	4049
42. Wildcat "E"	4041	—
43. Owl's Head	4023	4025
44. Galehead	3948	4024
45. Isolation	4005	—
46. Waumbek	4005	—
47. Tecumseh	4004	4003
48. Whiteface	4000*	—

---

[4] Elevations followed by an asterisk are highest contour elevations where no definite altitude is given.

** The US Geological Survey's new 7.5 min. quadrangles are in process of publication, and shown above are their elevation figures as received to date. In this book — text and maps — no change will be made until all the new quadrangles are available, except for Galehead.

*** See note above on addition of Bondcliff to list.

The New England Four Thousand Footer Club

Membership in the New England Four Thousand Footer Club is open to everyone who has climbed on foot to and from all summits designated official by the Four Thousand Footer Club of the White Mountains, as well as the twelve Maine peaks and five Vermont peaks listed below.

Upon completing the required list, contact the Four Thousand Footer Committee, Appalachian Mountain Club, 5 Joy Street, Boston MA 02108 for details about membership.

The official Maine and Vermont Peaks are:

MAINE

Mountain	Elevation (feet)
Katahdin, Baxter Peak	5267
Katahdin, Hamlin Peak	4751
Sugarloaf	4240*
Old Speck	4180
Crocker	4168
Bigelow, W. Peak	4150
N. Brother	4143
Saddleback	4116
Bigelow, Avery Peak	4088
Abraham	4049
The Horn, Saddleback	4023
Crocker, S. Peak	4000*

VERMONT

Mountain	Elevation (feet)
Mansfield	4393
Killington	4241
Ellen	4083
Camel's Hump	4083
Abraham	4006

New England's Hundred Highest Club

Any climber is eligible for membership in New England's Hundred Highest Club if he or she has hiked to and from the summits of all the following peaks, including the sixty-four mountains from the New Hampshire and New England Four Thousand Footer Clubs. These peaks have been designated official by the Four Thousand Footer Committee and the Council of the Appalachian Mountain Club. Ascent of any of these peaks can be made any time during the hiker's lifetime. New 7½-minute elevations are in this list. About half of the 36 peaks that follow have no trails.

Mountains in Maine	*Elevation (feet)*
Abraham, Middle Peak	3765
Baldpate	3812
Bigelow, N. Horn	3810
Bigelow, S. Horn	3831
Coe	3764
Elephant	3774
Fort	3861
Goose Eye	3860
E. Kennebago	3791
Mahoosuc Arm	3790
Redington Pond Range, N. Peak	3984
Snow, Chain Lakes quad.	3960
S. Brother	3930
Spaulding	3988
White Cap, Cupsuptic quad.*	3815
Peak between Boundary Monuments 445 & 446 Arnold Pond quad.*	3845

Mountains in New Hampshire	Elevation (feet)
Cannon Balls, N.E. Peak	3769
Horn, the	3905
Nancy	3906
Sandwich	3993
Scar Ridge	3774
Sleepers, the, E. Peak	3850
Tecumseh, W. Peak**	3790
Vose Spur (Mt. Carrigain)	3870
Weeks	3890
Weeks, S. Peak	3885
Peak on north ridge of N. Twin, S. Twin quad.	3813

Mountains in Vermont	Elevation (feet)
Big Jay	3800
Bread Loaf	3835
Dorset Peak	3760
Equinox	3840
Jay Peak	3861
Mendon Peak	3840
Pico Peak	3957
Stratton	3936
Wilson	3790

---

*Access through private lands, perhaps Canada. Check with Four Thousand Footer Committee.

**See note at beginning of chapter concerning deletion of W. Tecumseh.

New England Trail Conference

The New England Trail Conference was organized in 1917 to develop the hiking possibilities of New England and to correlate the work of local organizations. The Conference serves as a clearinghouse for information about trail maintenance and trail use both for organized groups and for individuals.

The annual meeting of this organization is held in the spring. Representatives of mountaineering and outing clubs from all over New England come together for a full day and evening program of reports, talks, and illustrated lectures on mountain climbing, hiking, and trails and shelters. All sessions are open to the public.

The work of the Conference is directed by the chairman, who is elected by the executive committee. For information, contact the chairman, Forrest House, 33 Knollwood Drive, E. Longmeadow, MA 01028 (203-342-1425 or 413-732-3719).

MEMBERS OF THE NEW ENGLAND TRAIL CONFERENCE

American Youth Hostels, Inc.
Amherst College Outing Club
†Appalachian Mountain Club
*ARACA, Inc.
*Ascutney Trails Association
*Bates College Outing Club
*Berkshire Chapter, AMC
Boy Scouts of America, National Council, Region I
*Camp Kawanhee for Boys
†Camp Union
†Chatham Trails Association
†Chocorua Mountain Club
*Colby College Outing Club
*Connecticut Chapter, AMC
*Connecticut Forest and Park Association
†Dartmouth Outing Club
*Franklin Pierce College Outing Club
*Friends of the Blue Hills

*Gould Academy Outing Club
*Green Mountain Club, Inc.
*Green Mountain National Forest
†Hutmen's Association
*Maine Appalachian Trail Club
*Maine Chapter, AMC
*Mass. Dept. of Natural Resources
*Mattawamkeag Wilderness Park
*Metawampe Club
*Mount Greylock Ski Club
*Mount Tom Citizens Advisory Committee
†Mowglis Camps
*Narragansett Chapter, AMC
*New Hampshire Chapter, AMC
*New London Conservation Commission
*Northfield-Mt. Hermon Outing Club
†Phillips Exeter Academy Outing Club
*Pioneer Valley Regional School Outing Club
†Randolph Mountain Club
  Sierra Club — New England Chapter
†Society for the Protection of New Hampshire Forests
†Squam Lakes Association
†Sub Sig Outing Club
*Taconic Hiking Club
  University of Maine Outing Club
*University of Massachusetts Outing Club
*Vermont Department of Forests, Parks and Recreation
†Waterville Valley Athletic & Improvement Association
  Wesleyan University Outing Club
†White Mountain National Forest
*Williams College Outing Club
†Wonalancet Outdoor Club
*Worcester Chapter, AMC

ASSOCIATE MEMBERS

*Adirondack Mountain Club
*Finger Lakes Trail Conference
*New York — New Jersey Trail Conference

---

†Organizations that maintain trails described in this *Guide*.
*Organizations that maintain trails elsewhere in New England.

Glossary

For abbreviations see page xxx.

blaze	a trail marking on a tree or rock, painted and/or cut
blazed	marked with paint on trees or rocks (blazes)
bluff	a high bank or hill with a cliff face overlooking a valley
boggy	muddy, swampy
boulder	large, detached, somewhat rounded rock
box canyon	rock formation with vertical walls and flat bottom
bushwhack	to hike through woods or brush without a trail
buttress	a rock mass projecting outward from a mountain or hill
cairn	pile of rocks to mark trail
cataract	waterfall
cirque	upper end of valley with half-bowl shape (scoured by glacier)
cliff	high, steep rock face
col	low point on a ridge between two mountains; saddle
crag	rugged, often overhanging rock eminence
grade	steepness of trail or road; ratio of vertical to horizontal distance
graded trail	well-constructed trail with smoothed footway
gulf	a cirque
gully	small, steep-sided valley

headwall	steep slope at the head of a valley, especially a cirque
height-of-land	saddle, col, or highest point reached by a trail or road
knob	a rounded, minor summit
lean-to	shelter
ledge	a large, smooth body of rock; or, but not usually in this book, a horizontal shelf across a cliff
ledgy	having exposed ledges, usually giving views
outcrops	large rocks projecting out of the soil
plateau	high, flat area
potable (water)	fit to drink
ravine	steep-sided valley
ridge	highest spine joining two or more mountains, or leading up to a mountain
runoff brook	a brook usually dry except shortly after rain, or snow melt
saddle	lowest, flattish part of ridge connecting two mountains; col
scrub	low spruce or fir trees near treeline
shelter	building, usually of wood, with roof and 3 or 4 sides, for camping
shoulder	point where rising ridge levels off or descends slightly before rising higher to a summit
a *slab* (n.)	a smooth, somewhat steeply sloping ledge
to *slab* (v.)	to walk across a slope
slide	steep slope where a landslide has carried away soil and vegetation
spur	a minor summit projecting from a larger one

spur trail	a side path off a main trail
strata	layers of rock
summit	highest point on a mountain; or, point higher than any other point in its neighborhood
switchback	zigzag in a trail to make a steep slope easier
tarn	a small pond, often at high elevation, or with no outlet
timberline	elevation that marks the upper limit of commercial timber
treeline	elevation above which trees do not grow

INDEX

B